PROVINC

Proving Shakespeare

Verifying BEN JONSON'S Vow
That EDWARD DE VERE Was
WILLIAM SHAKESPEARE

An Orvid Edition

An Orvid paperback

First published in the U.S.A. in 2008
by Lulu, N.C.
This revised and updated paperback edition published
in 2011
by Orvid Editions, www.orvid.co.uk

A CIP catalogue record for this book
is available from the British Library.

ISBN 978 0 9543873 4 1

Typeset in Plantagenet by Acumen

Printed and bound in Great Britain by
Lightning Source, Milton Keynes, UK.

Dedicated to the Memory

of

Hannah Northwood
Who made this book possible

Contents

Publisher's Acknowledgements

BENJAMIN JONSON, by Abraham van Blyenberch,
c. 1617: National Portrait Gallery, London.
BASILICON DORON, © British Library Board. All Rights Reserved
Harley 6855, 13.
PEACHAM MANUSCRIPT, Reproduced by permission of the
Marquess of Bath, Longleat House, Warminster,
Wiltshire, BA12 7NW.
HENRY WRIOTHESLEY, Attributed to JOHN De CRITZ Portrait of
Henry Wriothesley, 3rd Earl of Southampton (1573-1624), c.1592
Oil on panel 24in x 17 ¼ in reproduced under copyright from a
private collection.
EDWARD DE VERE, Miniature portrait by Nicholas
Hilliard, 1588. Previously unidentified, and referred to as:
'Unknown Man Clasping a Hand Issuing from a Cloud';
by permission of the Victoria and Albert Museum, London.

Acknowledgements

It is with the profoundest debt of gratitude that I wish to honour those who by the courage of their convictions and astute scholarship have made this book possible. It is no easy matter to publicly defy orthodox opinion by asserting views contrary to prevailing beliefs, as Galileo discovered to his discomfort. Yet, a sufficient number of worthy scholars, formidably endowed with the intelligence to combat error where it has been perceived, have emerged within the last hundred years and made known their deep disquiet at the poverty of information concerning Shakespeare's literary life. Chief amongst these of recent memory has been the late Charlton Ogburn jnr. His mammoth tome, published in the U.S.A. in 1984 as *The Mysterious William Shakespeare: The Myth and the Reality*, and four years later in England, as *The Mystery of William Shakespeare*, has been an inspiration to many, a turning point for the uncertain, and for myself, a source of constant references and quotations that have greatly helped to enhance the arguments I wished to propose.

Mention must also be made to Dr John Rollett for the excellent work he conducted in piercing the veil covering Thomas Thorpe's enigmatic dedication at the front of the Sonnets, and the suggestion made by Rae West, which led me to the Alternating Letter Sequencing encryption. Having laid the groundwork so well, this helped make the final solution to Thorpe's cryptogram that much easier to conclude.

A similar plaudit is due to the late Eva Turner Clarke for her work on Henry Peacham's illustration at the front of his book, *Minerva Britanna*. Once again, it was because of her sterling work in suggesting a solution to the riddle posed by Peacham that the matter can be explained in full.

Since the first publication of this book in 2008, other names have come forward to add to the revelations from cryptography, made necessary by late 16th and early 17th century censorship. Chief amongst these are Art Neuendorffer and Dr James Ferris, both of whom have found compelling proof that not only contemporaries of Edward de Vere were desperate in their effort to inform posterity that it was this member of Queen Elizabeth's court who wrote the works attributed to Shakespeare, but that de Vere himself admitted to being the poet. Their discoveries now join Ben Jonson's avowal identifying de Vere, which he encrypted into the six-lined verse beneath Shakespeare's effigy at Stratford-upon-Avon, and for which Dr Bruce Spittle has since provided the missing key that unlocks its secret.

Of the many others who have contributed towards this book, too numerous to be named without a fitting reference to the value of their input, they will find their acknowledgement within the pages that follow. Without their many hours of toil, and the labour of those, whose unpaid efforts to publish research against the trend in journals and newsletters continue to do so much to drive the authorship debate, this book could not have been completed.

To add to all these, it is with special gratitude that I acknowledge the splendid backing and encouragement, not to mention the many helpful suggestions, conveyed to me by Professor Albert Burgstahler. In fact, it was at his suggestion that the first edition of this book came to be written. Over the course of years he has supplied me with information that I would not otherwise have been aware of, and he has never hesitated to ensure that I received copies of the latest articles on matters that had a bearing upon my researches. I am therefore immensely appreciative for his suggestions, most of which I have been happy to embrace, although I hasten to add that any errors are entirely mine.

My final acknowledgement goes to my dear wife, and her unfailing and tireless support to see the successful completion of this book. To the many others, alas unmentioned, who have demonstrated their interest in the progress of this book over the years; they have not been forgotten; for in their own small way, they too have helped towards that day when Edward de Vere will again be reunited with his *nom de plume*, William Shakespeare.

LIST OF ILLUSTRATIONS

Author Profile

David L Roper has an Honours degree in Pure Mathematics, Statistics and Philosophy; combined with several decades of teaching experience at entry level to British universities.
During the past two decades he has been collecting evidence concerning the Shakespeare Authorship Dispute, to which he has added much, based upon certain numerical discoveries and the probabilities attached to their existence, which were not previously available to historians and the literati.
These discoveries have enabled him to lecture on both sides of the Atlantic, as well as participate in a documentary for German television.
His interest in the life and works of Shakespeare is exceeded only by a greater concern for the truth about this man.
Currently, he is engaged in research. He lives with his wife in the west of England.

INTRODUCTION

THE TITLE PROVING SHAKESPEARE was chosen because it is appropriate to the content of this book. The word *proof* has, at times, been used by academics for the purpose of propping up their particular argument; but later examination has shown it to be insufficient. In short, it was not a proof at all: merely evidence towards that goal and without any necessity it would actually lead to the desired result.

Proof in historiology is acceptable when it is founded upon reliable eye-witness accounts of an event, with more than one eye-witness reporting what happened. Even then, doubt may be cast upon these reports if contrary statements indicate a different outcome. In such cases the probity and reputation of the witnesses come under scrutiny, and the possibility of a motive or cause of error for what has been asserted by either party must be considered.

The present case at issue is that of the man recognised by the name William Shakespeare. For the past four centuries his work has been the source of continuous study, yet the man himself is an enigma. Vast amounts of money; unaccounted passages of time; and seemingly endless volumes of literature have been disposed to discover the man behind the poetry. Yet, despite this investment of money and human resources, nothing – absolutely nothing has ever come to light that *proves* this man wrote the plays and poems that bear that name.

The money, research and time spent on this endeavour has certainly *proved* that the subject of enquiry lodged in London for at least a dozen years; maintained a home in Stratford-upon-Avon where he was born and spent the first half of his life; but as far as actual evidence shows, his life was devoid of literature, or even literary connections. There is, however, substantial evidence that he occupied himself as a businessman; acquiring property, trading in malt and probably wool, and practising as a money-lender. His name, although only infrequently spelt Shakespeare, has been found appearing in several minor brushes with the law, and also as a plaintiff for the repayment of money owed to him. There is, however, no litigation involving literary work associated with him, even though Heminge and Condell, two members of the acting group, the Lord Chamberlain's Men, later the King' Men, declared that Shakespeare's work had been stolen by the frauds of impostors. This should raise a suspicion in the mind of anyone pursuing the truth about Shakespeare, especially when coupled with the undeniable fact that nothing has ever been discovered to *prove* conclusively that he had a hands-on connection with even one of the titles that Shakespeare wrote.

These arguments are not unfamiliar to those researching into Shakespeare's background. They are countered by several very weak arguments. Firstly, Shakespeare held shares in the Globe theatre, and his name occurs on several lists of actors who took part in performances. Apart from the fact that the name Shake-speare, when it does occur, is hyphenated: suggesting that the name is distinguishable, therefore separable from that of the other Shakespeare, neither acting nor the acquisition of theatrical shares confers the ability or talent to be a great playwright.

The second argument is actually an appeal. No one ever doubted that Shakespeare was the man from Stratford-upon-Avon until fairly recent times; therefore it is absurd to cast doubts upon a man acclaimed by past generations of scholars as both a poet and a playwright. But it is "*only in the last century, he has been subjected to the greatest battery of organized research that has ever been directed upon a single person. Armies of scholars, formidably equipped, have examined all the documents which could possibly contain at least a mention of Shakespeare's name . . . And yet the greatest of all Englishmen, after this tremendous inquisition, still remains so close to a mystery that even his identity can still be doubted.*" [Hugh R. Trevor-Roper: *What's In a Name? (Réalities)* Paris, November 1962].

Thus, no one doubted Shakespeare's authorship until the 19th century; because, until then, it was taken for granted that documentary evidence must exist to corroborate Shakespeare's authorship. But when the expected documents were not found – arguably, there were never any in the first place – honest men and women, with no vested interest in Shakespeare, began to raise questions.

The third argument is all that remains, and this has always been trumpeted as the strongest. It consists of four cornerstones. The first of these is the Stratford monument in the church of the Holy Trinity at Stratford-upon-Avon; it confirms Shakespeare's credibility as the writer he is believed to have been. The second is the First Folio of Shakespeare's Comedies, Histories and Tragedies, for it contains tributes to this man's memory. The third is given to Ben Jonson who famously called Shakespeare the Sweet Swan of Avon, thus alluding to the place of his birth and upbringing. Finally, there is Robert Greene's dying letter to three playwrights; which confirmed that Shakespeare was an actor and writer of blank verse who had recently arrived in the capital.

Impressive though these four cornerstones are, none are sufficient to constitute the proof that is claimed for them. This book will take each one in turn, and show the logic that undermines its acceptance is flawed. At the same time, it will be demonstrated how these four cornerstones have misled scholars by allowing their faithful willingness to accept Shakespeare without question, has either led them astray, or into blind alleys.

Let it therefore be understood that one can claim to have 'proved' anything if evidence to the contrary is deliberately omitted. The quest for proving Shakespeare's true identity is riddled with this fault, and led by those with what is tantamount to a religious devotion to the man, or a vested interest in maintaining the *status quo.*

This book treads new ground. For the first time it is possible to uncover statements made by Shakespeare's contemporaries that identified him by name. In fact, 'Shakespeare' does state very clearly, *"My Name's de Vere"*. Ben Jonson went further and said: *"I Vow E. de Vere is Shakespeare"*, adding that de Vere should be tested to verify it. Thomas Thorpe was another; he declared that Shake-speare's sonnets were written by de Vere, and that the 3rd Earl of Southampton was the fair youth. John Benson's edition of the sonnets added to this by proposing that some poems were addressed to Mary Sidney. Benson also included Leonard Digges' assertion that de Vere was Shakespeare. Nor must we forget Henry Peacham's illustration in *Minerva Britanna*, complete with Latin mottos; which, although offered as a conundrum, resolve into de Vere being named. From Peacham, this is not surprising. His book, *The Complete Gentleman*, was extremely popular in the seventeenth century, and is still considered to be a prime example of its genre. In his book, Peacham named those who had made Queen Elizabeth's England a Golden Age of literature. At the head of the list, he placed Edward de Vere, who had been dead for almost twenty years. As for William Shakespeare, his name is never mentioned; even though the book went through three reprints, thus allowing for corrections to be made and omissions to be inserted.

The naming of de Vere as Shakespeare, even by Shakespeare himself, as well as those who can be said to have been within his circle of influence, runs counter to orthodox opinion. Authority remains adamant that Shakespeare was the man who arrived in London from Stratford-upon-Avon, gained immediate access to the theatre, and more or less instantly began producing masterpieces of dramatic art; that is, without ever having undergone any proper training or apprenticeship. He was a genius, we are told, and needed no instruction. In this, he has a parallel. It is Athene plucked from the head of Zeus, ready and armed for battle, needing no instruction in the practice of warfare. Myth is also where this Shakespeare's genius is likely to be located. But to prove it, the declarations made by those named above, asserting that Shakespeare was de Vere, need to be validated. This takes us into the very heart of the contention, because it sets the science of cryptology against the conclusions reached by scholars of English Literature; numbers versus letters.

Anyone who has resorted to cryptology as a serious means for imparting secret information will have had a genuine reason for choosing this method of communication. When members of a particular group in society prefer this above all other means of making known the information they wish to convey, censorship, repression and punishment are likely to be the cause. In which case, where this occurs, a prediction can be made, and prediction is a powerful tool for validating a theory.

The prediction is that the information confined to cryptology will not be discovered, or referred to in documents written during the same period; the need for secrecy would prevent it. This is precisely the situation we find when inspecting the findings of researchers into the literary life of Shakespeare. There is a complete absence of any letters, sent or received, which would identify William Shakespeare of Stratford-upon-Avon as the real Shakespeare. There is also a complete absence of any writer from that period admitting to having spoken to Shakespeare, or having been approached by him. There are anecdotes about Shakespeare. There are references to Shakespeare. There is an abundance of praise for Shakespeare. But who was he? There, researchers hit a wall. No one in the past was prepared to say. Although one disgruntled resident in Stratford-upon-Avon greeted David Garrick's visit to the town in 1769, by continually interrupting his speech of acclamation with the assertion that Shakespeare was *"a provincial nobody"*.

In the present day, it is the convention to fall back upon reports of Shakespeare's commercial activities; his family life; his wife; his environment, and so forth, and onto this mundane existence, superimpose the works of Shakespeare in some semblance of order. This allows the suggestion that some plays were written after 1604: the year in which Oxford died. But this is mere supposition. There is no proof to confirm, definitively, the exact year when a play was written, nor even that the academics' Shakespeare was the actual author. In the past, it was this failure to secure proof of Shakespeare's authorship that caused such intense dissatisfaction amongst the faithful that more than one scholar resorted to forging it. Nowadays, this absence is filled by creative thinking, and the idle use of "certainly", to express what is in the author's mind, rather than he should admit to the uncertainty that exists elsewhere. And so we are told what could, or should, or would, have happened in circumstances thought to be certain; but for which no probative evidence exists.

Thus, Shakespeare's biographers count on the fact that most of their readers are unfamiliar with the full details, or lack of them, surrounding his literary life. They then feel free to either invent them, or offer facile interpretations to reassure their readership, while also ignoring troublesome facts or outright contradictions; which they themselves must be aware of. This may be a clever strategy for marketing, and appearing superior to doubts concerning Shakespeare's authorship, but it is an abnegation of scholarship; a complete disregard for truth, and an insult to those who pay to read what is essentially, junk biography. Only his commercial activities and the brief, dull account of his family life have any actual claim to reliability.

It is against this historical vagueness that any piece of cryptology asserting Shakespeare to be Edward de Vere must assert itself. In this, we are fortunate to have not just one piece but five; each of which, originated from the hand of a person intimately involved with the plays and poems of Shakespeare, and who lived in the age during which he flourished. To add to this, each piece of cryptology has been written in the same pattern: that of arithmetical letter sequencing. The positive aspect from this is that letters which comprise words, and words which comprise sentences, follow an arithmetic progression. Consequently, probability values can be assigned to their appearance, and assessed against a chance occurrence. This has been accomplished with a decisive result. Edward de Vere was William Shakespeare.

To refute this, a temptation exists to employ double standards. Probability calculations are used to resolve questions in every branch of science. One cannot therefore pick and choose on the basis of personal disbelief. Numbers do not discriminate, nor do they lie. They are impervious to the subject they attend. It is because of this that calculations supporting de Vere as Shakespeare are as acceptable to deciding the authorship question, as they are to deciding matters of scientific enquiry.

There are, of course, strict rules that need to be applied for the decryption of a piece of cipher-text. But when these conditions have been met, the result obtained will overrule any alternative to what has been revealed. Genuine criticisms – those apart from idle dissent – must be testable. Where tests are not provided, there is no requirement upon anyone to take this type of dissent seriously. Words come easy. A practical demonstration to support them is an entirely different matter.

It is on record that one of the greatest and most influential cryptologists of the last century, William F. Friedman, himself a Shakespeare prize winner, as well as having been decorated for his work in the Second World War, stated categorically: that if a decrypted statement met his criteria for validity, and it said that someone other than Shakespeare of Stratford wrote the works appearing under that name, he would accept it, no matter how much this might shock authority. Friedman believed in the superiority of a scientifically applied decryption process to that of conclusions drawn by scholars, however well qualified. As he remarked: *"the historical argument can never produce certainty ... there is always a counter-argument ... It is with relief that we turn to the more certain ground of cryptology."* [1]

It is this that forms the basis for a proof that Edward de Vere was Shakespeare. Jonson said he must also be tested as Shakespeare. This has been done. Fortunately, there are biographies of de Vere, and these allow a significant number of examples to appear that run parallel to the fate of the characters he created for his plays. By comparison, there are no such parallels, at least none of any value that exist between the life of Stratford's Shakespeare and characters from the plays he allegedly wrote. Moreover, successful writers tend to be those who write about what they know best. De Vere knew best about life at court, and it is titled characters and court scenes that occur most frequently in Shakespeare's plays. De Vere also knew about the customs of people in Italy and France, and again, these are to be found in plays written by Shakespeare. On the other hand, de Vere had little experience of the lower classes; and, as would be expected in this circumstance, the plays of Shakespeare show these people as simple and oafish. Jonson, on the other hand, lived amongst these people, he was therefore able to characterise them in a more realistic light.

With virtually every problem surrounding Shakespeare and his work solved, including the identities of the fair youth, the rival poet, his poetry, and the dark eyed mistress, the reader is entitled to ask – What is it that drives orthodox opinion to adopt such defiant opposition? The answer is disturbing. It is the universities and their system of engagement. Embedded within university departments are those appointed to positions of authority because they have followed the paradigm pursued by the board who engaged them. Anyone seeking a career in literary studies at a higher level, but with ideas of promoting an alternative to Shakespeare, will need to look elsewhere to further their ambitions. The strength of the paradigm is continually being reinforced by the system of 'embedding'; that is, engaging staff with a safe pair of hands, who can be relied upon to maintain the status quo. There is also a monetary aspect to this. Funding for research into Shakespeare is likely to be viewed favourably, whereas funding for research into an alternative author would almost certainly be rejected. Money from the funding agencies is therefore an incentive to suppressing the truth, and not only in literary departments. Embedding staff, for the sake of funding, as well as preserving an established paradigm, also occurs in the sciences. The effect of this is that media outlets, which rely upon the universities for authoritative statements to relay to the general public, are confined to publishing, as reliable, that which has been passed on to them by an embedded professorship that is unwilling to say anything that could be construed as a contradiction to their own priorities.

Let us take a critical look at this embedded professorship, and see the driving force behind it. It was Dr Lee Smolin who analysed the manner in which the system operates. Firstly, it requires tremendous self-confidence, accompanied by a sense of entitlement, and that of belonging to an elite community of experts. Secondly, those affected will see themselves as part of a monolithic community, with a strong sense of consensus, whether based upon evidence or not, and with a uniformity of views regarding open questions. These views are often related to the existence of a hierarchical structure in which the ideas of a few leaders have dictated that viewpoint. Thirdly, this group perceives a strong boundary existing between their own experts and those proposing alternatives. Fourthly, they disregard and treat with disinterest the ideas, opinions, and work of other experts who are not part of their group. Also, they prefer to discuss questions only with members of their community. Fifthly, they have a tendency to interpret evidence optimistically, and to believe exaggerated or incorrect statements, and never to allow these to endanger the commitment they have to how they view Shakespeare and his work. This often leads to an acceptance that evidence is true because it is widely believed to be true. One might also add to this a seventh driving force: it is that some approach Shakespeare in a manner similar to that of a religious faith, where the subject matter is beyond doubt, and research into Shakespeare's existence as a poet and author must never be pursued in any direction that would risk dethroning him.

Irving Janis, a psychologist at Yale, studied these attitudes in the 1970s and described them as *"goupthink"*. It is, he wrote: *"a mode of thinking that people engage in when they are deeply involved in a cohesive in-group, when the members' striving for unanimity override their motivation to realistically appraise alternative courses of action."*[2]

In recent times, *groupthink* has been held responsible for not preventing the *Challenger* disaster; for failing to foresee the collapse of the USSR; and for not anticipating the consequences of going to war in Iraq and Afghanistan. To this we may add a failing to comprehend the strength of the Oxford argument.

Where does this leave those who welcome any proposals that accord with the truth about Shakespeare's authorship? The answer, it would seem, is still very much on the defensive. The power of groupthink acts like a censorship to opposing views. It also has a readily available public stage on which to pontificate to the media, as well as an open door to the major publishing houses: both of which can be put to excellent use for the dissemination of pejorative opinions concerning alternatives to those held by the *groupthink* community.

A revolution in the way we think about what we are told to believe is required. And this must be accompanied by awareness that when an opinion is widely publicised, based upon money funded for research, the opinion received is bound to be biased in favour of the reasons given for that funding. Most times this is justified. Sometimes it is not. In the end, it is for the reader to weigh the balance, and to make personally sure, as far as possible, that the scales have not been previously weighted to obtain a desired result.

Provided that independent investigation shows an answer to be unique, and to have been reached by valid means, we shall accept it, however much we shock the learned world by doing so.

William F. Friedman &
Elizebeth S. Friedman

1

THE MONUMENTAL TRUTH

'Tis not the many oaths that make the truth,
But the plain single vow that is vow'd true.

All's Well That Ends Well

THE MONUMENT ERECTED in memory of William Shakespeare, emplaced upon the chancel wall inside the Holy Trinity Church at Stratford-upon-Avon, is one of the most frequently cited pieces of evidence given in support of the town's former resident having been England's greatest writer. Professor Alan Nelson, a prominent member of the Stratford orthodoxy, and an active contributor to conferences related to the authorship question, is unwavering in his attitude towards dissenting voices:

> *Let us quickly review the documentary evidence that William Shakespeare wrote the plays traditionally assigned to him. In the First Folio of 1623, Ben Jonson famously calls the playwright 'Sweet Swan of Avon', while Leonard Digges ... names 'thy Stratford Monument'.* [1]

The First Folio, and Sweet Swan of Avon are the subject matter of separate chapters, and need not be of present concern. It is the Stratford monument that is the subject of this chapter, and the facts surrounding it are not viewed logically, either by Nelson or those inclined to follow his opinion. With a mindset that can only be compared to that of the medieval priesthood, insisting upon the genuineness of Holy relics, Nelson is not alone in declaring the present monument to have *"survived unchanged from the original except for its surface paint,"* (ibid.). After four centuries of wear, the structure is, to his mind, still immune from decay, unaffected by the elements, and unchanged through neglect. Historically, the facts tell a different story.

A Concise History of the Stratford Monument

Documentary evidence, combined with a basic knowledge of material science, unite in concluding that the statuary has been submitted to wear and tear across several centuries. To suppose it had emerged into the present day, unscathed by the ravages of time almost four hundred years after its emplacement is absurd.

To begin with, little regard was given to the monument in the years following its emplacement. The Reverend Thomas Wilson was vicar at that time and he remained in office until c.1640. But in 1635, following a visit from Archbishop Laud's Vicar-General, he was suspended from office for three months. Included amongst his demeanours were: *"That he allowed his maids to dry linen in the chapel, his fowls to roost, his pigs and dogs to couch there, and his children to play at ball and other sports."*[2]

At a later date, the residents at Stratford were to suffer occupation from the Parliamentary army during the English Civil War. Churches were regularly used as barracks, and this would explain the subsequent claims for damages made in 1645. E.g. *"In 1691 the Chancel was repaired, the contributors being chiefly the descendents of those who had monuments of their ancestors there."*[3] However, there is no record of any contribution made towards this end by Shakespeare's Warwickshire descendants.

By the middle of the 18th century, years of neglect had taken their toll. A band of players visiting Stratford in 1746 observed how much the monument had decayed. Led by John Ward, the group decided to play *Othello*, directing that the proceeds be: *"Solely Appropriated to the Repairing [of] the Original Monument".*[4] The playbill advertising the performance explained the reason:

> *And as the Curious Original Monument and Bust of that incomparable Poet, erected above the Tomb that enshrines his Dust, in the Church of Stratford upon Avon Warwickshire, is through length of Years and other accidents become much impair'd and decay'd.*[5]

Had this 'decay'd' state and 'other accidents' been untrue, the residents of Stratford would have been aware of Ward's inaccuracy. Instead, John Hall, a visitor to the town, was engaged to carry out the repair work, *"and (provided he takes care, according to his ability, that the monument shall become as like as possible to what it was, when first erected) that the money already raised shall be forthwith paid him upon finishing the work."*[6]

John Britton, F.S.A., was another person who has left record of his interest in the monument. In 1849 he recalled that:

> *In Dec. 1814 I incited Mr. George Bullock to make a cast of the monumental bust. ... He was much alarmed on taking down the Effigy to find it to be in a decayed and dangerous state, and declared it would be risking its destruction to remove it again.*[7]

As a result of mounting alarm at the monument's precarious decay, Britton was made honorary secretary of a Society engaged to oversee its restoration. A public subscription was raised. Money soon arrived. *"The King subscribed £50, the Borough of Stratford the same. Many sent their subscriptions 'only for the restoration and preservation of the Monument'."*[8] At its close, the total raised was £5,000 (≈£525,000 in 2010 – Bank of England inflation calculator). But, *"The cost of restoring both the Shakespeare Monument and the Chancel"* was estimated to be only £1,210. 12s. (≈£127,000).

Britton had already referred to the original monument as, *"a small and comparatively trifling tomb ... [that] failed to attract anything like critical or literary notice."*[9] What emerged from this surplus of available funding is now described as a fine . . .

> *polychrome sculptured monument set on the chancel's north wall, within a few feet of his grave. Set against a background of white marble, with black marble Corinthian columns, and black touchstone panels, surmounted by the earliest surviving example of usage of the Shakespeare arms, appears a painted bust of Shakespeare, made of Cotswold limestone.*[10]

> *Modern experts have closely examined the bust which is made from one block of stone, and find no evidence that it has ever been substantially repaired . . . those who dispute the authenticity of the Shakespeare memorial at Stratford are either misguided or simply out to make mischief.*[11]

Disregarding this ignorant admonishment, which ignores the obvious fact that it is the replacement, not the original that has avoided repair: the original having long since crumbled away, those viewing each version of the monument for the first time, and having received only an elementary introduction to William Shakespeare, may be surprised to observe that the effigy which first appeared did not depict Shakespeare in a scholarly pose.

Many present-day scholars are also surprised by this and rarely advertise their confusion. When they do acknowledge it, it is to claim that either the sculptor or the artist must have made a mistake. Yet, conversely, and far more evidentially . . .

"Dr Whitaker has told us that Dugdale's 'scrupulous accuracy united with stubborn integrity' has elevated his Antiquities of Warwickshire 'to the rank of legal evidence.'"[12]

The Encyclopaedia Britannica (1973) took a similar view:

Sir William Dugdale ... one of the most distinguished antiquaries ... was a pioneer in the technique of historical research and his works display an accuracy and insight of unusual order for this period.

Professor Samuel Schoenbaum, formerly the foremost authority on all matters Shakespearian, did not agree with either of the above reports. In *Shakespeare's Lives* (1970), he stated . . .

As represented in (Dugdale's) engraving the monument differs strikingly from the artefact we know ... The best and simplest explanation is that this illustration, like others in the ('Antiquaries'), misrepresents the object, in keeping with the freedom exercised by seventeenth century engravers.[13]

Schoenbaum, despite the aura of infallibility surrounding his reputation, was wrong on two counts. The original pen sketch drawn by Sir William Dugdale in 1634 still exists as a family heirloom, and it shows in detail the monument with all its most important features to be exactly as it later appeared on Wenceslaus Hollar's engraving.

Schoenbaum's second blunder was the attempt he made to include the Stratford monument amongst the few errors that do occur on a small number of illustrations in Dugdale's book. These, notably, Schoenbaum did not blame the engraver for: as he did when referring to the Stratford monument; and for which he blamed Dugdale's artwork.

It was the Shakespearian scholar Francis Carr, who looked more deeply into the question of Dugdale's competence: he concluded: *"where inaccuracies occur in Dugdale's books, the drawings were supplied by the families concerned, and were not drawn by Dugdale himself."*[14]

For example, the Carew Clopton monument, although frequently cited as Dugdale's failure to copy precisely what was before him (there being differences between this monument and its engraving), was not of his hand. His sketchbook contains no drawing of the Carew Clopton artefact. It was the deceased's family who had sent the illustration that Dugdale used for his book, and which he accepted on trust. The only sketches which Dugdale was responsible for were those he drew in the absence of any sent by the families invited to submit their own. Those he drew are sufficiently accurate representations of what he saw.

Schoenbaum's impotent protest apart: in later years the monument's appearance was reaffirmed, independently, by the following personages: Thomas Betterton, the foremost actor of his day and a man distinguished for his integrity; Nicholas Rowe, a barrister who subsequently became England's poet laureate; the Reverend William Thomas, doctor of divinity and rector of St. Nicholas, Worcester, and Sir Thomas Hanmer, who included a copy in his 1744 edition of Shakespeare. All five had the opportunity to question the more *"curious"* details of the original monument for themselves, before publishing and republishing its likeness in the years that followed. The Reverend Thomas actually said he *"visited all the churches"* prior to editing his reprint of Dugdale's *Antiquities* (Title page, ix). Moreover, while the original monument stood, no one ever came forward to openly refute these illustrations. The protests only began to gather force after its neglected state precipitated its replacement by a new monument that was markedly dissimilar; 'Shakespeare' had been given a face-lift, a cushion, and a quill and paper.

It is in this respect that we now consider the drawing made by George Vertue in 1723, which he completed for Alexander Pope's edition of Shakespeare's plays. His engraving, which appeared two years later, bespeaks the frustration he must have experienced at observing the decaying remnants that Rowe had faithfully reproduced in his edition of Shakespeare's plays sixteen years earlier, and which Hanmer would himself repeat nineteen years later when compiling his own edition of the Shakespeare canon. Sandwiched between these two editions, and in obvious protest, Vertue designed his own ideal monument.

> *George Vertue was enchanted by the Chandos portrait and when he was commissioned to provide a drawing of the Stratford monument for Pope, he took the liberty of substituting the Chandos head for the one on the monument. ... in every other respect, Vertue's illustration depicts the monument we see today. Its columns are not, as in Dugdale, topped by lions' heads; the putti of Labor and Rest sit comfortably on the top of the monument rather than balanced precariously on it edge. Most of all, except for its face, the figure too is the same, one hand holding a pen, the other resting on a sheet of paper.*[15]

Despite this glowing attribute, the reality is different. Vertue did not visit Stratford-upon-Avon to see the monument (Stopes, 1918, p.110), but used Rowe's engraving, which he liberally embellished with his own ideas as to how he thought it should look. So well did he succeed, that its architecture, referred to above, became the *blueprint* for the monument that replaced the original in 1814. By then, it had become so dangerously fragile that to even remove it would *"threaten its destruction"*.

Vertue's illustration, showing the figure holding a quill and paper was in all likelihood drawn from the memory he held of a similar monument inside the Tudor church of St. Andrew Undershaft in the City of London. This still shows the historian John Stow (1525–1605) at his desk, with quill in hand, penning his *Survey of London*, (1598). [*"The quill is replaced at regular intervals to affirm that the surveying of London is a continuous task."*]

Vertue adopted a similar stance for his picture of the monument, endowing the figure with pen and paper, like that of Stow, and inclining the bust at a slight angle. He replaced the sack with a flat cushion. Then, to achieve some consistency with Shakespeare's features, he removed the figure's head, replacing it with one similar to that shown on the Chandos portrait.

Note how much the statuary has changed. The cherubs are no longer left perched on the edge at the top, with their legs dangling in space, but have been moved to safer ground, where they now sit alongside the central edifice bearing the family coat-of-arms. Particularly observe how the curvature of the arch above the figure's head has also been altered. This differs from the original. Both these points alone are evidence that the modern monument is a reconstruction based upon the idealised engraving made by Vertue in the previous century. Then there are the two side columns: originally, these were inset away from the edge of the monument. But now, as with Vertue's drawing, they define the actual sides of the structure.

The £5000 raised by the Stratford Society for the restoration of the monument and refurbishment of the chancel appears to have been put to good use. The evidence that a completely new monument replaced the old dilapidated one is unavoidable. And with almost £400,000 by current reckoning available, what alternative existed? Previous representations of the monument, made independently by, or for, Dugdale, Rowe, Hanmer, and Grignion, are essentially identical in their design, and together form a consensus regarding its original appearance. Yet, it was Vertue's idealised version that was selected as a replacement. Presumably, members of the Stratford Society found it convenient to reject the other engravings for reasons very similar to those proposed today, even though the committee members must have been perfectly aware of the monument's original appearance, having once witnessed its dilapidated state for themselves. For this, after all, had been the reason for raising subscriptions.

Also, from the evidence now available, it must have been the decision to rebuild the monument that encouraged members of the Stratford Society to withhold announcing, publicly, that the replacement was a new sculpture modelled upon the drawing made by Vertue, and was therefore not a true copy of the one it replaced. This was not, strictly speaking, what the money had been donated for, hence the need for silence to avoid a possible outcry.

In a very real sense, the actions of the Stratford Society differ very little from the forgeries perpetrated by John Payne Collier. Here was a scholar, dismayed to find that evidence for Shakespeare's authorship was either absent or of the wrong sort. His preferred solution was to provide it himself, or else alter it, so as to make it agree with his idea of how Shakespeare was to be understood, which is also what has happened with the bust on the present monument.

There are also other observable discrepancies in design, once attention has been drawn to them. For example, the nineteenth-century sculptor has neglected the doleful, cadaverous face of the original figure in order to give it a younger appearance. The cheeks have been puffed out, and the moustache ends turned up to give the image a merry, self-satisfied countenance.

This divergence from the original has not gone unremarked. With the addition of quill and paper, and a cushion replacing the sack, arguments suggesting it has been altered have never been far away. It has also resulted in some 'scholars' defending their idol with the quite preposterous proposal that apart from a lick of paint, it has never been repaired.

Nonetheless, the present effigy is without the least doubt a replacement of the original: to believe otherwise carries the implication that members of the monument's preservation society embezzled the King's money, as well as that donated "*solely*" for the restoration of the *"original monument.* And since a harder wearing stone was used for this new construction, there are no longer signs that any major repair work has ever been necessary.

Even so, one can already hear Shakespeare's Stratford advocates insisting that the present-day monument is the same one that Vertue sketched in 1723. In which case, it must have been done clairvoyantly, since Vertue made the drawing without having visited Stratford to see it in person. As for it being a replacement, after almost four centuries of neglect, bar John Hall beautifying it in 1748, some will affirm the monument is original, and remains as good as new. Will they also explain what happened to the £5000 and why a committee was convened to raise money for the monument's restoration, if the one existing was unmarked?

The Monument Reveals its Secret

Let us now look at the words on the monument and ask: Why does the inscription occupy valuable space (two and a half lines

IVDICIO PYLIVM, GENIO SOCRATEM, ARTE MARONEM,
TERRA TEGIT, POPVLVS MÆRET, OLYMPVS HABET

STAY PASSENGER, WHY GOEST THOV BY SO FAST?
READ IF THOV CANST, WHOM ENVIOVS DEATH HATH PLAST,
WITH IN THIS MONVMENT SHAKSPEARE: WITH WHOME,
QVICK NATVRE DIDE: WHOSE NAME DOTH DECK Y TOMBE,
FAR MORE, THEN COST: SIEH ALL, Y HE HATH WRITT,
LEAVES LIVING ART, BVT PAGE, TO SERVE HIS WITT.

OBIIT AÑO DO[I] 1616
ÆTATIS 53 DIE 23 AP.

from a total of six) in order to issue a challenge to each passer-by, when these same lines would be better employed by providing biographical details of the subject? Could something have been written into the inscription, which those having regard for it are invited to discover? This is by no means unreasonable. The age of Shakespeare was particularly noted for its addiction to codes, puzzles, and the like.

Authority for the prevalence of coded writing among Shakespeare's contemporaries comes from Christian humanist writers of the time, for whom civilised literature was coded by its very nature, and from the many allusions by Elizabethan poets and dramatists to the way they exploited this allegorical tradition ... to dodge political censorship.[16]

If the inscription does contain a code, its existence may be indicated by the presence of irregularities in the text. The discovery of any obvious inconsistencies in the way that the words are presented could be a possible sign that the text has been deliberately manipulated in order to conceal a secret. Careful examination of the monument's inscription reveals the presence of seven unnecessary deviations in the lettering.

- WHOM in line 2 is spelt differently to WHOME in line 3.
- THIS in line 3 is written in full, but in line 4 it is abbreviated to Y^{S}.
- THAT is abbreviated to Y^{T} in line 5.
- The words, SHAKSPEARE MONVMENT, have been inverted in line 3 to read, MONVMENT SHAKSPEARE.
- The name SHAKESPEARE has been spelt SHAKSPEARE.
- The German word, SIEH, has been used in line 5 instead of SEE.
- WRITT has been completed with an additional T.

The misspelling of words, the use of variants or archaic forms, and an occasional abbreviation: each one of these constitutes a sign that a piece of text may have been deliberately tampered with in order to conceal an encrypted message. But with so many occurring together, as they do above, suspicions beg indulgence.

The reason for changing words in a piece of text is one of necessity. That is to say, words that conceal a hidden meaning need to be tailored to accommodate the encrypted phrase or sentence, and, ideally, without attracting suspicion. This presents a difficulty that is only overcome by the word-power and the ingenuity of the encoder. Sometimes this entails certain liberties being taken with the cipher-text: a fact recognised where decryption processes are studied. As David Kahn, an authority on the history of cryptology, aptly noted in his reference to ELS encryptions (Equidistant Letter Sequencing is the method of encoding a secret by embedding it within a piece of text, referred to as cipher-text, so that each letter of each word is an equal distance apart):

> *... the method's chief defect, of course, is that awkwardness in phrasing may betray the very secret that that phrasing should guard: the existence of a hidden message.* [17]

What Kahn has correctly pointed out is very much apparent within the wording of the inscription. It indicates that an encrypted message may possibly be concealed within the sixaine. A further hint that this indication is likely to be correct can be inferred from the information—or lack of it—that actually appears within the three couplets comprising the inscription. As the late Charlton Ogburn observed: *"the Stratford monument, though wordy, cites no biographical fact about the deceased whatever."* [18]

Consequently, in line with what has been said concerning an encrypted message inside a piece of text: and as there are clear signals that this may have actually occurred, the next task is to discover what that secret is. The most appropriate method for exploring an ELS encryption without the aid of a computer is to number the letters in the inscription, and then search among them for Arithmetical Progressions. If any exist—the criteria being that the letters represented by numbers form phrases or sentences with a connection to Shakespeare—then whatever is revealed must stand as evidence that an encryption has been uncovered, and its content is genuine.

Once a table of numbers has been constructed beneath the letters of the alphabet (see appendix B) a simple technique for discovering hidden words from the assembled numbers is straightforward. It simply requires the choice of a *probable word.* The probable word is an important aid in code breaking, and once one has been identified, it acts as a crib, enabling the rest of the message to be decrypted *viz:*

> *Once ... the code breaker has a crib: a word or piece of text that they know is already repeated somewhere in the encrypted message ... the code breaker can then search for patterns that relate to it.* [19]

The paragraphs that now follow are based upon this method and represent a rigorous and scientifically valid approach to solving a problem in cryptology. As Eric Sams remarked: *"cryptanalysis, that is, the methodical application of techniques which permit decipherment without the key ... has become first mechanized and then computerized ... But far simpler methods can yield effective and even impressive results." (Cryptanalysis and Historical Research – Archivaria 21*, Winter 1985-86 p.87).

Let it therefore be assumed that 'Bacon' is the crib, and two alternate letters are chosen, such as the first and third, that is, 'B' and 'C'. Then, by adding each number in the 'B' column to each number in the 'C' column (see table: Appendix B), and dividing each sum by 2, a search can be conducted to see if the result appears in the 'A' column. If it does, then BAC suggests it may respond to an ELS decipherment of Bacon. For when a successful outcome is registered, the possibility of an extension to the sequence is indicated; thus requiring further inspection.

Because the monument has challenged passers-by to read if they can, who has been placed within it, the probable word is likely to be a name. Historically, the first name to test is the one chosen above, Francis Bacon. For more than a century he was thought by some to have been Shakespeare, and his name responds easily to this test, since there are only three 'Bs' and four 'Cs' available on the table. Hence:

$\frac{1}{2}(26_B + 44_C) \neq 35_A$; $\frac{1}{2}(26_B + 114_C) \neq 70_A$;
$\frac{1}{2}(148_B + 44_C) \neq 96_A$; $\frac{1}{2}(148_B + 114_C) \neq 131_A$;
$\frac{1}{2}(200_B + 44_C) \neq 122_A$; $\frac{1}{2}(200_B + 114_C) \neq 157_A$.

This proof by exhaustion eliminates the possibility that the name Bacon has been encrypted into the inscription using an ELS cipher.

The same test can also be applied to another candidate for Shakespeare's crown, Christopher Marlowe. This time, using 'L' and 'W': $\frac{1}{2}(X_L + Y_W) = Z_O$, produces just a single possibility $\frac{1}{2}(70_L + 14_W) = 42_O$. The numbers taken from this equation, 70_L 42_O 14_W reveal an ELS of 28 letters (Mar·L·O·W·e in reverse). This implies that E = 14 – 28 = –14. But negative numbers do not appear on the table, and further considerations of Marlowe's name having been encrypted by the ELS method are soon abandoned. Alternative ways of spelling Marlowe's name likewise fail to satisfy the ELS test.

The next probable name to be tested is that of Edward de Vere. In recent times a very strong case has been advanced for his authorship of Shakespeare's work. Moreover, as 17th Earl of Oxford and Lord High Chamberlain of England, there were valid reasons, according to the mores of Elizabethan society, for concealing his identity as a playwright: the more so, had he been active in writing for public entertainment. Consequently, by using the formula: $\frac{1}{2}(X_E + Y_E) = Z_R$, six possibilities occur.

$\frac{1}{2}(98_E + 206_E) = 152_R$; $\frac{1}{2}(110_E + 130_E) = 120_R$;
$\frac{1}{2}(121_E + 189_E) = 155_R$; $\frac{1}{2}(149_E + 213_E) = 181_R$;
$\frac{1}{2}(156_E + 206_E) = 181_R$; $\frac{1}{2}(186_E + 210_E) = 198_R$.

Taken in the order they occur, the first has a sequence of 54. This implies 'V' is either 260 or 44, since the name can be read in either direction. But numbers above 220 are impossible, and 44 does not occur under 'V', thus the sequence truncates at both ends. Similar truncations are found in all but one of the remaining five cases. $\frac{1}{2}(121_E + 189_E) = 155_R$ is the one outstanding, and it reveals a sequence of 34, from which 121 – 34 = 87. And since 87 is found under 'V', an ELS of 34 completes the name V E R E in ascending, numerical order (87, 121, 155, 189). We have therefore found a possible crib.

To test its validity, the next stage is to construct a grid of 34 columns, and thereafter examine each column for phrases or sentences that may have meaning in connection with de Vere and Shakespeare.

When this has been completed, the result revealed by this Equidistant Letter Sequencing of 34, is undeniably explicit: as are the initials, I. B. These belong to the person who was apparently responsible for guaranteeing the truth of the encoded statement. It is especially noteworthy that these initials have also been placed next to 'ME', (a pronoun that *"refers to the speaker or writer;" Collins English Dictionary*), and that ME and IB in the plain-text (the cipher solution) are positioned together so as to adjoin the word NAME in the cipher-text (the text containing the cipher). To have achieved this level of positioning is normally the mark of an accomplished and knowledgeable cryptographer. It was also common in that era to undersign one's self as *me* followed by the writer's name, or in this instance, initials. Shakespeare's will provides a good example of this, since it closes with a similar assertion: *"By me William Shakspeare"*.

It was Ben Jonson who habitually identified himself by using the Latin alphabet in which 'I' is used instead of the non-existent 'J' (compare his initials in the First Folio). Importantly, too, since the message is vertical, it implies that it should be read from top to bottom, according to the numerical order of each row. This is because, starting with the first row, and finishing in the last row, is quite the simplest way of inserting the encryption into the cipher-text. Furthermore, since the plain-text appears in clusters, these should be read one at a time, from left to right; for once again, this would have been the manner in which the encoder completed his enciphered message. When these simple instructions are followed, the ELS encryption reveals: –

SO TEST HIM, I VOW HE IS E DE VERE

AS HE, SHAKSPEARE: ME I. B.

S	T	A	Y	P	A	S	S	E	N	G	E	R	W	H	Y	G	O	E	S	T	T	H	O	V	B	Y	S	O	F	A	S	T	R
E	A	D	I	F	T	H	O	V	C	A	N	S	T	W	H	O	M	E	N	V	I	O	V	S	D	E	A	T	H	H	A	T	H
P	L	A	S	T	W	I	T	H	I	N	T	H	I	S	M	O	N	V	M	E	N	T	S	H	A	K	S	P	E	A	R	E	W
I	T	H	W	H	O	M	E	Q	V	I	C	K	N	A	T	V	R	E	D	I	D	E	W	H	O	S	E	N	A	M	E	D	O
T	H	D	E	C	K	Y	S	T	O	M	B	E	F	A	R	M	O	R	E	T	H	E	N	C	O	S	T	S	I	E	H	A	L
L	Y	T	H	E	H	A	T	H	W	K	I	T	T	L	E	A	V	E	S	L	I	V	I	N	G	A	R	T	B	V	T	P	A
G	E	T	O	S	E	R	V	E	H	I	S	W	I	T	T																		

What you now see above is an excellent example of a sixteenth century Cardano grille. *"This code was invented by an Italian doctor and mathematician called Girolamo Cardano in 1550 and is known as a Cardano grille."* [20]

To understand more fully how this type of encoding works, as in the present case, with an ELS of 34, imagine the wording on the inscription is written out as a single string of 220 letters. The 8th letter is 'S', therefore the 42nd letter must be an 'O' and the 76th letter a 'T'. By continuing to count to 34 each time, the remaining letters of the word, 'E', 'S', and 'T' also occur. The total number of letters in the cipher-text determines the number of rows available and the ELS used; in this case, 220 divided by 34 equals 6 · 47: requiring 7 rows. The encoder always has complete freedom to start at any letter, but once chosen, that freedom ends, and the encoder must ensure that after 33 spaces the 34th letter is the one that continues with the word being encrypted. However, if too much freedom is employed at the commencement of each new word, then the result will be dispersed across the resulting grille, inviting doubt concerning its genuineness.

To overcome this, the encoder must seek to cluster the words of the plain-text together. This can be achieved by using clock arithmetic. Each time the hands of a clock complete a full circle, counting begins again. In the present case, the encryption began with the 8th letter, and the second set of encryptions began with 'H', the 41st letter. But using clock arithmetic with an ELS of 34, 41 becomes 7, and 7 is next to 8, which began the first run of encryptions, thus producing a clustering effect. When completed, the 220 letters can be placed one-by-one onto a 34-column grille.

From this it can be seen that the 8th letter occurs vertically above the 42nd, which occurs vertically above the 76th, and so on down to row 7. The end result is a grille with three vertically aligned clusters, each in numerical order: the first run commencing at [8] **So Test** [41] **Him** [78] **I Vow** [179] **He** [182] **Is**; the second run beginning at [53] **E Vere** [122] **de**, and the third starting at [62] **As** [64] **He** [92] **Shakspeare** [133] **Me** [166] **I B.**

Even so, Jonson was not averse to commencing a sentence with a subordinate word or phrase: as when the plain-text is read from left to right. Examples of this can be found easily enough in his plays; e.g., *"From the bordello, it might come as well;"* (*Every Man In His Humour*, Act 1: sc. ii. 82). Or, *"The Doctor, he shall hear of him at Westchester;"* (*The Alchemist*, Act 5: sc. v. 121).

Those inclined to protest at Jonson's grammar, whether in the plays or the plain-text, should first be aware that the monument's inscription, with its deliberate inversion of MONVMENT SHAKSPEARE and its inexplicable inclusion of the German imperative, SIEH, pose questions of far greater significance and importance.

The medium for this encryption has been the three iambic pentameter rhyming couplets that form the cipher-text. Attention was previously drawn to the anomalies in its composition, and the failure to define its subject, as would normally be expected for the memory of so illustrious a writer. This is precisely the weakness pointed out by Kahn, when seeking a suitable cipher-text capable of accommodating letters at equal intervals, so that when joined together, they divulge the hidden message. Nevertheless, the achievement of the encoder in having had to constantly refer back and make suitable amendments to the poetic content of the inscription he was composing, so as to ensure that each letter was set in place at precisely the correct interval, has withstood almost four centuries of scrutiny; this, despite the visible use of several verbal tricks to engineer the secret concealed.

This type of encryption unfortunately produces the side effect known as 'background chatter'; these are the occasional words that are formed coincidentally outside the clusters that produce the main message. Observe how 'tin' and 'go' occur between the first two clusters, and 'tin' and 'hot' between the second and third cluster. Isolated, randomly occurring words like these help to disguise the fact that an encryption exists. They are also rightly ignored by the professional cryptanalyst because they are not part of a cluster, and they contribute nothing to the syntax within the clusters that do exist.

Apart from the clustering effect of the message revealed in the plain-text, there are several other signs that point to the existence of an encryption. MONVMENT SHAKSPEARE in the middle of the third line, as remarked above, is unnatural. The encoder has deliberately transposed these words so that SHAKSPEARE, minus the middle letter 'E', will interlock with AS and HE to produce the subordinate clause: AS HE SHAKSPEARE.

The second giveaway is the use of SIEH: a German verb in the middle of an English inscription. This does, however, ensure that the letters, 'I' and 'E', required for ME B.I., are present, and that they fall into place below NAMED. This doubly authenticates the truth of what the encoder has said, for the initials are instantly recognisable as those belonging to Ben Ionson, who often began his surname with 'I'. *

If Ben Jonson vowed that Edward de Vere was Shakespeare, and he should be tested to prove it, then the authorship controversy is at an end. All that remains is a revised view of the history surrounding de Vere, and a reinterpretation of the evidence allegedly given in support of Shakespeare's authorship. The purpose of this book, as will be seen from the chapters that follow, is to take the first step towards achieving that goal.

---

* An inspection of 41 grilles (10 – 50 columns) reveals that AS HE interlocks with SHAKSPEARE only twice: on this 34-column grille and one other. ME adjoining the initials B I, occurs only once; i.e., on this 34-column grille.

However, before commencing this task, there is still more to be gleaned from the grille.

> *Grilles of the kind just described and especially the question of the number of different grilles that can be made with a fixed number of squares, have been the subject of detailed study, first by C. F. Hindenburg [Archiv der reinen und angewandlen Mathematik, Heft III and Heft V (1796)] and later by M. de Prasse [De reticules cryptographics, Leipzig, 1799]. J. H. Klueber, in his Kryptogrphik [Tuebingen, 1809; p.195-225] gives De Prasse's calculations with observations of his own. F. von Wostrowitz, in his Handbuch der Kryptograhie (Vienna, 1881), and General Luigi Sacco, in his Manuale di Crittografia (2nd edition, Rome, 1936), are outstanding writers on the grille among modern cryptographers.*[21]

The inscription on the Stratford monument, which has been composed in what is called cipher-text, sits potently beneath the bust of the man assumed to be William Shakespeare, the supposed literary genius of Elizabethan England. The plain-text (the encrypted statement), insists instead that Edward de Vere must be tested for that honour, and this directive may actually be linked to a similar one inserted by B. I. accompanying the Droeshout's engraving of Shakespeare at the front of the First Folio: *"Reader, looke Not on his Picture, but his Booke."*

The two commands are unlikely to be coincidental, since both the Stratford monument and the First Folio made their first appearance within the same brief timeframe of 1623, and both are initialled by B. I.

Let us therefore look again at the grille and its decoded message. A Cardano grille can be read in two separate ways. If the person sending the encrypted message knows the receiver, then the receiver can be issued with a template covering the cipher-text, with suitable openings that reveal what has been encrypted. If the sender does not know who the receiver will be, as in the present case, the message must conform to an equidistant letter cipher, based upon a mathematical rule. For example:

> *To decipher a message [of this type], the recipient must either have a grille identical to the sender's, or must know the spacing rule that created it, if it conforms to a rule. An equidistant letter cipher ... is the equivalent of a 'simple' Cardano Grille. Note that although the rule is simple, the encryption process is more difficult since the encoder must*

devise a sensible-sounding message that accommodates encrypted letters at fixed positions: for a complex message, an exceedingly challenging problem in combinatorics.[22]

Significantly, the choice of a Cardano grille for concealing information was, at the time, entirely modern, and *"a number of countries made use of the Cardano grille in their diplomatic correspondence in the 1500s and 1600s."*[23] By 1623, it had become so popular that Cardinal Richelieu, newly established in the French court, is reputed to have preferred it for his more sensitive communications. In fact, even as late as the twentieth century, during World War II, similar devices to the grille were still in use. (S. Pincock & M. Frary: *The Code Breaker The History of Secret Communication*, London, 2007, p. 69).

The grille has had a considerable vogue in cryptography. Cardan's method is not limited to the insertion of whole words in the slits, as the usual descriptions of it would indicate, but inserts units of different size, varying from a single letter to a whole word or parts of different words. The development of the system has been, however, in the direction of slits to admit a single letter only.[24]

Slits, as we have said, would not have served the encoder's purpose, because it would require a future decoder to possess a template composed of identical slits. The logical alternative had to be Equidistant Letter Sequencing, which has the same effect, but with letters occurring in strict mathematical order, thereby opening it up to decipherment by anyone discovering the key, in this instance, 34. *

Insufficient space exists on the grille for the name E. DE VERE to appear vertically; hence DE has been placed adjacent to VERE.

* Following publication of the First Edition of this book, it was pointed out that although the Key to the Cardano grille had been discovered by the application of a mathematical algorithm, it should, nevertheless, be subject to a more immediate means of discovery. Even before this point had been made, Dr Bruce Spittle wrote to notify me that the Key could be found in Jonson's Latin distich, which occurs immediately above the six lines of cipher-text. This line, he said, is the only one on the inscription that has been inset. It also leads immediately onto the cipher-text, and consists of 34 letters. As Dr Spittle had discovered, this sentence would normally contain 35 letters, but through the use of a digraph in the word MÆRET, the count is reduced to 34: the exact number required for the construction of the 34-column Cardano grille, which reveals in plain-text, the identity of William Shakespeare.

According to the professional cryptologists, William F. and Elizebeth S. Friedman, simple adjustments to the plain-text are allowable so long as they are kept to an absolute minimum.

> *[A] temptation presents itself, which the professional cryptologist rgards as the great betrayal: exceptions are made to the rules, and these permit the 'right' kind of message to be extracted. This tactic is acceptable to the professional cryptologist only if the exceptions do not exceed a certain maximum.* [25]

William F. Friedman was renowned for his code-breaking ability during the Second World War, having led the team that broke Japan's Purple Code. He also continues to be a posthumous voice in the Shakespeare authorship debate, having set the ground rules for a decryption to be declared valid.

With the Cardano grille and its plain-text before us, we can now refer to the anomalies in the cipher-text bulleted above, and observe how each one has been instrumental in making a vital contribution to the formation of Jonson's declaration.

The additional E added to WHOME has provided the E in the word TEST.

The change of the word THIS to its abbreviated form Y^S has provided the S in the word TEST.

The abbreviation Y^T has ensured the letters T, H, W, and I, each fall into their correct position.

The transposition of SHAKSPEARE MONVMENT has provided the V in VERE,

By omitting E from SHAK(E)SPEARE, the letters, S and E correctly align with S and E in AS HE.

The I E in SIEH provides an I for the initial of Ionson's surname, and an E for the word ME.

By adding an extra T to WRIT(T), the final E in VERE and the initial B for Jonson's first name fall into position.

Each of these deviations from the norm has added some form of input to the final form of Jonson's avowal, thus insuring the words appropriate to his declaration are correctly aligned, while also avoiding the charge that the plain-text has been 'cherry-picked' for effect. Notably, an ELS of 34 is significant: its prime factors being 2 and 17. 2 is inconsequential, since it is the factor of all even numbers, but the number of de Vere's earldom was 17. An ELS of 34 is therefore appropriate for a Cardano grille involving the 17th Earl of Oxford.

Friedman's advice for a suspected decryption was sound.

This may be a good place to point out that a valid or authentic cryptanalytic solution cannot be considered as being merely what the cryptanalyst thinks or says he thinks the cryptogram means, nor does the solution represent an opinion of the cryptanalyst. Solutions are valid only insofar as they are objective and susceptible of demonstration or proof employing scientifically acceptable methods or procedures. ... namely, observation, hypothesis, deduction, induction, and confirmatory experiment.[26]

David Kahn, former editor of *Cryptologia*: a journal specialising in the secret science of cryptography, subsequently endorsed these requirements in *The Codebreakers The Story of Secret Writing*. In a passage specifically aimed at pseudo-cryptanalysts, he made it perfectly plain exactly what the Friedmans required for a valid cryptanalytic solution.

Anti-Shakespearean "claims based on cryptography can be scientifically examined, and proved or disproved." Because of this certainty, they [W. F. & E. S. Friedman] agreed, unconditionally, [to] accept as valid any cipher that fulfils two conditions: that its plaintext makes sense, and that this plaintext be unique and unambiguous—that, in other words, it not be one of several possible results.[27]

There can be no doubt that Jonson's avowal, committed in plain-text, meets the first of these requirements: his declaration is both grammatical and intelligible. But more importantly, it also answers the much-debated question concerning Shakespeare's true identity. And it does so, on the very artefact that was erected to commemorate the life of this great poet—the Shakespeare monument, thus, ensuring it would endure until discovered. In every respect, Jonson's use of a Cardano grille satisfies the first of the necessary conditions required by the Friedmans—*"its plaintext makes sense"*.

Additionally, the decryption process has followed a strict scientific process, thus ensuring that independent investigators, competent in mathematical procedures, will inevitably arrive at the same 34-column grille.

Firstly, each letter was numbered in the order of its appearance, and filed under the appropriate letter heading. Secondly, a probable word was chosen. Thirdly, alternate letters taken from the probable word were subjected to an arithmetical test to discover if the number assigned to the letter in between, formed an Arithmetical Progression. Where this result proved positive, further tests were suggested to see if the letters identified by the numbers appearing in the A.P. was part of a meaningful and grammatical sentence. It can be seen from this, that the Cardano grille above completely satisfies the requirements needed for independent, scientific evaluation.

Jonson's encryption also fulfils the second requirement insisted upon by the Friedmans and emphasised by Kahn. It is that the solution is unique. No alternative to Jonson's avowal exists. Professor A. W. Burgstahler, of the University of Kansas, has proved this uniqueness with a set of computer-generated grilles (see Appendix A for a selection of alternative grilles).

The conditions necessary for a genuine decipherment, as set by the Friedmans, have decidedly been met. Consequently, the admission that they would *"unconditionally accept as valid any cipher that fulfils [these] two conditions"* can only mean precisely that. Objectors to the grille and its solution, who persist in using the name Friedman to support their own inability to accept the content of Jonson's avowal, are therefore misusing the war hero's name in a most regrettable and inappropriate manner.

William Friedman did have something further to say during his lecture on encrypted messages. *"Mathematical and statistical considerations play an ever-increasing and prominent role in practical cryptology."*[28]

And so, as a further demonstration that Jonson's encrypted statement is consistent with a scientifically derived probability of it occurring outside the range of chance, the following odds are open to examination. The numbers 1 – 14 can be rearranged in more than 87 billion different ways. (14! = 87,178,291,200). For each number, 1 to 14, substitute a word or initial(s) appearing vertically in Jonson's avowal (SO TEST HIM, I VOW HE IS E VERE DE AS HE ... ME I.B.). From this, it must follow that these same clustered words and initials have just one chance in 87,178,291,200 of occurring in this one grammatical order, if subjected to chance. It is also this one grammatical order that allows AS HE to correctly interlock with, SHAKSPEARE, and for Jonson's initials, I B, to fall into position next to M E.

Immense though the odds are against these fourteen words and initials appearing in the order observed, even this statistic is dwarfed when the next calculation is undertaken. The letters forming the words can be calculated for the randomness of their occurrence.

Note particularly, how all the words occur in the same downward direction, and that they are clustered together. Take for instance the first cluster – So Test Him I Vow He. This consists of 15 letters spread over four columns before breaking off.

If it could be demonstrated mathematically that these letters were intentionally encrypted into the monument's inscription, it would then alert the reader to search for the continuation of the encrypted statement, knowing that whatever was found was part of the same purposeful intention.

Fortunately, the mathematics with which to apply this test exists. It consists of 10 tasks. These have been set out below. They cover all possibilities, and result in a probability value for the expectation of a single event in a given number of trials.

1. Find the number of ways the target words can occupy 3 adjacent columns; then multiply the result by 14; since there are 14 sets of 3 adjacent columns within the first 16 columns with 7 rows of letters.
2. Find the number of ways the target words can occupy 3 adjacent columns, for which the first 2 columns consist of 7 rows and the third column consists of 6 rows.
3. Find the number of ways the target words can occupy 3 adjacent columns, for which the first column consists of 7 rows and the second and third columns consist of 6 rows.
4. Find the number of ways the target words can occupy 3 adjacent columns and 6 rows; then multiply the result by 16; since there are 16 sets of 3 adjacent columns within the 18 columns remaining.
5. Find the number of ways the target words can occupy 4 adjacent columns in 7 rows; then multiply the result by 13; since there are 13 sets of 4 adjacent columns in the first 16 columns with 7 rows of letters.

6. Find the number of ways the target words can occupy 4 adjacent columns, for which the first 3 columns consist of 7 rows and the fourth column consists of 6 rows.
7. Find the number of ways the target words can occupy 4 adjacent columns, for which the first 2 columns consist of 7 rows and the third and fourth columns consist of 6 rows.
8. Find the number of ways the target words can occupy 4 adjacent columns, the first of which consists of 7 rows and the remaining 3 columns consist of 6 rows.
9. Find the number of ways the target words can occupy 4 adjacent columns and 6 rows; then multiply the result by 15; since there are 15 sets of 4 adjacent columns within the 18 columns of 6 rows that remain.
10. Calculate the probabilities of each letter that forms the target words, based upon the number of letters available and the frequency with which they occur on the grille.

The calculations are set out in the table below.

Composition	Letters	Arrangements	Total
[so test] [him I vow] [he]	6, 7, 2	3, 1, 6	18
[so test] [him I] [vow he]	6, 4, 5	3, 10, 6	180
[so test] [him] [I vow he]	6, 3, 6	3, 5, 4	60
[so] [test him] [I vow he]	2, 7, 6	6, 1, 4	24
Task 1, indicates there are 14 X 282 = 3948 possible arrangements of the target words in the first 16 columns.			
[so test] [him I vow] [he]	6, 7, 2	3, 1, 5	15
[so test] [him I] [vow he]	6, 4, 5	3, 10, 3	90
[so test] [him] [I vow he]	6, 3, 6	3, 5, 1	15
[so] [test him] [I vow he]	2, 7, 6	6, 1, 1	6
Task 2 indicates there are just 126 possible arrangements for this set-up.			
[so test] [him I] [vow he]	6, 4, 5	3, 6, 3	54
[so test] [him] [I vow he]	6, 3, 6	3, 4, 1	12
Task 3 indicates there are just 66 possible arrangements for this set-up.			
[so test] [him I] [vow he]	6, 4, 5	1, 6, 3	18
[so test] [him] [I vow he]	6, 3, 6	1, 4, 1	4

Task 4 indicates there are 22 X 16 = 352 possible arrangements of the target words in the remaining 18 columns.

[so test] [him I] [vow] [he]	6, 4, 3, 2	3, 10, 5, 6	900
[so test] [him] [I vow] [he]	6, 3, 4, 2	3, 5, 10, 6	900
[so test] [him] [I] [vow he]	6, 3, 1, 5	3, 5, 7, 6	630
[so] [test] [him] [I vow he]	2, 4, 3, 6	6, 4, 5, 4	480
[so] [test] [him I] [vow he]	2, 4, 4, 5	6, 4, 10, 6	1440

Task 5 indicates there are 4350 X 13 = 56,550 possible arrangements of the target words in the first 16 columns.

[so test] [him I] [vow] [he]	6, 4, 3, 2	3, 10, 5, 5	750
[so test] [him] [I vow] [he]	6, 3, 4, 2	3, 5, 10, 5	750
[so test] [him] [I] [vow he]	6, 3, 1, 5	3, 5, 7, 3	315
[so] [test] [him] [I vow he]	2, 4, 3, 6	6, 4, 5, 1	120
[so] [test] [him I] [vow he]	2, 4, 4, 5	6, 4, 10, 3	720

Task 6 indicates there are 2655 possible arrangements for this set-up.

[so test] [him] [I] [vow he]	6, 3, 1, 5	3, 5, 6, 3	270
[so test] [him] [I vow] [he]	6, 3, 4, 2	3, 5, 6, 5	450
[so test] [him I] [vow] [he]	6, 4, 3, 2	3, 10, 4, 5	600
[so] [test him] [I vow] [he]	2, 7, 4, 2	6, 1, 6, 5	180
[so] [test him] [I] [vow he]	2, 7, 1, 5	6, 1, 6, 3	108

Task 7 indicates there are 1608 possible arrangements for this set-up.

[so test] [him] [I] [vow he]	6, 3, 1, 5	3, 4, 6, 3	216
[so test] [him] [I vow] [he]	6, 3, 4, 2	3, 4, 6, 5	360
[so test] [him I] [vow] [he]	6, 4, 3, 2	3, 6, 4, 5	360
[so] [test] [him] [I vow he]	2, 4, 3, 6	6, 6, 4, 1	144
[so] [test] [him I] [vow he]	2, 4, 4, 5	6, 6, 6, 3	648

Task 8 indicates there are 1728 possible arrangements for this set-up.

[so test] [him I] [vow] [he]	6, 4, 3, 2	1, 6, 4, 5	120
[so test] [him] [I vow] [he]	6, 3, 4, 2	1, 4, 6, 5	120
[so test] [him] [I] [vow he]	6, 3, 1, 5	1, 4, 6, 3	72
[so] [test] [him I] [vow he]	2, 4, 4, 5	5, 3, 6, 3	270
[so] [test] [him] [I vow he]	2, 4, 3, 6	5, 3, 4, 1	60

Task 9 indicates there are 642 X 15 = 9630 possible arrangements for the target words in the remaining 18 columns.

The number of arrangements for the words: 'So Test Him I Vow He', occupying 3 or 4 adjacent columns anywhere on the grille, and read in a single direction, is 76,663. Task 10 requires that the probability for each letter in this phrase be calculated.

$S = \frac{19}{220}$; $O = \frac{14}{219}$; $T = \frac{27}{218}$; $E = \frac{25}{217}$; $S = \frac{18}{216}$; $T = \frac{26}{215}$; $H = \frac{20}{214}$;

$I = \frac{14}{213}$; $M = \frac{7}{212}$; $I = \frac{13}{211}$; $V = \frac{11}{210}$; $O = \frac{13}{209}$; $W = \frac{8}{208}$; $H = \frac{19}{207}$;

$E = \frac{24}{206}$.

The product of these probabilities is 1•329438172 X 10^{-17}, or 0.000,000,000,000,000,013 (2 significant figures).

Since it is required that these letters should appear in word perfect form, in one of the probability spaces, for which there are 76,663 available, there are this number of opportunities for it to occur. The product of these two statistics results in the expectation that 'So Test Him I Vow He' will occur by chance.

Thus, given these parameters, the result is 0•000,000,000,001 (1 significant figure); or once for every trillion trials.

A clock set to tick indefinitely, with each second ticking off one possible outcome at a time, would need 31,688 years for the first expected appearance of these words to occur by chance.*

A calculation for these words to appear in the position they actually occupy on the grille is $\frac{1}{76,663}$, multiplied by the frequencies of the letters available, which excludes those in use. At the 8th cell on the grille, 7 letters have been used, including 2 'S's and 1 'T'. The new calculation therefore begins with $S = \frac{17}{213}$, with the 3rd letter $T = \frac{26}{211}$. By completing this calculation in the manner set out at the top of the page, and making the necessary alterations: the result, after multiplying by $\frac{1}{76,663}$, permits one random success in more than 4 billion–trillion trials.

The implication from these probabilities is unavoidable. The words were encrypted deliberately. In which case, it implies there must be a further part to the message still to be read. There is! It is the identity of "He": "E. de Vere As He Shakspeare." Moreover, we also have the identity of the encoder; it is "Me I. B." These are the initials of Shakespeare's literary companion, Ben Ionson: a writer, who wished to be remembered for his honesty,

* No allowance has been made for the words to convey the same meaning in a different formation. This is over-compensated for by the absence of probability that the chosen letters will actually occur in an intelligible order.

and who often wrote his initials using the Latin alphabet, in which 'J' is written as 'I'.

From a purely scientific perspective, the statement arising from the monument's inscription is genuine. It is therefore the result of intelligent thought. Hence, Edward de Vere, 17th Earl of Oxford, was indubitably William Shakespeare.

Those sceptical of Oxford's role as Shakespeare are at a loss. A probability value of one trillion excludes chance, and affirms an intelligent intention. To overcome this, it would need a probability model that allowed the encypted words to be acceptable to chance. But this could be tested on other texts for comparative results. If none were forthcoming, the objection is disproved.

Those remaining defiant in their dissent are most likely to be amongst those suffering from *"confirmation bias"*. This is a psychological condition in which *"enough research will tend to support your theory"* (see *Murphy's Law of Research*).[29] Those affected will always seek to *"interpret new information in a way that confirms [their] preconceptions and avoids information and interpretations which contradict prior beliefs:"* (ibid.).

The departments of academe, specialising in Shakespearian studies, are populated with sufferers from this condition. It is infectious, and has been passed onto generation after generation of students who came into contact with those infected.

With the availability of scientific proof that Shakespeare was the penname used by Oxford, confirmation bias will have to be set aside. If not, then research into Shakespeare must be redefined, so as to allow facts to be set aside in favour of traditional beliefs. It is uncertain for how long such a prejudicial practice would be likely to endure. The quest for truth forms a seemingly unstoppable force in pursuit of progress. Indeed, it has always been the inspiration that drives scholarship.

One further consequence of significance is that the discovery of Jonson's encryption explains the statement made by Leonard Digges. His tribute to Shake-speare, which appeared in the First Folio, contained the thought provoking words: *"And Time dissolues thy Stratford Moniment."*[30] By writing 'Moniment' — the archaic spelling for 'monument' [*Chambers English Dictionary*, p. 928] — Digges has adopted the usage of a much older form of English. The employment of this particular word has therefore allowed an equally archaic meaning to be given to the line as a whole. In this respect, the now outdated definition of the verb 'dissolve'; *"to resolve (as doubts, riddles; arch.),"*[*Chambers* p. 112], places 'Stratford Moniment' as the direct object of this Old English verb. This means, Digges was looking to a future age, when: – *"Time [resolves the riddle of] thy Stratford Moniment, / Here we alive shall view you still."* Needless to say, that time has arrived; the riddle of the 'moniment', to which Digges so artfully referred, has at last been solved.

Another matter of considerable interest is the presence of Ben Jonson's initials: identifying him as the author of the encrypted avowal. This implies he was the poet who wrote the three couplets forming the cipher-text. A long-standing tradition already exists that Jonson composed the monument's inscription. His initials, placed so appropriately, now support that belief. There is also the fact that at the time of the monument's construction, he was involved in preparing the First Folio of Shakespeare's collected plays for publication; his hand in this work is rather obvious from the tribute he wrote, which precedes the plays. Hence, his participation in both of these projects is evident.

Apart from the presence of Jonson's initials, there is also the style of the monument's epitaph, and this, too, favours his authorship. Its opening words begin in a similar fashion to one he later composed for Henry West, 13th Lord La-ware, which begins: *"If Passenger thou canst but read / Stay drop a teare for him that's dead."*[31] In fact, the words 'stay', and 'read' or 'reader', each appear to have the making of a byword for Jonson when he was called upon to write memorials. Apart from the Stratford monument and Lord La-ware, these words appear on the epitaph he composed for *"Elizabeth, L. H."*: this begins: *"Wouldst thou hear what man can say / In little? Reader, stay... "* The words *"Reader stay"* also appear on Jonson's epitaph to Philip Gray.

Another who was remembered in Jonson's verse was Cecilia Bulstrode, her epitaph also includes these same two words; *viz: "Stay, view this stone; and if thou beest not such, / Read here a little."* The similarity these remembrances have to the words on Shakespeare's monument, which commences: *"Stay Passenger, Read... "* is inescapable, and greatly strengthens the conclusion that the encoded inscription was indeed the brainchild of Ben Jonson.[32]

Jonson's interest in code making can also be discerned in his two plays, *Volpone* and *The Alchemist.* Both summarise the plots with an acrostic poem. It was *"his cleverness at devising appropriate anagrams and impresas for his symbolic characters [that] was to be one of the bases of his success as a masque writer."*[33] Nor should it pass notice that Jonson's Book of *Epigrammes* (1616), dedicated to William Earl of Pembroke contains the sentence: *"For, when I made them, I had nothing in my conscience, to expreßing [sic] of which I did need a cypher."*[34] It may therefore be inferred from this that when Jonson's conscience was put to the test, he resolved his dilemma by resorting to the use of a cipher. Jonson's hand in devising the monument's Cardano grille is quite evidential.

What then is to be made of Jonson's double standards? In the First Folio his words are usually taken to imply praise for the dominant view of Shakespeare. Actually, a careful reading of the text reveals that Jonson was praising Shakespeare the artist, not Shakespeare the man, for whom biographical details are completely absent. It is Jonson's encryption on the monument that represents the truth, and this is expressed in the strongest possible manner as a personal vow: made at a time when vows were considered sacred.

It is an avowal that not only declares Edward de Vere to have been Shakespeare, but it even anticipates scepticism by urging that de Vere be tested to prove the truth of the vow. Which of these is to be believed, the encryption, or several notably ambiguous statements appearing in the poem he wrote for the First Folio?

To resolve this dilemma, one need attend to the actual words used by Jonson, for then there is no contradiction. This has been made plain in Chapter 9, which analyses the clever use he made of ambiguity in the First Folio.

Secrecy also explains why the original monument presented the bust in a merchant pose. Its purpose was to avoid raising incredulity amongst the deceased's neighbours. These were people that knew the literary limitations of their former neighbour and his daughters, neither of whom could read nor write. The four knotted corners of the sack, upon which the hands of the effigy originally rested, identify its commercial purpose to have been the packaging of wool. This was a valuable commodity that both Shaxperes, father and son, had dealt in. Even an enthusiastic supporter of the traditionalist view, like Charlotte Stopes, was forced to admit this resemblance to a woolsack.

> *The arms are bent awkwardly, the hands are laid stiffly, palms downward, on a large cushion, suspiciously representing a woolsack.*[35]

Apparently the town knew nothing of Shaxpere's ability to write the most deeply moving poetry known to man until it was pointed out to them in 1769. This was when the actor David Garrick organized a three-day jamboree inside Stratford-upon-Avon to celebrate the arrival of Shakespeare's statue: it having been modelled upon the one at Westminster Abbey. From that time onwards, the people of Stratford quickly adjusted to the commercial advantages that were to be gained by recognizing their former citizen as *the* William Shakespeare of literary fame. It had taken the town where he was born, raised and 'educated', 153 years to come to terms with the enormity of what London, and by extension, the entire world had been led to believe since the early 1590s.

Upon further inspection of the inscription, Jonson can be seen to have inserted another cryptic sentence into the text: one that proves to be an antecedent to his avowal, for it reaffirms the identity of HIM in the plaintext of the Cardano grille as DE VERE.

To unravel this, we must consider QVICK NATURE; i.e., the two words bridging the separated clusters of: SO TEST HIM, I VOW HE IS, and E. VERE DE. QVICK NATURE, we are told, DIDE (that is, DIED). Similar phrases to this can occasionally be seen as clues occurring in cryptic crossword puzzles. For example, one that appeared in the *Today* newspaper read: *"Diane and Edward faded away."* The answer to which, was *Died*, since this word is produced by joining together the remaining letters of *Diane* and of *Edward* after their second syllables, 'ane' and 'ward' have died or faded away. There is no reason to believe that such riddles were beyond the intelligence of earlier scholars.

> *Late sixteenth century England was a country that provided a ready audience for dissident codes: its people were addicted to hidden meanings. Codes, devices, and punning allusions were everywhere–in street songs and ballads, conversation, poems, plays, woodcuts, portraits,*

jewellery, costumes. Entire buildings were constructed in the form of riddles. ... Queen Elizabeth herself delighted in wordplay, setting the emblematic tone at court with teasing nicknames for her courtiers. ... There were literary codes, too, accessible only to a sophisticated elite.[36]

As long ago as 4 AD, the *Kama Sutra,* contained instructions for developing skills in cryptography:

Number 41 on the list of essential arts is the ability to solve riddles, enigmas and use covert speech. Following it is Mlecchita vikalpa, "the art of understanding writing in cipher and the writing of words in a peculiar way" ... including the verbal tricks of changing the beginning and end of words or adding letters between syllables.[37]

In which case, by treating QVICK NATURE as a potential suspect, and translating it into a Latin equivalent — Latin grammar is indicated by the inversion of the noun and adjective; that is, MONVMENT SHAKSPEARE — it becomes: SUMMA DE VELOCIUM RERUM NATURA. This is derived from Titus Lucretius' much acclaimed work on Nature, *De Rerum Natura,* which was widely read at that time. The poem, in six books, described the universe according to the atomic theory proposed by Epicurus, who viewed Nature as the sum (Latin - *Summa*) of its working parts, and operating without divine intervention. Therefore, by taking the title of Lucretius' poem on 'Nature' and adding to it the Latin for 'Quick', it becomes *De Velocium Rerum Natura.* Next, by adding 'Summa' to qualify the insertion of 'Quick', we obtain *Summa De Velocium Rerum Natura.* If these Latin words are viewed after they have 'DIED', or faded away, as with the Diane-Edward example, we obtain: SUM DE VE RE NATU, which combines to form, SUM DE VERE NATU: in English, this reads: I AM DE VERE BY BIRTH. It also provides the perfect antecedent to Jonson's avowal: indicating for a second time the name of the person he identified as HIM.

Importantly, by repeating for a second time the encrypted name, VERE, but using a different method of encryption, Jonson has employed the familiar strategy of repetition: a tactic intended to avoid the dissenter's charge of coincidence.

It is also, no less significant that this identification has been inserted beneath the bust of 'William Shakespeare': for he is now being identified as the man who took Oxford's place as poet and playwright: the man to whom Oxford's persona was temporarily transferred: the man who was therefore *not* de Vere by birth. And, as John Ruggero pointed out in a private correspondence, this further assertion of de Vere's identity has been strategically placed on the Cardano grille to form a bridge between its two leading clusters: the first of which: SO TEST HIM, I VOW HE IS, now becomes united to: E VERE DE, by the further assertion: I AM DE VERE BY BIRTH.

Jonson was noted during the time he lived for the pride he took in his knowledge of the classics, and this explains his use of 'velox' for 'quick'. When placed in conjunction with 'blood' (see *Henry V*, 3:v), or next to 'sense' (see *Troilus and Cressida*, 4:v), it means something animated. One would need to have been conversant with the writings of Quintilian, Pliny, Cicero, Horace, Tacitus &c, to know that precedents existed for using 'velox' in this particular sense: as for example, when Tacitus wrote *"velox ingenio"* in his *Agricola*, or when Horace referred to *"velox animus"* in his *Epistulae*, 1, 12, 13.

And so, by adding this further revelation to the effigy of Shakespeare, Jonson has provided a remarkably explicit piece of dialogue that embellishes de Vere's claim to authorship, raising it from a straightforward proof, as with the Cardano grille, to one of literary acclaim.

I AM DE VERE BY BIRTH !

SO TEST HIM: I VOW HE IS E DE VERE AS HE,
SHAKSPEARE: ME, B. I.

It is a sensational declaration and perfectly explicit: the 17th Earl of Oxford, Edward de Vere, was William Shakespeare.

The construction of a Cardano grille, according to the mathematical principle upon which this one was constructed, is not easy to achieve; the more so in this case, because the plain-text has to marry with the three couplets that are used for concealing the hidden sentence. The work entailed would have been laborious and time consuming. The hours required for its completion would have had to be a labour of love: perhaps indicative of the admission Jonson made in *Discoveries. De*

Shakespeare Nostrati, "for I lov'd the man, and doe honour his memory (on this side Idolatry) as much as any." [38]

It also tells us there was a need for the utmost secrecy concerning de Vere's authorship, and that a censorship existed: one so tightly imposed around the man's writing, it could only be breached by the very latest system in cryptography. Some idea of what was involved can be discerned from the following account.

> *The Privy Council, acting as the spokesman of royalty, planned and initiated all legislation ... the goal of Tudor government was benevolent paternalism in which the strong hand of authoritarianism was masked by the careful shaping of public opinion.* [39]

We may form some judgement as to how efficiently public opinion was shaped by censorship, through the disappearance of his original manuscripts and letters; which, if found, would connect Shakespeare's plays with the identity of their author.

In the absence of these papers, and with the compliance of those who knew the truth—Vere's family, friends, and literary associates who had been forced to remain silent—there was no longer anything to contradict what was taking place. The general public had no reason to doubt what they were told, nor did they. But, by accepting it, and with no possibility of a contradiction, the myth of Shakespeare, as a man having risen from humble beginnings to the peak of literary acclaim, entered English history.

As for historians of that age, they too were blinkered by necessity. As Sir Walter Raleigh commented when writing *The History of the World* in 1614, during his term of imprisonment, *"whosoever in writing a modern history, shall follow Truth too near the heels, it may haply strike out his teeth".* [40] It was advice that William Camden followed when writing his *"Tacitean history of Elizabethan England".* For although he asserted in his Preface: *"As for danger, I feared none, no not those who think the memory of succeeding ages may be extinguished by present power."* He also admitted: *"things secret and abstruse I have not pried into."* And, by adopting the same prudent attitude, he cautiously withheld publication of the second half of his *Annals* until after his death. [41]

Jonson, a former student of Camden, knew very well that the memory of succeeding ages was deliberately being extinguished with regard to Oxford's authorship. And he was also aware of the consequences this would have for literature. This clearly riled him. Hence his boldly encrypted avowal to posterity, which reveals the truth in a concise, informative sentence that tells a future generation to test Oxford as Shakespeare, and thereby confirm it. Notice how this appeal mirrors his introductory poem placed in the First Folio, immediately beneath the Droeshout engraving: *"Reader, looke Not on his Picture, but his Booke. B. I."*[42]

Many people of intelligence, which includes scholars from different walks of life, have been pleased to do as Jonson directed. They have discovered for themselves how consistently Oxford has written his biographical details into 'Shakespeare's' plays. Chapters 6 and 7 inform upon this aspect of Shakespeare's writing in detail.

But the poet also has his die-hards, and with an outlook comparative to the religious zeal of those who opposed Galileo, they blatantly deny the obvious: firstly, by blinding themselves to what, in any other circumstance, would be quite manifest to their understanding, and secondly, by forging imaginary explanations for the otherwise inexplicable, which sadly satisfies no one but themselves and their co-thinkers.

> *Rarely has so much been written about a man whom so little is known. Indeed, biographers are forced to invent their own Shakespeare, just as he created characters on stage. The extreme position is that "Shakespeare" was not written by Shakespeare at all, but by another author who preferred to hide his name.*[43]

What the authors of the *Essential Shakespeare Handbook* call *"the extreme position"* has now been scientifically verified: *"Shakespeare … written … by another author who preferred to hide his name."* But the reasons for this are complex, and must be deferred until later chapters.

Jonson's Latin Distich

Shakespeare's death in 1616 provided just the opportunity Jonson needed to begin considering how best he could signal to posterity the deception that had taken place. The Stratford monument was to be a time capsule into the future. Visually, it would be designed to satisfy the deceased's family and those who knew him as a man of commerce; linguistically, it would assure visitors acquainted with the works of Shakespeare that this was their man. But most importantly, it gave Jonson an opportunity for concealing within its sentences the truth about Oxford's pen-name. Not only could he now reveal the true author's identity, using the latest method for encrypting secret information, which had been published in 1550 by Girolamo Cardano, he could also expose Shakespeare as an allonym, and the role this man had played in disguising the truth.

Jonson therefore set about complementing the information contained in the Cardano grille by composing an ambiguous tribute in Latin to the counterfeit Shakespeare. He achieved this by drawing parallels to three men from antiquity: men whose reputations, when seen together, would outline the truth played by Stratford's William Shakespeare.

IVDICIO PYLIVM GENIO SOCRATEM, ARTE MARONEM
TERRA TEGIT, POPVLVS MÆRET, OLYMPVS HABET

[The judgement of Nestor, the genius of Socrates. the art of Virgil: the earth encloses, the people sorrow, Olympus possesses.]

Jonson's first choice, Nestor King of Pylos, was the mythical character described by Homer as having fought at Troy. This same individual also makes a rather lame appearance in Shakespeare's *Troilus and Cressida*. In the play, THERSITES refers to him as: *"old Nestor, whose wit was mouldy ere your grandsires had nails on their toes,"* [act 2 sc. i, 106-7]. And again: *"that stale old mouse-eaten dry cheese Nestor ... is not proved worth a blackberry"* [act 5 sc. iv, 10-12]. Jonson eagerly seized upon this JUDGMENT OF NESTOR from Shakespeare's own pen, and used it to form the first line of his Latin tribute, *viz*: IVDICIO PYLIVM.

The comparison cannot have been intended as a compliment to Shakespeare. For, by comparing Nestor to the bust situated immediately above the distich, the mythical nature of the Pylosian King becomes transferable to that person, causing him to be seen in the same light of myth.

Jonson's second choice fell to the philosopher Socrates. But, whosoever thinks that Shakespeare was another Socrates either knows nothing about this philosopher, or nothing about Shakespeare. The GENIUS OF SOCRATES has nothing remotely in common with the genius of Shakespeare. Nevertheless, Jonson has used this philosopher for a comparison, *viz*: GENIO SOCRATEM.

What is it that Socrates and Shaxpere have in common? From what we now know of this Greek philosopher, the one thing that defined him, apart from his reasoning ability via inductive arguments, was the fame attributed to him by Plato and others. This was necessary because Socrates wrote nothing himself. His fame and wisdom only became known to the world when Plato published impressive dialogues describing in detail his predecessor's powerful ability to analyse problems in order to arrive at the truth. Since this was achieved by adopting a probing question and answer dialogue, it has nothing to do with the prose, poetry, or drama that is uniquely Shakespeare's. We are therefore left with the Athenian's fame as the one remaining link uniting the two men; a link based solely upon third-party hearsay.

The third figure from antiquity is Virgil. But, by comparing the ART OF MARO (Maro was Virgil's surname) with that of Shakespeare, Jonson was ignoring the fact that this Roman's *"influence on the dramatist was negligible."* [44] Are we to believe Jonson was unaware of this?

> *L. P. Wilkinson, in the best book we have on Ovid, reminds us that Shakespeare echoes him about four times as often as he echoes Virgil, that he draws on every book of the Metamorphosis, and that there is scarcely a play untouched by his influence.* [45]

Jonson was a classical scholar, and he would have been perfectly aware of this fact. He would have also known that during the sixteenth century, it was said that a spirit, whose identity was a carefully guarded secret, transferred his gift of poetry to Virgil. Details relating to this gift of poetic ability are described in an early biography of Virgil (*Een Schone Historie Van Vergilius*, 1552).[46]

The reason for this mythical story was a religious one. Virgil was a pagan, having been born before Jesus Christ. Hence, to make his work acceptable reading for Christians, the story of his triumph over forces of darkness was invented.

A similar story is repeated about Shaxpere: that he, too, was the recipient of the poetic gift belonging to Oxford; and, like Virgil, he guarded the identity of his benefactor.

These three parallels define Shaxpere's role in the story of Shakespeare, and explain why it became surrounded by so much secrecy. Nestor, Socrates and Virgil, impart something of their personal stories towards unravelling that secret. Nestor tells us that the story surrounding Shaxpere is as mythical as his own. Socrates informs us that, like himself, Shaxpere never put pen to paper. And finally, Virgil explains how this came about. For, as mentioned in one of his early biographies, the gift of poetry was transferred to Shaxpere by a more gifted spirit: one who owned it, but who wished, or was required, to remain anonymous.

The Latin distich therefore explains in cryptic fashion the story behind the mystery of Shaxpere's role as Shakespeare. It also complements the name of Edward de Vere as Shakespeare, which has been encrypted in the Cardano grille contained within the inscription beneath the distich. In this important respect, both the three English couplets and the two-lined distich are in complete harmony with the carved figure of Shaxpere above them. For this originally showed the man to be a dealer in wool: something to which his mostly illiterate neighbours would have readily given their nodding assent.

The Final Secret?

Does the monument's inscription conceal one final secret? Immediately following QUICK NATURE DIED are the words: WHOSE NAME DOTH DECK YS TOMBE. This statement is puzzling. There is no tomb. Will Shaxpere's body was *"laid in the ground in a wooden coffin"* (M. M. Reese, 1980), close to the rail of the chancel inside the town's parish church. But, not only is there no tomb, Shaxpere's name does not even mark the spot where he was interred. Instead, a ledger stone covers the grave, upon which four lines of verse plead for the bones of the departed to be left undisturbed, while cursing those who ignore this appeal.

To this puzzle we can also add the peculiarity of abbreviating THIS TO YS. We know that the 's' in YS was necessary to form part of the plain-text in Jonson's Cardano grille. But for traditionalists, unable to accept de Vere's authorship, YS TOMBE should really read HIS TOMBE.

By referring to 'this' rather than 'his', the author has not confined the whereabouts of Shakespeare's tomb to the Church of the Holy Trinity. Instead, the possibility exists that it may refer to a tomb elsewhere: one decked by a name whose value was esteemed far greater than the cost of the monument on which it is found. With de Vere now definitely identified as Shakespeare, it is tempting to consider YS TOMBE to be his.

The words that follow actually support this possibility, since FAR MORE THEN COST compares the value of the tomb with that of Shakespeare's name, or in this case, his real name, de Vere. In 1623, when this inscription first appeared in public, there was more than one tomb carrying the name of Vere.

Oxford's family vault inside St. Nicholas Church at Castle Hedingham is one. It was last opened in 1562 to receive the 16th Earl, who was buried close to the black marble tomb on which carved effigies of the 15th Earl and his wife Elizabeth lay, with figures of their four daughters kneeling in prayer on the side panel. *"The usual burial place of the de Veres seems to have been the Earls Colney Priory, where several fine tombs have been preserved (now removed to a building at Bures)."*[47]

Edward de Vere is not amongst them. He was buried at the church of St. Augustine in the village of Hackney. When his wife died in 1613, her will requested *"a tomb fitting our degree, and of such charge as shall seem good to mine executors."*[48] But here there is a mystery. Oxford's cousin, Percival Golding, later wrote an unpublished history of the Vere family (*The Armes, Honours, Matches and Issues of the Ancient and Illustrious family of Veer*), in which he recorded: *"Edward de Veer ... died at his house at Hackney in the month of June Anno 1604 and lieth buried at Westminster."*[49]

Without the least shadow of doubt, Oxford fully deserved to be honoured with a burial in Westminster Abbey, along with England's literary elite. This would not have been difficult to arrange, secretly, in the early seventeenth century, especially if it had the blessing of King James. But did it really happen?

Golding's reference to Westminster certainly focuses attention upon the Vere tomb erected in the Abbey in 1609: it having been financed by the grieving widow of the soldier-knight, Sir Francis Vere.

> *Sir Francis (1560-1609) commanded the English troops in the Netherlands that fought against Spain in the service of the United Provinces, while his younger brother Sir Horace (1565-1635) fought in Germany during the Thirty Years' War.*[50]

Francis and Horace were cousins to Oxford, and it is Horace

who is held by many to be Horatio in *Hamlet*, and to whom the prince appeals at the end of the play with words that are equally appropriate to the Earl of Oxford.

> *O God! Horatio, what a wounded name,*
> *Things standing thus unknown, shall live behind me!*
> *If thou didst ever hold me in thy heart,*
> *Absent thee from felicity awhile,*
> *and in this harsh world draw thy breath in pain,*
> *To tell my story.* (Act 5: sc.ii).

The tomb commissioned by Lady Vere to commemorate her husband's gallantry on the field of battle took the form of a hugely expensive monument made from marble, with the carved figure of her husband recumbent at the base. Above him is a platform supported on the shoulders of four men-at-arms: one at each corner. Upon its surface are the carved accoutrements of war. The sculpture was modelled from a similar one existing in the Dutch town of Breda, and designed by Maximilian Colt for the Count of Nassau. (*Westminster Abbey,* Walter Annenberg, 1972 p. 225).

The expense involved in material and workmanship would undoubtedly justify the reference to its comparison with the worth of Shakespeare's authorship. Moreover, having been commissioned in 1609, it would have still been fresh in the mind of Jonson when he referred to *"this tomb"*. On the other hand, if the reference was intended for the tomb at Hackney, then sadly, it no longer exists, if indeed, it ever did.

Doubt exists that Henry, the youthful 18th earl, carried out his mother's wish. But if the young man knew that his father was to be reinterred at Westminster, this would help explain his apparent negligence. In any case, *"The Tudor church was destroyed in 1798, having fallen into irremediable disrepair."*[51]

The next phrase on the inscription states imperatively: SIEH ALL THAT HE HATH WRITT. The use of the German word SIEH, as noted above, was introduced to provide an 'I' and 'E' in the plaintext reading of the Cardano grille, to identify the author of the inscription as Jonson. But reference to the Vere tomb at Westminster (it having been copied from a Dutch original), also suggests a link with SIEH. This is because, *"In the European Middle*

Ages, the [Dutch] language was called Dietsc, or Dutsc, historically equivalent to German Deutsch."[52]

Was the German imperative, SIEH, intended as a linguistic clue to direct attention towards the costly *Deutsch* tomb at Westminster? If so, then presumably only after de Vere's name had been re-established as the author of Shakespeare's work. And did Jonson, and those involved in producing the complete volume of Shakespeare's collected plays, really intend to secrete *all that he hath writ*—that is, the manuscripts used for compiling the First Folio—inside the Vere tomb at Westminster Abbey? Or did they have in mind Vere's intended tomb at Hackney? The original papers have never been found: something must have happened to them, and Jonson certainly had his hands on them when the First Folio was being prepared.

Of these alternatives, Westminster Abbey must be favourite, because SIEH can also be translated as, LOOK THERE! in which case, one would have to ask, where? The most plausible answer is the one supplied by the monument; to wit, this tomb, whose name doth deck it far more then cost.

But, could all of this be just too speculative to be true? Let us put it into context. First of all there is the bust of the counterfeit Shakespeare clutching a sack of farm produce: very likely wool, a commodity which he and his father had dealt in. Secondly, the Latin distich beneath the bust likens the figure to three men from antiquity; neither one of which is the obvious exemplar of the true Shakespeare, but whose combined attributes, conveyed to the merchant figure, suggest he was acting as an allonym for the poet. Then there are the six lines of non-biographical verse beneath this distich, written in English, and containing two encryptions declaring Edward de Vere to have been Shakespeare. Against this background, is it likely, or perhaps unlikely, that the Stratford monument has one final secret to reveal – the whereabouts of Shakespeare's missing papers?

A fibre optic cable inserted into the Vere monument at Westminster might resolve that question. Until then, we have only Golding's word that Oxford was buried at Westminster, and this implies his remains were re-interred inside the tomb of Sir Francis Vere. Official records of reburials were not kept at that time. And in the secret manoeuvrings of that age, especially where the Earl of Oxford was concerned, anything seems possible. Certainly, if it were true, this would be because it provided the perfect opportunity for the Shakespeare manuscripts to be disposed of at the same time, alongside the body of their author.

Interestingly, we know the tomb was opened in 1635 for Oxford's cousin, Horace, Sir Francis' brother. This reopening of the tomb, three years after publication of the Second Folio of Shakespeare's collected plays, would have provided an opportunity for Oxford to be interred at Westminster, if that was the intention, but it is too late to account for Jonson's reference to *"this tomb"*.

It has also been claimed that the tomb was reopened in 1625 for Oxford's son, who died from wounds inflicted while serving his country. The Abbey's burial records (letter to author from the Assistant Keeper of Muniments at Westminster) confirm Ruth Loyd Miller's discovery (*Oxfordian Vistas*, p.42) that Henry de Vere, the 18th Earl of Oxford, was buried in St John the Baptist's Chapel on 15 July 1625; although the stone covering the vault was only put in place by Dean Stanley during the latter part of the nineteenth century. The confusion concerning the burial of Henry may have occurred because the tomb of Sir Francis Vere lies in the Chapel of St John the Evangelist, not the Chapel of St John the Baptist.

The inscription on the Stratford monument concludes with the words, LEAVES LIVING ART BUT PAGE TO SERVE HIS WITT. Once again, there is a double meaning to contend with. Page means a man, invariably a boy, who attends a member of the nobility. Allowing for a little poetic licence, the *page* in question, given the context referred to above, could very easily refer to the author of the inscription, Ben Jonson.

By writing this inscription, filled as it is with cryptology and double meanings, it can be said Jonson was in service to Oxford. Importantly, he was the only person at that time in a position to adequately serve Oxford's genius. This opportunity arose from the freedom he received to participate in the tributes appearing in the First Folio. And these date precisely to the time when the wording on the Stratford monument first appeared in public.

Failing this explanation, the meaning of 'page', as a leaf from a book, makes no sense at all. What page is indicated? There is no single page as far as can be determined from reading the inscription to which this could possibly refer.

Were Shakespeare's manuscripts concealed inside the Vere tomb at Westminster? This may have been the intention. But whatever was suggested at the time, regarding the fate of these valuable papers, others may have had similar thoughts. By a strange coincidence, in 1623 when the First Folio was ready to go on sale, Jonson's study was set ablaze. All his papers and books were lost. If the source material used for the Folio edition of Shakespeare's plays was amongst them at that time, they were almost certainly lost to the flames.

By the time the fire took hold, the Stratford monument had already been set in place. If it did have a secret to tell about the intended whereabouts of Shakespeare's lost manuscripts, then its message may no longer apply. In which case, the mystery of the missing Shakespeare papers would appear to have been solved. They were burnt. Unless…

Jonson's response to the frustration of losing so much learning gave voice to a protest against *"Vulcan's injustice"*. In *An Execration*, which he wrote in response to the conflagration, David Kay believes the work betrays *"the satirist's anxiety about overstepping limits"*.[53]

Jonson had certainly done so by encrypting the Stratford monument with the truth about Shakespeare. *"Did I"*, he asks perhaps self-admonishingly, *"itch to defame the state? Or brand the times?"*[54]

Perhaps Jonson was thinking of his recent work on the First Folio and the Stratford monument, and been keen to protest his innocence, so that he might distance himself from the life-threatening disclosures they contained, were they to be discovered before his demise. We shall never know.

As mentioned at the commencement of this chapter, the monument to Shakespeare at Stratford-upon-Avon is often cited as evidence guaranteeing Will Shaxpere's authorship of Shakespeare's work. This is no longer credible. No intelligent person, conversant with the full facts, can ever again with total confidence refer to the monument as an unambiguous tribute to the genius of Stratford's poet. In all three languages, visual, Latin, and English, the monument has declared this man to be an impostor: a sanctioned impostor, but an impostor nevertheless.

Even so, the revelations appearing within the inscription on the Stratford monument should not be thought of as a thunderbolt sent from the heavens to admonish a largely unsuspecting academia. Nothing, either historical or factual, has ever been discovered about Shakespeare that is not equally applicable to Oxford, and often more so. The reason for this is straightforward. There *is* nothing that has ever been discovered about the literary life of Will Shaxpere that unequivocally justifies belief in his recognition as England's greatest literary genius.

Whilst referring to this dearth of information, the acclaimed, former, Oxford historian, Hugh Trevor-Roper wrote:

> *Since his death, and particularly in the last century, he has been subjected to the greatest battery of organized research that has ever been directed upon a single person. Armies of scholars, formidably equipped, have examined all the documents, which could possibly contain at least a mention of his name.* [55]

Yet, there has been nothing: nothing of any literary value, because there is nothing to find. Walt Whitman was of a similar opinion: *"the record is almost blank–it has no substance whatever."*[56]

Ben Jonson was wholly aware of this when he conveyed to posterity the true identity that lay behind the works attributed to William Shakespeare, carefully placing his avowal in the one location where it would last for as long as Shakespeare's fame endured—the Stratford monument.

POSTSCRIPT: William and Elizebeth Friedman co-authored "The Shakespearean Ciphers Examined", published in 1957 by C.U.P. The book was re-issued in April 2011, claiming to be: "An Analysis of Cryptographic Systems Used as Evidence that Some Author other than William Shakespeare Wrote the Plays Commonly Attributed to him". However, the authors neglected both Cardano grilles and ELS encoding. They also disregarded the anagram of Vere, which occurs in Henry Peacham's "Minerva Britanna", made public at the time by Eva Turner Clark. But with exemplary foresight, the Friedmans did accept the possible, future discovery of a code that met their criteria, which they agreed to accept, should one be found. This has now been achieved through Ben Jonson's Cardano grille, along with others by Oxford, Thorpe and Digges.

2

REINTERPRETING SHAKESPEARE

Nemo dat quod non habet.
(No-one can give what he does not possess)

IN THE PREVIOUS CHAPTER it was asserted that because Jonson had made a vow that Oxford was William Shakespeare, the authorship controversy must eventually draw to a close. In which case, what now remains is a revised view of the history surrounding Oxford, together with a reinterpretation of the evidence that up until now has supported the counterfeit poet Shakespeare.

The purpose of this chapter is to meet that need by critically assessing the statements appearing in conventional biographies of Shakespeare, and to demonstrate cogently, with full compliance to historical and documentary evidence, that alternative explanations to those proposed do actually exist. At the same time, it will be necessary to reveal how these alternative explanations also support Jonson's declaration that Shakespeare was Oxford's penname, and the man from Stratford-upon-Avon, with a similar sounding surname, was paid to act as the poet's allonym, as the Latin distich's subtlety has declared was the case.

In the process of completing this task, the reader will discover that the lack of substantive evidence for the conventional idea of Shakespeare has allowed traditionalists to fabricate much of what has been written about their man: sometimes with inferences derived solely from imagination.

Thus, not only are there errors of omission, where evidence has been deliberately abandoned because it failed to fit the image being created, but there are also illogicalities. Circular reasoning, for example, has been introduced as fact, in order to fill the gaps occurring in the man's life story. Added to this, are errors of commission, where statements have been introduced, based solely upon false inferences.

If one wonders why this has gone on for so long, licensed as it is by authoritative assertions, it is because until now, there has been no actual proof that someone other than Shaxpere wrote the works that carry Shakespeare's name. There certainly exists a great deal of circumstantial evidence, but there has been no actual document to prove it. This has changed. There now exists such a document, and it is written in stone, and made with the assurance of a person who knew the truth. Ben Jonson not only insisted that de Vere was Shakespeare; he also demanded that he be tested to prove his authorship. And so he will be, but first the man from Stratford-upon-Avon has also to be tested, to show, and in many cases prove, that he was not the great genius of literature that he has been made out to be.

To begin with, no one doubts that Shakespeare existed. The doubt is that Shakespeare, arguably the greatest poet and playwright of the modern world, is the same person that rose to manhood in the small market town of Stratford-upon-Avon during the second half of the sixteenth century. If so, then his name amongst local residents was commonly pronounced and spelt with a short 'a', as in axe: hence Shaxpere.

As late as 1598, supposedly at the height of his fame, the chamber accounts of the town council, when recording a payment made to him of ten-pence for a load of stone, still referred to him as *"Mr Shaxpere"*. Six years further on, when issuing a summons against local resident Philip Rogers for non-payment of a debt incurred over the sale of malt, he was referred to as *"Willielmus Shexpere"*. In June 1607, his daughter married John Hall at Stratford-upon-Avon. The marriage register confirmed her name as *"Susanna Shaxpere"*.

It is therefore the style of address this book will adhere to when directly referring to the man whom tradition believes was better known as William Shakespeare; for this reason, the name has been spelt in this book exactly as it was recorded on his application for a marriage licence in 1582—*"Shaxpere"*.

Since the intention of this chapter is to examine whatever doubts may be deemed appropriate when viewed against the credentials of this man Shaxpere, considerable care and attention is required. For it is upon this man's brow that a poet's crown of bays has been bestowed: placed there by a longstanding tradition of accepting him as England's most gifted exponent of the written word. To prove otherwise is an onerous task because the prevailing view has always strongly affirmed the validity of his qualification to receive the accolades that greet Shakespeare's work. Nevertheless, within this certainty lies a potential weakness: it is the fragility of evidence underpinning the weight of the governing authority. If that should prove supportive, all doubts must evaporate. But if it is less than sound, the authority upon which it is supported collapses. What then does that say about the man, about the age in which he lived, and about those who refuse to acknowledge doubt, where doubt overrides all else?

Birth Date Uncertain

The first move towards transforming Shaxpere, with his rustic upbringing, into the mature gentleman and playwright known as William Shakespeare, must belong to his date of birth. Unfortunately, it is not known. However, the baptismal date was recorded in the parish register as 26 April 1564 (Old Style): equivalent to 6 May (New Style). And since the high rate of infant mortality in that age was responsible for many hasty christenings, and since the feast day of St George, the patron saint of England, is celebrated on 23 April, this date is assigned as Shakespeare's, or rather, Shaxpere's, birthday.

However, right across Christian Europe at that time, the Julian calendar was in force. This means that dates given in 1564 were reckoned according to the Old Style of numbering months; hence, dates from that time are ten days behind those that now occur on the Gregorian calendar. St George's Day in 1564, for example, would now be recalculated as 3 May. Consequently, when today's admirers of Shakespeare celebrate his birthday on 23 April, they are ten days too early, for this is equivalent to 13 April according to the calendar operating in Shakespeare's age. In fact, there is evidence to show Shaxpere was born some time before that date.

In England, according to the Julian calendar, New Year's Day was sometimes celebrated on 1 January, but for legal purposes and Church celebrations, each New Year was counted from 25 March. This allowed a nine-month pregnancy period to elapse before celebrating the birth of Jesus Christ on 25 December. 24

March would therefore have been the last day of 1563: the next day, 25 March, became the first day of 1564. This fact is of considerable importance when the age of Shaxpere is taken into account. The Stratford monument states clearly that Shaxpere was 53 at the time of his death, and this occurred on 23 April 1616. Simple arithmetic therefore proves he was born in 1563.

According to the Julian calendar, this places his true date of birth on or before the last day of 1563, which occurred on 24 March. It is therefore a birth date that has no connection whatever with St. George's day. In terms of the present day Gregorian calendar, Will Shaxpere was born at the very latest, on 3 April, and very probably, some time before that date.

This exposes the first myth of those who are intent upon creating the perfect image of Shaxpere: his date of birth was, at the least, weeks away from St George's Day.

A Dubious Education

The next point at which the transition of Shaxpere into Shakespeare draws interest is that of his education. But, to be blunt, there is not one single scrap of documentary evidence to satisfy an enquiry that his schooling ever took place. It is a stark fact that stands out in complete contrast against that of his literary contemporaries: men who shared a similar background to Shaxpere's upbringing.

We know, for example, that Ben Jonson was educated at Westminster School; Christopher Marlowe was sent from King's School, Canterbury to Corpus Christi College, Cambridge; Edmund Spenser was taught at Merchant Taylors' Grammar School before being admitted to Pembroke College, Cambridge; Thomas Nashe also went to Cambridge, as did Robert Greene, who also attended Oxford; Francis Beaumont was another who went to Oxford, and the man often mentioned alongside him, John Fletcher, studied at Cambridge too. Thomas Kyd attended the Merchant Taylor's' School in London, as did Thomas Lodge, although unlike Kyd, he continued his education at Oxford. But about Shaxpere's education, the record is blank. This is excused on the grounds that although King's New School in Church Street, Stratford-upon-Avon, did exist at the time of Shakespeare's youth, the records for this period are now missing.

Against this absence, one is bound to mention that records do exist, showing the list of tutors employed at the school at that time, as well as a reference to the educational advancement of one, William Smith, born in Stratford-upon-Avon in the same year as Will Shaxpere. Smith, it is recorded, was sent to Winchester College, and from there to Oxford. Smith's flair for advanced scholarship therefore stands out in stark contrast to the imaginary scholarship bestowed upon Shaxpere. But, then, with no records to support them, Shaxpere's scholarship has to be imagined.

It is at this point that Shaxpere's biographers develop their illogical argument. He is given a first class education. The argument goes as follows: for him to have written the works of Shakespeare, he must have received an education. Shaxpere wrote these works; therefore he attended King's New School, where he received his grounding in scholarship.

In terms of formal logic, the works of Shakespeare are used as a premise, from which it is inferred that he attended his local grammar school. But the argument quickly becomes circular, because his education at King's New School is then used as a new premise to justify his becoming Shakespeare the author of the books from which it was deduced he received an education. Those who understand the fallacy of circular reasoning will easily recognise what has happened.

An attempt has been made, firstly, to 'prove' Shaxpere's education by deducing it from the plays Shakespeare wrote; secondly, this deduction is then used to deduce the educational ability needed for him to have written the plays. The argument is circular because Shaxpere's education is inferred from the plays, and the plays are inferred from his education. But this circular reasoning is so central to Shaxpere becoming Shakespeare that his biographers, who abandon academic rigour in favour of 'special pleading', repeatedly embrace it: otherwise it would be impossible to establish a basis for Shaxpere having written the plays of Shakespeare.

Actually, a local resident did refer to Will Shaxpere having briefly been a pupil at a local School, but his attendance was said to have been so extremely brief, that reference to it is ignored. Such little time at school would not have provided the education needed for him to have begun so quickly writing the works of Shakespeare. Indeed, it would not even have been sufficient time for him to have learned how to read and write.

This report of Shaxpere and his short-lived education at the free schoolhouse was discovered during researches made on behalf of the lawyer and poet Nicholas Rowe, who included it in *Some Account of the Life &c. of Mr. William Shakespeare*: a six-volume publication of the poet's collected works.

To make the *Account* as factual as possible, Rowe sent his aid, Thomas Betterton (1635-1710), *"into Warwickshire on purpose to gather up what remains he could, of a name for which he had so great a veneration."* [1] Betterton returned with a report gleaned from someone who was obviously well informed about the Shaxpere family. For what Betterton was told is quite clearly an account relayed to him from the perspective of Will Shaxpere's father . . .

> *tho' he was the eldest son, he could give him no better education than his own employment. He had bred him, 'tis true, for some time at a Free-School, where 'tis probable he acquir'd that little Latin he was master of: but the narrowness of his circumstances, and the want of his assistance at home, forc'd his father to withdraw him from thence.*[2]

This narrative account, emanating from Shaxpere's native town by someone still familiar with the family history, even after a century or thereabouts, suggests that a descendant of Joan Hart, William's sister, relayed it to Betterton.

Consider, for example, the contacts sought by anyone sent to Stratford-upon-Avon at that time, in order to obtain information concerning Shakespeare. Would they neglect to call upon Shaxpere's descendants? While this does not prove that a member of his sister's family made the report, it would be absurd to suppose that Betterton did not interview those who were alive at the time. Rowe certainly had no qualms about accepting the report as true. Conversely, if this report did not originate from Joan Hart's family—what did? There is nothing in Rowe's biography of Shakespeare to indicate the wealth of detail that one would expect from an interview with—let us say—the son of this great writer's nephew. The upshot is that Betterton's report provides clear evidence, probably from a family source, confirming that Shaxpere was withdrawn from school before completing even a preliminary education. The argument sometimes heard that

Shaxpere was illiterate is therefore not without substance.

It is at this point that Shakespeare's biographers are forced to apply the principle of selective thinking. The person interviewed by Betterton was mistaken, they say. Why was he/she mistaken? Because they failed to confirm what every biographer of Shakespeare *knows*, even though there is no evidence to support what they *know*.

Circular reasoning together with special pleading, stemming from confirmation bias, is all that is required to rescue them from their plight. Most, if not all accounts of Shakespeare's life story will readily confirm this has happened: enhanced by imaginary tales of the books he read, and how he mastered the full curriculum. The biographers of Shakespeare have been very busy infilling history with imagined scenarios. This has helped establish, with the firmness of academic authority, their creation: William Shakespeare; a man of the people, dwelling in an environment constructed out of wishful thinking.

A Marriage of Uncertainties

Factually speaking, the only existing documentary evidence relating to William Shaxpere, between the time of his birth and his arrival in London, are three baptismal entries in the church register and a marriage licence.

The baptisms occurred in 1564, 1583 and 1585, with the first of these referring to his christening. The second entry records the baptism of his daughter Susanna, and the third relates to the same ceremony performed for his twins Hamnet and Judeth: both of these forenames belonged to his neighbours, Hamnet and Judith Sadler, and have nothing whatever to do with Shakespeare's *Hamlet*.

In addition to these church records are two others made at the Bishop of Worcester's office in 1582. The first of these refers to Shaxpere's application for a marriage licence: *"inter Willelmum Shaxpere et Annam Whateley de Temple Grafton"*[3] (between William Shaxpere and Anne Whateley of Temple Grafton). The entry remains a mystery, even today.

However, in 1836, a second document was uncovered, dated the next day, 28 November 1582, but signed by a different clerk at a separate office. This referred to a bond for £40 (≈ £11,000). The amount was the measure of indemnity judged appropriate to protect the Bishop should a later claim be made to suggest that the marriage between *"William Shagspere"* and *"Anne Hathwey of Stratford in the Diocese of Worcester, maiden"* [4] was invalid. The sureties to the bond were two rustic husbandmen, both illiterate, Fulk Sandells and John Richardson.

What happened during those two days in November 1582 to cause the bride's name and residence to change overnight is never likely to be known for certain. Suffice to say, William Shaxpere emerged with a licence to marry Anne Whateley of Temple Grafton, a village situated some five miles outside Stratford-upon-Avon. And his two companions returned to Shottery having given the Bishop of Worcester a surety for £40 to the effect that if their young companion, who was a minor, married Anne Hathwey, and the validity of the marriage was tested in court, the Lord Bishop would be exempt from blame.

To add further to the mystery, no record of Will Shaxpere's marriage has ever been discovered. It clearly did not take place in Stratford-upon-Avon. But a curious discovery did come to light some time later. Two leaves were found to be missing, cut out from the registry of St. Martins Church: both containing the marriage entries for 1582.

St. Martins was a small church in Worcester. One is therefore left to wonder what dark secret those pages divulged that required such drastic action. For, recall, Shaxpere's marriage licence was to wed Anne 'Whateley', *not* Anne 'Hathwey'. Whereas, on a different day and before a different clerk, the same three men had obtained a proviso that were William Shagspere to wed someone else, namely Anne Hathwey, and should the said union be declared invalid, the Bishop of Worcester would be indemnified against having had knowledge of this impropriety. For this, the two husbandmen agreed to a bond of £40: a huge amount, for them to have given their names to.

So what on earth was going on? Why should there be any doubt concerning the marriage status of Anne Hathaway? Could it be that the bride married under an assumed name? Perhaps, that of Anne Whateley, exchanging vows at a distance from the town and county where they were known? Could it be that Anne Hathaway was already married, and her husband had either left her, or otherwise disappeared, permanently, and without record?

Anne was, after all, twenty-six years of age when she married her eighteen-year-old husband; there must have been other suitors before him. This was rural England in the sixteenth century, when it would have been unusual for a woman of her age not to be already married.

Perhaps the answer can be found from an entry in the Stratford parish register recording the marriage of *"Anne Hathaway of Shottery to William Wilson on Jan. 17, 1579"*[5] That is, less than four years before *"Anne Hathaway ... the daughter of Richard Hathaway of Shottery"*[6] married William Shaxpere, at a date and place that has never so far been positively identified. This earlier entry in the parish register would certainly explain why the couple avoided the Stratford parish church, if the bride was getting married under the name of another woman.

The question marks existing over this affair may be in part due to the machinations of John Payne Collier. This once able scholar devoted the best part of his academic life to forging and destroying records so that the world would have a near perfect vision of the man he believed Shakespeare to have been. It is certainly believable that while looking through church records in the county of Worcestershire, Collier, or some like-minded individual, came across the entry of Shaxpere's marriage, and with a sudden churning of the stomach, realised the truth of what must have happened, and the subsequent harm this would do to 'Shakespeare's' image, were it to become known. Desperate to conceal the truth, the offending page was cut from the church register.

Speculative though this may appear, it is nevertheless quite certain that there was at least one important reason, undoubtedly ulterior, causing William Shaxpere and his bride to avoid Stratford's parish church, or any other church in the immediate vicinity; and an equally ulterior motive for the removal of two pages from St Martins' record of marriages.

> *Reputed scholars such as John Payne Collier and James Halliwell-Phillipps, who dedicated their lives to consolidating the legend of the English Bard, are known to have stolen, forged and destroyed numerous documents as they worked their way unsupervised through various libraries and private collections.* [7]

Naturally, Shakespeare's image-makers will have nothing to do with any suggestion of impropriety on the part of their man, and they quickly gloss over the problems that in other circumstances would be of genuine concern. Their main worry is to ensure that *their* Shakespeare emerges without taint; that is, beyond the evidential fact that Anne was pregnant at the time of her marriage, and that she had conceived within a few weeks of her father's death. In this respect, there is a touch of humour in the way Shakespeare's inventors prefer to see the two illiterate yeomen, Sandells and Richardson, as accompanying the bridegroom to give him support. More realistically, it was a shotgun wedding, and they were there to see that a local rascal did not dishonour the daughter of their recently deceased friend, the bride's father.

The Lost Years

Quite clearly, with only four documents covering the first half of Shaxpere's life—in fact, the same four documents that must have covered literally hundreds, if not thousands of young men in a similar situation—there is an enormous gap to fill, and absolutely nothing whatever to fill it with, nor to distinguish Shaxpere's life from that of anyone else of a similar age and circumstance. His image-makers quickly rise to the occasion. Their strategy is similar to the one that was adopted to cover his 'education'. They indulge in another round of circular reasoning. Not surprisingly, this causes more problems than it solves.

The difficulties begin to mount up when a list of Shaxpere's accomplishments is compiled; the idea being that these should indicate what he was doing before he arrived in London. Charlton Ogburn captured the essence of the problem in a single paragraph.

> *What was Will doing in the years before his appearance in London? Various stories have filtered into the vacuum, the best known involving deer poaching, but they are without substantiation or even plausibility. He 'may or may not have travelled to Europe, either as a touring actor or in the company of a noble patron', Ivor Brown theorizes. Louis P. Bénézet of Dartmouth College has garnered a fine crop of postulations all designed to endow the young Will in some measure with the range of knowledge and experience clearly possessed by the author of the dramas. Among the conjectures are: the Encyclopaedia*

> *Britannica (1894 edition), which suggests that Shakespeare must have spent much time in the 'forest of Arden ... picking up his remarkable knowledge of forest law'; J. Dover Wilson, who has him acting from 1581 to 1599, except when he was tutoring the Earl of Southampton 'in a country school' and taking a trip to Italy with the Earl and John Florio, a writer and teacher at Magdalen College; Joseph Quincy Adams, who also believes that he was teaching in a country school and in addition had been hunting to hounds and practising falconry; Edgar I. Fripp, who is convinced that he was studying law till 1587; Karl Elze, who believes that he was travelling in Italy; Edward Garnett and Edmund Gosse, who favour his travelling and fighting in the Low Countries; Caroline F. E. Spurgeon, who sees him spending his time in deer-hunting, horseback riding, hawking, bowling, tennis-playing, and engaging in other sports; Churton Collins, who is sure that he was working in an attorney's office; William Allen Nielsen, who is sure he filled his waking hours with the devouring of books. To these, Samuel Schoenbaum adds Arthur Gray of Jesus College, according to whom the young Stratfordian was a page to Sir Henry Goodere of Polesworth Hall and there acquired his knowledge of Latin and of polite society; Francis Yates, who has him teaching in a secret Catholic institution, and others more eccentric.*[8]

The impossibility of filling the seven lost years between 1585 and 1592 with a consistent explanation is much in evidence. In fact, it was inevitable from the very beginning, because the history of the real Shakespeare is not the history of Shaxpere. The essential fact remains that not one single record has ever been discovered concerning Shaxpere's activities during this seven-year period, and that is because there are none to be found. Whatever he was doing at this time was commonplace. He was a husband, a father, and a trade employee: as such, no record was made of these mundane activities.

The speculative attempts made by those attempting to fill these lost years with their own personal ideas are nothing more than assumptions derived from the content of Shakespeare's plays. This allows speculators to complete yet another exercise in circular reasoning, by deducing from the plays the information required for Shaxpere to have written about them. They then use this inferred knowledge as a fresh premise to describe him as a specialist in that subject, who transferred this knowledge to the plays.

Once again, without this circular reasoning there is nothing to substantiate Shaxpere's acquisition of so much detailed knowledge in so short a space of time: the extent of which covers politics, court etiquette, hunting, continental travel, ships, the army, legal matters, botany, &c. Dr Levi Fox seemed dazed by the sheer variety of possibilities, and was compelled to remark:

> *Yet in its way, this tantalizing seven-year gap is rather attractive, allowing everyone to construct an apprenticeship to his or her own mind, unfettered by the inconvenience of recorded fact.* [9]

In other words, an admission from one of 'the Bard's' most fervent admirers that it is all fantasy; there is not one jot of evidence to even suggest this man ever left Stratford-upon-Avon. Indeed, with a new wife and three infants to bring-up, there were four good reasons to keep him at home. Yet, between 1564 and 1592, one half of his lifetime had already passed by without the slightest indication that he was in any way different from other men who were leading ordinary, everyday lives: they were christened, they married; they laboured; they begot children who were also christened; they died.

Just occasionally, their names may have appeared in a court case, or on a legal document, as when William and his father engaged in litigation to recover land and property in Wilmcot. The building and ground had been passed to John Shaxpere through his marriage to Mary Arden, but he had subsequently mortgaged the property in 1578 for a cash sum of £40. The loan had then been left unpaid. A quarrel ensued, and the title to the estate passed to John Shaxpere's brother-in-law, who had provided the loan. In 1589, Will's father sought to recover the property by offering to repay the amount, naming his eldest son, William, as the beneficiary. But the lawsuit failed and the Arden inheritance was lost.

Why did John Shaxpere attempt to recover the Arden property by naming his son as a beneficiary to the inheritance? A possible reason is because the two families had outgrown their single household. Eight children were born to John and Mary, although by 1589, childhood deaths had reduced this number to five. Added to this number were William, his wife Anne, and their three children. With both families sharing the same home, and the house being used to run the family business, space would have been severely limited. An obvious solution was to seek repossession of the mortgaged property so that William's family could have a place of their own. To accomplish this, John Shaxpere needed to go to court to re-establish title. If this was the reason behind John Shaxpere's litigation, it raises an important question: Was it the loss of the court case that finally motivated William to leave home and seek a better fortune in London?

According to his biographers, Will Shaxpere's arrival in the capital city does, indeed, coincide with the loss of this court case. It is also an explanation that fits the account given by a certain Mr Dowdall, who visited Shaxpere's grave in 1693. He made conversation with the church sexton, an octogenarian who knew something of the town's history and its residents. Dowdall was told that as a young man, Shaxpere had been apprenticed to a local butcher, but he later escaped to London where he found employment in one of the theatres (Michell: 1996, p.57).

This narrative comes remarkably close to another report told to John Aubrey, who wrote in his *Brief Lives* a short biography of many prominent people of that time. Upon Aubrey's arrival in Stratford-upon-Avon, for the purpose of enquiring about Shakespeare, he learned that . . .

> *His father was a Butcher, and I have been told heretofore by some of the neighbours, that when he was a boy he exercised his father's Trade, but when he kill'd a Calfe, he would do it in a high style, and make a Speech.*[10]

There is every likelihood this was actually how Shaxpere spent his lost years. It would also explain why no better report of them has ever been discovered. And it provides a reason for him leaving home to seek a better fortune in the capital city; something that people still do, especially when they migrate to more prosperous countries.

But this explanation is not one favoured by Shakespeare's biographers. Although they have no objection to him arriving in London in 1589, they cannot afford to connect it with the loss of his father's court case, and especially not with him having been a butcher's apprentice. Instead, they sanitize his life. One popular way of achieving this has been by repeatedly referring to Shaxpere's father as *"a glove-maker"*. John Shaxpere did once describe his occupation as such, but that was eight years before William was born. His subsequent occupation, which caused him to be prosecuted for illegal dealings, was through trading as a wool merchant.

Perhaps John Shaxpere continued to make gloves, although for this he would have had to strip the carcasses and cure the hides; and this, quite apart from his other means of obtaining money, which included usury: a practice for which, once again, he was prosecuted.

After the birth of his twins, Shaxpere's transition to poet and dramatist requires that he did something scholarly; working in the family abattoir is out of the question, otherwise it would be impossible to justify his almost instant recognition in London as a highly educated young man, and an accomplished poet, actor and playwright.

Readers will no doubt be conversant with television 'Soaps', where characters are created with instant attributes, together with a ready access to any career or profession their creators wish to impose upon them. Shaxpere's biographers have dealt with his arrival in London similarly. Yet, realistically, not one iota of evidence exists to identify him as anybody other than a young man from the provinces: someone who arrived in the capital city with little or no money, and neither recommendation, nor education, but who was nevertheless determined to use his wits to do well. This brings to mind a quote from the *Satires* of Juvenal, which translated from the Latin, reads: *"Difficult indeed it is for those to emerge from obscurity whose noble qualities are cramped by narrow means at home."* Even if Shaxpere had possessed any of the noble qualities to which Juvenal was referring, the way ahead would have been far from the easy manner described by his biographers.

But his image-makers have to think differently. They reason *a posterior* from Shakespeare's plays, to deduce what Shaxpere was capable of, and then argue *a priori* to justify what Shaxpere accomplished through these inferred abilities. For example, the Shakespeare plays indicate their author to have been exceptionally knowledgeable with regard to English law.

> *No dramatist of the time, not even Beaumont, who was the younger son of a Judge of the Common Pleas, used legal phrases with Shake-*

speare's readiness and exactness … legal phrases flow from his pen as part of his vocabulary, and parcel of thought.

Richard Grant White,
William Shakespeare – Attorney in Law, (1865)

This can be taken as genuine evidence that Shaxpere had previously worked in a lawyer's office. Consequently, because he had previously worked for a lawyer, this in turn can be used to explain why he was so adept at introducing so much legal knowledge into his plays. It is, however, still circular reasoning. In fact, this argument can be applied to every single one of the proposed occupations that Shaxpere was allegedly involved in during his lost years. Without evidence to support his whereabouts during this seven-year period, circular reasoning has to be the mainstay of every biographer.

Someone arguing from the dominant view of Shakespeare could be tempted to persist, by claiming that his plays offer a sound basis for deducing the author's earlier learning experiences. This is quite true, but the argument is only credible if there exist separate and unambiguous evidence supporting Will Shaxpere's actual participation in such activities. Clearly, none has ever been found. If it were otherwise, there would be one less reason to question his authorship of the poetry and plays that carry Shakespeare's name.

In complete contrast, let it be claimed that the 17th Earl of Oxford wrote the works of Shakespeare, as Ben Jonson vowed was true; the situation then becomes quite different. All the activities that Shaxpere is said to have engaged in during his lost years would then be attributed to Oxford. But in Oxford's case, there exists evidence that he was definitely engaged in precisely these very same activities.

Consequently, when considering Shakespeare's lost years; that is, isolated from all other considerations, it is far simpler to show that Oxford was Shakespeare, than it is to justify the view that Shaxpere, in some unexplained manner, and in so short a space of time, achieved the same educational advantages as Oxford.

These advantages, befitting a nobleman's education, involved private tuition, a university education at Cambridge, a course of legal studies at Gray's Inn, continental travel, a spell with the army, an introduction to politics, familiarity with Court protocol, and a detailed knowledge of hawking and hunting; everything, in fact, that can be found in Shakespeare's plays.

There is another problem with Shaxpere's supposed activity during his lost years. To place him in a lawyer's office excludes him from having been a schoolteacher; excludes him from having been in service to a nobleman; excludes him from having travelled abroad; excludes him from having taken part in active service on the continent; excludes him from having learnt woodcraft in the Forest of Arden, as well as a number of other imagined occupations conjured up by his advocates.

Those who attempt to make a case for what Shaxpere did before arriving in London, invariably fall into the trap of excluding him from so much else that is of equal importance, especially when seeking answers for so much learning in such a brief space of time. The result is that Shakespeare becomes a soap character. Anything can be said of him, and his skills are those imparted by his image-makers.

> *Known as Shakespeare's 'lost years'; there is absolutely no documentary evidence about the poet's life between 1585 (the baptism of his twins as registered in Stratford-upon-Avon's parish records) and 1592 (the first time he was mentioned in print as an actor in London). Various theories seek to explain his activities during these seven years, including ... that Shakespeare was occupied as a schoolmaster during this time ... E.A.J. Honigmann offers a different interpretation of the schoolmaster theory. He believes that Shakespeare's employers were the powerful Hoghton family ... Others have speculated that Shakespeare passed this time working as a conveyancer's clerk in the office of a prosperous lawyer, that he served as a military foot soldier in the low countries, that he was a scrivener, a gardener, a sailor, a printer, a money-lender, a coachman, or that he simply went on an extended holiday to Italy.* [11]

Consequently, before reaching London, and with so many diverse opinions fastened to him, Shaxpere can comfortably be said to have accomplished everything necessary for him to begin writing the plays of Shakespeare. He can speak French fluently, he knows the geography of Italy's major cities, he is familiar with the etiquette of aristocratic households; he is accustomed to the terminology of the hunt, and the language of seamen; he knows what it is like to be in an army camp before battle; he is an accomplished attorney at law; he can read Latin and Greek in the original; he has read all the classical authors, and the popular plays of the Renaissance; he understands art and the artists, and appears conversant with many masterpieces displayed on the Continent.

In 1589, four years before Shakespeare's name emerged in public as the poet who wrote *Venus and Adonis*, the 17th Earl of Oxford was in his fortieth year, and had, by then, accomplished all that is listed above. Everything that Shaxpere supposedly did during his *lost years*, in order to be seen as publicly qualified for the authorship of Shakespeare's greatest works, had, by then, been integrated into Oxford's learning experience. And, it is this massive display of knowledge and education that Shaxpere's biographers condense into those seven absent years when Shaxpere's name disappeared from the records, and Shakespeare was still a name that no one had yet heard of. The word 'fantastic' appears to fall short of the imagination needed to accept this, whether in the writing or the reading of it.

Greene's Groats-worth of Wit

The exact year when Shaxpere arrived in London is not known. Betterton did, however, obtain an account of what happened upon his arrival in the capital, and this was included in Rowe's book. Betterton's informant was Sir William Davenant (1606–1668), England's poet laureate in 1638, and son of John Davenant, an innkeeper and former Mayor of Oxford. It was at Davenant's Crown tavern that Shaxpere stayed during his many journeys between London and Stratford-upon-Avon, and while there, the story he once related to the elder Davenant sounds appropriate enough for a countryman newly arrived in London. It is quite without airs and graces, and more believable because of that, especially since Shaxpere's country upbringing would have prepared him for the job he recalled having performed.

> *[His] first expedient was to wait at the door of the playhouse and hold the horses of those that had no servants, that they might be ready again after the performance. In this office he became so conspicuous for his care and readiness, that in a short time every man, as he alighted, called for Will. Shakespeare, and scarcely any other waiter was trusted with a horse, while Will. Shakespeare could be had. This was his first dawn of better fortune. Shakespeare finding more horses*

put into his hand than he could hold, hired boys to wait under his inspection, who when Will. Shakespeare was summoned, were immediately to present themselves, 'I am Shakespeare's boy, sir! In time Shakespeare found higher employment; but as long as the practice of riding to the playhouse continued, the waiters that held the horses retained the application of Shakespeare's boys.[12]

The part of London where Shaxpere operated as horse attendant is likely to have been Shoreditch. Both the Curtain, built in 1577, and the Theatre raised one year earlier, were in that vicinity, and the possibility of serving those arriving on horseback at either playhouse was an obvious incentive. In addition, there was a popular watering hole for horses nearby. The added security of having someone like Shaxpere to guard against horse thieves would have ensured the demand for his services remained high.

The lack of any alternative account relating to Shaxpere's arrival in London places his biographers at a great disadvantage. Davenant's story is rejected because it fails to fit in with the premise that governs what is acceptable fact and what must be discounted. The reader should therefore be aware that it is possible to prove anything when evidence is only accepted if it suits the premise it supports.

In the present case, it is conjectured that Shaxpere arrived in London c.1589, as a fully accomplished poet and playwright, with a sheaf of plays under his arm and an education to match the learning and experiences required to have written these. Will Shaxpere, the butcher's apprentice turned horse attendant, does not fit that role at all, and so it is dismissed. In its place, Shakespeare's image-makers project onto their ideal model of the man whatever is deemed necessary to facilitate the literary abilities of their invention.

It is at this point, with Shaxpere in London, supposedly possessing all of the accomplishments of a scholarly poet and dramatist, that his image-makers deliver what they believe to be their trump card. It is Robert Greene's dying rant against a man called Shake-scene, published in 1592 by Henry Chettle under the title: *Greenes Groats-worth of Witte Bought With A Million of Repentance*. Here, or so we are told to believe, is proof positive that by 1592, Shakespeare was already recognised by a leading writer of the day as an actor and playwright.

There is a problem with this so-called 'proof'. It does not stand inspection. Its survival as the prevailing view exists solely because it is repeatedly given unquestioned support by Shakespeare's advocates: academics, who read everything connected with Shakespeare through lenses that consistently distort the light of reason. These lenses are ground from the premise that Shaxpere of Stratford-upon-Avon was the same person that penned plays and poetry under the name of William Shakespeare. Once that premise has been accepted, it governs the interpretation of everything associated with the life and works of Shakespeare. Nothing, thereafter, is too fantastic that the word genius cannot overcome.

Nevertheless, once this premise is set aside, and the intellect is freed from its constraint, a quite different interpretation takes form: one, based upon factual evidence, and which unerringly draws the 17th Earl of Oxford into the picture.

In the summer of 1592, four men of literary standing met for a meal together at a tavern in east London known as *"The Steelyard"* (Nashe called it the 'Still Yard'). One of them was the playwright Robert Greene who died shortly after the meal: his death being cruelly attributed by Gabriel Harvey to: *"a surfeit of pickle herring and Rhenish wine."* [13] Two weeks after the funeral, a pamphlet was published that claimed to be his dying repentance. This was the now famous *Groats-worth of Witte.* Inside the pamphlet, Greene identified his three dining companions by their nicknames; one he called 'gracer', another, he named 'young Juvenal' and the third, he referred to as 'St George'. [14]

'Gracer' has been reliably identified as Marlowe; the Privy Council had intervened on his behalf to ensure that he received special grace while at Cambridge in order to receive his degree (the 'Grace Book' held at Cambridge refers; see Carroll, 2004, p.284 fn.34). Marlowe was also known for his violent temper, and his subsequent confrontation with Chettle, who he appears to have recognised as both editor and part-author of *Greene's Groats-worth of Witte,* led the publisher to afterwards declare: *"With neither of them that take offense was I acquainted, and with one of them I care not if I neuer be"* [15]

Marlowe had reason to take offence. Greene's pamphlet contained several slurs against his character, which, he thought, made him too easily recognizable. He was also quite certain Greene, who shared many of his vices, would never have penned these insults.

Chettle also claimed he was visited by the other person that took offence. It is this man's identity that is of considerable importance to anyone attempting to understand the subsequent events that followed the meeting of these four writers.

Further clues identifying Greene's other two companions became evident when Thomas Nashe published *Strange News*: a pamphlet that attacked Gabriel Harvey for the remarks he had made against the deceased Greene. In mid-flow, Nashe identified the other two men as: *"I and one of my fellows Will Monox."* [16] Nashe was therefore the third member of the quartet, and since *"tender Juvenal"* was the nickname for young Nashe,[17] we are left with 'Will Monox' as 'St George'.

Now, it happens to be a matter of unquestionable fact that 'Will Monox' is an anagram of 'M. Will Oxon.' And, as every Latin scholar knows, 'Oxon.' is the long established abbreviation for *"Oxonia latinized name of Ox(en)ford"* (OED).

When Nashe mentioned Will Monox to Harvey, he did so to raise Greene's esteem in Harvey's eyes. In an age of anagrams, he wanted Harvey to understand who was behind the name. He knew that Oxford and Harvey had been students together at Cambridge, and it was during their time there that Oxford had given Harvey *"gold angels"* (gold coins worth between one third and one half of a pound, embossed with the figure of Saint Michael) to help him through some financial difficulty. Harvey was therefore obligated to Oxford, and consequently at fault for insulting one of the earl's dinner guests. But in 1592, Harvey would not have understood why Oxford's abbreviated Latin name, Oxon, was prefixed by M[aster] Will. So, to make doubly clear who Will Monox was, and leave Harvey in no possible doubt as to the identity of Robert Greene's host, Nashe added: *"Hast thou never heard of him and his great dagger?"* [18] Harvey would then have understood this to be confirmation of the part of the anagram involving Oxon., even if he remained mystified by the prefix, 'M. Will'.

Will Monox's great dagger was Nashe's satirical reference to the great Sword of State. As Lord High Chamberlain of England it was Oxford's responsibility to carry this before the Queen on state occasions (see figure).

This takes us to the next question, which is why had Oxford been given the designate St. George? The answer is that it was simply harmless flattery, and in line with the grievance made by Oxford's father-in-law, Lord Burghley.

In a letter written to Walsingham in 1587, the Lord Treasurer had complained of *"[Oxford's] lewd friends who still rule him by flatteries."* [19] Greene, Marlowe, and Nashe would come under that definition in Burghley's estimation. However, the patriotic connotation attached to St George counted for more than flattery, because it could not possibly be construed as giving offence to a person of Oxford's standing, as some other nickname might very easily have done.

Although Oxford may have occasionally socialized with men like Greene, Marlowe and Nashe, talented writers though they were, it is certain that he insisted upon his own position in society being respected, especially in the class-structured age of Elizabethan England.

By the summer of 1592, 'Shakespeare' had recently completed *Henry VI Part III*, for it was being staged at that time. This play is noted for the many times it rings out with patriotic cries of Saint George, as does Part I, and *Richard III:* two plays that were part of the same tetralogy.

Henry VI Part I

[The English scale the walls and cry '**Saint George**!']
(Act 2: sc. i)

God and **Saint George**, Talbot and England's right,
Prosper our colours in this dangerous fight. (Act 4: sc. ii)

Saint George and victory! Fight, soldiers, fight.
(Act 4: sc. vi)

The thrice victorious Lord of Falconbridge,
Knight of the noble order of **Saint George**,
(Act 4: sc. vii)

Henry VI Part III

Then strike up drums. God and **Saint George** for us.
(Act 2: sc. i)

Unsheathe your sword good father; cry '**Saint George**!'
(Act 2: sc. ii)

For Warwick and his friends, God and **Saint George**.
(Act 4: sc. ii)

Lords to the field, **Saint George** and victory!
(Act 5: sc. I)

Richard III

God and **Saint George**! Richmond and victory!
(Act 5: sc. iii)

This and **Saint George** to boot! What think'st thou, Norfolk?
(Act 5: sc. iii)

Our ancient word of courage, fair **Saint George**,
Inspire us with the spleen of fiery dragons!
(Act 5: sc. iii).

Saint George also occurs in *The Taming of the Shrew*; said to have been written in 1591, at about the same time as *Henry VI: "Now by Saint George I am too young for you."* (Act 2: sc. i).

Robert Greene fell ill and died, soon after attending the banquet hosted (as it now appears) by Oxford – alias M Will Oxon, aka St. George. It is clear from the circumstances of Greene's death that he had little or no money with which to provide for himself, and it was entirely due to the charity of a shoemaker and his wife that his end came with a modicum of comfort.

Harvey referred to having called at the shoemaker's house in Dow-gate after Greene died, to be told that on his deathbed, Greene had called for *"a penny-pot of Malmsey"*, and had then scribbled a final note to his abandoned wife, begging her to repay the kindness of his two comforters. Harvey, it is assumed, copied the note.

Doll, I charge thee by the love of our youth, and by my soul's rest, that thou wilt see this man paid: for if he and his wife had not succoured me, I had died in the streets.

Robert Greene.[20]

Oxford, for it could hardly have been 'Shake-scene', the man Greene allegedly raged against in 'his' *Groats Worth of Wit,* committed the dead man's final hours to the pages of *Henry V.* And by doing so, immortalised his former companion's final moments through the mouth of SIR JOHN FALSTAFF.

> BOY: Mine host Pistol, you must come to my master;
> and your hostess—he is very sick, and would to
> bed. (Act 2: sc. i)

The HOSTESS is referred to by PISTOL as DOLL in the quartos, also in the First Folio, but some editors have since changed this to NELL.

> PISTOL: Fortune play the housewife with me now?
> News have I that my Doll is dead I'th'spital
> Of malady of France, (Act 5: sc .i)

The HOSTESS recalls FALSTAFF'S death, but is interrupted by NYM.

> NYM: They say he cried out of sack.
>
> HOSTESS: Ay, that 'a did. (Act 2: sc. iii)

Professor Jonathan Bate, an uncompromising advocate of Shaxpere's role as Shakespeare, also recognised the connection between Greene's and FALSTAFF'S deathbed scenes, although not without discernible unease.

> *Sir John Falstaff—who dies in Hostess Quickly's tavern, calling out for sack and remembering a woman called Doll in an uncanny replication of Greene's death in Hostess Isam's house calling out for malmsey and writing to a wife called Doll.* [21]

For Bate, this dramatisation of Falstaff's death retains an *uncanny* similarity to Greene's demise. Had Bate, and those of a like mind, not become so mesmerised by the attractive tales that govern Shakespearian study, and remained dispassionate scholars, there would not be the slightest problem in recognizing Oxford's final bow to Robert Greene. But, as it is, yet another error of omission is added to a multiple of others in order to shore up the unstable premise that Will Shaxpere wrote the complete works of William Shakespeare.

Bate was rather less coy when referring to Marlowe's death, which is referred to in a passing remark made by TOUCHSTONE to the unlettered AUDREY in *As You Like It.*

> *When a man's verses cannot be understood, nor a man's good wit seconded with the forward child, understanding, it strikes a man more dead than a great reckoning in a little room. Truly, I would the gods had made thee poetical.* (Act 3 sc. iii).

Bate saw little difficulty in Shakespeare having recalled that Marlowe, too, had been *"struck dead in a little room"* whilst quarrelling with his two companions over a *"great reckoning";* although whether this was for food or some other matter is left to conjecture (Bate, 1998 p.123).

One can therefore see how easily the premise that Shaxpere wrote Shakespeare controls what is acceptable and what must be omitted. Greene had insulted Shakespeare; therefore Shakespeare cannot be allowed to honour Greene, especially not with FALSTAFF'S death scene. On the other hand, traditionalists believe that Marlowe's work instructed Shakespeare; therefore it is perfectly acceptable that Marlowe's death should be acknowledged with a suitable poetic line.

We now come to the reason for Nashe having prefixed 'Oxon.' by 'Master Will' when taking Harvey to task in *Strange News.* Plainly, Nashe could not name Oxford without betraying a confidence. Fortunately, Nashe was a satirist, and in this lies the reason for his having referred to Oxford as 'Will'.

The explanation arises from the reason why Oxford had invited three of the capital's leading writers to join him for a banquet. His motive was straightforward. He needed to tell all three, Nashe, Marlowe, and Greene that there would soon be a new arrival on the literary scene: a person masquerading as the author of his poetry and plays.

This work would be presented to the public under the name William Shakespeare; but it was not to be attributed to Oxford because a certain William Shaxpere, recently arrived from the county of Warwickshire, had agreed to be his allonym. To every outward appearance, this Will Shaxpere would be a new poet named William Shakespeare. Hence, Nashe's satirical reference to 'Master Will Oxenford'—a hybrid of the two names, which he scrambled into the cryptically condensed form of 'WILL MONOX'.

By calling these three writers together, and treating them to a meal, Oxford was also appealing to them not to reveal his plan by seeking out this newcomer Shakespeare, for he easily recognised they would discover the deception, and likely commit it to a satirical pamphlet—as actually happened soon afterwards with the anonymously written *Willobie His Avisa* (1594). It is also possible that he asked the three men dining with him to support his plan, since it would enable his work to be made public for as long as the ruse could be maintained.

Apart from Nashe's reference to Will, Oxford may also be said to have acknowledged his acquired cognomen, for he used it in a sonnet, although not without a touch of that characteristic humour for which he was renowned.

> *Make but my name thy love, and love that still,*
> *And then thou lov'st me, for my name is Will* (cxxxvi).

It can be appreciated just how vital it was that Oxford should explain to his guests what was about to happen, and so prevent the deception being discovered as soon as *Venus and Adonis* went on sale. Oxford was using his class superiority, coupled with the respect his writing attracted, to ensure that Nashe, Marlowe and Greene, three leading lights in the literary world at that time, did not give the game away too soon by discovering for themselves that he was using Shaxpere as an allonym, while writing under the penname of Shakespeare.

Oxford needed these three men to remain silent about his plan: even, possibly, to the extent of deflecting questions from the curious, who might be expected to make enquiries about this newcomer Shakespeare. Oxford's plan to publish his work and seek a wider audience for it by employing Shaxpere as his allonym was about to be released in public, and although no one realised it at the time, it was to mark the beginning of one of literature's greatest mysteries, and eventual embarrassment.

The idea for getting his poetry into print had likely been on Oxford's mind for some time. Unfortunately, it was considered inappropriate for a titled nobleman to publish verses. Much lower members of England's class hierarchy, such as Raleigh and Donne, were content to circulate their poems in manuscript. Oxford was not so minded; what he needed was the right sort of person to act in his stead. Someone with no known educational background in London would be ideal, for otherwise the person could be checked out and found wanting. But the person did need to be intelligent and forcefully blunt, since he would have to respond to questions about his supposed art. Someone unable to write would also be acceptable, because anyone previously having put pen to paper might attract unwelcome comparison.

The person required, also had to be someone associated with the theatre, especially a person who could be trusted for a price. William Shaxpere, recently arrived from Stratford-upon-Avon and attached to the Theatre in Shoreditch, came close to these requirements: although his gruff Warwickshire burr was probably not what Oxford had in mind. Nevertheless, the similarity between Shaxpere's name and that of Shakespeare allowed Oxford the use of this more literary *nom de plume*, and one that could easily be confused with Shaxpere, Shagspere, Shakspeare, Shackspeare &c.

Thus, William Shaxpere, at a time no later than 1592, had graduated from horse attendant outside the playhouses to odd-job man in either the Curtain or the Theatre, and from thence to employee of the Earl of Oxford. Edmund Malone stated: *"there is a stage tradition that his first office in the theatre was that of Call-boy or prompter's attendant; whose employment is to give the performers notice to be ready to enter."* (Chambers, *Shakespeare: Facts and Problems* vol. 2 p. 296). This is another piece of evidence that is quietly brushed aside by orthodoxy.

The 3rd Earl of Southampton, for long under the influence of Oxford, as we shall later see, had agreed to participate in the scam by acting as 'Shakespeare's' patron; thus providing the cover of nobility for the 'embryo poet'. Although how this new, and as yet unheard-of, arrival from an obscure market town in the Midlands was supposed to have had almost instantaneous access to this pampered young Earl, and then to have persuaded him to become his patron, is just as fantastic as his supposed activities during the so-called 'lost years'.

Oxford would have realised this presented a potential obstacle to what he was planning, and he overcame it by writing the two grovelling letters, ostensibly composed by a man of his allonym's lower class, prefacing *Venus and Adonis* and *Lucrece.* In retrospect, one may suppose how amused Oxford would have been, could he have foreseen the legions of scholars who have since fawned over these same two letters.

Such then was the plan involving Oxford in his pretence to be William Shakespeare, and his nineteen-year-old companion, the Earl of Southampton, pretending to be his patron. It was the gist of this plot that was relayed by Oxford to Greene, Marlowe, and Nashe on that late summer evening of 1592.

We know this because Greene took notes of what was said, perhaps with the idea of writing something suitable in the near future, and it is this that takes us to the actual content of the letter published under his name in the *Groats-worth of Witte.* It commences:

> *To those Gentlemen his Quondam acquaintance, that spend their wits in making plays, R. G. wisheth a better exercise, and wisdom to prevent his extremities.*
>
> *Base-minded men all three of you, if by my misery you be not warned:* [22]

Greene would never have dared call Oxford 'base-minded', which confirms Chettle's hand in the affair. Although, let it be said, Chettle's input was entirely due to a misunderstanding on his part when reading the notes Greene had left behind. As for Nashe, he never once doubted Chettle's part in the matter, and vehemently denounced the publication as *"a scald trivial lying pamphlet, cald Greens groats-worth of wit".* [23] Even the publisher had been worried, and with considerable forethought added a disclaimer to the entry he made in the *Stationers' Register*; this read: *"upon the peril of Henrye Chettle."* [24]

Greene's letter continues: bewailing the fate of authors; for he had been abandoned while *in extremis* by players who had only recently been feeding off the words he put into their mouths. Then came the all-important sentence:

> *. . . there is an upstart Crow, beautified with our feathers, that with his Tygers hart wrapt in a Players hyde, supposes he is as well able to bombast out a blanke verse as the best of you: and being an absolute Johannes fac totum, is in his own conceit the onely Shake-scene in a countrey.* [25]

When Oxford read this, he must have recognised at once what had happened. After the banquet, Greene had jotted down some notes relating to their earlier conversation involving the planned launch of William Shakespeare onto the literary scene. Perhaps Greene had had it in mind to prepare the way for Shakespeare with a suitable introduction. But, alas, before he could commit his notes to a full article, he had fallen ill, and on 3 September 1592 he breathed his last. Chettle, having recently begun business as a hack writer, and being an acquaintance of Greene's, acted as the deceased man's literary executor. It was while in the employment of this office that he came upon the notes scribbled by Greene, and which he later acknowledged to have been . . .

> *il written as sometime Greenes hand was none of the best, licensd it must be, ere it could bee printed which could never be if it might not be read. To be brief I writ it over, and as neare as I could, followed the copy.* [26]

Unable to entirely decipher Greene's scribbled notes, and being unfamiliar with what was meant by the parts he could read, Chettle had pieced together what he believed would make a good death-bed repentance, written ostensibly in the words of a man widely acknowledged for his amoral life. It was the stuff that today's tabloids feed upon, and guaranteed to sell.

When the pamphlet was published, Oxford could only have been aghast. His carefully laid plans to present William Shakespeare to the public as a clean-cut, talented poet, with Lord Southampton as his patron, had been hopelessly compromised: misconstrued by Chettle's cock-eyed editing of the situation. Shakespeare was now being described by the pen of one of London's best known writers as a thieving magpie and a Jack-of-all-trades: a totally different person from the one Oxford had intended to portray.

Using richly cultured phrases that carried the suggestion of a classically, educated poet, Oxford had painted the picture of Shakespeare as a scholar wishing to dedicate the first heir of his invention, *Venus and Adonis*, to his newly acquired patron, the young Earl of Southampton: who had graciously agreed to become his sponsor.

Worse was to follow. Chettle's criticism of Shakespeare also included the phrase: *"his Tygers hart wrapt in a Players hyde"*, which he had unwittingly paraphrased from: *"O tiger's heart wrapt in a woman's hide": (3 Henry VI,* Act I: sc. iv). Incidentally, this is the same play that rings out with cries of Saint George, thereby confirming that it would have been fresh in the minds of Greene and his three companions. Thus, if *Henry VI* was to be attributed to the author of *Venus and Adonis,* as was likely, then without realizing it, Chettle had mauled Shakespeare with a phrase taken from what was intended to be 'his' own play.

Chettle did confess later that he had never heard of Shakespeare until that time; but, then, neither had anyone else: other than those involved in the plot. Even those who support the orthodox view are forced to admit that this was the first known reference to Shakespeare as an actor and man of literature.

Elsewhere in the Groats-worth letter, Shakespeare is rebuked for his resemblance to Aesop's crow: the bird that adorned itself with fine feathers taken from other birds, so that it might appear like them. The allusion to Shaxpere donning the literary plumage of Oxford is most appropriate. When drawing attention to this parallel in his notes, Greene would have been thinking of a play he had written, called *Never Too Late,* in which Cicero employs the same allusion to Aesop. *"Why Roscius are thou proud with Esops Crow, being pranct with the glorie of others feathers?"* [27]

Roscius was Rome's most celebrated actor during the time of Julius Caesar, and his name has since entered the English language to describe similarly gifted players (OED refers).

'Shakespeare' had also made mention of this actor in *3 Henry VI,* performed earlier that year: *"What scene of death hath Roscius now to act?"* (Act V: sc. vi). With so recent a reference to Roscius, the connection Greene made to Shakespeare and Aesop's crow would have been up to date at the time.

It is now an easy matter to see how Chettle had got hold of the wrong end of the stick. Greene had made notes after dining with Oxford, to the effect that by masquerading as a poet and a playwright, Shaxpere—or Shakespeare as he was now to be recognised—was really like Aesop's crow: pretending to be the person he was not. Oxford would write the work, Shaxpere would adorn himself with the airs and graces of the poet and playwright, as though he was the author; that is, *"in his own conceit",* which means in his own personal play. Oxford's close literary associates would maintain the deception by humouring Shaxpere in his pretence as a poet ape.

As if to confirm this, Chettle unconsciously allows Greene's letter to state the truth, when he notes how this upstart *"supposes he is well able to bombast out a blank verse as the best of you."*[28]

This can only mean that Chettle had managed to decipher Greene's scribble with moderate success, but without understanding the underlying story behind it. He not unnaturally took Greene's words at face value when editing them, believing that what he wrote down was a true account of the matter as seen by Greene before he died. Regrettably, this has had a similar effect upon scholars ever since: each one following the other into the wilderness.

Chettle's letter placed Oxford in a dilemma. His plan to launch Shakespeare's career under the patronage of the Earl of Southampton had met a huge setback. What could be done to remedy the situation? The solution he chose was to seek an apology from Chettle. The publisher was to be left in no doubt regarding the probity of 'Shakespeare's' character, and the esteem in which gentlemen of the highest rank valued his writing.

The strategy worked. On 8 December 1592, an entry appeared in the *Stationers' Register,* advertising a pamphlet to be published under the title *Kind-Harts Dreame.* This was to be the medium through which Chettle conceded ...

> *With neither of them that take offence was I acquainted, and with one of them I care not if I never be. The other, whome at that time I did not so much spare, as since I wish I had ... because my selfe have seen his demeanor no less civill than he exelent in the qualities he professes: Besides, divers of worship have reported his uprightness of dealing, which argues his honesty, and his facetious grace in writing, that aprooves his Art.*[29]

Who were the two who took offence? Distinguished Regius Professor of English Language and Literature at Glasgow University, Peter Alexander, provided the customary answer.

> *It is clear from Chettle's own reply that he is referring to Marlowe and Shakespeare. ... Chettle, however, feels he owes no apology to Marlowe ... To Shakespeare Chettle offers a full and frank apology.*[30]

Certainly, there is little cause to doubt Marlowe's belligerent attitude, which must have frightened Chettle, for he admits that he does not care to meet with one of them again. But, logically, how can the other person be Shakespeare; unless, that is, Shakespeare and Oxford were the same person? Remember, Greene had supposedly complained to his three companions about the *"upstart crow ... the onely Shake-scene in a countrey"*. Had one of the diners been Shakespeare—for it was he, to whom Chettle apologised for having given offence—then how could Greene be thought to have been referring to Shakespeare? For Greene would then be complaining to Shakespeare about this upstart crow called Shakespeare? It is sheer nonsense.

Yet, students of Shakespearian studies, without so much as a blink of the eye, repeatedly embrace it. One also wonders whatever became of those *"divers of worship"*: a mysterious band of men who suddenly appeared at the onset of Shakespeare's career, and then, just as suddenly, disappeared: never to be heard of again. Their names certainly do not appear in any of the conventional biographies.

It is now open to reason what had happened. In *Greene's Groats-worth of Witte,* Chettle used Greene's death to put into the dead man's mouth words intended to persuade Marlowe away from his atheism. While, in the letter he addressed to Greene's fellow diners, he had misread the deceased's notes, believing that they were intended for use *against* this newcomer, called Shakespeare. To both men he had therefore given offence.

Marlowe's reaction was predictable; he scared the life out of the poor little publisher. Oxford's reaction was different. He acquired some excellent references for his 'man' Shakespeare, and used them to persuade Chettle to print an apology.

Consequently, in *Greene's Groats-worth of Witte,* the connection between the covert references to 'WILL MONOX', 'his great dagger' and 'St George' leave no obvious room for doubt that Oxford was the chief diner at that ill-fated banquet, so quickly followed by Greene's death. And by exploring in greater depth the reasons for the Chettle-Greene letter, it quickly becomes apparent that the banquet was specifically held to prepare the way for William Shaxpere's arrival onto the literary scene, although not as a writer, but as a person specifically engaged to provide a living presence to the authorship of Oxford's poetry.

We shall later discover how Chettle exacted his revenge for having been duped into writing his apology.

There is still one further point that is often missed in the Chettle-Greene affair. It concerns the storm that broke out after the *Groats-worth* was published. Why should the brief ramblings of a dying man, writing about a person no one had heard of, cause such a rumpus? It is perfectly clear that at the time of Chettle's publication, Shakespeare was an unknown name, therefore of no importance. Chettle had certainly never heard of him, nor until then had the name ever been made public. It did not even appear on any actors list. And Henslowe made no record of him in his journal, despite having already staged several plays that are now attributed to Shakespeare. The name was simply unknown to the public until it suddenly emerged, some months after the Chettle episode, as the poet who had just published *Venus and Adonis.*

Insults against writers were far from unknown at that time, and when they occurred, the offended party was usually quick off the mark to print a suitable retort. Where was Shakespeare's reply? Why did this master of the ready response and clever insult not put Chettle in his place with a pamphlet of his own, and have done with it? The answer is because Shakespeare, as an actual person, never existed; he is either the Earl of Oxford or he is Will Shaxpere, depending upon the situation. To use William Shakespeare's name on a published pamphlet, when he had yet to emerge as a writer, was clearly a non-starter; it would also accentuate the deception. A personal appeal to Chettle for a public apology was the only logical course of action available.

VENUS AND ADONIS & THE RAPE OF LUCRECE

Oxford's plan to launch William Shakespeare as a penname for his allonym, Will Shaxpere, succeeded. *Venus and Adonis* was published to great acclaim in April 1593, and was followed a year later by *The Rape of Lucrece.* Two obsequious letters of dedication from the lower-class 'William Shakespeare' to his patron, Henry Wriothesley, 3rd Earl of Southampton, prefixed both poems respectively.

Plays, such as *Titus Andronicus, Henry VI Parts One, Two and Three, Richard III, Comedy of Errors,* and *Taming of A Shrew,* which, before 1593, had simply been anonymous, may have slowly begun to be associated with this new arrival from the country. Although proof is lacking, this has not prevented traditionalists from accepting it as fact.

Circumstantial evidence supporting a connection between these anonymous plays and Shakespeare's *Lucrece*, which was entered in the *Stationers' Register* in May 1594, appears to be reflected in Henslowe's Diary.

Almost immediately after this entry appeared, Henslowe staged three plays in quick succession at the Newington Butts theatre; each with titles recognizable as Shakespeare's.

5 of June	1594	Rd at andronicous	xij s
9 of June	1594	Rd at hamlet	viij s
11 of June	1594	Rd at the tamynge of A shrowe	ix s
12 of June	1594	Rd at andronicous	vij s

What now seems apparent is that Henslowe was intent upon profiting from the popularity of Shakespeare; who, in the year before, had written *Venus and Adonis*, and was now about to publish *The Rape of Lucrece*. Two of his plays, *Titus Andronicus* and *The Taming of a Shrew*, actually include references to LUCRECE, her chastity and her subsequent rape.

AARON: Take this of me: Lucrece was not more chaste
Than this Lavinia. (Act 2: sc. i: *Titus*)

...

TITUS: What Roman lord it was durst do the deed.
Or slunk not Saturnine, as Tarquin erst
That left the camp to sin in Lucrece bed?
(Act 4: sc. i: *Titus*)

...

MARCUS: And father of that chaste dishonoured dame,
Lord Janius Brutus sware for Lucrece rape,
(Act 4: sc. i: *Titus*)

ꕥ

PETRUCHIO: For patience she will prove a second Grissel,
And Roman Lucrece for her chastity.
(Act 2: sc. i: *Shrew*)

Hamlet is the other play in Henslowe's Diary, and it contains biographical details of the man who wrote all three of the plays performed at Newington Butts that June month in 1594. This was a particularly sensitive issue for the author of *Lucrece*, since he had recently published this poem under the fiction it had been written by the non-literate William Shaxpere.

It is also noteworthy that two months earlier, Henslowe had recorded the following entry: *"Rd at Kinge leare the 8 of apr ell 1594 xxvj s"*. This, he wrote, was performed by the Queen's Men and those of Lord Sussex together. Whereas, the plays performed in June were acted by the Lord Admiral's Men together with the Lord Chamberlain's Men.

To a man of Oxford's sensitive nature, the connection between these plays and his poem, *Lucrece*, was too obvious to be ignored. In his mind he may have feared his authorship was about to be revealed, and the pseudonymous Shakespeare, whom he had invented as a mask for his work, was in danger of being ridiculed. There was also an obligation to protect the young Earl of Southampton, who had lent his name to the deception by playing the role of Shakespeare's patron. Immediate action can be discerned from what happened the very next day.

> *[O]n 13 June, 1594, Henslowe drew a line across the page, and from this time on … No Shakespeare or Shakespeare-associated plays ever again appeared in Henslowe's listings.* [31]

Once again, as with Chettle's publication of *Greene's Groatsworth of Wit*, Oxford had foreseen the danger to his plans, and appears to have taken action.

Those advocating the traditional view of Shakespeare are alert to the fact that Henslowe's failure to enter Shakespeare's name in the daybook he kept is a weakness to their position of authority, and difficult to explain away without revealing just how fragile each explanation they offer must seem. But now we have a possible reason for knowing why Shakespeare's name never appeared in Henslowe's journal. Unwisely, the diarist had given offence to the Earl of Oxford by cashing in on the popularity of *Lucrece*, by staging plays referring to her rape, and with a subtle hint at their author, caricatured in *Hamlet*.

Oxford was an aloof and unforgiving man, and would likely have seen these productions as unauthorised and offensive to his status as their author. Henslowe must have bowed to the pressure exerted upon him, for he ceased to produce plays by Shakespeare from that time onwards.

Advocates of Shaxpere's authorship are quick to respond; they denounce any suggestion that either *Hamlet* or *King Lear* could have been written by Shakespeare so early in his career as a dramatist. Someone else must have written the plays. In that case what possible reason could Henslowe have had for never again staging *Hamlet, King Lear* or any other Shakespeare play after the cut-off date of June 13th?

For Shakespeare's image-makers, the period under review is something of a golden age. With little comprehension of the back-ground to what they write, and with a lack of knowledge as to how Shaxpere achieved instant recognition, or acquired the proficiency to write accomplished histories, comedies and tragedies without any known apprenticeship in drama or the theatre, they nevertheless indulge in the naiveté of face-value evidence. They are not alone, as E. T. Castle, QC pointed out.

> *A whole succession of writers, Malone, Steevens, Dyce, Collier, Halliwell, Knight and a host of minor authors, are so blinded by the admiration for Shakespeare, that they cannot read a simple document correctly, or are such simple followers of Malone that they have adopted his mistakes and made no enquiry for themselves.*[32]

This lack of any realistic idea—at least, none that does not incorporate contradictions—as to how Shaxpere could have achieved instant success as an accomplished poet and playwright, without undergoing some form of apprenticeship, has led to his supporters inventing a scenario in which he was instantly welcomed into the theatre, and his plays produced and circulated amongst several acting troupes as a matter of course. Yet, history speaks differently of such matters.

> *In Shakespeare's day the writer was commonly a drudge, obliged to hire out his services to anyone in a position to pay him money or house him in return. There were no newspapers, and the writer's craft was unprofitable.*[33]

We may recall how Shaxpere, upon his arrival in London, began life by offering himself to the gentry as a horse attendant: stationing himself outside the two playhouses in Shoreditch. From this situation, he soon became acquainted with the men who worked inside the playhouses, and from his association with them, found employment inside as a Call-boy. Greene was not the only one to refer to him as a Jack-of-all-trades.

> *It is at this Time ... that he is said to have made his first Acquaintance in the Play-house. He was receiv'd into the Company then in being, at first in a very mean Rank; But his admirable Wit, and the natural Turn of it to the Stage, soon distinguished him, if not as an extraordinary Actor, yet as an excellent Writer.* [34]

Here, we are presented with a more realistic picture of Shaxpere's entry into theatrical life, *"in a very mean Rank"*. Only later, after accepting an offer he could hardly decline, did his fortune change. Thereafter, he answered to William Shakespeare, the author of *Venus and Adonis*, and *Lucrece*, as well as the rumoured author of several plays attributed to that name.

As part of this subterfuge, he was encouraged to acquire a shareholding with the Lord Chamberlain's Men. This was later exchanged for a ten percent holding in the Globe theatre, for it was the place where 'his' plays were being performed, and it was necessary that he be seen to have a presence there

To the less inquisitive, this tended to satisfy his credentials as a playwright. It has also had the same effect upon the many scholars who have since been drawn to accept the same conclusion. But it was all an act, and one which required Shaxpere to constantly guard against becoming unmasked, so as not to jeopardise his source of income; for his employment by Lord Oxford was likely to have been profitable.

In preparing his book, *Brief Lives*, John Aubrey provided a clue as to how Shaxpere deflected attention away from his inability to write; it was discovered in a personal memorandum amongst his papers; *viz: "The more to be admired q[uia] he was not a company keeper lived in Shoreditch, wouldn't be debauched, & if invited to writ[e]:* he was in paine."*[35]

Aubrey, without realizing it, has confirmed Shaxpere's need to avoid the company of literary figures, lest he reveal himself as a deceiver. It was also from reports, contemporaneous with the time of Shakespeare, and handed down by word of mouth, one to

* The colon is authentic. This is sometimes omitted and a comma inserted after the word 'to', thus wrongly implying that he wrote he was in pain. Although why he should want to confess this in writing, instead of saying it, especially when he was supposedly complaining of pain from having written so much, contradicts the ailment he was protesting about. It is just another thoughtless attempt by doters at finding any excuse to avoid embarrassing evidence, even if it means changing the punctuation to satisfy their belief.

another, that Aubrey learned from Christopher Beeston's son William, how Shaxpere managed to evade discovery.

One can now better see how Shaxpere maintained the deception for so long. He repeatedly avoided invitations to write by pleading pain: no doubt excusing himself through having strained his writing hand. I say 'repeatedly pleading pain', because this excuse had become so well known, that it was still remembered when Aubrey made his enquiries some sixty years after Shaxpere's death. Understandably, therefore, as long as Shaxpere kept to this strict formula, and avoided drinking in public—which contradicts the tales of his time in the Mermaid—he was safe. The payment he received for his role as Shakespeare would have proved a lucrative incentive for him to keep up the pretence.

The next glimpse of Shaxpere we have at this time concerns his participation in a commercial activity for which records do exist—money lending. Within this environment he could be his natural self, moving amongst a non-literary set of people who would never give a thought to him being the poet, Shakespeare: assuming they had even heard of him. To ensure this situation continued, he retained the pronunciation of his surname with its short 'a', thereby distancing himself, when in company with the people he moved amongst, from the poet, Shakespeare, as pronounced with a long 'a'.

In 1592, the year when it is proposed that Shaxpere was persuaded to act as Oxford's allonym, a down payment would have been made to secure his compliance. The exact amount cannot be known, but a fee of £10 is not unreasonable. Were that so, it would have allowed Shaxpere to start a career of his own as a moneylender.

This idea would not have been new to him. His father had been engaged in this *"vice most odious and detestable"* for some years, and more than once, the elder Shaxpere had been brought before the court as a result of illegally lending money.

Coupled with this, we know that in 1598, Shaxpere was so well established as a moneylender that a fellow townsman, Richard Quiney, while in London on the behalf of Stratford-upon-Avon to plead the town's case for a tax reduction, wrote him a letter asking for a loan of £30; Quiney's request still exists.

Six years before, when Shaxpere seems to have begun lending money, a man named John Clayton became indebted to *"Willelmus Shackspere"* for the sum of £7 (≈ £2000). It was the result of a transaction, which Clayton acknowledged to the court, had taken place in Cheapside. But he had failed to repay the money, and as the court record for 1600 indicates, Shaxpere was compelled to wait eight years before he could get Clayton into court and sue him for repayment of this outstanding debt.[36]

Although Shakespeare's image-makers have much to work upon, through having adopted Chettle's misunderstanding of *Greene's Groats-worth of Wit,* further problems soon emerge.

> *The poem [Venus and Adonis *] had a growing success with the public as time went on: ten or eleven editions in his own lifetime, twenty before the fatal Civil War struck at culture. Venus and Adonis made its appeal to the cultivated, to the Court and fashionable society; it found its audience especially among the young men of the Inns of Court and the universities, who found it stimulating.* [37]

It was not only *Venus and Adonis* that received acclaim. By the year 1616, *Lucrece* had itself gone through six reprints. Yet, remarkably, having reached the pinnacle of success as a poet, the name William Shakespeare disappeared from view as suddenly as it had arrived. It would not surface again until 1598. For four years the name of Shakespeare is seen no more in print, save on the two poems already published. As for his supposed patron, Henry Wriothesley, 3rd Earl of Southampton, he is never heard of again in that capacity.

Shakespearian scholar Marchette Chute was totally baffled by this, as can be discerned from her following comment.

> *Whenever any promising young aristocrat made his debut at Court there was a rush of poets dedicating books to him, and a stupid youngster*

* Professor James A. Morgan was a Shakespeare scholar, and baffled by *Venus & Adonis.* Morgan's expertise was the English dialect. It was while studying the patois of Warwickshire, which was part of Shaxpere's formative years that he discovered there was not one single word of this dialect in *Venus & Adonis,* the so-called "first heir" of the poet's "invention". Morgan considered it "absolutely impossible that the lad Shakespeare acquired or used any other dialect than the Warwickshire he was born to, and that his father, mother and neighbours spoke." The poem's composition was therefore the source of an unsolved mystery.

(*A Study in the Warwickshire Dialect,* New York, 1900).

> *like the Earl of Southampton could hardly come of age before there was a cluster of anxious writers hoping to be admitted to the magic circle of his purse strings. The case of William Shakespeare who succeeded in getting this particular earl for his patron and then abandoned the relationship is so exceptional as to stand alone in the history of Elizabethan letters.*[38]

Chute had clearly failed to realise that the Shakespeare-Southampton connection was simply a light-hearted hoax, perpetrated by two peers of the realm, and with no thought to its future outcome. As soon as the ruse was discovered, authority must have stepped in and called the two wayward earls to book.

Once their ruse was uncovered, the Shakespeare penname was abandoned. No one had been hurt by the deception, Shaxpere had prospered, and the literary world was richer by two narrative poems. The subterfuge had simply been a strategy by which Oxford had been able to steer his poems into print without giving offence to his peer group: members of the ruling class who looked down at the idea of publishing one's thoughts for the public to read.

The nobility believed that for a member of their class to publish verses, worse still write plays for public entertainment, was totally repugnant. It was not only the upper class that thought this. *"Playwrights, especially in the increasingly Puritan world of the late 1580s, were counted worthless at best."*[39]

It was fear of rebuke that caused John Donne to forego the satisfaction of seeing his verses in print. As a consequence, his poems remained unpublished during his lifetime, *"lest he lose his dignity as a gentleman."*[40]

By engaging a tradesman's son, such as Will Shaxpere, and using him as an allonym to imply he was the author of both *Venus and Adonis* and *The Rape of Lucrece*, Oxford expected to avoid censure. What he failed to realise were the consequences. For his deception released into the world a genie, whose misunderstood association with the author, was to mislead scholars for generation after generation.

Four Years of Silence

From 1594 until 1598, the name William Shakespeare almost disappeared from public life. Had Shaxpere been the true author of the two poems, *Venus and Adonis* and *The Rape of Lucrece,* his fame and popularity would have translated itself into a lucrative opportunity for pleasing public demand by supplying more of his poetry. That he, a man renowned for his mercenary attitude to life, and with a history of poverty as well as a wife and three children to feed back home, would have neglected this golden opportunity set before him is not credible, and totally conflicts with the man's attitude towards money.

The standard response to this is that Shakespeare gave up writing poetry so that he could concentrate on an acting career whilst writing for the stage. The problem with this explanation is that researchers have toured England searching for his name amongst the visiting players who toured the country at that time and, predictably, have returned empty-handed. In short, there is no evidence to support the explanation. Secondly, the briefest look at the chronology of Shakespeare's plays indicates that they would have been composed at a non-stop rate from the time he apparently arrived in London up until the time he left. It has to be a non-stop rate because there are so many to squeeze into so short a time frame.

There is also associated with this frenzy of creative writing the fact that it was during this same period of time, when 'Shakespeare' was writing up to three masterpieces a year for the stage plus the two narrative poems already mentioned, that he was completing his sonnet sequence; this would result in 154 examples of the most sublime poetry known to man.

Some commentators have claimed these sonnets tell only a fictional story, because there is no discernible connection between their content and the life story of the man who wrote them. They are, so it is alleged, merely exercises in this particular form of verse. But, if so, why did Shaxpere not publish them and improve his income at the same time? With two major narrative poems already the talk of the literary world, a sonnet sequence to follow would have been in great demand, especially at that time when sonnets were in vogue. Their sale would have lined his pockets with gold. But since this question is quickly abandoned for want of a rational answer, one is free to conclude the sonnets *were* biographical—although evidently not Shaxpere's biography—and their content was sufficiently confidential to keep them from the public eye. The reason for maintaining this secrecy will become evident in later chapters.

In order to cover these years of obscurity, Shakespeare's image-makers concentrate upon the anonymous plays that were appearing during this time, and which were to become part of the Shakespeare canon. But why should they be anonymous when his name had become so famous? Stratford thinking has no reliable answer to this either, and merely comments upon plays that are *supposed* to have been written during this period. The dates, however, are nothing more than guesswork. But a consensus based solely upon Shaxpere having been the author, and the narrow margin of time in which reports of these plays appeared, ensures they receive the widest possible acceptance.

Their composition also accounts for what Shaxpere was doing at a time when his name had disappeared from public view. The busy little man was writing virtually non-stop, year after year, with no authorial credit for even one of his plays.

It was in the midst of this period of incessant composition that Shaxpere's name did appear on a number of occasions, but not in the context of literature. On 15 March 1595, in the Accounts of the Treasurer of the Chamber, his name is included amongst those having received £20 (≈ £5500) for performances before the Queen three months earlier, in late December 1594:

> *Will Kempe Will Shakespeare & Richard Burbage servants to the Lord Chamb[er]lain ... for two several comedies or interludes shewed by them before her Ma[jesty] ... upon St. Stephens day & Innocents day.*[41]

In the context of Shaxpere's role as the allonym for Oxford's compositions, the appearance of his name as a member of an acting company is only to be expected. It was fundamental to his role as Oxford's 'ape', for it lent substance to his connection with the theatre. Coincidentally, or otherwise, in the same year that *Lucrece* was published (1594), Henry Carey, Baron Hunsdon, the new Lord Chamberlain, became patron of the Lord Chamberlain's Men. This was the opportunity Oxford needed for his protégé, William Shaxpere, to buy himself into the theatre with a 10% shareholding. Thereafter, his presence in the playhouse was to form a natural bridge for the introduction and performance of the plays attributed to him.

It is in this capacity that it becomes possible Shaxpere played an occasional bit-part on stage: there being no report of his acting any major role. However, it is as an actor that his image-makers—who subtly change 'The Lord Chamberlain's Men' to 'his' company—embark upon another misdirection.

> *His company put on about fifteen new plays a year and Shakespeare, as a regular acting member of the company, must have appeared in most of them ... [Dover, on the Kent coast is added to his itinerary because] Shakespeare visited this district more than once with his company.* [42]

But when J. O. Halliwell-Phillipps visited Dover, expecting to find Shakespeare's name amongst the players who had visited the harbour town, it was absent One can see how easy it is to *imagine* a 'fact' about Shakespeare: in this case, that he was an actor who went on tour with *his* company. What one cannot do is provide evidence to support it.

Quite often these imagined 'facts' pass unnoticed, to become assimilated into the body of evidence supporting belief that Shaxpere was Shakespeare. However, when they are checked, where this is possible, such 'facts' may be discovered as no more than some author's wishful assumption. Consider the following paradox, which occurs in all major Shakespearian biographies.

An actor's life was a busy one. Everything had to be done in daylight hours. Rehearsals were held in the morning to prepare for the afternoon performance.

- Wake at dawn, eat breakfast, get to the theatre.
- Learn and run though any fights or dances needed. Check you have all your props and costume.
- Perform around 2 o'clock in the afternoon.
- Get your scroll for the play to be performed tomorrow.
- Find your props and costume for that play, and learn (or finish off learning) your scroll. Ensure that this is done by nightfall, because the poor quality smoky candles afforded by actors would make it difficult or impossible to read at home.
- Visit an ale-tavern (some things don't change).
- To bed, then the same again. [43]

[T]he Henslowe Diary reveals, it was commonplace for a London-based theatrical company to put on six different plays during a working week of six afternoons, and over a period of six months to stage some thirty different plays. About half of these new titles. Many would contain complicated action, sword fights, fits of madness, rapid changes of costume, mood and tempo, etc. As any present-day professional actor will instantly recognise, the pressures of such a programme would have been intense, demanding the strongest concentration, physical agility, personal self-discipline, and closest interdependence between performers. [44]

An actor's life, and the busy schedule that had to be followed are quite incompatible with the prolific output of plays required from Shaxpere during those four hectic years, when it must also be supposed that his copy was written at night by the light of a smoky candle, along with the dialogue that his fellow actors would need for their parts: for these were required whenever a new play was to be performed. But his image-makers never dwell upon such practical considerations. Their flights of imagination soar high above matters of realistic fact.

The next reference to Shaxpere's whereabouts, during his 'silent' years, occurred in August 1596, when he was informed of the death of his son Hamnet, aged eleven. Two months later, the parish of St. Helens in Bishopsgate named him on a tax assessment for the sum of five shillings. He did not pay, and in November 1596, he was posted as a tax defaulter. Then, in the same month, his name once again appeared, this time alongside that of William Wayte, a stepson of the Surrey gangster and loathed local judge, James Gardiner.

Be it known that William Wayte craves sureties of the peace against William Shakspere, Francis Langley, Dorothy Soer wife of John Soer, and Anne Lee, for fear of death, and so forth. Writ of attachment issued to the Sheriff of Surrey, returnable on the eighteenth of St Martin [i.e. 29 November 1596]. [45]

Gardiner was a Bermondsey leather merchant who had *"enriched himself by criminal dealings, swindling even his own family and oppressing the tenants in his slum properties."* [46] Wayte, too, had gained a bad reputation for being the local bullyboy, and was described as *"a certain loose person of no reckoning or value."* [47]

Professor Leslie Hotson delved into this squalid affair, as far as records permitted, and discovered that *"Francis Langley was an older man who had made his money by crooked means and had previously been charged with violence and extortion"* [48] Some type of feud had clearly developed between these underworld figures, Gardiner and Langley; as a result, their henchmen, Wayte and Shaxpere had become involved. The presence of the two termagants on the writ indicates this altercation between the gang leaders was for control of a vice ring – *"wife of"*, at a court hearing had become a defensive term used by some prostitutes.

> *The most notorious brothels were densely clustered on the Southwark Bankside. These were the 'stews'–so named from the original meaning of a heated room used for hot air or vapour baths, and formally controlled by the Bishop of Winchester (hence 'Winchester goose' the Elizabethan slang for a diseased Southwark whore or an infected client).* [49]

The fact that William Shaxpere returned to his native Stratford a very rich man, after only a few years in the capital, is not disputed, the evidence being undeniable; that he made his fortune from pimping is deemed too outrageous for even a moment's consideration. Yet, consider: his contemporaries in the theatre never achieved riches; in fact, the opposite was more often true. Greene, the top writer of his day, with degrees from both Oxford and Cambridge, died penniless in the care of a poor but charitable cobbler and his wife; Kyd died in debt and Nashe in destitution. Even Jonson died with little more than £8 to his name. One could barely scratch an existence from the pen unless there was a wealthy patron on hand to lend support. But, apart from the two letters that preface *Venus and Adonis* and *Lucrece*, which lack validation from the Southampton archives, and for which, an alternative explanation exists, there is neither evidence nor indication that Shaxpere ever had such a patron. And, even if it is believed otherwise, no patron did more than support an artist; this is far from being the same as bankrolling him.

> *The income from thirty-seven plays would barely have enabled the author to make ends meet over a twenty-year period, and certainly Shakspere did not make sufficient mark as an actor to have prospered in that capacity. The renowned Richard Burbage at his death held*

> *property worth £300, in addition to personal possessions. Shakspere put down £440 in one investment, to purchase tithes.* [50]

Could it be that the unnamed naval officer, who wrote *The Story of the Learned Pig* in 1786, hit the mark when he referred to 'Pimping Billy'? The author, calling himself TRANSMIGRATUS, recounted the story of the transmigration of his soul along the timeline of history. It was in Elizabethan England that he first became . . .

> *a horse-holder to those who came to visit the play-house, where I was well-known by the name of 'Pimping Billy.' My sprightly genius soon distinguished me from the common herd . . . I soon after contracted a friendship with the great man and first of geniuses, the 'Immortal Shakespeare.'* [51]

Here we have a story that repeats what has been said heretofore. Shaxpere arrived in London and became a self-employed horse-holder. His sprightly wit soon brought him to wider notice. As a result of which, he came into contact with the 'Immortal Shakespeare' (Edward de Vere). The author then denies that 'Shakespeare' had *"to run his country for deer-stealing"*. This was alleged in Rowe's *Life.* [1709]. After setting the record straight on that point, the author reveals . . .

> *With equal falsehood has he been fathered with many spurious dramatic pieces."Hamlet, Othello, As you like it, the Tempest and Midsummer Night's Dream," for five; of all of which I confess myself to be the author.* [52]

With an admirable twist to be appreciated by those who understood his meaning, the author explains what every supporter of Oxford already believes. It is he, 'Pimping Billy', the 'horse-holder', who confesses to have authored the 'Immortal Shakespeare's' plays, for that was the role he had been employed to play after meeting *"the first of geniuses, the immortal Shakespeare."*

Pimping would certainly help explain Shaxpere's otherwise unexplained wealth; it also fits the character traits of his life in London and in Stratford; that is, as a grain hoarder, tax evader, moneylender, and debt collector.

We shall discover Shaxpere later on, yet again in contact with the London underworld, when at the turn of the century he shared accommodation with the brothel-keeper, George Wilkins.

With such a background, and acting as henchman for Langley, he was unlikely to be seen as a man over-willing to engage in polite conversation regarding the finer points of iambic pentameter.

All of this may sound extreme, but Wayte's appeal to the judiciary for protection must be seen in the context of this man's, background and reputation. Wayte was not some innocent simpleton caught up in matters for which he had no part to play. He was a member of a powerful criminal gang, whose members were more than capable of taking care of their own. In modern day parlance it sounds as if a contract had been taken out on Wayte's life amidst a mild outbreak of gang warfare. And he had been forced to seek protection from the law. Control of the vice trade was likely to have been the reason.

Shakespeare's image-makers naturally put a different spin on the affair. They believe Langley's quarrel with Gardiner was over a business venture. One year before the writ was taken out, Langley had set up business in the style of Henslowe, and built the Swan theatre on the Surrey side of the Thames. At that time, this shoreline bustled with 'entertainment', with theatres, brothels and a bear pit all competing with each other. As part of this low life were gangsters seeking control: men like Langley and Gardiner. Shaxpere's presence in their midst suggests he was either part of that scene, or at the very least, on its periphery.

On 4 May 1597, Shaxpere was reported to be in Stratford-upon-Avon: this time with the purpose of acquiring two cottages, two barns, and New Place, the second largest house in the district. The purchase price was £60 (≈ £16,750). The house had once belonged to Sir Hugh Clopton, Lord Mayor of London, and at that time Stratford's most illustrious son. It was during negotiations for this purchase that a further shadow was cast upon Shaxpere's suspiciously dissolute character. Prior to his interest in the property, the house had been sold to William Bott, a lawyer and Alderman of Stratford, notorious for having swindled his son-in-law out of his property. Bott had poisoned his daughter inside New Place by feeding her ratsbane, which he kept concealed beneath a green carpet. His motive for the murder was to ensure he obtained sole possession of the property.

From Bott, the house passed to William Underhill, *"a subtle, covetous and crafty man"* [53] whose son, Fulke, acquired an even worse reputation. Two months after Underhill had sold New Place to Shaxpere, he was dead: poisoned by his son Fulke, to whom he had promised the inheritance of all his lands. The crime was uncovered and Fulke was hanged at Warwick. But his brother Hercules Underhill remained suspicious, and believed that Shaxpere had been involved in collusion over the purchase price of the property. The matter went to court, but there being no proof of any collusion, other than the ridiculously low price paid for such a large house, meant that Shaxpere was able to secure a warranty from the court making him the legal owner.

Despite the many researches into Shaxpere's background, and in contrast to the defamatory information which is found, but is then set aside almost as soon as it is discovered, for it does nothing to enhance his character beyond what has been contrived, there is not one reference to his having written anything between 1594 and 1598. Yet, we are told, not only did he compose many of his most enduring works of literature during that time, he was also regularly acting and directing plays in the daylight hours. Some even believe he was still in attendance to the 3rd Earl of Southampton, widely regarded as the inspiration for his sonnets.

The problem is that different writers concentrate upon different aspects of the Shakespeare myth, and it is only when these are viewed together that the contradictory nature of what is alleged becomes evident. In brief, there was never enough time for Shaxpere to have done all that has been claimed for him.

There is also another problem, barely mentioned by his image-makers; it is the dispersion of Shakespeare's plays almost as soon as they were written. Henslowe's Diary reveals that on 3 March 1591 (Old Style), Lord Strange's Men performed *Henry VI* and the receipts taken were £3.16s.8d (≈ £1000). The play was repeated on 7 March and again on the 11th; the 16th, and the 28th of the month, after which it was performed in April on the 5th; the 13th, and the 21st. This implies that Shaxpere was employed to write plays for Lord Strange. But, contrarily, *Titus Andronicus* was first staged by Henslowe at the Rose for Lord Sussex's Men on 23 January, 28 January, and 6 February. After a short break, when the theatres were closed because of fear of spreading the Plague, *Titus Andronicus* was again performed, this time on 5th and 12th of June, but it was then recorded as having been performed by the joint companies of the Admiral's Men and the Lord Chamberlain's Men. One is therefore entitled to ask: Just who was 'Shakespeare' writing for? Not for Henslowe, because no money changed hands. And why, at the outset of his career, was this unrecorded actor (for he appeared on no lists) so liberally allowed to work in this freelance fashion, supplying plays for different companies? Freelance writing was the prerogative of aristocrats, who naturally received no payment for their work. This would then explain the total absence of Shakespeare's name in Henslowe's accounts, and perhaps the curious inclusion of *"ne"* (Latin for 'not') that Henslowe recorded against certain plays, especially those that have become associated with Shakespeare.

These earlier plays also present other problems. *Titus Andronicus*, for example, has a chapter to itself, because of the vital information it provides in *proving* that Oxford was its author. Other plays, such as the *Histories,* can be examined for the interesting peculiarities exposed in their composition. *Richard II*, for instance, is claimed to have been written in the year following publication of the *Rape of Lucrece.* It is said to be the first of the author's second tetralogy; that is, *Richard II; Henry IV, Part One; Henry IV, Part Two; Henry V.* According to orthodox dating, which is forced to operate within a very tight timeframe, these four plays were completed between 1594 and 1599. This is not an unreasonable claim to make, until that is . . . betwixt these same years, Shakespeare is also said to have completed *Titus Andronicus,* (1594); *The Taming of the Shrew,* (1594); *The Two Gentlemen of Verona,* (1594-5); *Love's Labour's Lost,* (1594-5); *A Midsummer Night's Dream,* (1596); *King John,* (1596-7); *Romeo and Juliet,* (1596-7); *The Merchant of Venice,* (1596-7). And in 1599, when he was putting the final touches to *Henry V,* (1598-9), *Much Ado About Nothing* was completed (1598-9); after which, he began writing *Hamlet* (1599-1600); *Twelfth Night;* (1599-1600), and *Julius Caesar* (1599-1600). In the midst of this frenzy of activity, he had even begun *As You Like It,* (1596), *The Merry Wives of Windsor,* (1597), and *Troilus and Cressida,* (1597). And this is without mentioning the 154 sonnets, written, it is said, during the same period.

This exhaustive schedule of work requires the research and writing of each play to be accomplished at the rate of one play every three months: written, of course, during the evening hours by candlelight. It is therefore of some interest to recall what we know of Shaxpere during this period of between fifty and sixty months, when all this creativity was supposedly undertaken.

We know that in December 1594 he was involved with the Lord Chamberlain's Men in the production of two comedies or interludes; that in August 1596, he travelled to Stratford-upon-Avon after learning of his son's death; that in October and November he was being pursued for the non-payment of tax; that in the same month of November he was again in trouble with the law, when a writ was issued against him for the surety of the peace; that in May 1597, he had returned to Stratford-upon-Avon, this time negotiating the purchase of New Place, for which he had to obtain a warranty from court to secure ownership of the property: this necessity having arisen because he had been accused of fraud. One year later, in 1598, 'his' name, or rather that of Shake-speare, appears on the cast list of Jonson's *Every Man In His Humour*. But since the name is hyphenated, one may assume it was *not* Shaxpere. In January of that same year, two local businessmen, Abraham Sturley and Richard Quiney, discussed together whether Shaxpere might be interested in *"the matter of our tithes [10% of the income obtainable from land]."* [54]

It was also in this year, when famine struck parts of England that Shaxpere, once again, became involved with the law. This was the year when the name Shakespeare became even more famous, having been identified by Francis Meres as the previously unnamed author of twelve plays. Shaxpere's presence in Stratford, away from the glare of publicity, is recorded at Stratford in an entry made by the Justices of the Peace, who had been ordered by the Privy Council to investigate those hoarding grain. Concerning this misdemeanour, we learn that . . .

> *in the xl^th yeare of the raigne of our moste gracious Soveraigne Ladie Queen Elizabethe ... Wm Shackespere of Chapple Street Ward, Stratford [held] x quarters of grain [640 gallons ≈ 2910 litres]."* [55]

> *Hoarding drove up the price of wheat and barley (called corn and malt respectively in Elizabethan times) and the shortages led to brawls and open revolt, and the hoarders were condemned as 'wicked people in*

conditions more like to wolves and cormorants than to natural men.'.[56]

This led one enraged citizen to publicly express the wish that – *"God send my Lord of Essex down shortly, to see them hanged on gibbets at their own doors."* [57] But Essex stayed away and 'Shackespere' was saved from the noose. Irvin Matus, attempted to diffuse the situation by comparing 'Shackespere' to other local hoarders, thus allowing that he was no better than they. Well, yes! But, then we are talking about greedy, opportunistic vermin that preyed on the needy. This description is not far removed from his known activities in the capital. While *"in London he repeatedly failed to pay the taxes that supported the poor and aged."* (*Shakespeare's Life and World*, 2004 p.164) In these two instances, we see Shaxpere true to life: a dishonourable man, so very different from the *"Sweet Master Shakespeare"* of literary fame.

In October of the same year, having returned to London, Shaxpere was once again listed as a tax defaulter, this time for the sum of thirteen shillings and fourpence. Later that month, Richard Quiney, upon arriving in London to conduct legal business on behalf of Stratford-upon-Avon, and while staying at the Bell Inn in Carter Lane, wrote a letter: *"To my Lovinge good ffrende & countreymann Mr Wm. Shackespere,"* [58] requesting a loan of £30, *"uppon Mr Bushells & my securytee or Mr Myttons with me."* [59] But the letter was never delivered. Or, perhaps it was delivered and returned to sender unopened, the messenger having discovered that 'Wm. Shackespere' had left town. For, several weeks later, his name reappeared in the Stratford records, this time in receipt of ten pence for payment of a load of stone. Would it not have made more sense for him to receive a better return by publishing his sonnets, assuming they were his?

Shakespeare's literary silence during these four years, and the reason for it, did not go unnoticed.

To Mr William Shake-speare
Shake-speare, we must be silent in thy praise,
'Cause our encomions will but blast thy bays
Which envy could not, that thou didst so well;
Let thine own histories prove thy Chronicle. [60]

The first thing to notice is that the author addresses Shakespeare directly; that is, in the same way a living person is addressed. Yet, factually, these words did not appear in print until 1640, when it was reproduced as an anonymous epigram in *Wit's Recreations Selected from the Finest Fancies of Modern Muses.* Since Shaxpere had been dead for the past twenty-four years, and Oxford, half as long again, the epigram makes better sense if it was originally written while both men were still alive. This may have been the case, as Clare Asquith pointed out (see note 7): there were manuscripts circulating in the late fifteenth and early sixteenth century, which included *"double and triple meanings within printed texts"*. Had this verse been written while both men were still alive, it would then explain its author's anonymity.

The second point to notice is the hyphenated surname. The name Shake-speare does not appear hyphenated in either *Venus and Adonis* or *Rape of Lucrece.* By twice hyphenating it, the anonymous author is sending a signal to Shakespeare, whom he is addressing; and of course to each reader, assuming they are sufficiently awake, that he has special knowledge regarding the person behind the name. Why else hyphenate it, especially in the context of an epigram, where subtleties anticipate discovery?

Apologists for Shaxpere say there is nothing extraordinary in the hyphenation of his name; it was not unusual. It certainly was unusual, because no record exists of his name having been hyphenated in connection with his business transactions. Only when someone slyly refers to the name in a literary context is the name hyphenated, thus drawing attention to it.

Thirdly, in the opening line, the author divulges a need for silence when praising Shake-speare's work. Orthodox opinion remains non-committal when asked to explain the reason for this. But 'silence' is in fact, what the epigram is about: especially where it concerns the identity of Shake-speare.

This need for silence was particularly appropriate during the four years of quiet that followed publication of *Venus and Adonis* and *Lucrece.* These two long narrative poems met with extraordinary success, thereby suggesting that the author's silence, which followed their publication, was enforced by censorship. What other reason could there be for his failure to capitalise on this literary breakthrough? That is, if Shake-speare was the man that orthodoxy supposes him to have been?

The fourth point has the potential to be even more revealing, because the author gives his reason for silence. It is, he says, because our expressions of high praise (encomiums) might *"blast thy bays"*. What 'bays' are these? The only bays referred to in this context are those claimed by the 17th Earl of Oxford, when he offered them to any poet capable of defeating him in a rhyming contest. His challenge appeared in a collection of poems called *The Paradise of Dainty Devices.* Oxford was apparently so adept at impromptu rhyme that he took part in several rhyming duels with other poets; and it is his personal exclamation of triumph that connects him to the anonymous epigram under discussion:

A Crown of Bays shall that man wear
That triumphs over me: [61]

These lines were among those first published in 1576, and the entire collection proved so popular with the public that it was reprinted at least eight times, taking it well into the seventeenth century. This being so, the anonymous epigram writer can be seen alerting *"Shake-speare"* (i.e. Oxford) to the need for care where praise is being apportioned.

This warning had apparently become necessary, because too much praise was likely to have the effect of blasting – blowing open, blazing, revealing – him to the public as the true owner of that crown of bays. The epigram writer had evidently realised that Shaxpere, through his employment as Oxford's allonym, was on the receiving end of this honour. Care was therefore needed, lest the praise he was receiving should overflow, and in doing so, unmask him to reveal Shake-speare's true identity.

The epigrammatist then provides further information by disclosing that *"envy"* had previously failed to *"blast"* 'Shakespeare's' *"bays"*. This comment is in keeping with human nature; it being natural to suppose that some writers, with limited means of support and an awareness of what had happened, had become envious of Shaxpere acting as a counterfeit poet. But their desire to reveal the truth had been forestalled; presumably by an awareness of the painful and punishing consequences.

Envy, therefore had the potential to produce the same effect as too much praise; both were capable of unmasking Shakespeare, and revealing his secret identity to the public. This is why the epigram had very likely been circulating during his lifetime, and became revived in 1640, to coincide with the publication of

Poems by Wil. Shake-speare; issued by John Benson that year.

The epigram concludes with a further expression of its author's wit. It suggests that Shake-speare's *Histories* should be examined in order to prove his own *"Chronicle"*. The *Histories* dramatised by Shake-speare do, in fact, provide a rich source of information that presents difficulties for the Stratford theory. For example, *Richard II,* allegedly begun in 1595 and completed a year later, was described on 6th February 1601, by Augustine Phillips, as *"so old, and so long out of use that the house would be poor and the takings thin"*. The Queen, too, was able to recall – *"this tragedy was played 40^tie^ times in open streets and houses."*[62]

These references conflict with the suggested date of the play's composition, as posited by traditionalists, and this is not helped by further knowledge that the play contains information from two documents that were not in circulation. One of these, *La Chronicque de la Traison et Mort de Richart Deux roy Dengleterre* [The chronicle of the treason and death of Richard II, king of England] was owned by John Stow, and the other, *Histoire du Roy d'Angleterre Richard* [History of King Richard of England] was owned by astrologer, Dr. John Dee. *"These accounts were not easily come by in England, for their anti-Lancastrian sentiment was not acceptable to Henry the Fourth and his descendants."*[63]

Oxford knew Dee personally, but how Shaxpere could have known about them is left to the invention of his image-makers: a branch of 'pseudo-scholarship' where no invention is ever too preposterous to be rejected.

King John, a play allegedly begun the year that *Richard II* was finished is another that gives pause for thought. An earlier play called *The Troublesome Raigne of King John,* for which a quarto edition had been published in 1591, is claimed with justification to be the forerunner of Shakespeare's historical drama.

> *[F]or its author ... reveals, were he indeed its creator, powers of construction and invention that Shakespeare himself was to acknowledge in what is regarded as his rehandling of the work. ... the author of The Troublesome Raigne may be fairly held to have anticipated Shakespeare and even to have instructed him; for Shakespeare's King John follows The Troublesome Raigne almost scene for scene.*[64]

A more realistic interpretation suggests that Lord Oxford wrote *The Troublesome Raigne* during the late 1580s; in fact, a clue to its date of composition has been written into the text:

KING PHILIP: So by a roaring tempest on its flood
A whole armado of convicted sail
Is scatter'd and disjoin'd from fellowship.
(Act 3: sc. iv)

By any consideration, this represents an apt description of the fate that befell King Philip's Armada in the summer of 1588. Nor can the writing of *Love's Labour's Lost* be exempted from an equally early date. The character, *"Don Adriano de Armado, a fantastical Spaniard"*, would have been extremely topical as a figure of fun, especially with a name connecting him to the recently defeated Spanish Armada. Seven years later, the joke would have been so stale as to be barely noticeable.

Moreover, the repeated staging of *The Troublesome Raigne* would have provided the reason needed for its publication in 1591. Later, into the mid-1590s, with the leisure to rework his earlier plays, Oxford revised it. After appreciating its strengths, which were left in, and correcting its weaknesses, one of which was to eliminate the play's anti-papist sentiment, it received the shorter title of *King John*. But after Francis Meres reported its attribution to Shakespeare in 1598, nothing more was heard of it, either in performance or print; that is, until it re-emerged in the First Folio edition of 1623.

So troublesome has *The Troublesome Raigne* proved to be for the dominant view of Shakespeare, that some have resorted to supposing it was actually he who wrote both plays: the un-known author being too talented to be anyone other than himself.

> *It is however difficult to attribute to an unknown dramatist the powers characteristic of a born playwright, especially as he was never, so far as we know, to exercise them again in so remarkable a fashion. It is simpler to suppose he took his framework from the one man whom we know excelled in such constructions.* [65]

This, of course, requires orthodox opinion to push back the authorship of Shakespeare's plays into the *lost years*—the 'Black Hole' of Shakespearian study that swallows up everything which cannot otherwise be explained. In other words, Shakespeare copied from Shakespeare: he, having learnt all the accomplishments required for stagecraft and dramatic construction previously during his *lost years*. This is almost identical to the explanation that it was Oxford who copied from Oxford: except he had learnt the art of stagecraft and dramatic construction at an earlier time, in the conventional fashion: from actual experience.

Attention was previously drawn to performances of *Henry VI*, in which St. George was called upon a sufficient number of times for it to be seen as an appropriate address for the author. It was also from this same *History* that the Greene-Chettle letter obtained the phrase: *"Tygers hart wrapt in a Players hyde"*. *Henry VI* was first staged by Lord Strange's company at the Rose theatre on 3 March, 1592: its popularity thereafter being measured by the fourteen repeat performances made during the spring and summer months. Parts 2 and 3 of *Henry VI* were also played in London that summer, although by Lord Pembroke's company.

The topicality of this historical drama was undoubtedly the reason for the references made to it in the Greene-Chettle letter. It is also important to note: once again, 'Shakespeare' is operating as a freelance playwright by writing for two separate acting companies, despite the fact that this option would have been the prerogative of the nobility. It is also noteworthy that despite *Henry VI's* huge popularity, Henslowe stopped producing it, along with the other plays by 'Shakespeare' he had been staging. This followed in the wake of Oxford's pseudonymous publication of *Lucrece*, and Henslowe's stage production of *Hamlet*, with its characterisation of *Lucrece's* author (p.76); a step too far.

Turning directly to this play, we discover that *Henry VI* was preceded by two anonymously written histories: *The Contention Between the Two Famous Houses of Yorke and Lancaster* and *The True Tragedy of Richard Duke of Yorke*. Concerning these plays, Professor Alexander wrote:

> *They treat of the same action as 2 and 3 Henry VI, introduce the same characters, and contain much verse in common with the Folio texts; 3 Henry VI has about 2,900 lines, and of these some 2,000 on Malone's reckoning are found, sometimes word for word, sometimes in various transformations, in the True Tragedy.*[66]

When seeking an answer to what is at face value a blatant piece of plagiarism, the intelligent course of action would be to recognise the similarity this has with *King John* and *The Troublesome Raigne*, where the former followed the latter *"almost scene for scene"*. The simplest explanation for what is otherwise a case of patent duplication on the part of Shakespeare is that Oxford wrote *The Troublesome Raigne, The Contention,* and *The True Tragedy* as early court dramas during the 1580s. He later revised and updated them for further showing as *King John,* and *Henry VI.* This would explain the two pirated editions of *The Contention,* and *The True Tragedy,* both of which, appeared as 'Bad Quartos' in 1594 and 1595 respectively.

> *The Contention, and The True Tragedy belong to the group of texts Pollard called the Bad Quartos and show all the marks of plays put together from memory and odd players' parts.* [67]

Neither one of these two plays was challenged legally, nor did the author come forward to identify himself and exercise his right to 'stay' their publication, if only to protect his reputation against the indiscriminate use of his work—a trait shared in common with the poet of *Shake-speare's Sonnets,* and with the pirated quartos that were printed with Shakespeare's name as the author. One may therefore reasonably ask: — "Why this silence?" Was there a common bond between the anonymous author, who, prior to 1598, never complained, and the author post 1598 that was named, but likewise never protested?

The impressive popularity achieved by *Henry VI* also provided a financial incentive for rogue publishers to profit from its success. The way available for this, apart from the companies who owned the rights to the play and also possessed the relevant costumes, was by pirating it. This could be done if enough actors remembered their lines. A scribe could then make copies ready for the printer. In this respect, *The Contention,* and *The True Tragedy* were used, simply because the actors who had performed these plays were available, and because the plays told a similar story to the later version titled *Henry VI.*

It is an explanation that fits all the facts. But, if we omit Oxford and see only Shakespeare – as his biographical image-makers insist – then there is no single explanation that covers all the facts. In its place are a variety of speculations: each one beloved by its sponsor. Different writers are proposed for each of the plays upon which 'Shakespeare' modelled his own version, but without any single conjecture carrying a lasting conviction. Hence, there is no conclusive agreement as to the identity of the mysterious playwright of *"The Troublesome Raigne [who] is supposed to have shown the way to Shakespeare"*, and then disappeared from the scene, never to be heard of again. But Shakespeare's image-writers prefer it that way.

Quite whether the anonymous writer of the epigram who linked Oxford with Shake-speare had all of this in mind, when he suggested that *"thine own histories"* would prove *"thy Chronicle"*, is left for the reader to contemplate. Unfortunately, it is a feature common to the human race that when a belief has become entrenched within a person's mind (especially an academic's mind with a reputation to protect), it is there to stay. Those who have denied Oxford's authorship of the Shakespeare plays and poetry from their elevated seat of authority, will not flinch from a resolve to continue in the same vein: seeking to support their views with fresh energy, and by infusing each new generation of scholars, over whose minds they exercise control, with a theory of Shakespeare's identity that fails so many tests. But truth is truth for all eternity, and though it is buried, it will always resurface in some later age: as it has done in this present time.

A further matter of interest with regard to Shaxpere at this time concerns the coat of arms that John Shaxpere applied for *circa* 1568.

The Clarencieux King-of-Arms at that time was Robert Cook, and he refused the application. There the matter rested until October 1596, when William revived his father's request for arms. The application was founded upon a false claim that the family's antecedents had been rewarded for services to Henry VII.

The new Garter-King-at-Arms, William Dethick, approved the grant, and Shaxpere and son became entitled to call themselves Gentlemen; the exact date on which this was approved is unknown. In the event, however, the application and subsequent granting of arms to Shaxpere became a key piece of evidence when prosecuting Dethick for fraudulent practices.

> *It is an authentic fact that Sir William Dethick, who was Garter-King-at-Arms in 1596 and 1599, was called to account for having forged pedigrees and granted coats to persons whose circumstances and station in society gave them no right to the distinction; the case of John Shakespeare was expressly charged against him.* [68]

Since it is unlikely that John Shaxpere travelled four days to London in order to appeal an application for arms that had been turned down more than thirty years earlier, especially when he had then been younger and more affluent, attention focuses upon his son William.

What had changed to instil the necessary confidence that a new application made at this time would be more successful than the last? The answer is the adjudicator had changed. Dethick's reputation for accepting bribes, by inventing pedigrees in exchange for money was undoubtedly the reason why Shaxpere renewed his father's claim for a coat of arms.

As Jonson remarked about SOGLIARDO (apparently with Shaxpere in mind) he was *"so enamoured of the name of a gentleman, that he will have it though he buys it,"* (*Every Man Out Of His Humour*). Then, piercing the wound further still, Jonson suggested his motto should be *"not without mustard."* Shaxpere's motto was actually *"not without right"*, and his coat of arms was described as being: *"in a field of gold upon a bend sable;"* in short, mustard-coloured.

No one other than John Shaxpere's son could have revived the application for arms. In which case, bribery and fraud have to be added to his list of vices: with pretentiousness included for good measure. Not one jot of evidence exists to suggest that Henry VII rewarded Shaxpere's great-grandfather with "*lands*" and *"tenements"*: yet these were the reasons for Dethick approving the application.

Amazingly, Shaxpere's adulators actually boast about their idol having obtained a coat of arms; thus subscribing to the myth that this had been legitimately obtained. Instead, it is just another addition to the 'legend of the Bard'; one that helps sanitize the image of 'Shakespeare', thereby separating him from the flaws and frailty of his true character

It is of interest to note Jonson's complete lack of respect for Shaxpere. This came one year after *"Shake-speare"* was given first place on the list of actors who played *Every Man In His Humour*. It therefore presents a curious contrast to his characterisation as SOGLIARDO; unless the William Shake-speare leading Jonson's cast list was not the William Shaxpere he ridiculed as SOGLIARDO!

Recalled to Life

In 1598, the name Shakespeare re-emerged to publicly fulfil the literary acclaim that had once seemed imminent four years earlier. What had happened to bring this about? Logically, the answer is likely to be linked to the reason for its suppression.

Coincidence perhaps; but in that same year Oxford's father-in-law Lord Burghley, director of censorship, took ill and died.

> *As a statesman Burghley saw that his duty was to give the Queen his best advice and then to carry out whatever policy seemed expedient to her. ... His patronage in church and state enabled him to harness the clergy, the gentry, and the nobility to the tasks of administration. His attendance in council and Parliament was constant, and he understood how to manage both. He directed censorship.* [69]

The full explanation of Lord Burghley's role in the suppression and censorship of Oxford's plays and poems has been left to a later chapter, since it concerns a range of matters that have yet to be introduced. For the present, the important fact to note is that in the spring of 1598, Lord Burghley fell ill. His condition continued to worsen, and on 5 August he breathed his last.

The head of censorship in England was no longer a potent force. Any embargo he had imposed upon Shakespeare's name appearing on newly published work was diminished. A month after the Lord Treasurer's death, Cambridge graduate Francis Meres entered *Palladis Tamia, Wit's Treasury* in the *Stationers' Register*. In the book he named Shakespeare as the author of some twelve plays, all of which, up until then, had been staged anonymously. Shakespeare had been recalled to life.

> *The English tongue is mightily enriched and gorgeously invested in rare ornaments and resplendent abiliments by Sir Philip Sidney, Spenser, Daniel, Drayton, Warner, Shakespeare, Marlowe and Chapman.* [70]

The name Shakespeare had only thrice before appeared in public, in 1593 and again in 1594. On the first two occasions it was as the signature on letters of dedication to Henry Wriothesley, when introducing his two narrative love poems, *Venus and Adonis* and *The Rape of Lucrece*. In this respect, it is interesting to observe that 'Shakespeare' had been shy of drawing too much attention to the name, and had twice omitted it from the title pages of the two poems, leaving it for others to discover by reading the dedication.

This had been a wise but ultimately ineffective strategy, because on the third occasion when the name appeared in print, the anonymous author of *Willobie His Avisa* satirically hyphenated it to Shake–speare, describing W.S. as *"an old player"* (Oxford was then forty-four) while alluding to H.W.'s youth: *"If years I want"* (Southampton was then twenty, rising twenty-one), and had thus far in his life, rejected marriage. The *Avisa* poem declared him as one *"that never loved before"*.

However, by 1598, given that William Shakespeare had been the pseudonym used by Oxford, it remained essential that this name continue to be mentioned in books like *Wit's Treasury,* so as to allay any suspicions that may have been circulating regarding doubt about the author. For, it had been in 1593-94, within the space of little more than twelve months that this new poet, named William Shakespeare, had arisen like a celestial comet, illuminating the literary scene, with two magnificent narrative poems. But, as suddenly as Shakespeare appeared, his name disappeared from view. Four years were to elapse without a single new poem to his name. Then, in 1598, the name Shakespeare blazed forth: again in triumph, but not as a poet. He was now being acclaimed as a major playwright with at least a dozen works to his name. Why had this revelation taken so long?

The apparent suppression of Shakespeare's name on new publications between 1594 and 1598 had finally ceased. But any hint of a connection across the class-divide, between a high-ranking earl and an uneducated actor and moneylender, was strenuously to be avoided. Consequently, with the re-emergence of Shakespeare's name, it has become possible to understand how a simple prank begun in 1592, with Oxford and Southampton joining forces to get the senior Earl's poems into print was, six years later, about to begin a different life form.

Meres' book divided the waters between Oxford and Shakespeare. Oxford was already well known as a highly respected doyen of the literary world. In his early years, poems had been written and published against his name or occasionally just his initials; books had been dedicated to him, and glowing commendations were in print, extolling the virtues of his poetry.

> *I may not omit the deserved commendations of many honourable and noble Lords and Gentlemen of Her Majesty's Court, which, in the rare devices of poetry, have been and yet are most excellent skilful: among whom the right honourable Earl of Oxford may challenge to himself the title of most excellent among the rest.* [71]

The Art of English Poesie published in 1589 took up the same theme:

> *And in her Majesty's time that now is are sprung up another crew of courtly makers [poets], Noblemen and Gentlemen of Her Majesty's own servants, who have written excellently well as it would appear if their doings could be found out and made public with the rest, of which number is first that noble gentleman Edward, Earl of Oxford.* [72]

> *"Puttenham's second mention of Oxford associates him publicly with plays:"* (Nelson, 386) . . .

> *Th'Earl of Oxford and Master [Richard] Edwards of Her Majesty's Chapel for comedy and interlude.* [73]

Thus, by 1589, Oxford was already being publicly acknowledged as both a poet and a writer of comedies. Moreover, he was also named as one who wrote secretly.

Between 1594 and 1598, the London stage was the scene of a succession of plays by an unnamed author, all of which involved a royal setting complete with characters drawn from the nobility. In retrospect, traditionalists refer to these plays as those written by a shareholder and member of the Lord Chamberlain's Men: the same man, they say, who wrote *Venus and Adonis* and *The Rape of Lucrece.* However, apart from these two poems, this person's name had ceased to appear openly in public. That was reason enough for any person of intelligence to harbour suspicions, especially if they had read *Willobie His Avisa.* Could Oxford, known for the outstanding merit of his plays and poetry, be writing these unattributed works secretly?

Meres' timely book allayed all further doubts, and he did it with panache.

> *As the soul of Euphorbus was thought to live in Pythagoras, so the sweet witty soul of Ovid lives in mellifluous and honey-tongued Shakespeare: Witness his Venus and Adonis, his Lucrece, his sugared sonnets among his private friends, etc.*

> *As Plautus and Seneca are accounted the best for comedy and tragedy among the Latins, so Shakespeare among the English is the most excellent in both kinds for the stage. For comedy, witness his 'Gentlemen of Verona', his 'Errors', his 'Love's Labours Lost', his 'Love's Labour's Won', his 'Midsummer Night's Dream', and his 'Merchant of Venice'; for tragedy his 'Richard II', 'Richard III', 'Henry IV', 'King John', 'Titus Andronicus', and his 'Romeo and Juliet'.*
>
> *As Epius Stolo said that the Muses would speak with Plautus' tongue, if they would speak Latin; so I say that the Muses would speak with Shakespeare's fine filed phrase, if they would speak English.* [74]

It is noteworthy that Meres included *Love's Labour's Won,* a title lost, or still to be positively identified, while also omitting *Taming of the Shrew,* and *Henry VI Parts 1, 2* and *3.* Some may also wonder why Meres has concentrated so much upon Shakespeare's plays by naming twelve of them. It was an exceptional thing to have done, as Marchette Chute remarked: *"Meres mentions a great many playwrights in his book... Shakespeare was the only one he singled out for extended comment."*[75] Author Charlton Ogburn also remarked upon this oddity.

> *There must be a reason for all this, and the only realistic one I can find is that the decision had been reached that the author of the hitherto unattributed dramatic masterpieces was to be 'Shakespeare', and Meres had been selected to launch the artifice unobtrusively.* [76]

Granted this is speculation, but the appropriate timing of *Wit's Treasury* certainly fits well with Ogburn's explanation. There is also the fact that the plays mentioned above were sufficiently popular as to excite curiosity about their author: a playwright who, up until Meres' publication, had remained anonymous, but whose plays had been regularly pirated for publication without a single objection ever being made. What did the author have to hide; if, that is, he were other than the Earl of Oxford? But *Wit's Treasury* settled any question of attribution by naming Shakespeare, alongside a dozen titles he had written that were previously unidentified: the name that appeared on the dedication page in both *Venus and Adonis* and *the Rape of Lucrece* had now been safely united with the twelve anonymously written plays mentioned by Meres.

This was an enormous revelation that Meres implanted into

the public consciousness, and without any fanfare. Up until 1598, the name of Shakespeare was limited to the two popular poems published in 1593 and 1594. Thereafter, for four years no more was heard of the name. Now, with Burghley recently entombed, suddenly, Shakespeare was to be acclaimed the author of a dozen previously unattributed plays. London was suddenly filled with works bearing the name Shakespeare.

Although Burghley's reasons for suppressing Oxford's association with the poems and plays he had written ran much deeper than giving offence to the upper classes, or to the religious leaders who were striving to preserve morality, the censorship he imposed did serve this purpose. In England at that time, Puritan pressure was attempting to close the theatres by condemning the immorality associated with the stage. A letter sent from the Lord Mayor of London to the Archbishop of Canterbury, John Whitgift, on 25 February 1592, expressed this sense of repugnance.

> *[By] the daily and disorderly exercise of a number of players and playing houses erected within this City, the youth thereof is greatly corrupted and their manners infected with many evil and ungodly qualities by reason of the wanton and profane devices represented on the stages by the said players, the apprentices and the servants withdrawn from their works ... To which places also do usually resort great numbers of light and lewd disposed persons, as harlots, cutpurses, cozeners [cheats] pilferers and suchlike, and there, under the colour of resort to those places to hear the plays, devise divers evil and ungodly matches, confederacies and conspiracies which by means of the opportunity of the place cannot be prevented nor discovered, as otherwise they might be.* [77]

Geoffrey Fenton was similarly persuaded to pen his distaste.

> *Players ... corrupt good moralities by wanton shows and plays. They ought not to be suffered to profane the Sabbath day in such sports, and much less to lose time on the days of travail.* [78]

Wit's Treasury excused Oxford from these associations, and instead, passed them on to his allonym, William Shaxpere. But Oxford had already acquired a place in the public mind, and Meres could not ignore this, neither could he overlook the Earl's known literary output without raising questions. Oxford was therefore given a mention: one that simply confirmed what had previously been reported in *The Art of English Poesie.*

> *... so the best for Comedy amongst vs bee, Edward Earle of Oxforde, Doctor Gager of Oxforde, Maister Rowley once a rare Scholler of learned Pembroke Hall in Cambridge, Maister Edwardes one of her Maiesties Chappell, eloquent and wittie Iohn Lilly, Lodge, Gascoyne, Greene, Shakespeare, Thomas Nash, Thomas Heywood, Anthony Mundye our best plotter, Chapman, Potter, Wilson, Hathway, and Henry Chettle.*[79]

Not unnaturally, traditionalists see this to be documentary proof that Oxford was not Shakespeare. Proof, it is not. Proof has to be both necessary and sufficient to be afforded that highly prized title. Meres' reference to Shakespeare alongside Oxford certainly satisfies the condition of necessity, but not of sufficiency.

Several cases are known from the past, where two names appearing on a list have implied they were different persons, but upon closer inspection both names have been discovered to apply to the same individual (Ogburn, 1988 p.142).

More to the point is the fact that when an author ceases to write under his or her own name, and thereafter secretly or otherwise transfers all new work to that of a penname, both names need to be listed in order to identify which work is assigned to which. And that is precisely what Meres has achieved. He first acknowledged Oxford for his early Comedies, which were already public knowledge (Puttenham, 1589). He then granted Oxford's allonym William Shaxpere, known to some as William Shakespeare, concessionary title to the work produced under that name. To outward appearances, Oxford and Shakespeare were two different persons, whereas it was Oxford and Shaxpere, who were two different persons; Oxford and Shakespeare were the same man—all very clever, but also very devious.

It may be instructive to note that some, e.g. Professor Alan Nelson – the only academic ever to have written a biography of Shake-speare without realizing it – wrote: *"Meres (for one) knew that Oxford and Shakespeare were not the same man."*[80] Almost right; it was of course, Oxford and Shaxpere who were not the same man. In an endnote, Nelson referred to this as an *"obvious inference"*. But, of course, obvious inferences are not always true. One has only to watch the daily progression of the sun across the sky to understand the need for caution when judging the obvious. Nelson has simply displayed a similar lack of insight. The Shakespeare authorship question, as he well knows, is a complex problem, and requires deeper levels of thought, dare one say a greater application of intelligence than that being applied by those defending the Stratford position. As Aesop famously said: *"Men often applaud an imitation and hiss at the real thing."* Nelson has proved himself to be no exception.

It is also to the point that Meres has mentioned Shakespeare's *"sugared sonnets"* in the same breath as he referred to his two narrative poems and twelve plays. The sonnets are a biographical record of the poet's experiences and encounters: some of which were with the Queen of England, others, much more intimate, were with the 3rd Earl of Southampton. Whatever one may say about Will Shaxpere as author of the plays, there is no possibility whatever that he could have had such a poetic discourse with the reigning monarch, or indeed with any other member of the nobility. Consequently, when Francis Meres mentioned Shakespeare, as he did when recording the plays and poetry he had written, he can have had only one person in mind, and that was Edward de Vere, the pseudonymous Shakespeare.

The Elizabethan age was the most devious in the history of England. And Nelson's failure to penetrate its depths, particularly regarding his 'proof' (or spoof?) is understandable. The inefficient premise, upon which so many errors have arisen, requires more than the mutterings of off-the-cuff explanations to cover-up its deficiencies. Sadly, the prospect of this happening from the top downwards is not promising. Shakespearian studies, based upon the existing paradigm have long since become a means to aggrandisement in academe. Each scholar's motives in the search for truth inevitably become governed by the reality of their position, and their prospects for advancement. As Nelson was forced to admit:

> *I agree that antagonism to the authorship debate from within the profession is so great that it would be as difficult for a professed Oxfordian to be hired in the first place, much less gain tenure, as for a professed creationist to be hired to gain tenure in a graduate-level department of biology.*[81]

Much the same could have been said for a professed Copernican espousing the views of Galileo. Truth, it would seem, is sometimes barred from the universities when it threatens to replace the dominant paradigm.

SHAKESPEARE RESURGENT

After four years of absence, during which the name of Shakespeare appeared only as a signature on two letters of dedication prefixed to *Venus and Adonis* and *The Rape of Lucrece*, England awoke to discover that the author of these two poems was now being named as a playwright; in fact, as the author of twelve previously anonymous plays. The fame earlier achieved by Shakespeare for his two poems had never once been used during those four years to attract attention to any other written work; even the quartos of these plays failed to, or dared not mention the author's name, although it must have been on the lips of many who had read his *Venus and Adonis.* But from 1598 onwards, a change occurred; thereafter, it became quite acceptable to mention the name Shakespeare, and it was soon to be seen frequently in print. *Wits Treasury* can be said to have sanctioned its use by attributing a dozen previously unattributed plays to Shakespeare. And, as for his *"sugared sonnets",* also referred to by Meres, these, too, were now credited to him. From a poet, having written just two narrative poems four years ago, Shakespeare had suddenly been transformed overnight into a major playwright and sonneteer.

Meres' reference to Shakespeare was soon followed by another. In June 1599, John Weever published his *Epigrammes in the oldest cut and newest fashions.* Amongst its many verses was a sonnet in Shakespeare's verse form that twice named him.

Honey-tongued Shakespeare when I saw thine issue
 I swore Apollo got them and none other.
Their rosy-tinted features cloth'd in tissue,
 Some heaven-born goddess said to be their mother:
Rosy-cheek's Adonis with his amber tresses,
 Fair fire-hot Venus charming him to love her,
Chaste Lucrece, virgin-like her dresses,
 Proud, lust-stung Tarquin seeking still to prove her:
Romeo, Richard, more whose names I know not,

Their sugared tongues and power attractive beauty
Say they are saints although that saints they show not
For thousands vow to them subjective duty:
They burn in love thy children Shakespeare het them,
Go, woo thy Muse more nymphish brood beget them.[82]

Weever had drawn upon Meres' account and substituted *"sugared tongues"* for *"sugared sonnets"*; and with a nod to Shakespeare, he composed the verse in sonnet form. It is noteworthy, too, that after six or seven years, the barriers had finally begun to be removed, and Shakespeare's name could at last be openly lauded in print. Weever also mentioned *Romeo and Juliet* and *Richard II,* both of which had been entered in the *Stationers' Register* two years earlier. The public need no longer be in doubt that William Shakespeare was a writer of repute: a man known to both Meres and Weever as a sonneteer and author of *Venus and Adonis* and *The Rape of Lucrece:* as well as being the accomplished playwright who had authored a whole raft of work anonymously during the past decade.

Some months earlier, Richard Barnfield had published a verse in his final book, *A Remembrance of Some English Poets* (1598). This, too, reflected the anticipated flow of references to Shakespeare that were about to commence.

And Shakespeare thou, whose honey-flowing Vein,
(Pleasing the World) thy Praises doth obtain.
Whose Venus, and whose Lucrece (sweet and chaste)
Thy Name in Fame's immortal Book have placed.
Live ever you, at least in Fame live ever:
Well may the Body die, but Fame dies never.[83]

Poems in Divers Humors, 1598

The astute reader may inwardly question the repeated use of the word 'ever'. If Barnfield was aware of Shakespeare's true identity, its deliberate inclusion will have signalled to others who were in on the secret that E. Ver—an alternative spelling, and phonetically correct pronunciation of E. Vere (rhymes with 'air')—was the poet.

In the same year, John Marston published *Scourge of Villainy,* which contained a verse quite unconnected with the theme of his book. But it did provide him with the opportunity for a double meaning: – *"I ever honour"* for 'I E Ver honour' – to which he added a further clue concerning his intended subject.

> Most, most of me beloved, **whose silent name**
> **One letter bounds**. Thy true judicial style
> I ever honour, and if my love beguile
> Not much my hopes, then thy unvalu'd worth
> Shall mount fair place when Apes are turned forth.[84]

Marston has dispensed a number of clues concerning his intended subject. The man he is addressing is a person whose name is known for the silence surrounding it. Recall, this is the same report made by the anonymous epigram writer in *Wit's Recreation* – *"Shake-speare, we must be silent in thy praise"*.

Marston also says the name begins and ends with the same letter. The person whose name has greatest claim to this clue is, **E**[DWARD DE VER]**E**. We therefore have a common link between these two verses: it is the need for 'silence' concerning the subject of the poems. But, whereas *Wit's Recreation* actually names Shake-speare, *Scourge of Villainy* simply provides a hint that it is **E**[DWARD DE VER]**E**. Importantly, however, it is the need for *silence* surrounding this man that both poets were writing about.

Marston also suggests that this person's worth as a writer has been undervalued. This echoes Shake-speare's plaintive protest in Sonnet 72: *"For I am shamed by that which I bring forth / And so should you, to love things nothing worth."*

It was, of course, members of Oxford's own elitist class that poured shame upon him for his neglect of state duties, through devoting so much time to poetry and plays. George Puttenham captured the essence of their dissatisfaction in *The Arte of English Poesie*. His words having been written at about the same time as the Sonnets were being composed.

> *The credit and esteem [in which poets were held] was formerly not small. But in these days (although some learned princes may take delight in them) yet universally it is not so. For as well poets as poesie are despised & the name become of honourable infamous, subject to scorn and derision, and rather a reproach than a praise to any that use it ... Among the nobility or gentry ... especially in making poesie, it is to come to pass that they have no courage to write & if they have are loathe to be known of their skill.* [85]

Puttenham was simply repeating what the author of Sonnet 72 had confessed, concerning how his poetry had brought shame to his name. The two quotations complement each other, with the sonnet writer confirming what Puttenham said. For Oxford to have admitted to shame: as in Sonnet 72, makes sense; but written by an actor from the lower classes, it is quite ridiculous and totally inconsistent with Shaxpere's station in life.

Another cryptic reference to de Vere as Shakespeare may be determined from: *"the oddly phrased preface to the 1609 edition of Troilus and Cressida"*, which announced: *"A neuer writer, to an euer / Reader. Newes."*[86] Again, the same question arises – Was this the punning alert of 'An E. Ver writer', to an 'E. Ver Reader'? There are grounds for believing so, because the title page was quickly 'pulled' and a second title page substituted: the replacement now advertised the author's name: *"Written by William Shakespeare"*, as if to allay any lingering doubts introduced by the enigmatic expression contained in the first edition.

The publisher's *"Newes"* also disappeared, to be replaced by a revised Epistle. Presumably, the first edition had been too revealing, not only because of what it said, but also what it omitted.

> *The Epistle strongly implies that the play had never been acted in a public theatre, and (in order to appear in print) had made some kind of 'escape', since the 'grand possessors' would have prevented publication of it (together with other comedies [sic] by the same author) had they been able.*[87]

In addition, the original 'News' had included the sentence: *"And believe this, when he is gone, and his comedies out of sale, you will scramble for them, and set up a new English Inquisition."*[88]

Since this was written at a time when the infamous Spanish Inquisition was in full force: interrogating suspects in order to arrive at plots and conspiracies against Catholicism, the publisher's words, if taken literally, indicate he believed that another type of Inquisition would take place in England. This one, however, would be to enquire about the plays and their author, who in the first Epistle is unnamed, although there is that 'knowing wink' in the opening address that he was 'E Ver'. This must have been all too much for the authorities, and a new title page with Shakespeare's name as the author was firmly inserted.

In the same year that Meres' 600-page book sanctioning Shakespeare's name was published, a quarto edition of *"A Pleasant Conceited Comedie Called Loues Labours Lost"*[89] appeared on the booksellers' stalls, printed by William White, and full of typographical errors. It was the first play to carry Shakespeare's name. Word of Meres' book mentioning the play's author by name had got out. Nevertheless, it was not included in the *Stationers' Register*. Fear of the censor was still an inhibiting force.

The publisher, Cutbert Burby, emphasised his good fortune in acquiring the book by describing it: *"As it vvas presented before her Highnes this last Christmas. Newly corrected and augmented By W. Shakespere"* [90] From Burby's description, it would appear there had previously been an anonymous edition of lesser worth, for this one now bears the author's name as an incentive to purchase. However, with so many errors, it would be ludicrous to suppose that Shakespeare prepared this quarto for publication; but nor did he stay its printing; and for that matter, neither did the Chamberlain's Men.

William Jaggard, in 1612, was to repeat the same expression: *"Newly corrected and augmented by W. Shakespeare"*, for his third edition of *The Passionate Pilgrim*. For this falsehood he was brought to book, and made to issue a replacement title page with the author's name removed. Traditionalists are wont to claim that Shakespeare must have been responsible for forcing Jaggard to do this. But it was Thomas Heywood, another author offended by the publication, who protested the matter. He also claimed that he did this on Shakespeare's behalf. Oxford was then dead, and Shaxpere never once uttered a word concerning work connected with Shakespeare. Also, unlike Jonson, he never published a single one of his plays for profit.

On the other hand, he made no attempt to deny that he was the acclaimed poet and playwright, Shakespeare. There is a subtle difference between these two states; silently acknowledging a lie by refusing to deny it, allows it to be true. But making an outright claim of a false achievement is an open declaration of that lie. This difference between the two positions is repeatedly overlooked by those who engage in a study of Shakespeare's life and work. And though it is a distinction never remarked upon; it lies at the heart of the authorship question.

Love's Labour's Lost was originally believed to be the first of Shakespeare's comedies, written about 1588, when Shakespeare was twenty-four. *"The comedy of Love's Labour's Lost belongs indisputably to the earliest dramas of the poet, and will be almost of the same date as the Two Gentlemen of Verona."* [91]

> *[T]his was one of the earliest of Shakespeare's plays, if not the very earliest, a beginners clumsy effort, full of stilted rhyming couplets and over-elaborate puns, the characters unlife-like.* [92]

However, once it was realised that the play mirrored a little too closely the court of Henri III of Navarre (1572-1589), before he became Henri IV of France in 1589, and that the characters' names were actually based upon royal attendants at the court of Navarre, including the Princess of France, Marguerite de Valois, who became Henri's wife in 1572, Shakespeare's image-makers panicked and changed the date. It is now said to have been written in the mid 1590s.

As we shall later discover, Anthony Bacon resided in the region known as Navarre during the 1580s. It was where he set up part of England's spy network. His reports back to Walsingham are without doubt the source of the historical accuracy found in this play.

> *In the early Shakespeare play, Love's Labour's Lost, Lefranc recognised an author who understood the spirit of France, spoke cultured and colloquial French and knew at first hand the manners of court life. He must have spent some time at the Court of Navarre, for his allusions to it showed intimate knowledge available only to the privileged few. The play was evidently not written for public performance but for entertaining the English court, where these allusions would be recognised.* [93]

Love's Labour's Lost would, indeed, have made an excellent first effort when attempting a new style of writing for Court entertainment. Re-assigning the play's date to the mid 1590s does not seem a particularly intelligent move, since this places it in the midst of when Shakespeare was actively writing his second tetralogy:

> *Shakespeare with wonderful skill faithfully uses the historical material, even in the most minute touches; the comic and serious parts of Prince Henry's youthful extravagances, and his quarrel with his fa-*

> *ther, are worked out with poetic freedom from a few vague indications in the Chronicle.*[94]

Strange though it may seem to all but the Stratford orthodoxy, the *"wonderful skill"* Shakespeare exhibited while writing the *Henriad* tetralogy, stands out in total contrast to his *"beginner's clumsy effort, with characters unlife-like"*, when writing *Love's Labour's Lost:* both plays, so it is now claimed, were written at the same time. If you can still believe it!

This sudden naming of Shakespeare in 1598, as the author of plays previously thought to be anonymous – *Richard II, Richard III* and *Love's Labour's Lost* were the first plays printed with Shakespeare's name on them – was quickly seized upon by William Jaggard. In 1599 he published the first edition of *The Passionate Pilgrim,* ascribing the content to W. Shakespeare.

> *In fact only five of its 20 poems are Shakespeare's. Two are sonnets from the famous sequence that would be published in 1609 (Sonnet 138 and Sonnet 144). The remaining three poems were lifted from Act 4 of ... Love's Labour's Lost.*[95]

Yet, despite this, Shaxpere still took no action. It is therefore a fair question to ask: Is this really the same man that never once hesitated to apply to the courts for repayment of debts that occurred from the sale of malt?

Jaggard's publication of Sonnets 138 and 144 was the first example the world had of Shakespeare's sonnet sequence, although Meres had referred to these verses in *Wits Treasury.* It would be another ten years before the complete sequence of 154 was printed. But Shaxpere would remain quiet about these too, which raises interesting questions concerning his silence: questions that will bear closer scrutiny as we progress.

1599 also saw the erection of the Globe theatre on the south bank of the Thames: the work apparently being carried out by carpenter-builder Peter Street and his labourers, who used the timber brought over from the demolished Theatre at Shoreditch. Twenty years later, Heminge and Condell testified at court (*Witter v. Heminge and Condell*) that William Shakespere (sic) held a ten percent shareholding in the Globe: the same as he had held in the Lord Chamberlain's Company.

The circumstances surrounding the fifty percent shares held equally by Shaxpere, Phillips, Heminge, Pope, and Kemp are of some interest. It appears that these were sold to two financiers, William Leveson and Thomas Savage *"who regranted and reassigned to every of them severally a fifth part of the said moiety."* [96] In other words, their holding was returned, but under conditions that left Leveson and Savage with rights to the shares.

The land on which the Globe was built belonged to Nicholas Brend; he had inherited it from his father Thomas, who died in September of the previous year. Amongst the deceased's assets was listed – translated from the original Latin – *"One house, newly built, with a garden pertaining to the same in the parish of St Saviour's aforesaid ... in the occupation of William Shakespeare and others."* [97] Since the list of assets was compiled in May 1599, it is probable that Shaxpere moved in as a security guard at the time of the Globe's construction; some believe the house and the Globe were the same building.

Five months later, and the authorities were once again chasing Shaxpere for unpaid taxes: this time it was for a dwelling in the parish of St Helen's, in Bishopsgate. Presumably, this was from where he had transferred his lodgings prior to occupying the Globe. However, the tax record reported that he had moved to Sussex; no doubt a mishearing for Southwark.

The tax remained unpaid for another year, because it was not until October 1600, when the amount owing was referred to the Bishop of Winchester for collection that the sheriff was able to record a lump sum payment had been received to settle the debt.

To Shakespeare's admirers, the period between 1597 and 1600 must appear like a golden age. After a four-year period of unbroken silence, during which nothing bearing the name Shakespeare had been printed, although several anonymously written plays later identified as Shakespeare's were performed during this break, things started to happen.

Firstly, Meres launched *Wits Treasury,* this would herald Shakespeare's pre-eminence as an author of a dozen plays: all of which had been performed anonymously up until then. During that time there must have been numerable enquiries concerning the name of the unknown author. Secondly, William Shaxpere, for no known reason connected with either literature or the theatre, became rich enough to return to his hometown and buy two cottages, two barns, and a dominant mansion in the locality.

Thirdly, Shakespeare's plays began to slowly emerge as pirated quartos, often badly put together, but which, nevertheless, he always let pass: neither taking action, nor staying publication; although the latter action was a legal entitlement for any author (see Detobel, R. *The Oxfordian*, vol. 4: 39).

1598 *29 Aug. Richard II* entered in Stationers' Register.
20 Oct. Richard III entered in Stationers' Register.
15 Nov. Romeo and Juliet entered in Stationers' Register.
Richard II and *Richard III* published.
25 Feb. Henry IV, Part I entered in Stationers' Register.
10 Mar. Love's Labour's Lost published, the first of Shakespeare's plays to carry his name on the title page.
22 July. The Merchant of Venice entered in Stationers' Register.
7 Sept. Francis Meres' *Palladis Tamia* entered in Stationers' Register, providing a list of at least some of the plays Shakespeare had written thus far.
Dec. Richard III (Q2) published. Likewise *Richard II* (Q2 and Q3) and *The Rape of Lucrece.*

1599 *June.* John Weever publishes an Epigramme with the first allusion to Shakespeare's *Sonnets.*
Oct. Romeo and Juliet (Q2) and *Henry IV, Part I* (Q2) published. Also *Venus and Adonis* (Q3).

1600 *22 July. The Merchant of Venice* entered in the Stationers' Register.
4 Aug. Henry V, As You Like It, Much Ado About Nothing entered in the Stationers' Register.
23 Aug. Much Ado About Nothing and *Henry IV Part II* entered in the Stationers' Register as 'by Shakespeare'.
8 Oct. A Midsummer Night's Dream entered in the Stationers' Register.
28 Oct. The Merchant of Venice entered in the Stationers' Register.[98]

By 1600, as a direct result of these publications, which had flooded the market after Meres' book publicly acknowledged Shakespeare as a playwright, his reputation grew so great that . . .

anthologies began to appear containing excerpts from his work. Many extracts appear in three collections all published in 1600 – John

Flasket's England's Helicon, John Bodenham's Belvedere or The Garden of the Muses, and Robert Allot's England's Parnassus, whose subtitle was 'The Choysest Flowers of our Modern poets'. [99]

Bodenham's first choice of title is interesting. 'Belvedere', in both modern French and English is 'a turret': so called because it provides a fine (*bel*) view (*videre*). However, in the French language, up until publication of Randle Cotgrave's *Dictionary of the French and English Tongues* (1611), 'belvedere' *"is a shrub that grows to a man's height ... full of pleasant green boughs resembling branches of Hysope."* The Italian language also contained 'belvidere', which is used for the shrub called 'broome'. This may or may not be significant, but 'belvedere' is a perfect anagram for *Bel de Vere.* 'Bel' is the French alternative for 'beau', masculine form of the English 'fine'; 'glorious'; 'noble' &c. Hence: 'Noble de Vere'.

John Weever, the author of *Epigrammes in the oldest cut and newest fashions* (p.108), has also been credited with having contributed to the writing of the *Parnassus Plays:* a trilogy produced between 1598 and 1602 by the students of St. John's College, Cambridge. The plays were full of contemporary satire and, because of Meres' *Palladis Tamia,* Shakespeare's name was able to become part of the banter, without fear of redress. In the *Return From Parnassus, Part 2,* two characters called Kempe and Burbage – names that also identify two actors belonging to the Lord Chamberlain's Men – enact the following dialogue.

Why, here's our fellow Shakespeare puts them all down, I (Aye) and Ben Jonson too, O that Ben Jonson is a pestilent fellow; he brought up Horace giving the poets a pill, but our fellow Shakespeare hath given him a purge that made him bewray his credit. [100]

The author twice refers to Shakespeare as *"our fellow"*, in apparent recognition of Oxford's degree, which he obtained at St John's College in 1564. Jonson's *Poetaster* had been performed in 1601. It concerns the poetaster, CRISPINUS, who is forced to take a purge to relieve him of the nonsense he instigated by attempting to defame HORACE. The *Poetaster* is also said to contain a jibe at 'Shakespeare's' character, FALSTAFF. It has been suggested that 'Shakespeare' responded by characterising Jonson as the slow-witted AJAX in *Troilus and Cressida.* (Act 1; sc. ii). This could then explain the humour expected to be understood by the university audience.

In Part One of the *Return From Parnassus,* a character – aptly playing the part of a literary critic – with the revealing name of GULLIO is introduced with the words: *"Now, gentlemen, you may laugh if you will, for here comes a gull."* [101] A gull, of course, is someone easily gulled into believing anything they are told (some literary critics appear not to have changed much since then). GULLIO then gives voice to his gullibility by exclaiming: *"O sweet Master Shakspeare! I'll have his picture in my study at the court."* [102] (A sentence intended to be followed by laughter and applause from the audience.) Not only has GULLIO been made to pronounce Oxford's allonym with a short 'a' in the dialect spoken naturally in Shaxpere's native Warwickshire, but he has also drawn attention to *his* picture: surely a taboo subject.

There were, of course, no pictures of Shakespeare, nor could there be. A picture of Edward de Vere as Shakespeare would have revealed the nobleman behind the name. A picture of the counterfeit Shakespeare would have made him instantly recognizable to those who were aware of his literary limitations: especially people from his hometown in Warwickshire who had known him all his life. Any suggestion that John Shaxpere's apprentice son was London's and the world's great literary genius, as well as having fathered three children, none of whom could read or write, would have had the whole of Stratford bent double with laughter for weeks, and the truth about Oxford's penname, which the Court was desperately anxious to censor, would have been quickly revealed to all England.

As for GULLIO'S suggestion that he might hang Shakespeare's picture up at Court, where it could be seen by all, this was one more joke to delight the audience with, since it was the Court that was franticly attempting to prevent Shakespeare's identity from ever becoming known.

As satire, which it was, this scene was perfect. It also tells us that the university audience understood the truth behind Shakespeare's allonym, and this implies that an open secret already existed. The strategy of using Francis Meres' *Palladis Tamia* to establish Shakespeare's credentials within the community had been given licence, and a point of no return had been passed.

The three barren years, 1595, 1596, and 1597 were followed in 1598 by three years of plenty. Shakespeare's works became the talk of London's literary life. Yet, despite this rise in grandeur, the actual link connecting Shaxpere, the shareholder in the Globe theatre, to his near namesake, the incomparable genius *par excellence*, is extremely fragile. It is based solely upon an association of ideas. William Shaxpere's name is sufficiently like that of William Shakespeare to pass muster. Secondly, the Lord Chamberlain's Men performed William Shakespeare's plays at the Globe theatre, where Shaxpere held a financial investment. It is largely upon this basis that Shakespeare's image-makers transform Oxford's allonym, Will Shaxpere, into their invention of a self-made literary genius who rose from humble beginnings.

It is an appealing story, but strip away every innovation that his image-makers have applied, and what remains is somebody very ordinary. In fact, someone so very ordinary that neither the people of Stratford-upon-Avon, nor those in London whom he met with and lodged with, seemed even for one moment to consider that he might be the famous William Shakespeare. And why should they? In every recorded incident of his life, he was always reported to be doing what most other ordinary people might themselves be doing under similar circumstances. A case in point may better illustrate this truth.

At some time during the first years of the seventeenth century, William Shaxpere was lodging in Silver Street, inside the walls of the City of London. His accommodation lay directly to the east of Aldersgate, and south of Cripplegate. The house belonged to a French Huguenot headdress maker and his wife, Christopher and Mary Mountjoy. *"The Mountjoys regularly took in lodgers and for a number of years one of these was William Shakespeare."* [103] The actual house, which was situated on the corner of Silver Street and Muggle Street (later Monkswell Street), is pictured on Ralph Agas' map (1560). It shows a property not unlike the two-up, two-down terraced houses that were still, in the twentieth century, a familiar sight in many working-class areas.

> *His shop was on the ground floor, sheltered by a pentice, which had been a feature of the house for forty years. Upstairs the Mountjoys lived under a pair of gables that covered their end of the building.* [104]

Apart from his wife, and the lodgers he took in, Mountjoy also had three apprentices, a daughter also Mary, and a maid called Joan Johnson. One of the apprentices, Stephen Belott, the son of a French widow, subsequently married Mary Mountjoy, and it was through discussions concerning a pre-nuptial agreement that the future groom's fellow lodger, Shaxpere, was brought into the discussions, for *"they had amongst themselves many conferences about the marriage."*[105]

It must have been a lively and somewhat notorious household; for the elders of the French Church in London formally reported that the Mountjoys lived "a licentious life" and that both Mountjoy and his daughter's husband were "debauched".[106] *

Two years later, the bride's mother died and the Belotts set up a business of their own in opposition to Mountjoy. This resulted in acrimony between the two halves of the family, with the Belotts claiming against Mountjoy for the balance of the promised marriage portion. He refused to pay, and the dispute was referred to the Court of Requests; whereupon, Shaxpere was called from his home in Stratford-upon-Avon to bear witness.

William Shakespeare of Stratford upon Aven in the Countye of Warwicke gentleman of the age of xlviij [48] yeres or thereabouts sworne and examined the daye and yere above said deposethe & sayethe ... he knoweth the parties plaintiff and deffendant and hathe know them bothe as he now remembrethe for the space of tenne yeres or thereaboutes.[107]

Little was achieved by his appearance. The court passed the case over to the French Church in London for arbitration, where Belott's case was partly upheld, for which he was awarded twenty

---

* Charles Nicholl discovered from court records that Mountjoy ran a vice ring, controlling several brothels. It is also on record that "Mountjoy fathered two bastards and was excommunicated for his dissolute life." (*William Shakespeare,* Peter Holland, 2007, p.44)

Shaxpere's choice of companions, in this case residential ones, also included George Wilkins, who controlled several prostitutes. This fact cannot be separated from Shaxpere's former association with the doubtful profession of Dorothy Soer and Anne Lee, in what appeared to be an outbreak of gang violence for control of the vice trade in Southwark. Nor can the fact be excluded that Shaxpere inexplicably became extremely wealthy in a very short space of time, having allegedly acquired the nickname, "Pimping Billy".

nobles; but this, Mountjoy refused to pay. As for the witness, apart from not remembering the year in which he was born . . .

> *Shakespeare also pleaded inability to remember exactly "what implements and necessaries of household stuff" had been given. Nor did he know what sum of money had been promised to the couple.* [108]

At the close of the hearing, Shaxpere was required to sign a deposition. It is the first of his six known attempts at writing his name and displays the inevitable beginner's blot.

> *As remarked by Norman Evans of the Public Record Office: the dramatist's signature appears in the contracted form Willm Shkp. The 'p' is usually regarded as a form of the common abbreviation 'p' for 'per', which would make the signature 'Shakper' ... All six of the known signatures differ from each other in some particular and this example is the most awkward of them all.* [109]

Belott v. Mountjoy was also instrumental in bringing to the fore another lodger in the house, mentioned in the footnote above, this was George Wilkins, with whom Shaxpere shared accommodation.

> *In touch with the underworld and reputedly a brothel-keeper, Wilkins in his late twenties, clearly had some acquaintance with Shakespeare ... He brutally kicked a pregnant woman in the belly: he beat another woman, and then stamped on her so that she had to be carried home. We know of his behaviour from legal records.* [110]

It is debateable whether Wilkins' brief effort to earn money as a playwright was influenced by having once shared lodgings with Shaxpere. Were this so, he certainly acquired nothing of Shakespeare's art. What is not debateable is his record of criminality, which extended from 1610 up until his death in 1618. During that period he was continually brought before the court on charges of assault and battery; mostly, on account of his connection with prostitutes. One may also recall the similarity this has with William Wayte's application for *"sureties of the peace against William Shakspere ... for fear of death and so forth."*

Unsurprisingly, Shaxpere's time in the Mountjoy household is an extreme embarrassment to his image-makers. There is not only his inability to recall either his age or the relevant details of an agreement he had earlier been asked to advise upon, but also the company he was keeping. Wilkins, who was living off the immoral earnings of several prostitutes, eventually obtained enough money by this means to run his own brothel, which he fronted as a licensed alehouse located in a notorious red light district.

Shakespeare's traditionalists attempt to counter this with the suggestion that the poet was residing in this house of ill fame in order to receive French lessons from the debauched householder. They do not, however, indicate the nature of these French lessons.

In March 1603, at the same time Shaxpere was living in the Mountjoy household, Queen Elizabeth died.

> *The event stirred the Londoners to a flood of poetry. Everyone from Lord Burghley's elder son to the least of Henslowe's hacks rushed into print with combined wails for the death of the Queen.* [111]

Everyone, that is, except Shakespeare. His advocates are nonplussed. While it is fairly easy to invent situations surrounding Shakespeare; for example, to fill in his education, his lost years, his playacting, etc., using one's imagination coupled with the authority to package it all together as fact, it is quite impossible to invent his poetry. Why, then, did Shakespeare choose to remain silent; or, at least, not go public?

There are several plausible answers, for which, either one or a combination will serve to explain what happened. To begin with, there is no rational explanation as to why Shakespeare – if he had been the poet proposed by the dominant view – should have declined to add to the tributes that were being written by a woeful nation. Henry Chettle was fully aware of this at the time, for he remonstrated publicly with Shakespeare over this sad omission.

> Nor doth the silver-tonguèd Melicert,
> Drop from his honeyed Muse one sable tear
> To mourn her death who graced his desert,
> And to his lays opened her royal ear.
> Shepherd, remember our Elizabeth,
> And sing her rape, done by that Tarquin, Death.

> *As most scholars are agreed, Chettle's 'honey' imagery and clear allusion to Lucrece strongly indicate Shakespeare to have been the subject of this rebuke.* [112]

Chettle had a score to settle with *Shakespeare*. Some ten years before, he had been persuaded to publish an apology to this man in *Kind-Harts Dreame;* this was because of a letter he had included in *Greenes Groats-worth of Witte*, which ridiculed Shakespeare. Since then, he had learned that 'Shakespeare', as a flesh and blood person, did not exist. It was really Lord Oxford who was writing under that penname, and it was Shaxpere, with his connections to the Globe theatre and the Lord Chamberlain's Men, who was employed by the Earl to assume their authorship. As a result, Chettle must have felt foolish at having been gulled so easily.

As a publisher, Chettle knew that after *Venus and Adonis* and *The Rape of Lucrece* had been made public, 'Shakespeare' never again published any of his work. This undoubtedly meant he had been forbidden to do so, and ever obedient to a directive from the Queen's council, he had complied. Chettle's revenge was to publicly rebuke 'Shakespeare' for this silence, knowing, as he clearly did, that Oxford was unable to respond.

How can we be sure that Chettle knew Shakespeare was really the 17th Earl of Oxford? Chettle admits it in the first line of his verse, although careful to cover himself in language too erudite for the uneducated commoner. He calls the subject of his rebuke 'the silver-tonguèd Melicert'. Melicertes was the surname of Simonides, whom Plato had described as the best poet of the age. But, more than that, in the mythology of Plato's Greece, Melicertes was the *"the god of harbours"*. [113] By any stretch of imagination, this latter attribute cannot apply to Shaxpere of Stratford-upon-Avon. However, both these references fit Edward de Vere to a T.

Oxford's association with harbours began at Harwich in 1588. *"The seacoaste is here and ther furnished with harbours for shipping, whereof the principall is Harwiche."* [114] This was the year when the Spanish Armada invaded the shores of England. The battle at sea was fought during July (Old Style), and by the end of that month English ships, aided by gale force winds, had driven the remainder of the Spanish fleet to Calais, and from there, back into its own waters. In the aftermath of the first wave of battle, Oxford received the Governorship of Harwich, as corroborated by the Earl of Leicester in a letter he addressed to Walsingham.

1 August 1588.

> *I did as hir maiestie liked well of deleuer to my Lord of Oxford hir gratious concent of his willingness to serve her. And for that he was content to serve here amonge the formost as he semed, she was pleased that he shuld have the gouerment of Harwich & all those that ar[e] appointed to attend that place which should be ijM [=2000] men. A place of trust & of great daunger.* [115]

Oxford's active role at Harwich is also suggested in the following report.

> *[W]hen old Harbottle Grimston was writing from Bradfield in 1643 asking for £100 to fortify Harwich, he recalled that in 1588, the year of the Armada, new defences were constructed 'with not less than 46 great guns upon them', and there were 17,000 soldiers.* [116]

The Spanish fleet entered the English Channel on 19 July (O.S.). There then followed a number of naval battles, the final one being decisive, with the result that the foreign invader . . .

> *was forced to make the passage back to Spain around the northern tip of Scotland. The English fleet turned back in search of supplies when the Armada passed the Firth of Forth and there was no further fighting, but the long voyage home through the autumn gales of the North Atlantic proved fatal to many of the Spanish ships.* [117]

With the danger having passed, Oxford saw no further need to be away from London and his literary interests. He therefore asked to be relieved of his duties. Leicester commented upon this in his letter to Walsingham.

> *My Lord semed at the first to lyke well of yt, afterwards he cam to me & told me he thought that place of no [further] servyce nor credytt, and therefore he wold to the court and vnderstand hir maiesties further pleasur.* [118]

Although Harwich remained strategically important, it being opposite the Low Countries, Leicester was pleased to agree his request, and Oxford, whose wife had died the month before the Armada reached England, returned to the capital to arrange his daughters' future under the guidance of their grandfather, Lord Burghley. A pamphlet that was published at the time, and which reported Spain's threatened invasion of England, confirmed that "*the Erle of Oxford also in this tyme repayared to the sea co[a]st, for se-*

ruice of the Queen in the navy."[119]

Chettle's rebuke to 'Shakespeare', for not marking the mortal moon's eclipse (Elizabeth I was eclipsed by King James VI of Scotland) by penning a suitable tribute, appeared in a pamphlet entitled: *England's Mourning Garment.* Its theme was the reign of the recently deceased Queen Elizabeth. It therefore dealt with England's war against Spain, and the Queen's complicity in breaking a truce between the two countries that had served to further inflame the dispute. Chettle took up this question by debating it through the mouths of two shepherds, COLLIN and THENOT. COLLIN remarked:

> *I know some (too humorously affected to the Roman government) make question in this place, whether her highness first break not the truce with the King of Spain:*
>
> . . .
>
> *O, saith Thenot, in some of those wrongs resolve us, and think it no unfitting thing, for thou hast heard the songs of that warlike Poet Philesides, good Melúbee, and smooth tongued Melicert.* [120]

The references to Melúbee and Philesides, alongside Melicert, are called upon to provide support for England during its conflict with Spain. Sir Philip Sidney has been identified as the *"warlike Poet Philesides"*, for he was the *"courtier, statesman, soldier, poet,"*[121] who died fighting in the Spanish Netherlands; Melúbee is applicable to Sir Francis Walsingham, who was given this cognomen by both Thomas Watson, in his elegy to the statesman, and by Edmund Spenser, in *The Ruins of Time.*

Chettle's attempt at settling his score against Oxford, having been gulled by him at the time of Robert Greene's death, was given added emphasis by the title he chose for his rebuke: *England's Mourning Garment.* Oxford could not have failed to notice this title was almost identical to the *Mourning Garment,* written by Robert Greene more than a decade earlier. Touché.

Greene's novel, *Menaphon,* published in 1589, the year after Spain's Armada attacked England, had also included a character called MELICERT: a name associated with both poetry and the governorship of harbours. It was therefore a topical allusion to the recent royal appointment of Oxford as commander of Harwich. Aptly, therefore, it is into MELICERT'S mouth that Greene placed *"the best poetry in the book".*

Stratford's *literati*, whose intellect is often paralysed by their indoctrination into an acceptance that Shaxpere is equivalent to Shakespeare are baffled by Greene's choice of name; witness I. C. Elliot Browne's attempt at explaining it, as he is drawn inevitably towards observing Shakespeare as Greene's idol, MELICERT. And this, despite the fact that three years later, Greene supposedly ranted against the same man: denouncing him as an *"upstart crow"*. How often does inconsistency come into conflict with arguments directed against truth!

> *The character was evidently a favourite with Greene, who has put into his mouth the best poetry in the book. There are certainly some points of resemblance between Melicertus and the traditional idea of Shakespeare. Melicertus is a great maker of sonnets, and after his poetical excellence, the leading quality ascribed to him is the possession of a very ready and smooth wit, which enables him to shine in the euphuistic chaffing-matches with which the work is interlarded.* [122]

It is of particular note that the author of this excerpt, Elliot Browne, has referred to MELICERT'S *"euphuistic chaffing-matches"*. Euphuism was a linguistic movement aimed at refining the vocabulary and syntax of the English language, and which later spread to the continent where its influence is still apparent in the literature of many European countries. It was not, however, the form adopted by Sidney, whose writing pursued the reforms advocated at Cambridge by Gabriel Harvey.

> *[At] the head of the other literary party was Edward, Earl of Oxford ... a great favourer of the Euphuists, and himself a poet of some merit in the courtly Italian vein ... He was not only witty himself but the cause of wit in others.* [123]

It is noteworthy that W. J. Courthope, in his *History of English Poetry* (1920), has inadvertently credited Oxford with the very same qualities that Elliot Browne recognised as belonging to Greene's MELICERT.

It is often asserted that no evidence exists to link William Shakespeare with Edward de Vere. On the contrary, while it is acknowledged that a need for secrecy certainly existed concerning Oxford's later work being identified as his; nevertheless, it must have soon become an open secret amongst those close to him in the literary world. This naturally presented a challenge to some writers. If they could not acknowledge this truth, then it must be declared covertly. In Chapter 1, it was shown how Ben Jonson rose to this challenge with a personal avowal that Edward de Vere was William Shakespeare; and how he then succeeded to achieve this disclosure in a manner that is so remarkable in its intellectual cleverness that the result meets the requirement of an ineluctable statement of Shakespeare's true identity.

Early Retirement

It is a habit of mankind, easily recognizable in the present day, that the death of a famous actor or film star heralds the televising of those films in which the deceased had played a leading role. Edward de Vere died on 24 June 1604, and was buried twelve days later. Some unknown hand, perhaps with the presentiment that much greater attention would later focus upon the life and death of this man, was said to have added a margin note to the church record: *"The plague"* (Ogburn, 1988, p. 692); although this entry has since been questioned.

As summer turned to autumn that year:

> *James began his first season of extended Christmas revels, watching the King's Men in at least twelve performances, eight of which were of Shakespeare's plays. He saw Othello in the Banqueting House at Whitehall on 1 November, and The Merry Wives of Windsor three days later. Measure for Measure was performed on 26 December, and The Comedy of Errors was revived on the 28th. In January, Love's Labour's Lost and Henry V were staged. Shrove Sunday was celebrated with The Merchant of Venice, which proved so appealing that it was "Again Commanded by the King's Majesty" on Shrove Tuesday.*[124]

There is an interesting postscript to these performances. Amongst *"Entries in the Revels Accounts of 1604-5 recording performances by the Kings Men … Under the column of poets, 'Shaxberd is one of the more striking variants of Shakespeare'."* [125] 'Shaxberd' has been written twice: each time against *The Merchant of Venice.* No other named author appears on that page.

A further interesting fact to emerge following the death of Oxford is that King James permitted his coat of arms to be engraved on the flyleaf of *Hamlet,* as may be confirmed by its imprint in the second quarto (1604). Advocates for de Vere have always recognised Hamlet as a pen-portrait of the author. It was therefore fitting that the King should agree to acknowledge the passing of this great English dramatist by marking the year of his death with a sign of approval against the one play that most characterised the deceased.

Another interesting event that occurred at the time of Oxford's death was the immediate imprisonment of the 3rd Earl of Southampton, together with some of his former conspirators: men, who, at the time of Essex's rebellion, had been seized and imprisoned for their part in the plot. The events surrounding this tend to confirm the close bond that existed between Oxford and Southampton; it suggests, too, that Oxford had pledged Southampton's good conduct in return for his release. James I had apparently agreed to this condition, and released the errant earl into his safekeeping.

However, with Oxford's death, the King's fear at losing his crown, possibly with his head still attached, was revived and he took urgent measures to avert the danger. But on the next day, after a night of reflection, Southampton was brought before the King and required to personally pledge his loyalty to the Crown. This, Southampton did, and in return he was released for a second time from the Tower.

Oxford's death in 1604 also coincided with Shaxpere's retirement from the stage. From this year onwards, up until the time of his death twelve years later, his name disappears from the cast list of plays. In fact, his role as an actor has always been problematic.

> *Nicholas Rowe in 1709 asserts that he played the Ghost in Hamlet, and others have suggested Duncan and some of the Henrys. Other reports mention him playing Adam in As You Like It. And Ben Jonson lists him along with other actors as a player in Every Man In His Humour (1598) and as a 'Principall Tragœdian' in his play about Sejanus, Seianvs his Fall (1603).* [126]

Yet, contrary to this information there are the diary entries made by Shakespeare's contemporary, Edward Alleyn:

> *The Elizabethan actor, Edward Alleyn, noted in his diaries the names of all the actors and dramatists of his time, and those connected with the production of plays at the Fortune, Blackfriars, and other theatres. Shakespeare is not mentioned once.* [127]

Another peculiarity is that a study of the records of forty-six towns, including Stratford-upon-Avon and seventy municipal records in which acting companies played at the time of Shakespeare, show his name to be absent on every occasion.

> *Hopeful of finding traces of Shakespeare's footsteps, Halliwell-Phillipps personally examined the records of Banbury, Barnstaple, Bewdley, Bridport, Bristol, Cambridge, Canterbury, Coventry, Dorchester, Dover, Faversham, Folkestone, Hythe, Kingston-on-Thames, Leicester, Leominster, Lewes, Ludlow, Lyme Regis, Maidstone, New Romney, Newcastle-on-Tyne, Newport, Queenborough, Rye, Sandwich, Shrewsbury, Southampton, Warwick, Weymouth, Winchelsea, and York.* [128]

Despite all his travel and efforts, Halliwell-Phillipps could find no trace of Shakespeare's name. In this regard his failure was similar to that of Charlotte C. Stopes, another researcher seeking the ever-elusive *Shakespeare*. She spent more than seven years of her life sifting through the archives of the Southampton family seeking just one reference to Shakespeare. She found nothing: deeming her work a failure (Ogburn: 1988, pp. 206-7).

Perhaps the truth of the matter is that Shake-speare never acted in public, and only visited Southampton's home under his own name of de Vere: his stage performances being reserved for the privacy of court performances and private houses, as other noble ladies and gentlemen were apt to do at the time.

The Shake-speare of the Sonnets certainly admitted to acting: *"Alas, 'tis true, I have gone here and there, / And made myself a motley to the view"*. (Sonnet CX). But was it only in private? And why should he regret it? Acting privately at court would certainly explain Alleyn's failure to mention Shakespeare's name amongst those he listed. It would also account for the theatrical entrepreneur, Philip Henslowe, recording in his daybook some eight or nine plays that were Shakespeare's, but never once naming the author, and certainly never having made any payment for them. It would, of course, have been unthinkable in Elizabethan England for a nobleman of Oxford's pedigree to receive money for labour of this kind.

Professor Louis Bénézet confirmed the extraordinary oddity of Shakespeare's absence from such a comprehensive set of records, especially since they covered the years between 1592 and 1609: the time when *Shakespeare* is recorded by his biographers to have been most active, and at his peak of inventiveness.

> *The diary begins covering Henslowe's theatrical activities for 1592. Entries continue with varying degrees of thoroughness, until 1609 ... Henslowe recorded payments to twenty-seven Elizabethan play-wrights. He variously commissioned, bought and produced plays by, or made loans to Ben Jonson, Christopher Marlowe, Thomas Middleton, Robert Greene, Henry Chettle, George Chapman, Thomas Dekker, Anthony Munday, Henry Porter, John Day, John Marston and Michel Drayton. The Diary shows the varying partnerships between writers, in an age when many plays were collaborations. It also shows Henslowe to have been a careful man of business, obtaining security in the form of rights to his author's works, and holding their manuscripts, while tying them to him with loans and advances. If a play was successful Henslowe would commission a sequel ... Plays with Shakespearean titles like, Hamlet, Henry VI, Henry V, Taming of the Shrew and others, are found in the diary ... However, there is no mention of William Shakespeare in Henslowe's diary.* [129]

Shakespeare's advocates do not have a plausible explanation for this apparent paradox, and quickly bypass it: perhaps, they subconsciously realise that the absence of Shakespeare's name would be a predictable outcome if it were the penname of Lord Oxford. Instead, the dominant view maintains that Shaxpere responded to this flood of adulation by returning to Stratford-upon-Avon to pursue life as a merchant: trading in malt and wool; speculating in real estate, loaning money, and collecting tithes.

In 1601, while still in London, a different causal factor occurred to impel Shaxpere to return home; it was the death of his father. The funeral took place on 8 September.

With Oxford's health also now weak, Shaxpere appears to have prepared himself for a prolonged stay in Stratford. It may even be that he had been told to stay away from London, unless needed; which, of course, would make perfect sense, if he had been secretly acting as Oxford's allonym. For had he stayed in London, he would have to fend off questions concerning a future in which he would no longer have any part to play. There is also the possibility that were Oxford to die, Shaxpere might not remain completely silent about his part in the deception. In far off Stratford-upon-Avon, these issues would disappear.

In May 1602, Shaxpere arranged for his brother Gilbert to purchase, on his behalf, 107 acres of land north of Stratford. The vendors were William and John Combe, and the asking price was £320 (≈ £90,000). The title deed described Shaxpere as: *"of Stratford upon Avon"*. The reason for him dealing through the agency of his brother was presumably to lull the Combes into believing it was Gilbert they were selling to; this would have kept the price lower than if they had known it was his wily brother William who was behind the deal.

Four months later Shaxpere increased his property holding by purchasing a cottage in Walkers Street, also known as Dead lane. On the deed his name appears as *"Shackespere"*.

Apart from increasing his property portfolio, Shaxpere still continued to trade in malt. His purchase of two barns, for so it must be supposed, was to use them for storage.

We know of his trading activities because in July 1604, the month of Oxford's funeral: *"Willielmus Shaxpere"* took Philip Rogers, an apothecary working in Stratford, to court. The plaintiff's plea was that Rogers had been supplied with a quantity of malt in the previous March, but had failed to settle the bill: his indebtedness to Shaxpere was for £1. 15s. 10d plus charges. By contrast, a year later: —

> *On 24 July 1605 he paid £440 [≈ £123,000] to buy a half interest in tithes of crops ['corn, grain, blade and hay'] from Old Stratford, Welcombe and Bishopton, as well as certain tithes in Stratford parish.* [130]

These purchases can be interpreted as the action of a person intent upon establishing a permanent residence in the area where his fortune is invested. From which it may be inferred that Shaxpere had retired from theatrical life in London, and was making ready to settle down in the town of his birth. Indeed, most scholars supporting the dominant view of Shakespeare also infer this to be the case: especially since *"he does not appear on any of the surviving actor-lists after 1603"* (M. M. Reese, *Shakespeare: His World and His Work,* 1980, p. 252).

It is therefore important to follow this line of thought, and to discover how life in rural Stratford would have affected him; if he was the great author whom various vested interests attest was the case. Consider, firstly, Shaxpere in retirement.

> *The playwright's reputation was then at its height. Much adulated and enjoying the patronage of influential friends, he was called "gentle Shakespeare" or, more familiarly, "good Will".* [131]

Any retirement at the peak of his popularity must therefore be considered suspect. For consider, he had first been heard of in the autumn of 1592, at the age of 28. Ten years later, at the age of 38 he is preparing for retirement. In fact, Shaxpere was not beginning retirement at all; he was simply exercising a career change, to coincide with the redundancy he expected, due to Oxford's failing health and approaching demise. In doing so, he left London: leaving behind the theatre and the men of literature, with which and with whom, traditionalists suppose he had enjoyed a common bond, but which would be entirely absent in his hometown. He also said goodbye to the King's Men, who were performing the plays for which his name was known, particularly at court: thereby avoiding hearing James I's applause and the monarch's wish to see more of 'his' work. He also left Ben Jonson to take centre stage in all matters literary. This included the writing of Masques for Queen Anne, together with a long-standing collaboration with the scenery expert, Inigo Jones. *The Masque of Blackness* (1605) was to begin a new era of spectacle in the theatre (Wilson, 1993 p.464).

> *Ben Jonson … increased his reputation in the reign of James I, who commissioned him to write librettos for masques to amuse the Court in the winter months. His vast classical knowledge, his reputation as a poet and his friendship, not untouched by rivalry with Shakespeare, gave him prestige.* [132]

But there was no rivalry. King James, though a great admirer of plays by Shakespeare, never once commissioned him, as he did Jonson, to write plays or masques for his entertainment. This omission is accountable if he knew that *Shakespeare* was dead.

> *Ben Jonson produced some thirty masques in collaboration with Inigo Jones, who was responsible for the sets and equipment. In general these sumptuous shows were only performed once … [and] were financed by the nobility, or even by the king or queen, who would take part in the spectacle.* [133]

Away from this hive of theatrical activity, Shaxpere's choice of occupation was to sell malt, collect rent from his tenants, and indulge in land speculation with local businessmen. To put it bluntly, this is so far from normal behaviour as to suggest a split personality: unless, that is, Oxford's recent death had prevented Shaxpere from being seen habiting the Globe theatre.

The Stratford orthodoxy suggests a different explanation. Shakespeare combined his business activities with playwriting. And they name a dozen or so plays they allege were written between the time he left London and his death in 1616. But, once again, circumstances indicate otherwise. His deposition in the *Belott v. Mountjoy* case suggests that at the early age of 48, he was already suffering memory loss.

His contorted signature at the same time does nothing to persuade that he still had control of a pen. His house was also bookless. There were no references to call upon as an aid to his failing memory. And although New Place remained a family residence up until the death of his granddaughter's husband in 1674, not one single book, letter, or manuscript has ever been discovered there that could help to validate Shaxpere as Shakespeare.

This lack of evidence is most curious, because between the years 1616 and 1674, Shakespeare's collected plays were published several times: initially in the Folio edition of 1623, then in the Second Folio edition of 1632, which included Milton's *"An Epitaph on ... Shakespeare"*, and in a Third Folio printed in 1663, with a second impression issued the following year containing *Pericles* and six other plays considered to be apocryphal. Yet, contrary to the nation's interest in the Shakespeare family's deceased ancestor, his descendents retained a blissful—dare one say, ignorant—silence.

Also to be considered are Shaxpere's two daughters, Susanna and Judeth. Susanna did not leave home to marry John Hall until June 1607, and Judeth remained a spinster until 1616. Let their father now be imagined, seated at home, writing *Antony and Cleopatra, "a tragedy driven by politics and passion"*, and allegedly begun by the author in 1606. Is it not immediately obvious that his daughters would enquire of their father what he was writing? Are we to suppose that Susanna and Judeth, the natural stock of the finest brain in England, would not want to read some, if not all of this play? Alas, they cannot; neither one can read a word. But, would these two fine young ladies not have twisted their father's arm and asked him to give them some lessons in reading and writing? Are we to suppose they were both imbeciles? Is it conceivable that their father was too busy with his commercial activities to find enough time even to teach his two daughters how to write their names? Orthodoxy believes this to be the case.

"Judith, evidently took after her mother–she couldn't write," wrote A. L. Rowse, one of 'Shakespeare's' most fervent admirers, and a man who busied himself by adding as many inventions to the character of *his* Shakespeare as he thought appropriate. Judeth was only ever able to mark her name with a cross. Susanna fared a little better, but only after she married. Her husband was an educated man, practising medicine for his living. It was he, apparently, who taught her to write her name.

> *Shakspere's parents, his candid biographer Halliwell-Phillipps concedes, were 'absolutely illiterate'. His wife was illiterate. Of his two daughters, Judith was illiterate and Susanna, so far as is known, could do no more than sign her name.* 134

Yet, female literacy was never a problem in Shakespeare's plays, and is clearly something he took for granted, for he lived at a time when Mary was Queen of Scotland, Catherine de' Medici was Regent of France and Elizabeth was Queen of England. As early as *Titus Andronicus,* the dramatist has dumb amputee, LAVINIA, signalling her torment from a passage in Ovid's *Metamorphosis:*

TITUS: Ah, boy, Cornelia never with more care
Read to her sons than she hath read to thee
Sweet poetry and Tully's Orator.

. . .

TITUS: Soft! So busily she turns the leaves! Help her.
What would she find? Lavinia, shall I read?

MARCUS: See, brother, see! Note how she quotes the
leaves. (Act IV: sc. i)

Another early play by *Shakespeare* was *The Taming of the Shrew.* In act 3 scene i, HORTENSIO discusses BIANCA'S learning: to which KATHARINA'S sister responds by reading out aloud from her tutor's notes. In *Timon of Athens,* supposedly written in 1605, when Shaxpere was in Stratford and about to embark upon a massive investment in tithes, we are led to see the dramatist seated at his writing desk with – let it be suggested – Susanna and Judeth at his shoulder, while disparaging those unable to read. Has the man no conscience?

PAGE:	Prithee, Apemantus, read me the superscriptions of these letters; I know not which is which.
APEMANTUS:	Canst not read?
PAGE:	No.
APEMANTUS:	There will little learning die, then, that day thou art hang'd. (Act 2: sc. ii)

In 1609, a major event in the life of Shaxpere occurred. On 20 May, a book of *Shakespeare's Sonnettes* was entered in the *Stationers' Register.* Yet, strangely, these poems, undoubtedly the labour of so many memorable hours spent in their composition, were utterly and completely disregarded by the resident of New Place, Stratford-upon-Avon.

John Addenbrooke, another resident of Stratford, was not so fortunate. At that same time, he was being pursued through the courts by an irate William *"Shackspeare"* for non-payment of £6 plus costs of 25 shillings. Addenbrooke skipped town after having first persuaded a neighbour, Thomas Hornby, to stand surety for him. But Addenbrooke never returned; and so *"Shackespeare"* began legal proceedings against Hornby, just one month after *Shake-speare's Sonnets* had been registered for publication.

Should this not strike any normal, intelligent reader as odd? Why was *"Shackespeare's"* malt so much more important than 'his' sonnets that he would go to court for one but not for the other? Or should we conclude that the *Sonnets* were not his? But, if they were not his, then neither were the thirty-seven plays that custom has so far attributed to him. And here, too, we find a similar pattern emerging. Before Shaxpere's death in 1616, eighteen plays by 'Shakespeare' were published as quarto editions. But on no occasion did the author stay their publication. Instead, the plays became public, allowing rival performances to be staged. Why did Shaxpere not seek legal redress for his loss? The ridiculous answer proposed for this is that Shaxpere had sold these plays to the Globe theatre, and they were no longer his.

Firstly this explanation contradicts the one given earlier, when Shaxpere supposedly left Philip Henslowe in 1594, and took his plays with him; as if such a smart operator as Henslowe would not have secured the rights to these plays from a then unknown writer from the provinces. At a later date, Shaxpere was a shareholder in the Globe; he therefore had reason to stop the illegal printing of his, or the Globe's plays. But he never did, nor did the other shareholders at the Globe ever initiate legal proceedings; it was left to the Lord Chamberlain (3 May 1619), the brother-in-law of Oxford's daughter, to prevent the publication of Shakespeare's plays.

Even before then, the law had protected an author. Authority for this statement is found in the case of *Millar v. Taylor*, which was decided by the Court of King's Bench and reported in *4 Burrows Reports*, pages 2303 to 2407, in which it was reported . . .

> *That at common law an author of any book of literary composition had the sole right of first printing and publishing the same for sale; and might bring an action against any person who printed, published and sold the same without his consent.* [135]

Is this not totally inconsistent with Shaxpere's unhesitating reaction against those defaulting on their payment for malt supplied by him? And why should that be, other than that he had legal backing for supplying malt: while in literary matters, he had no legal right to anything written by Shakespeare?

In this respect, consider still further the plays and poetry that were published with Shakespeare's name on the title page, but which had not been written by him.

> *He made no audible protest when seven contemptible dramas in which he had no hand were published with his name or initials on the title page.* (Sir Sidney Lee, *A Life of William Shakespeare*, New York, 1909).

Why did he not take action against the publishers, or at least complain? Compare this with the protest 'he' (or was it Oxford) made to Chettle over the Groats-worth incident. Where are all those divers of worship that had once rushed to his defence over that incident? The difference is that in 1592, Oxford was planning to establish his penname Shakespeare, as an emerging poet, and Chettle had nearly ruined the plan. Much later, when his identity as Shakespeare had become sufficiently known, he could no longer protest under that name.

Thomas Heywood, as we have seen (p.112), certainly took action against Jaggard in *Apologie for Actors,* when Jaggard included some of his poems in a third edition of *The Passionate Pilgrim.* In a lengthy tirade against injustice, Heywood complained of *"manifest injurie"* (Crystal, 2005 p. 129). Shaxpere, as always, remained silent, even though Jaggard had included five poems attributed to him amongst twenty pieces that appeared under 'his' name. The intelligent conclusion to be drawn is that Shaxpere had no claim to title, and was therefore unable to bring a legal action against the publisher.

Shaxpere's final years in Stratford did not completely divorce him from London. There were several instances when his presence in the capital was either recorded or else is implied. But on none of these occasions did he make the journey in response to a writing engagement. On 19 May 1603, the Lord Chamberlain's Men became the King's Men, licensed by James I.

> *Wee ... doe licence and authorize theise our Servauntes Lawrence Fletcher, Willm Shakespeare Richard Burbage Augustyne Phillippes Iohn Heminge henrie Condell Willm Sly, Robt Armyn, Richard Cowly, and the rest of theire Associates freely to use and exercise the Arte and faculty of playing Comedies, Tragedies, histories, Enterludes, morals, pastorals, Stageplaies ... for the recreation of our loving subjects as for our solace and pleasure.* [136]

This appointment is of special interest. Almost immediately upon arriving in London as the country's new monarch, James I abolished all troupes of players; this was a concession to the prevailing Puritan view against actors. The King then reserved for himself the right to appoint one company for his own household: (Wilson: 1993, p.296).

> *Through what can only have been a special recommendation by someone of influence, on 17 May James instructed his Keeper of the Privy Seal to draw up for Shakespeare's company Letter Patent under the Great Seal of England appointing them the King's Men, that is his own company of players, a title they would carry throughout the rest of James' reign and beyond that into the reign of Charles I.* [137]

The recommendation *"by someone of influence"* seems most

likely to have been the man James referred to as *"Great Oxford"*, and who, by the King's generosity, was able to retain his £1000 annuity granted by Elizabeth in 1586, and still with no accounting required.

It is also to be noted that Lawrence Fletcher heads the list of men licensed by King James.

> *Lawrence Fletcher had been the King's favourite actor in Scotland. He had to receive the perquisites of royal patronage in the new kingdom, and so, although Fletcher never acted with Shakespeare and his fellows, he was officially numbered among them.* [138]

This tends to suggest Shakespeare's name was also included on the list of actors for appearance's sake. For it coincides with the year of his retirement from acting. But since the public had been given assurance in Meres' *Palladis Tamia* that Shakespeare was the author of a dozen plays, previously thought to be anonymous: it follows from this that his name was expected to be amongst members of the company staging 'his' plays. This does not mean – as with Lawrence Fletcher – that his presence on the King's list required him to play a role in the Company's performances; indeed, cast lists show this to have been the case; while his continued presence in Stratford confirms its truth.

The published list is also interesting from another viewpoint. Heminge and Condell are the first two names on the list of those still living when the First Folio was being put together for publication; Phillips died in 1605; Fletcher died in 1608; Burbage died in 1619. What is also interesting to note is that Heminge and Condell only appeared on Shaxpere's will as an afterthought—an interlineation that was made even after the will had been revised for its final completion. Burbage's name was also part of this afterthought, perhaps because his name was first on the King's list next to Shakespeare's, and he was still alive in 1616. But was this interlineation made after Shaxpere's death? It could very easily have been: although this cannot now be proved. It is, however, noteworthy that Shaxpere's will was first drafted in January 1616. Then after several revisions had been made, as evidenced by the different types of paper used, the final version was put together three months later. Consequently, the three actors' names were never considered for inclusion, either in the first draft, or in any later draft, otherwise they would not have been inserted at the end as an interlineation.

This fact does make it appear their inclusion only became necessary when it was realised that Shaxpere needed to have acknowledged, *beforehand*, the immense sacrifice in time and money that Heminge and Condell were required to make after his death, when they allegedly collected, edited and prepared his plays for publication. This is especially apparent when they justified their efforts by referring to Shakespeare as *"a Friend and Fellow"*. Consequently, it can be seen that without this interlineation in Shaxpere's will, the professed friendship of Heminge and Condell to the poet would have sounded completely one-sided.

Following their royal appointment as The King's Men, *"the playwright and eight of his fellows were each given four-and-a-half yards of cheap red cloth for gowns."* [139] This is frequently cited by Shakespeare's image-makers because it suggests evidence for their man's theatrical career (the term 'playwright' has been deliberately employed by Park Honan as reinforcement for the image he is creating for his readers). In point of fact, this record simply reaffirms Shaxpere's connection with the King's Men, which is not doubted. Nor is it doubted that Shaxpere may have occasionally performed as an extra, or even a bit-player.

The record cited above also implies that Shaxpere, in company with other men, received a red gown to celebrate King James' entry into the City of London. In fact, the planned entry for the 15th March was cancelled because of a severe outbreak of Plague. This forced the King to avoid London and seek refuge by way of a progress across southern England.

It was during this interlude that James visited Wilton House, the Wiltshire home of Lord Pembroke, and his scholarly mother the Countess, Mary Sidney, sister of the deceased Sir Philip. After a short stay at Wilton, the King crossed over to thc Isle of Wight. It was upon his return to the mainland that he unexpectedly changed direction, and retraced his steps back to Wilton. Many years later, the historian and lyric poet William Cory visited Wilton House and was shown a letter by his hostess, Lady Elizabeth à Court, the widow of Sidney Herbert, 1st Baron of Lea, which confirmed that King James had been invited back to the House because *"Shakespeare"* had since arrived as a house guest.

What followed, it is told, was a period of festivity during

which the King's Men were summoned from their winter retreat at Mortlake (then a Thames-side village on the outskirts of London), in order to perform *As You Like It* for the royal party. Unfortunately, the letter Cory was shown is another casualty to be counted amongst the lost papers of Shakespeare. It, too, has vanished; appropriately enough at the time Halliwell-Phillipps was engaged in combing through archives of the great houses, to construct evidence that would accord with his personal idea of the man he so idolised.

If Halliwell-Phillipps ever saw the letter, and he would have been drawn to it like a magnet, then he would have realised that William Shaxpere had not the social leverage to divert the King of England away from his itinerary. For, as Katherine Duncan-Jones correctly pointed out: *"Shakespeare was the King's Man, not the Countess of Pembroke's ... he was hardly in position, either socially or legally to stay at Wilton House as an independent guest, as if for a country-house weekend."* [140]

Yet, it is on record that King James did break his journey and *return* to Wilton House; it is also on record that the King's Men were summoned from Mortlake to perform for James I during his return visit to Wilton. Of course, the 17th Earl of Oxford at Wilton House, the home of his daughter's fiancé, explains everything. More will be said about Oxford's connection with Wilton in a subsequent chapter.

As for Shaxpere, there is one further reference to his association with the business end of theatre life. In 1619, three years after his death, his name was mentioned in a lawsuit involving the leasing of the Blackfriars theatre. It appears that a syndicate amongst the King's Men had been formed in the summer of 1608, for the purpose of obtaining the Blackfriars premises after the Children of the Chapel had been barred from performing there. Their offence was to have given performances that poked fun at the French ambassador and King James. The seven men named in this new syndicate were Cuthbert Burbage, Richard Burbage, William Shaxpere, John Heminge, Henry Condell, William Sly and Thomas Evans; each were required to pay one seventh part of the annual rent of £40 (≈ £11,200), in return for which, each investor received a seventh part of the shares.

The agreement was drawn up on 9 August, during an outbreak of the Plague and the inevitable closing of the theatres. The King's Men therefore went on tour, reaching Coventry by the end of October. But Shaxpere was not one of them; he returned to Stratford-upon-Avon where, on 9 September, he attended the funeral of his mother Mary Arden. The parish register recorded her burial as *"Mayry Shaxpere wydowe"*. It appears that her grieving son stayed on in Stratford, for on 16 October, he became godfather to William Walker, son of Henry Walker, a prosperous mercer in the town. Whereafter, from December until June of the following year, he was involved in proceedings against local man John Addenbrooke (p. 135).

For the remaining years of Shaxpere's life, records continue to show only his involvement in commercial activities. For example, in 1610, he was involved in *"further legal action with respect to New Place ... [in the same year] buying an additional twenty acres [from William and John Combe]."* In the following year, *"William Shackspeare, of Stratford uppon Avon"* together with two other leaseholders of the tithes he had acquired, *"submitted a bill of complaint in the Court of Chancery in Stratford seeking relief from having to make good the non-payment of rents by fellow leaseholders."* Later, that same year, the name of *"Mr William Shackspere"* was added to the margin of a document that listed seventy-one citizens of Stratford who were *"prosecuting the bill in parliament for the better repair of the highways."* Shaxpere, so it would appear from the margin entry of his name, was only later cajoled (shamed?) into joining in with his fellow residents.

His close association with the businessmen in that region was again confirmed in January 1613, when he was named as a beneficiary in the will of John Combe, who died soon after making the bequest, having left *"to Mr William Shackspere five pound."* In the autumn of 1614, a group of landowners in Stratford attempted to enclose, for their own purposes, an area of common land belonging to the Stratford Corporation. *"Shackespeare, as he is called in documents bearing on the case, was involved as owner of 106 acres in the area and as part owner with Thomas Greene [the Town clerk] of the tithes from neighbouring lands;"* (Ogburn, 1988, pp. 33-4).

Shaxpere apparently knew about this attempted seizure of land, for he was required to give evidence in the case, but further documents relating to his culpability in the matter have since been removed from the official proceedings, and are no longer to be found. It is an unfortunate feature of Shakespearian scholarship that documents, which have the potential of marring the image of this man, vanish with a regularity that belies coincidence. The hand of Collier is suspected, but not exclusively.

Although firmly entrenched in matters local, Shaxpere did make one final trip to London. His business in the capital was to purchase a property known as the Gatehouse, which was situated approximately where the foot of Blackfriars Bridge now stands.

> *On 10 March 1613, "William Shakespeare of Stratford upon Avon … gentleman" bought a house in Blackfriars near Blackfriars Theatre (both once part of a large Dominican priory) for £140 [approximately £40,000] … The next day he mortgaged it back to its previous owner for £60 [£17,000]. The device barred inheritance of any part of the property by his wife, who would otherwise have been entitled to her dower right of a third of its value.* [141]

By barring his wife from inheritance, he also distanced her from his connection with London and the theatre, which could have resulted in approaches being made to her as the widow of the late, and greatly respected 'poet', Shakespeare. It was something she would have found unbelievable; exceeded only by the disbelief of those she conversed with, who learned for the first time that the husband of this woman was illiterate, without any formal education. Consequently, Shaxpere's move was shrewd; it protected the secret he had been paid to keep. This could imply that payments were still being made from the estate of Oxford's late widow to retain his silence. For this reason, it is believed he was the Countess of Oxford's *"dombe man"*, mentioned in her will, and to whom she bequeathed a quarterly sum; any charity bequest would likely have been a one-off payment.

While in London, Shaxpere was one of four men investing in the Gatehouse, with its hidden rooms and a secret passage down to the Thames. The other three were William Johnson, *"citizen and vintner of London"*; John Jackson, *"a Hull shipping magnate"*; and John Heminge, *"a grocer* and theatrical shareholder. Smuggling contraband is one reason that binds these three professions to the house with its special features.

Shaxpere's name appears on the Gatehouse deed as *"William Shakspẽ"*, and is again repeated on the form of indenture as *"Wm*

Shakspẽ". Both Jackson and Johnson were able to sign their names in the normal manner. Shaxpere's six attempts at writing his name on various legal documents, all of which occurred between 1612 and 1616, represent the only evidence we have that this man ever picked up a pen, and even this is suspect. For this reason these six signatures have attracted expert criticism. Jane Cox of the Public Records Office in London, and an experienced expert in the field of signatories, wrote:

> *It is obvious at a glance that these signatures, with the exception of the last two [appearing on the will], are not the signatures of the same man. Almost every letter is formed in a different way in each. Literate men in the sixteenth and seventeenth centuries developed personalized signatures much as people do today and it is unthinkable that Shakespeare did not. Which of the signatures reproduced here is the genuine article is anybody's guess.* [142]

This account conflicts with a lecture given in 1919 to the Royal Society of Medicine by Dr. R. W. Leftwich, an authority upon the subject of physical handicaps but not an expert on handwriting; he accepted the traditionalists' assurances that the signatures were all perfectly genuine, and justified their form by saying that the hand that wrote them was *"spastic".*

> *In this the pen is not completely under the control of the writer* [as is the case with the beginner]. *Against his will it makes little jerks, unduly long strokes, or unintended marks; and though a good beginning may be made, the hand very soon tires and refuses to write at all* [as is also true when a complete beginner cannot remember what comes next]. [143] (Author's comments added.)

One may recall Ben Jonson's remark about Shake-speare's penmanship: *"that in his writing, (whatsoever he penn'd), he never blotted out a line."* Yet, Shaxpere's six attempts at a signature comprise *"no less than four blots in fourteen words".*

Last Will and Testament

The penultimate episode in examining the evidence upon which so many inventions have been concocted, in order to form a favourable image of Shakespeare, as the William Shaxpere of Stratford-upon-Avon, concerns his last will and testament. It was begun in January 1616, but not concluded until March. The final draft is *"unusual among legal documents for its large number of alterations, substitutions and interpolations."* [144] There is also the fact that it has been written on three sheets of paper, each of a different size, and from different batches. This said, what does it tell us about the man, apart from bequests to the surviving members of his family and his business acquaintances? In short, what does it say to confirm the life story invented by his biographers? For, were their inventions true, we have before us the last will and testament of the foremost genius of the written word in the history of western culture.

Consider first, his library. One room set aside in New Place to house his books is not an unreasonable speculation to make. Indeed, is there a single writer of prominence anywhere to be found in the world that does not have an array of books to call his or her own, and to dispose of at their time of departing?

> *For instance Stratford vicar John Bretchgirdle bequeathed his Latin-English dictionary to scholars of Stratford school; his Horace and Virgil to a godson, and works by Aesop, Cicero, Sallust, Erasmus and others to the five sons of Alderman William Smith. John Florio, who although he died in poorer estate than Shakespeare, left to William Earl of Pembroke: "all my Italian, French and Spanish books, as well printed and unprinted, being in number about three hundred and forty, namely my new and perfect dictionary, as also my ten dialogues in Italian and English, and my unbound volume of divers written collections and rhapsodies ..." Likewise the scrivener Humphrey Dyson, who wrote the wills for Shakespeare's fellow actors Henry Condell and Nicholas Tooley, in his will required his executor to "have a care to put off and sell my books to the most profit that he can".* [145]

Books were a very valuable commodity at that time. When Heminge wrote his will, he not only referred to his own collection, but also left five pounds for the purchase of new books for the education of his grandchild. The 3rd Earl of Southampton, supposedly Shaxpere's patron, bequeathed his entire library to Cambridge University. But when the biographer's invention of 'William Shakespeare' is put to the test, and compared with real, flesh and blood people, he is found to be deficient in the very substance that breathed life into his being—his books. For the will, which has *not* been invented, discloses no mention of a book: this fact alone must surely help vindicate those who have always argued that this man was as illiterate as were the rest of his family, both past and present.

But this revelation should not strike a reasonably intelligent person as at all surprising. While authors often invent fables about real people, as in historical romances, they cannot produce, from their imagination, the tangible evidence to support what they write. William Shaxpere is a case in point. He has been given, *via* the imagination of his biographers, everything necessary to stand before the public as an unparalleled man of genius. What these biographers cannot do is produce the tangible assets required for their invention; the simplest example of which is the abject failure to find just one single book that he bought or owned. By contrast, Ben Jonson had a study full with books that he had acquired over time.

William Shaxpere is not William Shakespeare. He has simply been dressed up by his inventors in imaginative clothes, which are often ill-fitting because of this, but which the public has been persuaded to agree are real.

Those amongst his believers who have risked going in search of tangible evidence in support of this man's credentials have wasted years of their lives. The evidence they seek does not exist; nor has it ever existed. Doubt this, by all means; search the records of William Shaxpere, and there you will unfailingly find the trappings of his life: church records, lawsuits, tradesman's debts, his property deeds, etc. But in terms of acknowledgement or money relating to anything he had written or published, there is nothing, and there never has been.

Consider, too, the difference between the bequests made by this man Shaxpere and the will of a genuine theatrical, such as Augustine Phillips of the King's Men. Having first provided for his wife and their four daughters, he next attended to his friends in the theatre.

> *I give and bequeath ... amongst the hired men of the company which I am of, the sum of five pounds to be equally distributed amongst them. I give and bequeath to my fellow William Shakespeare a thirty shilling piece in gold, to my fellow Henry Condell, one other thirty shilling piece in gold, to my servant Christopher Beeston, thirty shillings in gold; to my fellow Lawrence Fletcher twenty shillings in gold; to my fellow Robert Armin ... [ditto]; to my fellow Richard Cowley ... [ditto]; to my fellow Alexander Cooke ... [ditto]; to my fellow Nicholas Tooley ... [ditto] ... I give to Samuel Gilbourne, my late*

apprentice, the sum of forty shillings, and my mouse coloured velvet hose, and a white taffeta doublet, a black taffeta suit, my purple cloak, sword and dagger, and my brass viol. I give to James Sands, my apprentice, the sum of forty shillings and a cittern, a bandore and a lute. [146]

How does this compare with the bequests made by the man, whom biographers portray as a leading figure of the King's Men: even going so far as to describe the players as *his* company? Well, in the midst of Shaxpere attending to his daughters, their husbands, his neighbours and his business acquaintances – his wife is mentioned only once as the inheritor of his second best bed, and even then, only as a last minute insertion between the lines of the final draft – he goes on to say: *"and to my fellowes, John Hemynges, Richard Burbage, and Henry Cundell, xxvj.s. viij.d, a peece to buy them ringes."* [147] This amounted to £4 (≈ £1100) shared equally between them.

The fact that after three months of deliberation, between January and March, this bequest appeared on Shaxpere's will only as an afterthought, a late inclusion that had to be inserted between the lines, gives pause for thought. Was it inserted posthumously? Alas, we shall never know. But the fact that this question is left open for speculation serves to endorse the fact that although it is easy to invent the attributes of a character from imagination, it is entirely a different matter when it comes to validating the imagination with tangible evidence.

Another remarkable fact arising from Shaxpere's will are those plays which were at the time unknown. Thus, *Timon of Athens, Coriolanus* and *All's Well That Ends Well,* were totally ignored by the testator at Stratford-upon-Avon, and would remain unknown until publication of the First Folio seven years later. Florio, recall, made a bequest of his unprinted books. Shaxpere, though far more prolific than the Italian, left none.

To these previously unknown plays there are also a further seventeen, which had never been published. Yet, the law protected an author's right to the income from unpublished work.

[A]t common law an author of any book or literary composition had the sole right of first printing and publishing the same for sale: and might bring action against any person who printed, published and sold the same without his consent. [148]

So, once again, although Shaxpere never wavered from prosecuting tradesmen for non-payment of their dues, he always steered well clear of everything remotely connected with plays and poetry when it appeared as work by Shakespeare, however it was spelt.

The first draft of Shaxpere's will was drawn up by lawyer Francis Collins in January 1616, and was followed by a final draft on New Year's Day, 25 March. Beneath what passes for Shaxpere's signature on the final page is a note in Latin declaring that John Hall proved the will on 22 June and that an inventory would follow. Undoubtedly, the inventory failed to meet the requirements of the deceased's image-makers, for like every other document that would have cast doubt upon this man's literary and educational background, it, too, has vanished.

The Stratford fraternity have an explanation for the absence of manuscripts; at least, they are pleased to call it an explanation. Shakespeare, they say, disposed of his plays by selling them to a theatre company, and that is why they are not mentioned in his will. The response to this is that Shaxpere must therefore have sold them to Burbage. And where can one find Burbage's records confirming ownership? Alas, one cannot; like so many other crucial documents in the Authorship debate, they, too, are missing. However, *"The renowned Richard Burbage at his death held property worth £300 [≈ £84,000], in addition to personal possessions."* But there is no mention of the missing plays.

Heminge and Condell provide a much better idea of how Shakespeare's plays fared. In their letter *To The Great Variety Of Readers,* with which the First Folio commences, they explain to their audience that prior to this publication of Shakespeare's collected plays: *"you were abus'd with diuerse stolne, and surreptitious copies, maimed, and deformed by the frauds and stealthes of iniurious imposters that expos'd them".* [149]

In other words, William Shaxpere had done nothing to prevent the stealing, the misuse, the maiming and abuse of his plays; the law was there to protect him, but despite this, he declined to take action: simply ignoring what was happening, just as he ignored the publication of the *Sonnets,* for which, by law, had they been his, he was entitled to receive the benefits of *"first printing and publishing the same for sale."* [150]

How does the professional scholar reconcile Shaxpere's incredible inactivity at the hands of these fraudsters, with his no-nonsense approach towards those in default of payment for the malt he sold? It is impossible to say; a reasonable explanation has never been given.

The truth is that the plays and poems of Shakespeare were not those of Shaxpere. They were, instead, the property of the Earl of Oxford, for whom the receipt of any financial reward for writing plays or poems was a social anathema. For this reason, although acting in good faith as Oxford's allonym, Shaxpere was unable to obtain justice from the law; he was not the author, and that fact would quickly be established, were this question to be raised at a court hearing. The fraudsters knew this, and they took every advantage they could to profit from it. This left 'Heminge and Condell' to bewail the mischief that had befallen the plays in their letter to the *"Great variety of Readers"*.

Ignored Demise

William Shaxpere passed from this life on 23 April 1616 (O.S.), or 3 May (N.S.). According to the inscription on his monument, set in place inside the Church of the Holy Trinity; he was aged 53: *"ÆTATIS 53"*. His funeral, two days later, serves to focus attention once again upon the diversity between that of filling in a blank life with imagined scenarios and a person's situation in real life.

Shaxpere's spin doctors regale the reader with tales of how he performed before Queen Elizabeth and then King James; how he excelled at lessons; how his plays were eagerly seized upon; how and by whom he was praised, and much more. But when it comes to an event like his funeral, reality takes over, and the contrast between imagination and truth is exposed. Not one single person from the theatre; and especially not from the world of letters, nor from the world of learning, took the slightest notice of his death: let alone bother to attend his funeral.

This was not the case with the passing of Francis Beaumont, who died seven weeks before Shaxpere. In total contrast to the passing of Shaxpere, he was remembered in the many eulogies written about him. And his body was conveyed from Kent to London for burial inside Westminster Abbey. Yet Beaumont's literary ability was well below the level attained by 'Shakespeare'.

The funeral of Edmund Spenser was the scene of great mourning, and attended by poets who, at his burial, cast their quills into his grave. Francis Bacon's death was honoured by thirty-two Latin elegies. Ben Jonson's death was followed by a book of verses composed by the leading poets of the day. For Michael Drayton, an escort of gentlemen from the Inns of Court *"and others of note"* attended his final journey to Westminster Abbey. Even the actor, Richard Burbage, who died in 1619, was remembered by throngs of Londoners who lined the streets as his cortege made its way across the city. But the death of Shaxpere was completely ignored. Not one single person amongst those who, it is alleged, had so greatly admired him and his writing, took the slightest notice of his death.

Sceptics may point to a similar silence that greeted Edward de Vere's funeral. But silence was to be expected, since for him to be honoured in death as Shakespeare, raises the question why he was not similarly honoured in life? In point of fact, James I commemorated Oxford's passing by putting on a show of *Shakespeare's* plays. He also allowed his royal coat of arms to preface a quarto edition of *Hamlet*, the author's most biographical play (p.127); but beyond that, silence. Oxford met his end in 1604 exactly as he had predicted, in Sonnet 81 – *"I, once gone, to all the world must die"*.

When, twelve years later in the town of Stratford-upon-Avon, William Shaxpere, too, was laid to rest in a grave prepared for him beneath the floor of the chancel: the Church Register recorded the day's event under burials in a manner appropriate to this man's recognised station in life: *"April 25 Will. Shakspere gent."*

A ledger-stone was then laid over the grave, upon which, four lines of trivial verse were inscribed.

GOOD FREND FOR IESVS SAKE FORBEARE,
TO DIGG THE DVST ENCLOASED HEARE:
BLESTE BE Y[E] MAN Y[T] SPARES THES STONES,
AND CVRST BE HE Y[T] MOVES MY BONES.

These words have teased the imagination of his admirers ever since. A longstanding tradition maintains that the deceased wrote the words himself.

I think it fair to say that no known grave of a person, in whatever field of endeavour they have excelled, be it literature, music, politics, art, war, exploration &c., has had anything other than a suitable epitaph placed on their memorial stone. 'Shakespeare' is the one exception: and this begs many questions.

In ordinary circumstances, there can be no obvious reason whatever for any deviation from the norm. On the other hand, if Shaxpere was not the great genius of English literature, but a man with a similar name who had agreed to be identified as William Shakespeare, then circumstances would indeed be other than normal. It would certainly help to explain the bizarre lines covering his grave, as well as the total indifference afforded him by every person of letters at the time of his death.

There is, however, a more sensible explanation for the lines appearing on the gravestone. The verse demands that the body should never be removed. Those who dared to ignore the deceased's wishes would be cursed. When Anne Shaxpere died in 1623, these words generated such trepidation that rather than risk disturbing the grave, she was buried separately.

It has been suggested that the reason for this curse was to prevent his bones from being dug up and sent to the charnel house. But this indignity does not await those whose tombs lie inside the church, especially not those of the great Shakespeare, already recognised in England as a literary genius; so the reason for the curse must be other than this.

What the curse did was to express in the strongest possible words the wish of the deceased, which was that his body was not to be disturbed. Why should anyone think of disturbing it? The answer is, surely, to re-inter it inside Westminster Abbey at some later date; that he might also share eternity with the nation's other great writers. His dying wish therefore acted as a deterrent to anyone nurturing that idea.*

Unless Shaxpere was struck by pangs of conscience before he died, the more likely event was that he had been persuaded to ask for these lines to be carved on his gravestone; hence the tradition that he wrote them himself. But if illiterate the words would have

---

* It would appear that to make doubly sure Shaxpere's body was never transferred to Poets Corner, it was secretly removed. In 1796 his grave was accidentally penetrated: but it was empty.

been written for him, by someone desperate to ensure that this licensed imposter, this counterfeit playwright, did not carry his deceit into the hallowed ground of Westminster.

This explanation is considerably reinforced by the action of William Basse. He was alone in acknowledging the death of Shaxpere, albeit six years later. It was Basse who pleaded that Shakespeare should be re-interred inside Westminster Abbey, alongside the other great men of literature. Basse was careful to make sure there would be no mistaking the man he was referring to, by deliberately naming the year in which he died; thus distinguishing it from Oxford's death—the real Shakespeare.

Basse was anticipating that the forthcoming publication of the First Folio might inspire demands for the author to be buried in company with the nation's other great men of literature, at Westminster Abbey. In fact, Basse's purpose was opposed to this; it was, instead, intended to pre-empt this expected outcry. The strategy was remarkably simple. By making an early appeal, it blocked further demands from being proposed. It also gave Ben Jonson the opportunity he needed to deny the request by writing a specious denial, which he inserted inside the First Folio. It then became possible for everyone to understand why the re-burial of 'Shakespeare' inside the Abbey was unnecessary.

On Mr William Shakespeare
who died in April 1616

Renowned Spenser lie a thought more nigh
To learned Chaucer and rare Beaumont lie
A little nearer Spenser to make room
For Shakespeare in your threefold, fourfold tomb.[151]

Jonson replied:

I will not lodge thee by
Chaucer, or Spenser, or bid Beaumont lie
A little further, to make thee a room:
Thou art a monument, without a tomb,
And art alive still, while thy book doth live,
And we have wits to read, and praise to give.[152]

In modern parlance, it was a put-up job, contrived between Jonson and Basse. Basse was acting as the 'feed' so that Jonson could use his greater authority by responding with a measured rebuttal.

The timing was perfect. In 1622, when both verses were written, Shake-speare's collected plays were on the verge of being published in what was to be known as the First Folio. The sheer beauty of the poet's collected verse, and his depth of thought would undoubtedly revive interest in Shakespeare's work. This would lead to calls from the masses that Shaxpere be buried alongside the other 'immortals' of literature; that is, in Poets Corner in Westminster Abbey.

Those who knew of Oxford's secret life as Shakespeare were aghast at this prospect, fearing the public voice would be impossible to resist without divulging the truth. The Jonson-Basse strategy was designed to pre-empt the expected clamour by pointing out before-hand that Shakespeare was too great a person for a lesser honour: he was a monument in himself, and in no need for stone or marble inside Westminster Abbey to make it known.

The strategy succeeded. Compare this praise with the seven years of neglect at Shaxpere's death. However in 1740, the public did manage to achieve some success with their demand that Shakespeare receive recognition inside Westminster Abbey for his inestimable contribution to England's literary heritage. The statue of a man modelled on the Chandos Portrait was commissioned: it having been paid for by public subscription. The statue was then placed inside the Abbey as a permanent memory to Shakespeare, where it now stands; as much a memorial to the great poet as to the charade that brought it into being.

There was, in fact, a connection between Basse and Jonson, which can be traced back to Oxford's daughter Bridget, the sister of Susan Vere. Susan had married the Earl of Montgomery in 1605: one of the two brothers to whom the First Folio was dedicated. In 1599, Bridget married Francis Norris, Baron of Rycote. Among the family's retainers was William Basse. It would appear from research conducted by Ruth Loyd Miller that shortly before Norris's death in 1623, Basse had dedicated his poem *Polyhymnia* to Lady Bridget. This likely drew attention to him as a poet, worthy to prove compliant with Jonson's projected plan. It is therefore conceivable that Basse was persuaded to further serve his employers by participating in an arranged poetic exchange with Jonson; an exchange of words, as explained above, that was designed to prevent the illiterate and undeserving Shaxpere from becoming commemorated in Westminster Abbey. It is even possible that Jonson was the author of Basse's poem and that Basse's name was simply used as a ploy to provide authenticity to the plan.

Hence, in 1622, just prior to publication of the First Folio, Jonson's strategically placed obstacle, designed to forestall the expected outcry for Shaxpere to be re-interred inside Westminster Abbey, was inserted at the front of the forthcoming tome of Shake-speare's collected plays. There, it accomplished its purpose by preventing Shaxpere's re-interment.

1622 was also a time when it is believed that the monument to Shaxpere was set in place on the chancel wall of Holy Trinity Church. In which case, there is no better demonstration concerning the failure of Stratford-upon-Avon to recognise their local citizen's genius than the town's reaction to the arrival of the King's Men.

This was the same company of actors that Shaxpere had supposedly spent his working life with. These were the players that had performed many of 'his' plays: plays that were being published to eventually bring wealth and renown to the people of Stratford-upon-Avon. Yet, the accounts for that year, published by the Stratford-upon-Avon Borough Chamberlain, record the following entry:

> *To the King's Players for not playing in the Hall, 6/-* [6 shillings is approximately £80].[153]

'Shakespeare's' local Council at Stratford-upon-Avon actually made a payment to *"Shakespeare's company"* (as so many biographers love to call this body of actors) to go away. Members of the Council could not actually refuse them, because the King's Men had a royal licence from James I to freely use their art for performances *"within any town halls or moot halls or other convenient places within the liberties and freedom of any other city, university, town (&c.)."*[154] It is perfectly evident that the people of Stratford knew very well who Shaxpere was, and it certainly was not the great literary genius known as William Shakespeare.

> *For almost fifty years after Shakspere's death nothing personal was written about him. No one appeared in Stratford, notebook in hand, to find out what locals thought about the great man commemorated in their parish church. Shakspere's sister, Joan Hart, outlived him by thirty years, his younger daughter, Judith, by forty-six years, and his last descendant, granddaughter Elizabeth, lived on to 1670. Yet no writer interviewed them, and no one from Stratford who had known William Shakspere recorded any statement about him.* [155]

In response to this apathy, some defenders of Shaxpere's Stratford image point out that a certain Lieutenant Hammond visited the town in September 1634. After visiting the church and observing the monument, he made an entry in his diary, which confirmed that he knew the statuary had been put there in memory of Shakespeare, the famous English poet.

> *In that dayes travell we came by Stratford upon Avon, where in the Church in that Towne there are some Monuments which Church was built by Archbishop Stratford; Those worth observing and of which wee tooke notice were these ... A neat Monument of that famous English Poet, Mr. William Shakespeere; who was borne heere.* [156]

What does this prove? Hammond was simply confirming what he had been led to believe. This was essentially the stratagem agreed by Oxford, to cover-up the fact that Shakespeare was his penname and Shaxpere his allonym. Most of London's population would have said the same. What this does, is demonstrate that if documents are censored, and information suppressed in one age, the generation that follows will have no reason not to accept as certainty, the documents left for them by this previous period.

William Camden, author of a history of Elizabethan England, obviously knew of this when he expressed his awareness of higher authority and its censorship, and how *"those who think the memory of succeeding ages may be extinguished by present power."* [157] Camden was aware that future history was being manipulated to present Oxford's plays and poems, written under the penname Shakespeare, as having been the work of Stratford-upon-Avon's William Shaxpere; which is why he never acknowledged Shakespeare in his *Britannia*, as a resident of Shaxpere's birth town.

In 1603, the antiquarian and historian William Camden, in his Remains Concerning Britain, included 'William Shakespeare' as one of the 'most pregnant wits of these our times, whom succeeding ages may justly admire'. Yet Camden omitted Shakespeare when discussing the worthies of Stratford-on-Avon in his later work, Brittannia.[158]

The Reverend Richard Hunt noted Camden's omission. He was a Gloucestershire man who received his M.A. from Oxford in 1608, and became vicar of Itchington in Warwickshire in 1621. His life therefore overlapped that of Will Shaxpere's in nearby Stratford-upon-Avon. In his copy of William Camden's book, *Britannia* (1590 edition), wherein the author had mentioned that *"the little market town of Stratford"* was distinguished through the reputations of two of its residents, John of Stratford, former Archbishop of Canterbury, and Hugh Clopton, former Lord Mayor of London; Hunt, in an effort to correct Camden, added: *"and to William Shakespeare, certainly our Roscius."*

Quintus Roscius Gallus was the Roman actor referred to by Robert Greene (p.71). His name subsequently became synonymous with any actor whose talent was seen to be outstanding. Cicero had even extended the attribute to cover other occupations, so that one might, for example, become a Roscius of springboard diving. The point about extending this cover – as Canadian scholar and researcher Nina Green, so aptly indicated – was that it has to be qualified by the profession to which it applies: as with the springboard diving example. Hunt, however, offers no such qualification. He refers solely to *"our Roscius"* which, without qualification, can only mean Roscius the actor.

One is therefore led to believe that Hunt had recently heard that Will Shaxpere and his brother had been players in London, and the former had returned to Stratford a very wealthy man as a result. It was surely this that motivated the vicar to claim for his locality that Shaxpere must certainly be our own Roscius.

In 1662, the Reverend Doctor John Ward accepted the post of vicar in Stratford-upon-Avon. He was thirty-three years of age and an Oxford University graduate. Interest in Ward is derived from the memo he made in his notebook covering the years 1661–1663: *"Remember to peruse Shakespeare's plays. And be versed in them, that I may not be ignorant in that matter."* [159] Thus, Ward was well placed to furnish other notebooks with anecdotes or stories relating to his parish's famous author.

Yet, during the nineteen years that he remained vicar of the town, and though his notebooks increased in number to sixteen, his resolve to discover more about Stratford's famous resident lapsed to a single paragraph. It begins: *"I have heard that Mr Shakespeare was a natural wit"*. This does seem to have been an attractive feature of Shaxpere's personality; one may recall how neighbours remembered his speeches being made in high style when slaughtering a farm animal. Ward then continues with a surprising revelation: *"without any art at all."* The memory that the people of Stratford retained of William Shaxpere explains exactly why his bust on the monument inside the parish church had to depict him as a man of commerce. To have shown him as a writer, as it presently does, would have reduced it to mockery.

The reports Ward had received from those who remembered Shaxpere were obviously incompatible with the author of the plays that Ward had perused. The diary note continues: *"he frequented the plays all his younger time."* This can only relate to a time after Shaxpere arrived in London, since the opportunity to visit plays was not available in his hometown. In which case, it must refer to his career as a horse attendant outside the Curtain and Theatre, and from thence to his employment as a general factotum inside one of these playhouses.

Ward's next phrase harbours no doubt: *"but in his elder days he lived at Stratford."* The next comment is illuminating: *"and supplied the stage with 2 plays every year"*. A supplier is not necessarily an author; more often he or she is simply an agent, an intermediary who is paid to act on behalf of the provider. Shaxpere was a shareholder in the Globe theatre, also Oxford's allonym; he may therefore have quite legitimately *supplied* the Globe with Oxford's edited plays at the rate suggested by Ward's notes.

The report continues with words that certainly relate to Oxford: *"and for that had an allowance so large, that he spent at the rate of a thousand a year, as I have heard."* Oxford, did in fact receive an allowance of one thousand pounds annually from the royal purse, and appears to have spent at the same rate. Shaxpere also spent money liberally, but on the purchase of property, although this only became possible during the eventide of his life. (Ogburn, p.20).

The final line in Ward's single reference to Stratford's famous son, notes that, *"Shakespeare, Drayton, and Ben Jonson had a merry meeting, and it seems drunk too hard. For Shakespeare died of a fever there contracted."* [160]

Unfortunately, not knowing Ward's source for this last piece of information, it is impossible to be certain to whom it refers. Oxford would have had no problem drinking with Jonson and Drayton in London or at his home in Hackney. Whereas, Shaxpere, playing host in Stratford to these two men as late as 1616, especially after their four day journey from London, strains belief to breaking point; the more so, because neither Drayton nor Jonson took the slightest interest in this man at the time of his death; and this, according to Ward's statement, occurred just a few days after their drinking spree. Presumably, Drayton and Jonson having travelled for some three or four days to get to Stratford, would have stayed long enough before setting off for the return journey: in which case, they would have been aware of Shaxpere's illness. And since his death followed soon afterwards, they would have stayed for the funeral and returned to London with the sad news. London would have been in mourning. But since this never happened, we can add yet another myth to the Shakespeare story.

In conclusion, writers in the past who have stretched their imagination to write biographies about William Shakespeare have universally failed to understand that the few facts available – and they are so very few indeed – are capable of an alternative and far more realistic interpretation. That alternative, completely coherent in all its aspects, has been introduced above, and the consequences arising from it will be pursued in the chapters that follow.

3

THOMAS THORPE'S CRYPTOGRAM

With one day's reading a man may have the key in his hands.

Ezra Pound

ALTHOUGH BEN JONSON has declared that Edward de Vere was William Shakespeare, he was not the first to encrypt this secret information into a Cardano grille. More than a decade earlier, Thomas Thorpe, publisher of SHAKE-SPEARES SONNETS *Never Before Imprinted*, had done the same.

Up until 1609, Thomas Thorpe had been a minor figure in the publishing world. But his place in literary history changed dramatically when he acquired the manuscript collection of Shake-speare's Sonnets. Although from where these were obtained has always been a mystery, and one that will be discussed later. As the holder of the manuscript, and under the law of copyright then in force, Thorpe was entitled to publish them. His entry in the Stationers' Register for 20 May, reads: *"A Booke called Shake-speares sonnettes"*.[1] Printing was to prove a hasty affair, for the poems, replete with many errors, were on sale *"by 19 June because Edward Alleyn … recorded purchasing a copy on that date."* [2] However, the probity of this entry has since been questioned as a possible forgery by Collier.

These errors, however, do tend to suggest the publisher was anticipating a swift reaction to his enterprise: perhaps even before the printer had had time to typeset them; as Ian Wilson remarked: *"some form of suppression has to be suspected."* In this respect, it may be called to mind that a further thirty years were to elapse before a second edition of the Sonnets found its way onto the London bookstalls; yet Drayton's sonnets of much less literary appeal were repeatedly being reprinted.

The mystery is: why "SHAKE-SPEARE'S SONNETS *neuer before imprinted*" should have been subjected to a suppression order:

if that was indeed the case, and why did three decades elapse before a second edition was released for sale? These questions become even more pertinent when the peculiar manner in which Thorpe presented his publication is considered.

> *Contrary to all custom, the publisher T. T. (Thomas Thorpe) wrote a dedication to them, and this indeed to an individual designated only by the initials Mr. W. H., whom he styles "the onlie begetter of these sonnets" and to whom he wishes "all happinesse and that eternitie promised by our ever-living poet."*[3]

In short, Thorpe wrote a public dedication to an associate of his, using another author's book. And that someone else – Will Shaxpere, so we are asked to believe – was very much alive at the time. Strange, therefore, that this living author took not one jot of interest at this insult, nor to the fact that Thorpe was profiting from his poems! Compare the ruction over the Groats-worth letter.

Quite simply, none of this rings true. Thorpe would never have dared perpetrate such a public insult: much less to the famous author of *Venus and Adonis* and *Lucrece*. The whole idea is preposterous. Yet, something must have happened to explain it, and the only rational explanation is that the author was dead.

William Barkstead, who acted in Jonson's play *Silent Woman* at the Whitefriars in 1609, confirmed this was so. In November 1607, he entered his poem, *Mirrha the Mother of Adonis,* in the Stationers' Register. The poem contains a verse, which removes all legitimate doubt that Barkstead knew Shakespeare had died.

> *But stay my Muse in thine owne confines keepe,*
> *& wage not warre with so deere lov'd a neighbor*
> *But having sung thy day song, rest & sleepe*
> *preserve thy small fame and his greater favor:*
> *His song was worthie merrit (Shakspeare hee)*
> *sung the faire blossome, thou the withered tree*
> *Laurell is due to him, his art and wit*
> *hath purchast it, Cypres thy brow will fit.*[4]

Note that Barkstead does not say *"His song is worthie merit",* which would have come naturally to him, had Shakespeare been alive. Unsurprisingly, this is one piece of documentary evidence that scholars regularly omit when writing about Shakespeare. As the late Joseph Sobran carefully noted: *"Lee, Adams, Chute, Bentley, Quennell, Halliday, Rowse, Schoenbaum, Levi, Fraser, Kay, and O'Connor all fail to mention Barkstead's tribute."*[5] The list continues into the present time. Each new book that comes onto the market to extol the life and work of Shakespeare is careful to avoid Barkstead's poem. Were it not for pro-Oxford literature, the poem would have been airbrushed from the pages of history before now. Is it therefore not truly remarkable that those same people who refuse to accept that the evidence for Oxford's authorship was covered up; are guilty of doing precisely that?

THE SIX–TWO–FOUR KEY

In common with most traditionalists, Professor Gervinus, remarked upon the peculiarity of Thorpe having written the dedication himself, but remained silent about the meaning of *"our ever-living poet"*. Perhaps he recalled that from 1608 to 1610, Will Shaxpere was in his native Stratford, immersed in litigation for the purchase of land, while also attempting to recover some bad debts relating to the sale of malt. In short, he was very much alive, for which reason the epithet *ever-living*, which is always said of the famously dead, is not appropriate to this man's situation. It also confirms what Barkstead had earlier said about Shakespeare: he was no longer alive when his book of sonnets went on sale in 1609.

TO.THE.ONLIE.BEGETTER.OF.
THESE.INSVING.SONNETS.
Mr.W.H. ALL.HAPPINESSE.
AND.THAT.ETERNITIE.
PROMISED.
BY.
OVR.EVER-LIVING.POET.
WISHETH.
THE.WELL-WISHING.
ADVENTVRER.IN.
SETTING.
FORTH.

T. T.

Thorpe's use of 'ever-living' can therefore be acknowledged as a legitimate signal for the need to take care when reading what he wrote. Not only has he cast doubt upon the author by hyphenating his name, he has aroused further suspicion by alluding to the author as deceased. Thorpe was treading on dangerous ground.

For those committed to the dominant view of Shakespeare, worse follows. The source of this further dismay arises from the words in Thorpe's dedication. They are: *"commented [Sir Sidney] Lee ... fantastically arranged and in odd grammatical order."* [6] John Leslie Hotson was of a similar mind, and concluded the dedication was so *"preposterous"* that it could only be *"a cryptogram"* (*Mr W. H.* London, 1964). Louis Gillet also dismissed them as a *"few lines of gibberish"* (*Shakespeare*, 1930). For Dr. John M. Rollett, Hotson's remark did not pass unnoticed, and it is due to his excellent work that the following demonstration has come to light.

Why, he asked, has Thorpe presented his dedication in the form of three trapeziums, each consisting of six, two and four lines? And why have the words that are not hyphenated been separated by a point?

He was to later discover that the number of lines in each trapezium is the same as the numbers of letters that occur in the name, Edward de Vere, 6, 2, and 4. Although unaware of this connection at the time, Rollett's initial response was to apply this 6-2-4 sequence to each separated word in the dedication. What he discovered was to provide an explanation for Thorpe's use of 'ever-living', and the contorted form of the syntax. For the words that are revealed by applying this 6-2-4 sequence read:

THESE SONNETS ALL BY E VER THE FORTH. [7]

The initials, **T**[homas] **T**[horpe] are not part of the trapeziums, but have been set apart. They have also been typeset in a larger case. The reason for this is of considerable importance, as will become evident further down.

'EVER' is a perfect anagram of 'VERE', because it also allows the letters to regroup as E Ver: 'Ver' being a variant form of 'Vere' (both are pronounced 'Vair'). Oxford's name 'Ver' was derived from the *"town of Ver in Normandy where his family originated before the Conquest."* [8] It will also be recalled that this variant form of Vere has been used several times before in enigmatic phrases that implied Edward de Vere was the intended subject; c.f. the epistle to *Troilus and Cressida* that was hurriedly replaced following its first printing, *"A never (An E. Ver) writer, to an ever (E. Ver) Reader."* or Barnfield's, *"Live ever you, at least in Fame live ever."* or Marston's, *"Thy true judicial style I ever honour."*

In the present case, the revealed message, although lacking a verb, is sufficiently direct to prevent any misunderstanding. The rules governing encryptions of this type are quite clear. The meaning must be unique, and it must make sense in whatever language it is displayed.

Thorpe has therefore provided the key to unlocking this concealed statement via the number of lines in each trapezium, and using these as distance markers in the cipher-text. This strategy then ensures that the words revealing his plain-text message will stand out. And because he has signalled the breaks by a judicial use of points and hyphens, the criteria required for a genuine encryption have been met. No English-speaking person could fail to understand the import of these words, for they are the equivalent of today's media headlines. It is also important to attend the advice given by that eminent pair of cryptologists, W. F. and E. S. Friedman . . .

> *a temptation presents itself, which the professional cryptologist regards as the great betrayal: exceptions are made to the rules, and these permit the 'right' kind of messages to be extracted. This tactic is acceptable to the professional cryptologist only if the exceptions do not exceed a certain maximum.* (p. 18)

In the present case, the missing verb is sufficiently implied by the words of the announcement, and whether it is present or absent, it makes no difference whatever to the sense of the statement.

Unfortunately, Rollett later came to believe *"that a three-element key is far too ingenious or sophisticated for the Elizabethan or Jacobean period,"* [9] and he reluctantly abandoned his discovery. His lack of confidence in the devious, subtle practices of that period was unfounded. For what he had unknowingly discovered was a variant form of the Cardano grille.

As reported in Chapter 1, this method of conveying hidden messages was made famous during the 16th and 17th centuries through the diplomatic use it was put to when concealing state secrets in dispatches. Whereas the original grille, invented by the mathematician Girolamo Cardano in 1550, had employed only single letters, a subsequent variation of this same idea employed selected words, thus hastening the encryption process.

> *This code was invented by an Italian doctor and mathematician called Girolamo Cardano in 1550 … [it] allows for reading only single letters at a time, but it can be adapted … so that* ***whole words*** *or syllables* ***appear.***[10] [Author's emphasis]

Thorpe's address, when broken into a sequence comprising every sixth, second and fourth word, contributes towards the reason behind this *"fantastically arranged"* textual tribute. It was his way of concealing the hidden name of the poet who wrote the Sonnets: a man otherwise known to the world only as William Shakespeare.

In fact, had enthusiasts for Will Shaxpere's authorship of the Shakespeare canon attended to this convoluted text seriously, they, too, would have realised that its tortuous form was what David Kahn had been referring to when he described the weakness of the Cardano grille: *"the method's chief defect, of course, is that awkwardness in phrasing may betray the very secret that that phrasing should guard: the existence of a hidden message."* (p. 10).

This 'awkwardness of phrasing' in Thorpe's dedication has always been evident. The remarkable fact is, that such has been the mesmerising effect Will Shaxpere's story has had upon the minds of those willing to believe, uncritically, everything they read about this man, that they become intellectually numb to anything that might discredit him. Quite literally, they have adorned him from their imagination with everything he lacks, so that he may appear as they wish him to be seen. Consequently, in each personal reality, he possesses everything they wish for, and they protect their creation by attacking disbelievers with the only armaments available—invective, scorn and ridicule.

The next part of Thorpe's 6-2-4 identification of Edward de Vere as the author of the Sonnets refers to him as *"the forth"*; i.e., 'the fourth' (spelling had not yet been standardized in England, hence the many variations in the way words were spelt; c.f. 'onlie' in the cipher-text). As biographer Bill Bryson observed:

> *Elizabethans were as free with their handwriting as they were with their spelling ... You could write St. Paul's or St. Powles, and no one seemed to notice or care … Perhaps nothing speaks more eloquently of the variability of spelling in the age than the fact that a dictionary published in 1604, A Table Alphabeticall of Hard Words, spelled 'words' two ways on the title page.*[11]

The OED records several different forms of 'fourth', including 'fowerth', 'feorthe', 'foerth', 'forthe', 'furth' and 'firth'. We therefore take note that . . .

E. Oxenforde, 17th Earle of Oxforde, was the fourth ranking member of Queen Elizabeth's Privy Council at the time of King James' accession, and had been for an (as of now) undetermined number of years before. [12]

A fire at the Palace of Whitehall destroyed most of the records kept there, covering the latter period of Elizabeth's reign as well as the commencement of James I's succession. Nevertheless, several documents did escape the blaze. Amongst these: –

. . . records show that Lord Oxford's name was fourth on the proclamation of the accession and succession of King James of Scotland to the English throne on the death of Queen Elizabeth, proclaimed by the Lord Mayor of London, and the Privy Council on March 24th 1603. Other manuscripts show his signature coming fourth on an order and proclamation of the Privy Council, April 8th 1603. [13]

The positioning of signatories on documents recording the motions and proceedings of the Privy Council was considered of great importance. The first three signatures were always those of *ex officio* officers: the Archbishop of Canterbury, the Lord Keeper, and the Lord Treasurer. After these came members of the nobility according to rank. Oxford, as the senior earl and Lord Great Chamberlain, was first among the rest of the nobility, and therefore always fourth on the list of signatories. Had there been a marquis or a duke amongst the members of the Privy Council, as happened after Oxford's death, he would have given place, and moved down to the next position.

This became evident following Oxford's death, for an extant document shows the newly appointed Ludovick Stuart, the Duke of Lenox, immediately occupying fourth place amongst the signatories.

The Folger Shakespeare Library owns an original document of the Privy Council's proceedings for 8 April 1603 concerning the dispatch of boats between Berwick and London. The first signatures occur in order of rank, and stretch from left to right across the page. The councillors' names appear in the following order: Archbishop John Whitgift, Sir Thomas Egerton, Lord Buckhurst, the Earl of Oxford, the Earl of Nottingham, the Earl of Sussex, the Earl of Pembroke, the Earl of Worcester, the Earl of Rutland, Lord Howard of Effingham, Bishop Richard Bancroft, Thomas la Warre, Ro. Riche, T. D'Arce, William Sandys, Lord Windsor, G. Chandos, Fran Norreys, Sir W. Knollys, Sir Edward Wotton, Sir Robert Cecil, and Sir John Popham.

This information was presumably missed by Rollett, and may have contributed towards him renouncing, as genuine, the partial message he discovered, which he read only as far as: *"These Sonnets All By E. Ver"*.

It was, however, to Rollett's credit that while still persuaded his discovery warranted acceptance, he set about attempting to find a similar occurrence, where a 6-2-4 sequence of words formed a similar phrase, sentence, or announcement. He was to be disappointed. As he later remarked: after having examined . . .

> *many thousands of paragraphs, probably well over 20,000 I have only ever found one sentence that even remotely made sense at all . . . 'London was not built before.' It comes out of Boswell's Life of Johnson (an abridged version, I hasten to add).* [14]

The lack of discovering any comparable phrase led him to eventually conclude that the expectation of his discovery occurring by chance was approximately *"1 in 100 million"*, which he said, coincided with the level suggested by the cryptologists, William and Elizebeth Friedman.

HENRY WRIOTHESLEY REVEALED

Rollett's attention was next drawn to the rarely used spelling of the word 'onlie'. The absence of an 'e' between the 'n' and the 'l' restricted the number of letters in the address to 144. This suggested to Rollett that a 12 X 12 square grille might be worth looking at. In fact, it was only when he constructed the rectangular grille of 18 X 8 that he made a truly significant discovery. Running vertically down the centre of his 18 column grille were a cluster of nine letters: four adjacent to another five which, together, but for the absence of the first two letters, spelled the surname of the youth most associated with the sonnets: i.e., (WR)_IOTH_ESLEY. *"At that moment,"* Rollett wrote, *"I knew with absolute certainty that I would find the letters 'WR' somewhere."* [15] He was right, WR occurs vertically together, but several columns apart from the main cluster.

When all three are combined in boustrophedon order (see figure), they correctly spell WRIOTHESLEY. The boustrophedon style of writing dates back to ancient times, and relates to: *"Lines written alternately from right to left and left to right, as in ancient Greek inscriptions."*[16] Further searches conducted by Rollett led to his detection of the name HENRY, which he found in a 15 X 10 grille.

Dr. Bruce Spittle has since pointed out that the two grilles of 15 and 18, summing to 33, is equivalent to the number of letters

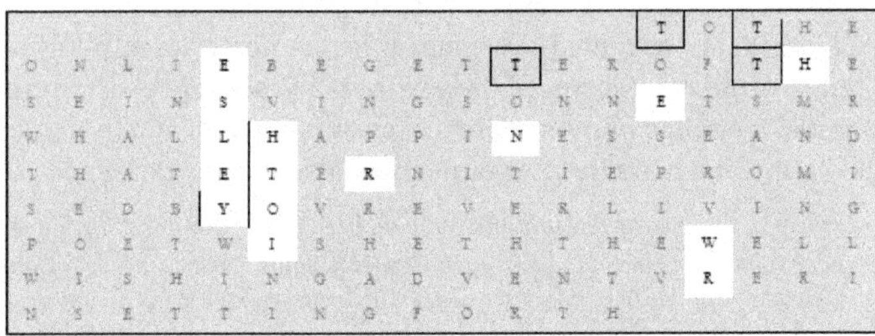

that occur in the name and title of the encrypted subject; that is, 'Henry Wriothesley, Earl of Southampton'. The interesting part about this observation is that 3, the number of his earldom is omitted between his name and title. But, if the number 33 is also partitioned, so that 3 is the difference between the two parts, the result is 15 and 18, which are the required keys for creating the two grilles that identify Henry Wriothesley.

The difficulty Thorpe had in constructing this cryptogram can be well understood. His first priority was to establish Edward de Vere as the author of the sonnets. Having achieved this with his selection of words at intervals of 6-2-4, in keeping with Edward de Vere's name, his next task was to signal to posterity the missing name of the youth, to whom the poetry was mainly addressed. Unfortunately, both Wriothesley and Southampton contain eleven letters, and so the name had to be broken up. Ideally, two parts would have been more efficient. Although this was not achievable, Thorpe has managed to cluster nine of these letters, IOTH and ESLEY, together: thereby signalling his intent.

To prove Thorpe's intention, note particularly that HENRY and ESLEY both end with 'Y'; and only one 'Y' exists in the 144 letters used for the cipher-text. Since this occurs as the 82nd letter:

what is the probability that 2 Equidistant Letter Sequences of 5 letters will occur within the first 82 letters, both of which end at the single letter 'Y'?

Since all grilles originate from a single ribbon of letters, the fact that HENRY and ESLEY occur on different grilles is irrelevant to the following calculation. Thus, on a single ribbon of letters containing Thorpe's words, it must be established how many sequences of 5 letters, equally spaced apart, are possible within the first 82 letters. For instance, 5 letters, 1 letter apart, occupy 9 cells. These 9 cells can be moved 73 times along the ribbon to arrive at the 82nd cell. Including the starting position, there are then 74 positions for this 9 cell sequence to occur. The same calculation is necessary for 5 letters inter-spaced by 2, and then by 3 and so on until 19. Thus 5 letters, 19 letters apart, occupies 81 cells, for which there are only 2 possible positions available.

Because these results follow an Arithmetical Progression, and the first and last result is known; the formula for summing the 19 results: $S_n = ½ n (F + L) = 722$, applies. Of this number, there are 19 that end on the 82nd letter 'Y' (one for each of the 19 changes of space between letters).

The probability of two 5-letter ELS's both terminating at 'Y' is therefore: $\frac{19}{722} x \frac{18}{721} = 0.000,657$ (3 significant figures). It is now necessary to calculate the probability that the letters in HENRY and ESLEY will occur by chance to meet at 'Y'. This can be determined by the frequencies in which H,E,N,R,Y,S,L occur within the first 82 letters, and then calculating for HENRY ESLE[Y].

$$\left(\frac{5}{82} x \frac{14}{81} x \frac{8}{80} x \frac{4}{79} x \frac{1}{78}\right) x \left(\frac{13}{77} x \frac{7}{76} x \frac{3}{75} x \frac{12}{74}\right) 0.000,657 = 4.53 x 10^{-14}$$

HENRY and ESLEY will therefore meet at 'Y' once in 22•2 trillion trials, or once in 704,180 years (at 1 trial per second). And this is without including IOTII also occurring by chance, with its ELS of 18, and positioned so as to accompany ESLEY.

Doubts concerning the identity of Wriothesley as the 'Fair Youth' are now likely to be entertained only by the innumerate; amongst this number will be those advocating William Herbert. Mathematical proof has now eliminated him—permanently.

> *The 'lovely boy' and object of the poet's passion has been identified with the earl of Southampton. In the late sixteenth century, however, the impropriety of addressing a young earl in that manner would have*

been quite apparent; to accuse him of dissoluteness and infidelity, as Shakespeare accuses the unnamed recipient, would have been unthinkable.[17]

Quite so, but Thorpe *has* identified the object of the poet's passion as HENRY WRIOTHESLEY. He has also identified the author of the Sonnets as Edward de Vere. This obviates Ackroyd's objection. It also makes redundant Ackroyd's admission: *"Wherever we look in Shakespeare's work, we see the impossibility of assigning purpose or unassailable meaning."*[18]

VERE'S EPIGRAM

Although Rollett pierced the veil of secrecy covering the first parts of Thorpe's dedication, the 144 letters still had one further secret to reveal: a hidden assertion that has remained undetected until recently. Proceeding as before, and numbering each letter as described in Chapter 1, it is possible to discover that the name VERE, in reverse order of lettering, has been encrypted into the dedication with an Arithmetical Progression of 19: the same number of the letters that occur in the book's title, *Shake-speares Sonnets*. The name VERE is also accompanied by a simple anagram of 'HIS' and the letter 'R'. Further investigation reveals a second and third Arithmetical Progression, also of 19, this time producing the letters 'S W' and 'G M A T O'.

By considering this 19-letter progression mathematically, it is possible to discern its construction has been based upon an Alternating Distance Letter Sequence of 9: 10: 9: 10: 9: 10: 9: 10: 9: 10: 9: 10: 9: 10: 9. Apart from its mathematical significance, Thorpe has taken the number of Oxford's earldom, 17, and split it into 8 and 9 to produce the alternating spaces that occur between each letter on the grille. Each letter in the sequence can then be read as the following plain-text message:

TO VERE HIS W S GRAM.

'GRAM' may be seen as a suffix for 'epigram': the letters, E P I actually occur adjacent to W S. as though to confirm this. Moreover, for a third time in the same number of grilles, the initials, T.T. can again be seen to confirm the statement's authenticity.

In the light of Ben Jonson's similar avowal, this statement acts as confirmation. Thorpe is informing those who have suspected Vere to be Shakespeare that they are correct. At the same time, he is satisfying those already aware of this. And, of course, he is also confirming the other assertions he has concealed within his dedication: principal amongst which is: THESE SONNETS ALL BY E VER THE FORTH.

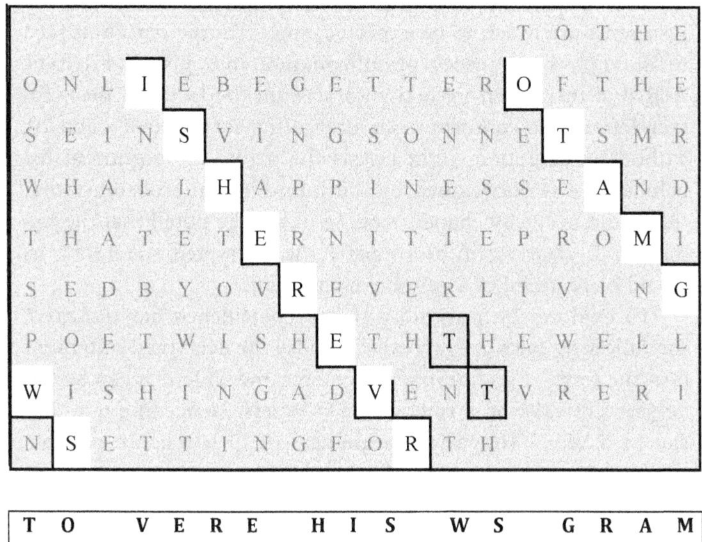

T	O		V	E	R	E	H	I	S	W	S	G	R	A	M
T	O	R	V	E	R	E	H	S	I	S	W	G	M	A	

Thorpe was risking serious harm to himself if the authorities discovered his method of concealment. And this may help explain the haste in which the Sonnets were printed. Let us therefore take a closer look at how Thorpe's new tribute to Vere has been constructed.

Although there is a perfectly acceptable objection to treating a string of letters as an anagram, and then deriving from them a phrase or set of words that serve a set purpose, that objection does not apply in the present case. Of the 15 letters, 60% have already been correctly placed, (TO VERE H · · · · G · A ·). After 'H', a simple transposition of 'I' and 'S' has become necessary, because Thorpe has already encrypted the E <u>**S**</u> L E Y part of Southampton's surname, for which he needed the 'S' in HIS. This forced him to transpose 'I S' in the word HIS in order to leave the 'S' in ESLEY untouched (see grille above and p.166).

The transposition of initials to read S. W. instead of W. S. is inconsequential, since Shakespeare, William carries the same meaning as William Shakespeare.

Thus, of the fifteen letters in Thorpe's phrase, only 2 letters, 'R' and 'M', are not subject to a transposition. These slight adjustments are much to be expected, since Thorpe has attempted to encrypt three pieces of information into just 144 letters. Added to this, when we take into account the fact that these fifteen letters also conform to an alternating sequence of 9 and 10, without interruption, right across the grille, the argument for coincidence is outweighed by the numerical improbability that this could occur by chance. And, let it also be noted that the initials T. T. once again accompany the decrypted statement, as would be required of a genuine encryption.

To explore the possibility that a coincidence has occurred, the following facts are relevant. Because the decrypted statement is in the form of an unbroken sequence, the 15 letters can be understood to exist on a ribbon of 144 letters. Hence, the question can be asked: – How many sequences of 15 letters are possible on this ribbon, which are either equidistant, or possess an alternating distance between letters? When that answer is known, it can be multiplied by the probability that the 15 letters in the decrypted statement have occurred by chance. The result will provide the expected number of times the statement, 'TO VERE HIS W S GRAM' will occur by chance in a given number of trials.

The grille overleaf sets out, in order, the total number of possible sequences that can be contained on a ribbon consisting of 144 letters. Since there are 15 letters in the encrypted statement, there must be 14 spaces between each letter. And since alternating distances occupy these 14 spaces, it implies that 7 will occupy one half of the available distances and the remaining 7 will occupy the other half. For the ELS, both halves will have the same distance between each of the fifteen letters.

Note that the first column of the grille overleaf contains 2 numbers. Thus, the fourth row of the first column is (4, 1). This represents a space of 4 cells, followed by a space of 1 cell repeated 7 times. Hence the total number of spaces is 4 + 1 seven times, or 35 spaces. Add to this 15: the number of letters that border these spaces, whereupon the sequence covers 50 cells.

Since there are 144 letter cells available, and 50 of these are occupied by the sequence of 15 letters and 35 spaces, it follows there are 144 – 50 = 94 further possible positions in which to place this sequence of 50. But since the sequence is already occupying a position, the total number of possible positions for an alternating sequence of 4 spaces followed by 1 space is 95.

The single numbers in the remaining columns represent the second space; the first space remaining constant for the entire row. Thus (4, 1) 2, represents a space of 4 then 1, repeated: followed by a space of 4 then 2, repeated. The procedure for calculating the possible number of positions remains the same.

Fortunately, the tedium of calculating for every cell on the grid is overcome by the formula for summing an Arithmetical Progression, and this gives the total number of positions for each row. Equally impressively, each sum is also the result obtainable from the quadratic formula: $\frac{1}{2}\,(7n^2 + n)$. This means the formula for summing quadratics can be employed. Hence, the total for n = 17 is the result of $^1/_{12}[n(n + 1)(14n + 10)] = 6324$.

1,1	2	3	4	5	6	7	8	9	10	11	12	13	14	15	16	17	Total	1020
2,1	2	3	4	5	6	7	8	9	10	11	12	13	14	15	16			904
3,1	2	3	4	5	6	7	8	9	10	11	12	13	14	15				795
4,1	2	3	4	5	6	7	8	9	10	11	12	13	14					693
5,1	2	3	4	5	6	7	8	9	10	11	12	13						598
6,1	2	3	4	5	6	7	8	9	10	11	12							510
7,1	2	3	4	5	6	7	8	9	10	11								429
8,1	2	3	4	5	6	7	8	9	10									355
9,1	2	3	4	5	6	7	8	9										288
10,1	2	3	4	5	6	7	8											228
11,1	2	3	4	5	6	7												175
12,1	2	3	4	5	6													129
13,1	2	3	4	5														90
14,1	2	3	4															58
15,1	2	3																33
16,1	2																	15
17,1																		4

(Note, the sum of each pair can never be greater than 18, for the sequence would then overrun the length of the ribbon.)

The only task remaining is that of calculating the probability of the letters required to fill the 15 spaces, given they occur by chance. The probabilities can be calculated from the 144 letters supplied by Thorpe.

$T = \frac{17}{144}$; $O = \frac{8}{143}$; $V = \frac{6}{142}$; $E = \frac{23}{141}$; $R = \frac{9}{140}$; $E = \frac{22}{139}$; $H = \frac{10}{138}$; $I = \frac{14}{137}$; $S = \frac{10}{136}$; $W = \frac{4}{135}$; $S = \frac{9}{134}$; $G = \frac{5}{133}$; $R = \frac{8}{132}$; $A = \frac{5}{131}$; $M = \frac{2}{130}$.

The product of these fractions is: $6{\cdot}714405123 \times 10^{-19}$, which represents the probability these letters will occur by chance, *in any order.* The fact that they can be read in an order that is intelligible, extends the probability value very much further. But we will stay with this result. Hence, there are 6324 opportunities for these letters to be placed in a mathematical sequence. When this number is multiplied by $6{\cdot}714405123 \times 10^{-19}$, the result is: 0•000, 000, 000, 000, 004 (1 significant figure).

Translated into words, this result indicates that the 15 letters comprising TO VERE HIS W S GRAM can be expected to occur by chance in an arithmetical sequence, once in 250 trillion trials. Even then, the letter order need not represent an intelligible statement, since the probability value of $6{\cdot}714405123 \times 10^{-19}$ is obtainable no matter in which order the letters are arranged.

Returning to the clock example (p. 25), with one trial taking place each second, it would take almost 8 million years for this sequence of letters to make just one appearance. So, yet again, the court poet de Vere is authenticated as the pen behind Shakespeare's plays and poems: using a valid scientific method of approach for solving the authorship problem.

Some may demur at such large numbers, believing this could not apply to such a small sample. But let physicist and cryptologist Dr Simon Singh (Ph.D Cambridge) correct this belief; keeping in mind that Thorpe's sentence contains 144 letters.

> For example consider this short sentence. *It contains just 35 letters, and yet there are more than 50, 000, 000, 000, 000, 000, 000, 000, 000, 000, 000 distinct arrangements of them. If one person could check one arrangement per second, and if all the people in the world worked night and day, it would still take more than a thousand times the lifetime of the universe to check all the arrangements.*[19]

What impelled Thorpe to go to such extraordinary lengths as to construct this cryptogram? The answer is that it was a time when *"writing . . . went into code."* The year 1609 came in the wake of an extremely punitive period of censorship.

> *Never have books or writing or letters been as dangerous as they were between 1581 and 1606: proclamation after proclamation forbade seditious writings; books were seized in midnight raids, and men were questioned for copying poems. Stephen Vallenger lost his ears for printing one work ... and subsequently died. Writing went underground, between the lines, into the paper and into code; far from suppressing language, the state's actions seemed merely to put value on writing.* [20]

It is understandable that those who have been persuaded to adopt the view that Shakespeare was Shaxpere will seek every opportunity to reject arguments that contradict this belief. No one in a position of authority appreciates learning their judgement has been at fault. But numbers do not lie.

Unfortunately, those strongly inclined towards literature, by and large, are unhappy when faced with numbers. Something Galileo discovered to his cost and discomfort when trying to persuade philosophers and theologians that a mathematically based theory of the heavens, placing the Sun at the centre, was superior to the orthodox view, which insisted the Earth occupied centre stage. As we now know, Galileo eventually triumphed, and his opponents were compelled to yield to the power of numbers. It would appear that History is about to be repeated in this present century. Many academics will find themselves placed in the same position as Galileo's dissenters: being presently faced with a valid scientific proof that overturns former 'certainties'.

Part of that predicament is a set of very pertinent questions, which, by ascribing the poetry of the Sonnets to Shaxpere, cannot be satisfactorily resolved. Why did Thorpe compose the dedication himself? Shaxpere was alive and active in 1609. If he agreed to their publication, why did he not write it? At the same time, he could have overseen the editing, and eliminated the errors that occurred, as had previously been done for his two narrative poems, published fifteen years earlier. But, if he did not agree to their publication, why did he fail to seek legal redress from the publisher? Suing miscreants was a familiar remedy for him, even if the amount was quite small. Alternatively, he could have stayed publication once the printer's intention had been declared in the *Stationers' Register*. This was the legal right of an author with unpublished work.

We must also ask why Thorpe implied the writer was deceased, by naming the publication *Shake-speares Sonnets*. The title emits an air of finality, as if to signal the work of someone who was no longer alive. Was this connected to his description of their author as: *"our ever-living poet"*; for this again signalled the author was no longer living? On the other hand, if 'Shakespeare' was alive in 1609, is not Thorpe insulting him by dedicating his sonnets to the man who obtained them, Mr. W. H: one of the publisher's minor associates? Can you imagine—No! Really imagine—Shaxpere's reaction upon reading that his most intimate thoughts had been dedicated to the person who acquired them, surreptitiously as it would appear, and then discovering that all England was about to enjoy them, and fill the publisher's purse at the same time? I don't think so! Thorpe knew very well that de Vere had written the sonnets, and the author's death five years earlier meant he had to write the dedication himself.

And if this still fails to convince, then why did Thorpe resort to a cryptogram in order to say Shaxpere was not the author? And if the cryptogram is also rejected (and the only reason for that, as I can see, is one of limited education in the numerical sciences) then why is the dedication written in words that Lee described as *"fantastically arranged and in odd grammatical order"*? That, in itself, is certainly a sign that an encryption is likely to be present (p. 10). Even Hotson was forced to admit Thorpe's words were *"so preposterous"* they must conceal *"a cryptogram"*.

There is also the question of why the Sonnets took so long to become public, when it is generally agreed they had been written at approximately the same time as *Venus and Adonis* and *Lucrece*? Why did it take another thirty years before a second edition became available, when lesser talented poets had no difficulty in publishing several editions of their lower grade work?

The inevitable reaction to unanswerable questions is a refusal to even consider them; consequently, these dilemmas are ignored; and because they are ignored, they persist. Thus, over an extended period of time, the view of Shakespeare has become so completely associated with the pronouncements of academics and their imaginative excuses to cover-up the inadequacies of Will Shaxpere's authorship, that when confronted by perfectly valid reasons for considering an alternative author, the need to save face governs intellectual honesty. Refuge is then sought in censorship, ridicule and a blatant disregard for truth.

THE ONLY BEGETTER

One of the first questions to intrigue those who examine Thorpe's dedication concerns the identity of Mr. W. H. Gallons of ink have been used in attempting to arrive at a solution: one that is in agreement with what Thorpe meant by 'begetter'. In biblical terminology, 'begetter' refers to the creation of life. In grammatical terms, this word belongs to a set of Old English verbs prefixed by 'be'; e.g., bespeak, belittle, bedevil, and many others. In each case the sense of 'be' is to make someone or something the object of an action associated with the verb it prefixes. For instance, to belittle a person is to make that person the object of some deprecating comment or action. Hence, to beget is likewise to make someone or something the object of 'getting': c.f. beget, *"Old English, get, obtain by effort"* [Compact OED].

Thorpe's use of 'begetter' was intended to acknowledge Mr W. H. as the 'onlie' procurer of the Sonnets. Note that the adjective, 'onlie', spelt in this extremely rare fashion for that age – an 'e' following the 'n' was usually required – has also aided the compilation of the cryptogram, since it has provided the letter 'I' in, 'H I S'; re: 'HIS W.S. GRAM' and the first 'E' in Southampton's split name, 'E S L E Y'.

So, once again, it is worth pressing the point; imagine Will Shaxpere's reaction upon learning that his sonnet collection had been acquired for publication without his consent, and then, quite preposterously, finding that it had been dedicated to the rogue who had procured it. It is a remarkable person who can see this as occurring without producing any repercussions from the offended party: especially a man who, according to what we know of Shaxpere, not only sought justice from the courts at every opportunity, but who had once threatened the life of a petty gangster named William Wayte (p. 85).

At the time these Sonnets were acquired, there lived in the village of Hackney a certain William Hall. Like so many other villages that once lay outside London, it has long since been swallowed up by the capital's urban sprawl. But in Tudor and early Stuart times it was the favoured spot for nobles and courtiers, and was occasionally the destination for visiting monarchs. Amongst the residents of the village at that time were Elizabeth Trentham, dowager Countess of Oxford, and her son, Henry, the 18th Earl of Oxford.

Colonel Bernard R. Ward, in his book, *The Mystery of 'Mr W. H.'* (Cecil Palmer, 1923), has argued that Hall acquired the Sonnets at the time of the family's removal from Hackney. He suggested the disruption caused by packing the household contents together, prior to transporting them to Castle Hedingham, allowed some unknown person to 'liberate' the Sonnets, and, possibly the play, *Troilus and Cressida* too, for this was published in the same year as the Sonnets. This is the play with its interesting Preface referring to its liberated acquisition.

> *There is no mention of a company or a theatre; and indeed the Epistle [to the reader] strongly implies that the play had never been acted in a public theatre, and (in order to appear in print) had made some kind of 'escape', since the 'grand possessors' would have prevented publication of it (together with other comedies [sic] by the same author) had they been able.*[21]

From this, it is a simple matter to speculate that the Sonnets also 'escaped' their 'grand possessors' at the same time. It would also explain why the furtive removal of these manuscripts occasioned no outcry. To have done so would have drawn attention to the Oxford household, and the family's connection to the manuscripts of *Shakespeare*. This allows a further possibility to arise. Was it Oxford's son Henry who passed them over to Hall? At the time of their publication, the 18th Earl was sixteen years of age and undergoing a period of teenage rebellion.

> *Managing young Henry's estate was one thing, but managing "a young nobleman neither of years nor judgement to advise himself, wanting the guidance of a father and past the government of a mother ..." in the words of countess Elizabeth, [it] was evidently quite another once the sixteen year old Henry had fallen into the wayward company of his second cousin John Hunt.*[22]

It is not difficult to imagine the headstrong young man believing he was fulfilling his father's wish for publication by passing the Sonnets over for printing. And if he knew they had been forbidden to the public, then so much the better for satisfying his rebellious nature. Like father, like son, one could say.

Eighteen months later, the situation had grown so bad that his mother was forced to appeal jointly to Robert Cecil and Lord Henry Howard for their urgent assistance concerning the *"apparent danger of my son's ruin";* amongst his vices were the huge debts he had incurred.

This fact has the further appeal of fostering the possibility that he had been persuaded by a financial inducement into parting with his father's Sonnets and possibly *Troilus and Cressida* also. Although this is speculative, it nevertheless coincides with his financial predicament, which at the time was dire.

> *By the age of eighteen Henry had run up debts of £700 to £800, plus £150 (pledged against his pension), plus £200 (secured with £700-£800 worth of Oxford's sister's jewels), for a total of well over £1000. Henry's £200 pension was garnished for a year and a half (thus depriving him of the immediate benefit of the directive that the money should be paid to himself rather than to his mother). More recently he took a loan from the Low Countries.*[23]

Ward's argument for William Hall as the Mr W. H., to whom Thorpe was beholden, extended beyond the circumstance of just location. Amongst the entries in the parish church register for Hackney, he found that: *"William Hall and Margery Gryffyn were joined in matrymonye on the 4th Aug. 1608."*[24] It was an event that coincided both in time and in detail to the reference made by Thorpe in his dedicatory preface to the Sonnets, in which he wished the *"begetter Mr. W. H. All Happinesse ... In Setting Forth":* an apt expression for someone embarking upon married life.

Hall was also Sir Sidney Lee's choice for Mr W. H. This was because Hall had already earned a reputation for obtaining manuscripts and then either selling them on to interested publishers, or occasionally publishing them himself. He also had connections with both Thorpe, who was one of his *"occasional collaborators",* and with George Eld who printed the Sonnets for Thorpe.

In 1606, Eld had published *A Foure-fold Meditation.* This was a poem believed written by Father Robert Southwell, a Catholic priest who was betrayed in June 1592, and arrested by Richard Topcliffe, the recently made head of Elizabeth's secret police. After undergoing torture, Southwell was executed in February 1595 at Tyburn.

> *Father Southwell's writings, both in prose and verse, were extremely popular with his contemporaries, and his religious pieces were sold openly by the booksellers though their authorship was known.* [25]

When writing about these acquired poems, a certain *"W. H."* informed readers: *"A mere accident conveyed them into my hands".* Lee identified this W. H. as William Hall, and likewise assumed some other 'mere accident' had taken place with the Sonnets.

It is therefore of some interest to note that Southwell's capture took place at Uxendon Hall in Hackney, the home of Catholic sympathiser Richard Bellamy. It was Bellamy's daughter Ann who was arrested and repeatedly raped by Topcliffe in his private torture chamber until she betrayed Southwell's whereabouts. Consequently, it has been conjectured that Southwell left the *Foure-fold Meditation* at Hackney before his arrest, and this led Hall to assume Southwell had written it. In fact, its composition is now credited to a close friend of Southwell's, the Earl of Arundel.

Stratford based scholarship has never properly come to terms with Thorpe's dedicatory address. The oddly composed words with their lack of grammatical order, strongly suggest some secret has been concealed within their composition, and this bewilders orthodox thinking. The professorship sees no reason for secrecy where Shaxpere is concerned, and so those advocating his authorship, having committed their intelligence to the blindfold of a barren precept, are never able to see beyond the confine of this bleak outlook.

This is apparent from Professor Katherine Duncan-Jones' observation, concerning Jonson's *Epigrammes,* addressed to the Earl of Pembroke (1616). She noted how Jonson had remarked that his epigrams were not dangerous, and there was nothing *"to expressing of which I did need a cipher."* From this, she concluded he had in mind *"some other, more compromising or 'dangerous' form of poetry, which had indeed required use of a 'cipher'."* [26] She thought this might allude to Shakespeare's sonnet sequence, but carried the thought no further: perceiving no obvious reason within her understanding of Shakespeare's identity as to why a cipher would have been required.

It was the very real fear of a public scandal that gave reason to the furtiveness associated with the publication of the Sonnets; furtive, because haste soon led to an excess of printing errors, followed by the predictable disappearance of the poems from booksellers: an absence that was to last for more than three decades. Even thirty years later, in 1640, the fear of scandal caused the publisher to change the gender of the young man to that of a maid.

In a comprehensive analysis of the Sonnets' editions for 1609 and 1640, Dr. James Brooks was able to demonstrate:

> *That the Benson text has no independent textual authority and is indebted to Thorpe's volume as the primary source is supported by the results of all individual elements of the analysis. The similarities revealed by the detailed textual comparison point unambiguously to Q [the first Quarto of 1609] as the copy-text for Benson's volume.* [27]

The gender change that occurs in Benson's edition, concerning the 'fair youth', was therefore not instigated by access to a manuscript copy of the Sonnets, but made by editing Eld's printing of the 1609 edition.

A change of gender for the subject of the verses also helped safeguard the noble families involved, since it removed the suspicion of improper conduct between Oxford and Southampton and the involvement of Burghley. For the poems, in their original form, tell a story that was never to be spoken out loud: the reason why the 17th Earl of Oxford was barred from all association with their authorship, and by extension, from connection with the plays he had written. It was also the reason why Will Shaxpere was entirely unconcerned when the Sonnets were published—they were not his to be concerned about.

In summary, Thomas Thorpe's dedication is enigmatic, because—as the great Shakespearian scholar Leslie Hotson had realised—it conceals *"a cryptogram":* although one he would have found difficulty coming to terms with. For its decryption contains a different set of responses to the questions he would have expected to find answered: one being the author's name.

That name has now been exposed. But Thorpe, as Jonson would do later with the Stratford monument, was also saying something equally revealing. By referring this information to the secret science of cryptology, he was also covertly admitting to the pressure of censorship, which necessitated this form of communication. At the same time, he conceded to the inevitability that future generations, in common with popular belief at the time, would persist in the conviction that Will Shaxpere was the same man as William Shakespeare. So certain were Thorpe and Jonson that this was inevitable, they dared commit the truth behind this deception to two time capsules; each of which they believed would endure for as long as Shakespeare's name was given breath.

These time capsules were the dedication to the Sonnets, and the monument's inscription to Shakespeare's memory. Each one continues to complement the other by declaring without ambiguity that Edward de Vere was the poet and playwright known as William Shakespeare. Both sources strongly imply that until a scholarly appraisal of Oxford's life and Shakespeare's work are undertaken, and their concurrence obtained without it raising manifest contradictions, people will continue to believe wrongly about Shakespeare's true identity.

TO.THE.ONLIE.BEGETTER.OF.
THESE.INSVING.SONNETS.
Mr.W.H. ALL.HAPPINESSE.
AND.THAT.ETERNITIE.
PROMISED.
BY.
OVR.EVER-LIVING.POET.
WISHETH.
THE.WELL-WISHING.
ADVENTVRER.IN.
SETTING.
FORTH.

T. T.

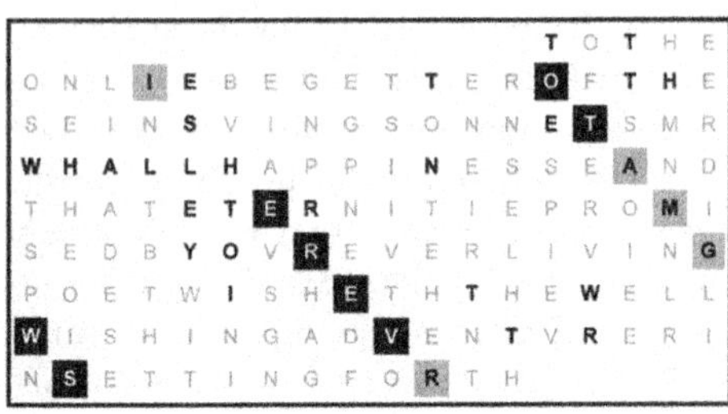

As an interesting postscript, three experts in cryptology from the United States National Security Agency examined Rollett's decryption, and recommended that it be published. It was subsequently featured in *The Times* newspaper (31/12/1997) having also appeared in *The Elizabethan Review* (autumn edition, vol. 5, No. 2). Additionally, it was submitted to *Cryptologia,* a journal specialising in cryptology, where it received the approbation of the review committee. But there the matter ended. The then editor-in-chief, David Kahn, vetoed publication; allegedly, in fear that any evidence contradicting orthodoxy's view of Shakespeare would damage the reputation of *Cryptologia.*

Those similarly persuaded by the traditionalist viewpoint concerning Shakespeare, will follow Kahn's lead and banish the evidence. For them, Thorpe's dedication must forever remain an enigma. Truth can sometimes be very confusing, even hurtful, when it contradicts everything one has been taught to believe about Shakespeare.

4

WHAT THE SONNETS TELL

Not a syllable of them but was lived, experienced, thought, enjoyed, suffered.

J. W. von Goethe

THE PUBLIC FIRST became aware of Shakespeare's Sonnets when Francis Meres published his *Palladis Tamia* in 1598, referring to the poems as *"sugared sonnets among his private friends"*. If William Shaxpere had written these, and shown them to his company of actor-friends, any number of enterprising publishers, at a fair price, would have quickly obtained the sonnets, and they would have been on sale within weeks of their acquisition. As it was, William Jaggard was the only person outside of *Shakespeare's* private audience to get near them.

In 1599, by means that remain questionable, he obtained two sonnets, 138 and 144. These, he quickly published in a collection of verses bearing the title: *The Passionate Pilgrim.* After that, no more was heard of them for an entire decade. Then suddenly, in 1609, the entire sequence of 154 sonnets, plus a lengthy poem called *A Lover's Complaint,* burst upon the public scene. *"[W]e know that it was on the bookstalls by 19 June because Edward Alleyn … recorded purchasing a copy on that date."*[1] But, as quickly as they appeared, they disappeared. It was not until 1640, thirty-one years later, that they re-emerged in print, although only after they had been edited to remove the scurrilous implication that their author was writing about a homosexual affair with a youth.

More than a century was to pass before a scholarly perusal of the original text revealed the truth of this gender change, and it led to a re-appraisal of the sonnets. Were they autobiographical, as it was believed, when they appeared to have been written to a woman; or were they merely poetic exercises, as perfecters of Shakespeare's image decided, when it was discovered they were addressed to a youth? This dichotomy has not gone away, and shows no present sign of agreement.

The nub of the problem is the beliefs adopted by advocates on each side of the debate. If someone subsumes an idolized view of Shakespeare, then it becomes impossible to assimilate into that belief system anything of a derogatory nature about the man. No amount of reasonable appeal will effect a change. (This also refers to the Authorship Controversy, and explains why Oxford has yet to be accepted as the pen behind Shakespeare's name.) Offering reason to Shaxpere's unflinching advocates is like administering medicine to the dead. Take for example the suggestion that the sonnets were merely poetic exercises. If so, there would have been no imperative for deferring publication: either in 1592/3, when the bulk of them were written or for the delay of thirty-one years after their brief emergence in 1609.

It is also clear from what *Shakespeare* wrote that he expected his sonnets would be read long after his own life had ended, for this is implicit within several of his lines.

So long as men can breathe and eyes can see,
So long lives this, and this gives life to thee. (xviii)

ꕥ

And thou in this shalt find thy monument,
When tyrants' crests and tombs of brass are spent. (cvii)

ꕥ

If I could write the beauty of your eyes
And in fresh numbers number all your graces,
The age to come would say 'This poet lies;
Such heavenly touches ne'er touch'd earthly faces.'
So should my papers, yellowed with their age,
Be scorn'd, like old men of less truth than tongue; (xvii)

Let us regard *Shake-speares Sonnets* in the context of what was happening at the time they were written. In 1591, Philip Sidney's *Astrophel and Stella* was published. This book of songs and sonnets was quickly followed by edition after edition of sonnets during the next seven years, with sequences *"by Samuel Daniel, Thomas Watson, Barnabe Barnes, Thomas Lodge, Giles Fletcher, Henry Constable, William Percy, Michael Drayton, Edmund Spenser,*

Richard Barnfield, Bartholomew Griffiths, William Smith, Henry Lok, Robert Tofte, and Nicholas Breton."[2] If Shakespeare's sonnets were truly just poetic exercises, and if their author was the son of John Shaxpere from Snittersfield, then why did he not take financial advantage of this popular form of verse and publish his poems? This, after all, was only a few years after John Shaxpere's appeal to the courts had failed in a bid to recover his wife's house, which had been forfeited after he mortgaged the property as security for a loan. But, through poverty, he had failed to repay the debt, and the house was lost. Money sent home by Shaxpere for his wife Anne and their children, who were still living off the proceeds of his father's work, should have been a priority. The public were then at his feet, following publication of *Venus and Adonis* and *Lucrece*. But it was an opportunity he declined, thus foregoing an opportunity that would have brought him a nice sum of money. That an astute businessman like Shaxpere should have neglected such a readily available means to increase his income does not ring true; and that is, because it is untrue.

The Fair Youth

Clearly, there was an insurmountable obstacle preventing publication of the Sonnets. Firstly, Shaxpere was not the author, despite claims to the contrary; it is therefore pointless looking to him for an explanation as to why these poems were not sold to the public. Secondly, the sonnets were autobiographical. They revealed in language, too passionate to be mistaken for anything else, the true feelings held by the author for a boy less than half his age. And, when one identifies the sonneteer as Edward de Vere, 17th Earl of Oxford and Lord Great Chamberlain of England, and Henry Wriothesley, 3rd Earl of Southampton, as the object of his passion: both being elite members of Elizabeth's court, as well as their lordships having a close and legal connection with the Queen's chief minister Lord Burghley, a need for silence and the utmost secrecy concerning the illicit nature of this relationship was as obvious as it was essential.

Burghley, in particular, was Master of the Queen's Wards and guardian to Southampton, with the responsibility for the young lord's safety and moral upbringing; he would therefore be publicly culpable for any immorality on the part of his ward's behaviour. To make matters worse, the author of the sonnets was actually confessing, in written verse, his most intimate feelings for the youth.

In a poetic confession to Queen Elizabeth, Oxford remarked upon the scandal that his affair with Southampton had brought upon him, while also acknowledging her support and declaring his love and loyalty to her.

Your love and pity doth th'impression fill
Which vulgar scandal stamp'd upon my brow;
For what care I who calls me well or ill,
So you o'ergreen my bad... (cxii)

This part of the sonnet, which uses *"you"* instead of *thou* indicates it was addressed to Queen Elizabeth: as do the remaining lines, which touch matters inappropriate to a youth. Oxford may not have cared about the consequences attendant to his actions, but others did. Silence regarding 'Shakespeare's' name was therefore crucial; it even became a theme for the two commendatory poems referred to in Chapter 2: *"Shake-speare, we must be silent in thy praise,"* and *"most, most of me beloved, Whose silent name one letter bounds."*

Some idea of the passion contained in these sonnets, and their wider implication is clear from the lines that commence Sonnet 20.

"A woman's face, with Nature's own hand painted, Hast thou, the master-mistress of my passion;"

The painting shown here of young Henry Wriothesley, was discovered as recently as the end of the twentieth century. It had lain neglected in the Cobbe household for three centuries until a chance inspection identified the sitter as the 3rd Earl of Southampton: aged between 17 and 20. The Cobbe family household, during the seventeenth century, lived in property adjoining the Earls of Southampton at Titchfield in Hampshire, and it is presumed that the 4th Earl, who died childless, passed the portrait on to the Cobbes. Prior to this discovery, the picture was surmised to be Lady Norton, daughter of the Bishop of Winton; proof, indeed, that Southampton did possess what *Shakespeare* described as: – *"A woman's face with Nature's own hand painted.*

> *Experts who have studied the facts now agree that the portrait is undoubtedly the earliest known image of the third Earl of Southampton – Shakespeare's patron, the 'fair youth' addressed in his sonnets – somewhere between the age of 17 and 20 and painted exactly the time those first few sonnets were written.* [3]

Upon reading *Shake-speare's Sonnets*, one is soon struck by the frequency of the poet's expression of love for this young man. The examples are many: *"O, know, sweet love, I always write of you,"* (lxxvi); *"Dear my love,"* (xiii); *"O, therefore, love, be of thyself so wary,"* (xxii); *"Take all my loves, my love, yea, take them all;"* (xl); *"Thou canst not, love, disgrace me half so ill,"* (lxxxix).

They are, commented, C. S. Lewis, former Cambridge professor of medieval and renaissance literature, *"too lover-like for that of ordinary male friendship."* Joseph Pequigney, in his detailed study of the Sonnets, reached a similar conclusion. The relationship, he wrote, *"is decidedly amorous-passionate to a degree and in ways not dreamed of in published philology, the interaction between the friends being sexual in both orientation and practice."* He then went on to say, *"that verbal data are clear and copious in detailing physical intimacies between them."*[4]

Despite the obviousness of what Lewis, Pequigney and others see as poetry describing a homo-erotic liaison, it has many times been pointed out that although Shakespeare does admit his 'passion' for this boy, he also makes it quite plain, in the concluding lines of Sonnet 20, that his love stopped short of intromission. Recall the portrait of Southampton, above.

A woman wert thou first created;
Till Nature, as she wrought thee, fell a-doting,
And by addition me of thee defeated
By adding one thing to my purpose nothing.
  But since she prick'd thee out for women's pleasure,
  Mine be thy love, and thy love's use their treasure.

This claim may well have been true at the time it was written; although Southampton's effeminate appearance and his activities in Ireland with Captain Piers Edmund do nothing to encourage confidence in the lasting truth of this statement. It has also been pointed out that *"nothing"* was formerly a slang word for female genitalia.

There is also Oxford's own past to be considered. His return from Italy in 1576 with Orazio Coquo, a sixteen-year-old choir boy, whom he engaged as his page, but who escaped the Oxford household and fled back to his native Venice after only eleven months is very possibly significant; the more so, because Coquo was said to have *"complained howe horribly my Lord had abusid him, and yet wold not giue him any thinge."*[5] Presumably, this 'abuse' was sexual abuse, and the 'thing' was a salve to ease his discomfort

Elsewhere, Oxford had enemies anxious to condemn him for the same crime, but against other page boys he employed.

> *Howard and Arundel were bent on having Oxford tried for the specific crime of pederasty. To this end they offered testimony from nearly a dozen victims, near victims, and non-victim witnesses. They charged Oxford with the sexual abuse of 'so many boyes that it must nedes come out' especially of pages* (LIB-3.6.1/3).[6]

But the charges levelled against Oxford by Howard and Arundel were not subjected to prolonged scrutiny, and he was never brought to trial. Was Oxford entirely innocent of these accusations? Had it not been for his infatuation with the teenaged Southampton, it would be much easier to give him the benefit of doubt, notwithstanding Sonnet 87.

> *Thy self thou gav'st, thy own worth then not knowing,*
> *Or me, to whom thou gav'st it,*

Any woman who has *given* herself will know immediately what this means. But because it was said of a man, is it then to be interpreted differently?

Sonnet 121 is another poem that arguably contradicts the earlier claim made by the poet that his love was based solely upon admiration for the youth, with no sexual impropriety having taken place between them.

> *'Tis better to be vile than vile esteemed,*
> *When not to be receives reproach of being,*
> *And the just pleasure lost, which is so deemed*
> *Not by our feeling, but by others' seeing.*

It is difficult to see this declaration as anything other than a reference to the accusations made against the poet regarding his homosexual relationship with the youth. The forcefulness of the word 'vile', as understood by a country that looked to the Bible for moral guidance, is especially indicative. Let us see how the verse continues.

For why should others' false adulterate eyes
Give salutation to my sportive blood?

It is interesting to see the poet excusing himself because of his 'sportive blood'. In 1594, when the satirical poem *Willobie His Avisa* was published, the anonymous author made a similar reference to 'sport': connecting it with sodomy.

Our English soil, to Sodom's sink,
Excessive sin transformed of late,
Of foul deceit the loathsome link,
Hath worn all faith clean out of date,
The greatest sins mongst greatest sort,
Are counted now but for a sport. [7]

Was this a covert reference to Oxford's relationship with Southampton? The author does deal with their togetherness elsewhere in the storyline. Also, its date of composition coincides with the received opinion as to when the Sonnets were written; that is, when Southampton was still a youth. There is also this mention of 'sins amongst the greatest sort'. That too fits the picture, since both Oxford and Southampton were highborn. Then there is the reference to the affair being excused as 'sport': a term used in the sonnet.

The word 'sin' has now lost its impact. In the sixteenth century, it held deadly implications, and was never used lightly.

It was also at this time that the Earl of Essex gathered around him a companionship of *"scholars, statesmen, spies and sodomites"*, [8] included amongst whom were Anthony and Francis Bacon, and Southampton. These men cannot therefore be excluded from the possibility they, too, were objects of Willobie's disgust.

Returning to Sonnet 121, several lines further down, the poet makes a revealing confession. *"No!"* he exclaims, *"I am that I am; and they that level / At my abuses reckon up their own."* The reason why this is particularly revealing is because Oxford had used the same expression in a letter of protest (October 1584), addressed to Lord Burghley. *"I serve Her Majesty, and I am that I am—and by alliance near to your Lordship, but free."* [9] Under duress, it seems,

Oxford was apt to resort to the same figure of speech, and this has found its way into both his letter and his sonnet. Other similarities occurring between Shakespeare's language and Oxford's letters can be found in *Shakespeare Revealed in Oxford's Letters* (W. P. Fowler, Portsmouth, N.H. 1986).

Burghley's own thoughts at what was happening between his son-in-law and the youth under his protection may be judged by the events that followed. Evidence for believing Southampton's behaviour 'womanish', and that the Master of the Queen's Wards was attempting to cure the situation by marriage, is indicated in the Latin poem, *Narcissus,* written by Burghley's secretary John Clapham: no doubt, composed under orders from his employer.

The verse was intended to persuade Southampton to marry; it also contained: *"galling hints that the youth might be lacking in manliness:"* [10] an accusation that was intended to rile any normal red-blooded male into action. Burghley must have been complicit in the poem's terminology, for he was responsible for the welfare of his young charge, and the earl's tendency towards homosexual practices would explain this otherwise unnecessary rush towards finding him a suitable bride.

Oxford, too, was drawn into making his own poetic appeal for Southampton to wed, thereby adding to Clapham's poetry by using his personal influence over Southampton. The result was a succession of sonnets, seventeen in number, urging the young earl to marry and beget children.

The subject matter of *Venus and Adonis* and *Lucrece,* with its erotic content, would also seem to have been part of a more involved plan, and this would explain the astounding fact that a certain 'William Shakespeare': hitherto unknown as a writer anywhere in England, was immediately, and without difficulty, able to obtain a licence for the publication of two poems whose sexual content would, in different circumstances, have secured the Church's censure and instant condemnation.

> *Observing that the printing of Venus and Adonis—which for explicit eroticism can be exceeded by few literary works openly published and sold in the English-speaking world for the next 350 years—was personally authorized by the Archbishop of Canterbury, George Philip, V. Akrigg comments, "We have lost a good story concerning Archbishop Whitgift's licence."* [11]

Perhaps not altogether lost, if it is understood that Lord Burghley had explained to Whitgift the need for the licence was to save young Southampton from a life of sin and damnation: *"sodomy was a capital offence and religious people of all persuasions regarded it as an instant passport to hell."*[12]

Burghley's anxiety, and his solution to settle the problem of Southampton's sexuality, can also be seen as a desire to save his own position, which both his ward and son-in-law had clearly jeopardised by their affair together. To his mind, any threat to his position as the Queen's closest advisor, was also a threat to the nation's security, and must be dealt with as such. Divorcing Oxford from his confessional sonnets, and pinning the author's artistic output onto a member of the lower classes, was merely a step necessary to ensure the protection of the state, with which he identified.

A direct if circumstantial link between Shakespeare's verses urging matrimony and the controversy surrounding the teenage Southampton has been the subject of speculation for many years. It has also led to the suggestion that Lord Burghley and Southampton's mother, Lady Mary Browne, agreed to their private affairs being made known to a tradesman's son, recently arrived from the midlands, so that he might achieve some influence over the young nobleman.

Let it quickly be understood, even as late as the 19th century, trade was still looked down upon by the English upper classes; - how much more this would have been so in the 16th century can easily be imagined. Moreover, how could it even be suspected that such an arrangement, involving advice from a man of Shaxpere's class, would be contemplated for a moment by the most powerful man in England? And how could this be supposed to have taken place without considering the wishes of the 17th Earl of Oxford, himself a poet, and whose daughter Elizabeth, was to be the temptress leading Southampton to the altar? Yet, the marriage sonnets have to be explained by traditional thinking. And so, based upon the premise that Shaxpere wrote Shakespeare's Sonnets, nonsense turns to stupidity as an explanation is concocted involving Queen Elizabeth's principal advisor, Lord Burghley, seeking advice from an untutored member of an uneducated and illiterate family— *"Pimping Billy"* if his occupation as a horse attendant holds true.

In fact, the sonnets do give advice to Southampton on the subject of marriage and his need to procreate. But the reason for Southampton's marriage was so sensitive, that it could never be discussed by anyone outside the class of nobility to which Southampton, Burghley and Oxford belonged. Those apt to think differently know nothing about the English aristocracy and the privacy they demand for conducting their affairs.

Although Oxford's daughter Elizabeth was Southampton's prospective bride, the arguments in the sonnets are far broader. The young man is urged to consider marriage in general, and to continue his family line. Oxford's contribution to this was the composition of 17 sonnets on the subject of matrimony; 17 being the number of his earldom.

> *Would any self-respecting Elizabethan have written a sonnet sequence around a prime number, save for a very good reason . . . The number of sonnets in an Elizabethan sequence always had a mathematical significance. Yet the marriage sonnets are indivisible in number. Not only do none of the notable Elizabethan sonnet-sequences that precede Shakespeare's total seventeen, no other important sequence deals in units of seventeen.*[13]

Had Clinton Heylin exercised greater perspicacity, he might have understood that 17 represented the number of the author's earldom. Instead of which, he was persuaded to latch onto Dover-Wilson's suggestion that this number was connected to William Herbert's seventeenth birthday, and the marriage sonnets were written in response to his having broken off an engagement to Bridget Vere. This was not the case. William's father had negotiated the marriage with Bridget's grandfather, Lord Burghley. Bridget's father had no money for her dowry, so Burghley offered £3000 (≈ £850,000) plus an annuity that would commence after his death. Pembroke declined, demanding that the annuity commence on the day of the wedding. Both men refused to give way, and further negotiations ceased. Hence, there was no cause for the marriage sonnets. Those who believe these verses were written for William Herbert and not Henry Wriothesley have therefore lost a major part of their argument. Later, at the age of twenty, William impregnated Mary Fitton, but the baby did not survive. Four years later, having inherited his father's title, he married Mary Talbot.

We now know from Thomas Thorpe that the Fair Youth was Henry Wriothesley (p.167); and he was under the strongest pressure to marry. These sonnets add to this growing persuasion.

Now stand you on the top of happy hours,
And many maiden gardens, yet unset,
With virtuous wish would bear your living flowers, (xvi)

ꕥ

Be not self-willed, for thou art too fair
To be death's conquest and make worms thine heir. (vi)

At this point the astute reader may have noticed a change in the poet's form of address.

In Old English, thou was singular and you was plural; but during the thirteenth century, you started to be used as a polite form of the singular – probably because people copied the French way of talking, where vous was used in that way. English then became like French, which has tu and vous both possible for singulars. So in early Modern English, when Shakespeare was writing, there was a choice: [14]

Opener	Situation	Normal reply
you	upper classes talking to each other, even when closely related	you
thou	lower classes talking to each other	thou
thou	superiors to inferiors, such as:	
	• parents to children	you
	• masters to servants	you
thou	special intimacy, such as	
	• talking to a lover	thou
thou	• addressing God or a god (e.g. Jupiter)	you
thou	character talks to someone absent	—

In Sonnet 16 above, the poet has addressed the prospective bridegroom as *you.* But *you* is employed as an opening address between members of the upper classes, as would be the case with Oxford talking to Southampton. However, *you* and *your* are also employed by an inferior talking to a superior, as made to appear in the opening epistle to *Venus and Adonis.* This latter usage in the Sonnets is naturally the preferred choice of those believing Shaxpere to be Shakespeare.

But in Sonnet 6 above, the poet addresses his subject as *thou.* Since this is neither the lower classes talking poetically between themselves, nor master to servant, we are left with 'special intimacy', as when one talks to a lover.

The thought of Shaxpere, with his uncouth background and his arrival in the capital, unrecognised and without contacts, to suddenly be found cuddling up to a young nobleman for an intimate and improper relationship is frankly ludicrous. Yet, the poet's persistent usage of *thee* and *thou* when addressing Southampton is clearly evident throughout the sonnets.

> *Shall I compare thee to a summer's day?*
> *Thou art more lovely and more temperate.* (xviii)

Other sonnets addressed to Southampton follow a similar pattern of delivery, and by doing so, betray the intimate relationship that existed between man and boy.

Nothing seems to have been achieved by the verses advising matrimony, other than to enrich the English language. But it did enable Oxford to develop a particular theme with considerable effect. The poems also served to distance him from the rumour of his homosexuality, by their recommendation that his young friend should behave as nature had intended and beget children.

This may, in some way, have helped dispel the scandal of his illicit relationship with the youth: as it still does to some readers of the sonnets. But, perversely, Southampton remained unreceptive to the sonnets' appeal and the reasons given. He would eventually marry, but not until 1598, when in secret, he returned from Paris to wed Elizabeth Vernon, the Queen's lady-in-waiting, who was both impoverished and pregnant. She was also cousin to the 2nd Earl of Essex, with whom, at a later date, Southampton would conspire in their attempt to overthrow Robert Cecil's hold over the Queen.

Southampton's timely return from France did manage to save Elizabeth Vernon from social disgrace. But, interestingly, in all his affairs only two women are ever mentioned in connection with his private life—his mother and Elizabeth Vernon.

Eight years earlier, Burghley's options to obtain a bride for his ward had been seriously limited, not least because of Southampton's affinity with his feminine side. A shortlist of nubile young ladies may have failed at every approach. Lady Bridget Manners said Southampton was not eligible as a husband because he was *"so fantastical and would be so carried away."* This may explain why the responsibility for preserving the honour of both families fell to Lady Elizabeth Vere, Oxford's eldest daughter and Burghley's granddaughter.

In the same year that *Venus and Adonis* was published: dedicated to Southampton, and which, despite its forbidding sexual content, it had still managed to receive Archbishop Whitgift's approval, Burghley added one further inducement. This was the unprecedented nomination of his ward for election to the rank of Knight of the Garter.

> *In 1593 Southampton was mentioned for nomination as a knight of the garter, and although he was not chosen the compliment of nomination was, at his age, unprecedented outside the circle of the sovereign's kinsmen.*[15]

But even this honour proved ineffective. Southampton remained stubbornly opposed to matrimony, even preferring to pay the enormous fine of £5000 imposed upon him for breach of promise. This was a large amount of money to forego (approximately equal to £1·4 million in 2010*), and a sum the young Earl's inherited estate could ill afford to lose. But against the Lord Treasurer's hope and expectation, his ward remained obstinately opposed to taking a wife, and so the engagement to Oxford's daughter was abandoned, and with it, his nomination as a knight of the garter was withdrawn. Conventional thinking fails to understand why this reversal in Southampton's fortune occurred.

---

* Based upon statistical information available in the U.K. since 1750, the sum of £5000 in 1590 would be equivalent to £864,607 in 2010. A linear model of the inflation rate between 1590 and 2010 is estimated to be 27,933%.

The rejected bride's father received better fortune. Oxford succumbed to the prospect of an enforced marriage. His bride, however, was untitled and far below the dignity and expectations of his own high birth. In different circumstances, the wedding would have been judged entirely unworthy of his family name. One must therefore suppose that no small pressure was exerted to achieve this union. Only the Queen could have applied the force necessary to impel a penniless Oxford towards another period of matrimony: the first having proved so disastrous.

The Queen's involvement in this arranged marriage may be concluded from her lack of objection to Oxford's new wife. Elizabeth Trentham was one of her Maids of Honour. Hence, the Queen's silence was quite exceptional, and this indicates just how damaging the threatened scandal was perceived at the time.

> *It must be remembered that the maids of honour could not marry without the consent of the queen, which Elizabeth was always most reluctant to give and would be particularly unwilling to give when the husband was an old favourite of her own.* [16]

Oxford fell into the category of an old favourite: a friendship that dated back to 1571, when as an accomplished courtier, with an intellect to match the Queen's, he had caught the royal eye.

> *Elizabeth certainly delighted in his company ... there was something appealing in his eccentric, dissolute ways, and after anger and tears would come reconciliation.* [17]

The continuation of Sonnet 112 (p. 185), addressed to Queen Elizabeth goes some way towards confirming what history had to say regarding the often fraught relationship between the monarch and her poet-earl.

> *For what care I who calls me well or ill,*
> *So you o'ergreen my bad, my good allow?*
> *To know my shames and praises from your tongue;*
> ...
> *You are so strongly in my purpose bred*
> *That all the world methinks are dead.*

Oxford was the beneficiary of an annuity from Elizabeth's private purse of £1000 (≈ £280,000), which had been awarded to him in June 1586, with no accounting required. If the Queen remained true to form, she would be expected to have withheld her consent to this marriage. Very likely, she did the opposite.

Sharing Burghley's concern for the danger Oxford's intimate relationship with Southampton was placing them in, and by implication those connected with both families, she must have 'suggested' he redirect his attention to the fairer sex. In this respect, she had at her bidding Elizabeth Trentham. Unlike the adolescent Southampton, both Oxford and her Maid of Honour were sufficiently adult, and loyal, to understand that any 'suggestion' from a Tudor monarch was something that required unquestioning obedience.

With virtual certainty, it can be said this was a marriage of convenience: Oxford being impoverished at the time. They were married – the actual record is missing, but it is believed it took place during the final weeks of 1591 – about five months after their engagement, when property rights were being negotiated for the benefit of Oxford's widow in the event of his death.[18]

As a concession to taking on Oxford as a husband, the bride was allowed the company of her brother, ffrancis Trentham: a person skilled in financial matters and estate management. This was essentially a move to safeguard their family fortune. Together with help from his uncle, Ralph Sneyd, the two men took control of the finances, including Oxford's heavily mortgaged estate. This curtailed the poet's extravagance, but also freed him from financial worry. He was therefore able to commence the mammoth task of editing and rewriting plays that had only previously been seen at Court, while presumably adding to their number, at such times his muse inspired him.

It is also clear that the Trentham family's hand of constraint upon Oxford's financial situation soon led him to make several appeals to the Queen for a monopoly: several requests for this preferment were made after his marriage. Control of the Cornish tin mines would have provided a lucrative source of income, had he obtained the concession. But his application was declined, as were his requests to become President of Wales, and then Governor of Jersey. It is not impossible that he believed the Queen might be sympathetic to his plight, he having agreed to take her maid of honour as a wife. If so he was mistaken. He would have to await the change of monarchy before his fortune recovered.

The assumed chronology attributed to the composition of

Shakespeare's plays during the 1590s – through Oxford having had time to revise and re-edit his earlier productions – was to eventually become the hallmark of Shaxpere's genius. One play written every thirteen weeks without a single break, year in, year out, while acting and rehearsing during the day, and travelling to and fro between London and Stratford-upon-Avon to conduct his many business ventures, is something that never causes Shaxpere's enthusiasts to bat an eyelid: so mesmerised are they by their idol. Yet that is what was required of their playwright. And this is without mentioning his detours to please his patron, Lord Southampton, by composing the majority of his 154 sonnets. Time also has to be found for the composition of three thousand lines of verse that make up his first two narrative poems, *Venus and Adonis* and *Lucrece.*

And when he was not writing, he was reading books: many books. These were to become the sources he used for his plays; some of which were still in the foreign language of their first printing.

Is this unbelievable? Is it ridiculous? Not at all; read Shakespeare's 'biographies'; it is there to be found in expanded form, but not in words that reveal the absurdity of what passes as *thinking* in the minds of those who believe Shaxpere capable of so much activity within such a limited time span.

To add to this injury to common sense, his biographers also require readers to accept that the full range of the Histories and Tragedies were composed anew; fresh from the learning of a man without any *known* education or theatrical background, and that his Comedies were the inspiration of a man never once known to have made a single person laugh—unless it was in the yard of the slaughterhouse, where he worked as a butcher's apprentice before relocating to London; but, this is denied by his biographers, and so even that has to be discounted.

Astonishingly, the perpetuation of this self-imposed deceit is so infectiously gratifying to Shakespeare's admirers that it dulls the critical ability of even the most intelligent amongst them. It certainly draws Shaxpere's biographers into a world of make-believe: amongst whom, there can sometimes be discerned a slight tremor of unease at what they are required to profess.

What has helped to bring this strange situation about can be traced to the impassioned words and phrases of the sonneteer, which many have attempted to dampen down or diffuse, in order to preserve the author's reputation. Yet, occasionally, the truth is allowed to break through:

> *'Pederastic infatuation' sums up very well what confronts us in the sonnets. No amount of hot air about Elizabethan friendship can evade the fact that no other Elizabethan wrote a long sequence of sonnets to a boy.*[19]

In fact, Oxford actually does refer to the object of his passion as *"a boy"* in Sonnets 108 and 126.

> . . .
> *What's new to speak, what new to register,*
> *That may express my love or thy dear merit?*
> *Nothing, sweet boy; but yet, like prayers divine*
> *I must each day say o'er the very same;*
> *Counting no old thing old, thou mine, I thine,*
> *Even as when first I hallowed thy fair name,*
> *So that eternal love in love's fresh case*
> *Weighs not the dust and injury of age,*
> *Nor gives to necessary wrinkles place,*
> *But makes antiquity for aye his page . . .* (cviii)
>
> ꙮ
>
> *Oh thou, my lovely boy, who in thy power*
> *Dost hold Time's fickle glass, his sickle hour;*
> *Who hast by waning grown, and therein show'st*
> *Thy lovers withering as thy sweet self grow'st;*
> . . . (cxxvi)

This love for a *"sweet boy"* by an older man, whose countenance shows the wrinkles of time, is expressed in the lines of Sonnet 108. A prematurely balding Shaxpere in his late twenties is the supposed explanation for the poet believing himself to be old. But, wrinkled? Surely not!

The final couplet confirms *"time and outward form"* would normally prevent love from developing between the poet and a boy less than half his age, but this has been overcome; *viz.*

> *Finding the first conceit of love there bred*
> *Where time and outward form would show it dead.*

The poet has also given praise to the *"lovely boy"* who presently holds the advantage of *"Time's fickle glass."* And while he increases in complexion, Time withers those who are his lovers. But, in this there is warning.

Yet fear her, O thou minion of her pleasure!
She may detain, but not still keep her treasure;
Her audit, though delay'd, answer'd must be,
And her quietus is to render thee. (cxxvi)

In June 1590, Oxford celebrated his fortieth birthday; Southampton was only sixteen. The following sonnet seems to sum up the poet's feelings upon reaching this milestone in life. It also has particular relevance to the marriage plans proposed by Lord Burghley at that time, since the verse draws to its end by urging the youth to beget a child, thereby *"Proving his beauty by succession"*.

When forty winters shall besiege thy brow,
And dig deep trenches in thy beauty's field,
Thy youth's proud livery, so gaz'd on now,
Will be a tatter'd weed of small worth held.
. . .
How much more praise deserv'd thy beauty's use,
If thou couldst answer 'This fair child of mine
Shall sum my count, and make my old excuse,' (ii)

The entire thrust of this book has been to prove that the 17th Earl of Oxford wrote plays and poetry under the pen name of William Shakespeare. The close attachment between *Shakespeare* and Southampton, or alternatively between Oxford and Southampton, is verified by their partnership when posing as poet and patron for the publication of *Venus and Adonis* and *The Rape of Lucrece* (Chapter 2 refers to this in detail).

This collusion between a man past forty and a youth still not twenty, which also involved a hoax performed upon the buying public, implies a past between the two participants. That past is expressed most notably in *Shake–speare's Sonnets.*

Equally notably, the content of the more revealing poems proved to be a *cause célèbre* in the eyes of their peer group. And it was for this reason that every effort was made to force Oxford into disowning what he had written. The persuasive force of higher authority succeeded, and a stand-in from the lower classes was paid to adopt them by name only. It was therefore through Shaxpere's participation in this pretence that the written and revealing record of Oxford's relationship with Southampton was able to disappear from public record.

Sceptics are apt to protest at the absence of any supporting documents—apart from the sonnets, of course. Yet, while aware that scandals in high places are inclined to produce a vanishing effect with regard to incriminating documents, lest they fall into the wrong hands, the same voice of dissent fails to admit this would also be an inevitable consequence of a paederastic affair between Southampton and Oxford. Let us again recall the words of William Camden, who referred to: *"those who think the memory of succeeding ages may be extinguished by present power."*

The facts about the two men cannot be easily extinguished. We know that both Oxford and Southampton were addicted to plays and to literature. To this effect, there exists an early 18th century drawing and set of plans relating to Southampton's home at Titchfield Abbey (also known as Titchfield House or Place House), which describes a Playhouse room. Guides to the House continue to show visitors where it existed. Moreover, since there have been no major structural alterations to the House since Southampton's time, the plans can be considered authentic.

Southampton also bequeathed his library, valued at £300 (≈ £85,000) to St. John's College, Cambridge. We know, too, that upon reaching the age of eight, he became a ward of Lord Burghley, who was then responsible for his care, education and moral welfare.

Between the ages of twelve and sixteen, Southampton was studying at Cambridge, and it was after his return to the Burghley household, in order to enrol at Gray's Inn in February 1588, that Oxford's fascination for this youth must have begun.

That same year Oxford's wife died, and Nicholas Hilliard painted the portrait of a man, identifiably that of Oxford, dressed in mourning black, implying recent bereavement. A legend on the painting's perimeter describes the subject as a captive of *"Attic love"* – a euphemism for pederasty. A woman's outstretched hand reaches down from heaven to clasp the man's right hand. It appears the bereaved man's wife is lovingly reaching out to him in an effort to support him against his sin. In every single respect, these facts fit de Vere as Hilliard's subject, and Queen Elizabeth as the commissioner, for only she could have done this without offending the sensitivity of Oxford (p.266).

Like many Elizabethans of his day, Oxford was not averse to a punning reference when the opportunity arose. Thus in Sonnet 76, he alludes to his name three times as the author of this verse.

Why write I still all one, euer the same,
And keep inuention in a noted weed,
That euery word doth almost fel my name,
Shewing their birth and where they did proceed?

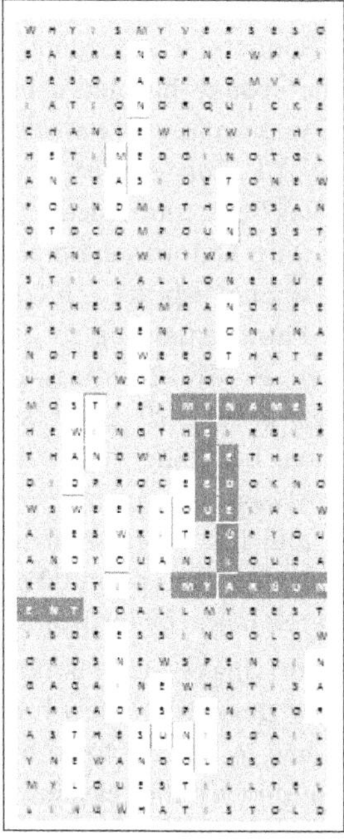

"Euer the same" can be rearranged to mean *'the same ever'*; that is, 'the same E Ver.'

A different method used by Vere to identify his authorship set a trend that others were to follow. He encrypted LO E. DE VERE, between the words "MY NAME" and "MY ARGUMENT"; using 14 columns as the key, in place of a template, so as to coincide with the number of lines in a sonnet *(1609 text used).

The median expectation that these words will occur by chance on any grille, in either one or two columns, above or below the words MY NAME, and with at least one of the encrypted words abutting MY NAME, has been calculated to occur just once in more than 9¼ million trials.

Hence, with a magnitude of 9,259,259 to 1, the encryption must be considered genuine. The probability supporting this calculation is given in Appendix B.

The third line to the verse overleaf is also the third reference to de Vere's name. By transposing just two words, the line reads:

* Dr J. S. Ferris independently arrived at a similar conclusion, although his preference was to include S on the end of NAME, and to use the ED beneath VERE. The result then reads "MY NAME'S DE VERE".

"That word 'every' doth almost tell my name." This has the same meaning as if the words had remained in place. All it requires is emphasis to be placed upon 'every'. For then, that word *every* does *almost* spell 'E Vere'; which, as he remarks in his 14-column encryption, is *"my name"*. Nor must we overlook the fourth line of this excerpt. When questioning his *every word*, the poet, knowing well the answer, asks – *"Shewing their birth and [from] where they did proceed?"* Their birth, and from where they did proceed was from his mind and pen as he has emphatically made clear. *

So much of what Oxford did was original. This example was also a 'first' in using Cardano's method of encryption to conceal the truth of his authorship. The idea was copied by Thorpe for his introductory remarks prefacing the Sonnets. It was adopted next by Jonson for his encryption in the sixaine he placed beneath the bust of Shaxpere at Stratford-upon-Avon. It was also employed by Digges in *Poems Written by Wil. Shake-speare, Gent.* In each of these cases, de Vere's identity has been confirmed by a second method of encryption, thus following Oxford's example. For Digges, it was the caped engraving of 'Shakespeare', clutching a sprig of belvedere and the poet's name emerging in the seventeenth column of an ELS of eighteen; for Thorpe it was his 6-2-4 encryption coupled with his alternating 9-10 letter sequence, both confirming de Vere to have been the author of *Shake-speare's Sonnets.* And for Jonson, it was his personal vow that Edward de Vere was Shakespeare, and his appeal that he should be tested: confirmed, also by his second encryption taken from the classics, which referred to de Vere's name by birthright.

De Vere's right to be known as William Shakespeare is now established by his own hand, as well as by those who knew him personally. The fact it was a secret that had to be encrypted for future generations to find, has as much to do with the reason for its secrecy as for the threat against those who wanted to reveal it.

---

* The words surrounding LO E. DE VERE on the 14-column grille, which read upwards, in the direction of "My Name", indicate the lack of any coherence expected from their random distribution. It is virtually impossible that a randomly produced cluster of words composed in the present manner could make an informed, grammatical statement about the theme of the original text. Hence, encrypting the author's name – his name being a major theme of the sonnet – signals a deliberate intention on the part of the sonneteer.

Torture, mutilation, imprisonment and possible death awaited those who thought to act differently. But now the truth is out. The 17th Earl of Oxford was William Shakespeare.

"Ever the same" is the English translation for SEMPER IDEM, Queen Elizabeth's motto. It would have been impossible for a scholar of Oxford's standing not to have realised this. In which case, one can discern the poet acknowledging that Her Majesty would read his verse, and that she would see herself addressed in these terms, where *you* in place of *thou* would also be obligatory.

Wriothesley's name, too, is alluded to in the sonnets; when it is pronounced with a short 'i' and a long 'o', it becomes 'Roseley'. Bate confirmed this pronunciation as fact, adding that Southampton's descendants attested to it during the 19th century (Bate, 1997 p. 47). It is therefore not surprising to find that no less than six sonnets play on the word 'rose'.

From fairest creatures we desire increase,
That thereby beauty's rose might never die, (i)

This is the first of the sonnets urging matrimony. Southampton's reading of *"beauty's rose"* could hardly fail to strike him as a deliberate play upon his name. Another sonnet that draws its inspiration from the rose occurs in No. 54.

The rose looks fair, but fairer we it deem
For that sweet odour which doth in it live.
...
But for their virtue only is their show,
They live unwoo'd, and unrespected fade;
Die to themselves. Sweet roses do not so;
Of their sweet deaths are sweetest odours made.

Then, in the final couplet, the poet issues his denouement.

And so of you, beauteous and lovely youth,
When that shall vade [fade], my verse distils your truth.

Within this verse, it can be seen how the rose has been used to provide for the conclusion in the final couplet. Once again, Wriothesley, the *youth,* could hardly avoid acknowledging that this was deliberately intended to play upon his surname.

By the time we reach Sonnet 95, there are signs of a growing disappointment in the poet's perception of the youth.

How sweet and lovely dost thou make the shame
Which, like a canker in the fragrant rose,
Doth spot the beauty of thy budding name!

The youth's reputation has been marred by some recent activity, and this has brought shame upon him. The poet likens it to *"canker in the fragrant rose"*. The analogy between the *rose* and the youth's name therefore seems inescapable.

In the fourth line the connection receives further emphasis, when the poet addresses the young man, referring to his *"budding name."* At the time these poems were composed, Wriothesley, *"the rose"*, was still *"budding"*.

Thomas Nashe had also divined the connection between Wriothesley's name and the rose bud. And he must have been one of those to whom Meres referred in *Palladis Tamia,* when he gave the world its first report of Shakespeare's *"sugared Sonnets among his private friends"*.

Nashe's inclusion amongst 'Shakespeare's' *"private friends"* is to be expected, since he was in company with *"my Lord"* upon his return from the country in 1592, when the two joined Marlowe and Greene for a banquet at the Steel Yard one late summer's day. This meeting of minds was to precede Greene's death and herald the emergence of *Shakespeare* as the poet who wrote *Venus and Adonis.*

Nashe's Prologue to his *Choice of Valentines,* dedicated to Southampton also include lines referring to him as a 'rose'.

Pardon, sweet flower of matchless Poetry
And fairest bud that red rose ever bore
...
Ne blame my verse of loose unchastity
For painting forth the things that hidden are.

That Nashe sees Southampton as the *"sweet flower"* of Oxford's *"matchless Poetry"* suggests he had read the Sonnets. This tends to confirm he was one of the *"private friends"* mentioned by Meres. But Nashe never once mentions Shakespeare.

Nevertheless, we see that Nashe has identified the flower as a budding rose: thereby repeating 'Shakespeare's' own means of identifying Southampton. Nashe then addresses the young nobleman with a plea not to be blamed for the composition of his verse: which, he suggests, appears to bring to the fore, *"things that hidden are."*

From this, we are again made aware that Shake-speare's Sonnets are focussed upon Henry Wriothesley, and both author and youth were involved in some dark secret known to only a few.

When we arrive at Sonnet 109, the poet finally and unmistakeably reveals that the rose is, indeed, metaphorically, the youth.

O, never say that I was false of heart,
Though absence seem'd my flame to qualify!
...
For nothing this wide universe I call
Save thou, my rose; in it thou art my all.

Henry Wriothesley (compare W-**R**-i-**O**-t-h-e-**S**-l-**E**-y), was known privately as 'Rose': the teenage 3rd Earl of Southampton. Henry was also a name the poet *"hallowed"*; that is to say, a name to which he was devoted. He entered Oxford's life in the late 1580s, which coincides, time wise, with Oxford's preparations in 1592 for publication of *Venus and Adonis*; in which Southampton was to play the part of patron to a poet, newly arrived in the capital city from the midlands—William Shakespeare.

Further confirmation that the youth was Southampton can be found in Sonnets 3 and 13, where the poet correctly refers to the youth's parents. The 2nd Earl of Southampton died in 1581, which is why his eight-year-old heir to the title came to be a ward of Lord Burghley's. But the boy's mother, who was quite a beauty in her day, was very much alive when the bulk of these sonnets were composed, and Oxford, who had known her in her prime, makes this reference to her early glamour (picture 284).

Thou art thy mother's glass, and she in thee
Calls back the lovely April of her prime; (iii)

ꙮ

... *Dear my Love, you know*
You had a father: let your son say so. (xiii)

The fact should not be missed that the poet is able to refer back in time, with a naturalness born from familiarity, to when the youth's mother was in the springtime of her life. This must exclude Shaxpere as the sonnet writer. At the time of Southampton's birth and infancy, he would have been at home in Stratford-upon-Avon, still in his boyhood. The poet also refers to the youth's mother in the present tense, indicating that she was still alive. But he refers to the youth's father in the *past tense*, thereby indicating he had died.

The relationship between de Vere and Wriothesley was to have two further effects. In February 1593, Oxford's second wife gave birth to a son. His name, new to the Oxford line of succession, unbroken for five hundred years, was Henry.

This has caused some to consider if Henry de Vere was truly the son of Oxford. It is not a totally idle thought, since Oxford had declined the marital bed of his first wife because he resented the marriage. Did history repeat itself? Did he choose the name Henry in the fashion that Anne Vavasor named her son Edward to identify the father? Oxford should have delighted in the late arrival of an heir to his name and family line. Yet, the evidence is that he rejected his son to such a degree that as soon as Henry became sexually active, he turned to homosexuality.* Thus, we find his mother complaining bitterly at his frequent bedding of John Hunt, a cousin.

The second effect emerged much later, when Henry had succeeded to his father's title. Many reading this will be aware that a lasting friendship between two families can sometimes perpetuate itself into the succeeding generation. In this respect,

there survives an equestrian etching by Thomas Jenner, dating from about 1620 (Walpole Society Vol. Viii, G xxviii), which shows Southampton and the 18th Earl of Oxford together (see picture). A caption declares: *'the two most noble Henries revived.'* *"One of the two meant by that phrase must be Henry V."*[20] In which case, the title is acknowledging the close relationship that had existed between the author of *Henry V* and Henry Wriothesley. If the 18th Earl and Henry Wriothesley were actually father and son, this would also account for their togetherness.

* Joseph Nicolosi: *Reparative Therapy of Male Homosexuality*, Lanham, 1991

Further indication of the friendship existing between Oxford and Southampton occurs in *Willobie His Avisa:* a book that was *"called in"* after a pirated version re-appeared at the turn of the 16th century. It may therefore be concluded that with the sudden emergence of books, poems and pamphlets openly naming Shakespeare – Meres' book having given the green light to this name appearing in print – it suggested to a wily publisher that he, too, might profit from the name. But *Avisa* went too far in the eyes of the censor. For although the book was not about the earls of Oxford and Southampton, the hoax played by Oxford in publishing *Venus and Adonis* and *Lucrece* under the authorship of William Shakespeare, was alluded to in *Avisa:* even to the extent of identifying the two earls by their initials.

> *[Willobie His Avisa was] one of the books ... called in by the High Commission in 1599. The poem, first published in 1594, consists of 74 serviceable but uninspired songs and a few other poems. They narrate the unsuccessful courting of Avisa ... by four foreign suitors [after her marriage]. The last of these [identified as H.W.] has a "familiar friend W.S." as a companion; he has been identified with Shakespeare, who is also mentioned as author of The Rape of Lucrece in prefatory verses.* [21]

In fact, apart from these initials, and the *familiar* friendship between the two, to whom this poem refers, *Willobie* provided the first known reference to Shakespeare's name in print. And it did so by hyphenating the name, just as Thorpe would do 15 years later when the Sonnets were published.

> *Yet* Tarquyne *pluckt his glistering grape,*
> *And* Shake-speare *paints poore* Lucrece *rape.*

The name was also hyphenated in two of the tributes to 'Shakespeare' appearing in the First Folio. One can only look in vain for similar hyphenations at that time addressing, perhaps, Beau-mont, or Mar-lowe, or Spen-ser, or Flet-cher, or Jon-son, or Hem-inge, or Cond-elle, or Burb-age. The reason these names never appeared hyphenated is because they were people who were known by their unhyphenated names, just as Shaxpere's name was never hyphenated in his business dealings; for in the commercial environment where he operated, he was known by his unhyphenated name.

In 1594, the Sonnets were still unknown to the public, and their revealing content would remain hidden for another fifteen years. One can therefore see a possible connection between the pirated publication of the two sonnets 138 and 144 that did make it into the public domain in 1599, and the banning of satire in June of that same year. *Willobie*, as we shall discover, was more than a little involved in what was happening *"amongst the greater sort."* Placing this poem on the list of books to be burnt in 1599 could therefore be construed as the censor's response to Sonnet 144, wherein the poet makes a most compromising admission: *"Two loves I have, of comfort and despair ... / The better angel is a man right fair."*

The censor's action in banning *Willobie* can therefore be seen as the best means available for preventing the poem's reference to W.S. and his familiar friend H.W. becoming identified with William Shakespeare and Henry Wriothesley, the *"man right fair"*. For behind this banning of *Willobie* was a desperate attempt to protect the three noble families of Burghley, Southampton, and Oxford, which were in danger of becoming embroiled in a scandal involving homosexuality, and even pederasty.

The fact that a scandal was avoided, although hardly without an undercurrent of rumour, speaks volumes for the power of censorship and the warning, which the burning of books sent out to the public.

Apart from the initials W.S. and H.W. being those of William Shakespeare and Henry Wriothesley, *Willobie* also referred to H.W. as having had a *"fantastical fit"*. This adjective is the same one that had greeted Lord Burghley during his search for a suitable bride for Southampton; he is *"so fantastical"*, Lady Manners told the Lord Treasurer, when rejecting her own daughter as a suitable match.

Elsewhere in the poem, H.W. confesses to his youthfulness, *"If years I want ..."* At the age of twenty, Southampton could still, with justification, make this remark. H.W. also admits, *"I love, that never loved before."* This, too, identifies Southampton: Burghley had been trying to find a suitable wife for his young ward for some time, but without success. In the process of considering his options, Elizabeth Vere had been proposed, but Southampton declined to go through with the marriage. The author of *Willobie* has clearly seized upon Southampton's opposition to a woman's love, and used this as an indicator to further identify H.W. as Henry Wriothesley.

Oxford, who only one year before publication of *Willobie His Avisa,* had begun publishing his own poetry under the guise of William Shakespeare, was then forty-four years of age. In the continuing satire of *Willobie,* W.S. is described as: *"the old player."* Average life expectancy for a man during the 16th century was less than fifty. Apart from which, Oxford had, by 1594, already acquired a reputation for court performances: something he refers to in Sonnet 110, where he describes himself as having *"made myself a motley to the view"*, and which Albert Feuillerat also referred to in his treatise on John Lyly, in 1910, citing Oxford as *"le meilleur acteur comique de son temps"* [22] [the best comic actor of his time].

By considering Sonnet 29, we learn something of Oxford's reaction to his inner turmoil and the threat of public scandal.

When in disgrace with Fortune and men's eyes,
I all alone beweep my outcast state,
And trouble deaf heaven with my bootless cries,
And look upon myself, and curse my fate...

Yet, despite these feelings of remorse, he continued to seek consolation from the cause of his public disgrace, as the rest of the sonnet reveals.

Yet in these thoughts myself almost despising,
Haply I think on thee, and then my state,
Like to the lark at break of day arising
From the sullen earth, sings hymns at heaven's gate;
For thy sweet love rememb'red such wealth brings
That then I scorn to change my state with kings.

This final line confirms his resolve to continue the intimate relationship he enjoyed with Southampton, despite his inner anguish and the shame accompanying it.

After the death of Queen Elizabeth in 1603, the pressure on Oxford's association with Southampton found better sympathy with her successor. This may have been because of James I's own sexuality; he was bisexually inclined, and therefore likely to take a more lenient attitude towards Oxford and his relationship with Southampton. This was certainly evident from the financial benefits Oxford received from the newly appointed monarch.

> *Oxford's … claims to Waltham Forest and Havering House were confirmed on 18 July. A major goal of his life had finally been achieved. Yet another piece of good news came on 2 August, when James issued a reconfirmation of Oxford's £1000 annuity.* [23]

Oxford's rise in fortune came in the wake of even better news. Three months earlier, Southampton had been released from the Tower, where he had been imprisoned to live out the remainder of his life for the part he played in Essex's rebellion of 1601. But, after just two and a half years he was once again a free man.

It is not wholly unusual for political prisoners to be given their freedom when a new leader succeeds to power, but in Southampton's case, it would appear that Oxford had agreed to stand guarantor for the Earl's future loyalty to the crown. This became evident when, fifteen months after his release from prison, news of Oxford's death was brought to the King. That same evening Southampton was re-arrested and placed under guard.

> *Southampton's papers were seized and scrutinized. He himself was interrogated. According to the French Ambassador, King James had gone into a complete panic and could not sleep that night even though he had a guard of his Scots posted around his quarters. Presumably to protect his heir he sent orders to Prince Henry that he must not stir out of his chamber.* [24]

What other circumstance could conceivably have motivated King James into ordering the imprisonment of Southampton just hours after being informed of Oxford's death? It can only have been the removal of the one man who was known to have control over this rebellious young earl.

With Oxford's demise, the guarantee he had given to James for the safe conduct of Southampton expired, and the control he exercised over this former rebel and men under his command, expired with him. The King's state of panic was understandable.

According to this scenario, Oxford's relationship with Southampton had endured from the time when the latter was still a boy; that is, no later than 1588, and had lasted up until Oxford's death in 1604: a space of sixteen years.

In 1603, after Southampton's release, the stress of his trial and the threat of decapitation must have left their mark on his features. His death sentence had only been commuted to life imprisonment after Cecil succumbed to pleas made by the condemned man's wife and mother. One therefore suspects that upon his release, he looked far more careworn than before his imprisonment. Sonnet 104 has all the correct ingredient to have been Oxford's response to his friend's liberation. It is also in the grammatical form of one nobleman talking to another.

To me, fair friend, you never can be old,
For as you were when first your eye I ey'd,
Such seems your beauty still. Three winters cold
Have from the forests shook three summers' pride,
Three beauteous springs to yellow autumn turn'd
In process of the seasons have I seen,
Three April perfumes in three hot Junes burn'd,
Since first I saw you fresh, which yet are green.

The emphasis is upon three years of absence. Southampton was arrested on 8 February 1601 and released 10 April 1603: a total time of two years and two months, but which includes the "*three April perfumes*". The missing time can be accounted for by Southampton's involvement with the Essex clan, which included his brief return from France to wed Robert Devereux's pregnant cousin, Elizabeth Vernon. Southampton knew that Oxford's loyalty to the Queen would never allow him to remain silent if it became known that Essex and he were involved in a rebellion against the Crown. Secrecy was paramount, and this adequately explains Southampton's absence from Oxford during the months before the rebellion.

Oxford's opening words in the sonnet appear to be his reaction to the younger man's own awareness that he had aged since they last met. One would expect some change in appearance after three years absence, but the poet's remark, and his reassurance, when dismissing his friend's concern, can be interpreted as more than casual. There is also an emphasis upon the change of seasons. This, too, is indicative of someone who has recently been incarcerated, and had only the progression of the seasons, seen through the bars of a cell window, by which to judge the passage of time.

When Southampton was released from the Tower, he was not yet thirty. Oxford's observation he was still *"green"* is therefore appropriate. Had Queen Elizabeth lived, Southampton could have expected to remain imprisoned indefinitely. This is indicated in Sonnet 107.

Not mine own fears, nor the prophetic soul
Of the wide world dreaming on things to come,
Can yet the lease of my true love control,
Suppos'd as forfeit to a confin'd doom.

Oxford is talking about his *"own fears"* for the future, which he associates with those of the *"wide world";* that is, not only those prevailing in England, but the similar fears that existed abroad, and which were giving rise to prognostications from pundits concerning the future, and what it may hold when the Queen died without heir. Yet, these thoughts, he says, are downplayed by the recent release of Southampton, his *"true love",* freed from *"a confined doom"* inside the Tower. Reference to the death of Elizabeth follows: symbolized by her love for lunar analogies.

The mortal moon hath her eclipse endur'd,

'Eclipse' is from the Greek 'ekleipō' *"fail to appear"* OED. No one at that time could have failed to understand who was meant by this expression, for it was *"Queen Elizabeth I* who *was often depicted with a crescent moon as her headdress."* [25] At the height of his attachment to Elizabeth, Raleigh wrote of *The Ocean's Love to Cynthia. "Cynthia. The moon; a surname of Artemis or Diana. The Roman Diana who represented the moon was called Cynthia"* [26] 'Shakespeare' was therefore referring to the Queen's demise, which occurred in the early hours of 24 March 1603.

Some have disputed this meaning, believing that 'her eclipse endured' is an inappropriate use of language for expressing the Queen's death. Instead, they believe it refers to the formation of the Spanish Armada in 1588, which from an aerial view was said to be likened to a crescent. But quite why an armada should be referred to as 'her' and not 'it' is left unexplained. 'Shakespeare' would presumably agree, for both 'endure', and 'eclipse', are employed by him when referring to the death of a person.

EDGAR: Men must endure
Their going hence, even as their coming hither,
Ripeness is all.

King Lear (Act 5: sc.ii)

TALBOT: Then here I take my leave of thee, fair son,
Born to eclipse thy life this afternoon.
Come, side by side together live and die;
And soul with soul from France to heaven fly.

1 Henry VI (Act 4: sc.v)

Thus, too, did Queen Elizabeth 'endure her eclipse', when her soul from England to heaven flew.

Note how TALBOT'S words imply a biblical connotation, and it is this, presumably, that often impedes the understanding of Sonnet 107. *Shakespeare* lived in an age immersed in religious thought. Secular teaching offers poor preparation for understanding any text that refers to the Christian beliefs of those who lived at that time, especially when it refers to death.

There is also a special political meaning to the Queen's mortality. *"When she ascended the throne ... the queen's whole being was profoundly altered: her mortal 'body natural' was wedded to an immortal 'body politic'."* This, she acknowledged in her succession speech: *"I am but one body, naturally considered, though by [God's] permission a Body Politic to govern".* [27] When she died, it was her mortal self that was eclipsed by the immortal Body Politic, who emerged in the form of James VI of Scotland, to become James I of England.

The sonnet then continues by recalling how *"the sad augurs mock their own presage."* The doubts and uncertainties that preceded Elizabeth's demise were caused by the absence of an obvious successor to the throne. Asking Elizabeth to decide the regnal consequences of her passing was illegal. This led to much private speculation at home, also abroad, for England was still at war. But to be at war without a recognised leader bred thoughts that soon gave way to dire possibilities of the consequences.

> *In the mean time several serious deliberations were held in the council with regard to the succession ... great numbers of idle and suspected persons, who swarmed in the metropolis and adjacent villages, were seized and sent to Holland, for the Dutch service. The fleet which lay ready equipped was ordered to guard the mouth of the Thames: the sea ports were all shut, and the lady Arabella Stuart taken into custody. It was also resolved to summon all the peers to town, and if any commotion should happen on the queen's death, which was now hourly suspected, to make the earl of Northumberland general of the forces.*[28]

However, once the smooth transition of power was successfully accomplished, the pessimists were reduced to laughing off their fears; seeing instead, how *"Incertainties now crown themselves assured / And peace proclaims olives of endless age."*

Uncertainties were crowned, literally, in the form of James I, King of Great Britain and Ireland. The King was given every assurance of loyalty from the nobility, as he journeyed south to the capital.

In Church affairs, the *Millenary Petition* of 1603 led to the King arranging the *Hampton Court Conference* in which he played a leading role, threatening to *"harry from the land"* those who were opposed to the established church. At the same time he entered into negotiations with Philip II to end sixteen years of warfare between Spain and England.

> *James showed his abilities from the first. In the counties through which he passed on his way to London he lavished royal bounty upon the elites who had been starved for honours during Elizabeth's parsimonious reign. He knighted hundreds as he went, enjoying the bountiful entertainments that formed such a contrast with his indigent homeland.*[29]

His efforts proved highly successful, and the *Treaty of London* was signed in 1604 shortly after the death of Oxford, who, as a member of the Privy Council, would have had prior knowledge of the forthcoming negotiations for peace. This would explain the next passage:

Now with the drops of this most balmy time
My love looks fresh, and Death to me subscribes,
Since spite of him I'll live in this poor rhyme,
While he insults o'er dull and speechless tribes.

As part of James' efforts to turn over a new leaf in England's political life, he released the 3rd Earl of Southampton from the Tower, where he had been *"forfeit to a confined doom"*. Oxford then remarked how fresh his love looks: recalling a similar expression in Sonnet 104: *"Since first I saw you fresh, which yet are green."*

But it was a view he held in direct contrast to a presentiment he had of his own approaching end. One can see from this simple comparison why traditionalists shy away from the Sonnets as biography, preferring to see them as poetical exercises, born from imagination, rather than factual experiences of the author.

In 1603, Will Shaxpere was 38 rising 39: he had nearly one third of his life ahead of him. It was Oxford who was entering his final year in this life. It was also Oxford, his name obliterated from all association with the plays and poetry he had written, who was now reduced to the sad reality that, despite his approaching death, his words would live on in the memories of succeeding generations: fulfilling the promise he made to Southampton.

And thou in this shalt find thy monument,
When tyrants' crests and tombs of brass are spent. (cvii)

Self-revealing Lines

The Sonnets are also a rich source for providing other clues to Oxford's authorship. Professor Alan Nelson, a well-known anti-Oxford campaigner, recorded Oxford's lameness in his book, *Monstrous Adversary*. The reference to this disability occurs in a letter from Oxford to Burghley, in which he offered to attend *"at yowre house ('as well as a lame man may')."*[30] We know from this that Oxford was lame. But we also know from Sonnets 37 and 89 that *Shakespeare*, too, was lame.

Say that thou didst forsake me for some fault,
And I will comment upon that offence;
Speak of my lameness, and I straight will halt; (lxxxix)

ꕥ

As a decrepit father takes delight
To see his active child do deeds of youth,
So I, made lame by Fortune's dearest spite,
Take all my comfort of thy worth and truth;
. . .
So then I am not lame, poor, nor despis'd (xxxvii)

When Oxford wrote *Othello*, he included a scene in which IAGO stabs CASSIO in the leg from behind, before running away. CASSIO is left to cry out: *"I am maim'd for ever, light, ho, murder, murder!"* The leg wound was held to be so serious that CASSIO was thought to have died at one time. The same was believed about Oxford who also received a near fatal injury.

> *In England of late there hath bene a fray betwene my Lord of Oxford and Mr Thomas Knyvett of the Priuy Chamber, who are both hurt, but my lord of Oxford more dangerously:* (Nelson, p. 280).

The sonneteer records a similar outcome.

> *The earth can have but earth, which is his due;*
> *My spirit is thine, the better part of me.*
> *So then thou hast but lost the dregs of life,*
> *The prey of worms, my body being dead;*
> *The coward conquest of a wretch's knife,*
> *Too base of thee to be remembered.* (lxxiv)

The 17th Earl of Oxford, also the Lord Great Chamberlain of England was descended from one of the noblest families in the land, with an ancestry that went back to France before 1066. A sense of his pedigree and *"high birth"* are revealed in Sonnet 91, wherein he speaks of the trappings of the nobleman:

> *Some glory in their birth, some in their skill,*
> *Some in their wealth, some in their body's force;*
> *Some in their garments, though new-fangled ill;*
> *Some in their hawks and hounds, some in their horse;*

But these are mentioned only that the poet may denounce them in favour of his love for the youth. They are therefore not the words of a loving father to a son, nor are they in any sense paternalistic, as may be determined from what follows.

> *But these particulars are not my measure:*
> *All these I better in one general best.*
> *Thy love is better than high birth to me,*
> *Richer than wealth, prouder than garments' cost,*
> *Of more delight than hawks and horses be;* (xci)

Nor can it be overlooked that when the poet speaks of growing old, Oxford would have then been past his fortieth year. But in 1590, when Oxford was forty, Shaxpere was only twenty-five.

> *Sin of self-love possessive all mine eye,*
> *And all my soul, and all my every part;*
> ...
> *But when my glass shows me myself indeed,*
> *Beated and chopt with tann'd antiquity,*
> *Mine own self-love quite contrary I read;* (lxii)

Only special pleading by the Stratford fraternity can explain this as anything other than the mirror telling the poet the truth about himself. Moreover, Sonnet 2 not only confirms his age by recalling: *"When forty winters shall besiege thy brow, / And dig deep trenches in thy beauty's field,"* but, in Sonnet 63 he acknowledges how time's injurious hand now contrasts his features with the youth's fine looks: *"Against my love shall be as I am now, / With Time's injurious hand crush'd and o'erworn."* In this we see the poet confessing to being old at a time when Southampton was in his youth, and Shaxpere, a mere nine years older.

The low point in Oxford's life came after his wife's death in 1588. Some indication of his state of mind is provided in Sonnet 66, wherein a list of his woes is provided line by line. He begins with a despairing look at suicide: seeing himself in the deserted state of *"a begger born"*. One cannot help but recall HAMLET in a similar frame of mind, as he juggled with the big question in life – *"To be, or not to be?"* And, *"Whether 'tis nobler in the mind to suffer the slings and arrows of outrageous fortune, or to take arms against a sea of troubles, and by opposing end them?"* (*Hamlet:* 3. i).

Some notion of the slings and arrows that beset Oxford is given in the lines of this sonnet. High on the list is *"purest faith unhappily forsworn."* About *Shakespeare*, of whom one has reason enough to call Oxford, Ian Wilson writes:

> *[H]e must have attended many Protestant services for his subsequent plays are full of allusions to Protestant homilies and the words of the Protestant Prayer book – though this proves nothing as he would simply have been fulfilling what everyone was required to do to comply with the law.* [31]

Elizabeth Cottle and Christopher Dams in Chapter 18 of *Great Oxford* (Parapress, 2004) have described some of the biblical allusions that occur in *The Merchant of Venice.* Dr Roger Stritmatter, who had access to Oxford's *Geneva Bible* for his doctorate studies, made a long list of the Earl's annotated phrases, which he encountered amongst its pages: a considerable number of which subsequently appeared in Shakespeare's plays. (Refer: *The Marginalia of Edward de Vere's Geneva Bible: Providential Discovery, Literary Reasoning and Historical Consequence,* University of Massachusetts, 2001).

According to a report made by the French ambassador to England, Oxford converted to the Catholic faith at the age of twenty-six or thereabout.

> *On his return from Italy, [de Vere] made profession of the Catholic faith together with some of his relatives among the nobility and his best friends and had sworn, as he says, and signed with them a declaration that they would do all they could for the advancement of the Catholic religion.* [32]

Recalling his religious enthusiasm of earlier years, Oxford next confided to his sonnet the unhappiness he has come to feel at having renounced his faith. His dismay is followed by a further regret concerning: *"gilded honour shamefully misplaced."*

Unlike Shaxpere, the supposed author of this phrase, Oxford's noble ancestry, combined with a privileged education, had prepared him for entrance to any one of the highest offices in the land. But instead of serving Queen and country in a political capacity, he had chosen to use his intellect for the advancement of a profession that, in the eyes of his peer group, made him a figure of scorn and which humiliated him amongst the nobility. It also invited pity for his long-suffering family.

Writing plays for release in public, and placing one's self in the proximity of actors, hack writers and the lower classes, as those who frequented the theatre were deemed to be, was not considered suitable occupation for a senior member of the court. And the nobility will have left Oxford in no doubt concerning their disdain for his wayward connections with the public stage.

Oxford's next disfavour with himself was *"maiden virtue rudely strumpeted."* This must surely hark back to his seduction of Anne Vavasor. *"In 1580, aged fifteen she came to court under the tutelage of her Knyvet relatives, especially her aunt, the widow of Lord Henry Paget (d. 1568)."*[33] She soon became a target for conquest by both Walter Raleigh and de Vere; both wrote poems about her. One year later she gave birth to a son fathered by Oxford. It would appear this was her second pregnancy by Oxford: the first having ended abruptly in a miscarriage.

> *Ann Vavasour fared less well, having inconveniently given birth to a son in the chamber allocated to the maids of honour; Elizabeth was incensed and Ann was hauled off to the Tower in March. Oxford tried to smooth over the birth with a gift of £2000 [that is ≈* £560,000] *to*

the mother and property for the baby.[34]

It did nothing to appease the Queen, and Oxford joined Anne in the Tower. After their release, according to historian Gwynneth Bowen (Nelson, 2003, p.5), Anne, *"after a series of illicit love affairs ... married a sea captain named John Finche."*[35]

Another, counted amongst Anne's illicit lovers, was the elderly Queen's Champion at tilt, Sir Henry Lee, whose mistress she became, *"by pushing aside his wife–also Anne (née Paget)."*[36] In 1589, she gave birth to their son, Thomas Vavasor, who later became known as Thomas Freeman (Ogburn, 1984, p.661).

Interestingly, in a letter to Christopher Hatton, pleading for Oxford to be restored to Court, Burghley called Anne Vavasor a *"drab"*; i.e. a strumpet. Oxford's sonnet echoes this sentiment with his usage of *"strumpeted"*; for it had been his wilfulness in first bringing disgrace upon her that destroyed her reputation; thereafter, setting her on the path of social disgrace.

Oxford's next complaint was that of *"right perfection wrongfully disgrac'd."* One suspects this alludes to the charge made against him in 1581 by Charles Arundel.

> *Thus Arundel accuses Oxford of (1) atheism, (2) pathological lying, (3) subornation, (4) murder by hire, (5) sedition, (6) sexual perversion including pederasty, (7) chronic inebriation, (8) nursing of private grudges (especially against members of the Howard family), and (9) lèse majesté. Arundel follows up with one or more paragraphs on each accusation in turn.*[37]

Yet, despite the gravity of these accusations, which included No. 9, high treason, *"no one ever pressed charges, no lawsuits came out of the libels, no investigations were called, no further accusations emerged, no other scandals arose."*[38]

Let us therefore pursue Oxford's next grievance. It is his *"strength by limping sway disabled."* The poet's lameness has already been referred to in Sonnets 37 and 89, where he described the cause as, *"Fortune's dearest spite"*. Beyond that, there is only speculation. We are told that while in Italy, he cracked his shin in a boating mishap; as to whether the injury worsened, or whether he suffered a sword or dagger thrust from some assailant, as happened to CASSIO in *Othello*, these are conjectures. Suffice to say this reference to lameness is found in both the sonnets and in Oxford's letters; it was therefore understandably of major concern in his life, since he mentioned it several times.

We now come to a protest that was most dear to him: *"art made tongue-tied by authority."* This has echoes from an unnamed writer who declared: *"Shake-speare, we must be silent in thy praise."* And from Marston, who wrote of a poet, *"whose silent name one letter bounds."* It also reminds us of the censorship at that time, and the 'stigma of print', which gentlemen writers were bound to respect, if they wished to retain the title of gentleman. Thus, in a single phrase, Oxford bewails the silence imposed upon his art, especially by his own class, and by government authority.

Another bone of contention immediately follows this protest by singling out *"folly, doctor-like, controlling skill."* Oxford's greatest skill was that of a poet and playwright. His remark implies some form of control, or censorship, had been imposed on his artistic output. This is not at all remarkable. He lived in an age of censorship, and even though he was a high-ranking nobleman, the authorities would still have been anxious to vet his plays. The poet's reference to this being *doctor-like* would seem to refer to the surgeon's knife, and is a metaphorical reference to excising material considered injurious to the State.

Some evidence of censorship emerges in *Hamlet*, wherein CORAMBIS (Latin, Two-hearted) was seen as a too obvious pun on Burghley's family motto (One heart, One Way). People were bound to recognise this and connect the two. Steps had to be taken to avoid this happening. To prevent the possibility, Oxford changed the name to POLONIUS. It is wholly inconceivable that a similar request would have been so politely put to Shaxpere, had he been Shakespeare, and because of this, the Stratford professorship ignores it. This clears the way for them to protest there is no similarity between Burghley and POLONIUS.

> *... it is absurd to suppose that any Elizabethan play might contain satiric references to particular aristocrats of the day. Polonius cannot be a satirical portrait of Lord Burghley for the simple reason that if it were, the author of the portrait would have found himself in prison before he could turn around.*[39]

Absolutely true, if the poet were Shaxpere, but untrue if he were an earl married to Burghley's favourite daughter. Oxford was ahead of the game, and remained determined to associate the Lord Chamberlain in *Hamlet* with Lord Burghley. His second choice of name was POLONIUS: an epenthesis of Polus; that is, POL–oni–US. *'Polus is thrice applied to him [Burghley] in Gabriel Harvey's address at Audley End of 1578."* 40 Incidentally, the use of epenthesis as a coded reference dates back to the *Kama Sutra*.

Consequently, whether it is CORAMBIS or POLONIUS, it is still Lord Burghley, and the characteristics of both these officials are sufficiently alike as to be undeniable. Shaxpere would never have got away with this impudence against Elizabeth's Lord Treasurer: nor would he have dared try, even if he had been the great dramatist: as Professor Bate is persuaded to believe. On the other hand, Oxford, as a former ward of Burghley, then son-in-law, and finally father to his three grandchildren would have escaped all but a stern rebuke.

Evidence for the composition of *Hamlet* close to the time when the Sonnets were believed to have been written exists. We may recall (page 75) that a play called *Hamlet* was staged in June 1594 at the theatre in Newington Butts. A plaque on the wall of the Royal Crown Hotel in Oxford (recently removed by order of the town council, despite it being a tourist attraction akin to JULIET'S balcony in Verona) asserted that Shakespeare's *Hamlet* had been performed there in 1593. Four years before that, in his Epistle to Robert Greene's *Menaphon*, Thomas Nashe referred to *"whole Hamlets, I should say handfuls of Tragicall speeches."* Moreover, as pointed out by Ogburn *et al* (Ogburn, 1984 pp. 339-40), a speech by MARCELLUS is best understood as a witness's account of the preparations being made to meet the threat of Spain's Armada in 1588.

> Why this same strict and most observant watch
> So nightly toils the subject of the land;
> And why such daily cast of brazen cannon,
> And foreign mart for implements of war;
> Why such impress of shipwrights, whose sore task
> Does not divide the Sunday from the week; (Act I: sc. i)

Thus, HAMLET'S explanation that actors *"are the abstract and brief chronicles of the time,"* suggests it is to 1588 that one should turn for Oxford's composition of this play. This, of course, fits perfectly with Sonnet 66, for both sonnet and play deal with the subject of suicide: the former, with the author's thoughts on a self-inflicted death: the latter with a caricature of himself as HAMLET, who is also dwelling upon ending his life.

The father of psychoanalysis, Sigmund Freud, comfortably recognised the character of HAMLET as a self-portrait of Oxford. Pequigney followed this lead by acknowledging *"that the psychological dynamics of the poet's relations with the friend comply in large measure with those expounded in Freud's authoritative discussions of homosexuality."*[41]

Despite Freud's expertise in psychoanalysis, efforts were made to dissuade him from pursuing this line of enquiry, even displaying contempt towards him for maintaining it; for such has been the mesmeric effect that 'Shakespeare' exercises over his followers, it often translates into an impulse for verbal attack.

As the play unfolds, HAMLET mocks POLONIUS with banter that borders on his supposed madness. One suspects Burghley had levelled the accusation of madness against Oxford on account of his disreputable affair with Southampton, and for advertising his love for the youth to his friends, in what must have seemed a never-ending sequence of sonnets. Burghley must have been in total despair at what he conceived to be the madness of the situation, and doubtless said as much to Oxford.

His son-in-law's response was to allow HAMLET the vicarious pleasure of teasing POLONIUS by falsely feeding the ageing Lord Chamberlain with a speech affecting madness. In fact, HAMLET'S 'moment of madness' carries with it subtle undertones, which appear to stem from a deeper truth: as when he calls POLONIUS a *"Fishmonger"*. At its worst, this means a man who sells 'fish': the slang word for prostitutes. A depressed Oxford in a hateful disposition may well have seen his wife Anne as her father's pawn in a political power game: one in which she had been used to promote her father's dynastic ambitions by marrying into one of England's noblest families. But it is also true that Burghley had been responsible for adding Wednesday to Friday as a day for eating fish. J. Dover Wilson called him *"the fishmonger Secretary of State"*, because of his plan to enlarge the fishing fleet by urging people to eat fish twice a week. But his reasoning may have been to increase the number of ships available for war.

In the play, it soon becomes apparent that OPHELIA'S love for HAMLET is based upon Anne Cecil's love for Oxford. Hence,

LAERTES is seen as a hybrid of Anne's brothers, Robert and Thomas. Even the naming of LAERTES contains a touch of Oxford's darker humour. LAERTES was the name of Hercules' father: the progenitor of the strongest man in Greek mythology. By contrast, Robert Cecil was both frail and hunchbacked. The plays of Shakespeare, in reality are a treasure trove of Oxford's biographical details; which is the reason why Ben Jonson urged that he be tested to prove his authorship of Shakespeare's work.

Before ending his grievances, Oxford added two more; *"simple truth miscall'd simplicity,"* and *"captive good attending captain ill."* The meaning of the former would be self-explanatory if we knew what was in Oxford's mind at the time. Its significance seems bound up with what he had already complained about; which was, that his plays expressed simple truths, and his so-called simplicity existed in making these known with little regard for the consequences that might follow.

Authority, as it would appear, did not appreciate any simple truths, when they put civil order at risk. The deposition scene in *Richard II* expresses a simple truth, but not one that authority wished to see staged in public.

> *[B]oth the Queen herself and the Essex party ... regarded the play as a vehicle of political instruction ... When the play came to be printed in Quarto in 1597 the deposition scene, which may be regarded as the very heart of the action, was omitted, doubtless because the official licenser disapproved of it.* [42]

There is no suggestion that the scene deposing the King was written to incite similar thoughts amongst Elizabeth's subjects. It was, instead, composed solely as the dramatisation of an event that had passed into history. Nevertheless, it was cut from public performances; although, one presumes, not when Essex and Southampton commissioned it, for they wanted to prime their audience for the rebellion that was to follow next day.

Oxford's final objection to his reduced state of being was what he called a *"captive good attending captain ill."* One suggestion, as to its meaning, may be the suddenness of his second marriage, which was being planned at about the time this sonnet was written. Elizabeth Trentham would then be seen as the *"captive good"* – captive, because deprived of any real choice, she was pressured to leave court and take Oxford as a husband. By doing so, her role in life changed to one of *"attending"* her husband's 'chief' ill – *"captain ill"* – a desire, much despised by his family; that of continuing his intimate relationship with Southampton.

The concluding couplet does nothing to suggest a different explanation. Instead, Oxford expresses no pleasure at becoming a bridegroom for a second time. Instead, he bewails his situation: confessing it to be only the wish of not leaving the youth alone in the world, which prevents him from ending his life.

> *Tir'd with all these, from these would I be gone,*
> *Save that, to die, I leave my love alone.*

Oxford survived his forlorn state, and lived. A number of his close associates in the world of literature were less fortunate. Robert Greene died a pauper's death in September 1592. Christopher Marlowe, also close to Oxford, was murdered in a tavern brawl eight months later. Incidentally, the pierced eye that ended Marlowe's life, far from being accidental, was a known method of assassination. Thomas Kyd, Marlowe's fellow lodger, a dramatist and inciter of public outrages following the 'invasion' of Dutch shopkeepers, was pronounced dead in the following year. Thomas Watson, poet, classicist, and friend of Oxford and Marlowe he had dedicated his *Hekatompathia, The Passionate Century of Love* to Oxford in 1582 – was also in his grave by 1593, aged only thirty-six.

All, at one time, had been writers closely associated with Oxford, but within the space of two years, they were dead. And, by a curious coincidence, this was also the time when extreme measures were being undertaken to prevent the scandal of Oxford's relationship with Southampton breaking out into the public domain. Was there a connection? Three close contemporaries that did survive this period were Tom Nashe, Anthony Munday and John Lyly, all three had once served as trustworthy secretaries to Oxford. Such coincidences have a tendency of adding suspicion to these events.

In Sonnet 36, we catch a moment of reflection, when the poet looks back upon his departed friends.

> *When to the sessions of sweet silent thought*
> *I summon up remembrances of things past,*
> *And with old woes new wail my dear time's waste.*
> *Then can I drown an eye, unus'd to flow,*

For precious friends hid in death's dateless night,
...
But if the while I think on thee, dear friend,
All losses are restor'd, and sorrows end.

Assuming that this sonnet was composed in or after 1594, it confirms that Oxford's marriage to Mistress Trentham had not quenched his love for Southampton. Nevertheless, the newlywed Countess did produce the long-awaited male heir to the Oxford line. And since the wish she expressed in her last will and testament was to be buried alongside her husband, we may assume she possessed a forgiving streak: as did Anne Cecil.

It is with the subject of death that we arrive at what must be the most often quoted verses in the authorship debate, numbers 55, 72, and 81. While the first of these expresses *Shakespeare's* self-awareness of his literary gift and his confidence of having written verses that will endure for eternity, the other two sonnets state, with equal conviction, that he, personally, will very soon be quite forgotten.

It is a paradox for which no sensible solution exists, other than that Oxford was the poet in question. In fact, the nonsense of supposing that Shaxpere, with perverse vanity, wrote these lines, can be exceeded only by the slump in critical thinking from those who promote it as an explanation.

Not marble nor the gilded monuments
Of princes shall outlive this pow'rful rhyme; (lv)

ℵ〇ʒ

My name be buried where my body is,
And live no more to shame, nor me nor you! (lxxii)

ℵ〇ʒ

From hence your memory death cannot take,
Although in me each part will be forgotten.
Your name from hence immortal life shall have,
Though I, once gone, to all the world must die;
The earth can yield me but a common grave,
When you entombed in men's eyes shall lie.
Your monument shall be my gentle verse,
Which eyes not yet created shall o'er-read;

And tongues to be your being shall rehearse,
When all the breathers of this world are dead,
You still shall live, such virtue have my pen, (lxxxi)

Within these autobiographical announcements is yet further proof of Shakespeare's true identity. How is it possible for an artist: one who is fully cognizant of his own exemplary gift and knowing that because of it, his work will endure to the farthest reach of time; yet also know his name will never be associated with what he has written? It will be altogether forgotten; that upon his death, he will be buried, as are hosts of other unexceptional people, in a grave that will soon become neglected and ultimately ignored. There is only one true answer. It is because he knew, at the time of writing, that his work was being reassigned to another person, William Shaxpere of Stratford-upon-Avon: a literary nonentity who would bear his penname William Shakespeare. This person would live on, and by doing so would give immortality to Southampton: the inspiration of so many sonnets.

We shall conclude this section with one further statement by the poet that definitely alludes to his nobility. It is sonnet 125, which begins with a question the poet poses to himself, as much as to another person. *"Were't aught to me I bore the canopy, / With my extern the outward honouring?"* Canopies are the privilege and priority of a monarch. To openly contemplate carrying a canopy over the head of a king or queen, reveals the questioner to be a man of title. Shaxpere was not a man of title, nor does the verse suggest he had reached the age of dotage, which might be an excuse for his having dreamt of possessing one.

There were at least three occasions when a canopy was on view during Oxford's adult life – at the trial of Mary Stuart, when a canopy was erected to symbolise the presence of Elizabeth, and which the former Scottish Queen thought was there for her benefit; at the funeral of Elizabeth, and at the coronation of James I. The responsibility for carrying the canopy over a monarch at a coronation ceremony was a prerogative claimed by the barons of the Cinque Ports,[43] and not by the Lord Great Chamberlain. Oxford was therefore not asking: *"Was it aught to me . . ."* Instead, he was using the subjunctive, in the sense it was used in his plays.

HOTSPUR: O gentlemen, the time of life is short!
To spend that shortness basely were too long.
(*1 Henry IV*, Act V. sc. ii.)

Fowler's Modern English Usage gives 'would be' as the modem equivalent of 'were'. Hence, the poet is asking: *"Would it be anything to me (if / that) I carried the canopy?"* He then extends the question, by adding: *"Or laid great bases for eternity, / Which proves more short than waste or ruining."* Oxford has returned to a former theme, in which time reduces everything physical to waste and ruin. This leads him to the next part of his verse.

Have I not seen dwellers on form and favour
Lose all, and more, by paying too much rent,
For compound sweet forgoing simple savour—
Pitiful thrivers in their gazing spent?

As Gwynneth Bowen pointed out (*The Shakespeare Fellowship News-letter* : Spring 1956), *"The Lord Great Chamberlain was no dweller on form (ceremony) and favour—an expression which exactly describes the reciprocal arrangement of Grand Serjeanty."*

> *In medieval times the tenure of a Manor by virtue of rendering some personal service to the King was not uncommon. Such tenures, by Grand Serjeanty as it was called, were abolished in the 17th century, but the actual service continues to be rendered in two notable instances at a Coronation.*[44]

Oxford was therefore referring to a medieval practice, which allowed some manorial owners, who had once served the king in some way, to participate with a small gesture at his coronation. Essentially, it was a reciprocal *"favour"* granted by the monarch. The poet calls those favoured in this way: *"Pitiful thrivers"*. To thrive, at one time meant: *"to clutch, grip, seize for one's self,"* (*Concise Etymological Dictionary of the English Language,* Skeat, 1936). It would seem from this outburst that Oxford was thinking of the graspers, who overspent to obtain a favour at the King's coronation, which was no more than a vainglorious indulgence, to be pitied as such. This led him to protest, which is the point of his verse.

No, let me be obsequious in thy heart,
And take thou my oblation, poor but free,

Which is not mix'd with seconds, knows no art
But mutual render, only me for thee.

... the hereditary Lord Great Chamberlain, whose coronation services, which are connected with the charge of the King's bedchamber, the handing of a basin and towel at the banquet, and the preparation of the royal oblations.[45]

Gwynneth Bowen recognised the importance of the phrase 'royal oblations' and this led to her researching the coronation ceremony in detail. It was there she learned that *"the royal oblation consisted of bread and wine, an ingot of gold of a pound's weight ... and it was the duty of the Lord Great Chamberlain to pass these things to his sovereign as required."* [46]

We therefore have a sonnet, written by 'William Shakespeare' referring to the *"oblation"*, which was reserved for the Lord Great Chamberlain (17th Earl of Oxford) to administer personally to the King during his Coronation. This, the poet declared, was his personal privilege, *"poor but free"*; that *"knows no art"*; in other words, devoid of wiliness, as practised by those seeking favour. And, which is 'rendered mutually' between *"me"* and *"thee"*. In this, he was comparing his office at the coronation with *"favours"* obtained by estate owners, for duties they performed during the same ceremony.

The phrase: *"not mixed with seconds,"* as Canon Gerald Rendall indicated, was a reference to *"the sacrificial cake of pure wheaten flour,"* served to the King during the part of the service reserved for the *"bread and wine"*. [47] Professor Peter Alexander, in his Shakespeare glossary defined *"seconds"* as *"flour of second quality, so inferior elements"*. Hence, everything, this far, remains consistent with the sonnet's usage of words and duties connected to James I's coronation; and it takes us to the final couplet.

Hence thou suborn'd informer! A true soul,
When most impeach'd, stand least in thy control.

A *suborned informer* is a lawyer's term. C. K. Davis provides its legal definition in *Law in Shakespeare* (1884, p. 282) – *"The person who informs against or prosecutes in any of the king's courts those who offend against any law or penal statute."*

Gwynneth Bowen looked into de Vere's history at the time of James' coronation, and discovered that shortly before the death of Elizabeth: the Earl of Lincoln had dined with Oxford at Hackney. Over dinner, the subject of the succession had been discussed privately. However, Lincoln later informed Sir John Peyton, Lieutenant of the Tower, what had been said. Peyton then reported what he had been told in a letter dated 10 October 1603. Oxford, so it was claimed, had named Lord Hastings, the great-nephew of Lord Lincoln, as successor to the Queen. He had also suggested that *"there should meanes used to convaye him over into France, where he should fynde friends that wolde him a partye, of the which there was a precedent in former times"*.[48]

It transpires that Lincoln had claimed the right to bear the ball and cross at James' coronation, and to be the carver. But his claim was rejected. To recover his reputation, he wrote a letter, dated 21 September 1603, informing upon the dinner conversation he had had with Oxford, in which, he claimed, his host had offended against the statute forbidding discussion of the Queen's succession.

> *And those speeches of the Erles of Ox that yf any were sent into France (how small soever his title were) . . . made me feare, and think that thes men might doo the kyng good servyce in bewraying their knoledg, which I though my dyeuty to ympart, if I had any possible meanes to enforme hys maiestie. But it so pleasyd god that withyn few days after afore any advertisement culd be sent, I saw hys quyet entry and yet nevertheles went to the toure afore her maiesties death, I told Sir J. Peyton thereof . . . and others, beside my letters to hys maiestie.*[49]

It is noteworthy that Sir John Peyton's letter was sent three weeks after Lincoln's letter.

Oxford's sonnet complains of a perjured informer, thus denying the charge made against him. If Lincoln was meant to read this verse, then he would be reminded that a true person, when impeached, will no longer be under the control of whosoever had been manipulating him. But Lincoln's mental state was in doubt. When writing about this period, N. J. O'Conor, referred to Lincoln as *"almost insane"* (Godes Peace and the Queenes Vicissitudes of a House, 1539 – 1615).

The reader will be aware that many books have been written about Shakespeare's sonnets, in an effort to discover Shaxpere's 'fingerprints'. Yet, those found do not match the prints of Shaxpere; they are of another. Sonnet 125 reveals the identity of that other as the nobleman whose privilege it was to provide the ceremony of *"oblation"* at the King's coronation. And we know the identity of that nobleman to have been Edward de Vere. The sonnet he wrote referring to his privilege was therefore likely to have been the last he wrote, for he died in the following June.

This misidentification of Shakespeare was eventually to find substance as the statue now standing in Poets' Corner inside Westminster Abbey, despite Jonson's plea in the First Folio to prevent it. And it is this counterfeit figure, which has become established in the English psyche as the immortal genius of English literature. It is perhaps ironic that Shakespeare's comedies, noted as they are for characters causing confusion by exchanging identities, should now have mirrored his own life; for he has himself become a figure of mistaken identity.

When George Bernard Shaw remarked: *"with the plays and sonnets in our hands we know more about Shakespeare than we know about Dickens and Thackeray,"* he was anticipating a similar opinion expressed by Louis Auchincloss, who observed that the sonnets *"constitute the only hint or fragment of an autobiography that we have."* [50] Johann Wolfgang von Goethe was of a similar mind (see epigraph to this chapter). Consider, too, Edward Dowden's comment, when writing his Introduction to the Sonnets in 1881.

> *With Wordsworth, Sir Henry Taylor and Mr Swinburne; with Francois-Victor Hugo, with Kreyssig, Ulrici, Gervinus and Hermann Isaac; with Boaden, Armitage Brown, and Hallam; with Furnivall, Spalding, Rosetti and Palgrave, I [too] believe that Shakespeare's Sonnets express his own feelings in his own person.*[51]

The peril this has for the Stratford position is clear. Dr. Levi Fox was evidently aware of the contradiction this posed, for he knew the man's life was devoid of the dramatic experiences related by 'Shakespeare'. Fox's disagreement was correspondingly blunt: *"these Sonnets are not rooted in Shakespeare's own experiences but essentially they are autonomous dramatic meditations."* [52]

This, most certainly, they are not! Because Fox has expressed the view of a committed believer, wedded to the dominant view that Shakespeare was the famous son of an illiterate merchant from Stratford-upon-Avon, he is perfectly correct to say that the Sonnets are not rooted in this man's experience. The content of the poems have nothing whatever in common with the life of this man. But when Fox added that they were simply this man's dramatic meditations, he was endeavouring to explain how they came into existence, while knowing, as he admitted, that their creator had not actually experienced the emotions involved; in reality, a contradictory explanation.

This is because it is impossible to bring into one's imagination an emotion that has never been experienced. In the same way, it is impossible to imagine the colour red, if one has never seen this colour. Deprived of their emotive quality, the Sonnets are drained of their life-blood.

Consequently, if the emotions expressed in the Sonnets are not rooted in Shaxpere's experience, as Fox admits, then they must belong to another sonneteer; that is Oxford, who definitely had experienced these emotions. That is why it took ten years for a publisher to lay hands on them? And why it took another thirty years before a second edition was published?

There is no truly sensible solution to this paradox involving Shaxpere, unless one agrees to accept that the Earl of Oxford was the poet in question, and that he had been put to shame by the love he wrote about, which was unbiblical and scandalous in the eyes of the moral multitude.

The alternative position, preferred by Fox, who was for many years director of the Shakespeare Birthplace Trust, and therefore highly motivated to defend Stratford's tradition, is a last gasp effort to protect an unworthy idol.

The Rival Poet

An acknowledgement that Oxford was William Shakespeare suggests an entirely fresh approach now be adopted when seeking identities for the poet's mistress and the rival poet: both of whom figure prominently in the Sonnets. In the case of the rival poet, the problem has been obfuscated by what appears to be two rivals, each competing for attention under different circumstances. Fortunately, Oxford has distinguished between the two men with sufficient clues to make discernment possible. Sonnet 79, for example, makes it plain that the subject matter is addressed to Southampton, and concerns a rival pen.

Whilst I alone did call upon thy aid,
My verse alone had all thy gentle grace;

But now my gracious numbers are decay'd,
And my sick Muse doth give another place.
I grant, sweet love, thy lovely argument
Deserves the travail of a worthier pen;

Thomas Nashe dedicated *The Choice of Valentines* to Southampton in late 1593. The work was inspired by *Venus and Adonis*, but was more sexually explicit; this may have been why it remained unpublished until much later. In the same year, Barnabe Barnes dedicated a sonnet to Southampton. Nashe then sought better success with *The Unfortunate Traveller*, (1594), which he also dedicated to the Earl, declaring it to be *"a cleane different vaine from other my former courses of writing."* (*Oxford Companion to English Literature*)

> *[Southampton] was early the patron of all scholars; the excellent Chapman calls him in his Iliad 'the choice of all our country's noblest spirits;' Nash, in speaking of him, says: 'Incomprehensible is the height of his spirit, both in heroical resolution and matters of conceit.' Beaumont asks, who lives on England's stage and knows him not? All poets and writers vied with each other in dedicating their works to him.* [53]

This, presumably, was the reason behind the composition of Sonnet 78, which precedes the one above, and begins:

So oft have I invok'd thee for my Muse,
And found such fair assistance in my verse,
As every alien pen has got my use,
And under thee their poesy disperse.

Since the identities of Southampton's aspiring hopefuls offer nothing of material substance to the naming of Shakespeare, they need be pursued no farther. The second rival is far more interesting, and the sonnets that refer to this poet are abundant with his characteristics: leaving room for doubt as to who was intended by these references at an absolute minimum.

After Oxford's return from Italy, and having also been immersed in French culture, he turned this knowledge into good effect by attending to the Queen's entertainment at Court. The sudden appearance of so many *Shakespeare* plays that flooded the stage during the 1590s, many reflecting life in renaissance Italy, is indicative of their composition by Oxford a decade or more earlier. *Titus Andronicus, The Taming of a Shrew, King Lear, and Hamlet,* which appear as entries in Henslowe's daybook dated 1594, support this inference.

It was in the midst of this theatrical activity during the 1580s that a new poet appeared at Court; this was Walter Raleigh. As Sir Robert Naunton (1563-1635) observed:

> *True it is, he had gotten the Queen's ear in a trice, and she began to be taken with his elocution, and loved to hear his reasons to her demands. And the truth is, she took him for a kind of oracle, which nettled them all.*[54]

Raleigh then began plying the Queen with his poetry.

> *Now we have present made*
> *To Cynthia, Phoebe, Flora,*
> *Diana and Aurora,*
> *Beauty that cannot fade.*
> ...
> *So her celestial frame*
> *And quintessential mind,*
> *Which heavens together bind,*
> *Shall ever be the same.*
>
> *Then to her servants leave her,*
> *Love, nature and perfection,*
> *Princess of world's affection,*
> *Our praises but deceive her.*

In another poem, Raleigh confided: *"In heaven Queen she is among the spheres:"* and in another: *"Those eyes that hold the hand of every heart,"* and yet one other: *"Those eyes which set my fancy on a fire."* To these accomplishments, he added: *"Praised be Diana's fair and harmless light,"* followed by *"Wrong not, dear Empress of my heart, / The merit of true passion"*. And the Queen loved it.

This passionate display of words was quickly recognised by watchers at Court as an attempt by Raleigh to play court to Elizabeth. Indeed, his ambitious enterprise even found its way into Spenser's *Faerie Queen* (Book III canto 5; Book IV canto 7). There, he is portrayed as TIMIAS, the lowborn squire who loves BELPHOEBE: a thin disguise for Elizabeth in her virginal role.

It was during this time that Raleigh completed a long sequence of verses entitled: *The Ocean's Love to Cynthia,* which he addressed to Elizabeth. In fact, her nickname for Raleigh was *"Water"*, and since she was his *"Cynthia"*, the title speaks for itself.

Oxford was aware of the Queen's new favourite, and his poetic courtship of the Queen, for this is admitted in Sonnet 80.

O, how I faint when I of you do write,
Knowing a better spirit doth use your name
And in the praise thereof spends all his might
To make me tongue-tied, speaking of your fame!
But since your worth, wide as the ocean is,
The humble as the proudest sail doth bear,
My saucy bark, inferior far to his,
On your broad main doth wilfully appear,
Your shallowest help will hold me up afloat,
Whilst he upon your soundless deep doth ride;
Or, being wreck'd, I am a worthless boat,
He of tall building and of goodly pride. ...

The poem is flooded with allusions to the sea, and by inference to Raleigh: he having identified himself with *"the Ocean"* in his love for *"Cynthia of the Sea"*.

Reference to the rival poet's superior ship also appears in the poem, as confirmed by the 800-ton *Ark Raleigh,* launched at Deptford in June 1587. The vessel was subsequently sold to the Queen for £5000 (≈ £1·4 million) to become the first *Ark Royal.*[55] Oxford's own ship, the *Edward Bonaventure* – his *"saucy bark"* – was inferior in build, and less expensive, as he admitted in the sonnet.

Oxford then refers to his rival's *"tall building"*. Raleigh had tried several times to obtain possession of Sherborne Castle in Dorset, with its impressive four, huge Norman towers. He had wanted to make this his family home, but it was not until 1592 that Elizabeth was able to acquire it for him as a present. In addition to this gift, Raleigh was appointed Admiral, *"in full command of an expedition of thirteen ships to attack the silver fleet and sack Panama."*[56]

The rival poet, we are told, was also a man of *"goodly pride"*. John Aubrey, in *Brief Lives* ascribed this same word to Raleigh: *"His naeve was that he was damnably proud."*[57] It was a sentiment expressed, too, by an anonymous epigram writer: *"Raleigh doth time bestride ... For all his bloody pride."* Charles Cavendish, in a letter to the Countess of Shrewsbury was another who remarked upon Raleigh's pride.[58] A similar accusation was made by the correspondent, *"A.B"*, in a letter of protest written to Lord Burghley (7 July 1586), in which he maintained: *"His pride is intolerable, without regard to any, as the world knows ... "* [59]

In his sonnet, Oxford compared his own circumstances with that of his rival. In this, he would have had in mind the aid he received from the Queen six years earlier, when she had given him an annuity of £1000 to add to her gift of the Manor of Rysing. *"Your shallowest help will hold me up afloat,"* he wrote.

Raleigh, by comparison, fared very much better. Apart from Sherborne Castle, a knighthood in 1584, several leases from All Souls College at Oxford, and a monopoly on wine, he was also given the lease of a manor formerly owned by the Bishop of Bath and Wells, and appointed, firstly, Lord Warden of the Stannaries, and secondly, Vice-Admiral of Cornwall and Devon. This joint position made him the most powerful man in the west of England, with charge over the lucrative tin industry and control of both the army and navy in Cornwall. In addition, he also held the licence to export cloth. In Ireland he received 42,000 acres of land in Cork and Waterford: previously the property of the Earl of Desmond, and to this bounty was added the land and manors of the Babington Estate in the Midlands. *"Whilst he upon your bounteous deep doth ride,"* remarked Oxford in recognition.

The Ocean's Love for Cynthia is now lost, which may have something to do with its author having impregnated Elizabeth Throgmorton, while perhaps dreaming of a different Elizabeth. The Queen was understandably furious. Raleigh did the honourable thing, eventually, and married Bess. And for his deceitful protestations of love for CYNTHIA, 'Cynthia' sent him and his wife to the Tower. *"Ma sœur s'en alla à la Tour, et Sir W. Raleigh."* (Diary entry by Sir Arthur Throgmorton, 7 August 1592) [60]

'Shakespeare' cryptically referred to Raleigh's betrayal of the Queen by likening it to the infidelity suffered by OTHELLO, when the Moor learned that DESDEMONA had been unfaithful to him. *"She was false as water,"* OTHELLO tells EMILIA, in an attempt to justify the murder of his wife (act V: sc. ii). The Queen could not have missed the significance of this remark: likening it to her own situation, with this reference to *"water"*. It was the name she had given Raleigh, only to be repaid by his unfaithfulness to her, despite the gifts she had lavished upon him.

Elizabeth's reaction to the loss of Raleigh's attention was to turn to Oxford, demanding from him the reason why he had remained silent, allowing Raleigh to gain the upper hand in her affections. Oxford's response can be judged from those Sonnets referring to his rival, in which the Queen is addressed as *"you"*.

> ...
> *I found, or thought I found, you did exceed*
> *The barren tender of a poet's debt;*
> *And therefore have I slept in your report*
> *That you yourself, being extant, well might show*
> *How far a modern quill doth come too short,*
> *Speaking of worth, what worth in you do grow.*
> *This silence for my sin you did impute,*
> *Which shall be most my glory, being dumb;*
> *For I impair nor beauty, being mute,*
> *When others would give life, and bring a tomb.*
> *There lives more life in one of your fair eyes*
> *Than both your poets can in praise devise.* (lxxxiii)

Raleigh, it will be recalled, had written several poems in praise of the Queen's eyes. Oxford's response was to exceed his rival in disseminating praise. The opening two lines to this sonnet are also revealing. They begin: *"I never saw that you did painting need, / And therefore to your fair no painting set"*. Elizabeth was noted for her daily application of face paint: *"Her face paint was a mixture of white-of-egg, powdered egg-shell, alum, borax and poppy-seeds moistened with mill water."*[61]

Needless to say, the thought of Will Shaxpere referring to the Queen's personal use of cosmetics is too ridiculous to even contemplate. It is also noteworthy that Oxford has used the words, *"you yourself"*. This appears to hark back to the speech made by Elizabeth at Tilbury, when she appeared there on horseback to rally her troops in preparation for the arrival of Spain's armada.

> *I know I have only the body of a weak and feeble woman; but I have the heart and courage of a king, and even of a king of England, and think foul scorn that Parma, or Spain, or any prince of Europe, should dare invade the border of my realms; to which rather than any dishonour shall grow by me, I myself will take up arms, I myself will be your general, judge and rewarder of every one of your virtues in the field.*[62]

That she should repeatedly refer to herself as *"I myself"* was at that time a quite novel form of expression. Was Oxford employed to write her speeches one wonders? The reference to *"you yourself"* has, however, captured an echo of the Queen's Tilbury speech.

Shortly before his disgrace, Raleigh had left England to lead a fleet of thirteen ships with the purpose of intercepting a silver fleet and sacking Panama. But during the voyage, he heard from a Spanish informer that no treasure ships were to sail that year. He therefore instructed Martin Frobisher to alter course and intercept Portuguese carracks returning from the East Indies, while he returned to London.

It therefore befell Sir John Burroughs in the *Roebuck*, under Raleigh's command, to seize one of the prize vessels making for the Iberian coast, the *Madre de Dios*, which he escorted into the port at Dartmouth.

> *She was the largest ship that had ever entered an English port, seven decks high, the most valuable single prize ever taken, with 537 tons of pepper, cloves, cinnamon, cochineal, mace and nutmegs, and as well jewels, gold, ebony, carpets and oriental silks.* [63]

ꕥ

> *The crewmen who boarded it had immediately begun stuffing their pockets, and the pillaging resumed when the ship reached Dartmouth harbour. The lure of spices and gems attracted merchants, jewellers and goldsmiths, who descended on the port to purchase plunder from sailors at a bargain … The queen claimed as her share … far more than her actual investment. Some of what she garnered came at Raleigh's expense, who though nominally entitled to at least two-thirds of the loot, had to settle for about one fourth.* [64]

The reason for Elizabeth's indifference to Raleigh was that she had, by then, discovered his secret marriage. As punishment for deceiving her, she confined him first to Durham House, and then to the Tower. Oxford's response to this sudden downfall of his rival at Court is remarkably apt, and not without a few of those poisonous barbs for which he was noted. He asks . . .

> *Was it the proud full sail of his great verse,*
> *Bound for the prize of all-too-precious you?* (lxxxvi)

In the sonnet's opening line, Raleigh's *"pride"* is instantly referred to, coupled with his *"full sail"* as a seaman, privateer, and latterly, Admiral of the fleet. By uniting this nautical analogy to his *"great verse"*, Oxford draws upon Raleigh's poetic love for Elizabeth, as contained in the *Ocean's Love for Cynthia.*

The second line to the sonnet refers to the recent capture of the prize ship, *Madre de Dios,* treating it as an allegory for the Queen, with Raleigh intent upon capturing Elizabeth as his *prize*.. The sonnet also reveals the reason for its author's silence.

> *That did my ripe thoughts in my brain inhearse,*
> *Making their tomb the womb wherein they grew?*

These words continue to excuse Oxford for his recent silence, and for which he offers several explanations. His thoughts, he admits, were enclosed as in a tomb. But now, with Raleigh in prison, the tomb inside his brain has become a womb, wherein new thoughts are able to develop. Note, especially, that Oxford has coined his own word for this recent burial: it is *"inhearse"*. One does not have to look far for the reason. In Raleigh's postscript to *The Ocean's Love to Cynthia,* which he penned while in prison, these lines occur:

> *But my loue's wounds, my fancy in the hearse,*
> *The Idea but restinge, of a wasted minde,* [65]

Raleigh's *"fancy"*; his mental imagery, like Oxford's thoughts, lay entombed *"in the hearse"*. One might dismiss this connection as coincidence, except that Oxford has deliberately coined the word *"inhearse"*, thus drawing upon his rival's own expression for a similar entombment. Further allusions to Raleigh follow.

> *Was it his spirit, by spirits taught to write*
> *Above a mortal pitch, that struck me dead?*

Oxford is again questioning his recent silence, but now with a note of sarcasm. Raleigh was known to have been conducting séances at Durham House, hence the reference to *"spirits"*. As historian, Norman Williams remarked: *"It is widely held that a free-speculating group around Raleigh was known by the name of 'the School of Night'."*[66]

In 1592, a pamphleteer had referred to this assemblage as, *"Sir Walter Rauley's Schoole of Atheisme."* George Chapman had even composed a poem, *The Shadow of Night*, in honour of Raleigh's circle of mathematicians and philosophers who attended these meetings. Chapman's poem was entered in the Stationers' Register in December 1593 and published the following year.

By 1593, Raleigh's nocturnal activities had also come under the surveillance of Lord Burghley.

> *... he was looking askance at the activities of a loose club or gathering of scientists, mathematicians, astrologers, astronomers and writers, who met under the joint aegis of Sir Walter Raleigh, and Henry Percy, Earl of Northumberland, nicknamed "the Wizard Earl". It was known as the School of Night.* [67]

Robert Parsons, an Oxford University Jesuit, living in exile in Augsburg, was aware of Raleigh's occult practices, and wrote condemning them. *"Certainly if the school of atheism of Sir Walter Raleigh flourishes a little longer—which he is well known to hold in his house, with a certain necromantic astrologer as teach."* [68] Parsons was voicing his fear that Raleigh might be appointed to the Council, where he could conceivably be influenced to draw up *"a proclamation by that Magus and Epicurus, Raleigh's teacher, and published in the name of the Queen ..."* [69]

As the sonnet continues, Oxford once more refers to his silence. But now, it is with an air of boldness. In a defiant, ringing tone he aims a verbal blow at Raleigh, and to what Parsons had called Raleigh's *"Magus"*.

> *No, neither he, nor his compeers by night*
> *Giving him aid, my verse astonished.*
> *He, nor that affable familiar ghost*
> *Which nightly gulls him with intelligence,*
> *As victors, of my silence cannot boast:*

Amongst Raleigh's *"compeers"* were several mathematicians, Thomas Harriot, Walter Warner and Thomas Hughes. Marlowe also attended, as did Chapman and the minor poet Matthew Roydon. It was later revealed that *"Marlowe had boasted he had 'read the atheist lecture to Sir Walter Raleigh and others', and had said 'that Moses was but a juggler, that one Harriot, being Sir Walter Raleigh's man, can do more than he.'"* [70]

This sonnet does reveal how well informed Oxford was regarding the séances taking place inside Durham House. The *"familiar ghost"*, for example, would be what is now called a spirit guide, but in earlier language was called 'a familiar'.

Oxford's attitude towards Raleigh's activities in the School of Night was completely sceptical, for he dismissed it as something that *"gulls him with intelligence"*; in other words, his rival, Raleigh, was being deceived by the information he received, or so Oxford asserted.

With such historically accurate evidence for Raleigh being the rival poet, it is difficult to see how those confined to interpreting the Sonnets from a Stratford perspective, with its many restrictive possibilities, can respond. They would certainly need to produce a recognised man of letters, together with his poetry and the competitive lines of verse that revealed the rivalry. Added to this, there is the requirement that they produce fitting historical episodes to match the lines of the relevant sonnets. Then there is the valid question as to just who was it that Shaxpere and his rival were addressing? It seems unnecessary to point out that close to four centuries have now passed by without achieving any mentionable success in that direction.

THE DARK LADY

In sonnet 144,published in 1599 by William Jaggard, Oxford had confessed to having two loves.

Two loves I have, of comfort and despair,
Which like two spirits do suggest me still;
The better angel is a man right fair,
The worser spirit a woman colour'd ill.

There is no thought within these lines of love for his wife, Elizabeth Trentham: only for his male friend Southampton. The story of Oxford's shame, and his separation from the plays and poetry he had written, emerge from these four lines. But as the sonnet progresses, the story they relate becomes ever more sensational. His mistress has, or so he believes, seduced his male friend: and both are now betraying him.

To win me soon to hell, my female evil
Tempteth my better angel from my side
And would corrupt my saint to be a devil,
Wooing his purity with her foul pride.

Even though the poet suspects this has occurred, he remains uncertain that the seduction has yet been accomplished.

Yet this shall I ne'er know, but live in doubt
Till my bad angel fire my good one out.

So Oxford must wait until the passion between his two friends has cooled, and confessions are made. It cannot pass notice that there is an obvious similarity between the subject referred to by the author, and the person described in *Willobie His Avisa.*

> *H.W. being suddenly infected with the contagion of a fantastical fit, at the first sight of A, pineth a while in secret grief, at length not able any longer to endure the burning heat of so fervent a humour, bewrayeth the secrecy of his disease unto his familiar friend W.S. who not long before had tried the courtesy of the passion.* [71]

Past commentators of this passage, notably Schoenbaum and Chambers, are in agreement that H.W. and W.S. are Henry Wriothesley and William Shakespeare, respectively. But who is A.?

At the commencement of 1592, Oxford was forty-one years of age, Southampton was eighteen, and Anne Vavasor was twenty-six. For several years after joining the Court at the age of fifteen she had been Oxford's mistress, and had subsequently given birth to his illegitimate son as a result of their liaison. The question this now poses is whether Oxford renewed his affair with the mother of his son after the death of his first wife in 1588, or did he take a new mistress? The author of *Willobie* has certainly provided the correct initial for Anne, but are there other clues to be found?

In Sonnet 138, the age difference between Oxford and his mistress is exposed and this corroborates what is known about Anne Vavasor and Oxford in 1591.

When my love swears that she is made of truth,
I do believe her, though I know she lies,
That she might think me some untutor'd youth,
Unlearned in the world's false subtleties.
Thus vainly thinking that she thinks me young,
Although she knows my days are past the best.

Further clues supporting the proposition that Vavasor is the aforementioned mistress are forthcoming in Sonnet 152, where the poet's conscience becomes a factor in the action taking place.

In loving thee thou know'st I am foresworn.

Oxford's marriage to Elizabeth Trentham occurred towards the end of 1591. It would therefore still further appear that the marriage was one of convenience and certainly not the result of a love tryst (p.195).

In the next line of his verse, Oxford provides another piece of damning evidence. He accuses his mistress of *"swearing love to me"*, as well as to her husband.

But thou art twice forsworn, to me love swearing;
In act thy bed-vow broke,

As Gwynneth Bowen discovered:

[Anne Vavasor] after a succession of illicit love affairs had married a sea captain named John Finche, but left him about 1589 for the redoubtable Queen's champion, Sir Henry Lee, then nearly 60 years old and on the point of retiring. Nevertheless, with Sir Henry Lee she continued to live, steadfastly if not faithfully, to his dying day, 21 years later. [72]

By piecing together the evidence concerning Anne Vavasor as Oxford's mistress, it can be inferred that the poet was referring to John Finche and Sir Henry Lee, so that she, by swearing her love for Oxford, has renounced whatever vows of love she made to these other two men. In this sense, she was *"twice forsworn"*. And her *"bed-vow broke."* Oxford then pursues her dishonesty with a question concerning his own morality.

But why of two oaths' breach do I accuse thee,
When I break twenty? I am perjur'd most;

This is a plain admission of guilt on Oxford's part for his own infidelities, which he weighs against the two breaches of oath committed by his mistress. But he then goes on to explain why he has lost faith in what she says.

And all my honest faith in thee is lost,
For I have sworn deep oaths of thy deep kindness,
Oaths of thy love, thy truth, thy constancy;

There is so much here that Oxford is referring to, and to have then discovered much of this was false, implies their affair had sustaiined a long and troubled history. Once again, Oxford's involvement with Anne Vavasor, which began in 1580, is right on target.

The poet concludes with a neat couplet that summed up his feelings.

For I have sworn thee fair—more perjur'd I,
To swear against the truth so foul a lie.

The reason why Vavasor left her husband to live with Lee as his mistress, was because she was pregnant by him. *"Their son, Thomas Vavasour, (later known as Thomas Freeman), was born in 1589 when his half brother, Edward Vere, was eight years old."* [73] Presumably her husband, who was a sea captain, had been away at the time of conception, and she was unable to pass it off as his.

Oxford alludes to an illegitimate birth in Sonnet 127. The first three lines of the verse also introduce the colour black as a new definition for beauty: poetically claiming it to be the successor of fair.

But now is black beauty's successive heir,
And beauty slander'd with a bastard shame:

Both of Anne's children were bastards, but equally, she too was illegitimate (Haynes, 1997, p. 39). The sonneteer also paints a pen picture of his mistress, and in doing so he provides a brief account of her features. These bear resemblance to the portrait of Anne Vavasor owned by the Master and Wardens of the Armourers & Brasiers' Company in London.

Therefore my mistress' brows are raven black,
Her eyes so suited, and they mourners seem
At such who, not born fair, no beauty lack,
Sland'ring creation with a false esteem.
Yet so they mourn, becoming of their woe,
That every tongue says beauty should look so. (cxxvii)

This conflict between black and fair is resumed in Sonnet 131. Oxford, although confessing a love for his mistress, now begins to question the reason.

For well thou know'st to my dear doting heart
Thou art the fairest and most precious jewel,
Yet, in good faith, some say that thee behold
Thy face hath not the power to make love groan,

To say they err I dare not be so bold,
Although I swear it to myself alone.

In the concluding couplet, the poet wraps up his dilemma in a single sentence. He is under the dark spell of a woman he cannot resist, even though he knows her motives to be evil. It is also because of her immorality, for so he believes, that others have defamed her looks.

In nothing art thou black save in thy deeds,
And thence this slander, as I think proceeds.

Evidence of Anne Vavasor's immoral behaviour has already been given above; for instance, her taking Sir Henry Lee as a lover, despite both she and he being otherwise married at the time. Then, after giving birth to Lee's son, as it would now appear, returning to Oxford's arms to renew their affair together.

There are also references to her illicit lifestyle occurring between the birth of her first son and her marriage to Finche. But to cap these, she turns her attention to Oxford's young friend, Henry Wriothesley, and, as it would appear from the Sonnets, successfully seducing him. Oxford contemptuously writes of this in Sonnet 135

Whoever hath her wish, thou has thy Will,
And Will to boot, and Will in over-plus;

The word 'will' has a double meaning, for it refers to both desire and the organ through which it is achieved. In short, the poet is implying that his mistress was a nymphomaniac.

In 1592, Vavasor was twenty-seven, Southampton was nineteen, and an object of temptation too urgent for her to resist. Oxford had already suspected what was happening behind his back, and he voiced his suspicion in Sonnet 144. His misgivings were justified, as we are drawn to discover in Sonnet 42, which the poet addressed to his male friend; also from Sonnet 134, which he directed at his mistress.

That thou hast her, it is not all my grief,
And yet it may be said I lov'd her dearly;
That she hath thee is of my wailing chief,
A loss in love that touches me more nearly.
Loving offenders, thus I will excuse thee: (xlii)

So now I have confess'd that he is thine,
And I myself am mortgag'd to thy will;
My self I'll forfeit, so that other mine
Thou wilt restore to be my comfort still.
...
Him have I lost; thou hast both him and me;
He pays the whole, and yet am I not free. (cxxxiv)

There is in these verses a weary resignation concerning what has befallen the poet. In danger of losing both those whom he loves, he is forced to concede defeat, and preserve what he still cherishes. The poet's fiery youth of former years has been mellowed by age and bitter experience. This change was to prove dramatic, and its effect soon came to reveal itself in the revisions he made to his plays during the 1590s, which have come down to us in a more polished form than when they were first performed.

Some commentators have wondered at this development of Oxford's verse, from a brash young aristocrat with the world at his feet to that of the mature and worldly-wise poet of later years. The answer lies in his life story. He had become something of a misanthrope: reflected to some extent in *Timon of Athens*. Like TIMON, he, too, became disillusioned by the deceits of fair-weather friends and the betrayal of those close to him, not to mention his impoverishment and being pursued by angry creditors. But, as he approached the final decade of his life, through the use of his intellect combined with his art, and by learning from the many experiences he had lived through, he took a more detached view of people and the inner working of their minds. These inner workings he saw as the driving force behind all human striving, and with the aid of his agathodaimon he made it the motivating force of his characters.

Thus, in many ways the characters he created are an embodiment of the emotional highs and lows that structured his own life story. For having learned the ways of the world from bitter experience, while also being gifted with the ability to write verse almost at will, he seems to have experienced a metanoia late in life, causing his artistic nature to respond. Thereafter, the world's cultural heritage became hugely enriched with a whole raft of insight into human behaviour; which, having been set to verse, is never likely to be equalled.

The author of *Willobie His Avisa* may be said to have had the betrayal of Oxford, by his friend and his mistress, in mind: for he refers to the poet as W. S., the initials of the pseudonym adopted by Oxford for his two poems: *Venus and Adonis* and *Lucrece. Willobie's* author takes up the story.

> *W.S. who not long before had tried the courtesy of the passion, and was now newly recovered of the like infection, yet finding his friend [H.W.] let blood in the same vein, he took pleasure for a time to see him bleed, & instead of stopping the issue, he enlargeth the wound...* [74]

Willobie His Avisa is not principally a book central to matters involving Oxford and Southampton. Its satirical nature, and the fact that it was banned, but remained for many years undercover reading, is testament to the secrets it contained; that is, for those who understood them. The book's author, according to Professor Barbara de Luna, (*The Queen Declined,* 1970), was for the most part hinting at the *amours* of Queen Elizabeth, who though 'married' to the nation was courted by many.

But, in the course of writing his satire, the author of *Willobie* was unable to resist introducing a similar romance, current at the time, and sufficiently similar to the one that was central to the theme he was developing. It involved a love triangle between W.S. (whom he recognised as Oxford's recently adopted pen-name of William Shakespeare, which he then hyphenated to signal recognition), H.W. (Henry Wriothesley) and A. (Anne Vavasor: fortunately possessing the same initial as Avisa). In a brief interlude within the main storyline, the passions of these three become integrated into the theme of the book.

Willobie was first published in 1594, shortly after *Lucrece* became available. In fact, the poem is referred to in the second stanza, along with its pen-named author, again suitably hyphenated to distinguish it from the unbroken form it takes in the dedications to both *Venus* and *Lucrece.*

> Yet *Tarquin* plucks his glistering grape,
> And *Shake-speare* paints poor *Lucrece* rape.

One might reasonably suppose that this recognition of Shakespeare by another poet as early as 1594, together with the mention of only his second published poem, and this in close proximity to the appearance of his initials and those of Henry

Wriothesley: the patron to whom the poem was dedicated, would supersede Robert Greene's reference to *"Shake-scene"* in importance. But this is not the case, and with good reason. *Willobie* refers to W.S. not as an upstart crow, nor as a Jack-of-all-trades, as the Chettle-Greene letter had identified this new arrival on the literary scene, but as *"the old player"*, which at the age of forty-four, fairly described Oxford.

There is also a further embarrassment for orthodoxy. In the poem, W.S. greets the arrival of H.W. with the expression: *"friend Harry"*. Only those entirely lacking critical ability can imagine the 3rd Earl of Southampton agreeing to this familiar greeting by a man of Shaxpere's upbringing. Hence, to avoid attention being drawn to this conundrum, *Willobie*, if it is mentioned at all, is speedily passed by.

Mary Sidney

The mystery of Shakespeare's mistress has a long history of speculation, but no one has seriously considered that two women were involved. Art. Neuendorffer, who was searching for possible ELS encryptions involving the name Vere, using material associated with the work of Oxford's contemporaries, made an interesting find, which strongly suggests Edward de Vere had enjoyed a brief liaison with Mary Sidney, Countess of Pembroke. If true – and one is reminded of W. F. Friedman's assertion that evidence from cryptology takes precedence over history, when records are capable of more than one interpretation – then it would also have been a marriage of minds.

Mary Sidney was in so many ways Oxford's second self. She was born at Ticknall Place in Bewdley, in the county of Worcestershire on 27 October 1561. Her uncle was the Earl of Leicester and her knighted brother, Philip, was the soldier poet whose life was tragically cut short from a wound suffered at Zutphen. Like Oxford, she received an excellent education, and was proficient in the classics, as well as in French and Italian. As a woman, she was taught needlework and music. Her artistry with the needle earned her considerable admiration; and her singing was acclaimed by the composer Thomas Morley, who set the words from *It was a Lover and his Lass,* in *As You Like It,* to music. Mary Sidney's ability with both lute and virginals would undoubtedly have impressed Oxford, who was reputed to have participated in the composition of a March by William Byrd.

> *Among close to three hundred pieces contained in the most famous keyboard manuscript of the English Renaissance, now known as the Fitzwilliam Virginal Book, is William Byrd's "The Earl of Oxford March" (Fitzwilliam II 402). The Oxford March has become well known to present-day early music enthusiasts, and apparently was well known at the beginning of its life ... In Thomas Morley's The First Book of Consort Lessons of 1599, an unsigned, truncated version of the march, arranged for a mixed group of instruments, appears as "My Lord of Oxenfords Maske" (Morley 134). Anthony Munday's 1588 A banquet of daintie Conceits, a collection of his lyrics for various well known tunes, contains verses to be sung to a melody he describes as "a gallant note" called the "Earl of Oxenford's March" (Munday 227). Circumstances surrounding the Oxford March and the battle pieces suggest an association of at least ten years between the Seventeenth earl of Oxford and William Byrd.*
>
> (*The Oxfordian*: Vol. 1, 1998).

A particular sonnet written by Shakespeare has always set its readers pondering upon the possible identity of the player. It is generally thought to have been his mistress, but there is no record that Anne Vavasor had received this level of tuition on the keyboard. Mary Sidney was noted for her ability, and this sonnet may have been the poet's acknowledgement of her talent.

How oft, when thou, my music, music play'st
Upon that blessed wood whose motion sounds
With thy sweet fingers, when thou gently sway'st
The wiry concord that mine ear confounds,
Do I envy those jacks that nimble leap
To kiss the tender inward of thy hand,
Whilst my poor lips, which should that harvest reap,
At the wood's boldness by thee blushing stand!
To be so tickled, they would change their state
And situation with those dancing chips
O'er whom thy fingers walk with gently gait,
Making dead wood more blest than living lips.
Since saucy jacks so happy are in this,
Give them thy fingers, me thy lips to kiss. (cxxviii)

There can be no room for doubt this sonnet was written by the poet to a lady: both of whom were on intimate terms. It is also interesting to see how the sonneteer refers to *"my music"*. This may simply mean they were his favourite pieces, but the possibility he had written some minor compositions is an alternative explanation; not least, because Oxford had written several excellent songs for inclusion in his plays.

In November 1588, following the defeat of Spain's armada, when celebrations included a service of thanksgiving at St Paul's Cathedral, Mary was twenty-seven years of age and Oxford thirty-eight. Both were in mourning despite attending the victory jubilations. In 1586, Mary had suffered the loss of her mother (5 May) and father (9 August) as well as that of her brother Philip (17 October), who died from a Spanish musket ball to the thigh. This triple tragedy had caused Mary to distant herself from society, and she had remained apart: isolated at her marital home in Wilton. Oxford, in the July of 1588, had lost his wife Anne. There can be kinship in mutual commiserations, and Mary's overriding interest in literature would also account for her seeking to converse with Oxford.

What is known for certain is that from this time forward, the Countess of Pembroke turned over a new leaf. She returned to her home at Wilton, intent upon promoting literature, for which she soon acquired considerable fame. It was also at this time, with Oxford raising money from the sale of his estates to pay his massive debt that he disappeared from the London scene, causing Spenser to remark: *"Our pleasant Willy, ah! is dead of late."*

Oxford eventually re-emerged in 1592 with Tom Nashe, who declared he had been *"with my Lord in the country"*, and had dwelt in a *"Nobleman's house"* where there were gathered many *"rare qualified men and selected good scholars."* This would refer to the Wilton Circle, which Mary Sidney started at Wilton House. In its heyday, it became a *"paradise for poets"*, attracting Edmund Spenser, Michael Drayton, Sir John Davies and Samuel Daniel amongst other notables. In this respect, it bore some similarity to the writing circle that flourished under Oxford's guidance during his occupancy at Fishers Folly. It is tempting to suggest that Lady Pembroke obtained this idea from Oxford after returning to Wilton, but expanded it to include musicians, artists and architects. Lord Pembroke was one of the wealthiest men in England, and could afford to indulge his wife in her preferred choice of companions.

Coincidentally, before Oxford's return to London in 1592, Mary Sidney had published two translations from French. These were *A Discourse of Life and Death,* which she inscribed: *"The 13 of May 1590. At Wilton".* The other was *Antonius,* dated *"At Ramsburie. 26. Of November 1590".* Her translation of Philippe de Mornay's thoughts concerning Life and Death was sufficiently popular to be reprinted three times. It may also have helped to free her from continuing to mourn her parents and brother. But coming so soon after her visit to London, and her proximity to de Vere, it is an open question as to whether he had been the person who introduced her to de Mornay's work, and then offered to assist her with the translation.

Antonius became an even greater success. This was a translation of Robert Garnier's *Marc Antoine,* and was the first dramatic account in England of *Antony and Cleopatra.*

> *[It was also] one of the first English dramas in blank verse ... to introduce the continental vogue for using historical drama to comment on contemporary politics ... Antonius also seems to have inspired a vogue for drama primarily intended to be read or performed in private.*[75]

The work can be seen to embody characteristics that are later observed in the plays of 'Shakespeare.' A joint enterprise between Oxford and his hostess at Wilton can therefore be said to have laid the foundation for 'Shakespeare's' more accomplished play, *Antony and Cleopatra,* which was completed after 1594. This was the year that a member of Mary Sidney's Wilton Circle, Samuel Daniel, wrote *Cleopatra:* a sequel to his patroness's *Antonius.* In 1607, Daniel re-issued a revised edition of *Cleopatra, "which reflects Shakespeare's in phrases, names and stage business, as the earlier edition of 1594 did not."* Shakespeare's *Antony and Cleopatra* was one amongst several plays unknown to the public until these were featured in the First Folio. Nevertheless, Daniel clearly had access to the play at least sixteen years before it was published in 1623.

Of all the Countess of Pembroke's writing, one work stands out above the rest, and it was accomplished very soon after her return to Wilton at the end of 1588. Her brother Philip had begun translating the *Psalms*, but had managed only the first 43. Mary completed the task by writing 44 to 150 *"in a dazzling array of verse forms"*.

> *She employed a dazzling array of some 126 different verse forms, including ottava rima, rime royal, terza rima, two sonnet forms, and some highly original stanzaic forms. Samuel Woodforde's transcription of her working papers (Bodl. Oxf., MS Rawl. poet. 25) gives a glimpse of her process of poetic composition. She typically began with a paraphrase of the Book of Common Prayer or the Geneva Bible, and then consulted other psalters and scholarly commentaries, expanded metaphors, added rhetorical flourishes, and improved the rhyme, metre, and phrasing.* [76]

> *In these Psalms ... The consensus of critical opinion seems to be that her part shows more literary merit than her brother's, especially in the skill and ingenuity of the versification.*[77]

Never again would she achieve the heights of literary invention and expression that she achieved with her translation of the *Psalms*. After reading them, John Donne was compelled to remark that God *"hath translated the translator [and] We thy Sydnean Psalms shall celebrate."* [78] Yet, for the two years since her brother's death, she had lived the life of a recluse, moping for the loss of her parents and brother. What can account for this sudden uplift into the realm inhabited by genius, especially at a time when according to Nashe's account, Oxford was a guest at Wilton House?

> *It is hard to believe that a woman of so much literary ability, living in an age when poetic expression was not only the fashion, but a matter of course, did not do a greater amount of original composition than we find now remaining.*[79]

In the years beginning 1589 and ending 1592, Mary Sidney celebrated her 28th, 29th and 30th birthdays. Her marriage to the 2nd Earl of Pembroke in April 1577 had been politically motivated. Henry Herbert had been married before. At the age of nineteen he was wedded to Catherine Gray, sister of the ill-fated Lady Jane Gray. But after the Queen's execution and the disgrace of her family, the marriage was annulled. This left him free to remarry, and in 1562 he chose Lady Catherine Talbot for his new wife. Their union lasted thirteen years up until her death in 1575. Two years later at the age of 43, he married for a third time. His bride was Mary, aged fifteen and a half: the daughter of Sir Henry Sidney and Lady Mary Dudley. Thus, by the year 1592, Lord Pembroke was in his fifty-eighth year.

John Aubrey, in his *Brief Lives*, is unkind to Lady Pembroke's reputation in the matter of her sexual life. Aubrey's method of obtaining information was to enquire personally from those who were closest to his subject, and what he was told he reported as fact, even though it would often be no more than gossip. We therefore learn from him that . . .

> *a royalist friend had told him that he had heard old men say that 'there was so great love' between Sir Philip Sidney and 'his fair sister that ... they lay together, and it was thought the first Philip Earl of Pembroke was begot by him'.* [80]

Mary Sidney's niece, Mary Wroth, later wrote a prose romance with the title *The Countesse of Mountgomeries Urania.* The Countess of Montgomery was Lady Susan Vere, daughter of the 17th Earl of Oxford, Edward de Vere. However the subject of *Urania* was based upon her aunt Mary, whom she depicted as a lover and writer of secular verse.

The vivaciousness of Lord Pembroke's young wife and the fear held by her father-in-law that she would disgrace the Pembroke family with an adulterous relationship are reasons why she was kept on the Wilton estate instead of receiving the freedom of London society. This constraint seems to have given credibility to the story Aubrey recounted of her interest in the coupling of horses during the mating season; to which, he added that she had slept with Lord Burghley's son Robert, after his wife died. It is, however, with greater certainty one can report that after Lord Pembroke's death in January 1601, following a long illness, she moved from Wilton House. And, at the age of 43, began a love affair with a man ten years her junior. This was Dr Matthew Lister, whom she never married, but with whom she remained for the remainder of her life.

It is against this background that Oxford's visit to Wilton House, following soon after he and Lady Pembroke had attended the victory celebrations in London, is initially to be judged. One could easily dismiss the idea that a relationship had occurred between the two, on the grounds there is no physical evidence to suggest it ever happened. But this is to miss a most important point: one vouchsafed by William Friedman, who maintained that evidence from cryptology carries certainty whenever an historical dispute is at issue. Art. Neuendorffer's discovery involving cryptology reveals that Mary Sidney and Edward de Vere did have an affair. It therefore cannot be ignored, especially as it now appears, they were both working together for long periods on her brother's *Psalms.*

In 1639, John Benson entered in the Stationers' Register the forthcoming publication: *Poems Written by Wil. Shake-speare.* The edition duly appeared in 1640. The present enquiry will confine itself to the opening introduction. Elsewhere in this book, reference will be made to Leonard Digges' poetic tribute to Shakespeare; also to William Marshall's new etching of the Droeshout engraving, Both of these make contributions to the hidden identity of de Vere as Shakespeare, and both appear in Benson's 1640 publication.

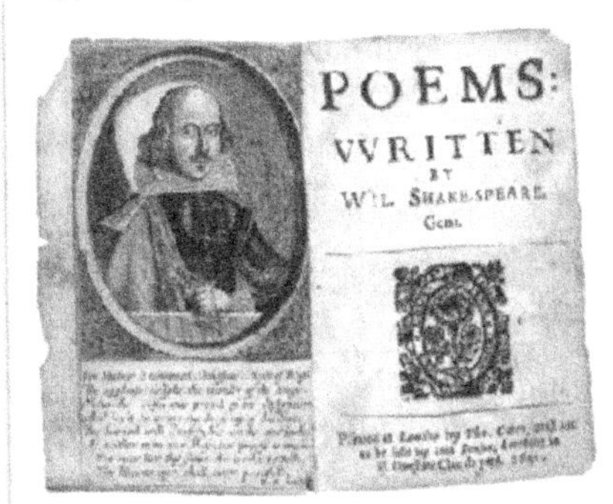
POEMS:
VVRITTEN
BY
WIL. SHAKESPEARE.
Gent.

At the front of this book, in the form of an introduction, is a letter to the reader. It is the opening words, as one would expect, to which attention is required. Special note should be taken of the title, and how the word WRITTEN has been given a capital W typeset as VV; whereas the W for Wil. is printed in normal type. It will be recalled from Chapter One that just one line in the inscription on the Stratford monument was deliberately inset, and that a digraph had been used to reduce the number of letters in that line from 35 to 34. This contrivance served to direct attention to the formation of a 34-column grill, which revealed the hidden sentence – SO TEST HIM, HE I VOW IS E. DE VERE AS HE SHAKESPEARE: ME I.B. We are now presented with something similar. The word WRITTEN has 7 letters, but by writing W as VV, the number increases to 8. If this is significant, then an 8-column grille may be expected to add to the proof that earlier encryptions have already established: to wit, E de Vere was Shakespeare. Benson's letter, which introduces the poem, begins:

To The Reader

I Here presume (under favour) to present to your view, some excellent and sweetely composed Poems, of Master William Shakespeare . . .

T	O	T	H	E	R	E	A
D	E	R	I	H	E	R	E
P	R	E	S	U	M	E	U
N	D	E	R	F	A	V	O
U	R	T	O	P	R	E	S
E	N	T	T	O	Y	O	U
R	V	I	E	W	S	O	M
E	E	X	C	E	L	L	E
N	T	A	N	D	S	W	E
E	T	E	L	Y	C	O	M
P	O	S	E	D	P	O	E
M	S	O	F	M	A	S	T
E	R	W	I	L	L	…	

By applying an ELS of 8, the result produces the statement: **Lo! E. Vere: Re, Mary S. Wed.** This sentence comprises a single cluster of words; within which, occurs a run of 5 letters adjoining another of 7 letters. It is a very positive signal that the decrypted statement is genuine; for it is difficult to find even one 5-letter word occurring by chance. To find two in a single cluster, and again involving the same name Vere alongside another writer of his acquaintance—the future mother-in-law of his daughter Susan, is too remarkable to be ignored. When Friedman was lecturing on acrostics, he suggested that where a word or name occurs with 5 or more letters, it is worthy of serious investigation.

Let it also be observed that this decrypted sentence satisfies the earlier criteria laid down by William and Elizebeth Friedman. The words form a grammatical sentence, and the sentence conveys meaningful information, as well as being unique. No other such sentence is to be found in the grid.

The meaning of 'wed' may cause comment. But given the constraints of ELS cryptology, it is difficult to imagine a more succinct way of describing an intimate affair between two consenting adults.

When Lord Pembroke wrote out his will, leaving Mary £3000 in plate, jewels, etc., and an interest for life in several properties he owned, he also stipulated that it was only for so long as she remained *"solo and unmaryed"*. It is unknown whether she forwent her inheritance after uniting with Dr Lister. Alternatively, her decision not to marry may have had something to do with the loss of income that would have resulted from legitimising the union.

We now have strong cryptographic evidence that Edward de Vere was at Wilton House, together with the Countess of Pembroke, in a relationship that must have been intimate. What is more to the point, this revelation is made in a book of Shake-speare's Poems. Note particularly the hyphen; for this confirms that where it has been used, when referring to Shakespeare, it applies to the Earl of Oxford. It is not some printer's device for separating letters, as some bewildered commentators have been compelled to conjure up for an explanation. Secondly, to have proof that Oxford was at Wilton House under circumstances of intimacy with the Countess of Pembroke, reinforces Jonson's description of Shakespeare as *"Sweet Swan of Avon"*, for the river Avon flowed across the extensive parkland of the Pembroke estate. We shall return to this topic once more in chapter 10.

It now remains only to suggest which sonnets Oxford may have written in praise of Mary Sidney. Sonnet 99, which draws the poet's inspiration from the flowers in order to compare them with his love, is too girlish, even for Southampton, too tender for the way he treated Anne Cecil, too intimate for the Queen, whom he would not have addressed as 'thou', and too full of admiration, to be for Anne Vavasor: which leaves Mary Sidney.

To this, one may possibly add Sonnet 88. The poet is aware that he may be exposed over some misdemeanour – *"my merit in the eye of scorn"* – but he is prepared to remain true to the one he loves, even if she exposes him – *"Upon thy side against myself I'll fight."* It is tempting to think this might be appropriate to Southampton and the charge against both men for their indecent behaviour together. But against this the poet remarks that he will *"prove thee virtuous, though thou art forsworn."* In order to achieve this, he will disclose *"faults concealed, wherein I am attainted."* By taking this action, he believes the accusations against his loved one will change to sympathy for her, at having been wronged by him. He then wraps this up in the final couplet by expressing the reason.

Such is my love, to thee I so belong,
That for my right, myself will bear all wrong.

This is not the love he had for Anne Vavasor. Nevertheless, it was an illicit love, for the woman was forsworn. The scandal that threatened to expose them both would thus appear to be the woman's adulterous relationship with the poet. For that, he was prepared to take the sin upon himself: certain in his mind that his disreputable affairs in the past would sway the attitude of her accusers to one of sympathy.

Perhaps that is how the brief affair between Oxford and Mary Sidney ended. After 1592, Oxford settled down with his second wife, and we do not learn of his return to Wilton House again until 1603, two years after Lord Pembroke's death. The £3000 her husband bequeathed to her is approximately £838,000 by today's reckoning. It is a paltry sum compared to his wealth, and leads one to suspect he held a grievance against her.

Mary Sidney's one last tribute to Oxford, shortly before he died, was to erect a little 'temple' – for many years called Shakespeare's House. It commemorated the festivities that took place in the final months of 1603, when 'Shakespeare' arrived, joined later by King James and his court: and *As You Like It* was performed (see p. 496)

5

A SHAMEFUL COVER-UP

He who controls the present, controls the past.
He who controls the past, controls the future.
George Orwell

IN AN ENTERTAINING BOOK by Bill Bryson 'suggestively' titled *Shakespeare*, the author makes an interesting admission about his subject.

We don't know if he ever left England. We don't know who his principal companions were or how he amused himself. His sexuality is an irreconcilable mystery. On only a handful of days in his life can we say with absolute certainty where he was. We have no record at all of his whereabouts for the eight critical years when he left his wife and three young children in Stratford and became with almost impossible swiftness, a successful playwright in London. By the time he is first mentioned in print as a playwright, in 1592, his life was already more than half over. For the rest, he is a kind of literary equivalent of an electron – forever there and not there. [1]

Bryson has identified a problem that both frustrates and bedevils everyone who undertakes to write about the life of this man as a poet and playwright. As Hugh Trevor-Roper, former Regius Professor of History at Oxford University was forced to admit: *"One hundredth of the effort devoted to one of Shakespeare's obscure contemporaries would have produced a respectable biography."* [2]

Consequently, everything we are told about Shakespeare's literary life, distinct from his commercial activities, has to be speculative. The speculation, long since petrified into tradition, is that William Shakespeare was the same person as William Shaxpere of Stratford-upon-Avon. He was not. He was, instead, a stooge paid by the Earl of Oxford to act as his allonym. This being true, the logical inconsistencies and unknowns mentioned by Bryson are all solved. It has been, however, this singular lack of any substantive evidence in support of Shaxpere as a writer, or even a book owner, along with the stubborn refusal to abandon belief that this missing evidence must once have existed, that has caused some 'bardolators' to resort to forgery, and to provide the 'missing' books and manuscripts themselves.

THE FORGERS

In the late eighteenth century, John Jordan, a local man from Shaxpere's hometown, capitalised on this lack of evidence by producing reading material once 'owned' by the author, and even inscribed *"William Shakespeare his Booke"*.

William Henry Ireland went much further by counterfeiting documents and letters that he said were found in an old chest shown to him by a *"mysterious rich man"*. Some of this forged correspondence, for so it was alleged, had once passed between Shakespeare and his patron Lord Southampton. Amongst which, was a love letter from the poet to Anne Hathaway. To Ireland's astonishment, he found *"some serious scholars surprisingly easily deluded by this."* [3] But Ireland eventually overstepped the mark when he added to his discoveries, the 'original' manuscript of the *Tragedye of Kynge Leare* together with fragments of *Hamblette*, and a previously unknown Shakespeare play, *Vortigern and Rowena*, which he had written himself.

In the wake of Ireland came John Payne Collier; a brilliant scholar in the field of Shakespeare studies, until frustration at the lack of facts got the better of him, and he threw his career and reputation into the dust of history by creating whatever evidence he imagined should have existed, but didn't.

> *Occasionally he would slip into a pile of genuine material a forged manuscript of his own creation. At other times he would simply add a 'Shakespeare' line or so to a document that was otherwise completely genuine.* [4]

Clement M. Ingleby eventually exposed this deception in 1861, by using chemical tests to prove the ink used by Collier was actually watercolour.

Like Collier, James Halliwell-Phillipps was another highly regarded scholar who dedicated his life to help substantiate *"the legend of the English Bard."* But, in the course of his endeavours, like Collier, his name is blemished by those accused of having *"stolen, forged and destroyed numerous documents as they worked their way unsupervised through various libraries and private collections."*[5]

It has been wholly to the credit of men like Ingleby, who exposed Collier; and Malone, who revealed Ireland's forgeries, that Shakespearian literature is now cleansed of its deceivers. Yet, the fact remains that highly educated men can sometimes become so irritated by the lack of documents supporting their beliefs that they become tempted to manufacture the evidence themselves; thus providing false credentials for a man that, in their estimation, was the immortal Shakespeare.

Psychologically, this is of some interest, with ramifications that extend even to the present day. Yet, whereas these forgers supplied material evidence in support of William Shaxpere's authorship, in an attempt to cover up the embarrassing fact that nothing similar to the documents they manufactured actually existed, modern-day scholars practise a different masquerade. They forge in their own minds the evidence they require, and then present it with the hallmark of their authority.

This is still, essentially, a type of forgery. For the fact is that no unambiguous evidence exists, which is capable of identifying William Shaxpere as the William Shakespeare of poetic acclaim. It is because of this gaping hole in Shaxpere's literary background that it has become necessary to forge it, albeit mentally. That is to say: it is forged by imaginative speculations derived from a false starting point. As long as everyone is willing to accept that false starting point, the deductions made from it by academics will be indulged by both the media and the public, because the conclusions bear the stamp of academic authority.

The authorship crisis occurs because not one of these deductions has been, or ever can be substantiated by actual evidence. And this is because the starting point is false. In certain types of mathematical proof, a false starting point leads by gradual deductions to a contradiction or absurdity. That is precisely the case with Shaxpere. One can make deductions by assuming Shaxpere held the pen in Shakespeare's hand, but this has never led to any actual evidence to guarantee it as factual.

Behind these failures to discover evidence for Shaxpere lurks a question at the heart of the matter. It is asked by those in sympathy with the doubts surrounding Shakespeare's authorship, but who also remain unable to accept an alternative to the man promoted by the traditionalists: – 'Why conceal the author's identity?' The remainder of this chapter is given over to answering that question.

SPECIAL PRIVILEGES

Oxford began his apprenticeship in drama by writing plays for the entertainment of Queen Elizabeth and her court (see Chapter 6). Inevitably, this resulted in a number of characters in his plays adopting certain characteristics of the courtiers with whom he was familiar. Shaxpere could not, and would not have dared do this, had he been Shakespeare. Apart from which, it had been made illegal. Hence, disbelief in Oxford as the author of the plays written by Shakespeare disables an in-depth study of the characters he created, for they cannot be likened to anyone at court.

As a woman in a man's world, the Queen would have been highly amused during these moments of entertainment, when observing members of her court fidgeting with embarrassment at recognizing themselves in a play: much to the amusement of others in the audience; yet, with the victims careful always to mask their inward irritation with enforced smiles.

The characteristics attributable to some courtiers would have likely become recognised if Oxford's penname became identified with William Shakespeare. Should this occur, it would have the potential of exposing some very elite members of the Queen's inner circle to the danger of mockery.

Elizabeth was well aware that ridicule was the forerunner of disrespect. This was evident in the reprimand she delivered to Sir Philip Sidney for an indiscretion involving the Earl of Oxford. Lord Brooke recorded the context of the Queen's displeasure in a letter concerning the incident.

> *... the Queen ... lays before him the difference in degree between Earls and Gentlemen, the respect inferiors owed to their superiors, as degrees descending between the people's licentiousness and the anointed sovereign of Crowns; how the Gentleman's neglect of the Nobility taught the peasant to insult both.* [6]

A further reason for concern about Oxford's plays was that their content occasionally overstepped the boundaries imposed by authority. Again, something that Shaxpere would not have dared do, had he been Shakespeare. This demanded that authors restrict political comment. Details of this restriction are referred to in the passage below.

> ... *the work of a new generation of Reformation scholars who paint a picture of widespread resistance, surveillance, coercion and persecution in sixteenth-century England ... years of censorship and propaganda during which the subjects of religion and politics were forbidden to dramatists.* [7]

Oxford had not only drawn his characters from dignitaries at court, his plays also included highly sensitive material, such as the usurpation of the throne and the deposition of a monarch (*Richard II*). This and other contentious issues were tolerated, but only because they were confined to private performances, and attended solely by sophisticated members of the ruling class. If let loose in the public domain, such content was considered dangerous—as proved to be the case when Essex commissioned the Lord Chamberlain's Men to stage *Richard II* for a performance at the Globe on the eve of his ill-fated revolt against the Queen.

As Elizabeth afterwards reflected (1601), when conversing with William Lambarde, the person in charge of records at the Tower of London: *"I am Richard the Second, know ye not that?"*[8]

The reader may very well wonder at this remark, as other scholars have wondered before. How was it possible, under such a repressive administration, that the author of *Richard II,* purportedly a member of the lower merchant class, could possibly write such a politically sensitive scene, leading as it did to a *coup* against the monarch – and then fail to receive even a reprimand for having done so? A prison sentence, the loss of a hand, even execution for treason would have been Shaxpere's fate, had he truly been Shakespeare. Amputation at the wrist was the fate that befell both pamphleteer John Stubbes and his publisher in 1579, because they dared print a politically sensitive plea that the Queen should withdraw from her proposed marriage to the French prince, the duc d'Alençon .

Consider, too, the fate of Dr. John Hayward. In 1600, just months before Shakespeare's *Richard II* was used for seditious purposes, Hayward was found guilty of treason and sent to the Tower for writing The First Part of the *Life and Raigne of King Henrie IV.* His book was also suppressed because it was deemed to contain seditious material. Despite its misleading title, Hayward retold the story of Richard II's deposition. Sauce for the Hayward goose was apparently not sauce for the Shakespeare gander.

Two years before this, Thomas Nashe had been sent to the Fleet Prison for his part in writing a *"slanderous and seditious"* play, called *The Isle of Dogs.* Edmund Spenser was another who fell victim to the censor; he was banished to Ireland for depicting Lord Burghley in an animal fable as a power-hungry fox. Strange, is it not, that the Stratford orthodoxy can accept Burghley caricatured as a fox, but baulk at conceding Burghley as POLONIUS in *Hamlet?* But, perhaps, not so strange when it is realised that to concede this latter characterization would require an explanation as to why Shakespeare was not dealt with in a similar fashion. The difference in degree between Spenser and the 17th Earl of Oxford provides the missing explanation.

John Marston and George Chapman were two other writers punished by the censor; they were arrested for just two paragraphs considered slanderous, which appeared in *Eastward Ho.* Later, they told how they were to have *"had their ears cut and their noses."*

Jonson, having already suffered imprisonment along with Nashe for his part in writing *The Isle of Dogs,* was once again brought before the Privy Council; this time accused by the Earl of Northampton of *"popery and treason".* His crime was having written and then published *Sejanus* (Conv., II. 325-7).

In the midst of this atmosphere of repression, John Stow's *Annales* for the summer of 1601 recorded the following event.

> *The last of June Atkinson a Customer of Hull, was set on the Pillory in Cheape, and with him three other, to wit, Wilkinson, Alson, & Cowley brought thither on horseback, with their faces towards the horse tails and paper on their heads. They were there whipped on the Pillory, and lost their ears, by judgement given in the Star Chamber, for slanderous words by them spoken & written against the Lord Treasurer [Lord Burghley] and others of the council.* [9]

The reason, discerned from these punishments, explains why orthodoxy refuses to accept POLONIUS as a caricature of Burghley. Shakespeare was not punished for writing *Hamlet;* therefore Burghley could not be a model for POLONIUS. Had it been otherwise, Shakespeare would have been severely dealt with: possibly been whipped at the pillory or else had his ears removed. Since nothing of the sort happened, ergo: POLONIUS could not have been recognizable as Burghley.

Of course, it is equally clear that by acknowledging Oxford as the author of *Hamlet*, this argument is overturned. A senior earl in the court of Elizabeth, who outranked Burghley through the longevity of his family's service, and who enjoyed the favour of the reigning monarch for the entertainment he provided, as did her jester Richard Tarlton, would be beyond the reach of the pillory. A frown from the Queen was sufficient for Tarlton. For *Shakespeare*, a polite but firm word was sufficient: as when the playwright abandoned CORAMBIS* as his choice of name for CLAUDIUS'S chief counsellor and renamed him POLONIUS.

This was not the only time Oxford had been asked to change the name of a character. FALSTAFF, in *Henry IV One*, had originally been named OLDCASTLE; but the Cobham family took umbrage at the antics of their ancestor on stage (Oldcastle had married into the Cobham family in 1408 to become Lord Cobham), and protested. Oxford responded, and bowed to their objection by renaming the character. But he did explain in the play's Epilogue that *"Oldcastle died a martyr and this is not the man."*

Nevertheless, the Cobham family did cause a rumpus at the time. Not only were they able to secure the character's name change, but the fuss they made allowed the Admiral's Men to cash in on the commotion, which had clearly gone public, by producing their own play, *The First Part of the True and Honourable History of the Life of Sir John Oldcastle, the good Lord Cobham.* But, ever careful not to anger the Cobham family, the Prologue explained to the audience:

It is no pampered glutton we present
Nor aged Councellor to youthful sinne
But one whose vertue shone above the rest
A valiant Martyr and a virtuous peere.

This brouhaha over Oldcastle's name must have still been in the

* Cor = a heart, amb/is = of two. By comparison, the motto of Lord Burghley, who is the widely accepted model for Polonius, began with Cor una = one heart; hence, this barbed pun by Oxford against his former guardian who later became his much despised father-in-law.

public domain in 1618, because Nathaniel Field referred to it in his play, *Amends for Ladies*, printed that year, in which a character says: *"Did you not see the piece in which the fat knight, named Oldcastle, told you truly what was honour?"* This was a reference to *Henry IV One,* (Act 5: sc. iii). (Gervinus, 1883, p. 299).

From this, it is very easy to discern the class distinction that existed between a highborn titled playwright and one from the lower strata of society. Whippings, imprisonment, amputation, exile, and facial mutilation were the punishments meted out to those from a working class background, if guilty of writing material thought to be defamatory, or seditious. But for a noble lord it was sufficient only that a quiet word from the offended party be made to the Master of Revels, requesting the author to omit from public performances, say: the deposition scene in *Richard II,* or to remove the part in *Henry V,* where the Lord Chancellor receives a box round the ears: lest these give unwelcome ideas to audiences from the lower classes.

Be this as it may, Lord Burghley's power at suppressing undesirable material, and punishing offenders was immense, and cannot be separated from his sanction of torture.

> *After careful examination of a considerable body of evidence ready to our hands, it is impossible to avoid the conclusion that Cecil must be held, in the main, responsible for the systematic use of torture, during the last thirty years of the Queen's reign, as a means of literally wrenching from men under accusation such information as might implicate themselves or others, and which was used by the prosecution as evidence against the accused ... The same authority tells us that the Rack-master, Richard Topcliffe, was actually licensed to torture his victims in his own house, and that he was regarded as an expert in extorting confessions.*[10]

Oxford's position amongst Elizabeth's personal retinue safeguarded him from any form of mutilation. Indeed, he could not be publicly admonished at all for his writing. It was for this reason that Shaxpere was never brought in for questioning: to have done so would have brought the truth of his secret employment by Oxford out into the open.

Censorship, for reasons of national security, is easy to comprehend, as too is the suppression of printed material, which, if made public, could reduce titled figures at court to ridicule. But blame for such peccadilloes as caricaturing senior members at court becomes irrelevant with the passing of time. Oxford's greater culpability was his disregard for the traditions of the age in which he lived. His ancestors had been feudal lords, and England was still trying to distance itself from its feudal past: a system wherein *"every man had a master"*. Oxford's position as the 17th Earl in his family line, with the hereditary title of Lord Great Chamberlain of England, placed him amongst the elite of society, subservient only to the Monarch and the directives of her Privy Council. Unfortunately, the penning of plays by which actors earned their living, and his contact with writers belonging to a lower class, caused him to overstep the boundaries that a person from his privileged birth and upbringing was meant to respect. That he recognised this is evident in the works of *Shakespeare*, where his cognizance and confession of the damage that was done to his noble name is heard more than once.

A Matter of Public Concern

From what has so far been said, it may reasonably be judged that persuasive reasons existed for preferring that Oxford should not be associated with the plays and poetry attributed to his penname of *Shakespeare:* at least, in the short term. But one stands out as being superior to all others. And it was this one reason that scandalised his own peer group, and to so great an extent that to save the honour of his family name, his daughters and their descendents, as well as that of other noble families caught up in his activity, it required he be forever dissociated from the poetry to which this shame referred. That shame was his love for young Southampton, which began when Henry Wriothesley was still a boy, and which was openly confessed in the sonnets he wrote. The poet's often emotive words describe too well the innermost feelings he experienced for the youth.

In 1593 Oxford had published *Venus and Adonis* under the penname William Shakespeare, calling it: *"the first heire of my invention"*. [11] Although it was sold to the public as a poem written by a Warwickshire man, it contained not a single word from that dialect; a dialect that would have been natural to Shaxpere in his part of England (p. 80). The 3rd Earl of Southampton had been party to the ruse: acting as patron to the mythical Shakespeare.

From their well conceived plan, it must follow that this friendship between man and youth had been formed some time ago.

In fact the closeness of their relationship had become a matter of concern as early as 1588, when Southampton was only fourteen. The Queen's artist, Nicholas Hilliard, was apparently commissioned by a person of rank close to the developing scandal, and asked to paint a reminder to Oxford of his recently deceased wife, and to signal the unfaltering love she had had for him despite the tribulations she endured during their marriage. Hilliard responded by painting an appropriate, symbolic picture that called attention to the late Countess of Oxford's great desire to see her husband join her in Heaven, and not be pulled down by the pederasty that was obsessing his mind.

Hilliard's miniature of Oxford depicts him sad-faced, and dressed in mourning black. To his right and reaching down to him through the *"clouds of heaven"* (*Matthew*, 26:64) is the delicate hand of his recently deceased wife, seeking to lend support and prevent him from slipping into the disgrace that was threatening his future: both in this world and the world to come.

As she liv'd an Angel on the earth
So like an angel doth she sit on high,
On his right hand . . . [12]

Hilliard has reproduced these words, by Wilfred Samonde, with telling effect. The painting is also suitably inscribed with the reason for its composition: *"Attici amoris ergo"* 'Because of Attic Love'. (*Attici* is an adjective in the genitive case for *Atticus*, the ancient district of east central Greece whose chief city was Athens; *amoris* is the genitive case for the noun, *amor*, meaning love or great desire; *ergo*, if accompanied by the genitive, as it is in this present case, means *because of*, or *for the sake of*). Also, the date is written *"Ano Dm 1588"* (In the Year of the Lord 1588), *Dm* being a reminder of the religious symbolism in the painting, for it is usually neglected in works of art.

Remarkably, despite the year 1588, some Stratford advocates have thought it appropriate to name the subject of this portrait as Will Shaxpere. The word preposterous is apparently absent from their vocabulary. For, not only has this caused them to abandon any commitment they may have had to the historical record of Shaxpere's life, meagre though it is, they have then been forced to mistranslate *"Attici amoris ergo"* in order to make it say something quite different to its literal meaning.

Consider the otherwise level-headed Leslie Hotson, who, when writing his *Shakespeare By Hilliard*, (California, 1977), said that the painting referred to the Greek god Apollo reaching down to the nimble Mercury in the form of Shakespeare. *

One can only assume the intellect of such people is made dysfunctional by the obsession they have with seeking reasons to support and maintain a cogent belief in Shaxpere, when none exists. Once affected by this delusion, almost anything must seem possible to them. Appalled by the suggestion of 'Attic Love', and the implication of pederasty this has upon the character of his idol, Hotson, declared the Latin to mean, *"Athenians because of love"*: in which 'love' is intended to mean only devoted friendship.

Apollo, let it be noted, was the sun god of Greek mythology, and a deity responsible for *"prophecy, archery, and music"*. He was also male, whereas the hand reaching down from heaven is decidedly feminine. The choice of Mercury fares no better. He was *"the Roman messenger god"* responsible for *"trade and commerce"*: Neither of the two were Athenians; indeed, the Latin expression for Athenian, would be 'from Athens': which translates as 'Athenis'. But, Hilliard did not write 'Athenis amoris ergo', which would in

* Although the Hilliard portrait contains the official description of a hand reaching from the clouds, this ignores the artistic conventions of that time. Henry Peacham's book, *Minerva Britanna* published in 1612, contains several similar illustrations; each one shows a hand reaching down *through the clouds* "from heaven".

any case make very little sense, either to the painting or to anything else; instead, he wrote *"Attici amoris ergo"*–*'Because of Attic Love',* and this carries a great deal of meaning in the context of Hilliard's subject – the bereavement suffered by the Earl of Oxford in 1588. For it comments upon his love for a youth less than half his age, and the concern felt by a person of obvious nobility, able to commission the Queen's portrait painter to complete this picture without reproach; especially since Oxford would recognise the symbolic hand of his wife reaching down to him from Heaven, to support him in his weakness.

Sidney, in contrast, was quite irritated by the subject of 'Attic love', and said so in his *Defence of Poetry*. He found the ease and freedom with which the Greeks wrote about male love repulsive. And he advised against reading Plato's *Phaedrus* or *Symposium*, to which he added the discourse of love in Plutarch. It was, he said, because of the unwelcome and unwholesome rhapsodising on boy love these contain. (Haynes, 1997, p. 101).

Since Hilliard's subject is not named in the portrait, and the Victoria and Albert Museum refers to it as *"Portrait of Unknown Man Clasping a Hand Issuing from a Cloud":* some justification for Oxford as the sitter is required.

Firstly, the face is of a similar structure to that of Oxford, as it appears in a copy of the Welbeck portrait, which was originally painted in Paris in March 1575. Secondly, the hair is light brown and curly: the same, in fact, as Nicholas Hilliard had previously painted Oxford's hair in the ceremonial parade of garter knights, where he is seen carrying the Sword of State, accompanied by Queen Elizabeth. This painting was subsequently engraved by Hogenberg, and is held by the British Museum. Thirdly, the eye colour and eyebrows match those of Oxford. Fourthly, there is the actual historical circumstance to be considered. Oxford's wife was known for her angelic spirit, and her forbearance at the wayward behaviour of her husband, even when he denied paternity of their eldest daughter Elizabeth. For her to be depicted in Heaven, while still reaching out for her husband below, would be recognised by those who knew her circumstances. Fifthly, the year 1588 corresponds precisely to the time Anne Cecil died; moreover, the man in the picture is dressed in mourning black; he also wears a sad expression as one who suddenly sees a life recently extinguished. Sixthly, the man is wearing a hat that recalls the Queen's gift to Oxford in 1581. To celebrate his reunion with Anne Cecil, Elizabeth presented him with a black taffeta hat in the Dutch style, enriched with pearls and a gold threaded hatband.* It would be an important reminder to Oxford, if seen wearing the Queens' gift in a portrait that reunited him with his wife; especially, if Elizabeth had commissioned it. Seventhly, the artist has given his reason for the hand reaching down from heaven: it is because of 'Attic Love', a cultured expression for pederasty. This ties in with the, then, thirty-eight-year-old Oxford and his love for Southampton: a boy who would not reach fifteen until 6 October 1588.

To add further to the correctness of this interpretation, it was not the first time Oxford had been accused of *"Attic love"*: although he was never brought to trial.

Elizabethan society remained firm in its opposition to homosexuality: perceiving it to be a threat to society's moral fabric.

> *To pursue a sexual relationship with a boy was disreputable and might be punished… [A]s Sidney put it, "abominable filthiness"…*
> *English law gave stern directions against a man having genital contact with another man or boy. Yet the noble and dignified friendship of love between men could never exclude such a possibility, while the accusation that a man had had sex with boys was a damaging one that the courts would punish variously … A prominent example was the Earl of Oxford, whose dealings with a pederastic coterie at court led to accusations and a blotted career.* 13

But a far worse situation had developed. Oxford's infatuation for this youth had become expressed in poetry; in lines of richly flowing verse. Some sonnets were even written as a confession of the author's intimate relationship with this young boy, and for which the effeminate appearance of Southampton made him the obvious choice of subject for these verses.

Shake-speares Sonnets teem with rapturous, homoerotic comment, directed at the object of the author's passion; honest to a fault, but potentially disastrous to an already blighted reputation. And to make the situation still worse, the sonnets were being circulated among his private friends, as Meres was to later

* Kurt Kreiler: "Der Mann, der Shakespeare erfand" Frankfurt, 2009, p.265

confirm in his *Palladis Tamia*. The prospect that they might find their way into the public domain, with untold consequences, required preventive measures to be put in force.

It was the very real possibility of discovery that marked the final downfall of Oxford becoming recognised for his unparalleled contribution to English verse. The potential of imperilling state security proved too great a risk to let pass. If the verses reached the public, and Oxford and his catamite Southampton were identified as the two male lovers in the verses, Burghley's position as virtual Head of State would be placed in jeopardy, and his hold on power might be irreparably damaged. Burghley had enemies, and they would not hesitate to prise some benefit from any scandal in which he stood accused. Elizabeth, too, must have feared the turmoil to her court, for this would certainly follow the loss of Burghley, if he was seen to be culpable in his neglect of the Queen's ward.

To add still further to Burghley's mounting problems, Oxford had littered his past with a string of indiscretions: many true, some rumoured, others false. Amongst the more serious, from a moral and legal point of view, were several accusations of 'Attic love', which he had been accused of committing with a kitchen boy. This complaint against his character was sworn by Charles Arundel.

> *I have sene this boye many a time in his chamber, t[w]o [h]ours doors close-lockied, together with him, namlie at Whitehall, and at his howse in Brodestrete. And finding it so, I have gone to the backe dore to satisfie my selfe; at the whiche the boye hath come owte all in a swete, and I have gone in and fownd the beast in the same plight.* [14]

When this charge was brought to Elizabeth's notice, it is said she thought it more of an entertainment than the basis for legal action, and so it passed into history without ever coming to court. But still, the threat of it being reintroduced, should a new and similar accusation be raised, needed to be avoided. To prevent this, a solution was desperately required.

The Solution

Preventing a catastrophe before it happens is better than remedying it in the mayhem that follows, and in this respect Burghley's response to the dilemma he faced still sends a faint echo down the corridor of time.

Before the age of twenty, Southampton was attiring himself in women's clothes. The recently discovered Cobbe portrait shows the young Earl at about seventeen or eighteen years of age in feminine attire. In fact, for the past three centuries, the sitter was mistakenly thought to have been Lady Norton, the Bishop of Winton's daughter. But the portrait is unmistakably that of Southampton, and it shows him wearing double earrings and a Venetian lace collar that was in vogue between 1590 and 1593. The curling tongs have been carefully applied to his hair, which has been styled like that of Juno, the Roman queen of womanhood. A long tress dangles down his left breast and is held in place by the slender delicate fingers of his right hand. He is clearly wearing lipstick, and rouge colours his cheeks. The eyebrows have been plucked with careful precision, and the eyes are bright: possibly due to the effect of belladonna. [15]

The Lord Treasurer's attempt to resolve the problem of his ward's transsexual behaviour took an all too familiar course; he must wed.

Burghley's activity in this direction first became noticeable when he attempted to marry the young Earl to his fifteen-year-old granddaughter, Lady Elizabeth Vere. We first hear of this proposed marriage in mid-July 1590 (Ogburn 1988, p. 648), at a time when Southampton was still just sixteen years of age.

It must have been an act of sheer desperation. No other rational explanation is equal to justifying the fervour Burghley poured into uniting these two children in matrimony. But, in order to proceed with his plan to marry the two, he had first to wait until his granddaughter celebrated her fifteenth birthday, which occurred on 2 July.

In the same month, he hurriedly arranged a meeting with Southampton's family: the actual details of the discussions that took place were never recorded, or if they were, they were destroyed. The object of this family meeting would have been to include a discussion of the proposed marriage between the two teenagers. Their betrothal would help dispel the damaging rumours circulating behind closed doors that Southampton had become Oxford's lover. No other motive serves to explain such an impetuous rush towards completing the nuptial agreement between these two youngsters.

It was very much in the interests of all three families, Southampton, Oxford, and Burghley, to agree the wedding, since it would defuse the threatening scandal. A further clue to the Lord Treasurer's nervousness can be discerned from his previously held view that fifteen was too young an age for marriage. His own daughter Anne had become engaged at fourteen. He had strongly urged against it. Yet, within days of his granddaughter's fifteenth birthday, Burghley was in dire need for her to wed a boy just one year older. As *Shakespeare* so eloquently explained: *"The appetite of our necessities is strange, and can make vile things precious."*

Burghley's marriage plan was designed to be a responsive countermeasure to rumours of Southampton's sexual deviancy; it would also help dispel the scandal building up around himself as Master of the Queen's Wards, which held with it a responsibility for the moral welfare of those placed by the Queen into his care. In this, his problem was compounded by the possible accusation that he was ignoring his ward's behaviour because of his relationship to Oxford. His position must have seemed tenuous, even menacing: fraught with risk to his political career and his dynastic ambitions. As Elizabeth's chief councillor, any serious damage to his reputation would be seized upon, and used as a source of criticism; even implicating the Queen for her closeness to him. The security of the nation, still in the throes of religious turmoil caused by Henry VIII's divorce, required firm government. Any perceived danger, however remote, could not be risked; preventive measures had to be put in place.

Oxford, having been brought to his senses, and realising the political situation that had begun to develop because of his relationship with Southampton, now circulating in his sonnets, admitted the merit of the proposed marriage, and offered no objection. Sonnet 111 confirms an awareness of how his own reputation had now suffered: *"Thence comes it that my name receives a brand, / And almost thence my nature is subdu'd."*

There can be no doubt that the Queen's approval for the marriage had been given. She may have also spoken to Oxford in order to personally express her deep concern at the risk of a scandal breaking out, for this could very easily affect her realm, even her own rule, if Burghley came under attack.

'Shakespeare's' seventeen sonnets urging Southampton to marry, were a response to the rumours then existing amongst those who had read them, that Burghley's ward was too effeminate to marry. They were also intended to dispel the suggestion, circulating at the time, that Oxford was homosexual. The reasoning for this was made clear in *The Sonnets of Shakespeare: A Psycho-Sexual Analysis* by Henry McClure Young (Wisconsin, 1937).

> *No homosexual ... would ever urge such action [as marriage] upon his love. The terror of his days and nights would be the fear of losing him through the wiles of a wife.* (pp. 8, 13)

Young was writing with a commitment to Shaxpere, believing him to be the author of the Sonnets. But, taken as a strategy to distance Oxford, from a charge of homosexuality, these marriage verses had the same effect.

The poems were quite likely to have been written at the suggestion of Lord Burghley for their possible twofold effect. On the one hand Southampton was susceptible to Oxford's poetry and might be moved to comply with their recommendation; while at the same time, they served to exonerate the author from any connection with a sexual desire for the youth.

As to whether these verses had much influence upon the young man's thinking, as had originally been hoped, seems unlikely. Southampton continued to baulk at the suggestion of marriage, and finally ended the engagement; ending too, the promise of his nomination to the prestigious Order of Knights of the Garter. This had been another strategy devised by Burghley, and offered as a bribe to Southampton; he having done nothing of worth to have earned such an honour.

> *He was not appointed, but the fact of his name having been proposed was in itself an honour so great at his early age that it had never before been paid to anyone not of Royal Blood.* [16]

Burghley was furious. Not only had his granddaughter been slighted, but still worse, his plan for dispelling the rumours that surrounded his teenage ward and his daughter's husband had collapsed. This failure would undoubtedly be interpreted as confirmation that the rumours about Southampton were true. In his anger, and perhaps as a last ditch attempt to force the wedding upon the reluctant fiancé, he imposed upon his ward a crippling fine of £5,000 (equivalent to approximately £2,500,000 according to Bryson, *Shakespeare*, Atlas Books, 2007, p. 86; but I believe a more realistic figure to be in the region of £1,400,000). But even this financial penalty was to no avail; Southampton stubbornly refused to marry Oxford's daughter, or any other bride, and the marriage plan was abandoned.

Burghley was not finished. If Southampton refused to marry and stifle the breath of scandal that he was attracting to himself, as well as those around him, then Oxford would have to remarry. In fact, the ideal plan may have been for them both to marry; that way, the heat of gossip would quickly disperse for lack of fuel. It can therefore be no coincidence that Oxford's second marriage occurred at precisely the time when Southampton was refusing to engage in a similar union.

Ever loyal to the Queen, a bride was found for him amongst her maids of honour, and his engagement to Mistress Elizabeth Trentham was announced. In terms of title and status, it was a mismatch. Oxford's bride was the eldest daughter of Thomas Trentham III, a wealthy but untitled landowner from Staffordshire. The Queen's maid had been in service to her majesty for more than ten years. But, at the age of thirty, or thereabouts, her prospects for matrimony had greatly diminished: the more especially because marriage amongst the Queen's personal ladies in waiting was actively discouraged. Those who disobeyed and wed secretly, hoping to avoid Elizabeth's displeasure, paid the penalty by accompanying their husband in prison. Mistress Trentham was most singularly exempt from Elizabeth's disapproval.

The fact that she was released from the Queen's service so readily, and received a wedding present from the treasury as well, argues that Elizabeth was fully apprised of the threatened scandal that might soon erupt, and the political damage this threatened in the aftermath. In short, she was complicit in recommending her maid-of-honour to Oxford.

There is another peculiar feature to this sudden marriage of convenience. Oxford was at that time virtually insolvent, and greatly in debt, not only to Burghley but also to other important creditors. He even owed money to Julia Penn, the woman from whom he had rented rooms; and he owed money, too, to his old retainer, Henry Lok. In short, he was in no position to support a wife, and was scarcely able to sustain himself. Added to this, his first marriage had been the source of much unhappiness, and to ease his sadness, he had found consolation in a close and particularly unwise friendship with the teenage Southampton.

The possibility that Oxford's marriage to Elizabeth Trentham was gently but insistently urged upon him, for the same reason Burghley had attempted to persuade Southampton to marry, becomes even more credible when it is realised how far Mistress Trentham was below her husband's level in society.

Under normal circumstances, the 17th Earl of Oxford would no more have entertained this marriage proposal than he would have considered wedding his former mistress, Anne Vavasor: a woman who had also been handmaid to the Queen, and was from the same class to which the Trentham family belonged. In fact, the Trenthams' position was little different to that of Will Shaxpere. For he, too, eventually acquired a coat of arms, the title of gentleman, and became rich as a landowner; although by comparison, he was less wealthy, and without the court connections that an ancestry on the fringes of upper-class society would have generated.

Unlike the immature Southampton, Oxford responded to the politically sensitive situation he was in, and with his usual volatile nature subdued; he became receptive to the effect a scandal was likely to have upon his daughters' future prospects, and upon Lord Burghley, who was now maintaining all three of his daughters at his personal expense. He must also have been made aware of the Queen's position, should any dishonour involve a senior member of her Privy Council.

On a more positive side, one may consider the possible benefits to Oxford that this marriage held. The Trenthams were a wealthy family. Marriage would not only help to remove the stigma of his suspected paedophilia with Southampton, but the bride's wealth would undoubtedly make available a stable and suitable dwelling place for them both: one, where he would be free from financial pressure, and the more able to indulge in his playwriting activities without interference from irate creditors.

The marriage between Lord Oxford and Elizabeth Trentham took place quite soon after it was proposed, and with so little fuss that the date and location have not survived. An entry in the

Queen's account book referring to her wedding present for the couple implies a date at the close of 1591.

As part of the marriage arrangement, and to end further speculations concerning allegations of his pederasty, Oxford was placed under pressure to sever all future connections with Southampton. Burghley's ward was likewise warned to stay away from Oxford. This separation, and its reason, is referred to in Sonnet 36: *"I may not ever more acknowledge thee, / Lest my bewailed guilt should do thee shame, / Nor thou with public kindness honour me."*

Despite Oxford's marriage, Burghley's plans to diffuse the threatened scandal were not completely successful. Southampton was still single, and his effeminate dress, his mannerisms, and his use of cosmetics could have only added to the rumours that continued to circulate. The Lord Treasurer therefore had reason to feel uncomfortable, perhaps suspecting that despite promises to the contrary, the relationship between his son-in-law and his ward was still continuing.

To satisfy these suspicions Burghley cunningly introduced a spy into the Southampton household: someone who could be depended upon to report back to him with news of what was happening there. The man he selected as undercover agent was John Florio who, between 1592 and 1594, entered Southampton's residence as the Earl's language tutor (Bate, 1998 p. 55).

The Allonym and its Effect on Present History

Burghley had still to deal with the Sonnets, which had all too openly expressed the heartfelt love Oxford felt for this womanly youth. These continued to circulate in private, fuelling further suspicion of Oxford's pederasty. Fortunately, the poet's 'private friends', as Meres would later call them, guarded their content from prying eyes. Publishers would have been only too eager to print the verses, had they been able to lay hands upon them. Will Shaxpere's private friends, assuming they were literate enough, would have been under no obligation to guard them, especially if they were poetic exercises, as his 'bardolators' prefer to believe: a point that is repeatedly overlooked by Shaxpere's biographers.

Because of these love poems and the bond of intimacy they spelt out between Oxford and Southampton, Burghley assumed others would soon become aware of their relationship, were the opportunity to present itself. Consequently, there was only one course of action to take in order to safeguard against this ever happening: Oxford must sever his association with the poems, which meant he must also relinquish authorship of the plays he had written, for their style and content would unfailingly connect the two. But this required the confidential service of another person. Fortunately, the choice was made easy, because Oxford had previously published two major poems, *Venus and Adonis* and *Lucrece*, passing them off as having been composed by the mythical William Shakespeare, for whom Will Shaxpere had stood in as an allonym. This stratagem was therefore revived. Henceforth, this man from Warwickshire would resume his former function as the acknowledged author of Oxford's literary work. Added to which, Oxford appears to have been placed under oath never again to publish, lest it lead to him becoming identified in public as Shakespeare, and the true author of the Sonnets with their guilty admission of Attic love.

In addition to this arrangement, a prohibition was placed upon the printing of the Sonnets. And it was not until 1599 that two found their way into publisher Jaggard's hands. Ten years later, Thomas Thorpe, operating under questionable circumstances, acquired the remainder. A small number of booklets were hurried off the printing press before they could be suppressed. Few survived compared with the number that survived John Benson's edition thirty years later. Thus, for the succeeding generation, *Shake-speare's Sonnets* disappeared from public view. The thirteen copies that have come down to us from Thorpe's first edition, confirm the haste in which they were printed, for they abound with typographical errors. As Ian Wilson remarked:

> *[N]o second edition was to appear ... for another thirty years. By contrast the altogether lesser sonnets of ... Michael Drayton, already six times printed by 1609, went into three further editions. Although hard evidence is lacking, some form of suppression has to be suspected.* [17]

The publishing prohibition placed upon Oxford was to have an embarrassing consequence. It occurred at the time of the Queen's death, when Henry Chettle issued his taunt to the *"silver tongued [poet and god of harbours] Melicert"* for not shedding a tear at Elizabeth's passing. But if Oxford had pledged never again to publish any of his work—it is then perfectly understandable, given the circumstances, that neither would 'Shakespeare'.

As a further measure, to ensure the success of his plan to disunite Oxford from his sonnets and his plays, Burghley had at his immediate disposal enormous control over the kingdom, backed by the undoubted sympathy of the Privy Council, and the approval of the Queen. In addition, he had a spy network; sufficient in its operation to bring to his notice anyone intent upon revealing that Oxford was author to the work of Shakespeare, viz *"Under the Cecils, a spy service grew up that became an invaluable tool of intimidation and suppression throughout the Elizabethan reign."*[18]

Yet, historians have been kinder to him than have those who did come under his suppression. Compare Spenser's opinion:

So did he good to none, to many ill,
So did he all the kingdom rob and pill
Yet none durst speak, no none durst of him plain,
So great he was in grace and rich in gain.[19]

Suppression and intimidation were to be the tools Burghley used to avoid the scandal that he feared might undermine his position; and which, if successful, could disrupt the smooth running of the State.

Even in the relaxed, secular age of the present day, sexual scandals can still cast a heavy sentence of disapproval upon leaders: as US President Clinton discovered through his dalliance with Monika Lewinski, which brought about calls for his instant removal from office. Four centuries ago, this reaction would have been just as evident to Burghley, accompanied, no doubt, by the fear of further repercussions due to the religious divide in England, and the anxiety caused by the country being still in a state of war with Spain.

It was, however, to Burghley's great advantage that not only was he able to influence the Queen in her decision-making (she called him her Spirit), he also exercised complete control in England upon matters of censorship.

The 1559 law re-imposing a uniform state religion headed by the Queen was passed. ... An era had begun which was to be known abroad as the 'Regnum Cecilianum', when for fifty-two years William Cecil and his son Robert effectively governed England. In the process, they created a dynasty so powerful that members of the Cecil family have remained a periodic force in British politics ever since.[20]

In his capacity as the virtual ruler of England, subservient only to Elizabeth, Burghley was determined to use the power of the State to save his family name from becoming tainted by scandal. Through his eyes, any harm done to his person would damage the nation by weakening the Queen's hold on power. The remotest prospect of that occurring was sufficient for him to take action. Nothing was thought too extreme. Oxford's loss of recognition as the author of his plays and poetry was a very small cost to pay if it helped ensure the smooth running of the State.

Oxford's acknowledgement that he was to be dispossessed of his plays and poetry is indicated in Sonnet 81 – *"I once gone, to all the world must die"* – and another in 72 – *"My name be buried where my body is, / And live no more to shame nor me nor you"*. Other than that, history has nothing to say beyond the fact that neither Oxford nor *Shakespeare* ever published again, thus bearing silent witness to what had taken place behind closed doors.

If there were any documents to identify Shaxpere's role in this deception, Burghley's aids would have located and seized them. But to explain Oxford's now orphaned plays became the next problem. Their enforced anonymity could not be expected to last. This difficulty was not resolved until after Burghley's death, when a graduate scholar from Cambridge, Francis Meres, noted only for his powerful sermon, *"Gods Arithmeticke"* (1597), was able to include an incomplete list of Shakespeare's plays in his *Palladis Tamia* (a book that would set out the literary situation in England from Chaucer up to the year of its publication in 1598).

His piece concerning *Shakespeare,* identified the man as an author of twelve plays: even more had the list been complete; all of which, up until then, had been presented anonymously; and this, despite the author's widespread fame as the poet of *Venus and Adonis* and *Lucrece*. Through this stratagem, the public were able to see from the printed word that Oxford, although known for his poetry and comedies, was not the same person as Shakespeare, as some people may have begun to suspect. It is also interesting to note that after having written his book, Meres retired to the tiny county of Rutland, where he spent a life in tranquillity as rector and founder of a small school.

With a paper trail connecting Oxford to Shakespeare severed, and the compliant or suppressed silence of his friends and family assured, it would take no more than a generation for the remembrance of his composition of Shakespeare's work to be forever lost.

There was also another reason for the silence of those who knew that Oxford's disgrace was responsible for the emergence of 'William Shakespeare'. When a threatened scandal affects one of the noblest families in the kingdom, and the governing body uses a spy system to ensure the subject matter is barred from discussion, members of the general public, suppressed to a state of ovine obedience, will do nothing overtly to oppose authority.

Historians have therefore been left with nothing to work upon that is sufficiently capable of contradicting the prevailing opinion left to them by that generation. Contemporary historian William Camden was aware of the problem this posed for future scholarship when he referred to members of the governing body as: *"those who think the memory of succeeding ages may be extinguished by present power."* [21] This is precisely what happened to Oxford's literary life. Whether intentional or not, Camden's words proved an apt description of the manner in which Oxford's work was separated from that of *Shakespeare's*, and all record of it ever happening was obliterated. Future scholars were therefore left to obey the conventions of their training, by accepting only such records that remained. These undeniably refer to a man named Shaxpere, variously spelt, with connections to the Globe theatre and to Stratford-upon-Avon, but also to some questionable characteristics and appreciable deficiencies, which continue to fuel doubts about his authorship. But equally, there are also undeniable records of the praise afforded to Shakespeare by writers who were his contemporaries. However, given that Shakespeare was the penname of Oxford, its use, in respect of praise, is understandable, given the circumstances of censorship. What scholars have therefore been left with are just a few scattered pieces of innuendo, with nothing of sufficient significance to restore what happened. Hence, the importance of Jonson's hidden vow that Edward de Vere was Shakespeare; of Thorpe's encrypted dedication that de Vere wrote the Sonnets, and Oxford's own cryptic reference to himself as author of Sonnet 76. These provide the much needed proof of what really did occur in the final decade of the sixteenth century.

Such, then, was the position regarding Oxford's authorship until Shaxpere's death occurred in 1616. Only then was it considered safe, by those who had shared in Oxford's secret, to publish a permanent record of his plays. With his allonym dead, there was no longer any risk this man might be lulled into betraying the shadowy role he had played as 'William Shakespeare'.

The Sonnets were, of course, omitted from the First Folio. The intimate details included in their content posed far too many embarrassing questions for those who knew the answers. Even three decades later, paedophilia proved a stumbling block to publication, and this was only overcome by changing the gender of the young man.

> *When Shakespeare's sonnets were re-edited in 1640, their publisher John Benson ... altered their language so that sonnets addressing a man spoke instead to a female beloved. ... His manipulation of the [gender] supports the theory that Jacobeans would have been shocked to discover love sonnets addressing a man.* [22]

The Elizabethan and Jacobean periods were times of devout religious observance. The Bible was very much seen as the Word of God and the doorway to salvation. The book of *1 Corinthians* (6:9) in the Geneva *Bible* of that period made no mistake upon the issue of homosexuality.

> *9 Knowe ye not that the vnrighteous shal not inherite the kingdome of God? Be not deceiued: nether fornicatours, nor idolaters, nor adulterers, nor wantons, nor bouggerers.* [23]

Acts of male homosexuality were taken very seriously. In 1563, Queen Elizabeth had decreed by statute that sodomy was a crime punishable by death (Crompton, L. *Homosexuality and Civilization*, Harvard, 2003, pp. 362-6).

A case involving the buggery of a boy at that time throws light upon the crime of male intercourse, which had obvious ramifications for Oxford's plight: *"Humphrey Stafford was tried by the Court of the King's Bench (1607–8) for just such a crime and executed."* [24] As the astrologer Simon Forman later remarked: *"his mistake was to choose a sixteen-year-old."* Oxford's relationship with Southampton covered that same age group.

Some there are, however, that are incapable of believing that such a cover-up could have remained concealed from the public for so long. They are mistaken in their belief. A similar cover-up, also involving Lord Burghley, his nephew and sodomy, was uncovered as late as 1973, after the passage of 386 years. Such was the power of censorship in these matters; especially those involving the Cecil dynasty and homosexuality, that every reference to it was removed from State records.

French records were beyond the power of Cecil's censorship. In 1973 Dame Daphne du Maurier was combing through 16th century records at Montauban in southern France, when, to her amazement, she uncovered a piece of history that had been denied to English historians. It was an account of Anthony Bacon's guilt in acts of sodomy he committed in France, while engaged in building up a spy network for Sir Francis Walsingham. As a result of this, he was . . .

> *charged with sodomy in the summer of 1586. His favourite page was Isaac Burgades, who himself would forcibly "mount" a still younger page in the household, David Boysson, and who told another page, Paul de la Fontayne, that there was nothing wrong with sodomy. One of the lackeys, Barthelemy Sore, had left Anthony's service because his master was wont to bugger all the boys and then bribe them with sweetmeats to keep quiet. In France, convicted sodomites were sentenced to death by le bucher* [the wood-pile; i.e. burnt at the stake].[25]

Anthony Bacon was the brother of Sir Francis, and the son of Sir Nicholas Bacon, one of the wealthiest men in England who shared power with Lord Burghley, with whom he was related by marriage. Anthony Bacon's high profile, which stretched to the very top of the English government, caused the King of Navarre to intervene. This was the future Henri IV of France, who was caricatured as FERDINAND in *Love's Labour's Lost.* Henri sent a letter to Burghley in England with a proposal for clemency.

> *I write now desiring you to bring his right of appeal promptly before the judge and have it granted as expeditiously as possible. ... He will know how to repay us in kind for mercy shown to him.*[26]

All account of what happened has been deleted from English records. Bacon left Montauban but remained in France until 1592. After returning to England, he settled first with his brother Francis, and later joined Robert Devereux at Essex House, where he became a witness for the prosecution at Essex's trial in 1601. In the same year he died in the home of Walsingham's daughter Frances.

Let it therefore never be said that Oxford's indiscretion with young Southampton was incapable of being covered-up. Since Burghley had successfully accomplished this for his nephew, he would certainly have set the same wheels in motion for his daughter's husband. In neither case did he want his family name tainted by paedophilia. But Oxford's case was more complicated. He had written about his love for Burghley's ward in sonnets that were already circulating amongst his private friends.

It was the poetic detailing of this irreligious and unlawful relationship between Oxford and Southampton that prevented the sonnet sequence from being published. And when Thorpe did lay hands on the verses in 1609, which he then published – so hastily they teem with uncorrected errors – it does indicate that Thorpe anticipated their sale would be stopped. While direct evidence for this is absent, the circumstance preceding their publication after nigh on twenty years, and then to be so quickly followed by their disappearance for another thirty years, is far from what would be expected of William Shakespeare, were he truly the uncomplicated, unassuming man from Stratford.

> *[Shake-speares sonnets] is now a very rare book; yet the natural presumption would be that in 1609, at the height of Shakepeare's contemporary fame, it would have found a considerable sale if it were not interfered with; and that a second edition would have followed in a few years ... There is fair ground for a presumption that ... [it] was stopped, whether through the intervention of Shakespeare or another.*[27]

A further point to note, but which is never addressed by expert opinion, concerns the lack of subsequent comment that would be expected from the publication of these Sonnets, had Shaxpere written them.

> *Unless Q [Shakes-speares Sonnets] was quickly suppressed, how can one account for the total silence of Sh.'s contemporaries about the mysterious figures of the dark woman, the male friend, and the rival poet? Surely the first of these would have attracted at least as much attention and comment from readers as Sidney's Stella or Daniel's Delia.*[28]

But nothing was forthcoming. In the rough and tumble of literary exchanges amongst pamphleteers, everyone remained as silent about this mysterious trio, as they had done about the man who wrote about them. Frankly, this lack of reaction is totally unbelievable, were Shaxpere the poet; whereas, non-reaction is to be expected if it meant commenting upon the private life of a senior member of the nobility; who, although deceased, retained powerful family connections in government and at court.

The suppression of the poems until 1609, followed by thirty years of silence, would be a natural consequence of their content. But in 1638, Sir William Davenant became England's Poet Laureate. In his imagination, built upon uncertain ground, he believed himself related to Shakespeare through Shaxpere's illicit union with his mother Jeannette. The two had supposedly consummated their friendship at the family-run tavern in the city of Oxford during one of Shaxpere's annual breaks, when he journeyed between London and Stratford-upon-Avon. And for this supposed moment of passion, Davenant lovingly referred to his mother as a whore.

Believing himself to be the 'son of Shakespeare', Davenant would have been highly motivated to see the Sonnets restored to public readership, so that he and his own poetry might glow in their reflected light. Moreover, as Poet Laureate, he would have had the necessary leverage to press for their publication. And so, whether due to coincidence or appeal, in 1640, Benson's expurgated version of the Sonnets, but now reduced from 154 to 146 and in a different order from that of 1609, was published. It would be another hundred years before eighteenth-century scholarship reversed Benson's editing of the poems' homoerotic content, and restored to the printed word the true object of the poet's passion: much to the dismay of readers.

The reason for their dismay was the suggestion of the poet's homosexuality lurking between the lines of many verses. This understanding, formed by the general public, was precisely what Burghley's censorship had intended to prevent. By the nineteenth century and into the twentieth, it was finally out in the open and the literary world in England, and beyond its shores, began candidly debating the question of Shakespeare's sexuality. Hyder Rollins, in Appendix VIII of *A New Variorum Edition of*

Shakespear – The Sonnets (1944), p. 232, discussed the pros and cons that were occupying the minds of those disposed to confirm or reinterpret more favourably the offending passages. The following extracts from Rollins, reveal the opinions of those moved to accept Shakespeare's homosexuality, long before Joseph Sobran (*Alias Shakespeare,* 1997) turned Oxford partisans livid by accepting the same conclusion.

"Good heavens," wrote De Wailly (*Revue des deux mondes,* 1834, 3d series, IV, 688), *"Shakespeare! Great Shakespeare! Did you feel yourself authorized by Virgil's example?"* But Conrad (*Archiv,* 1879, LXII, 16 f.) considered it to be *"our moral duty"* to disavow Shakespeare's complicity in that *"loathsome, sensual degeneracy of love among friends that antiquity unfortunately knew."* Not so, H. M. Stanley (*Essays,* 1897, p. 4), he believed them to *"celebrate a love ... dubious in its character."* Thomas Neal (*Marzocco,* December 19, 1897, p. 3) was more explicit, referring to them as *"forbidden love".* Samuel Butler (ed. 1899) was no less certain, remarking that the sonnets suffer *"from a leprous or cancerous taint ... [and tell] a very squalid [story] 86 ... more Greek than English." 122.* Jusserand, too, was unhappy with the tenure of the sonnets, and wrote: *"something morbid exhales ... [revealing] an unconscious and involuntary Platonism,"* (*Literary History,* 1909, III, 237). Albert Moll agreed (*Berühmte Homosexuelle (Grenzfragen des Nerven – und Seelenlebens,* 1910, XI, no. 75, 38 f.), *"one can scarcely deny the erotic nature of the sonnets."* A similar sentiment was repeated by G. W. Knight (*Holborn Review,* 1929, LXXI, 450 f.), *"One can say no more than that Shakespeare had probably at one time experienced a passionate love for some friend."* Thurston (*Month,* 1930, CLVI, 434) was dismayed at having reached the same conclusion: *"regretfully as we must say it, the Sonnets in their plain and obvious meaning point to a plague spot, which beginning in the neo-paganism of the Italian renaissance, had by degrees infected the more dissolute and godless among young men of fashion throughout Europe."* Three years later, Francis Birrell wrote to concur (*New Statesman,* 1933, n. s., V, 480): *"Such complete absorption in another person of the same sex, whether 'Platonic' or not, seems to me psychologically homosexual."*

The paedophilia implied by the Sonnets has therefore been an ongoing problem when commenting upon these poems. Lovers of Shakespeare's art, in the main, prefer not to see in them the autobiographical dark side of their idol, and are dismissive of the author's subjectivity, referring to it, if at all, as his *"imagined emotions"*. Others, such as Goethe, Wordsworth, Carlyle, and Raleigh (d. 1922) were far more alert, being of the same mind as Beethoven, who declared: *"What comes from the heart, goes to the heart"*.

Alternative Proposals

Advocates for Oxford's recognition as Shakespeare have had the same problem to contend with. In order to meet the challenge of sanitizing the sonnets some have resorted to theorizing that Southampton was Oxford's son by Queen Elizabeth; hence the poet's love for this young boy was strictly paternal.

To muster evidence for the theory, Sonnet 57 is often cited because it includes the line: *"Whilst I, my sovereign, watch the clock for you."* Southampton thus becomes the sovereign, because he was born of the Queen:. The problem with this interpretation is one of Tudor grammar (p. 192).

When a parent spoke to a child, the proper form of address was *thou.* And again, when two persons were involved in an intimate relationship, the proper form of address was also *thou:* as occurs in the majority of 'Shake-speare's Sonnets' to Southampton. But when members of the upper classes spoke to each other, the correct form of address was *you,* as in Sonnet 57. Hence, it may be concluded that Oxford, when addressing *"my sovereign"*, had Queen Elizabeth in mind.

This is evident from the excessively subservient expressions contained throughout the poem; it is the manner in which a noble subject is likely to address the monarch in poetic form:

Being your slave, what should I do but tend
Upon the hours and times of your desire?
I have no precious time at all to spend,
Nor services to do, till you require.
...

Nor think the bitterness of absence sour
When you have bid your servant once adieu;
Nor dare I question with my jealous thought
Where you may be, or your affairs suppose,
...

A further possibility is that the clock referred to by the poet was the astronomical clock, with its eight-foot diameter, which was made for Henry VIII by Nicholas Oursian in 1540. This was set in place at Hampton Court Palace above an archway leading into a small court. The clock directly faced what were to become Queen Elizabeth's private rooms.

One may therefore imagine an impatient Oxford standing at the window overlooking Clock Court, *"watching the clock"* while he waited for an audience with the Queen, daring not to *"question with my jealous thought / Where you may be, or your affairs suppose;"* and then, during his enforced leisure, penning this particular sonnet so that he might offer it to the Queen.

Once again, it can be seen how stifled Stratford scholarship becomes when thoughts are restricted to Will Shaxpere. It is impossible to understand this Sonnet, or any other for that matter, being addressed to Queen Elizabeth in such intimate terms by a man of Shaxpere's rank. The words had to come from a high-ranking member at Court. As for the nonsense that Shaxpere shared a cosy relationship with the pampered young Earl of Southampton, and that he could address him intimately and later admonish him for loose behaviour—then let it be said, class distinction would have positively forbidden such impertinence.

Nevertheless, there still exists several unanswered questions surrounding the birth of Henry Wriothesley. He was born on 6 October 1573: but in a seeming contradiction to this, nine months earlier, his 'father' was a prisoner inside the Tower of London. It is therefore unlikely that the 2nd Earl of Southampton was the father; apart from which, it was said that he had a preference for male company.

The second oddity occurred when Henry Wriothesley joined forces with the Earl of Essex in his ill-fated rebellion against the government in 1601, which led to their capture. On 19 February Essex and Southampton were arraigned before a jury of twenty-five peers. Both were found guilty and sentenced to death by beheading. Essex was executed on 25 February. His associate Meyrick and his secretary Cuffe, were hanged at Tyburn on 25 March, and Sir Christopher Blount and Sir Charles Danvers were also beheaded. Remarkably, Southampton's sentence was commuted to life imprisonment; although, it has been said, this was achieved only by the most tearful overtures to the Queen from the condemned man's wife and mother. Wriothesley was later released when King James came to the throne in 1603.

This curious episode has led to the argument that Queen Elizabeth could not sign the order for executing her own flesh and blood. The suggestion is certainly plausible, had Southampton been her son. But on its own it is not sufficient, since other persuasions appear to have influenced the Queen's clemency.

A major flaw to the suggestion that Queen Elizabeth was the mother of Henry Wriothesley is more obvious. It is the genetic

similarity occurring between the features of Lady Southampton and her son. Oxford made the same observation in Sonnet 3, when addressing his subject. *"Thou art thy mother's glass, and she in thee;"* (see also p.185). Added to this, the 2nd Earl of Southampton confirmed his wife's delivery in a letter sent to William More. He began by expressing regret that More's wife was not able to be present to assist at the birth, as had been desired . . .

> *Although it is so happed by the sudden sickness of my wife that we could not by possibility have her present as we desired, yet have I thought good to impart unto you such comfort as God hath sent me after all my long troubles, which is that this present morning at three o' clock my wife was delivered of a goodly boy (God bless him!) the which, although it was not without great peril to them both for the present, yet now I thank God both are in good state ... From Cowdray, this present Tuesday 1573. Your assured friend. H. Southampton.* [29]

It may also be recalled that in Sonnet 13, the poet remarks to young Southampton: *"Dear my Love, you know / You had a father: let your son say so."* Since Oxford was not speaking about himself from the afterlife, then this plainly spoken sentence, especially when emphasised with a pause after *know*, refutes the idea that he was the youth's father.

Despite these objections, yet another piece of 'evidence' is proposed to support Southampton's royal parentage. It is the so-called 'Persian Portrait', purportedly showing Queen Elizabeth *enceinte*. A long-standing tradition has always referred to Elizabeth as the Virgin Queen. In which case, the portrait would contradict that title. What also fascinate the observer are the clues put there by the artist, in line with the habit of that era. These have been painted over, thus obscuring their identification. Even more surprising, it seems this obfuscation was conducted in the twentieth century.

Quite naturally, some supporters of Oxford see this as further evidence that Elizabeth I bore an illegitimate son, and that the 2nd Earl of Southampton and his Countess, who had recently lost their own child, for so it is alleged, fostered the royal infant. In short, Southampton was a changeling.

The problem with this is not that it refutes Queen Elizabeth's virginity, but that her one-time pregnancy, as depicted by the portrait, was the result of an amorous liaison with Oxford, and not with her favourite, the Earl of Leicester. Historically, it was Leicester's bedroom that was moved to adjoin Elizabeth's—if not for night-time encounters, then why? Elizabeth claimed it was for expediency in State matters. If that were true, why did Lord Burghley, a statesman far more important than Leicester, never occupy a similar adjoining bedroom?

Determined attempts have been made in the past by experts to dismiss the idea that the woman in the *Persian Portrait* is pregnant. But the picture originally carried three announcements in Latin that appear to suggest otherwise: *Iniusti Justa querela* (A just complaint of a wrong); *Mea sic mihi* (Mine, as things stand, for me), and *Dolor est medicina editum* (Sorrow is the cure having given birth). The last word in these mottoes has since been altered from *editum* to read *ed tori*. A simple test with pencil and eraser proves how easy it is to change *editum*, a genuine Latin word, into *ed tori,* which then renders the motto meaningless: since 'ed' is not a Latin word; the dictum therefore becomes untranslatable, which, it must then be supposed was the purpose behind the alteration.

Nevertheless, the mottoes in their original form; the pregnant appearance of the woman; a weeping stag (an animal that was part of Leicester's subsidiary coat of arms); and a longstanding tradition of the title originally given to the painting; give credence to those suggesting that it refers to Queen Elizabeth I some months after conception. And, by the tenure of the three mottoes, her lover had something to complain about.

Let it be supposed that Leicester did lose a son by Queen Elizabeth, then, indeed, he would have had good reason to protest. This would certainly explain the motive for someone later altering the Latin text; and for painting over any relevant clues that might be considered too revealing if left uncovered.

Titillating though this may be, and there is a film, *Anonymous,* that repeats a similar storyline, no actual documentary evidence has ever been found to support it; rather the contrary. In 1584, Mary Stuart, imprisoned in England by order of Elizabeth, wrote to the Queen, touching indelicately upon her love life, and her virginity.

> *. . . the countess of Shrewsbury said to me about you what follows as nearly as possible ... Firstly that one to whom she said you had made a promise of marriage before of your chamber had lain many times with you with all the licence and familiarity which husband and wife can use to one another. But undoubtedly you were not as other women and for this reason all those who desired your marriage with the duke of anjou, considering that it could not be consummated were foolish and that you would never wish to lose the liberty of making love and gratifying yourself with new lovers ... even the count of Oxford dared not reconcile himself with his wife for fear of losing the favour, which he hoped to receive, by becoming your lover.* [30]

Attention is drawn to three major points in the letter. Firstly, there is the assertion that the Queen's marriage could never be consummated. Secondly, the Queen wished to retain the liberty of gratifying herself with new lovers. Thirdly, the Earl of Oxford had hoped to succeed where others had failed. Thirty-five years after Mary Stuart's letter was written, William Drummond of Hawthornden wrote down the conversations he had had with

Ben Jonson, who visited him in the previous year. Among these recollections, he provided the reason for Elizabeth's failure to consummate a marriage.

> *Queen Elizabeth never saw herself after she became old in a true glass; they painted her, and sometymes would vermillion her nose ... That she had a membrana on her, which made her uncapable of men, though for her delight she tried many. At the comming over of Monsieur [the duc d'Alençon] there was a French Chirurgian [surgeon] who took in a hand to cut it, yet fear stayed her.* [31]

The Countess of Shrewsbury's report to Mary Stuart in 1584, and relayed to Elizabeth, is explained in adequate detail from Drummond's meeting with Jonson in 1618.

Elizabeth was incapable of full sexual intercourse, and remained so for the remainder of her life. This did not prevent her enjoyment with new lovers. In fact, it must have acted as a contraceptive. Oxford had once been favoured by the Queen. He may have had visions of becoming her husband since his own marriage had not been consummated, which meant it could be legally annulled. But Elizabeth had no intention of marrying; to her, it was all a game.

Much has been made of her several visits to Archbishop Parker in 1573, accompanied by Oxford. Politically, this was a turbulent year. The Siege at La Rochelle was underway, with England's commitment to the Huguenot cause challenged by France, to the effect that ships with French and Flemish names were being prepared by the Queen to relieve the siege. An army was being assembled to march on Edinburgh. Charles IX had assembled a squadron of ships to sail to Scotland and aid Mary Stuart's supporters. The Earl of Shrewsbury had been implicated in a plot against the Queen. And amidst these state affairs for 1573, we learn . . .

> *Leicester was still considered as the principal favourite with the queen, and enjoyed more of her private conversations than any other person about the court.*[32]

Oxford was then twenty-three years of age, and the Queen in her forty-first year. In February 1559, Parliament had petitioned her to marry. Her response to the petition is instructive; the more so to those believing her to be a single mother.

In her response to Parliament she endeavoured to set out her thinking on the matter, touching as it did the private and public, shifting the matter to divine guidance rather than temporal need, and declaring that it was sufficient for her to have lived and died a virgin. She had been untutored in that general expectation of marriage which swamped all girls, as stepmothers came and went. (25)... With a teasing flourish she justified her single life by claiming the kingdom as her spouse, so "every one of you, and as many as are English, are my children, and kinsfolk," (31).[33]

The birth of Henry Wriothesley must therefore be divorced from any suggestion that he was the son of Queen Elizabeth. But the 2nd Earl of Southampton did accuse his wife, Mary Browne, of adultery with a retainer. And since the Earl had been locked away in the Tower at the time of his wife's conception, he seems to have had good reason. Conjugal rights were possible inside the Tower, but they involved a bribe paid to the gaoler; as was the case with the Earl of Hertford, who paid for *"procreative time with his wife"*[34]

Furthermore, to suppose that Henry Wriothesley had a claim to the throne requires some form of admission by him. The perfect time for this was during his part in the rebellion led by Essex in 1601. In fact, as heir to the throne, he should have led the rebellion himself.

A not too dissimilar situation occurred during the reign of King James's grandson, James II. His succession was challenged by the Duke of Monmouth, the illegitimate son of Charles II; although Monmouth did claim his mother had taken part in a marriage ceremony with the King. Monmouth conducted an armed rebellion against his uncle in July 1685, but was defeated, and suffered the same fate that befell Essex.

For 'Prince Tudor' theorists, the evidence for Queen Elizabeth having given birth to a child, fathered by Oxford, is elicited from the sonnets. Confirmation is then sought from historical records. But the sonnets make no such claim, and history does nothing to suggest otherwise. This mistake is easily rectified by attending to Elizabethan protocol. Sonnets addressed by Oxford to his sovereign, Queen Elizabeth, are those that use *you* instead of *thou*. Sonnets that use *thou* are primarily written to Southampton. Oxford may use *you* when addressing Southampton, but it will then be as one peer of the realm to another, and not as a love poem.

Had this simple rule been adhered to at the beginning, so much unnecessary disputation within Oxford circles could have been avoided; instead, it has led to pixilated theories being formed, involving incest at the highest level. Such suppositions are based upon each author's imaginative reading of the Sonnets, and a contorted view of how history might be interpreted differently, so as to coincide with their thoughts. Evidence to the contrary is always neglected, or else represented out of context.

Consider the proposal that Oxford was actually a love child of the Queen. The time for this adventure into the imaginative arts, centres upon Elizabeth's stepfather, Baron Seymour of Sudeley. He was known to have desired his stepdaughter, and had far too often frolicked with her inappropriately: especially in her waking hours. This led to rumours that he had made her pregnant. Elizabeth was outraged when it was brought to her notice, and vigorously denied it in a written letter to the Lord Protector: *"My Lord, these are shameful slanders,"* she said. This is not at all a statement that could ever be made by a woefully pregnant girl whose lie would very soon become exposed by the swelling in her womb.

On 22 February 1549, any ambitions towards the throne that Seymour may have cherished were brought to a close. He was tried before his peers on thirty-three counts of treason; and was executed one month later on 20 March: a full year, and more, before Oxford was born (12 April 1550).

Had this rumour been founded upon truth, and then united to the proposition that Henry Wriothesley was also a child of the Queen by Oxford, as some have thought proper to believe, the consequences are bizarre. It would mean that Queen Elizabeth wished to marry her son Henry – who was conceived after she had slept with her eldest son Edward – to her granddaughter Elizabeth Vere. Her son Henry would then be his wife's half brother, as well as being the half brother of his father.

The return to sanity takes us back to Oxford's homosexuality and Lord Burghley's ability to use censorship as a means of preventing this becoming public knowledge, as he had already done for his nephew, Anthony Bacon. But there are still dissenting voices. These come from those who refuse to concede 'their' Shakespeare could be defamed by either incest or the Attic vice.

It is their view that Oxford was forced to transfer his authorship to another, because the 'stigma of print' forbade a nobleman from publishing his writing. Added to which, the content of his plays were too great an embarrassment for some members of the court to accept. For example, if it were publicly known that Shakespeare was a pseudonym of Oxford, there would be a growing awareness of the personalities he had caricatured, leading to mockery by the under classes. But these are weak arguments. The latter would have lost force in step with the retirement or decease of each member of the court; whereas, Oxford's severance from his plays and poetry remained constant. The other suggestion has little relevance once King James set an example by publishing his own works, such as *Daemonologie* (1597), *True Law of Free Monarchies* (1598), and *Basilikon Doron* (1599). Moreover, in neither case does 'stigma of print' explain the explosive, significant consequences of the sonnets, and the homo-erotic love addressed to a youth.

In summary, Oxford was denied recognition as author of his plays and sonnets, and these became assigned to another. Why, if not because of their content? Was it because a few sonnets might be read to suggest the poet had fathered an heir to the throne through a clandestine affair with the Queen? Only by misreading certain lines in the sonnets can this attract followers. Was it to save face amongst courtiers who might protest at recognising themselves? Unlikely, in 1623 there were few still living. Was it the 'stigma of print'? Not when the King had removed this taboo by publishing his own works. This leaves homosexuality. Sonnet 144 records the poet's preference for the youth to his mistress.

In 1533, *"Buggery"* became a capital offence. Edward VI later repealed the law, but Elizabeth reinstated it in 1563. When James VI of Scotland became King of England, he had already stated in his *Basilikon Doron* that sodomy was a crime *"ye are bound never to forgive."* It was therefore a sin, for which Oxford's guilt required the cloak of censorship. It must never be made public. As a result, the Sonnets, in which his confession to this vice could be construed by readers, and which was presumably known as fact amongst his closest contemporaries, became a forbidden publication. The plays, too, written in his unmistakeable style were officially allowed to be known as the work of 'Shakespeare': a man by the name Shaxpere, who was a shareholder in the Globe theatre, and a sometime actor, in the pay of Oxford.

Like all good theories, this one allows predictions to be made. One of these is that Oxford's contemporaries: writers, who appreciated his genius, would use their talent to encrypt his name into tributes and inscriptions that referred to his work, and which were likely to endure long enough for a future generation to discover. For this was the only safe way to communicate the truth of what was a heavily censored piece of social history.

The theory also makes a second prediction: that every scrap of documentary evidence linking Oxford to the work attributed to Shaxpere, would be scrupulously gathered in and destroyed. The success of this operation is measured by the frustration felt by orthodox scholars, who have searched in vain for Literature's missing link – physical evidence that would connect the resident of Stratford-upon-Avon with an actual poem or play he is said to have written.

The third prediction is very obvious. Since Shaxpere did not write the works of Shakespeare, research into his background will indubitably fail to verify that he did. And that is precisely the position today. If it were otherwise, there would be no authorship problem.

6

SHAKESPEARE'S LEARNING CURVE

Exegi monumentum aere perrennius.
(I have reared a monument more lasting than brass.)

Horace

IS THERE SUCH A MISDEED as scholastic cowardice? One would like to think not; nevertheless, one does wonder why a well-documented event in the life of the Earl of Oxford, which was repeated in a Shakespeare play, is never mentioned in pro-Shaxpere commentaries that discuss this play. It is almost an invitation to believe that commentators are affected by collective amnesia; unless, that is, there is something they prefer not to make known?

HENRY V

The play referred to is *The Famous Victories of Henry the Fift.* It was published in 1598, with no author named, but its appearance coincided with Francis Meres' *Wits Treasury,* which identified William Shakespeare as the author of twelve plays that had previously appeared anonymously. *The Famous Victories of Henry the Fift* was in fact an old play. Richard Tarlton had once played the role of DERICKE long ago, and he had been dead since 1588. So, why was *The Famous Victories* suddenly thought to be a marketable commodity? The question appears to have more to do with Meres having brought Shakespeare's name into the public domain, rather than that of meeting an otherwise late and questionable demand.

Three of Shakespeare's plays, *1 Henry IV, 2 Henry IV,* and *Henry V,* draw upon actions occurring in *The Famous Victories of Henry the Fift.* A similar case occurs with *King John, 2 Henry VI,* and *3 Henry VI,* which draw upon *The Troublesome Reign of King John, The Contention Between Two Famous Houses* and *The True*

Tragedy of Richard Duke of York.

In the anonymous *Famous Victories,* scenes 1 through to 7 correspond to actions that have been transferred to Shakespeare's *1 Henry IV*; and the same can be said of scenes 8 and 9, which have been transferred to *2 Henry IV;* while scenes 9 through to 20 reappear in *Henry V.* These earlier plays therefore emerge as excellent examples of how the master playwright perfected his art.

There are no comparative examples for Shaxpere. The only similarity that does exist can be found in Greek Mythology, where the goddess Athene was plucked fully armed from the head of Zeus. Pro-Shaxpere academics prefer to believe this also applies to their man. He arrived in London from an obscure community in the Midlands, populated by less than 1500 people, having left behind an uneducated and illiterate family. Under his arm was a sheaf of plays, each one word perfect. And so fully compatible was each work with Italian life and the code of behaviour at court, as well as being near perfect for an immediate performance on stage, that both he and his plays were received with instant acclaim.

Those who decry this 'explanation', and prefer the reality of an apprenticeship for Shakespeare, will find it in the *Histories.* On Thursday 21 May 1573, two of Oxford's former servants, William Faunt and John Wotton (aka Clopton), wrote a letter of complaint to Lord Burghley, concerning an attack with light muskets that had been made upon them the day before, at or near Gads Hill, which is situated between Gravesend and Rochester.

> *... wootton and my sealfe, rydynge peasably by the hyghe way, from Grauesend to Rochester, had thre calyvers charged with bullettes discharged at vs by thre of my Lord of Oxenfordes men / Danye Wylkyns Ihon Hannam, and Deny the Frenche man vhoe lay preuylye in a diche awaytynge oure cumminge wythe full intente to murder hus.* [1]

As Professor Bate might have remarked, it is uncanny to discover this same scene at Gads Hill, also in the month of May, being exactly repeated in *The Famous Victories of Henry the Fift,* and then found to recur in *Henry IV, Part One;* where, this time it involves PRINCE HAL; who, as with the real life incident, also happens to be in company with *three companions*.

Another interesting fact found in *The Famous Victories* concerns the importance given by the author to the role of RICHARD DE VERE, the 11th Earl of Oxford. With no documentary support for the role of this nobleman, the anonymous author has nevertheless seen fit to promote him to a position of principal advisor and lieutenant to the KING. As Eva Turner Clark astutely remarked, this was . . .

> *in defiance of Hall, who, on historically accurate grounds, makes Exeter, York, and Westmoreland the principal councillors to both Kings. ... It is especially noteworthy that the organization of the palisade of stakes, which probably did more to win the battle than anything else, is definitely handed over to Lord Oxford.* [2]

Captain Bernard Ward, writing in July 1928 for the *Review of English Studies* proposed *"that The Famous Victories was based on an account in Hall's 'Chronicles', published in 1548 . . . the source of the historical facts used in the play,"* [3]

Nor must one overlook the controversy surrounding Sir John Oldcastle. This was a character appearing in *The Famous Victories*. In Shakespeare's later version of the play, *2 Henry IV,* he also included this character, OLDCASTLE.

> *One of Falstaff's speech prefixes in Act I, Scene ii is mistakenly left uncorrected, "Old." instead of "Falst." In III, ii, 25-6 of the same play, Falstaff is said to have been a "page to Thomas Mowbray, Duke of Norfolk" — which was true of the historical Oldcastle. In Henry IV, Part 1 i, ii, 42, Prince Hal calls Falstaff "my old lad of the castle."* [4]

Although the name, Oldcastle, survived unchanged while it remained part of *The Famous Victories,* this was not the case when it appeared publicly on stage in the *Henry IV* plays.

> *It may not be improper to observe that this part of Falstaff is said to have been written originally under the name Oldcastle; some of the family being then remaining, the Queen was pleased to command him to alter it, upon which he made use of Falstaff.* [5]

By good fortune, a letter remarking upon this change from OLDCASTLE to FALSTAFF has survived. The change is mentioned in a letter written by Richard James in 1625, and addressed to Sir Henry Bourchier. James also confirmed that Shakespeare was, indeed, the author of *The Famous Victories of Henry the Fift*.

> *A young gentle ladie of your acquaintance, having read the works of Shakespeare, made me this question: How Sir John Falstaffe, or Fastolf, as it is written in the statute book of Maudlin College in Oxford, where everye daye that societie were bound to make memorie of his soule, could be dead in Harrie the Fifts time and againe live in the time of Harrie the Sixt to be banisht for cowardice? Whereto I made answeare ... That in Shakespeare's first shewe of Harrie the Fift, the person with which he undertook to playe a buffoon was not Falstaffe, but Sir John Oldcastle, and that offence beinge worthily taken by personages descended from his title, as peradventure by manie others allso whoe ought to have him in honourable memorie, the poet was made to putt an ingonorant shifte of abusing Sir Jhon Falstophe, a man not inferior of vertue, though not so famous in piety as the other.* [6]

The truth of James's letter is unquestionable: *"in Shakespeare's first shewe of Harrie the Fift, the person with which he undertook to playe a buffoon was not Falstaffe, but Sir John Oldcastle."* The earliest known performance of the play predates the death in 1588 of Tarlton, one of the actors, who took the role of DERICKE. James obviously knew the truth about Shakespeare's playwriting career, which stretched back into the 1580s, and this awareness flowed easily from his pen. Moreover, to suppose the Queen *commanded* a man of Shaxpere's class *to be pleased* to change the name of OLDCASTLE is ludicrous. For Shaxpere to have lampooned a real knight, especially if it conferred mockery on the powerful Cobham family, would have brought him before the Privy Council. Libelling peers was deemed to be a serious offence, punishable under the decree *Scandalum Magnatum*, and the offending author may well have had his nose and ears slit.

The superior position held by the 17th Earl of Oxford at Court was different. His birth and title would have rendered him immune from the punishment meted out to the lower classes, but not for *"the Queen [to be] pleased to command him to alter [the name];"* thus sparing the Cobham family public embarrassment upon seeing their ancestor being publicly staged as a figure of fun.

This incident, almost insignificant when set against the larger picture of the authorship debate, is nevertheless a further indication that Shaxpere was not Shakespeare. Shaxpere's station in life would not have shielded him from the Cobhams in the way that Oxford's position protected him.

Oldcastle had married into the Cobham family in 1408 to become Lord Cobham, which was at the root of the protest. 'Shakespeare' responded to the Queen's command by renaming OLDCASTLE, FALSTAFF; but, in doing so, he also felt obliged to distance himself from any intentional offence, by declaring: *"Oldcastle died a martyr and this is not the man."*

No Elizabethan was better connected than members of the Cobham family. And the commotion they caused at the time not only secured the character's name change, it also allowed the Admiral's Men to cash in on the rumpus, which had clearly gone public. The result was a new play, *The First Part of the True and Honourable History of the Life of Sir John Oldcastle, the good Lord Cobham.* But, with care not to anger the Cobham family, the Prologue explained to the audience: —

It is no pampered glutton we present
Nor aged Councellor to youthful sinne
But one whose vertue shone above the rest
A valiant Martyr and a virtuous peere.

As previously explained (p. 263/4), the effect this had was far from short-lived. For, we may recall that as late as 1618, Nathaniel Field was referring to it in his play, *Amends for Ladies.*

In his play, a character says: *"Did you not see the piece in which the fat knight, named Oldcastle, told you truly what was honour?"* [7] This was recognised as a reference to *1 Henry IV* (Act 5: sc. iii).

There also exists a piece of dialogue in *The Famous Victories* indicating that it had been acted in the privacy of a court performance. Consider the scene at Gads Hill, which is followed in Scene 4, by PRINCE HAL giving the CHIEF JUSTICE a box round the ear, and for this, the heir to the throne is sent to prison. In *1 Henry IV* a similar scene at Gads Hill is repeated, but the box round the ears, which PRINCE HAL gave the CHIEF JUSTICE, is not performed; it is only referred to, and this occurs in the sequel, *2 Henry IV.*

JUSTICE: Your Grace hath said truth, therefore in striking me in this place, you greatly abuse me, and not me onely, but also your father: whose liuely person here in this place I doo represent. And therefore to teach you what prerogatiues meane, I commit you to the Fleete, untill we haue spoken with your father.

HENRY 5: Why then belike you meane to send me to the Fleete?

JUSTICE: I indeed, and therefore carry him away.

[*Exeunt Henry 5 with the Officers.*]

(*The Famous Victories of Henry the Fifth*: sc. 4)

FALSTAFF: For the box of the ear that the Prince gave you—he gave it like a rude prince, and you took it like a sensible lord. I have check'd him for it; and the young lion repents—marry, not in ashes and sackcloth, but in new silk and old sack.

JUSTICE: Well, God send the Prince a better companion!

(*2 Henry IV*: act 1, sc. ii)

These two excerpts are united by the single memory of their author. It is natural to the human mind; and, as seen above, this same naturalness also allowed James to unite the same two plays to Shakespeare when replying to his correspondent's question. Yet, Falstaff's conversation with the Chief Justice in *2 Henry IV* in which he refers to the *box of the ear* delivered by the Prince, despite its natural continuity from *The Famous Victories*, is ignored by the Shaxpere lobby. The stagnating effect that belief in Shaxpere has upon the intellect leaves no choice but for this man's admirers to admit 'their Shakespeare' was a plagiarist.

This same disturbing belief also requires care when referring to the Gads Hill incident. The reason for this is plain to understand. If too much attention is drawn to the fact that this scene originally occurred in *The Famous Victories of Henry the Fifth* it would invite a reference to the same event having been undertaken by the same number of participants, in the same month, at the same location by the Earl of Oxford's servants. Biographers are therefore careful to avoid any connection between William Shakespeare and the Earl of Oxford; which, in the circumstances is completely unreasonable. Consider, too: *The Famous Victories* was written by an unnamed author. How, then, can pro-Shaxpere academics *know* that this author was not the Earl of Oxford, especially since, contrarily, Oxford's ancestor has been glorified in the play: contrary to historical fact?

As for the difference in quality between the two plays, this is easily explained by the time difference occurring between each composition. The event at Gads Hill occurred in 1573; Oxford was then twenty-two: before he had embarked upon his mind-bending experience in Renaissance Italy. The later play reflected his greater maturity during the final decade of his life, when in retirement he had the leisure to edit, and improve upon his earlier work. Shaxpere had no earlier work to improve upon.

The Comedy of Errors

In addition to *Titus Andronicus* (which has a chapter to itself) and *The Famous Victories of Henry the Fifth,* both of which can be dated to before Oxford left for Italy in 1575, we may also add *The Comedy of Errors,* written after his return. E. T. Clark has drawn attention to the *Documents Relating to the Office of the Revels in the Time of Queen Elizabeth,* published by A. Feuillerat in 1908. These reveal that on Tuesday 1 January 1577 (N.S.) *"The historie of Error (was) shown at Hampton Court on Newyeres daie at night, enacted by the Children of Powles."* [8]

According to Sir Edmund K. Chambers . . .

> *the great choirs of St. Paul's and the Chapel Royal had been at least as conspicuous as the professional companies ... the Paul's boys appear to have joined ... a composite company, to which Lord Oxford's boys also contributed.* [9]

The Blackfriars theatre was converted from the former monastery of the Black Friars in 1576, and this was where the boy players performed. Oxford acquired the sublease for the theatre in 1583 and passed it to his secretary, causing Gabriel Harvey to comment that Lyly *"hath not played the Vice Master of Paul's, and the Fool Master of the Theatre for noughts."* [10]

Hampton Court Palace, the Children of St Pauls and *A History of Error* were united on New Year's Day, 1577. For, this play is surely *The Comedy of Errors,* and the parallels to Oxford that occur within it, plainly mirror his plight at that time.

BALTHAZAR: Have patience, sir: O, let it not be so:
Herein you war against your reputation,
And draw within the compass of suspect
The unviolated honour of your wife.
Once this,—your long experience of her wisdom
Her sober virtue, years, and modesty,
Plead on her part some cause to you unknown;
And doubt not , sir, but she will well excuse

Why at this time the doors are made against you.
. . .
For slander lives upon succession,
For ever hous'd where it once gets possession.
(Act 3, Sc. i)

Those aware of Oxford's situation upon his arrival back in England in the spring of 1576, after more than a year's absence, will immediately understand the similarity this has with the passage quoted above.

Oxford's reputation amongst members of the peerage was at its lowest ebb. He had separated from his wife Anne Cecil, believing that despite the many years he had known her for her wisdom, virtue, and modesty, her honour had nevertheless been violated during his absence, and the baby born to her on 2 July 1575 was not his.

He knew, too, that Anne was desperate to be reunited with him, and that she would, as the author of *Errors* made clear: excuse his behaviour, which had since caused the doors to be closed against him. That is to say, he was no longer an invited guest at the great houses that had once welcomed him.

The fault of this unwelcome disruption to Oxford's homecoming is indicated by the final two lines of BALTHAZAR'S speech. Anne had been defamed by a false accusation, and the slander made against her had taken root in Oxford's mind. The details of what he had been told, and by whom, were never revealed, and so the identities of the perpetrators remain unknown. However, for a proud young aristocrat descended from one of the noblest families in England, the suggestion that he had been cuckolded proved too much, and he had separated from his wife and child.

Some hint at the efforts made by Anne's family members to placate Oxford can be discerned in the dialogue that follows on from the last scene.

LUCIANA: If you did wed my sister for her wealth,
Then, for wealth's sake, use her with more kindness:
Or, if you like elsewhere, do it by stealth;
Muffle your false love with some show of blindness:
. . .
Then, gentle brother, get you in again;
Comfort my sister, cheer her, call her wife:

'Tis holy sport to be a little vain
When the sweet breath of flattery conquers strife.
(Act 3, sc. ii)

LUCIANA'S advice is of great interest, since no corresponding character occurs in the *Menaechmi* of Plautus, from which *The Comedy of Errors* is derived. (*The Menaechmi* is a Roman comedy with a story of long-lost twin brothers and confused identities.) And, Anne did have a sister, Elizabeth. The suspicion that Oxford had only agreed to marry Anne because of her father's wealth is also apparent. *"Burghley had agreed to provide Anne with a dowry of £3000* [≈ £840,000 in 2010] *which* [historian Lawrence] *Stone characterizes as a 'record sum'. Oxford's financial condition was nevertheless dire."* [11]

The remainder of LUCIANA'S advice is equally applicable to Oxford. His search for the feminine touch elsewhere, during his separation from Anne, is evident from the free-living style of life he exercised when competing with Walter Raleigh for Anne Vavasor's sexual favours in 1580. [12]

One year earlier, on 24 July 1579, John Lyly entered *Euphues and his England* in the *Stationers' Register,* with its dedication—

To the Right Honourable my
very good Lorde and Maister, Edward de Vere,
Earle of Oxenforde, Vicount Bulbeck, Lorde of
Escales and Badlesmere, and Lorde great
Chamberlaine of England, John Lyly
wisheth long lyfe, with en-
crease of Honour.

On a separate page to itself, immediately before this dedication, is the Oxford coat-of-arms, with the Vere motto, VERO NIHIL VERIVS. Oxford had been maintaining Lyly in his apartment at the Savoy, opposite Burghley House in the Strand. Gabriel Harvey would later remind Lyly of *"thy old acquaintance in the Savoy, when young Euphues hatched the eggs that his elder friends laid."* [13] Harvey was referring to Lyly's first book, *Euphues: the Anatomy of Wyt,* published in 1578.

Harvey's reference to Lyly's friends confirms that Oxford had been operating a school of writers at the Savoy, which would likely have included Kyd, Marlowe, Munday and Lodge. This activity apparently continued when Fishers Folly, with its more spacious accommodation, was acquired by Oxford in 1580.

It was also during this period of separation from his wife that Oxford became the subject of several more dedications. In 1579, Anthony Munday dedicated *The Mirrour of Mutabilitie* to Oxford, describing him as *"his singular good Lord & Patron"* [14] Others, favouring Oxford with their work at that time, were Geoffrey Gates, Gabriel Harvey, and John Brooke. [15] With so much flattery for his vanity to feed upon, Oxford was able to distract himself from the strife of his failed marriage. As LUCIANA so aptly observed: *"it is sport to be a little vain, when the sweet breath of flattery conquers marital strife."*

But Oxford remained unmoved: apparently happy with the thought that if a young man married is a young man marred; he, at least, was now free, and intending to remain in that condition. Similar thoughts intruded into the reply ANTIPHOLUS gave to LUCIANA.

ANTIPHOLUS: Your weeping sister is no wife of mine,
Nor to her bed no homage do I owe:
Far more, far more, to you do I decline:
O, train me not, sweet mermaid, with thy note,
To drown me in thy sister's flood of tears:

(Act 3, sc. ii)

Anne Cecil's plight can well be imagined. Her husband had left England to travel abroad, and during his absence she had borne his child. When, after more than a year had passed and he returned, it was to desert her once again, but this time without hope of return. LUCIANA'S weeping sister, drowning in a flood of tears, can have been in no worse state than Anne, Countess of Oxford.

Pro-Shaxpere scholars like to date their man's plays by recognising events that have been written into the dialogue. Using the same strategy, the first draft of *The Comedy of Errors* can be dated to the year of Oxford's return from the Continent. He was therefore able to stage its performance at Hampton Court on New Year's Day, 1577. He initially called it: *The historie of Error*, changing the title later. The Queen would have been especially pleased to note that Oxford had changed the play's location to Ephesius in her honour: a town dedicated to the goddess Diana, with whom she identified.

John T. Looney was the first commentator of *Errors* to draw attention to the similarity between one of Oxford's early poems and a piece of dialogue spoken in the play by Dromio. The style of Oxford in this early piece of verse and that of Shakespeare, which it predates, is quite irrefutable.

Dromio: She is so hot because the meat is cold;
The meat is cold because you come not home;
You come not home because you have no stomach;
You have no stomach, having broke your fast;
But we, that know what 'tis to fast and pray,
Are penitent for your default today. (Act 1, sc. ii)

The Grief of Mind

What plague is greater than the grief of mind?
The grief of mind that eats in every vein;
In every vein that leaves such clots behind;
Such clots behind as breed such bitter pain;
So bitter pain that none shall ever find,
What plague is greater than the grief of mind.

This verse was originally included amongst Sidney's sonnets, contained in his *Astrophel and Stella*. Many of the poems had circulated in manuscript form before the first edition was printed in 1591, by which time Sidney was dead. When published, it included verses from other poets including the Earl of Oxford. [16] *The Grief of Mind* was later republished in *England's Parnassus*, in 1600, where it was ascribed to: *"E. of Ox."* [17]

Love's Labour's Lost

One comedy that a consensus of scholarly opinion attributes to the embryo Shakespeare is *Love's Labour's Lost*, although it was not published until 1598. Professor Gervinus explained the reason for this.

> *The reiterated mention of mythological and historical personages; the air of learning, the Italian and Latin expressions, which here, it must be admitted, serve a comic end; the older England versification, the numerous doggerel verses, and the rhymes more frequent than anywhere else and extending over almost half of the play; all this places this work among the early efforts of the poet.* [18]

Two phrases in the extract above strike a nerve; *historical personages* and *Italian expressions*. Neither can be explained by the innate genius of the author. They both rely upon personal knowledge from a reliable source, together with an understanding that breeds familiarity. But this play is amongst the earliest written by a young man raised in a cultural backwater. There is no explanation worthy of that description which accounts for this acquisition of special knowledge by Shaxpere. Contrarily, Oxford spoke fluent Latin and Italian, and his Court connections allowed him access to the latest news from abroad. Consider, for example, how the content of the play conflicts with the early life of Shaxpere, particularly his culturally barren start in life.

> *In the burlesque parts of Love's Labour's Lost we meet with two favourite characters or caricatures of the Italian comedy; the Pedant, that is the schoolmaster and grammarian, and the military Braggart, the Thraso of the Latin, the 'Captain Spavento' of the Italian stage.*[19]

After Oxford had received permission from the Queen to travel abroad, especially to Italy, he would have witnessed these *two favourite characters of the Italian comedy*, thus enlivening his desire to share the entertainment in a play of his own, performed before Elizabeth and her Court. No such scenario exists for Shaxpere, beyond the pale shadow of his advocates' pleaded guesswork.

The historically accurate content of *Love's Labour's Lost* is a feature that is often remarked upon but never explained by pro-Shaxpere scholars, confined as they are to the dim light shed by the facts of his non-literary lifestyle. The play is set in the court of Navarre, which was a kingdom that lay to the south-west of France and its border with northern Spain. It was ruled over by the King of Navarre, the future Henri IV of France, who, after his succession, united both kingdoms. The play is therefore set before Henri III's assassination in 1589.

The composition of the play at a date close to this year finds support from Robert Tofte's *Alba* published in 1598. Tofte remarked: *"Loues Labour Lost, I once did see a Play / Ycleped so, so called to my paine."*[20] The phrase: 'once did see' implies the author was recalling an event that had happened many years past. In fact the basis of the play has been traced to the year 1583, when *"the English ambassador to the court of France reported to Walsingham that Navarre 'has furnished his Court with principal gentlemen of the Religion, and reformed his house'."* [21] This is reflected in the play when Navarre (he is named FERDINAND not Henri) also decides to reform his house by directing the minds of his courtiers away from revelry and the pursuit of women, in preference to a life of contemplation and study. There is a joke in this that would have caused laughter at Court. Henri IV was known as the *"impetuous, outdoor type, full of spirit and humour, keen on hunting and excessively fond of the ladies, he was known as the vert gallant – the gay spark... and had at least 56 mistresses."* [22]

A series of historical parallels between Henri and FERDINAND were discovered by Professor Abel Lefranc. These were characteristic of the living Henri. Lefranc particularly drew attention to the King's *"impetuous style of riding"*, which is repeated in *Love's Labour's Lost.*

PRINCESS: Was that the king, that spurr'd his horse so hard
Against the steep-up rising hill?

(Act 4, sc. i)

Henri of Navarre also had a habit when writing letters that displayed *"his covering of the whole sheet, 'margent and all'."* [23] Once again, this habit of the king finds expression in *Love's Labour's Lost,* when the PRINCESS receives a letter from the KING.

PRINCESS: Look you what I have from the loving king.

ROSALINE: Madam, came nothing else along with that?

PRINCESS: Nothing but this! yes; as much love in rhyme
As would be cramm'd up in a sheet of paper,
Writ o' both sides the leaf, margent and all,

(Act 5, sc. ii)

A passing remark made by Katharine (Act 2, sc.i) proves to be not without some further interest. She says of the character, DUMAINE, *"I saw him at the Duke Alençon's once."* Historically, the duc d'Alençon refers to Hercule (later François), the younger brother of Henri III.

Oxford was in Paris in March 1575. Nine months before his arrival, Charles IX died, and his brother Edouard, who was then in Poland as that nation's king, was recalled to accept the French crown; it was then that he chose to be called King Henri III, leaving his former title duc d'Anjou vacant.

Henri III's coronation occurred on 13 February 1575 at Rheims. Oxford would then have been in France, and it is difficult to believe England's ambassador to France would not have arranged for him to be invited to attend the ceremony unofficially. This would then account for KATHERINE'S reference to DUKE ALENÇON, for Henri III's brother did not assume the vacant title duc d'Anjou until May 1576,[24] following the *Edict of Beaulieu* by which time Oxford was back in England.

ALENÇON and KATHERINE are briefly mentioned for a second time, when KATHERINE is said to be the heir of ALENSON. This again proved accurate. [K]atherine de' Medici, Alençon's mother, became her son's heir following his death from consumption in June 1584. Henri III hated his brother, having previously threatened to kill him, and declined to benefit from his death. There being no other brothers surviving and no descendent: the inheritance went to his mother.

Another interesting connection between the play and historical fact occurs in the exchange made between ROSALINE and BEROWNE.

ROSALINE: Did not I dance with you in Brabant once?

BEROWNE: I know you did.

ROSALINE is the PRINCESS'S lady-in-waiting, and the inference to be drawn is that she had attended the PRINCESS at Brabant. Historically . . .

> *[Princess] Marguerite had made journeys exactly corresponding to those referred to by the Princess and her ladies in Act II, Scene i, of the play: to Alençon (Marguerite's brother François was Duc d'Alençon) in 1578 and to Liége (Brabant) in 1577.* [25]

Lefranc's researches also disclosed more parallels between *Love's Labour's Lost* and Henri of Navarre. In 1579, Marguerite de Valois, Princess of France, arrived in Navarre at the town of Nérac with the Queen-mother, Catherine de' Medici. Henri of Navarre had married Marguerite on 18 August 1572, making her Queen of Navarre, but the question of her dowry, which included Aquitaine, was still being disputed. An identical dispute is played out in *Love's Labour's Lost,* also involving Aquitaine and involving the exact sum of money that had led to the dispute.

BOYET: Now, madam, summon up your dearest spirits:
Consider who the king your father sends,
To whom he sends, and what's his embassy:
Yourself, held precious in the world's esteem,
To parley with the sole inheritor
Of all perfections that a man may owe,
Matchless Navarre; the pleas of no less weight
Than Aquitaine, a dowry for a queen.

It was in this regard that Joseph Hunter, (*New Illustrations, 1845)*, made known his discovery that in *Chronicles Johnes' translation,* i, 108 (1810), there is a written record of *"an engagement by Charles VI, about 1420, to pay Charles of Aragon, King of Navarre, 200,000 crowns."* [26]

KING: Madam, your father here doth intimate
The payment of a hundred thousand crowns;
Being but the one half of an entire sum
Disbursed by my father in his wars.
But say that he, or we, as neither have,
Receiv'd that sum, yet there remains unpaid
A hundred thousand more; in surety of the which,
One part of Aquitaine is bound to us,
Although not valued to the money's worth,
If then the king your father will restore
But that one half of which is unsatisfied,
We will give up our right in Aquitaine,
And hold fair friendship with his majesty.
But that, it seems, he little purposeth,
For here he doth demand to have repaid
A hundred thousand crowns; and not demands
On payment of a hundred thousand crowns
To have his title live in Aquitaine. (Act 2, sc. i)

Gervinus confirmed the problem this presents to the conventional view of Shakespeare.

> *... it is difficult to explain. No source is known for the purport of this piece, which, however (as Hunter has proved from Monstrelet's 'Chronicles'), in the one point of the payment of France to Navarre (Act II. sc. 1) rests on an historical fact, namely, an exchange of territory between the two crowns.* [27]

Unquestionably, someone had a very detailed knowledge of what was happening across the English Channel at the time this dispute relating to Princess Marguerite's dowry was still under negotiation, and that person was unlikely to be fifteen-year-old Will Shaxpere, buried away in the rural environment of a small Midlands community, with less than fifteen hundred residents (the size of a modern-day UK school). On the other hand, it is known that Anthony Bacon was in Montauban from 1580 until his downfall six years later, and that he built up a friendship with the King of Navarre. It would have been within the compass of Oxford's position as a senior member of Elizabeth's court to have learned of events relayed back to England by Bacon; and no better source exists than he, for the historically accurate content of *Love's Labour's Lost.*

In Act 5, Scene ii, the lords disguise themselves as Russians. For this, there must have been a reason that was topical when the play was first performed.

> *There had been an exchange of ambassadors between England and Russia and in 1583 a special envoy was sent by Czar Ivan the Terrible to ask for the hand of Lady Mary Hastings in marriage. The lady was nicknamed at court the 'Empress of Muscovia' and was much teased about the wooing, which was conducted with elaborate and, on the part of the English, mock ceremony. Sir Sidney Lee was convinced that this incident lay behind the scene in the play.* [28]

But after the death of Ivan in March 1585 (N.S.), this piece of comedy would have been in far too bad taste for it to be included in the composition of the play.

Further evidence of the author's personal acquaintance with French politics is indicated by the names appearing in the *Dramatis Personæ* of *Love's Labour's Lost.* In which instance, it is noteworthy that neither the King of Navarre nor the Princess of France is actually named in the play. The King of Navarre was identified as FERDINAND only because of Rowe in 1709, although no king by that name had previously ruled Navarre. As for the names of those who attended the King, it is these that attract attention. *"The Duc de Biron [Anglicised as Berowne] and the Duc de Longueville [Anglicised as Longaville] were his faithful supporters,"* [29] They are the names of two lords chosen by Shakespeare as attendants of FERDINAND. The third lord, the Duke DUMAINE, has been identified with Charles of Lorraine, the duc de Mayenne; the 'i' and 'y' were often interchangeable in Elizabethan English, hence, 'de Mai[en]ne' becomes DU MAINE, thus DUMAINE. In addition, *"the names Boyet, Marcadé, and de la Mothe appear in contemporary registers of court officials;"* [30] thus adding a further confirmation of the historical accuracy written into the play.

The inclusion of Mayenne is sometimes objected to, because after the assassination of Henri III in 1589, Mayenne took up arms against Henri of Navarre, hoping to win the right of succession to the Crown. This conflict resulted from the formation of the Holy Catholic League, which was set up in 1584 by the duc de Guise. The League was opposed to Navarre becoming King of France because he was a Huguenot. Mayenne's opposition to Henri IV is therefore dated to after 1584.

The composition of *Love's Labour's Lost* from the pen of Lord Oxford may now be confidently assigned to a period soon after his return from Italy in 1576, but not later than 1584.

TWELFTH NIGHT

Not all plays written by Oxford after his return from Italy are so easily identifiable. *Twelfth Night* is an interesting example. The composition of this play was originally assigned to 1613-14, upon the basis of internal evidence that had been identified by scholars relying upon certain references. Had Oxford been a contender for authorship at that time, he would have been dismissed as easily then, as scholars dismiss him today, and for the same reason: he died in 1604. But in 1831, John Payne Collier published an entry from John Manningham's Diary dated 2 February 1601 (O.S.) This was a report by the diarist describing his visit to a performance of *Twelfth Night.* Manningham was a law student at Middle Temple, and the description of the play he gave, leaves no doubt that this was the play he had seen. Scholars were therefore forced to tear up their account of the date they had given for the composition of the play, and start again. It is now thought to have been written between 1599 and 1601.

Many Oxford supporters believe the date of the original composition is much earlier. The reason for this is found in . . .

> *PECK'S "Desiderata Curiosa" [where] there is a passage in which he says that he proposes to publish a manuscript called "a pleasant con-*

ceit of Vere, Earl of Oxford, discontented at the rising of a mean gentleman in the English Court, circa 1580." [31]

The historical facts surrounding this date can, in fact, be applied to the composition of *Twelfth Night*. It was circa 1580 that Walter Raleigh's star began to rise at Court. An indication of this may be determined from a letter addressed to Lord Treasurer Burghley, dated 15 July 1580; it refers to the Acts of the Privy Council.

> *Walter Raleigh, gentleman, by the appointment of the Lord Grey is to have the charge of a hundred of those men presently levied within the City of London to be transported for her Majesty's service into Ireland, his Lordship is desired to deliver unto the said Walter Raleigh, by way of imprest, one hundred pounds.* [32]

It was at this time that Oxford had cause to be discontented with Raleigh.

> *Early in 1580 he was paying attention to a new young lady of the bedchamber, Anne Vavasour, Raleigh showed a protectiveness for her virginity which echoes his reluctance to lay siege to Elizabeth Knollys, and he bravely or foolishly put in writing his warning against the important and wild nobleman.* [33]

The warning he gave – *"Raleigh, advice to Anne Vavasour"* – came in the form of a poem of three stanzas of six lines: each commencing with, *"Many desire, but few or none deserve,"* and concluding with, *"farewell the rest ..."* [34] Oxford's discontent can be imagined at the impertinence of this *mean gentleman* who dared intrude into his personal relationship with Anne Vavasor. But, at the same time, this *mean gentleman* had caught the eye of the Queen, leading Raleigh to believe, misguidedly of course, that she was in love with him and could be wooed into marriage.

Oxford's response can be seen in the characterisation of MALVOLIO: *"A fantastical steward to Olivia."* [35] According to Farmer (1767), the name is a transposition of 'Malivolo'. As a figure of fun, he is shown to be *a kind of Puritan*. The advice given by Raleigh to Anne Vavasor, and the poem he slipped into the pocket of Elizabeth Knollys could have some bearing upon this. Despite MALVOLIO'S outwardly moral stance, he is made to look foolish by believing that OLIVIA is secretly in love with him, and that she has sent him a letter. This allows a capital piece of subtle, bawdy fun involving the 'C' word to be put into his mouth, effectively mocking his puritan attitude.

Elizabeth, upon seeing the play, would have looked for her own identity in the character of OLIVIA – *"A Lady of great Beauty and Fortune."* [36] In Act 3, scene iv: Olivia responds to *"Malvolio's fantastical wooing,"* by referring to it as *"very Midsummer madness."* MALVOLIO had been gulled into appearing before OLIVIA fantastically attired, which may have had something to do with Raleigh's first appearance at Court, dressed as a seaman.

Oxford completed his revenge by having MALVOLIO declared a lunatic and confined to a dark room. There, in darkness, he is tormented by FESTE and SIR TOBY into expressing the belief held by Pythagoras, with regard to the transmigration of souls. Pythagoras was said to have believed himself the reincarnation of Euphorbus, killed by Menelaus in the Trojan War. The story has been traced to *The Testament of Heraclides of Pontus* and was later confirmed by the biographer Diogenes Laertius, a third century biographer of Greek philosophers. It was in this same respect that Raleigh became a central figure for a group of free thinkers investigating spiritualism, discarnate souls and reincarnation. Not surprisingly, therefore, 'The School of Night' to which the group belonged, is actually referred to in *Love's Labour's Lost.*

It is with these connections: on the one hand Raleigh and Elizabeth, on the other hand MALVOLIO and OLIVIA, that when they are viewed alongside *PECK'S "Desiderata Curiosa",* concerning Oxford and a *mean gentleman in the English Court,* that a possible unity of purpose can be determined. This would then allow *Twelfth Night* to have been commenced in 1580; and for Oxford to have sought revenge against Raleigh, by mocking him as MALVOLIO. Certainly, Raleigh believed himself to be at the receiving end of Oxford's annoyance. In a letter he addressed to Burghley dated 12 May 1583, Raleigh did confess: *"myself may be most in danger of his poison and sting."* [37]

ROMEO AND JULIET

A quite different set of circumstances surrounds the composition of *Romeo and Juliet.* Commentators are unanimous in declaring that when Shakespeare wrote this work, he had by his side, and was indebted to, a copy of Arthur Brooke's edition of *The Tragical History of Romeus and Juliet.* Little of consequence is known about Brooke, other than this was one of two publications before he drowned at sea in the shipwreck of *The Greyhound,* between Rye and Le Havre, on 19 March 1564. Brooke's other publication in 1563 is a translation from an anonymous French author of 107 passages taken from the Bible. Lucas Harrison, the publisher, excused the book's inferior prose, on the grounds that Brooke was absent, because *"the realm thought good to command him"*. If Brooke had enlisted in the army in 1563, then it must have been within months of his having enlisted at the Middle Temple to study law, which occurred on 4 February 1563. (N.S.)

What interests supporters of Oxford, is that in Bandello's version of the story, he said JULIET was aged sixteen, 'Shakespeare' unaccountably changed this to fourteen, which was Anne Cecil's age at the time of her planned wedding to Oxford, scheduled for September 1571. But at the last moment the date was put back to 16 December, the 3rd Sunday in Advent.

It has also been observed that *Romeo and Juliet* contains *"many verbal resemblances"* to the poem of 3020 lines written by Brooke. Research has confirmed that there was a person named Arthur Brooke, born in 1544. In which case, he would have been seventeen or eighteen years of age in 1562 at the time of publication, and this would account for the poem's description as *pedestrian, prolix, leaden, inert,* and *wearisome.* J. J. Munro, in his introduction to a 1908 edition of *Romeus and Juliet,* stated that *"Brooke's story meanders on like a listless stream in a strange and impossible land."* It would also explain Oxford's role as the author, were it indeed he, writing under the pseudonym of Brooke, for he would have been barely twelve years old when the poem was published; but, nevertheless, a true prodigy in the mould of Mozart, Mendelssohn, Pascal, Gauss &c.

Oxford's youthfulness and his use of a pseudonym would also explain the need to ensure that any search made for Arthur Brooke would end in failure. His sudden death at sea answered that need. It has also been said that he was *en voyage* to take part in France's Religious Wars. This must be doubted. The First War of Religion began in April 1562 and was over in March 1563. Thereafter, Catherine de' Medici, the Queen-mother, took France's boy-king, Charles IX, on a grand tour of the country to introduce him to the French people, following the calamity of the recent civil war. The progress lasted one and a quarter years.

During that time France was at peace. The Second War of Religion was not expected, and did not begin until September 1567.

1567 was also the year that George Turberville published a collection of poetry entitled, *Epitaphs, Epigrams, Songs and Sonnets* which included *An Epitaph on the Death of Master Arthur Brooke Drownde in Passing to New Haven.* Turberville is described by Ogburn as a poetical disciple of de Vere's uncle, the Earl of Surrey, and by writing this tribute he was bolstering Brooke's authenticity, which helped divert attention away from the youthful Oxford having written under Brooke's name.

Romeo and Juliet in Shakespearian form appears to contain two significant clues, the first of which provides the date of composition, and the second the name of the playwright. The date is alluded to by the NURSE in act I, scene iii: *"'Tis since the earthquake now eleven years."* The question is – which earthquake is the NURSE referring to? If the NURSE is speaking true, then she is referring to the 'earthquake that devastated Verona in 1570. Joseph Hunter described it thus:

> *It will not be denied that Shakespeare might make an Italian story allude to an event that occurred in London; but the whole argument is of the most shadowy kind, and it seems to be entirely destroyed when the fact is introduced that in 1570 there did occur a most remarkable earthquake in the neighbourhood of Verona, so severe that it destroyed Ferrara, and which would form long after an epoch in the chronological calculations of the old wives of Lombardy.* [38]

However, there was a serious tremor felt in London in April 1580, although its epicentre was thought to be in northern France where greater damage occurred. This earthquake is preferred by conventionalists to the one felt in Verona, because it allows Shaxpere to have written *Romeo and Juliet* in 1591. The truth of the matter is that if Oxford wrote the play, he would have had Verona in mind, and his reference to eleven years dates its composition to 1581. If Shaxpere had written the play, he would have needed to refer back to several accounts written that Easter week, describing the apprehension felt in the capital.

Let us move from this and consider the greatly overlooked importance of an observation made by Admiral Hubert Holland in *Shakespeare Through Oxford Glasses.* Interest centres upon a remark made by MERCUTIO about ROMEO in act 2, scene iv.

MERCUTIO: O, here's a wit of cheveril, that stretches from an inch narrow to an ell broad!

ROMEO: I stretch it out for that word, broad:

Cheveril is soft flexible kidskin leather, but MERCUTIO refers to the word, not the skin, and emphasises its part in the *wit* that he and ROMEO are exchanging with each other. So, what is the *wit* contained in this word?

Holland, to his credit, took MERCUTIO seriously and narrowed the word 'inche' or 'ynche'; that is, according to Old English spelling, to 'che', which then accords with the first three letters of cheveril. He then focussed upon the last two letters, 'il', equivalent to 'ell', since 'cheverell' is an alternative spelling of 'cheveril' (ell was an English measurement of variable length); *ell broad* is also part of the word play. Thus cheveril *stretched* from an 'inche' *narrow* that is, 'che', to 'il' *broad*, becomes: che – ver – il, and this, when rearranged is: **IL CHE VER**. 'Ver' is a variant form of 'Vere'.

> *Albericus de Ver married ,Beatrice, half sister of King William, and they had five sons. He founded Earl's Colne Priory in 1105 ... [His son] Aubrey II was responsible for building the great castle-keep at Hedingham.* [39]

Having certified VER for Vere, this leaves CHE and IL: both are Italian words. But, much more importantly, *"il che is used to translate 'which' when it represents a whole idea, not just a specific noun."* [40]

Consequently, in this piece of dialogue, MERCUTIO'S *wit* has been used to direct attention at *the thought* behind 'VER'. But, why? What is the significance of these three letters? Indeed, what has VER to do with this play at all; unless, VER also happened to be the author? Most certainly, ROMEO accepted that the word CHEVERIL should be *broad*; that is stretched out, for he readily agreed to this in his response to MERCUTIO.

It seems Oxford was adding to the word play that had taken place in the preceding lines:

BENVOLIO: Here comes Romeo, here comes Romeo.

MERCUTIO: Without his roe, like a dried herring.

As Ogburn observed: ROMEO without his phonetic RO(E) is left with ME O. Oxford was wont to identify himself at the foot of his early poems with the initial letter, 'O': a reference to his title.

Also, the personal pronoun 'me' occurs in both the accusative and dative cases. This would be seen of significance to the Latin speaker, because it allows 'me' to be the object of MERCUTIO'S banter, with 'O' as the identifier, qualifying the pronoun, 'me'.

Thus, ROMEO *without his ro(e)* is 'ME O', which can be understood as Oxford identifying himself with ROMEO.

It was William Hazlitt who first pointed this out . . .

> *Romeo is Hamlet in love. There is the same rich exuberance of passion and sentiment in the one, that there is of thought and sentiment in the other. Both are absent and self-involved, both live out of themselves in a world of imagination. Hamlet is abstracted from everything: Romeo is abstracted from everything but his love, and lost in it.* [41]

This house is the "real" home of Juliet's family (the Capuleti). The building dates from the 13th century (Verona Tourist Board).

HAMLET has long been recognised by supporters of Oxford as a self-portrait of its author, surrounded by caricatures of the people closest to him at the time of his greatest, inner, torment.

One can anticipate the likely Stratford response. Complete disinterest. Yet, consider! CHEVERIL exists. The directions exist. Apply the directions to the word; translate this into the language of the play. The result is the solution to MERCUTIO'S wit. Oxford well knew that writing plays fell far below what was expected of his position and high birth. But his innate genius demanded he release his gift to the world, and this he did, anonymously at first: but later, using an allonym, whose name has ever since been given credit for the poems and plays that poured from his pen.

Just now and again he identifies himself. Here it is through the wit of MERCUTIO. In the sonnets, he secretly encrypted his name (No. 76) while also openly confessing to the ultimate disappearance of that same name after death, even though he knew his work would live on. Others took up his cause, like Ben Jonson who revealed the truth of the deception in the inscription he wrote for the monument in Stratford's parish church. Thomas Thorpe was another, with his cryptogram embedded in the dedication to the Sonnets. Leonard Digges was also amongst this group, with his reference to the 'moniment' confirming the secret it held. It was also he who encrypted de Vere's name into the first sentence of the poem that was originally intended for inclusion in the First Folio.

And so, was the teenage Brooke in reality the embryo Shakespeare? Quite probably; the faithful attention that Oxford gave to the childish verse in *Romeus and Juliet* is the love that an older person gives to the fruit of their youth. Did Oxford revise his earlier work written in 1581, eleven years after a giant earthquake struck Verona and destroyed Ferrara? Why not? It was within his power to have done so.

7

PLAYS SKETCHED FROM LIFE

Experto Credite
(Believe the man with experience)
Virgil

THE CATALOGUE AT THE FRONT of the First Folio lists thirty-five plays by Shakespeare, whereas the volume, itself, contains thirty-six. *Troilus and Cressida* appears to have been included too late to be listed. This was the same play that in 1609 made its 'escape' from certain 'grand possessors', and thereafter seems to have come late into the hands of those preparing Shakespeare's collected plays for publication. Of the plays appearing in the First Folio, eighteen had never before appeared in print:

Antony and Cleopatra, As You Like It, The Comedy of Errors, Cymbeline, Henry VI Part I, Henry VIII, Julius Caesar, King John, Macbeth, Measure for Measure, The Taming of the Shrew, The Tempest, Twelfth Night, The Two Gentlemen of Verona, the Winter's Tale;

Added to these, were another three; which, as far as is known, had never even been heard of until they emerged in 1623: *Timon of Athens, Coriolanus,* and *All's Well That Ends Well.*

THE DATING DILEMMA

One of the many problems confronting researchers is that of assigning to each play its date of composition. Upon what basis should one proceed? Scholars of different persuasions have their own ideas. The result has been a general compilation of dates, although not universally accepted, but mostly agreed upon and backed by the more powerful voices of authority; that is, those wholly committed to supporting the conventional view of

Shakespeare as the poet in residence at Stratford-upon-Avon. The factors relied upon when applying a date of composition are documentary evidence relating to the first known performance of the play, and/or the date of a title's entry in the *Stationers' Register*. Underpinning these methods is the evidence that Will Shaxpere arrived in London *circa* 1590, and immediately began producing plays of genius quality up until 1603/4; whereupon, he returned to Stratford-upon-Avon, changed his way of living, whereupon his play-writing all but ceased. Quite naturally, his advocates disagree. Instead, they maintain not only did Shaxpere continue writing after 1604, but the plays he wrote disprove Oxford's authorship; since, for so it is claimed, they were written after this particular earl's death. We shall see how this accords with the evidence.

Another way of seeking a probable date of composition is to consider the source(s) used by the author. This allows a solid conclusion to be reached, since a play cannot have been written earlier than the first appearance of its source. The following list of Shakespeare's sources leads to an interesting conclusion (see Joseph Sobran, 1997, pp. 156-7).

1516	Fabyan, *Chronicle*	*I Henry VI*
1529	More, *Dialogue*	*I Henry VI*
1532	Gower, *Confessio Amantis*	*Pericles*
1534	Polydore, *Vergil Anglica Historia*	*Richard III*
1542	Montemayor, *Diana Enamorada*	*Two Gentlemen of Verona*
1548	Halle, *Union of York and Lancaster*	*English history plays*
1549	Thomas, *History of Italy*	*Tempest*
1557	More, *Richard III*	*Richard III*
1558	Fiorentino, *Il Pecerone*	*Merchant of Venice*
1559	*Mirror for Magistrates*	*English History Plays*
1562	Brooke, *Romeus and Juliet*	*Romeo and Juliet*
1562	Secchi, *Gl'Ingannati*	*Twelfth Night*
1563	Foxe, *Martyrs*	*I Henry VI*
1565	Cinthio, *Hecatommithi*	*Othello; Measure for Measure*
1566	Painter, *Palace of Pleasure*	*All's Well That Ends Well*
1567	Golding *Metamorphosis*	*general*
1567	Fenton, *Bandello*	*Much Ado About Nothing*
1569	Grafton, *Chronicles*	*I Henry VI*
1570	Foxe, *Acts and Monuments*	*Henry VIII*
1573	Gascoigne, *Supposes*	*Taming of the Shrew*
1576	Belleforest, *Histoires Tragiques*	*Hamlet*

1576?	Twine, *Painful Adventures*	*Pericles*
1577	Holinshed, *Chronicles*	*Histories*
1577	Eden, *History of Travel*	*Tempest*
1578	Whetstone, *Promos and Cassandra*	*Measure for Measure*
1579	North's *Plutarch*	*Julius Caesar, Antony & Cleopatra, Coriolanus*
1582	Bretin's *Lucian*	*Timon of Athens*
1582?	*Rare Triumphs*	*Cymbeline*
1587	Holinshed, *Chronicles (revised)*	*English history plays*
1588	Greene, *Pandosto*	*Winter's Tale*
1590	Sidney, *Arcadia*	*King Lear, Pericles*
1590	Spenser, *Faerie Queen*	*King Lear*
1590	Lodge, *Rosalinde*	*As You Like It*
1591	*Troublesome Reign of King John*	*King John*
1591	Harrington's *Ariosto*	*Much Ado about Nothing*
1592	*Second Part of Coney-Catching*	*Winter's Tale*
1594?	*King Leir*	*King Lear*
1595	Daniel, *Civil Wars*	*Henry IV*
1598	Chapman's *Homer*	*Troilus and Cressida*
1603	Harsnett, *Popish Impostures*	*King Lear*
1603	Florio's *Montaigne*	*Tempest*

At this point, the sources used by Shakespeare cease. Oxford, it will be recalled, died in the summer of 1604.

THE TEMPEST

Attempts have been made to overcome the embarrassment this final date of 1603 has upon the traditional position. Sources have therefore been suggested that postdate Oxford's death. For instance:

> *"Geoffrey Bullough's eight-volume edition of Shakespeare's sources enumerates dozens printed during the 1580s and 1590s, but few after 1603 (Bullough further deems most of the latter only 'possible' sources)."*[1]

Chief amongst the obstacles raised against Oxford's authorship is William Strachey's account of the ship *Sea Venture*, which became separated in a storm from a fleet of nine ships carrying colonists to Virginia. On 25 July 1609, the *Sea Venture* was driven by adverse conditions towards the Bermuda shore; where, he says: *"We were inforced to runne her ashore, as neere the land as we could ... neither did our ship sincke, but ... fell in betweene two rockes, where shee was fast lodged and locked, for further budging."*[2] No lives were lost and most of the provisions that had not been jettisoned were later saved.

The Tempest is a play that begins with a storm. This has been responsible for attracting attention to the misfortune of the *Sea Venture*. The ship's fate has therefore been compared to the action occurring in the play, with parallels sought between the two accounts. No thought, however, has been given to other reports that were available, involving equally comparable shipwrecks that occurred before Oxford's death in 1604.

From these highly selective deliberations by Shaxpere's supporters, a convenient conclusion has been reached that the author must have drawn upon Strachey's report when writing *The Tempest*. Whence, Oxford cannot be the play's author, since he died in 1604. Let us therefore consider Strachey's description of an important part of what happened on that July day in 1609.

> *Sir George Summers being upon the watch, had an apparition of a* ***little*** *round* ***light****, like a faint Starre, trembling, and streaming along with a sparkeling blaze, halfe the height upon the* ***Maine Mast****, and shooting sometimes from* ***Shroud to Shroud****, tempting to settle as it were upon any of the foure Shrouds: and for* ***three or foure houres*** *together, or rather more, halfe the night it kept with us, running sometimes along the* ***Maine-yard*** *to the very end, and then returning* (Author's emphasis). [3]

The importance of this extract was indicated by Peter Moore. He referred to the same incidents having been reported during earlier voyages: notably two that appear in Richard Hakluyt's *Principal Navigations, Voyages, Traffiques and Discoveries*, Volume III (London 1600).

> *And straightaway we saw upon the shrouds of the Trinity as it were a candle, which of itself shined, and gave a* ***light*** *... which appeared on the* ***shrouds****.*
>
> (Account of Francis de Ulloa, p. 405).

❧

> *In the night, came there upon the top of our* ***mainyard*** *and* ***main mast****, a certain* ***little light****, much like unto the light of a little candle ... This light continued aboard our ship* ***about three hours****, flying from mast to mast, and from top to top: and sometime it would be in two or three places at once.*
>
> (Account of Robert Tomson, p. 450). [4]

Since Strachey's letter has much in common with what is contained in Hakluyt's 1600 volume, as does *The Tempest,* it is neither sufficient nor is it conclusive to maintain that this letter was the source of the play's storm scene. Instead, for the sake of truth, it is necessary to acknowledge that both the Shakespeare play and the Strachey letter have enough in common to suggest that both pieces of work could just as well have been sourced from Hakluyt, and quite possibly from Ulloa and Tomson too.

There is also another aspect to the borrowing of text; it is that Shaxpere died in 1616, and Strachey's account of the shipwreck was not published until 1625, two years after *The Tempest* appeared in the First Folio: time enough for Shakespeare's play to have influenced Strachey's prose account.

The Stratford response to this is that Strachey wrote a letter, dated 15 July 1610, addressed to an unnamed *"noble Lady",* describing the ship's misadventure. By some equally unnamed means, so it is alleged, Shaxpere saw this private copy and used it as his source. But who can say what was seen by Shaxpere in 1610? The records we have confirm only that he was in Stratford-upon-Avon in 1610 and 1611, immersed in various commercial enterprises. Are we to believe a messenger arrived in Stratford, all of a sweat, to deliver to the resident of New Place a copy of Strachey's letter to this noblewoman? Of course not, the Lady's letter would have remained private property. And so the situation remained until several years after the death of Strachey in 1621, when Samuel Purchas acquired the content of Strachey's letter from Hakluyt's papers, following his death five years earlier. It was then published in 1625 as the dramatic tale of a shipwreck, alongside other reports concerning the colony that had been established in Virginia.

To add to this, the discovery by Noël Hume of a 19th century copy of a rough draft of the letter proves it had been edited for publication. In short, some 'borrowing' has to be suspected; and since Harkluyt's role in editing Strachey's letter is evident, his retention of the earlier account he had written of a similar shipwreck would naturally have tended to influence his editorial input; there are also signs of borrowing from Ulloa and Tomson.

What is it, therefore, that connects *The Tempest* to the foundering of the *Sea Venture?* It is, we are told, occasional phrases in

Strachey's account that are descriptive of those Shakespeare wrote when describing the storm scene in the play. But Hakluyt's editing of Strachey's letter, based upon what he had written in 1600, easily accounts for these similarities. Thus, the sequence of events is as follows. It begins with Hakluyt's book; Oxford read it before writing *The Tempest* in 1602; Hakluyt later edited Strachey's letter, recalling what he had written in 1600. The notion that it was Shaxpere who copied from Stachey's letter; which, at the time of *The Tempest's* composition was unpublished, is far too improbable to be of serious merit.

Sir Charles Strachey, a descendent of his Stuart ancestor, has confirmed *"family rumours"* of a Shakespeare link. Strachey's connection with plays and the Jacobean playhouse is confirmed by his inclusion amongst the names of those supporting Jonson's play, *Sejanus.*

> *The publication of Sejanus, equipped with dedication, preface, argument, and commendatory verses, gives some insight into Jonson's standing at that time. Chapman for instance wrote a long poem of one hundred and ninety lines ... Many others of Jonson's well-born or scholarly friends also rallied round to contribute some line of verse to launch the publication on its way: Hugh Holland, Marston, William Strachey, 'Th. R.', 'Philos' and 'Cygnus', among others.* [5]

Strachey's connections with the theatre and dramatists of that time would certainly have provided him with the access he required to have read *The Tempest.* Thus, *Shakespeare's* richly coloured expressions can be seen as possibly having a more direct bearing on the letter of 1609, with its account of what happened to the *Sea Venture* off the coast of Bermuda.

It is also noteworthy that the name of Shakespeare amongst those promoting *Sejanus* is conspicuous by its absence. Yet, Ben Jonson's service to Shakespeare's memory in the First Folio suggests a bond between the two men, such, that had Shakespeare been alive when *Sejanus* was published, he would have added his commendation. Jonson does, however, make an interesting remark:

> *To the Readers ... this book, in all numbers, is not the same with that which was acted on the public stage, wherein a second pen had good share: in place of which I have rather chosen to put weaker (and no doubt less pleasing) [verses] of mine own (II. 37-40).*

Who was this mysterious pen that Ben Jonson was referring to but reluctant to name, while at the same time admitting his own inferiority in the presence of this playwright? And why was this better poet absent, or perhaps unnamed in 1605, when the commendations were made? Or could Oxford have been the man whose posthumous tribute to *Sejanus* was included, but under the title *"Cygnus",* the Swan: later to become Jonson's *Sweet Swan of Avon*?

The Tempest does, however, raise the question of where *Shakespeare* acquired his knowledge of shipwrecks, and the effect they had upon the crew and passengers; apart, that is, from Hakluyt. The *Bible* is one possible source, since St. Paul's account of his ship sinking off the coast of Malta bears some similarity with that appearing in *The Tempest.*

One also has to consider that Oxford was familiar with the sea. He owned a ship, the *Edward Bonaventure.* It was a heavily gunned craft that had crossed the Atlantic Ocean several times during the 1580s. Accounts of the voyages it made, either from word of mouth, or written by its captain, at one time Luke Ward, would have given Oxford background knowledge of the perils to be met during a return voyage to the Americas. Moreover, both Drake and Raleigh had lost family members to the destructive power of the sea whilst serving on board a stricken ship. Members at Court would have heard accounts of the circumstances responsible for these losses. Oxford would also have had access to Erasmus's *Naufragium*: an account that was to later persuade J. D. Rea (*Modern Philology,* xxii (1919), 279 ff) that this was the literary source for *The Tempest.* Joseph Hunter, in the first half of the nineteenth century, argued for *Orlando Furioso* as a source: believing that the play had stylistic similarities with Shakespeare's earlier period of romantic comedy.

Strachey's account has, instead, become the traditionalists' favoured source. This has become argued for with ever-greater insistency ever since Oxford's authorship of the Shakespeare canon began to gain momentum; gathering its converts from the more educated sections of society. Hence, if Strachey's influence upon Shakespeare should be confirmed, it would positively eliminate Oxford and his troublesome qualities from all further thought, and the professorship, with its limited factual knowledge of Shaxpere's literary life, would feel more secure when promoting their imagined scenarios to the public.

Yet, contrary to authoritative support for *The Tempest* having been written after Oxford's death, there exists *"evidence … purporting to show that the play existed many years before 1611 (the accepted date of its first production in something like its present form)"*[6] Parallels can be found between *The Tempest* and a German play called, *Die Schöne Sidea.* The author was Jakob Ayrer: well known for his adaptations of English plays. Hence, there is a more than likely possibility that *Die Schöne Sidea* was his version of *The Tempest,* which he adapted for the German tongue. From which it follows that since Ayrer died in 1605, the composition of Shakespeare's original version of this play would then fall into line with Oxford's life span.

One cannot leave *The Tempest* without mentioning ARIEL'S usage of the word, *Bermoothes.* It occurs only once (Act 1: scene ii), and is mentioned in reply to PROSPERO'S enquiry.

PROSPERO: Of the King's ship,
The mariners, say how thou hast dispos'd,
And all the rest o' th' fleet.

ARIEL: Safely in harbour
Is the King's ship; in the deep nook, where once
Thou call'dst me up at midnight to fetch dew
From the still-vex'd Bermoothes, there she's hid:
…
and for the rest o' th' fleet,
Which I dispers'd, they all have met again,
And are upon the Mediterranean flote [sea],
Bound sadly home for Naples;

Amazingly, Bermoothes, becomes the island of Bermuda in the North Atlantic, also known as the Somers Islands after Sir George Somers settled there in 1609.

Although the island home of PROSPERO and his daughter MIRANDA is unnamed in the play, the dialogue locates it somewhere between the north coast of Africa and Italy. To relocate it to Bermuda seems hardly credible until one realises that these are the same facile minds that believe the son of illiterate parents, raised amongst illiterate siblings, and with illiterate children of his own was the very same person who wrote the works of Shakespeare. The appetite for conjuring up imagined 'facts' about Shakespeare would seem to grow from what it feeds upon.

In the play, PROSPERO had once been the Duke of Milan, but his brother conspired with the King of Naples to replace him. As a result of this *coup* the Duke and his daughter were carried several leagues out to sea and set adrift in . . .

> A rotten carcass of a boat, not rigg'd,
> Nor tackle, sail nor mast; the very rats
> Instinctively have quit it: (Act 1: sc. ii)

They survived, thanks to provisions secretly supplied by a friendly counsellor. Eventually, their boat drifted on to the shore of an uninhabited island. It was from there that PROSPERO was able to exact his revenge. Twelve years later, he learned that the King of Naples was returning home from Tunisia, where he had been attending his daughter's wedding. Using magic, PROSPERO summoned up the tempest, which gives the play its title, and the King's ship was driven onto his island.

Now, according to the Strachey-Bermuda fairytale, PROSPERO and MIRANDA first drifted in their rotten and unrigged tub across the Tyrrhenian Sea into the Mediterranean, whereupon prevailing currents carried them to Gibraltar and out into the Atlantic Ocean, eventually drifting to the coast of Bermuda, eighty-seven degrees west of Naples, and just three degrees short of a quarter the distance to circumnavigate the globe: a trip that would have taken a good sized bite out of their water and provisions and the dozen years that PROSPERO was absent from Milan. It was also, we are told, a voyage that CALIBAN'S mother, SYCORAX had made many years before. Because ARIEL confirmed that SYCORAX had been born in Algeria (Act 1: sc. ii).

PROSPERO then recounts how *"This damn'd witch"* had, for her sorcery, been banished *"from Argier"* (ancient name for Algeria) and marooned by sailors on the island where he now dwelt. But she had died before he and MIRANDA arrived. Common sense suggests the island lies somewhere in the Mediterranean, between Italy and the north coast of Africa, and has nothing whatever to do with the island of Bermuda.

In the early nineteenth century, Joseph Hunter was of a similar mind, and proposed the island of Lampedusa as the setting for the play. The isle is situated in the Mediterranean east of Tunisia. This would have allowed PROSPERO to discover the King of Naples' departure from Tunisia on board a ship bound for Italy. To suppose otherwise is to assume the storm continued unabated for many months, and always following the fleet until it had forced the ships across the Mediterranean, and then across the Atlantic Ocean until reaching the shores of Bermuda.

In fact, it is really a crackpot notion, quite unnecessary to the plot, and worthy only of those who persist in the belief that Shaxpere, with no education that has ever been established, was the great mind that produced the finest flowers of English literature. Bermuda plays no part in the play, and is mentioned just that once. It is obviously a piece of humour, probably bawdy, inserted for the private amusement of the players.

The Bermoothes, or Bermudas . . .

> *(and variations of that spelling) was also a section of London notorious for harbouring thieves and prostitutes; Ben Jonson implied the Bermudas' nefarious character in Bartholomew Fair (6.57-8).*[7] *The area was apparently named for the islands because they attracted fugitives from justice during the early years of English settlement.* [8]

'Shakespeare's' description of it as *"still vexed"* would be appropriate to the continued depravity of that area, and was not directed at the North Atlantic Island of the same name. Some have disputed this, because John Stow failed to mention it in his *Survey of London*, published in 1598. But, in reality, Bermoothes was just a slang name given by the local community to a small ghetto: notorious for its depravity. Jonson lived in a street off the Strand. On the other side of the Strand, and to its rear, was the area called the Bermoothes. A similar slang name exists for a market area in South London called 'The Cut'; it is absent from any London gazette, but well known to the local community.

To judge from the dialogue in the play, it would appear that someone from the cast of the Chamberlain's Men had made a midnight visit to a brothel in the Bermoothes to relieve his passion. And in the course of what followed, had also obtained his dew (dew is the archaic form of due, also used by Spenser, but especially used by 'Shakespeare' for its double meaning); in other words, the man received his due, or reward, in the form of dew from the genital discharge of an infected prostitute. This would have caused considerable concern and embarrassment to the actor at the time, but was thought no more than an amusing part of London life by fellow actors.

Oxford, having heard this kafuffle, could not resist the temptation to remind the cast with a suitable reference at the actor's expense. In any case, it has nothing whatever to do with an island in the North Atlantic, where some allege the play's action takes place. Those who think ARIEL had been sent to Bermuda to *"fetch dew"*, supposedly for a magic potion, need explain what Bermuda has to do with the play, since it is never again mentioned. And, how can ARIEL be sent to *"the Bermoothes"* if he is already there, on the island, with PROSPERO? It is giddy logic, typical of the manner in which traditionalists create weak ideas to shore up the pretence of Shaxpere's authorship.

These occasional insertions, which contribute nothing to a play, can at times offer the best chance of eliciting further facts about the author and the date of composition. For example, by positing Oxford as PROSPERO and Susan as MIRANDA, we can reasonably date the play's composition to 1602. This allows Strachey to have used the text as a background for his own published account of the Bermuda incident much later, and for Oxford to have read Hakluyt in 1600.

The reason for proposing 1602 as the date of composition is because, in the play, MIRANDA is fifteen years of age. Oxford's daughter Susan Vere was born in 1587; therefore she, too, was fifteen in 1602.

PROSPERO also drops a truism about MIRANDA'S mother, which is equally applicable to Susan's mother, whom the girl never knew, for Anne Cecil died a month after Susan's first birthday. *"Thy mother was a piece of virtue,"* PROSPERO tells his daughter. Anne, Countess of Oxford, was exactly as described . . .

> *This Anna lived ever a modest maiden and a chaste wife, faithful in her love, a daughter wonderfully devoted to her parents in all exigencies, exceedingly diligent and devout in her devotion to God.* [9]

There is also a second reason to conclude that 1602 was the year *The Tempest* was begun; it is the air of finality in the closing speech. At the time of the play's composition, Oxford had not an able body, nor had he long to live. In April 1603, he confirmed his ill health in a letter addressed to Robert Cecil . . .

> *for by reasone of myne infyrmite, I cannot come amonge yow so often as I wishe, and by reasone my house ys not so nere, that at every occasione I can be præsent, as were fitt.* [10]

This infirmity conveniently coincides with PROSPERO'S farewell speech, which appears to have been the author's valediction.

> Now my charms are all o'erthrown,
> And what strength I have 's mine own,
> Which is most faint:

Before making this speech at the end of Act 5, PROSPERO again alludes to his approaching end: *"Every third thought shall be my grave."* To which, ALONSO replies: *"I long to hear the story of your life, which must take the ear strangely."* Oxford's life would indeed fall strangely upon the ear. The same cannot be said for Shaxpere. His life was plodding dull, enlivened only by the 'imagined facts', that embroider what is written about him. One such 'imagined fact' is that PROSPERO is Shaxpere. An odd suggestion, especially since PROSPERO was at pains to educate MIRANDA, whereas Shaxpere never lifted a finger towards that end for his own daughters; yet, the same man is believed to have written:

> And seeing ignorance is the curse of God
> Knowledge the wing wherewith we fly to heaven.
>
> (*2 Henry VI* (act 4, sc. vii)

An equally erudite dismissal of Strachey's letter as a source for *The Tempest* has been made by Roger Stritmatter and Lynne Kositsky in *The Oxfordian* ('*The Spanish Maze and the Date of The Tempest*', vol. X p. 10, October 2007). In their joint rebuttal of the arguments proposed by traditionalist journals, they make the following interesting observation.

> *Eastward Ho! (1605), known to parody Hamlet, Richard III, and other Shakespearean plays, also parodies The Tempest in an extravagant lampoon of a shipwreck in the Thames River that washes the survivors onto the Isle of Dogs. The evidence of these four plays overwhelmingly argues for a Tempest composition date at least as early as 1603 . . .*

The Isle of Dogs faced the Palace of Greenwich. *Eastward Ho!* was also the cause of Chapman and Jonson being imprisoned and sentenced to facial mutilation because of a passage considered derogatory to the Scottish (Act 3, sc. iii 40-7).

THE MERCHANT OF VENICE

Another connection between Oxford and Shakespeare that suffers the same fate of dismissal by the Stratford based fraternity is the dramatist's knowledge of Italy. The plays written by *Shakespeare* resound with references to Italian life, culture, and geography.

> *The author knows how to travel from town to town, knows the names of side streets and piazzas, he knows where the courthouses are, he knows where the harbours are, he names churches where people get married, he's familiar with the interior decoration of Italian houses, he uses colloquial Italian figures of speech and he can quote the inscription on Giulio Romanos grave.* (Der Mann der Shakespeare erfand: Kreiler, 2009).

But Shaxpere's life story, sparse though details are, provides not the slightest hint that he was ever attached to anything Italian. Biographers simply graft onto his commercial activities knowledge of Italian geography and society, in order to make their biographies believable. If asked: – 'Where did Shakespeare's knowledge of Italy come from?' The stock reply is the Mermaid tavern. 'Shakespeare' must have spent so much time in this hostelry taking notes from returning travellers that it is a wonder he found time to write so many plays.

The Italian scholar Dr. Ernesto Grillo had a more sensible explanation.

> *We have no hesitation in affirming that on at least one occasion Shakespeare must have visited Italy … We find such a wealth of precise and vigorous detail that we are forced to conclude that Shakespeare must have visited Milan, Venice, Verona, Paris and Mantua.* [11]

The cities mentioned are precisely those visited by Oxford during his year in continental Europe. Grillo then added: *"the topography is so precise and accurate that it must convince even the most superficial reader that the poet visited the country."* Grillo had obviously no experience of the xenophobic English scholar who believes there is nothing to be learned from continental travel that cannot be gleaned from an evening spent in a 16th century tavern. Despite this, it remained evident to Grillo, if not to the senior academics of the most prestigious universities in England and the USA that 'Shakespeare' had very definitely experienced life in the Italian cities he wrote about.

Dr. Cecil Roth was another who thought like Dr. Grillo. He believed that the author of *The Merchant of Venice* could not have written this play unless he had first visited the city. Other notable scholars such as Hugh Trevor-Roper, Pietro Rebora, George Greenwood and Karl Elze have likewise remarked upon the poet's remarkable knowledge of Venice. It is this familiarity with the city that allows Shakespeare to dramatise conversations amidst scenes of Venetian life with so much ease that they number more than sixty occasions in six different plays. Chief amongst these is *The Merchant of Venice,* where, in Act 3: scene iv, PORTIA sends BALTHASAR with a letter to her cousin in Padua:

> And look what notes and garments he doth give thee, —
> Bring them (I pray thee) with imagin'd speed
> Unto the tranect, to the common ferry
> Which trades to Venice...

The *tranect,* which appears in all the quartos and in the First Folio, was a misspelling for 'traject'; this remained unidentified until it was realised that *"the common ferry"* was known by the Italian word *traghetto.* The ferry conveys its passengers across the *laguna morta* and into the Grand Canal, which leads to the city. It is at the *Isola de Rialto, "where merchants most do congregate,"* not the *Ponte di Rialto,* thus confirming that 'Shakespeare' was perfectly aware of the difference.

For Oxford, who once resided in Venice, all this would have been common knowledge. The State Archives in Venice confirm that the Earl of Oxford made himself a home in the city *("et vi si fermò et vi fabricò anch' una casa"),* where he resided for three months or more.

The university at Padua was where Civil Law was studied, and this would need to have been known by 'Shakespeare', for it is where PORTIA'S cousin, the learned DOCTOR BELLARIO is to be found: it being he who suggests a solution to ANTONIO'S legal predicament.

LAUNCELOT GOBBO, the servant to SHYLOCK, has a name that is famous in Venice. It is derived from the *Gobbo di Rialto, "a stone figure ... from which the laws of the Republic were proclaimed."* And *The Merchant of Venice* is a play that depends upon the interpretation of law.

Such detailed knowledge tends to overwhelm even the most committed traditionalists, and they seek for different explanations. The *traghetto,* they point out, appears in Florio's *World of Words.* But they omit to mention this was not published until 1598, the same year that on 22 July, *The Merchant of Venice,* otherwise called *The Iewe of Venyce* was entered in the *Stationers' Register.* Florio's book is nevertheless held by some to also account for the name GOBBO, which is defined as *"crook-backt. Also a kind of faulkon."* Yet, there is no reference to SHYLOCK'S servant being either 'crook-backed' or a 'faulkon'.

These spurious explanations result from having adopted a false premise upon which to work, and thereafter suffering the confusion of what follows. The Oxford solution sidesteps this muddle; it is simple, elegant, and straightforward, which is only possible because it happens to be true. H. H. Furness, in a footnote to his *New Variorum Merchant of Venice,* included the following note by C. A. Brown (1888, 72-73).

> *The Merchant of Venice is a merchant of no other place in the world. Everything he says or does, or that is said or done about him . . . is, throughout the play, Venetian. Ben Jonson, in his Volpone, gives no more than can be gathered from any one book of travels that has ever been published; nothing but the popular notion of the city. Shakespeare, in addition to the general national spirit of the play, describes the Exchange held on the Rialto; the riches of the merchants; their argosies 'From Tripolis, from Mexico, and England; From Lisbon, Barbary, and India:' some with 'silks' and 'spices,' 'richly fraught; 'he represents 'the trade and profit of the city' as consisting 'of all nations;' he talks familiarly of the 'masquing mates,' with their 'torch-bearers' in the streets; of 'the common ferry which trades to Venice. .All this is written with a perfect knowledge of the place.*

How do Oxford's objectors' respond to this? What is the rationale they use to counter such intimate knowledge of a city that 'their author' never visited? How do they persuade students of Shakespeare, interested readers, and the inquisitive media that there is no need to doubt this play was written by a man who never left England? In as far as providing a genuine, believable explanation for such profound knowledge of a city, unknown to 'their author', all is silence. The old adage, 'where there's doubt, leave it out' is the academics' only refuge. Consequently, it is through this silence that the reading public and students alike are 'taught' to remain ignorant of the facts which undermine Shaxpere's presumed literary ability.

The Merchant of Venice is a play that, apart from its love interest, concerns a bond of 3000 ducats, which was guaranteed by the merchant ANTONIO to SHYLOCK, a Jewish moneylender. This sum has been advanced to BASSANIO, a friend, and kinsman of ANTONIO. But, if the loan is not settled on time, ANTONIO, as guarantor, must forfeit a pound of his flesh in lieu of the money. When ANTONIO'S ships fail to arrive with the promised merchandise, and he is unable to pay SHYLOCK, the Jew seeks justice from the law. But the court's judgement denies SHYLOCK his pound of flesh upon a legal technicality, and the play ends happily, although not for the Jew. Now let us compare the likely source.

In 1579, Oxford was persuaded to invest in one of Sir Martin Frobisher's voyages to the New World. The expectation was that the fleet would return laden with gold bearing ore. The merchant promoting the expedition was Michael Lok (compare Shylok: 'shy' meaning 'of doubtful repute', hence 'shyster'), in whose hands Oxford placed *"in bond"* 3000 pounds (≈ £838,000). The voyage failed, the ore proved to be fools' gold and worthless. Frobisher responded by accusing Lok of being *"a cozener of my Lord of Oxford"*, and the case went to court.

For Oxford, as for ANTONIO, the venture had proved to be a disaster. In neither case had their ships returned to erase their debts; one had lost 3000 pounds, the other 3000 ducats.

The main source for *The Merchant of Venice* is recognised to have been Giovanni Fiorentino's *Il Pecorone,* published in Milan in 1558. Oxford was fluent in Italian and no doubt acquired a copy during his tour of Italy in 1575. It is pointless to ask where Shaxpere acquired his knowledge of Italian, or where he picked up a copy of *Il Pecorone.* Fiorentino's play foreshadows that of Shakespeare's. It is set in Venice and has a Jewish moneylender who advances money to a rich merchant's godson, so that he might woo a lady in Belmont. The money is not repaid on time, and the Jew demands his pound of flesh. But he is denied by the same technicality in court that defeated SHYLOCK.

It is quite possible that Oxford wrote the first version of the play in 1579 as a response to his dramatic loss of £3000 when Frobisher's ships returned, minus their promised wealth. Stephen Gosson's pamphlet, *The School of Abuse,* published in 1579, referred to a play called *The Jew,* which has similarities to *The Merchant of Venice.* Gosson was no friend of the theatre, he believed actors to be responsible for corrupting the morals of the country. But he did make an exception for *"The Iew and Ptolome, showne at the Bull, the one representing the greedinesse of worldly chusers, and bloody mindes of Usurers."*[12]

The greediness of worldly choosers occurs in the casket scene in which the PRINCE OF MOROCCO chooses the gold casket in his attempt to win the hand of PORTIA. Inside, he receives a skull and a warning not to be deceived by outward appearances. The next to try is the PRINCE OF ARAGON. He chooses the silver casket, only to discover it contains the portrait of an idiot and a second warning.

Further indication that these two plays are one and the same occurs with SHYLOCK'S demand for human flesh, sliced from ANTONIO'S body in lieu of the unpaid debt. This echoes Gosson's reference to *"the bloody minds of usurers".*

The combination of the casket scene with the subject matter of *Il Pecorone,* both of which occur separately in the *Gesta Romanorum,* has proved too rich a fare for some commentators. Professor T. M. Parrott was one who spoke of his disbelief that an anonymous author could have written a play in 1579 that so accurately mirrored the genius of Shakespeare in 1598. It is a protest also heard in Shakespeare's *Histories.* Recall Professor Alexander (p. 95), who maintained . . .

> *the [anonymous] author of The Troublesome Raigne may be fairly held to have anticipated Shakespeare and even to have instructed him; for Shakespeare's King John follows The Troublesome Raigne almost scene for scene.*

Once again, it is possible to see how easily the brightest of scholars have allowed themselves to be misled by fastening their thoughts unquestioningly to a false premise. The simplest explanation remains, as it always has, that Oxford wrote the play seen by Gosson at the Bull. Much later, when in retirement and with the leisure to perfect it, he rewrote parts of the play, applying his greater experience to ensure it became another of his masterpieces. The most likely year for the revision was 1596; this being the time when an audience would recognise the appropriateness of a remark made by ANTONIO'S friend:

> ... my wealthy Andrew docke'd in sand
> Vailing [burying] her high top lower than her ribs
> To kiss her burial; (Act 1: sc. i)

The *Saint Andrew* was a Spanish galleon captured at Cadiz in 1596. It was brought to England as a prize ship but ran aground in the sands of the King's Channel, close to the port of Chatham. Amongst the collection of manuscripts at Hatfield House is a letter to the Queen, advising her *"how dangerous it will be for her great ships to go about the Sands this ill-time of the year, especially for the 'St. Andrew'."*[13]

In rewriting *The Merchant of Venice,* Oxford was not only able to incorporate the personal touches that came from having once lived in Venice; for example, the *traghetto* that ferries its passengers between the city and the mainland; the distance of twenty miles between PORTIA'S home in Belmont and the city of Padua; the *Gobbo di Rialto*, and *"the liberty of strangers"*, as set down in the Venetian constitution; he was also able to include his own experiences. For although *The Merchant of Venice* is based upon *Il Pecorone,* Oxford's adaptation has been tailored to meet his personal situation. This is particularly noteworthy when referring to the original play, where the bond between the merchant and the Jew of Mestri was 10,000 ducats, but which Oxford changed to 3000 ducats, in order to reflect his own loss of £3000.

The courtship scene between PORTIA and BASSANIO is also different from that between their counterparts in *Il Pecorone.* The legal help, too, received by ANSALDO, who is the precursor of Shakespeare's ANTONIO, comes from Bologna, not Padua: the city whose university actually teaches Civil Law. From these minor instances, it can be seen that Oxford's version of *Il Pecorone* is made more true to life by his personal knowledge of the locality: not the tavern talk that Shaxpere's advocates are compelled to offer, in what they are pleased to call explanations.

Finally, it cannot pass remark that in 1580, one year after Gosson's reference to the *Jew*, Anthony Munday, employed by

Oxford as his secretary, published *Zelauto*. This book is sufficiently close to the content found within *The Merchant of Venice* to support suggestions that it was a source used by 'Shakespeare'. Actually, it is entirely probable that Oxford suggested to Munday that he use *The Merchant* as a basis for *Zelauto*, since his own upper-class position in society prevented him from selling the play to the public.

Munday certainly responded as though this was the truth for he dedicated the story . . .

> *To The Right Honorable, His singular good Lord and Maister, Edward de Vere, Earle of Oxford ... And Ioe Right Honorable, among such expert heads, such pregnant inventions, and such commendable writers, as preferred to your seemely selfe, woorkes worthy of eternall memory.*

This was a fitting tribute to the author of *The Merchant of Venice* and worthy of one addressed to 'Shakespeare', who, as one is entitled to believe, was the source and inspiration for *Zelauto*.

ALL'S WELL THAT ENDS WELL

Love and marriage are central to many of the world's great stories. Oxford's married life was famous for its drama and its trauma, and it is difficult to retain intellectual honesty while refusing to recognise the similarity between certain events in his marriage and those dramatised in 'Shakespeare's' plays.

All's Well That Ends Well is an example. It is set mainly in France, but with an excursion to Florence. We have already learned from one Italian national that 'Shakespeare' possessed a detailed knowledge of that country; we now learn from a French national that 'Shakespeare' also had a similar understanding of France. Sir John Russell quotes below from Georges Lambin's book, *Voyages de Shakespeare en France et en Italie,* which was dedicated to the distinguished French scholar, and foremost authority on the French Renaissance, Professor Abel Lefranc.

> *[There is] overwhelming evidence that the Plays were written by a man who knew his Italy, his France, and the intimacies and intricacies of French politics personally and well. This claim is not based on a few, a dozen, or a hundred statements of fact, but upon a myriad, all pointing ... to a cultured gentleman, almost certainly of the highest grade in the aristocracy.* [14]

Evidence of the truth behind this statement can be found in abundance from plays that were written after Oxford's return to England, following the year he spent on the continent. To judge from a report pertaining to his one-time presence in Milan, dated 31 March 1576, it is assumed he passed through that city on his homeward journey from Venice; which he left on the 5th of the month. Milan lays to the west of Venice, and Lyons to the west of Milan, but the Alps rise up as a barrier to France, and in early March, crossing them could be icy and hazardous.

Oxford was an aristocrat, not a mountaineer. His simplest expedient would have been to travel south from Milan to Genoa, and from there, board ship to Marseilles. After disembarking, a pleasant journey to Lyons beckons: most of which occurs along the course of the Rhône.

'Shakespeare' certainly shows some familiarity with this journey. In Act 5: scene iii of *All's Well,* a gentleman arriving at Rousillon remarks: *"Here's a petition from a Florentine / Who hath for four or five removes come short / To tender it herself."* In other words, *"has failed to catch up with the King at halting places, for on each occasion when she arrived she found that the court had already removed on the next stage of its journey."*[15] These four or five removes were discovered by Georges Lambin to have been at Lançon, Avignon, Montelimar, and Valence, and they formed a direct line to Tournon-en-Rhône. At that particular time, the Château Tournon belonged to the Comte de Rousillon, who also held land and property in the nearby town.

For Oxford, travelling from the south of France, this would have been an obvious choice of where best to break his journey before arriving at Lyons, since Tournon is located only a short distance downstream from this city, and the Count's château would have afforded him the comfortable companionship of a titled family.

It is such a visit that appears to have inspired *Shakespeare* to convert the ninth novel of the third day of Boccaccio's *Decameron* into *All's Well That Ends Well.* The reasons for proposing this are clear. Much of the action in the play takes place at the Count of Rousillon's palace, *four or five removes* from Marseilles. However, this Rousillon should not to be confused with another Rousillon in the south of France, which was a Spanish possession at the time *All's Well* was written, and is referred to as Rossiglione by Boccaccio. France did not acquire this Rousillon until November 1659, when Philip IV was compelled to cede it to Louis XIV at the *Peace of the Pyrenees*. Needless to say, the characters in *Shakespeare's* play are decidedly French.

Another reason for positing the French Rousillon is that *Shakespeare* brings HELENA into the play. Hélène de Tournon was an actual person. She was the Count's youngest sister, and lived under the protection of the Countess of Rousillon. It is probable that Oxford met her during his visit. She was also the victim of a tragic love story. The year after Oxford's visit to the château, she died from a heart broken by her love for the Marquis de Varenbom, whose family had forbidden their marriage. The tragedy of Hélène's thwarted love was told by King Henri IV's first wife Marguerite de Valois, but it was not published until 1628: twelve years too late for Shaxpere.

Further similarities between Oxford's circumstances, prior to his continental travels, and Boccaccio's *Decameron* appear to have been triggered by Hélène de Tournon's fate. For *All's Well That Ends Well* contains yet more of those *uncanny similarities* to which Professor Bate drew attention, when he likened the final moments of Robert Greene to those of FALSTAFF (p. 65).

Consider, for example, this next passage, from which it can be seen where more *uncanny* similarities arise.

> *In delivering my son from me, I bury a second husband" laments the widowed countess...* [Act: 1 sc. i].

> *No romantic hero in Shakespeare's comedies is more offensive than Bertram, but even he has good reason for being odious: his mother clings to him, and just as he begins to live independently, the King of France forces him to marry against his will. Determined to forge his liberty, Bertram escapes from France as soon as he has obliged the King by marrying Helena. One is tempted to see Bertram as a villain but he is ultimately just a foolish youth making mistakes he will later regret. Helena, too, initially seems merely determined to have her way. But her love for Bertram, genuine and self-seeking, explains her campaign to secure him as her husband.* [16]

After her husband's death, the Countess of Oxford, while still suffering this bereavement, was compelled to release her son to be raised as a ward of Queen Elizabeth; this is mirrored in the opening words of *All's Well That Ends Well,* given above.

The description of BERTRAM (see above), as a foolish youth making mistakes that he will come to regret is as appropriate to Oxford as it is to BERTRAM. Nelson provides a sufficiently apposite account of this in his *Monstrous Adversary.*

> *Long before his seventeenth birthday ... Oxford evinced deeply rooted habits of self-importance and fiscal extravagance, spending heavily on clothes, personal weapons, horses and retainers...*
> *Apparently, writing from quarantine, Oxford concedes that he had disappointed Cecil, and begs him, "yf I haue done any thinge amise that I haue merited yowre offence", to impute any failings to his youth and "lak of experience to know my friendes" ... We have reason to suspect indeed that by this his nineteenth year Oxford had found companions in drink, riot, and sexual licence.* [17]

Nelson also refers to some interference in Oxford's affairs by his mother: a complaint similar to that made by BERTRAM. In a letter dated 7 May 1565, a month before her son's fifteenth birthday, the Countess of Oxford wrote to Cecil, making ...

> *requests that monies from family properties be guarded by friends during her son's minority ... Margery fears that her son's extravagance will pose a danger to the livery of his estates six years hence. She will assume responsibility herself with the assistance of Robert Christmas and others, offering bonds to guarantee honest performance.* [18]

Nelson readily concedes: *"Young Oxford cannot have appreciated this interference by his mother."* [19]

BERTRAM also protests that the King has forced a marriage upon him. At the age of twenty-one Oxford was unmarried, and the last male heir of the longest surviving earldom in England. Death came early in those days, either through war or disease, and the possibility that Oxford might die without a successor was seen as a matter of concern. This would also have been the main reason why his request for military duty was rejected.

Since it was in the interest of the Queen's ruling elite to see that the nation's titled nobility did not die out, the protocol would have begun with a royal reminder that a young courtier, such as Oxford, had reached an age when he might ask her majesty for permission to marry. This does seem to have been the case where Oxford was concerned. A retrospective note entered in Burghley's diary recorded that ...

> *The Erle of Oxford declared to the Queen's Majesty at Hampton-court his Desyre to match with my Daughter Anne: whereto the Queen assented.* [20]

Despite this note, their betrothal in December 1571 appears to have been due more to the desire of Anne than to a wish made by Oxford; a letter from Lord St. John to the Earl of Rutland explained the situation, as seen through his eyes.

> *Th' Earl of Oxenforde hath gotten hym a wyffe — or at the leste a wyffe hath caught hym — that is Mrs.* [= Mistress] *Anne Cycille, whereunto the Queen hathe given her consent.* [21]

Further evidence that it was an arranged marriage, at least as far as Oxford was concerned, is indicated by Nelson.

> *Burghley yearned for Oxford to command Anne to join him anywhere at all, for Anne had been married two and a half years and was not yet pregnant. To the extent that Oxford had been sexually active since December 1571, it was evidently with partners other than his young, pretty, and lawful wife.* [22]

From extant letters written by Burghley, and conversations held with the French ambassador, to whom he confessed: *"he was unhappy, given her age, for her to be brought to church to marry one the age of the Earl of Oxford, and that this could not transpire without criticism and regret"* (ibid.), it may be inferred that the two people who had pressed for this marriage were Anne Cecil, and Queen Elizabeth. This conclusion also ties in with BERTRAM'S situation:

> BERTRAM: Although before the solemn priest I have
> sworn, I will not bed her. (Act 2: sc. iii)

From this brief synopsis of *All's Well That Ends Well,* outlined above, we learn that after BERTRAM had satisfied the King's wish by marrying HELENA, he then fled the country to join the wars. Nelson gives a similar account of Oxford's actions in the summer of 1574, two and a half years after his marriage: time necessarily passing quicker on stage than it does in real life.

> *Oxford had been living at Lady Yorke's house in Walbrook Street, whence between two o' clock and three o' clock in the morning of Thursday 1 July, he went east by foot to Aldgate, secured a horse, rode the forty miles to Wivenhoe, and took ship to reach Flanders via Calais ... Oxford would later boast that he had taken part in the battle*

> *of Bommel ... Conceivably, Oxford witnessed the siege of Leiden, which lasted from June to October 1574.*[23]

From extracts taken from the play, it may be assumed that HELENA is modelled upon Anne Cecil. The fate of HELENA was to be abandoned soon after her marriage to BERTRAM. Nelson refers to the same fate having befallen Anne Cecil: *"within three months of his marriage rumour had reached as far as Antwerp that Oxford ... had separated from Anne."*[24]

Yet, of all *Shakespeare's* heroines, HELENA is Coleridge's *"loveliest creature"*, and for Jameson, *"it is the beauty of the character [that] is made to triumph over all."*[25] Nelson comments: *"Though not yet fifteen, Anne was, by all accounts, a nubile beauty"*. It is a description that also fits fourteen-year-old JULIET before her marriage to ROMEO. Interestingly, as we have seen (p. 315), *Shakespeare* deliberately altered JULIET'S age to fourteen, and by doing so, changed Bandello's version of the tale, where she is sixteen.

Nelson has also drawn attention to Wilfred Samonde's poem, written upon the death of Oxford's wife; what is . . .

> *startling in a memorial poem, is the characterization of Anne as "Another Grissel for her patience". The story of 'Patient Griselda' was one of the most popular of the European Renaissance, told by Boccaccio, Petrach, and Chaucer (Clerk's Tale), and dramatized in Patient Grissel (1603: STC 6518).*[26]

We therefore have before us a set of circumstances running sufficiently parallel to the leading characters and events in *All's Well That Ends Well,* to suggest that coincidence may be disregarded. Yet, remarkably, although Professor Alan Nelson is most frequently quoted, he has failed to see – or if he did see, failed to acknowledge – the *uncanny* similarities to BERTRAM and HELENA that his own narrative on Oxford and Anne has disclosed. This is all the more astonishing because the good professor has also produced a copy of the letter by Flaunt and Wotton, dated 21 May 1573, which complained to Lord Burghley that while . . .

> *rydynge peasably by the hyghe way, from Grauesend to Rochester, had thre calyvers charged with bullettes dyscharged at vs by thre of my Lord of Oxenfordes men ... vhoe lay preuylye in a diche awaytinge oure cummynge ... whervppon they mounted one [=on] horse backe and fled towardes London wythe all possible spede.*[27] (p. 297)

Despite the obvious similarity this has to the robbery scene at Gads Hill involving three men, also in May: FALSTAFF, BARDOLPH and PETO and which was dramatised in *The Famous Victories of Henry the Fyft,* and repeated in *Henry IV Part I,* Nelson made no attempt at mentioning this congruity of events either. One is therefore drawn to wonder: was it through an absence of intelligence upon his part, thus preventing these *uncanny* similarities from being noticed? Or was it a perverse attitude, contrary to all notion of true scholarship, which compelled him and possibly others of a similar standing, to fear a loss of face, were the truth about Shakespeare's identity to be publicly recognised? Could this be the motivating force causing academics to repeatedly distance Oxford from *Shakespeare ?*

Nelson's book, *Monstrous Adversary,* was intended to be a biography of the 17th Earl of Oxford, but omitting the slightest hint that he was, or could have been, William Shakespeare. No stone, it seems, was left unturned in presenting his subject in the worst possible light, especially if it involved some sexual scandal. Yet, oddly, one such stone has been entirely ignored. It involves the following passage, which first appeared in *The Traditional Memoires of the Reigns of Elizabeth and James I* by Francis Osbourne, published in 1638, page 79. Osbourne was Master of the Horse to Philip, 1st Earl of Montgomery, Susan Vere's husband and, posthumously, Oxford's son-in-law.

> *The last great Earle of Oxford, whose Lady was brought to his bed under the notion of his Mistris, and from such a virtuous deceit she is said to proceed.* [28]

Osbourne (1593–1659) was referring to the strategy that helped reconcile Oxford to his wife. It would appear that Anne Cecil played the well-known bed trick on her husband, which occurs in Boccaccio and other folk tales. It involves letting the husband believe he is in bed with his mistress, when in fact his wife has taken her place. Local historians Morant and Wright also referred to Oxford and the bed trick in their *History of Essex* published in 1836.

> *He forsook his lady's bed, [but] the father of Lady Anne by stratagem, contrived that her husband should unknowingly sleep with her, believing her to be another woman, and she bore a son to him in consequence of this meeting.* [29]

Osbourne's version of this story refers to Oxford's youngest daughter Susan: born the year before her mother died; this cannot therefore be Osbourne's subject. However, there was a son born to the Countess of Oxford following soon after reconciliation with her husband, but the child died shortly after birth. The parish church at Castle Hedingham registered the death as: *The Earle of Oxenfords first sonne … buried the 9th of May 1583.* [30]

Noticeably, the poet in Sonnet 33 appears to lapse into a reflective mood as his thoughts change from losing the sun to what appears to be a reference to the loss of a son. Perhaps, the child, sickly at birth, was quickly removed from the father to be nursed until its death a few days later.

Even so my sun one early morn did shine
With all triumphant splendour on my brow;
But out, alack, he was but one hour mine,
The region cloud hath mask'd him from me now.

The bed trick, which alludes to Oxford, if practised in 1582, was by all accounts the final push needed to bring a reluctant husband back into the bed of his long-suffering and ever patient wife. In the space of the next four years, three daughters would be born to Lady Anne of which two, Bridget and Susan, survived into adulthood.

One is therefore entitled to be suspicious of Nelson having omitted to mention the bed trick, especially as he had never flinched before from repeating rumours and reports of Oxford's sexual misadventures. Perhaps BERTRAM'S antics in *All's Well That Ends Well* caused him momentary amnesia.

Meanwhile Helena had decided on a trick of her own to win back her husband … She tells the whole story to Diana's mother, and Diana agrees to pretend to yield to Bertram … Bertram has been pleading with Diana to let him into her room at midnight, and she offers to do it … So Bertram spends the dark night with a woman he believes to be Diana but who is in reality his own wife Helena. [31]

As a result of this union, HELENA became pregnant (Act 5: sc. iii), thereby reflecting yet again the same course that Anne's life had taken after a similarly reported bed trick.

Nelson is a staunch defender of the old school approach to Shakespeare, as well as being the biographer of Edward de Vere, which some have thought too laced with spite to provide an accurate account of his subject. Yet, despite his being knowledgeable in both Oxfordian and Shakespearian studies, he has shown himself incapable, or unwilling, to refer to any connection between these two playwrights. It would be an insult to the intelligence of the reader to suggest that they too have been unable to appreciate the connections between *All's Well That Ends Well* and the biographical extracts above; these, apart from the bed trick, having been taken quite deliberately from Nelson's study of Oxford and Anne Cecil.

This begs two very important questions. Firstly, we may ask again, why has Nelson been unable to make these same connections? And secondly, if literary blindness can affect someone of Nelson's standing, may we not expect others of equal stature to be similarly affected?

Both questions thrust deep into the heart of the authorship controversy, for there exists a tacit understanding inside English Literature departments not to break ranks by admitting to a link between Shakespeare and Oxford. Like fish that swim in shoals for their defence, 'group-think' has the same pretence.

In his desire to disassociate Oxford from the works of Shakespeare, Nelson has written a life of Oxford, which deliberately downplays his literary talent, his education, and the respect in which contemporary writers held him. In place of these, he has emphasised at every opportunity Oxford's waywardness and the dissolute side of his life. The problem for Nelson is that Oxford had already done this himself, not least by writing *All's Well That Ends Well.* Towards the end of his life, and with the benefit of hindsight, his gift for looking into the recesses of the soul, including his own, enabled him to portray the worst side of his character by transferring it to BERTRAM.

> *Bertram's character is ... haughty, rash, and unbridled, assuming although ill-advised, influenced by the most wretched of society, and entirely devoid of judgement and reflection.* [32]

It has also been said: *"No romantic hero in Shakespeare's comedies is more offensive than Bertram".* Hazlitt also remarked upon this character's *"wilful stubbornness and youthful petulance."* In fact, there has always been a question mark as to why *Shakespeare* created such an unappealing hero for HELENA to fall in love with. The truth is that HELENA, ANNE PAGE and OPHELIA are the same person, but cast in different situations and at different times. On each occasion they have fallen in love with the same man. BERTRAM, FENTON, and HAMLET; for these in turn, represent Oxford as he saw himself at different times in his life, between the years 1570 and 1590. This would then account for the reason why *All's Well That Ends Well* and *Timon of Athens* remained unknown to the public until two decades after Oxford's death; he had characterised himself in them, to his embarrassment, in an all too recognizable and unappealing light.

THE MERRY WIVES OF WINDSOR

The date of composition for *The Merry Wives of Windsor* and the speed with which it was allegedly written is discussed in Chapter 10. The play, itself, contains a subplot involving the courtship of ANNE PAGE. She has three suitors, ABRAHAM SLENDER, DOCTOR CAIUS, AND MASTER FENTON. It is here that the similarity with Anne Cecil commences. She had three suitors, Philip Sidney, Edward Manners and Edward de Vere.

With regard to Sidney's marital prospects, Nelson discovered from the *Cecil Papers* that *"On 9 August 1569 … Anne had been pledged to Philip Sidney."* [33] In other words, ***this was her father's choice*** for her hand. Details of the prenuptial agreement made between the two families exist. Leicester, Sidney's uncle, *"who heartily approved the match undertook to provide Philip with an income of 266l. 13s. 4d. on the day of his marriage … Cecil agreed to pay … his daughter an annuity of 66l. 13s. 4d."* [34] Sidney's total annual fixed income, upon marriage to Anne, would therefore have been £333. 6s. 8d. Now compare this with the dialogue appearing in the play.

MISTRESS QUICKLY: [*To Anne*] Hark ye, Master Slender would speak a word with you.

ANNE: I come to him. [*Aside*] This is my father's choice.
O, what a world of vile ill-favour'd faults
Looks handsome in three hundred pounds a year! (Act 3: sc. iv)

As for the prenuptial agreement between Anne Cecil's *father* and Sidney's *uncle*, this too is referred to in the play.

ANNE: ... what would you with me?

SLENDER: Truly, for mine own part, I would little or
nothing with you. Your father and my uncle hath
made motions...
They can tell you how things go better than I can.
(ibid.)

Some idea of Oxford's barbed wit can be discerned from the names he gives the characters. A portrait of Sidney as a young man shows him to be of *slender* build: a fitting aptronym therefore to match the character SLENDER. From this it follows that Sidney's uncle, the Earl of Leicester, must be the country justice named SHALLOW. Leicester's grasp of intellectual and cultural affairs was considered by many to be *shallow* when one considers the important position he held at Court. Anne's father, Lord Burghley, is therefore GEORGE PAGE. Page is a servile name, especially when attached to Elizabeth's first minister. But as the most powerful man in England, his forename represents that status: it being that of the nation's patron saint.

Nelson has also given notice that Edward Manners, 3rd Earl of Rutland, and a ward of court in Burghley's house until 1570, was another suitor who had eyes for Anne Cecil. *"Taking pen in hand on 15 August, Burghley explained matters at length to the presumably disappointed Rutland."*

> *I think it doth seem strange to your Lordship to hear of a purposed determination in my Lord of Oxford to marry with my daughter ... Truly, my Lord, my goodwill serves me to have moved such a matter as this in another direction than this is, but having more occasion to doubt of the issue of the matter, I did forbear, and in mine own conceit I could have as well liked there as in any other place in England. ... Percase your Lordship may guess where I mean, and so shall I, for I will name nobody.* [35]

Nelson concludes from this that with Sidney out of the picture, Rutland would have been Burghley's preferred choice as a suitable husband for his daughter.

In the play, Manners, who at the time of Oxford's wedding preparations was living in France, is cast as DOCTOR CAIUS, a Frenchman. The name Caius is also an apt choice, for it refers to the famous Roman legislator Caius: responsible for preparing the *Institutes* in the reign of Justinian (483-565 A.D.). Under this emperor's rule, these became the legal foundation for the *Corpus Juris Civilis*, which not only codified Roman law, but also became the basis for much of European jurisprudence.

Manners, like CAIUS, also enjoyed a legal career. In 1587 he was on the threshold of attaining the title of Lord Chancellor, the most distinguished position in English law, but his death that same year ended that ambition.

There was also another man named Caius, and he is more often connected with the character of that name. This was John Caius, who founded Gonville Hall at Cambridge in 1557. He apparently disliked Welshmen to the extent of banning them from holding fellowships there. This friction between Caius and the Welsh is possibly reflected in the play, where a duel is arranged between CAIUS and the Welsh parson, SIR HUGH EVANS.

However, the naming of Caius after the Roman legislator should not be thought to exclude a connection with the Elizabethan of the same name. 'Shakespeare' was perfectly capable of entwining one with the other. However, according to the *Oxford Companion to English Literature* (p. 157), the re-founder of Gonville and Caius College Cambridge bears no resemblance to the character of DOCTOR CAIUS.

Let us not allow the name of Evans to pass without a further remark. For there existed a Henry Evans who was a Welsh play master and scrivener who worked for two years in 1583 and 1584 as a supervisor for the troupes sponsored by the Earl of Oxford (Anderson, 2005, p. xviii). Another who worked for Oxford as his amanuensis and secretary was Abraham Fleming, and it is his Christian name that was given to MASTER SLENDER.

As the play unfolds, ANNE PAGE rejects both SLENDER and CAIUS as potential husbands.

> *S]he begs her mother not to marry her 'to yond fool'; but, on hearing that her mother destines her for Caius, declares that she 'had rather be set quick in the earth, And bowled to death with turnips'.* [36]

ANNE, it transpires, has eyes only for her third suitor, MASTER FENTON: as indeed, her namesake had set her sights on Oxford to the exclusion of Sidney and Manners.

It will therefore come as no surprise to learn there was an actual person named Fenton living at that time (*DNB*), and that he had links with Anne Cecil and her father Lord Burghley. In a letter dated 22 July 1581, *"Geffray Fenton"* wrote to the Lord Treasurer confirming that after following a recommendation made by the Earl of Leicester, he had subsequently been sworn in as the Queen's secretary in Ireland.

Seven years before this appointment, he had addressed a written declaration of *A forme of Christian pollicie drawne out of French* to Lord Burghley, in which he confessed to the *"dutifull effection I haue always borne to your Honour."*

In the year before that, he had contacted Anne Cecil, Countess of Oxford, with a request for permission to dedicate his book to her. This was his *Golden Epistles, Contayning varietie of discourse both Morall, Philosophicall, and Diuine: gathered as well out of the remainder of Gueuaraes workes, as other Authors, Latine, French, and Italian.* Permission for the dedication was granted, and Oxford's wife was addressed as . . .

> *the right Honourable and virtuous Lady, Anne Countesse of Oxenford . . . [who] hath bene alwayes rightworthily noted a diligent follower of those Artes and studies which best serue to the declaracion and glory of true virtue and pietie."* [37]

The book proved popular and was reprinted in 1577 (Newly corrected and amended), and again in 1582.

As Christopher Paul correctly pointed out, *"Fenton's book contains a chapter titled 'A discourse of the Ages of mans lyfe'."* This is of special importance because Paul discussed the same question 'Shakespeare' answered through the mouth of JAQUES, in *As You Like It* (Act 2: sc. vii).

> All the world's a stage,
> And all the men and women merely players;
> They have their exits and their entrances;
> And one man in his time plays many parts,
> His acts being seven ages.

Paul noted that Fenton, too, had considered seven as being *"a number universal and accomplished,"* for describing the different stages through which a man's life progressed.

It is in character with Oxford that he would acknowledge Fenton's dedicatory address to his wife by using the man's name as a suitor to ANNE PAGE in *The Merry Wives of Windsor*. By doing so, and adopting Fenton's name, Oxford was able to complete the parallel between the three men courting *Anne Page* and the three who were considered for marriage to Anne Cecil. This arrangement was also especially appropriate, since both he and FENTON emerged victorious over their rivals.

There also existed a likeness of Oxford in FENTON: familiar to Burghley, and which caused PAGE to complain.

FENTON: He doth object I am too great of birth,
And that my state being gall'd with my expense,
I seek to heal it only by his wealth;
Besides these, other bars he lays before me—
My riots past, my wild societies—
And tells me 'tis a thing impossible
I should love thee but as a property.

ANNE: Maybe he tells true.

FENTON: No, heaven so speed me in my time to come!
Albeit, I will confess thy father's wealth
Was the first motive that I woo'd thee, Anne,
Yet, wooing thee, I found thee of more value
Than stamps in gold or sums in sealed bags;
And 'tis the very riches of thyself
That now I aim at. (Act 3: sc. iv)

This is Oxford speaking from the heart. It had taken his wife's recent death in 1588 for him to discover that only in parting does one really look into the depths of love. From that time onwards he honoured her memory, immortalising her as the virtuous and sometimes misunderstood heroine of his plays.

Before leaving *The Merry Wives of Windsor*, it is instructive to compare the traditionalist's opinion of a scene taken from this play.

In act four scene one of The Merry Wives of Windsor, a boy called William is given a Latin grammar lesson by Sir Hugh Evans, a Welsh schoolmaster. Was this scene written by an earl such as Oxford who never set foot inside a grammar school in his life? Or by a man called William who as a boy was entitled by virtue of his father's status as an alderman of the town to attend the grammar school at Stratford-upon-Avon, where there was a Welsh schoolmaster, one Thomas Jenkins? [38]

Appealing though this may sound, almost every statement in this excerpt is false. Firstly, SIR HUGH EVANS is *not* a *"Welsh schoolmaster"* he is a Welsh parson. Secondly, the Latin grammar lesson does not take place in a classroom, but is given as a one-to-one tutorial. Oxford's early education had been acquired by just such tutorials. Thirdly, at the age of eight, Oxford was sent to Queens' College, Cambridge, where one may reasonably suspect he *set foot inside* the rooms assigned for class teaching, in much the same way as other pupils did in the Stratford grammar school. Fourthly, and I quote from H. J. Oliver, editor of *The Merry Wives of Windsor:*

> *[EVANS] The character can hardly have been based on the Stratford schoolmaster of 1575-9, Thomas Jenkins, as is sometimes said. Jenkins was born in London (Mark Eccles, Shakespeare in Warwickshire, Madison, 1961, p.56).* [39]

Based upon this fabrication and the observation that *"The lesson of Sir Hugh Evans in Merry Wives is based on the Latin grammar book that was the standard school text of the period;"* Bate concludes: *"It is all the evidence we need that young William Shakespeare attended the King's Free Grammar School of Stratford-upon-Avon."*[40]

Emboldened by what he is pleased to call evidence for William Shakespeare's authorship, Bate further concludes:

> *The two characters called William stand as symbols for the essentials of Shakespeare's youth. William of Arden embodies his origins in rural Warwickshire; William of Windsor enacts his exposure to a grammar school and not university: the image precisely fits the earliest surviving allusions to William Shakespeare as dramatist.* [41]

In fact, WILLIAM of Arden does appear in *As You Like It,* but only as a clown:

> *A clown in love with Audrey* (Rowe), v. 1] *discovers Audrey in Touchstone's company, and intimidated by the latter, submissively departs.* [42]

Consider also, how the play abounds with French characters: AMIENS, JAQUES, LE BEAU, CHARLES, PHEBE, and JAQUES DE BOYS. This play is very far removed from the English Arden. Instead, the action is set in the French Ardennes, which once stretched from the Rhine to the Sambre.

As for WILLIAM of Windsor, he is a boy whose education is the despair of his mother: *"my husband says my son profits nothing in the world at his book,"* (Act 4: sc. i). Can Professor Bate seriously be suggesting that England's incomparable genius, Shakespeare, has falsely compared himself to a feeble minded, insignificant boy in one play and a dunce in another? I suggest most people, unaffected by the mythologizing of Shakespeare, would have difficulty in accepting that any man at the top of his profession would find reason to demean himself as either of these two Williams. Yet, these explanations are seen as all the justification Bate needs to persist with his nonsense of Shakespeare having left his mark in the plays.

The reader is therefore invited to compare Bate's examples with the similarities that exist between Oxford and BERTRAM, or Oxford and FENTON, or Oxford as HAMLET, and then make their own judgement as to how ill-informed professional scholars are when it comes to discussing the authorship question.

What seems to have happened is that Bate looked for some rationale between the content of the plays and the life story of the man he was taught to think of as Shakespeare but found nothing significant. Rather than abandon his search and settle for defeat, he opted for the best he could come up with, which were these two ineffectual Williams, whose only connection with Shakespeare happens to be their forename. Why, then, not also mention WILLIAM the cook, in *2 Henry IV*, (v. 1)? Noticeably, the one person Bate could not cite was ROBERT SHALLOW'S cousin WILLIAM, for he *was* a *"good scholar"* but at *"Oxford"* (III. 2).

If there is a lesson to be learnt from this, it is surely that most of the acclaimed spokespeople, who talk authoritatively about the works of Shakespeare, are almost wholly ignorant of the arguments concerning the authorship debate. This is because they have ignored the subject, and have only a superficial understanding of the problem's complexity and magnitude.

The sceptical position, as favoured by orthodox scholarship, is based solely upon a comprehensive knowledge of Shakespeare's plays and poetry. This is used to silence any dissenting voice suggesting some other author wrote Shakespeare's work. Yet, when questioned, say by media reporters attracted by doubts that have been raised, they immediately assume the role of an expert witness. And by using their authority concerning the literary merit of Shakespeare's work, they are able to deflect counter suggestions that Shakespeare was a penname used by another author. It is a comfortable position, but inevitably one wherein the wider aspects of authorship must eventually end with their defeat. One cannot fool people indefinitely.

Professor Bate, to his credit, is one who has deigned to write about the authorship controversy, having devoted a chapter to it in his book, *The Genius of Shakespeare*. Sadly, like most men of his mistaken persuasion, he has no understanding of the meaning of proof, and uses the word without sufficient warrant, as may now be demonstrated.

> *No one in Shakespeare's lifetime or the first two hundred years after his death expressed the slightest doubt about his authorship.*
> *That nobody raised the question for two hundred years proves that there is no intrinsic reason why there should be a Shakespeare Authorship Controversy.* [43]

Once again Bate commits inaccuracies with his statements. It is quite untrue to say nobody dissented to Shakespeare's authorship for two hundred years. Ben Jonson positively avowed that Edward de Vere was Shakespeare, and urged that he be tested to prove this. Thomas Thorpe also asserted that *Shake-speares Sonnets* were written by the Earl of Oxford; Henry Peacham was another who cryptically confirmed de Vere's hidden authorship by the use of a clever anagram on the cover page of his book, *Minerva Britanna* (Chapter 9 refers). Leonard Digges was also one who encoded de Vere's name into the poem he had intended for inclusion in the First Folio (Chapter 9 refers). And in Sonnet 76, which is specifically about the poet's name, Oxford, himself, admits to having written it (p. 201).

Apart from these instances, there are the subtle innuendoes contained in the comments made by Nashe, Chettle, Marston, Barnfield, who were so closely associated with Oxford at one time; they must have known his secret identity. There is also the oft repeated hyphenation of Shake-speare:, thus denoting the use of a penname. And let us not forget the irate onlooker at Stratford-upon-Avon, who repeatedly heckled David Garrick's closing speech at the 1769 jamboree, by repeatedly interrupting him in no uncertain terms to inform him that Shaxpere was a *"provincial nobody"*; a sentiment repeated by the anonymous author of *The Learned Pig* (1786). In point of fact, Stratford-upon-Avon had for the past 153 years treated their former resident, William Shaxpere, as exactly that – *"a nobody"*.

This changed after Garrick's three-day visit. From 1769 onwards, the people of Stratford-upon-Avon resolved to forget the stories about Shaxpere, passed down to them over the years, and to enjoy the benefits of his acquired reputation. First, the Shakespeare Club was formed; then a theatre was built. And in 1869, the Theatre Royal was adapted from the Shakespearian Rooms; to be replaced in 1879 by the Victorian Memorial Theatre.

Today, Stratford-upon-Avon is a thriving tourist town that welcomes visitors from every part of the world. It is a delightful place to visit. Understandably, its resident population and those concerned with the conventional story of Shakespeare are desirous, if not desperate, to see this should continue. But the 18th century also saw a growth in doubt concerning Shakespeare's credentials. With increased education and literacy, the ability to research into past lives afforded better opportunities. Also the new Enlightenment encouraged greater scrutiny into the claims made by previous generations. Bate should therefore not act surprised that two hundred years passed before a better educated people, influenced by the culture of the Enlightenment, began to re-think what they had been told about Shakespeare.

Bate's response to these doubts has been to raise a number of arguments intended to 'prove' that Oxford could not be William Shakespeare. It may come as a sad shock to this learned professor, but none of his objections actually constitutes a proof. For although Bate raises objections that are *necessary* to form a proof: none are actually *sufficient*. In every case he submits, it is perfectly possible to reinterpret the situation and show Oxford fits the situation described. Indeed, answers to most of the objections raised by Bate are to be found within the pages of this book.

Henry VIII

Let us consider an argument raised by Bate, which continues to be favoured by those disposed to believe the unbelievable, for it purports to be both *necessary* and *sufficient*.

> *Henry VIII was described by at least two witnesses as a "new play" in 1613. How de Vere managed to write [this play] from beyond the grave is a profound mystery indeed. …*

> *Henry VIII was one of Shakespeare's three collaborations with John Fletcher, who subsequently took over as house dramatist of the King's Men.* [44]

Apart from Bate's quirky comment about writing from the grave, there is nothing in the above statement that disqualifies Oxford from having written *Henry VIII.* All that is needed are the *complete* facts, and sufficient intelligence to see how they combine.

The first thing to look at is the piece of evidence provided in Sir Henry Wotton's letter to Sir Edmund Bacon, dated 2 July 1613, from which, I quote: *"The King's Players had a new Play called All Is True, representing some principal pieces of the reign of Henry 8."* [45] There is nothing conclusive to be drawn from the phrase 'new play'; the same could have been said about a number of Shakespeare's plays that had not previously been performed, and which only became known when the First Folio advertised them in its list of contents, a full decade after Wotton's letter was written. His epistle continues by describing the play as one . . .

> *which was set forth with many extraordinary Circumstances of Pomp and Majesty, even to the matting of the Stage; the Knights of the Order, with their Georges and Garter, the Guards with their embroidered Coats, and the like.*

Very clearly, Wotton was treated to a most lavish spectacle. And it is these remarks that open the way to accepting Oxford's authorship. As R. A. Foakes, editor of the Arden edition of *Henry VIII* commented: *"reference to the 'Knights of the Order, with their Georges and Garter, the Guards with their embroidered coats' [are observations] for which the play provides no evidence."* [46] In other words, the play seen by Sir Henry Wotton in 1613 is not the same play that was published in the First Folio under the title of *The Life of King Henry the Eight.*

This apparent contradiction is easily explained. Three days before Wotton wrote his letter; that is, on 29 June, the Globe theatre burnt to a cinder. In less than an hour the flames had consumed everything that had been abandoned in the rush to evacuate the theatre, and this included the theatre's wardrobe with its *"few forsaken Cloaks".* It is a persuasive thought that these were the robes of CARDINAL WOLSEY and HENRY VIII which appeared amongst a list of costumes compiled at the beginning of the century by Edward Alleyn. Alleyn was Henslowe's son-in-law and business partner; therefore the exchange of costumes between these two men cannot be discounted.

With the loss of the costumes, what could Henslowe do in order to produce this play in the future? He could order a new set of costumes to be made, but that would be very expensive, and the profit from the play would be unlikely to justify the cost. Another solution was much simpler and more to his liking. He would engage Fletcher to rewrite the play, being careful to avoid the scenes requiring an extravagant display of robes. This would then explain why the actual text of *Henry VIII* is so much better than that of other plays, and why it is accompanied by a most unusual display of act and scene divisions, together with a comprehensive set of stage directions. Fletcher must have begun rewriting it a few years before work on the First Folio began.

Cyrus Hoy's analysis of *Henry VIII* – the play that appears in the First Folio – concluded that Fletcher's style was discernible in 1: iii; 1: iv; 3: i, and in 5: ii, iii, iv. From this, it is easy to understand how the traditionalists' *rush to judgement* has prompted the conclusion that Fletcher must have collaborated with Shakespeare to write the play in 1613, when it was first produced under its original title, *All Is True*. In promoting collaboration as 'fact', Bate, together with those of a similar persuasion fail to mention that the writing of plays depicting English history was forbidden by law in 1613.

The reader should therefore beware; it is possible to 'prove' anything by ignoring alternative explanations, or by omitting pertinent facts that, if used, would contradict what one is trying to prove. Unfortunately, this has happened in attempts to find ways of justifying the belief that Oxford could not have written the plays and sonnets under the penname, *Shakespeare*.

But why should this be? Why has it been so difficult for those who teach, lecture, and write about Shakespeare to acknowledge alternative possibilities? The answer is surprisingly simple. Professor Alan Nelson, himself a traditionalist and fervent advocate of the Shakespeare-is-Shaxpere theory explained it to a packed audience when he addressed the University Of Tennessee College Of Law in 2004. Quite simply, the English departments, he admitted, operate a 'closed shop'.

> *[I]t would be as difficult for a professed Oxfordian to be hired in the first place, much less gain tenure, as for a professed creationist to be hired or gain tenure in a graduate-level department of biology.*[47]

Selecting for office only those who can be counted upon to maintain and defend the traditional position, safeguards the reputations of the professional scholars who have contributed so much of their lives to establishing the life and works of Shakespeare as a lower class boy, whose inherent genius allowed him to surpass all others in the field of dramatic art and poetic literature: an ideal founded in imagination, but for which no real evidence has ever been discovered.

The Two Noble Kinsmen is usually grouped with *Henry VIII* as a further example of the collaboration that took place between 'Shakespeare' and Fletcher. But *The Two Noble Kinsmen* was not listed in the catalogue of plays that appeared in the First Folio. A quarto edition of the play did become published in 1634, claiming to be a work by Shakespeare and Fletcher: however, both men had long since died. And not everyone accepts this attribution. Nevertheless, if it were true, the explanation would be that Fletcher had acquired one of Oxford's earliest plays, either whole or in part, and had reworked and added to it. The finished play would then be by Shakespeare and Fletcher, but not a collaboration as the word is understood.

HAMLET

We can now return to the plays that brought the courtship between Oxford and Anne Cecil into direct focus: particularly *Hamlet*. Oxford's sister was married to Peregrine Bertie, Baron Willoughby de Eresby, who in 1582 and 1585 was the English ambassador stationed at the Danish court in Elsinore, and he, if not his wife Mary, must be considered the likeliest source for the background to this play's location.

Sigmund Freud, the father of psychoanalysis, was left in no doubt that PRINCE HAMLET was a personification of Oxford. Lord Burghley, characterised as POLONIUS, reinforces this conclusion, for both men held similar positions at Court. As remarked before, POLONIUS is an epenthesis of POLUS; i.e. **POL**-oni-**US**: POLUS having been the name given to Burghley by Gabriel Harvey, who referred to the Lord Treasurer as *"Polus"* three times during his speech before Queen Elizabeth at Audley End in 1578.

However, it will be recalled POLONIUS had not been Oxford's first choice of name: this had been CORAMBIS (p. 263 fn, which appears in the first quarto. Burghley must have protested this was too obviously a pun on his family motto. As to whether the name was changed from POLONIUS to CORAMBIS, as some commentators have argued, or *vice versa,* is irrelevant; the fact is, either way, it is still Burghley, and Burghley never lifted a finger to reprove or punish the author for his audacity. The only explanation to account for this is that the audacious author was his son-in-law, and father of his three grandchildren.

The traditionalists' response to this is mute. They well know that inaction by Burghley for gross disrespect against his person by someone of Shaxpere's reduced standing was quite unthinkable. But there is a further problem for the traditional view; Burghley fell ill in the spring of 1598 and died on 5 August. His protest to have the name changed in *Hamlet* must therefore predate his last illness, which pushes back the writing of the play to before 1598. In fact, just two years earlier, Thomas Lodge had already made a reference to the title, even though *Hamlet* would not appear in the Stationers' Register until 1602. In his pamphlet, *Wit's Misery,* (1596), he referred to: *"The ghost which cried so miserably at the Theator like an oister-wife, 'Hamlet, revenge'."* [48]

Nelson, a firm supporter of orthodoxy's Shakespeare, did manage to let slip in his biography of Oxford that he was fully aware that a connection existed between his subject and 'Shakespeare'; this, despite his many affirmations to the contrary. The Freudian slip occurred when he included an excerpt from an historian who had no qualms when writing about Burghley's relationship, to POLONIUS.

> *A personal recklessness of behaviour ... grew up [amongst] a whole new generation of high-spirited young aristocrats in open rebellion against the conservative establishment in general and Lord Burghley [i.e., Cecil] in particular. Very many, like Oxford, Rutland, Southampton, Bedford, and Essex, had been wards of the old man and were reacting violently against his counsels of worldly prudence. Such a development is hardly surprising. To listen to Polonius for a few moments in a theatre is one thing; to have to put up with him pontificating at every meal-time for years on end is another.* [49]

Nelson was quoting from historian, Lawrence Stone's *Crisis of the Aristocracy 1558-1641* (Oxford, 1965, p. 582). It is of particular interest to note that Stone has unhesitatingly linked POLONIUS to Burghley, expecting his readers will themselves understand this connection. Not so, those indoctrinated with the old school of thought; this decries everything connecting Oxford with Shakespeare. Unanimously, they protest there is no connection between the two whatever. Nelson, however, has already let slip the fragility of this 'unanimity' by including Stone's opinion. Therefore, unless these dissenters wish to be counted amongst those unable to fully comprehend what Stone meant, the following assistance is intended to be helpful.

Stone had in mind both the *Certaine Precepts, or Directions* conveyed by Burghley to his son Robert, and those POLONIUS delivered to his son LAERTES. Stone rightly conceived that like POLONIUS, this was but one example of Burghley *"pontificating"* to his charges, and that it would have eventually grated the nerves of his wards who were forced to endure his meal-time lectures.

Felicia H. Londré has drawn attention to these precepts:

> *Let thy hospitality be moderate ... Beware thou spendest not more than three of four parts of thy revenue ... Beware of being surety for thy best friends ... Be sure to keep some great man thy friend ... Towards thy superiors be humble ... Trust not any man with thy life, credit or estate.* [50]

Londré correctly points out that these were not published until two years after Shaxpere's death. As Dr. Louis Wright, former director of the Folger Shakespeare Library has acknowledged, it is unlikely that Burghley's advice would have been available to a commoner of Shaxpere's class, before their publication.

Oxford, however, when released into adult life, could look back and mock his guardian through the mouth of POLONIUS. He certainly does so when HAMLET puns on the Lord Chamberlain's death – *"A certain convocation of politic worms are e'en at him. Your worm is your only emperor for diet"* (Act 4: sc. iii).

This sentence is most appropriate when directed at Burghley: 'convocation'; 'politic'; 'worms'; 'emperor', and 'diet' being the important words. Burghley was born on 13 September 1520. One month later, Charles V was crowned King at Aachen and made *emperor*-elect. Charles then proceeded to *Worms* to attend the *convocation* that had been arranged to confront Martin Luther in a specially prepared *Diet*. Luther should have been brought before Pope Leo X, who had condemned the Lutheran doctrine in 1520, but *"Because of the confused political and religious situation of the time, Luther was called before the political authorities rather than the pope or a council of the Roman Catholic church."*[51]

Unlike FENTON in *The Merry Wives of Windsor*, or BERTRAM in *All's Well That Ends Well*, HAMLET is a sombre, brooding almost suicidal figure that is out of step with the other characters in the play. OPHELIA, on the other hand, observes the same devotion towards the man she loves, as was apparent in both HELENA and ANNE PAGE.

The picture we see of Oxford, caricatured as HAMLET, is the person he saw himself to be, following the sudden death of his wife in 1588. This tied in with the sense of loss he displayed in Sonnet 66, written at about the same time.

It was actually Thomas Nashe who first referred to *Hamlet*. In his Epistle to Robert Greene's *Menaphon* of 1589: the year after Oxford's wife died, Nashe wrote . . .

> *Yet English Seneca read by candlelight yields many good sentences . . . and if you entreat him fair in a frosty morning, he will afford you whole Hamlets, I should say handfuls of Tragicall speeches.* [52]

It will be recalled that 1589 aligns perfectly with the play's reference to shipwrights having worked seven days a week in the year before; that is, during the time England was being threatened by Spain's great armada. Moreover, Nashe's early reference to *Hamlet* is very likely to have resulted from his employment as Oxford's secretary during the time he spent in the country with *"my Lord"* (Chapter 10 refers).

The first recorded performance of *Hamlet* was at Newington Butts on 9 June 1594, which was the second Sunday of Trinity, and this may have been the reason why Henslowe recorded takings of only 8 shillings. Two months before that, on Monday 8 April, he had produced *King Lear* when the receipts had been 26 shillings. Also in June that year, Henslowe produced two other 'Shakespeare' plays, *Titus Andronicus* and *The Taming of a Shrew*; noticeably, he recorded no payment having been made to the author(s) for these stage productions.

The dominant view, stitched together by traditionalists, is that *Titus Andronicus* was by Shakespeare; *The Taming of a Shrew* could be Shakespeare's, but *Hamlet* cannot be his: the date being far too early. They therefore *invent* another play, also called *Hamlet*, but to distinguish it from Shakespeare's, they refer to it as *Ur-Hamlet,* and allot it to Kyd, calling it his 'lost play'. Further references to this 'lost play' then fade into the background, it having served its purpose by removing an embarrassing reference to the Stratford bard's life story.

This anonymous play, invented by academics to cover their embarrassment, emerges later, as a suggested source for 'Shakespeare's' own *Hamlet,* thus 'proving' its prior existence. It then becomes a source: aiding the more accomplished Shaxpere in his writing career at the end of the century, at a time more in keeping with his greater maturity. One can see how easily Shaxpere has become 'created' as the mythical *Shakespeare.* Academics simply explain away any inconsistencies in the historical record by introducing what are, factually speaking, non-existent pieces of evidence designed to overcome their difficulties. John Payne Collier, a much regarded scholar of his day, was not alone in creating 'historical facts' to fill an absence in Shaxpere's record as a playwright. Those proposing *Ur-Hamlet's* existence, differ from Collier only because they pursue the same objective in a more careful manner.

With *Hamlet* still in mind, Gabriel Harvey made a marginal note in his 1598 edition of Chaucer's poems, to the effect that *"his Lucrece & his tragedie of Hamlet, Prince of Denmark, haue it in them, to please the wiser sort."*[53] Since marginal notes can be made at any time after publication of the book in which they occur, it allows for *Hamlet's* suggested date of composition to be 1599-1600. This neatly coincides with 'Shakespeare' having written at the same time, *Twelfth Night,* and *Julius Caesar,* both with dates of composition given as 1599-1600. But 1599 was also the year he is said to have written *Much Ado About Nothing* (1598-99), and *Henry V,* (1598-99). Sandwiched in amongst these are *Troilus and Cressida* (1597-1602), *The Merry Wives of Windsor* (1597-1601), and *As You Like It* (1596-1600). Moreover, let us not forget that 'Shakespeare's' daylight hours were filled with acting, learning his lines, attending rehearsals, and giving performances. As late as

1598, Jonson asserted in his folio *Works* that 'Shakespeare' had played a role in *Every Man in His Humour.*

In a study of *Hamlet* (*The Problem of Hamlet: A Solution*, London, 1936), Professor A. S. Cairncross attempted to rationalise the similarities of phrase and expression between Thomas Kyd's *Spanish Tragedy* and the first quarto edition of *Hamlet*, as published in 1603. He suggested that actors had remembered lines from one play and transposed them on to another. Bad quartos were sometimes cobbled together by actors reciting their lines in front of a scribe. It was therefore easy for an actor to err by substituting the gist of one speech in place of another, especially if there where similarities in scenes, or if the lines required had been forgotten.

At other times, quartos were copied from old discarded prompt books that may have had pages missing, requiring the memory of some player, if available, to fill the vacant gap. It is therefore noteworthy that the first quarto of *Hamlet*, entered in the *Stationers' Register* on 26 July 1602, as *Revenge of Hamlett Prince Denmarke*, contains little more than half the play.

As a result of his deliberations, Cairncross was able to insist that until evidence can be produced to the contrary, the play referred to by Nashe in 1589 and subsequently staged by Henslowe in 1594 was Shakespeare's *Hamlet* ... *"and no other"*.

Bate, together with others of a like mind, refuse to accept Cairncross' rationale, and together they view *Ur-Hamlet* with the same adoration the courtiers viewed the emperor's new clothes in Hans Christian Andersen's fairytale. Despite this adoration of the invisible, Cairncross was able to ...

> *show that by the latter date [1594] Hamlet had become familiar. The ridicule of euphemism in the play, as in the character Osiric, he maintains, dates it to shortly before or after 1590. He then narrows the date on the basis of the play's contents to the summer or autumn of 1588.*[54]

Autumn 1588 is precisely the time that Oxford would have begun writing *Hamlet* as a catharsis for the death of his wife earlier that year, and the disreputable way he had treated her during their marriage.

To succeed with his catharsis, Oxford first characterised the people involved, including himself, and brought them to life with all the art his genius could attain to, and he did this with such consummate skill, and such a charge of emotional energy that *Hamlet* has become, for the majority of theatre-goers, the greatest tragedy ever written.

Few people realise, however, that when watching *Hamlet* in performance, they are seeing a dramatisation of Oxford as *"a son struggling to find his place in a family disturbed as much by political events as by intimate relationships."* [55] His mother has become GERTRUDE, and his father, whom he dearly loved but who died when he was only twelve, is a ghost; POLONIUS is his father-in-law Lord Burghley, and the Lord Chamberlain's daughter, OPHELIA, is Anne Cecil; her brother LAERTES is Robert Cecil, and HORATIO is Horace de Vere, who was Oxford's cousin and *"most trusted relative"*. It is therefore to HORATIO that HAMLET makes his final aching appeal at the close of the play, echoing what must have been a terrible yearning, with each word wrenched from the depths of his soul.

> O God! Horatio, what a wounded name,
> Things standing thus unknown, shall live behind me!
>
> Act 5: sc. ii

His is a story narrated by the characters Oxford has introduced into the play, and with whom, as HAMLET, he interacts: weaving his emotions into the fabric of a tale first published in France in 1514 and then again in 1570 (*Histoires Tragiques* of Pierre de Belleforest): although it was not translated into English until 1608; but again, too late for Shaxpere.

In the play, we recognise snippets of Oxford's life from HAMLET'S perspective. One example occurs when he tells OPHELIA *"Get thee to a nunnery. Why wouldst thou be a breeder of sinners?"* (Act 3: sc. 1). It is Oxford, acknowledging Anne Cecil and her deep devotion to religion, which she combined with her love for him. Against her show of virtue, he recognises himself to be one whose standard of behaviour has fallen by the wayside. Lovers of Shakespeare see no objection to this 'confession' having originated in their hero's imagination, but for it to have been an actual part of his life experience, this has to be avoided. So they cling to their belief it was Shaxpere who wrote these lines; although his known association with members of the criminal class does little to justify that faith.

Consequently, when HAMLET recoils from OPHELIA'S attraction to him, it is Oxford, realizing that in real life his friendship with Anne had only brought her pain and misery, and that she would have been happier had she not loved him; his own assessment of himself being: *"I could accuse myself of such things that it were better my mother had not borne me."*

In the end, OPHELIA dies young: despairing for the love she wished to give but which was not received. It reflects Anne's marriage to Oxford and her own early death. But history does not record Anne's husband having been present amongst the mourners attending her funeral. HAMLET, too, was absent at the funeral of OPHELIA. He had been sent abroad on a mission, and upon his return was taken captive by pirates. Oxford, too, whilst crossing the English Channel, had twice shared the same experience: on one occasion, his ship was boarded by pirates, and: *"the young Earl of Oxford ... had been stripped to his shirt only six miles from Dover."*[56]

In another part of the play, HAMLET taunts POLONIUS with his feigned madness. It is not difficult to conceive of Burghley having also accused Oxford of insanity. His scandalous relationship with the teenage Southampton is a case in point, and more so because he committed this affair to poetry, which he then audaciously circulated amongst his private friends.

Burghley, however, had other reasons to condemn Oxford for his madness. In a fit of rashness, his son-in-law had invested heavily in Frobisher's north-westerly voyage to Baffin Island, in what is now Canada, hoping the voyagers would strike gold. They returned empty-handed. As a result, Oxford lost a significant part of his family fortune. HAMLET echoes this loss when he woefully confesses, *"I am but mad north-north-west."*

Elsewhere in the play, HAMLET again taunts POLONIUS with: *"Conception is a blessing, but not as your daughter may conceive."* This held a vibrant meaning in Oxford's once tortured mind. Burghley's daughter, while married to Oxford, had conceived her first child in a marriage of apparent conjugal neglect. This had the misfortune of becoming an issue when her husband was about to embark upon his tour of the continent. By the time of his return, more than a year later, word had reached him that his wife had conceived the child out of wedlock. He so believed the evidence put before him, that for a long time afterwards, he remained separated from his wife and daughter. It is this episode that is reflected in HAMLET'S quotation above. The question of Oxford's paternity, concerning the child born during his absence, is dealt with more fully in this chapter, under the section headed *Othello*.

Letters still extant tell of the friction that grew up between Burghley and Oxford, and the accusation he made that the Lord Treasurer was spying on him. In *Hamlet*, POLONIUS also spies on the PRINCE by concealing himself behind an arras; whereupon, his movements are observed by HAMLET, and these are mistaken for those of a rat, and he is slain. This must reveal what was going on in Oxford's mind after the death of his wife. Burghley was seen as a rat, by demanding to be repaid the marriage fee that had remained outstanding since the wedding, seventeen years ago. This would never have been asked for had his daughter lived. To satisfy Burghley's legal claim, Oxford was forced to part with his remaining homes, leaving him virtually destitute.

Professor Bate's response to these parallels (one presumes he is aware of them) is as follows:

> *Typically, the argument runs: Polonius is a satirical 'portrait' of Lord Burghley; therefore the Earl of Oxford wrote Hamlet. … since Shakespeare's range of characters and plots, both familial and political, is so vast that it would be possible to find in the plays 'self-portraits' of, once more, anybody one cares to think of.*[57]

In which case, where does the self-portrait of Bate's 'William Shakespeare' occur? Could it be WILLIAM, the ineffectual clown who is scorned by TOUCHSTONE, or is it the single appearance of the educationally challenged WILLIAM PAGE, or can it to be the cook named WILLIAM?

Let us now turn to ROSENKRANTZ and GUILDENSTERN, two inseparable courtiers that appear in the play, and who studied at the University of Wittenberg. Frederik Holgerson Rosenkrantz and Knud Henriksen Gyldenstierne were two sixteenth-century Danish noblemen, apparently cousins. Lowell James Swank has drawn attention to the comparisons these two courtiers have with the two courtiers in *Hamlet*. Drawing upon the researches of Af Palle Rosenkrantz's article of 1910, which was published in *Gads Danske Magasin*,[58] Swank pointed out that they, too, were students at Wittenberg. And in 1592, they travelled to England as members of a Danish legation, which would have brought them into the compass of the court and Oxford. One may well imagine the amusement it would have caused the Queen and her assembled audience, to see these two men reappear in a play set in their Danish court. Contrast this with the only known account we have of Shaxpere at that time, when it was said of him that he was employing a group of urchins as horse attendants outside the Shoreditch Playhouse, while he worked as a *"Iohannes fac totum"* inside.

We shall leave it to Cairncross to deal the fatal blow to those believing *Hamlet* and *Ur-Hamlet* were different plays. Cairncross drew attention to Richard Tarlton. His name appeared in the first quarto of 1603, but was subsequently deleted. In fact, Tarlton had died fifteen years earlier.

His death in 1588 once again focuses attention upon the plight of Oxford at that time. It was not unusual for the man who would be *Shakespeare* to name the actors he was writing for in place of a character's stage name. This would explain the appearance of Tarlton's name. It also implies the 1603 quarto had been copied from a 1588, or earlier, prompt book or manuscript copy.

Moreover, Tarlton's name also explains Nashe's reference to *Hamlet* in 1589: it being a natural reaction having read the play with its many fine tragic speeches: he may even have written them down at Oxford's dictation; for he was in the country with *"my Lord"* soon after 1588 (Chapter 10 refers).

Consequently, with these documented facts at hand, and nothing to suggest any contamination of this evidence between 1588 and 1603, it follows that *Ur-Hamlet* never existed. This conclusion is quite logical, because Tarlton's name, which originally appeared on the 1603 quarto, proves that this publication had been sourced from a copy that existed before Tarlton died. Hence, the play proposed as *Ur-Hamlet* can be none other than the *Hamlet* published in 1603: written in 1588-89, and staged by Henslowe in June 1594.

References to *Ur-Hamlet* are therefore all flim-flam, used to patch over what traditionalists admit is too absurd, even for them – the notion that Shaxpere commenced his career as a playwright, by writing his greatest and most mature drama.

The Winter's Tale

In several instances, Oxford anticipates Nelson's disparaging assessment of his character by personally committing some of his misdeeds to the confessional of his plays. Amongst what were seen to be his more deplorable acts was the denouncement of his daughter Elizabeth as illegitimate. The commotion this caused sent vibrations through the withdrawing rooms of the nobility, and it began when he returned from the continent in 1576; following more than a year's absence from England. Burghley, while in retrospective mood, recorded what happened:

> *The Erle of Oxford arryved being returned out of Italy, he was enticed by certen lewd Persons to be a Stranger to his Wiff.* [59]

The seeds of suspicion had been planted in Oxford's mind while in Paris, before embarking upon the final part of his journey home. He therefore arrived in England firmly convinced that the child, born to his wife on 2 July 1575 and baptised eight days later, was fathered by another man. This, despite later admitting to Lord Howard *"that he laye not with his wiff but at Hampton Court:"* [60] This was a reference to the attendance of the couple in 1574 at the palace during late September and early October, nine months before his wife gave birth.

Yet, despite this concordance in dates, Burghley had learned from his son-in-law that *"the child could not be his because the child was born in Iuly, which was not the space of twelve monthes."* [61] This has naturally puzzled commentators, and the reason for it will be given in the section headed *Othello*. Burghley, though, seems to have taken it as a thoughtless remark from his son-in-law.

In December 1577, more than eighteen months after he had separated from his wife and child, Lady Catherine Suffolk took the opportunity to intervene in their marital dispute. She was about to become related to Oxford through the marriage of her son, Peregrine Bertie, who had become betrothed to Mary Vere, Oxford's sister; presumably, she wished to see the matter of her son's future niece and sister-in-law resolved before the wedding.

In a letter addressed to Lord Burghley, dated 15 December, the countess outlined her plan. She would obtain the child without Oxford's knowledge, and whilst he and his sister were together, she would appear with the little girl as though it belonged to some friend of hers *"and we shall see how nature will work in him to like it, and tell him it is his own after."*[62] If the plan was intended to go further, and effect a reconciliation between Oxford and his wife. It failed. The exact details are unknown, except for the fact that Oxford remained separated for a further four years.

Criticism of Oxford for his autocratic arrogance in treating his wife and child this way has been unsparing. Yet, there is another side to his behaviour: not that it excuses him, but it does help one to understand why he remained unmoved by appeal. He had openly condemned his wife as an adulteress, and the child, a consequence of her extra-marital affair. Almost everyone who knew Anne and her little daughter disbelieved him.

It was also open to suggestion that his conclusions were based upon a calumnious report: one that in all probability was directed at the Burghley family. Even more remarkable, as it would seem from Burghley's note, Oxford had been misinformed about the time between human conception and birth. For an adult member of England's ruling class, brought up to recognize his superiority in the political order, it was unthinkable that he could be seen to have committed such a gross error of judgement. An admission of fault is an admission of fallibility; and to be steadfastly avoided in the class-structured society to which Oxford belonged.

Even in this present age, it is inconceivable that an outspoken advocate of Shaxpere's literary genius will publicly admit to having been mistaken in the belief that Oxford was not William Shakespeare. Pride will overrule truth most times. And Oxford was a very proud young man. Nevertheless, although he refused to effect an apology to his wife, he did allow the thoughts running through his head at that time, to be voiced by BALTHASAR in the aptly titled *Comedy of Errors* (p. 302). It was the closest he could come to admitting the possibility of a mistake.

For Lady Anne, there was to be no comedy from her husband's errors. During the entire period of their separation she bore her suffering with a fortitude that won sympathy from every quarter of the aristocracy. Though charged with adultery by her husband, she defended herself with eloquence: displaying a religious tolerance to the recognition of her fate. And, despite her husband's failings, she never wavered in her acceptance of him, forgiving him every injury to herself and child, and longing always for reconciliation.

This episode of betrayal, and its consequences, gave rise to other parallels: these occur in *Othello* and *The Winter's Tale*. Both plays concern jealousy: the emotional fuel that drives inner torment.

> *Shakespeare has in both instances shown us the origin of this passion out of a mere nothing, and its frightful consequences; the destruction of the whole happiness of life ... from the madness of a moment ... Othello, little disposed to jealousy by nature, is made susceptible of it by circumstances and situations, he is driven to it by a cunning whisperer and deceiver.* [63]

Dr. Levi Fox had previously remarked of *The Winter's Tale ...*

> *Shakespeare's play is a study in obsession, with the manic need for instant proof – as in Othello, but now without the villain. Appalling consequences for everyone follow this royal madness.* [64]

That Oxford also saw himself as the victim of an obsessional disbelief, similar to that occurring in both plays named by Fox, is even more evident when we learn from *The Winter's Tale* that HERMIONE has given birth, and her husband, LEONTES, is denying that he is the father. *"Hermione's noble presence makes no alteration in his impression; he insists that his child is a bastard."*[65]

Consider how appropriate these lines would be to the Oxford household, between April 1576 and December 1581.

"[Anne Cecil's] *noble presence makes no alteration in his impression; he insists that the child is a bastard."*

In a bid to restore order to a disintegrating situation,

> *The wife of one of the noblemen, a gallant and loving woman named Paulina ... brings the baby to the king, sure that the sight of his little daughter will release him from his restless and tormented imaginings.* [66]

Have we not read this before in real life?

> *The wife of one of the noblemen, a gallant and loving woman named* [Catherine] ... *brings the baby to* [Oxford], *sure that the sight of his little daughter will release him from his restless and tormented imaginings.*

As in life, so in the play: Lady Suffolk's strategy failed to bring about reconciliation between Oxford and his wife. In the play, this is only achieved towards the end, and coincides with the death of LEONTES' son, which he interprets as a punishment from heaven for his destructive obsession.

In real life, Oxford and his wife, too, were eventually reconciled and their daughter accepted without blemish to her birth. The manner of their reunion has already been discussed with reference to the bed trick, as dramatised in *All's Well That Ends Well* (p. 344). It is also of particular note that as a result of their reunion the Countess of Oxford gave birth to a son nine months later. But, as with MAMILLIUS in *The Winter's Tale*, this child, too, was claimed by death. We do not know if Oxford believed that the loss of his male heir was divine judgement, brought about by his destructive obsession, but he did allow LEONTES to believe it. (See Sonnet 33, p. 345).

OTHELLO

In 1575, Oxford was in Venice, where he stayed for a period of at least three months. During his time in that city he acquired a residence; it is actually recorded that he had one built, but the time span suggests this may have been a renovation rather than a construction. While residing in the city, it would have come to his notice that a wealthy Venetian nobleman had also built a house close by, but tragedy befell him when he was told his wife had been unfaithful. Overcome with emotion, and while in a fit of jealous rage, he murdered her. The nobleman's name was Otello: presumably a member of the family *"Otelli del Moro"*, for the house he built was the *"Casa Otello"*.

When we turn to Shakespeare's play, *Othello:* is not a similar story retold there? In a fit of jealous rage, OTHELLO murders his Venetian wife believing her to have been unfaithful. By what manner of creative reasoning can Shaxpere's apologists seek to explain how nine-year-old Will Shaxpere came by this precise knowledge? It cannot be from the seventh story in the third decade of Geraldo Cinthio's *Hecatommithi,* which is the primary source for *Othello*, because this was published in Venice in 1566, and no English translation existed before 1753. Furthermore, the Italian tale does not name OTHELLO: referring to him only as *"a Moor, handsome and valiant, and highly thought of by the Signory of Venice"* [67] In fact, the only person named by Cinthio is DISDEMONA, the Moor's wife, whose name 'Shakespeare' retained, changing the second letter 'i' to an 'e'.

As the play unfolds, the characters and plot take form and the failure of OTHELLO'S ensign, IAGO, to receive his expected promotion becomes a focus for his revenge. He will destroy OTHELLO by exciting him to acts of jealousy. The tool he intends to use is the Moor's wife. While playing the trusted servant to OTHELLO, he slowly begins sowing seeds of distrust regarding the faithfulness of DESDEMONA.

Something very similar can be discerned in the events leading to Oxford disowning his own wife while touring Italy. Upon embarking for his Grand Tour in 1575, he had taken with him a servant named Rowland Yorke, who may be Oxford's IAGO.

Yorke was the ninth son of Sir John York: –

> . . . *'well borne and of gentle blood' and benefited from his father's close association with John Dudley, duke of Northumberland, until the succession crisis of 1553 (Blandy, 27). The family was restored to favour at the accession of Elizabeth I.* (DNB).

Yorke's profession was that of a soldier. On one occasion he served as a lieutenant in Captain Thomas Morgan's English and Welsh force (the same rank to which IAGO at first aspired and then obtained) during conflict against Spain's ambitions in the Lowlands. In 1573, he joined George Gascoigne on an ill-fated voyage that ended in the ship's wreck with the loss of twenty lives. It was after surviving the sea that he joined Oxford's service: possibly with a commendation from Burghley, to whom he had been recommended by England's ambassador to Holland, William Davison. The diplomat described Yorke as a person of *'great value and reputacion'*. Yorke's military service and background would therefore have qualified him as a most suitable companion and bodyguard for any young nobleman about to travel across Europe.

The name IAGO is actually a phonetic anagram of Yorke, since 'Yrkoe' is capable of the same audible sound as IAGO. The name is also Spanish, and an incident occurred to connect him with Spain at Zutphen. Having been given a fortification to defend, he promptly surrendered it to Spain, and then joined the Spanish army in command of a troop of lancers (Ogburn, 515). For this act of treachery, he was condemned as a traitor to his country. This would account for his Spanish name in *Othello*.

Yorke was also responsible for introducing into England *"foining [thrusting] with the rapier"*. Camden commented . . .

> *the English till that time used to fight with long swords and bucklers, striking with the edge, and thought it no part of a man, either to foin or strike beneath the girdle.* (ibid. 515)

Iago, too, admitted to foining: – *"Though in the trade of war I have slain men ... nine or ten times I had thought to have yerk'd him here, under the ribs."* (Act I: sc.ii)

A further point of interest is that Gascoigne, Yorke's companion at sea, was both a soldier and poet, and author of *Hundredth Sundrie Flowres.* This was published in 1573, at a time when Gascoigne was on active military service in the Netherlands. Upon his return to England, he re-published the book as *Poesies of Gascoigne,* together with some deletions and an apology for the offence that the first edition had caused. It has been argued that Oxford covertly arranged publication of the first edition in Gascoigne's absence, so that he could include an exposé of Sir Christopher Hatton's love for Elizabeth, under their pseudonyms of Master F. I. (Fortunatus Infoelix) and Mistress Elinore.

Gabriel Harvey subsequently claimed Fortunatus Infoelix was *"lately the poesie of Sir Christopher Hatton"* (Ogburn, 461). Orthodox opinion remains baffled by the sudden appearance of Gascoigne's second edition and the apology and deletions it contained. To add to the mystery, in 1576 the Queen's ministers called in all unsold copies of this book, thus ending further distribution of its enigmatic references.

By then, Oxford had returned from his European Odyssey ablaze with anger. He had lately been told that his wife's child was not his. Echoes of the rage he felt appear to have been converted into what takes place between OTHELLO and IAGO, for the Moor, too, was told by his ensign that he had been cuckolded.

OTHELLO Villain, be sure thou prove my love a whore,
Be sure of it, give me the ocular proof,

...

Make me to see't, or at the least so prove it,
That the probation bear no hinge, nor loop,
To hang a doubt on: or woe upon thy life!

(Act III: sc.iii)

IAGO provides the evidence that sways OTHELLO to the tragedy that defines the play. But what was the evidence that convinced Oxford that his wife's child was by another man? It is not unlikely that his own guilty liaisons with the women he had lain with while absent from his wife had cultured his mind to suppose that his Countess had been a mark for similar flirtations, and this had led to an evening of abandonment, resulting in her pregnancy. In support of this possibility, there was the fact that she had kept her condition secret for several months. But Oxford was to learn more. It also transpired that his wife had attempted to abort the expected child. Was this the normal behaviour of a loving wife who had conceived a child by her lawfully wedded husband? If Oxford needed proof of this attempted abortion, it was available in a letter written to Burghley by Richard Master, physician to the Queen. In the letter, Master described attending Anne Cecil *"after schrovetyde."* * She asked *"me to prepare sum medicines,"* he wrote, that would enable her to resume her periods (*"ad menses promotions"*).[68]

Master declined Anne's request; instead, he bled and purged her. But he did inform the Queen of the circumstances, before reporting the entire matter to Burghley in a lengthy missive.

> *Her Majesty asked me how the young lady did bear the matter. I answered that she kept it secret four or five days from all persons and that her face was much fallen and thin, with little colour—and when she was comforted and counselled to be gladsome and rejoice she would cry, "Alas, alas! How should I rejoice, seeing he that should rejoice with me is not here, and to say truth, [I] stand in doubt whether he pass judgement upon me and it [the pregnancy] or not;" and bemoaning her case would lament that after so long sickness of body she should enter a new grief and sorrow of mind. At this Her Majesty showed great passion as your Lordship shall hear hereafter. And repeated my Lord of Oxford's answer to me, which he made openly in the presence chamber of Her Majesty, viz., that if she were with child it was not his.* [69]

The situation is a curious one. Oxford was to admit to Lord Howard that he had not shared the marital bed with his wife

---

* In the Church calendar, the first week in Lent follows Shrovetide, and is marked by Quadragesima Sunday; which, in 1575, occurred on 20 February.

since the festivities at Hampton Court in late September and early October 1574. One is therefore reminded of HAMLET'S comment to POLONIUS concerning OPHELIA: *"Conception is a blessing, but not as your daughter may conceive."* Burghley must have been greatly alarmed. His daughter was more than four months pregnant, and her husband still remained unaware of his approaching fatherhood. What is more, Oxford had already denied paternity in the Queen's presence, having made this quite plain before leaving for the continent. Burghley immediately put pen to paper, informing his son-in-law of the good news. We know this because Burghley's letter from Master is dated 7 March 1575, and Oxford's response to the news was dated ten days later.

> *My Lord, Your letters have made me a glad man, for these have put me in assurance of that good fortune which you formerly mentioned doubtfully. I thank God therefore, with your Lordship, that it hath pleased Him to make me a father, where your Lordship is a grandfather; and if it be a boy I shall likewise be a partaker within a greater contentation. (ibid. 486).* [70]

Oxford's delight at the expected birth remained undisturbed throughout the rest of the year, and it was not until 4 April 1576, four days after his arrival in Paris as he journeyed home, that a dramatic change to his peace of mind occurred. Burghley's account of this change was found amongst his notes.

> *No unkindness known on his part at his departure. She made him privy that she thought she was with child, whereof he said he was glad. When he was certified thereof at Paris he sent her his picture with kind letters and messages. He sent her two coach horses. When he heard she was delivered he gave me thanks by his letters for advising thereof. He never signified any misliking of anything until the 4th of April in Paris, from whence he wrote somewhat that, by reason of a man of his, his receiver, he had conceived some unkindness.*[71]

It is time to play the Devil's Advocate, and consider what could possibly have been said to Oxford to cause such a drastic change in his temper. For reasons that will become clearer, the informant is most likely to have been Yorke. Anyone of lesser standing in his retinue would not have dared repeat sensitive rumours heard against the Earl's wife.

The content of the letter sent by the Queen's physician to Burghley, and known also to the Earl of Leicester, as we shall discover, is most likely to have been the first injection of poison whispered into Oxford's ear. His wife had sought to procure a miscarriage in February. Moreover she had looked pale and tired at the time, even suggesting that her husband would not believe the child was his. But how could this be? When Oxford received the news, he expressed his delight at her pregnancy with the gift of a portrait and two coach horses? Secondly, why should pious Anne seek to procure a miscarriage, thus damning herself before God?

The obvious answer, and the one Yorke must have used, for it is a persuasive one, is that Anne's earlier suspicions about her pregnancy were either mistaken, or perhaps she miscarried. But at a later date she conceived a child out of wedlock, and under such conditions that can only be speculated upon. What *is* known with certainty is that by the end of February she was in a pitiful state, asking for medicine to resume her monthly cycle. Let this information be conveyed to Oxford in private, and one may begin to sympathise with his plight, especially if the source of the knowledge was believed reliable.

Even so, surely this slanderous accusation can easily be set aside by referring to the dates. Anne had possibly become pregnant at Hampton Court by 2 October. Nine months later, to the day, her daughter Elizabeth was born. How could Oxford deny the child was his? Reason requires he concur with his wife.

There is, however, an alternative to this scenario: one that is borne out by documentary evidence. Suppose the child was not born on 2 July, as claimed, but was delivered in isolation in September. If this were suggested to Oxford, it would contradict the information he had received concerning the birth of 'his' daughter. So when did Oxford learn that his wife had given birth? There is no record apart from the two notes that Burghley made to himself (and seemingly for posterity). From these jottings, a conclusion may be drawn.

2 July.	*The Countess delivered of a daughter.*	
24 September.	*The letter of the Earl by which he gives thanks for his wife's delivery. Mark well this letter.*	
3 January.	*The Earl wrote to me.*	(ibid. 513)

Because this has been written as a personal memorandum by Burghley to himself, it is readily accepted as documentary evidence. The date of the child's birth is given, alongside the father's acknowledgement of paternity. All is clear. However, it was not written at the time of the child's birth, but a full half year later. Secondly, is it not truly remarkable that 24 September is just eight days short of three months? A quarter of a year had therefore elapsed between the baby's birth and the father's response to his receipt of the news. Compare this with the speed, just days, which it took for Burghley to inform Oxford of Anne's pregnancy!

Once again there is an explanation, but it requires the birth to have taken place in September; before then it would have been impossible to report the birth. Anne would still have been pregnant, and the baby's gender would be as then unknown. For this reason, Burghley and his daughter would have to await the event before telling the 'father'. Only then could they declare the birth had happened in July, within the normal gestation time. Burghley's position was of such an order that he had the power to arrange a cover-up. He was also devious, and Anne was his favourite child, therefore to be protected.

Burghley's second note to himself was intended to verify the first, for it bears the same date as the third entry on his other memorandum.

> . . . *he confessed to my Lord Howard that he laye not with his wiff but at Hampton Court, and that than the child cold not be his, because the child was born in Iuly, which was not the space of twelve monthes.*[72]

The note contains two statements concerning Oxford's reaction to the birth. The first confirms that he did sleep with his wife at Hampton Court, in which case a child born to the couple on 2 July would be a natural outcome. So, again, Burghley's note reads like a vindication of his daughter; it was also intended to make Oxford look silly by reference to the second statement. This latter remark has puzzled past commentators. Was Oxford totally ignorant of the gestation period, and because of this, he added insult to injury by the total neglect of his wife and daughter? Or is there a deeper meaning to Oxford's comment?

I contend that what Oxford said to Howard was sarcastic; that because the child was born in July it could not be his, since his wife's gestation period was twelve months; that is from September 1574, when he last slept with his wife, to September 1575, when 'their' child was actually born. In other words, he was acknowledging, albeit sarcastically, that according to information received, Anne had actually given birth in September and not July. Burghley was notoriously poor at mental arithmetic, and likely missed the sarcasm in Howard's report.

This information, presumably sprung upon the unsuspecting traveller on his way home to greet his wife and child, would account for the rage that overtook him. He had been cuckolded and then duped into believing the baby born of this adulterous liaison was his. To add to this, his behaviour upon reaching England was not improved when the ship carrying him homeward was boarded by pirates. It is recorded that he lost his shirt, and might have lost his life, but for the intervention of a Scotsman who recognised him. It will be recalled how pirates in the English Channel also captured HAMLET on a similar voyage home.

Notably, after disembarking from the ship, and ignoring those who came to welcome him, Oxford accompanied Rowland Yorke by barge and wherry to York House in London's Walbrook Street. For the next five years he would be a stranger to his wife. The emotional build-up in his mind would find release in the plays he wrote; each time examining both sides of the argument. Was his wife innocent of the charge made against her, as her friends and family repeatedly maintained, or did she give birth in September, secretly, as he had been told? If so: Who was the father?

There is no answer to this last question, unless one is resolved to accept that Oxford embedded the answer in *Hamlet*, and in *Pericles*: a play that he never completed.

The clue found in *Hamlet* occurs in the accusation made by the PRINCE to POLONIUS (act II: sc. ii).

HAMLET: O Jephthah, Judge of Israel, what a treasure hadst thou!

POLONIUS: What a treasure had he, my lord?

HAMLET: Why—'One fair daughter, and no more,
The which he loved passing well'.

POLONIUS: [Aside] Still on my daughter.

HAMLET: Am I not i' th' right, old Jephthah?

POLONIUS: If you call me Jephthah, my lord, I have a daughter that I love passing well.

HAMLET: Nay, that follows not.

POLONIUS: What follows then, my lord?

HAMLET: Why—'As by lot, God wot' and then you know,
'It came to pass, as most like it was'.
The first row of the pious chanson will show you more; for look where my abridgement comes.

HAMLET was referring to Jephthah's vow to God, that if he triumphed over the Ammonites, he would offer up the first person he met upon reaching his door. The battle was won. But the first person he met at his door was his only daughter, whom he dearly loved, and who had come to greet him. When she learnt of his vow to God, she begged from him a promise. It was to be allowed to wander for two months in the mountains with her companions *"and grieve that I must die a virgin."* (*Judges*: 11-37). Jephthah agreed, and after two months his daughter returned, and her father dealt with her in obedience to his vow.

It can be seen from this that Oxford was alluding to Burghley's daughter, whom he had refused to bed, thus implying she remained a virgin. He then went further by referring to Lot, albeit without supplying a capital to the name. The allusion is to what occurred after the destruction of Sodom and Gomorrah. Lot's daughters were afraid their new life in hiding would leave them virgins; so first the elder daughter and then the younger daughter conspired to give their father wine, and then have intercourse with him while he was intoxicated; by this means they both became pregnant. (*Genesis*: 19: 32-35). As for Oxford's own situation, he added *"God wot;"* (God knows).

HAMLET then states his references were an *"abridgement"* to the 'first row of the pious song'. This must refer to the *Song of Solomon*: *"one of the most sensual and erotic love poems in world literature."* It begins with a woman saying: *"Let him kiss me with the kisses of his mouth: for thy love is better than wine."* Whereas Lot's daughters required *wine* to achieve their end, Solomon's woman knows that loving kisses are better than *wine* – "*he shall lie all night betwixt my breasts,"* she says. There can be no doubt Burghley loved his daughter, but whether he succumbed to incest, as implied by HAMLET'S *abridgement* of these three biblical passages: given Anne's unhappy state at the time, remains a tantalising and almost forbidding question. It is one; however, that Oxford, through the mouth of HAMLET, has indicated was the information that tormented him.

Consequently, this piece of dialogue from *Hamlet* can be seen as an *abridgement* of what Oxford may have learnt in Paris, before embarking for England. It has everything to do with the reason for him separating from his wife and child, and nothing whatever to do with Shaxpere or the play in which it occurs.

Pericles, which does not appear in the First Folio, and was left for another to finish, begins with an unsolved riddle. ANTIOCHUS, King of Antioch, declares that whosoever unravels the riddle's meaning will win the hand of his daughter.

> I am no viper, yet I feed
> On mother's flesh which did me breed.
> I sought a husband, in which labour
> I found that kindness in a father:
> He's father, son, and husband mild;
> I mother, wife, and yet his child.
> How they may be, and yet in two,
> As you will live, resolve it you.

PERICLES discerns its meaning. The King of Antioch has enjoyed an incestuous relationship with his daughter. But having learned the riddle's dark secret, it is one that he can never divulge for fear of his life. A good reason, perhaps, for Oxford to have abandoned the play, but only after having relieved his tortured mind of what most haunted it. In *Othello* he is less reticent, and expresses the range of his emotions through the speeches of IAGO, EMILIA and OTHELLO. Consequently, by the time the play was written, it can be seen that Oxford had begun to come to terms with the fact that he may have been misled.

First, there is IAGO'S formation of a plan to poison OTHELLO'S mind by leading him to suspect the infidelity of his wife. *"I have't; it is engendered. Hell and night / Must bring this monstrous birth to the world's light."* Oxford uses the birth of an idea as allegory for the birth of his wife's bastard child. Then, as IAGO'S plan nears fruition, he defames DESDEMONA with his devilish remarks: *"So will I turn her virtue into pitch, / And out of her own goodness make the net / That will enmesh them all."*

OTHELLO'S trust in IAGO is his undoing. But first he must be satisfied of the truth. IAGO begins by reminding him: *"She did deceive her father, marrying you ... She that so young could give out such a seeming / To seal her father's eyes up."* But OTHELLO'S trust in his wife is not yet broken, and so he asks for proof of her infidelity.

OTHELLO: By the world,
I think my wife be honest, and think she is not,
I think that thou art just, and think thou art not;
I'll have some proof:
. . .
Give me a living reason, that she's disloyal.

IAGO cunningly prepares the Moor for the lie he is about to tell, and the trap he has set by contriving to place a handkerchief given to DESDEMONA by her husband, as a love-token, into the hands of CASSIO, her supposed lover. OTHELLO is convinced. His faithless wife must die. *"Damn her, lewd minx: O damn her! ... I will withdraw / To furnish me with some quick means of death."*

It is only when the deed is done, and OTHELLO'S passion is spent that he learns the truth from EMILIA. But first he must suffer her judgement.

EMILIA: O gull, O dolt,
As ignorant as dirt; thou hast done a deed . . .

It was by such self-accusations that Oxford also came to judge himself. He eventually took back his wife, resumed married life, and accepted Elizabeth as his daughter.

Some indication of Oxford's state of mind, after Anne Cecil's death, may be discerned from OTHELLO'S curse upon himself, through having been the instrument of DESDEMONA'S brutal end. While this cannot be said of Oxford, there was still a great deal about himself to condemn. He allows OTHELLO to say it for him.

OTHELLO: O ill-starr'd wench,
Pale as thy smock, when we shall meet at count,
This look of thine will hurl my soul from heaven,
And fiends will snatch at it:
. . .

Whip me, you devils,
From the possession of this heavenly sight,
Blow me about in winds, roast me in sulphur,
Wash me in steep-down gulfs of liquid fire !

(Act V: sc. ii)

Despite Oxford's penance, there still remain many unanswered questions, and as many suggestive answers. What was the real truth about Lady Anne's pregnancy? Who supplied the 'poison' to Rowland Yorke, so that he could administer it to Oxford? And what motive lay behind the plan? History remains almost mute, but there are tantalising glimpses of some possibilities.

Lord Henry Howard's brother Thomas, 4th Duke of Norfolk, had been executed, and Burghley had remained opposed to his reprieve. To add to the family's downfall, the dukedom had been forfeited, depriving the successor of both lands and title. Howard therefore had a motive for infecting the House of Burghley with the bitter taste of revenge, either through a lie or the revelation of some hidden truth. But he was not alone in that wish.

The Earl of Leicester enjoyed a close relationship with Queen Elizabeth, and this allowed him to act as her advisor: a position occupied more cleverly by Burghley. Any deflation of the Lord Treasurer would help Leicester's ambitions. Conyers Read in 1925, described *"Leicester [as] a selfish, unscrupulous courtier and Burghley a wise and patriotic statesman."* It is not difficult to picture the friction occurring between these two courtiers, leading to Leicester's resentment against the Queen's chief counsellor.

According to reports, Leicester was also *"the most accomplished intriguer at court, and a model for manipulating the Queen."* [73] J. A. Froude described him as: *"Without courage, without talent, without virtue."* [74] In 1584, a book called *Leicester's Commonwealth* was smuggled into England, and sold by undercover booksellers. It exposed in detail his ugly private life, as well as accusing him to be an expert poisoner, responsible for a number of deaths.

When Richard Master was informing the Queen about Anne Cecil's pregnancy, the doctor recounted in his letter to Burghley, the part of their conversation in which Leicester entered the room and became a third party to what was being said.

> *Then sche [the Queen] askyng, and beyng answeryd of me ... caulethe my Lord of Lecyter [Leicester] and tellythe hym al.* [75]

So we know from this that Leicester was apprised of the situation this far. But he was to learn more as the conversation between Master and the Queen came to its conclusion. For it transpired that Burghley had not yet told the Queen that his daughter was pregnant, even though half her term had passed.

I told herre [the Queen] that thoughe your Lordship [Burghley] hade concelyd yt a whyle from herre yet yow lefthe [left] yt to herre [Anne Cecil] discretion eyther to reuele [reveal] yt or to kepe yt close. And here an ende was made, taking advantage off my last woords, that sche [the Queen] would be [wroth?] with yow [Burghley] for concelying yt so longe from herre.[76]

The mystery deepens. Was the reason for Anne saying nothing about her pregnancy because there was nothing to reveal; that is, until discovering her new condition in the middle of February? Then, instead of rejoicing at this late discovery, she sought a termination: contrary to her religious devotion: even declaring that her husband would not believe the child to be his.

Leicester must have been alert to the possibility that a marital indiscretion on the part of Oxford's wife had likely taken place. It required only that he play the waiting game, and determine the time of delivery, in order to confirm his judgement one way or the other. The fact that news of the birth was delayed until late September would have further convinced him, even if he were not Rowland Yorke's informer, that nine months earlier Oxford had been cuckolded. The child could not be his.

Years later, Charles Arundel would publish charges against Leicester, in which he made known the Earl's *"manifold crimes against his countrymen, God and England."*[77] Arundel was a Catholic and, at one time, a good friend to Oxford. A significant part of the charges in his denouncement of Leicester appears to refer back to the conversation that took place between the Queen, Dr Master, and Leicester in 1575. Arundel recounted the matter as follows:

[Leicester] hath ever used to sow and nourish debate and contention between the great lords of England and their wives, in which he always showed himself a good practitioner and very diligent ... The same he attempted between the earl of Oxford and his lady, daughter of the lord treasurer of England, and all for an old grudge he bare to her father the said Lord Treasurer.[78]

One further fact emerges to strengthen the suggestion that Yorke acted under information received from Leicester. It is that Yorke's brother, Edward, served as a servant to Leicester during that time.

This brings us to the expectant mother. What is to be said about Anne Cecil? At the age of fourteen, she is seen as a precocious young lady who wanted to marry the young man she had known since a child. Life expectancy was short in Elizabethan England, and the earliest a girl might marry was twelve: in line with that time when Nature began preparing the female body for motherhood. Oxford was no angel, and if OPHELIA'S bawdy talk is a reflection of Anne Cecil before her marriage, then she was no novice intent upon preparing for a life of religious devotion: as her later reputation attests. Did she deceive her parents, who wished her to marry Sidney or Rutland: perhaps suggesting that she had already succumbed to Oxford's advances? Despite her parents' known objections, she got her way; but it was to bring her much unhappiness.

That Anne Cecil later turned to a life of religious devotion raises another question. Could it have been guilt that converted her to a life of piety? Did she accept she was responsible for Oxford's outrage, brought about by her own actions? Did she then seek to salve her conscious and obtain forgiveness by devoting herself to the service of God? It is not an unknown reaction to some great sin, and Elizabethan society would certainly judge as sinful, the birth of another man's child, and to then introduce it into the family under the pretence it was lawfully conceived.

Oxford's neglectful treatment of the marriage bed from the time they were wed, and his continuation of the bachelor lifestyle he had previously enjoyed were possible inducements for her to give way to a moment's indiscretion, particularly at a time when she had been, to all intents and purposes, abandoned by her husband, both in the marital bed and by his absence abroad.

Her subsequent reputation as both PENELOPE and another GRISSEL [Griselda] appeared in Wilfred Samonde's elegy, written at the time of her death. The opening lines of Samonde's poem are an allusion to Anne Cecil's plight. But they also echo Shakespeare in act 2: scene i of *Titus Andronicus,* in which PETRUCHIO speaks of LAVINIA: *"For patience she will prove a second Grissel, / And*

Roman Lucrece for her chastity." Samonde was not going to let Oxford forget his wife was also the patient, chaste LAVINIA that he had characterised in *Titus Andronicus*; even so, he wisely changed LUCRECE for PENELOPE. Subtlety is never obvious.

> *For modesty, a chaste Penelope,*
> *Another Grissel for her patience,*
> *Such patience as few but she can use,*
> *Her Christian zeal unto the highest God,*
> *Her humble duty to her worthy queen.*
> *Her reverence to her aged sire,*
> *Her faithful love unto her noble lord,*
> ...
> *Who as she liv'd an angel on the earth,*
> *So like an angel she doth sit on high.*

According to Homer, Penelope was the wife of Ulysses. During his absence, while fighting at the Siege of Troy, she was approached several times by men wishing to enjoy her favour. But she remained chaste: excusing herself until the shroud she was weaving had been completed. Each evening she undid her day's work so that her task was never completed.

Griselda was a poor girl married to a nobleman who abused her in a most shameful and humiliating manner, to which she responded without complaint. It is to this feature that Samonde refers. The tale is the last of Boccaccio's *Decameron*. It is also the source of 'The Clerk's Tale' in Chaucer's *Canterbury Tales.*

The picture we are given of Anne, protests against Oxford's behaviour towards his wife. Undoubtedly, she had won the hearts and minds of the society within which she moved. Oxford appears to have capitulated in the end and accepted the official verdict of his wife's fidelity; although several 'Shakespeare' plays would thereafter reveal the ebb and flow of doubt the author felt at the time of their composition.

If we seek to discover what evidence may have convinced Oxford that he had been duped by Yorke, it could be the Queen's baptismal gifts. Nelson (p. 128) produces a quote from Stiffkey,* affirming that Elizabeth sent gifts to celebrate the christening of Elizabeth Vere on 14 July, four days after Burghley recorded the baptism had taken place at his Theobolds home. The gifts consisted of a piece of plate and a basin. Burghley also received a letter one day after the birth from Sir Walter Mildmay (Chancellor of the Exchequer), which congratulated the Lord Treasurer upon the birth of his grandchild (no gender mentioned).

> *I thanke God hartelie with your Lordship for the good delyvery it hath pleased hym to geve my Lady of Oxford, and I thank your Lordship that it like yow to let me vnderstand the same by your lettres which I received this mornynge / I trust God shall make hir a glad mother of many children, to your Lordships compfort and her mother's.* [79]

I must confess I do not find Mildmay's letter sufficient as evidence. He was an officer in Burghley's department, and subservient to the Lord Treasurer's wishes. There is also the haste in which the communication occurred; whereas, the father had to wait nearly three months before receiving a letter with the news that his wife had safely delivered her baby. And, why is it that Mildmay's letter is alone in offering congratulations? The evidence of Oxford's sister would be far more impressive, for she was the baby's aunt. Her presence at the christening, and her baptismal present would have been sufficient to convince Oxford of the truth. But it is without reference. Yet, she had almost three months in which to see her niece and confirm the child's birth with a gift. This raises the question – Who, amongst those Oxford could trust, did see the baby between July 2 and the third week in September? It would seem no one. Even the Queen's gift arrived too late to be delivered on the day of the christening, when she might have come to see the child for herself.

In *Hamlet,* we find Oxford reflecting upon the chastity of his PENELOPE through the lips of THE PRINCE; using for his purpose, a conversation HAMLET held with OPHELIA: *"be thou as chaste as ice, as pure as snow, thou shalt not escape calumny."*

---

* Although Nelson quotes from "Stiffkey, page 185", and elsewhere states that publications before 1640 can be accessed at EEBO, 'Stiffkey' is absent; neither is the name included in Nelson's Bibliography. Stiffkey is in Norfolk, the home of Sir Nathanial Bacon (d. 1622), half-brother of Sir Francis Bacon. It is also noteworthy that the Queen's gifts arrived four days late, which could imply the service of baptism was a sham operation, for which there were no invitations. When the Queen learned of it later, she responded conventionally. Nelson also noted that Stiffkey claimed Oxford's departure for Europe took place in February 1575, instead of 7 January. The references given by 'Stiffkey' cannot therefore be considered totally reliable.

There is an interesting postscript to this strange saga. In July 1577, with Oxford's mind still tormented by the question of his wife's fidelity and the paternity of the baby he had been told was his, he turned against Rowland Yorke. And, as documents appear to confirm, he ordered William Sankey, a man distantly related on his mother's side of the family, to murder Yorke.

In proceeding to carry out this commission, Sankey attacked and wounded another man called George Whitney: although for what reason remains unclear. The incident took place in Cheapside. Oxford thereupon paid a member of his retinue, William Weekes, to deal with Sankey. Weekes did so; but in the course of which, he fatally wounded Sankey. He was later arrested, after fleeing to Durham.

Before going to his execution for the crime, Weekes confessed to a church minister that he had been paid . . .

> *a hundred powndes in gold after the murder committed to shifte him a waye, and so muche was fownd abowte [him] when he was apprehended.* [80]

Rowland Yorke survived the attempt on his life and returned to the army.

It was during the fighting at Zutphen that Yorke managed to obtain from the Earl of Leicester the command of a fortification to be held against the Spanish. But, in what has been described by historians as: *"Yorke's revenge against Leicester,"* he surrendered this fortification to the Spanish army, and joined their company of lancers (p. 372).

Yorke died in 1588, shortly before the Armada sailed against England: poisoned by the Spanish who had learned not to trust him. The Dutch patriots, who had been betrayed by Yorke, later exhumed his corpse and hung it as a public spectacle.

This ends the sequence of events following Oxford's return from Europe, and the terrible homecoming that awaited him. We catch some glimpse of what occupied his mind during that period through OTHELLO'S personal torment. However, those amongst Shakespeare's more fervent admirers, who believe their idol to have been raised in Stratford-upon-Avon, they must, instead, suppose the play to be solely the result of their man's imagination. Oxford's support scholars are better informed.

TAMING OF THE SHREW

Reference has already been made to Henslowe's production of *The Taming of a Shrew* at the Newington Butts theatre on 11 June 1594, when it was described as an *"old piece"*. In the same year, *"A Pleasant Conceited Historie, called The taming of a Shrew"* was published, *"As it was sundry times acted by the ... Earle of Pembroke his seruants"*. Further editions of the play appeared two years later, and again in 1607; in both cases there were no significant differences in the text. It was not until the First Folio of 1623 that the indefinite article was changed to 'The'. The similarity between the two titles is reflected in the similarities between the pirated quartos and the text of the First Folio, as Dr. Levi Fox explained:

> *The relationship between The Shrew as we have it in Shakespeare's First Folio of 1623 and A Shrew as published in Quarto in 1594 has been at the root of most of the debates about the text, date and sources of the play. It was formerly thought that A Shrew was an independent work which preceded Shakespeare's The Shrew and was the main source of it, but most scholars now believe that A Shrew is some form of half-remembered, half-invented derivative version of it. Consequently, the date has been pushed back: instead of placing it in 1593-94, modern opinion places it in 1588-90 and one recent editor argues that it is Shakespeare's first play of any kind.* [81]

Ogburn has argued that the play echoes the time Oxford spent in Italy. Nelson unintentionally provides a possible reason. *"On 11 December money sent by Pasquino Spinola reached Oxford at Venice"*.[82] It was while in Venice that Oxford had written to Burghley explaining his need for this extra money: *"by reason of my great charges of trauell and siknes I haue taken vp of Mr Baptisto Nigrone 500 crounes, which I shall desire yowre Lordship to se ther[e] [i.e. in England] repaid."*[83]

Ogburn was cognizant of this and remarked upon the part in the play where BAPTISTA MINOLA is repeatedly mentioning his *crowns*. He then drew attention to this name, which appears to be a combination of BAPTISTO Nigrone and Pasquino SPINOLA.[84]

The *Shrew*, under both titles, is exceptional within the Shakespeare canon, in that it has an Induction scene. This unique example, first published in 1594, opens with a tinker from Warwickshire called CHRISTOPHER SLIE (later changed to SLY) having become the worse for drink. A visiting nobleman decides to have fun with the fellow and arranges for him, while in his drunken state, to be carried to his castle. There, he is put to bed so that when he awakens, he discovers his situation in life transformed from the meanest class to the highest. Servants are placed at his beck and call; a wife is produced who convinces him that his past life has been a dream.

Slowly, the lowly tinker begins to accept what he has been told and reacts to the advantages that this new position affords him. In the earliest edition of *A Shrew*, the tinker is eventually returned to his former state, but in the First Folio edition, the tinker's future is left unexplained.

This change, without any obvious reason for it, mystifies traditionalists. In point of fact, the explanation is quite simple: it is tied to Oxford's employment of Shaxpere in 1592. Originally, the transfer of Oxford's authorship to Shaxpere, the tinker from Warwickshire, was meant to be temporary: but later on, events took over and the transfer became permanent.

Oxford may therefore be understood to have taken his early play, *Taming of a Shrew,* and with his predilection for including bits of his life story in what he wrote, added an Induction scene. This, as we now know, occurred at the time he engaged an odd-job man from Warwickshire, in order to use him as the face behind his creation of William Shakespeare. In effect, Shaxpere was his own WILLIAM SLIE – a fitting name, considering his task.

Oxford must have been aware his plan would eventually be discovered; and everything would revert back to normal, and this is reflected in the play, with SLIE returning to his former station in life. However, at some later date, it was explained to Oxford that a change of circumstances required that he be permanently excluded from any connection with his Sonnets, and this would of necessity have to extend to his plays, since their style would testify to his authorship of the love poems with their homosexual content. It was for this reason that the part where SLIE returns to his humble beginnings was removed, so as to reflect what had taken place in real life.

For Shaxpere, like his counterpart SLY, in the revision of the play, there was to be no going back. Shaxpere would have to continue standing in for the nobleman as poet and playwright:

secure in the position Oxford had placed him, yet never actually claiming any of Oxford's work as his. But, on the other hand, careful never to deny it, should it be suggested; and never calling attention to himself by taking court action for the illegal acquisition of the literary titles associated with the name 'Shakespeare'.

We shall conclude by returning to *A Shrew:* described in 1594 as an *"old play"*. This fits in with it being one of Oxford's early Comedies, written after his return from Italy, and in its unedited form, of inferior merit to the version published in the First Folio. There is strong evidence it was written before 1587, and available to the group of writers that Oxford had assembled at Fishers Folly during the years leading up to 1588. For it was in that year, Oxford was forced to disband his group and sell the house.

The reason for reaching this conclusion relies upon Marlowe. In 1587, he arrived in London with an M.A. degree from Cambridge, and a reputation as a poet. Like John Lyly, Marlowe was born in Canterbury. He may therefore have seen Lyly's employment by Oxford as a means by which he could gain access to the writers' circle inside Fishers Folly. His subsequent acceptance by Oxford (he was a dinner guest at Oxford's table in 1592) helps to explain how *Doctor Faustus* and *Tamburlaine I* came to include parts taken from *The Taming of A Shrew.*

Now that the gloomy shadow of the night,
Longing to view Orion's disling looks,
Leaps from th'antarctic world unto the sky,
And dims the welkin with her pitchy breath.

(Taming of A Shrew, 1.8-11)

Now that the gloomy shadow of the night,
Longing to view Orion's dazzling look,
Leaps from the Antarctic world unto the sky,
And dims the welkin with his pitchy breath.

(Doctor Faustus, Liii.l-4)

Eternal Heaven sooner be dissolved,
And all that pierceth Phoebus's silver eye,
Before such hap befall to Polidoro

(Taming of A Shrew, 4.67-9)

Eternal Heaven sooner be dissolved,
And all that pierceth Phoebus's silver eye,
Before such hap fell to Zenocrate.

(Tamburlaine I, III.ii.18-20)

The persistent belief that Shaxpere wrote the poetry and plays of Shakespeare has inevitably led to the conclusion that it was 'Shakespeare' who first learned and then filched from Marlowe. Dr Sabrina Feldman has used these verses to make that case, although her own approved candidate for Shakespeare's laurels is Thomas Sackville. Sackville did collaborate with Thomas Norton in the writing of a play called *Gorboduc*, although it is thought he was responsible for only the last two acts (*Oxford Companion to English Literature*). The play was performed at the Inner Temple in 1561, three years before Shaxpere was born. Sackville also wrote several poems, three or four of which have survived. But after entering political life, he was recorded to have dismissed poetry as the *"folly of youth"*.

Summary

Occam's razor – *Entia non sunt multiplicanda* – 'Entities are not to be multiplied' is a much admired response to the unnecessary increase in explanations that are often given to bolster a belief; that is, when a much simpler answer to a problem is available. In this chapter, one has been faced with parallels between the plays of *Shakespeare* and the cameos they include that are also found in the life experience of the 17th Earl of Oxford. But, orthodox opinion maintains that this is all one enormous coincidence. To support this counter argument Shaxpere's advocates parade a multiple of reasons that *may have* occurred to cause these coincidences. Perhaps this; perhaps that; maybe he did this; maybe he did that; this could have happened; that could have happened; and so it goes on; creative reasoning at full pelt to save a longstanding belief, weighed down by the number of unprovable explanations it is forced to bear.

This is by no means an unusual response. It is found in all disciplines. Dr Lee Smolin explained:

Philosophers and historians of science, among them Imre Lakatos, Paul Feyerabend, and Thomas Kuhn, have argued that one experimental anomaly is rarely enough to kill a theory. If a theory is believed deeply enough, by a large group of experts, they will go to ever more extreme measures to save it. ... Sometimes the theory's defenders succeed, and when they do, great and unexpected discoveries can be made. But sometimes they fail, and then lots of time and energy is wasted as theorists dig themselves deeper and deeper into a hole. [85]

Shaxpere's authorship of the Shakespeare canon is theory, not fact. If it were a provable fact, there would be no authorship problem, and many fine intellects who have written in support of Oxford as Shakespeare, would have had no reason to doubt that it could ever have been thought otherwise. Thomas Kuhn, in his celebrated book, *The Structure of Scientific Revolutions* (Chicago, 1962), explained the dynamics of doubt and how these affect a theory.

According to Kuhn, a scientific revolution is preceded by the piling up of experimental anomalies. As a result, people begin to question the established theory. A few invent alternative theories. The revolution culminates in experimental results that favour one of the new alternatives over the old established theory.[86]

It is easy to see how this translates into discussion about the authorship of Shakespeare's written work. The experimental ('research') anomalies continue to pile up against Shaxpere, causing people to question the established theory ('belief'). A few invent alternative beliefs (Bacon, Marlowe, Oxford, &c). The revolution will culminate when research results favour one of the new alternatives over the established belief. Proof from cryptology has already decided the issue; apart from which, the evidence for Oxford having written under Shakespeare's name is greater than can be accounted for by reference to any other candidate.

The question as to why the authorship debate continues still to favour Shaxpere, while the known facts corroborate Oxford, is because the university system conducts a practice of embedded professors; the detail of how this operates was explained by Alan Nelson; himself, once an embedded professor, to an audience of lawyers in 2004 (p. 107).

The effect this has upon ambitious applicants hoping to obtain an academic post is predictable. There is nothing to be gained by promoting Oxford as Shakespeare, except unemployment; at least, within the halls of academe. Not surprisingly, the dissident voices who do argue for a rethink in what is taught about Shakespeare are those of well-qualified professionals, who are unattached to the English Literature enclaves of today's universities.

This has a knock-on effect in media presentation, and the publication of books and journals. Reporters rely upon the established order, which requires that the highest form of scholarship should come from experts at professorship level. But these are also embedded professors: men and women who have been given tenure because they proved themselves subservient to the beliefs required for the post to which their ambition aspired. Publishers also rely upon this source for their catalogues. And so the same junk biographies, based upon error and speculation, are yearly produced to shore-up the mythical ascendency of the rural Shaxpere from his drab beginning to genius level.

To understand how far this has stretched, factually speaking, it is important to understand there is no proof that Shaxpere was anyone other than the son of illiterate and uneducated parents. There is no proof that he ever had an education, beyond a month or two at a local school. There is no proof – in fact the opposite is true – that his children could read or write. There is no proof that the praise given to Shakespeare's literary work by his contemporaries actually refer to Shaxpere. There is no proof in Shaxpere's last will and testament that he was a writer. There is no record of Shaxpere ever having met a literary figure of his time. There is no record that any person from the world of literature paid the least attention to his passing at the time of his death, not even from the theatre. For close to two hundred years, no one in Stratford-upon-Avon acknowledged him as the famous William Shakespeare. To reverse this absence, a vast input of creative thinking has been required.

Chief amongst those who have risen to meet the challenge in modern times are Professor Jonathan Bate and Professor James Shapiro. It is therefore instructive to understand how they reply to the parallels that occur between those parts in Shakespeare's plays and sonnets that mirror the real life experiences of Oxford. Bate first: –

Don't be drawn into the trap of supposing that they are biographical: that is an allusion of Shakespeare's art. But it's very hard to stop yourself. When I worked on them for my book The Genius of Shakespeare *in the 1990s, I became convinced that I had identified the dark lady: she was the wife of John Florio, the Italian tutor in the household of the Earl of Southampton. When I returned to them recently for my book* Soul of the Age, *I became convinced that I had identified the rival poet: he was John Davies of Hereford, the greatest calligrapher in England and a hanger-on in the circle of the Earl of Pembroke.* [87]

Bate was employing his authority in the establishment Press, to assure readers that Shakespeare's Sonnets were not biographical; because he had twice been attracted to this idea, but without retaining any lasting conviction that the conclusions he reached were correct. Bate had naturally based his two theories of identity upon the blank canvas of Shaxpere's life, upon which almost anything of a literary nature can be painted, but never with the required evidence that would guarantee its truth.

Shapiro was likewise critical of the belief that Shakespeare used personal experience as the source of his poetic invention.

Those who believe that Elizabethan plays were autobiographical ought to be able to show that contemporaries were on the lookout for confessional allusions, as ... some were for topical ones. Yet not a single such contemporary observation survives for any play in the period, including Shakespeare's; however much on the minds of modern biographers, it doesn't appear to have occurred to Elizabethan playgoers. [88]

Unfortunately for Shapiro, his literary expertise is not best tuned to the authorship debate, where it is often observed to be wedged, and inert, on the periphery. Richard F. Whalen, author of *Shakespeare: Who Was He*? responded with devastating effect.

In [his] "Epilogue" *Shapiro returns to the argument that while fiction in recent centuries has often been autobiographical, that was not the case for Elizabethan-Jacobean writers. As it happens, however, Stratfordian scholars have argued that those writers did indeed draw on their life experience, their times and their reading. Professor David Riggs, the biographer of Ben Jonson, says that Jonson created his works out of his life and that* Volpone *in particular is a self portrait. Shakespeare editor, Harry Levin of Harvard says Jonson lampooned contemporaries and what he wrote drew on his observations of life in London. In her biography of Jonson, Marchette Chute says that many touches in Jonson's plays are based on literal fact. The Shakespeare scholar Edward Berry says that an autobiographical impulse characterizes many writers of the Tudor period, and for example, Philip Sidney identified himself and Penelope Rich in* Astrophel and Stella.

> *... As Professor Berry concludes in his book on Sidney, autobiographical touches in fiction were an integral part of Elizabethan culture.* [89]

In both cases, Bate and Shapiro represent the voice of an embedded professorship. Each defends the 'group-think' notion of who Shakespeare was by a *volte-face.* In the past, as Shapiro readily admitted, it was accepted that authors *had* relied upon personal experiences to convey realism to their work. But the authorship controversy has changed this. The personal experiences of Shaxpere are nowhere to be found in the Shakespeare canon. Hence, these could not have been Shakespeare's source of inspiration: and this means that personal experiences must likewise be denied to other writers of that era.

Both professors must surely be aware there is enough personal material relating to Oxford, occurring within the sonnets and plays of *Shakespeare,* to seriously question their authorship by anyone other than the person to whom these experiences apply. Could that awareness, accompanied by the risk of losing face, be the reason for their defensive strategy?

8

BACKDATING TITUS ANDRONICUS

New opinions are always suspected, and usually opposed, without any other reason but because they are not already common.

John Locke

A SUBSTANTIVE, SCIENTIFIC proof, accompanied by a literary proof, now exists: sufficient to establish William Shakespeare as the penname used by Edward de Vere, 17th Earl of Oxford; and that he employed an allonym with a similar sounding name to conceal his authorship. This, as we have now seen from the previous chapter, has far-reaching implications for dating the composition of the plays.

TIME AND THE SHAKESPEARE CANON

The present chronology for dating Shakespeare's plays consists of educated guesses based upon the first known reference to a surviving quarto, or to a performance mentioned at the time in an old letter or diary. Even so, there are still some plays that were unknown until they appeared in the First Folio of 1623.

The result of these uncertainties means that no definitive dates exist as to when even one of Shakespeare's plays was first written. Some plays, such as *Hamlet* and *King Lear,* have such early dates assigned to their performance in Philip Henslowe's daybook that it has been concluded they must have been written by someone other than Shakespeare, for they tend to predate the beginning of Shaxpere's career.

Other plays, such as *The Troublesome Raigne of King John,* published in 1591, are found to be so similar in content to a play later known to have been written by Shakespeare—in this case, *King John*—that it is said Shakespeare must have copied most of it: in many places, scene by scene and word for word. *'The Bard'* was therefore doubly fortunate; that is to say, in the first place he had the manuscripts of these earlier plays to use so freely, and secondly, to have escaped the wrath of the original, unnamed author and his friends: actors and men who would have recognized the same words, plots and scenes being performed, just as they appeared in the work of this other playwright.

The Stratford theorists remain largely mute in the face of this embarrassment. They dare not suggest these anonymous plays, from which Shaxpere copied so freely, may have been written by a nobleman who desired his name should remain undisclosed. To do so, might lead to further enquiries, with the suggestion that this unknown lord was the Court playwright, Edward de Vere. In which case, they would have to admit to a link between Oxford and Shakespeare, with the ultimate acceptance that these 'two' playwrights were actually the same person.

There is another problem with the chronology of Shakespeare's plays. The timeframe is too condensed to be realistic. Shaxpere's theatrical career amounts to little more than ten years. At some time close to 1590, he arrived in London, completely unknown; having no letters of introduction, with no university friends, and without a reputation to back his entry into the capital's theatrical life. He retired in 1603, returning to the same obscurity from which he had arrived. In between these years he is said to have worked full-time as an actor; written two very long narrative poems; 154 sonnets; several lengthy poems; travelled back and forth between London and his hometown to see and care for his family, and where he also found time to immerse himself in several business enterprises and law suits; read numerous books as sources for his plays, some of which were not available in English; * ingratiated himself with the Earl of Southampton to obtain his patronage; had at least one torrid

* German scholar, Kurt Kreiler, has identified the following authors whose untranslated work was read by 'Shakespeare' as sources for his plays. Accolti, Bernardo: *La Virginia* (All's Well That's Ends Well). Bandello, Matteo: *Le Novelle* (Much Ado About Nothing; A Winter's Tale; Two Gentlemen of Verona; Twelfth Night). Boccaccio, Giovanni: *The Decameron* (Measure for Measure; Cymbeline). Bruno, Giordano: *Il Candelaio* (Love's Labours Lost). Cinthio, Giraldi: *Gli Hecatommithi* (Othello; Twelfth Night). Fiorentino, Ser Giovanni: *Il Percorone* (The Mercant of Venice). Straparola, Giovanni Francesco: *Le piacevoli nocci* (The Taming of the Shrew). Vasari, Giorgio: *Le Vite de' più eccelenti pittori* (A Winter's Tale).

affair with an unknown mistress; whom, as the sonnets tell, he shared with Lord Southampton; frequented London's Mermaid tavern where he socialised with travellers from abroad; who, for so we are told, gave him detailed information about the places he had never visited; and in the midst of this, with no previous experience at playwriting and no recorded evidence of any education, he sat down at the end of a hardworking day to write, by candlelight, the masterly works that are attributed to him; these are almost entirely in verse, and teem with emotional situations he had never, personally, experienced.

The 'biographies' of Shakespeare refer to all these activities, either implicitly or explicitly, but because they are separated, chapter-by-chapter, they appear as everyday accomplishments.

Compare Shaxpere's alleged writing career with a timeframe pertaining to Oxford. De Vere would have begun writing plays in the years before leaving for the continent. He would have continued writing after his return. So that, broadly speaking, there would have been a period of creativity up until 1575, interrupted by a fifteen month period abroad, when he benefitted from the Italian Renaissance. Upon returning to England, he would have taken up the pen again; writing up until his death in 1604. He therefore had approximately forty years in which to write the plays and poems orthodoxy claims Shaxpere wrote in little more than a quarter of that time, and without having had Oxford's life and travel experiences, or his education.

Moreover, for the last ten years of Oxford's life he lived in secluded retirement with his second wife. It was during this time that the majority of Shakespeare's plays emerged: sometimes as pirated quartos, sometimes as performances. Those ten years in Oxford's life would have provided him with every opportunity to have revised his earlier plays, and also to have added to their number with an occasional new work. These revisions would also explain the sudden emergence of so many masterpieces in such a short a space of time: the earlier work having been written for Elizabeth's court entertainment during his learning period. This scenario not only fits a more reasonable timescale, it also allows for the plays to be correctly attributed to emotional experiences that occurred within the life of Oxford: a correlation that is impossible for Shaxpere's advocates to make.

Those committed to Shaxpere's authorship frequently argue that Oxford could not have written the works of Shakespeare because *The Tempest* was written after his death. This is a fallacious argument, and has been exposed as such in Chapter 7. But it does allow the same argument to be turned against traditionalist thinking. Thus, Shaxpere could not have written the works of Shakespeare, because *Titus Andronicus* was written in 1574, when William was still a child. No amount of genius can account for that. But what is also interesting is that *Titus* is a Shakespeare play entirely dissimilar to any other. Some have even argued that it could not be his, it is so different; but its inclusion by Francis Meres, and its entry in the First Folio contradict dissent.

Actually, the explanation for the play's lack of similarity to any other play he wrote is very simple: it was written before Oxford embarked upon his continental tour. Up until then, he had only the classics to guide him. *Titus Andronicus* is a tragedy in the style of Seneca, and was written no later than 1575, although it was certainly revised afterwards. What now follows is a proof that this explanation is factually correct.

The Titus Manuscript

At some time during the second half of the 16th century, a pen drawing in brown ink was made on a folded sheet of paper bearing a watermark in common use between 1523 and 1611. The illustration was that of a scene from Shakespeare's *Titus Andronicus.* Beneath the picture, the artist had included a short excerpt from the play involving several of the characters taking part. The Longleat Manuscript, as it is also known, represents the only copy of an original Shakespearian production anywhere to be found. But it is also the focus of several mysteries, not least of which is the date.

Unfortunately, the author chose to date the manuscript in the style of abbreviated Latin, instead of employing numbers. Normally, there would be no difficulty in interpreting this form of dating. But, in the present case, there is: the author having used a letter that appears to be a 'g' but which others believe is a 'q'; some even want it to be a '9'. None of these alternatives have, until now, provided a satisfactory resolution to the intended date.

Another uncertainty is the identity of the author. He has

written his name as Henry Peacham. Popular opinion asserts this to be the same author of several books that were published during the early part of the 17th century. But again, this is not certain. This Henry Peacham had a father of the same name who was also an author. As we shall later discover, there are compelling reasons to believe the manuscript was the work of Peacham senior, and not that of his son.

A third mystery occurs in the dialogue. It flows as a single tract, but in the earliest known publication of *Titus Andronicus* (1594), this same dialogue occurs in different parts of the play as well as displaying occasional differences to the wording used on the document. Strangely, too, there are several lines of dialogue written into the excerpt that do not occur in the actual play.

The fourth oddity involves the drawing. It shows players enacting a scene that does not take place in quite the same way as when the play is now performed. Taken as a whole, the manuscript appears to represent a performance predating the current play, and which, at some time past, underwent serious revision before finally emerging in its present form.

Tracing the Play's History

These queries are far from being all there is to consider. A further peculiarity is the style in which it was written. *Titus Andronicus* is the only play by Shakespeare that models itself upon the Roman tragedies of Seneca. As Gervinus, wrote: *"we do not feel at home in it; but if the piece is perused in turn with those of Kyd and Marlowe, the reader will find himself upon the same ground."* [1]

For reasons such as these, doubts have arisen that question its authorship. However, the play is part of Shakespeare's folio of collected works for the stage, and his contemporaries never questioned its attribution. *"The express testimony of Meres, a learned contemporary, who in the year 1598 mentions a list of Shakespeare's plays, places Titus positively among them."* [2]

If this were an early composition of Shakespeare's it would explain why the play was modelled upon the classical style, and why it may have needed revision after the playwright had acquired more experience in the execution of his art. It would also account for the unexplained differences appearing in the manuscript copy. One may note, too, Gervinus's reference to Marlowe and Kyd, for both were at their literary peak during the 1580s, and both faded at the time Shakespeare's career was commencing. Yet, in the First Folio, Jonson names them as 'his' peers!

The Most Lamentable Romaine Tragedie of Titus Andronicus was first published in 1594 by John Danter as a stitched, unbound pamphlet of 40 quarto leaves. The author's name was not given, but the fact it was deemed worthy of printing, confirmed the popularity it had by then achieved. The cover also advertised the play as having been previously *"Plaide by the Right Honourable the Earle of Darbie, the Earle of Pembrooke, and Earle of Sussex their Seruants."* [3] It therefore had a history of popularity going back a good number of years.

The first recorded allusion to the play may have been in 1592, when *A Knack to Know A Knave* was acted at the Rose theatre in London. However, this has allowed the suggestion to be made that lines, suggestive of *Titus*, actually refer to the lost play, *Titus & Vespasian*:

> As Titus was vnto the Roman Senators,
> When he had made a conquest on the Goths:
> That in requital of his seruice done,
> Did offer him the imperiall Diademe. [4]

Many years later, when Ben Jonson wrote his Introduction to *Bartholomew Fair* (1614), he included this statement:

> *Hee that will sweare Ieronimo or Andronicus are the best playes yet shall passe vnexcepted at heere as a man whose Iudgement shewes it is constant and hath stood still these fiue and twentie or thirtie yeeres.* [5]

Jonson was recalling that *Titus Andronicus* belonged to the same era as Thomas Kyd's, *The Spanish Tragedy:* a topical play set at the time of Spain's conquest of Portugal in 1580. Insofar as *The Spanish Tragedy* was concerned, Jonson's memory was accurate. Kyd's play is usually dated between 1585 and 1589. Jonson had previously mentioned it in *Cynthia's Revels,* published at the turn of the 16th century. There, he had referred to *The Spanish Tragedy* as: *"departed a dozen years since."* [6] In other words, by 1588, *Ieronimo* had completed its initial wave of popularity.

This places the theatrical performances of *Titus Andronicus,* to which Jonson also referred, within a timeframe that began in 1584. Assuming William Shaxpere was the author, it must have been written close to the time of his marriage, and the birth of his daughter Susanna. This is not something those educated in the belief that Shakespeare was Stratford-born can easily envisage. Conventional biographies place him and his family at home, sharing accommodation with his parents and his brothers and sisters. A house full with young children, frequent interruptions, and having to earn a living under needy, sixteenth-century conditions are not conducive to the peace and quiet required for writing a lengthy tragedy, especially if it is the budding playwright's first attempt.

Jonson's evidence for *Titus Andronicus* as a play belonging to the mid-1580s, combined with its publication in 1594, implies Shaxpere had completed it before he arrived in London. This raises a serious question. How could this unknown, still in his twenties and with his thick Warwickshire patois acquired from the rural community in which he grew up, having also neither a university education nor any previous attachment to players or the theatre, find instant acceptance as a playwright? And why was it, thereafter, that such a successful play as *Titus Andronicus* could be transferred from one company to another, until finally it was sold to the public as the first of what would be many more pirated editions from the pen of Shakespeare? How could publishers have possibly known they would not be held to account for stealing and selling his plays? This question becomes even more frustrating to answer when it is understood how often Shaxpere sought justice from the courts when one of his commercial transactions was at issue.

Let these concerns be added to the many other irresolvable problems surrounding the play and the life of Shaxpere, and perhaps it will be admitted the time has come to look outside Stratford-upon-Avon for a rational explanation to these unsolved questions.

DATING THE TITUS MANUSCRIPT

One key to resolving these issues is undoubtedly the Longleat Manuscript. It was discovered by E. K. Chambers in 1925. Of special interest is the unusual form in which the date is written. Three letters appear next to the Latin word for 'year': and with sufficient clarity as to leave no doubt as to their intended meaning: **Anno m^{o} q^{o} _ q^{to}**. The year 15?4 **m**illesim^{o} (1000);

quingentesim^{o} (500) **q**uar^{to} (4).[7] The implication is that someone who had received a classical education during the mid-sixteenth century, when abbreviations and superscripts were fashionable, wrote this date in a form still familiar to him.

> *In the Middle Ages, when costly parchment was the only available writing material, there was a strong motive for the packing of the greatest possible number of words into each line. As an aid in this compression there grew up a convention of copious abbreviation (the cutting off of the ends of words) and contraction (the omission of medial letters and elements) — devices to which Latin lent itself rather better than English did ... At the opening of the sixteenth century in England the general use of abbreviation and contraction persisted, like so much else that was medieval.*[8]

An explanation for this late medieval style of dating leads naturally to a consideration of the third letter in the given year. Chambers, without explanation, suggested it was a 9 (Chambers, 1930), but this can be questioned. Roman letters combined with Arabic numbers to provide a date are not used as combinations, because the result gives an absurd appearance to the text; apart from which, the symbol bears scant resemblance to a 9. In any case, if 9 had been the copyist's intention, he would have written **n**^{o} as the abbreviation for **n**onagesim^{o}. Or, he would have used four Arabic numbers. But he did neither. The dispute is therefore between 'g' and 'q'.

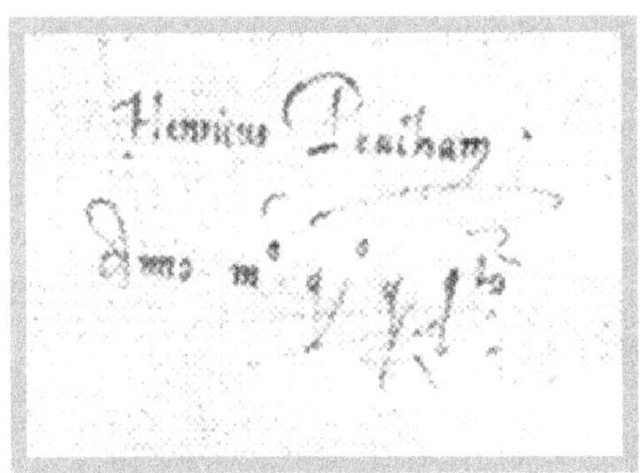

To begin with, there are two excellent reasons for rejecting 'q'. Firstly, the symbol is not the same as the first and fourth 'q', which argues its difference. Secondly, the use of 'q' contributes nothing of relevance to the date. It is neither 50 (**q**uinquagesim^{o}) nor 40 (**q**uadragesim^{o}), for that would make the date either 1554 or 1544, and a far cry from Shaxpere's year of birth. Finally, a trawl through the Latin dictionary under 'Q' reveals no hint of a possible word for which 'q' could be its abbreviation; the more so, because its position as the third figure in a sequence descending through 1000s, 100s to units, logically requires it to be a number in the 10s. For this reason alone, 'q' must be eliminated.

What then of 'g'? The first thing to notice is that the figure differs from the other letters in the chronogram, in that it lacks a superscript. This implies it is not – as the other letters are – an abbreviation for a word. In which case, it is a symbolic figure. This is more encouraging, especially since *"'G' is the seventh letter of the Roman alphabet."*[9] And, significantly, the *Oxford English Dictionary* states that *"g is used to denote anything occupying the seventh place in a series."* The classical languages are also well known for substituting letters in place of numbers, and the chronogram is a *series* of descending numbers in logarithmic order. In which case, 'g' represents 7, and the date can be read as 1574. However, William Shaxpere was then, at most, ten years of age; whereas Oxford was twenty-four, and soon to embark upon his journey into continental Europe.[10] There, under the influence of Renaissance artists and writers, he would take full advantage of this opportunity for improving his understanding of stagecraft, and the writing of plays. It was manna to his genius.

This earlier date for *Titus Andronicus* would also explain the occurrence of discrepancies between a 1574 manuscript and the later revisions to the play. These became evident when the three separate quartos of 1594, 1600, and 1611, together with the First Folio of 1623 were examined.

Remarkably, there does exist evidence for an earlier version of the play. Two entries in Henslowe's diary dated *"11 of apʳell 1591"* and *"20 of apʳell 1591"* (these dates are consistently referred to as 1592 on the reasonable presumption that Henslowe made a mistake) record a production with a similar title: *tittus & vespacia.*

June Schlueter makes a strong case from existing evidence that this play was translated into German as '*Eine sehr klägliche Tragœdia von Tito Andronico und der hoffertigen Käyserin, darinnen denckwürdige actiones zubefinden*' (A Very Lamentable Tragedy of Titus Andronicus and the haughty Empress, wherein are found memorable events) (Schlueter, 1999).

[An] intriguing possibility, however, encouraged by the prominence of Titus's son Vespasian in A Very Lamentable Tragedy, is that the German version is a translation of the lost 'tittus & vespacia' recorded in Henslowe's diary in 1592. [11]

To support her argument, Schlueter referred to the lack of correspondence between the illustration at the top of the Manuscript, which shows what was happening onstage, and the play in performance. She redressed this discrepancy by asserting that . . .

in A Very Lamentable Tragedy such a correspondence does in fact exist ... This correspondence between the Peacham drawing and A Very Lamentable Tragedy reawakens interest . . . that the German version is a translation not of Shakespeare's Titus Andronicus but of the lost Titus and Vespasian recorded in Henslowe's diary in 1592. [12]

But Jonson's avowal on the Stratford monument – that de Vere was William Shakespeare – does make perfect sense if it is allowed that *Titus and Vespasian* was the first version of Oxford's *Titus Andronicus,* written and performed in 1574, and seen by Henry Peacham.

The fact that Peacham had seen the play is doubted by only those few who believe the illustration on the Titus manuscript was drawn from the artist's *"mental theatre"* (Bate, 1995, 41). Others conclude differently.

[T]he Peacham drawing depicts an actual theatrical wardrobe . . . [and] show features that the artist was highly unlikely to have imagined and must therefore be assumed to have been seen and drawn upon a living actor. [13]

Albert Cohn was first to arrive at the same conclusion. In 1865 he wrote that *A Very Lamentable Tragedy* could be reliably identified with *Titus and Vespasian.*

. . . this Vespasian, like all other characters of the German piece, was taken from the original 'Titus Andronicus,' and thus we should have to acknowledge that 'Titus and Vespasian' as the original on which Shakespeare's play was founded. [14]

Schlueter obtained further evidence from Henry Morley, editor of *Titus Andronicus* prior to 1904, for he also agreed with Cohn.

[T]hanks to Mr. Albert Cohn, we have restored to us, in mangled form, the old play of Titus and Vespasian, with absolute certainty that it was the original of Titus Andronicus. [15]

From this, an intriguing fact ensues. By giving details of the correspondence existing between the Longleat manuscript and *A Very Lamentable Tragedy*, the figures in the Peacham drawing acquire different names to those which are presently assumed by reading the play in its present form.

Accepting the Peacham drawing as a literal rendering of this sequence requires that we discard the long-standing assumption that the figure in classical cuirass and buskins who wears the laurel crown and holds the tasseled ceremonial spear is Titus Andronicus ... for at this point in the German version, it is the Emperor who wears the Roman crown, and it is he, not Titus, whom the queen of Ethiopia addresses and to whom she and her sons surrender. [16]

Schlueter correctly points out that in the German version, this scene would be scripted with the queen exclaiming: *"we submit ourselves to your Majesty as your most humble servants. Dispose of us as you please."* [17] This differs from the stage direction on the manuscript, which announces *"Enter Tamora, pleading for her sons going to execution."* However, Schlueter's response to this, together with other points raised, was that . . .

any difficulties in the correspondence between the Peacham drawing and A Very Lamentable Tragedy derive from the stage directions. I make no claim that the lost Titus and Vespasian on which the German version was based was similarly annotated or that the production Peacham saw was staged, or blocked, in the same way. [18]

Schlueter's proposal has therefore been condensed to the following conclusions.

[T]he Peacham drawing depicts a sequence from A Very Lamentable Tragedy ... that the Peacham drawing, along with the autograph, is independent of the lines from Shakespeare's Titus Andronicus inscribed below it ... that A Very Lamentable Tragedy may well be a translation, with interpolated stage directions, of the lost 'tittus & vespacia' recorded in Henslowe's diary in 1592. [19]

But, if Schlueter had accepted Jonson's vow that Shakespeare was the Earl of Oxford, senior by fourteen years to the man she believed wrote *Titus Andronicus,* then a different proposal, with different conclusions would have had to be considered.

This would have suggested to her that the known facts are equally or better served by positing de Vere as the author of *Titus & Vespasian.* This would then serve as the original play from which the others were derived; one of which, found its way to the continent, as: *A Very Lamentable Tragedy*; it having been edited and reworked for greater ease of performance in translation, and to find acceptability amongst a culturally different audience. While back in England, the same play was revised by de Vere some years after his return from the continent. This became the *Titus Andronicus* that was printed as a pirate edition in 1594.

This explanation resolves the puzzle concerning the original work from which the German play was translated. It would explain, too, without raising fanciful conjectures, why Henslowe's diary records the performance of *Titus Andronicus* at Newington Butts in June 1594, alongside *Hamlet* and *The Taming of a Shrew.* Traditionalists find these last two plays incompatible with their supposition of who Shakespeare was at that time. But Edward de Vere having written these plays by the age of forty-four is so probable; it can be accepted with confidence.

A resolution to all these questions, and the problems that arise from them, can very easily be settled by agreeing that the date on the Peacham document is 1574. But, before accepting the symbolic 'g' as seven, one is bound to enquire why Peacham did not use the conventional form for seventy; i.e., **s**^{o} (**s**eptuagesim^{o}). The short answer is that **s**^{o} can also mean sixty; i.e., (**s**exagesim^{o}). Ambiguity between 60 and 70 needs to be avoided, and this is best accomplished by using the classical method; in this case, by adopting the seventh letter of the Roman alphabet.

It is of some relevance to note that the *Stationers' Register,* during the late sixteenth century, overcame problems of uncertainty where dating was concerned in a similar fashion; Roman numerals were employed when giving the day of the month, but appended with a Latin superscript afterwards; e.g., *"vi^{to} die ffebruarij"* [20] (sixth day of February; i.e., vi^{to} instead of **s**^{to}).

Peacham, it may be noted, having elected to use lettering for the first two digits of his date, no doubt felt it natural to continue using letters and employ a 'g'. Until numbers became the accepted form of dating, and spelling standardized, it was left to the idiosyncratic habits of each person as to how they expressed their thoughts on paper.

The Longleat manuscript was actually a personal document. It had originally belonged to Sir Michael Hicks, secretary to Lord Burghley. The document was discovered amongst Hicks's political correspondence as part of the Portland Papers. Lady Elizabeth Cavendish Bentinck brought these to Longleat House in 1759, following her marriage to Viscount Weymouth, later to become the 1st Marquis of Bath. Elizabeth Bentinck was the 2nd Duke of Portland's daughter, and granddaughter of Edward Harley, 2nd Earl of Oxford (from a second creation of the earldom).

This fact, however, serves only to introduce one further problem, and for which the Stratford faithful have no reliable answer – How did Hicks come to possess the manuscript in the first place?

In 1574 Michael Hicks was one of two secretaries employed by Lord Burghley. The knighthood Hicks received was not bestowed upon him until August 1604. At the beginning of 1574, Hicks was thirty years of age. He had been educated at Trinity College Cambridge, and from there, aged nineteen, he entered Lincoln's Inn to study law. Sir William Cecil quickly recognized Hick's potential, for the young man was invited to join the Cecil household long before he began training for the position of secretary.

At Court, Hicks was described as *"very witty and jocose."* He was also a noted collector of Roman memorabilia, and he filled many notebooks to that effect, for it was said he . . .

> *was well skilled in philological learning, and had read over the polite Roman historians and moralists; out of which authors he made large collections, especially of the moral and wise sentences out of which he filled divers paper-books, still remaining in the family.* [21]

The attraction of the Titus manuscript to a man of Hicks' taste, with its dramatic Roman content, is at once obvious. Moreover, as secretary to Lord Burghley, he would have been present at Hatfield House during the year 1574. It is from the recognition of these facts that the third player in this mystery comes under scrutiny—the copyist, Henry Peacham.

IDENTIFYING HENRY PEACHAM

In 1574, Henry Peacham was the curate – *curatum beneficium* – at St. Mary's Church in North Mymms. The parish is located adjacent to Hatfield House. The church still stands. Inside the porch is a wooden tablet dated 1604, acknowledging Henry Peacham's conveyance of a *"Messuage and Garden called Barefords with three crofts of land adjoining for the use of the Parishioners of North Mimms."*[22] Peacham was not only a generous benefactor to his parishioners, but also an author. His book, *The Garden of Eloquence conteyning the figures of Grammar and Rhetorick, from whence may be gathered all manners of Flowers, Colours, Ornaments, exornations, forms and fashions of speech* was published in 1576, two years after the date on the Longleat Manuscript.

Peacham dedicated the first edition of his book to John Aylmer, the Bishop of London, but when it was re-printed in 1593, he found a new dedicatee in Sir John Puckering.

Three years earlier, Peacham had published a sermon, which was devoted to the three last verses of the first chapter of *Job*, which he dedicated to the Countesses of Cumberland and Warwick. Quite clearly, Henry Peacham was a man of letters, and a scholar, with a particular interest in grammar and the English language. We may also discern that he was very well connected amongst the upper strata of society. It is also known that his authorial interest in the English language extended to plays and the theatre, for his son recalled having attended a performance in which Richard Tarlton, the principal comedy actor of his era, played a part.

Tarlton was Elizabeth's favourite clown and a member of her troupe. Thomas Nashe has left a record of his ability to entertain an audience just by appearing: *"people began exceedingly to laugh when Tarlton first peeped out his head."*[23]

Tarlton died during the summer of 1588, when Peacham's son was at most twelve. The fact that Peacham *fils* remembered having seen Tarlton on stage suggests a likelihood that the boy had seen him perform before the Queen at Hatfield House.

Hatfield was Queen Elizabeth's best loved residence, and there is no disputing that plays would have been arranged for her leisure hours inside the House, particularly those performed by her own company of players.

As was the custom at that time, an invited audience of court officials, together with elite members of the local community, would be invited to join the Queen for a particular performance. With his living as the parish priest in the grounds adjacent to Hatfield House, and having important connections in society, Henry Peacham was well qualified to have been among those invited to attend these theatrical interludes.

Michael Hicks would also have been amongst the guests. A meeting between Hicks and Peacham was therefore inevitable (possibly they had known each other while at university, for they were of a similar age). Both men also had a special interest in literature. To complete the picture, it requires no more than a consideration that the Earl of Oxford had recently completed the original version of *Titus Andronicus*, and was set to present it before the Queen.

Hicks' interest in Roman history would therefore seem to be the motivation for Peacham illustrating a scene from the play and accompanying it with the appropriate dialogue; presumably, the words were copied from an actor's script. This was then presented to Hicks by Peacham, who signed and dated it.

THE ERRORS OF ORTHODOXY

Shakespeare's conventionalists take a different view, as indeed they must; their preferred premise being that Shaxpere wrote *Titus Andronicus* at a much later date. Let us see how they argue their case, commencing with the date on the Titus manuscript.

Joseph Quincy Adams, writing in 1936, acknowledged the third letter on the chronogram to be 'g', but declined to offer a reason for it. Instead, he referred to the date given by the notorious forger of Shakespearian documents, John Payne Collier. Collier had written on the manuscript *"Henrye Peachams Hande 1595"*. Adams was forced to concede: *"[this] may be merely Collier's attempt to interpret the curious Anno* m° q° g q^to^ *"* which appears beneath the name *"Henricus Peacham."* 24

Eugene M. Waith (aka Douglas Tracy Smith), in his 1984 Introduction to *Titus Andronicus*, was another who declined to commit himself to an actual meaning for the third letter: preferring instead to describe it as a mistake.

> *Since a date in the 1590s is most probable, one would expect for the third letter an 'n' for nonogesimo (sic). A 'g' is unknown as a numerical symbol*[contradicted by the OED, supra]*, and another 'q' (as it is sometimes read) makes no sense. It is possible that the writer, intending to make an 'n', inadvertently repeated the 'q'.*[25]

But, as already pointed out, the third symbol does not resemble the manner in which Peacham has written 'q', where it appears in both the first and fourth position on his chronogram.

Waith then refers to Collier as possibly having attempted a forgery by adding to the manuscript *"in what resembles Renaissance handwriting 'Henrye Peachams Hande' 1595 ... [which] in any case is only a guess."*[26] Overall not very helpful; Waith remained baffled.

Jonathan Bate, a more audacious commentator than his predecessors, offered to interpret the date using a combination of mental arithmetic and Roman numerals. He agreed with Adams and Waith that the letter in question is a 'g'. *"I suspect that 'g' is intended to stand for gentesimo: if quingentesimo is 500, gentesimo is 100 (i.e. a variant spelling of centesimo)."*[27] From this, it can be seen that Bate has obtained this notion from *quin-gentesimo* (five-hundredth), although the conventional Latin word for 'hundredth' remains *centesimo.*

Two points need to be made clear. Firstly, the 'g' carries no superscript. Had Bate's suggestion been correct, the third letter would have been written g^{o}. Secondly, Peacham's chronogram would then read very awkwardly: 'In the year 1000 500 100 5' (Bate prefers to read q^{to} as 5). The mental arithmetic is then used to give a total of 1605. Bate justifies this hitherto unknown method of dating by referring to the Roman numerals, MDCV, the Roman date for 1605. In other words, M=m^{o}, D=q^{o}, C=c^{o} (but with 'c' written as 'g' and with no superscript), V=q^{to}.

There are objections to this. Firstly, had Bate's interpretation been the same as Peacham's intention, would the chronogram not have read MDCV, therefore avoiding the need for mental gymnastics? Then again, if 1605 was intended, using the Latin abbreviated form, why would Peacham not present the date as **m**^{o} **s**^{o} **q**^{to} (**m**illesim^{o} **s**excentesim^{o} **q**uin^{to})? An obvious choice, one would have thought. Thirdly, why write the Roman numeral for 'C' as 'g'? Bate has clearly raised more unanswerable questions than the one unanswerable question he sought to resolve.

Unsurprisingly, Schlueter bypasses Bate's interpretation, but without giving a reason. Instead, she suggests a different source:

> *In an analysis appearing in the Spring 1999 issue of Shakespeare Bulletin, Herbert Berry offers what will surely become the definitive reading of this elusive date … 1594.*[28]

What is it that Professor Berry has seen, that other eyes have so apparently missed?

Berry begins by rejecting the third symbol as 'g', insisting that it is a 'q'. He supports this opinion by referring to the text, where 'q' occurs twice: in 'conqueror' and 'quench'. Each 'q' has a firm downward stroke, as appears in the chronogram. But the two unquestionable 'q' letters that contribute to the date on the manuscript, **q^{o}** and **q^{to}** are completed by a downward stroke that turns sharply upwards with a noticeable ***convex*** arc. Berry argues the same can be seen happening to the third letter. This is untrue. But let Berry speak for himself. *"The upward stroke of the third **q** rises weakly and peters out about halfway up the downward stroke."*[29] (See picture).

Berry's anxiety to see the third letter as 'q' has caused him to overlook the glaringly obvious. The copyist has added several flourishes to the letter. One of these is a ***concave*** arc that starts to the left and well below the vertical stroke of the disputed letter; the arc then rises and cuts across the bottom of Berry's supposed 'q', transforming what can only have been intended as a 'g', into what careless observation might easily mistake for a 'q'.

In other words, Berry has referred to only the top half of the arc in order to make his case; and even there, the arc is ***concave***, not ***convex***, as with the second and fourth 'q'.

A second point to observe is that the squiggle beneath this character is reminiscent of the condensed squiggle that now forms part of the typographic '**g**'. Note the barb at the top of an enclosed space, a line dropping down, followed by a squiggle or flourish.

By dismissing the concave arc, which plays no part in the formation of the third letter, what remains is unquestionably a 'g', and very deliberate. Peacham has used the 'g' as a grammalogue for *septuagesimo* to avoid confusion with *sexagesimo*. Once this is understood, and careful examination of the manuscript confirms this to be true beyond reasonable doubt, the date is undeniably 1574. Thus Berry's analysis, which is based upon the letter being a 'q', can now be safely dismissed.

Berry then compounds his error by committing another.

> *Had the writer (who I assume, perhaps wrongly, was male) written out his abbreviations, therefore, his date would read 'Anno millesimo quingentesimo quinquaginta quadragintaquarto', the English is: 'in the 1594th year [of grace]'* 30

Let us pass over the triviality of why Berry should assume *wrongly* that Henry Peacham was male, and consider what his translation really says. Literally, word for word, Berry's date reads: '*in the thousandth, five-hundredth, a fifty, a forty in the fourth year.*'

This is a hotchpotch of totally absurd mental arithmetic and questionable Latin. Berry has mixed ordinal numbers with cardinal numbers. *Millesimo* and *quingentesimo* are both ordinal in the ablative case; quinquaginta is cardinal [cardinal numbers other than *unus, duo, tres* and *milia* are never declined], and *quadragintaquarto* is one half cardinal and the other half ordinal.

When Berry wrote 'quadragintaquarto', he presumably meant to say, as is said in English, 'forty-fourth' [quadragintaquarto!]. But the Romans used their ordinals differently. They would have spoken as Cicero did: *"quarto et quinquagesimo anno post primus consules."* (cic. Rèp. 2.60). Or, as Berry should have said: '*quarto et quadragesimo*'.

Even so, this does nothing to help a cause already lost. It simply allows the translation: '*in the one thousandth, five-hundredth, fiftieth, forty-fifth year of grace*'. This is nonsensical; apart from which, the third symbol is not the 'q' that is needed to support this proposed date.

It is safe to conclude that despite Schlueter's commendation that Berry's analysis of the date will be seen as *"definitive"*, the Stratford theorists are again left without any sensible idea to explain how the chronogram can be interpreted to support their conviction. Berry does, however, refer to one piece of information that supports the elder Peacham's hand as having been the author of the manuscript; it is his reference to the superscripts.

No fewer than eighteen of these occur in two consecutive pages of the elder Henry Peacham's dedication, dated 3 February 1593[/4?], to the second edition of his The Garden of Eloquence (London, 1593[/4?] … Eight occur in the four pages of his dedication to the first edition (1577). [31]

These indicate that the Reverend Henry Peacham had been overly fond of using the type of superscript that occurs in the chronogram on the Titus document

Comparing Hands

With no reliable alternative to the date of 1574 available, and with evidential grounds for asserting this year to be the correct interpretation, the person responsible for writing the manuscript can only have been the elder Peacham.

Stratford's professorship will object, drawing comfort from an unproven premise. But not all are so sure. Adams, who refrained from saying overmuch concerning the date, other than it was a 'g', had much more to impart when referring to the name, the handwriting, and the illustration.

The manuscript is written throughout in a small non-cursive upright secretary hand … But whether the drawing and the handwriting are the work of 'Henry Peacham—author of the Complete Gentleman' is hard to determine. A holograph manuscript of his, entitled Emblemata Varia … is written in both formal non-cursive and informal cursive italian hands, which reveal no points of similarity to the secretary hand of the Titus document. [32]

Although Adams attempted a half-hearted explanation as to why this could have occurred, he was forced to conclude:

. . . the quality of the handwriting in the Emblemata Varia seems to be distinctly inferior, and it is hard to conceive of one person being responsible for both manuscripts. [33]

The British Library possesses documents written by Henry Peacham *fils*: one of which is his manuscript copy and draft of *Basilicon Doron*. Dr. W. W. Greg, acting on behalf of Adams, examined this in London, but Greg could only confirm what the *Emblemata Varia* had already revealed.

The Titus drawing seems to me better done, and the writing, which bears no likeness to that of the emblems, is distinctly superior. [34]

Turning next to the illustration at the top of the Longleat Manuscript, Adams reached the same conclusion.

> *The elaborate and detailed drawing at the top of the Titus document seems to be not in the style of, and very distinctly superior in technique to, the numerous drawings we have from Peacham's pen.* [35]

Once again, Adams attempted a half-hearted excuse as to why this may have happened, only to conclude . . .

> *in the Folger manuscript of Emblemata Varia we have twenty pen drawings by Peacham, carefully executed for presentation to Sir Julius Caesar, which are, I think, quite obviously different in style and inferior in craftsmanship to the Titus drawing.* [36]

To support this assertion still further, Adams explained . . .

> *The faces in Peacham's work are entirely without character, the details often clumsy in execution, and the whole drawing lacking in vitality.* [37]

Berry's comments regarding the actual text of the document are meagre by comparison, but nonetheless for that, assertive:

> *Above the date is a signature, 'Henricus Peacham,' perhaps the younger, author of* **The Compleat Gentleman** *(1622). The note on the facing page reads* 'Henrye Peachams Hande. [/] 1595.' *Whoever wrote this note mistook the date beside the lines from* **Titus**, *and if he meant that Peacham wrote the date and speeches, he was also wrong. Nearly all the letters in the signature are decisively different from their counterparts nearby, whose rather solid formality and consistency suggest that a scrivener wrote them.* [38]

Dover Wilson was of a similar opinion. Bate disagreed . . .

> *The hand seems to be the same as that which copied the extracts from the play, though the signature is in Italic script whereas the transcription uses mainly secretary forms.* [39]

If Berry's explanation is correct, and the hand that wrote the dialogue is different to the hand that wrote the name and date, then why did Berry compare the letter 'q' in the speech made by TAMORA to argue these 'q's were of the same

form as the third letter in the date? Sidestepping this inconsistency, Berry has made an important point. If a scrivener had been instructed to copy the manuscript, and perhaps illustrate it, then the comparisons made by Adams, between the inferior work of Peacham *fils* and the superior execution of the manuscript would be explained. In which case, and because of it, attention must now focus upon the name, Henry Peacham.

Adams observed that the name, Henricus Peacham, on the *Titus* document . . .

> *shows some resemblance to, and also some very distinct differences from, the signature 'Henricus Peacham' affixed to the dedication of Emblemata Varia.* 40

These he annotated as being especially notable:

> *[1] The capital letter 'H' in the two signatures is quite different in formation. [2] The letter 'r' in the Folger MS. has a conspicuous right-hand stroke at the bottom. [3] In the Folger MS. the letters 'cu' are joined and the letter 's' is separate: in the Longleat MS. the letter 'c' is separate and the letters 'us' are joined. [4] The capital letter 'P' in the Folger MS. is made without lifting the pen, and is entirely different in form. In the Folger MS. there is no flourish attached to the final letter 'm'. The printed letters in both signatures, however, are so conventional that it is difficult to arrive at any conclusion.* 41

Despite these anomalies, Schlueter described Peacham's signature on the *Emblemata Varia* as *"strikingly like that of the Longleat manuscript."* Further examples of Peacham's signature appear among his notes concerning genealogy, and are presently included as a part of the Harleian manuscripts held by the

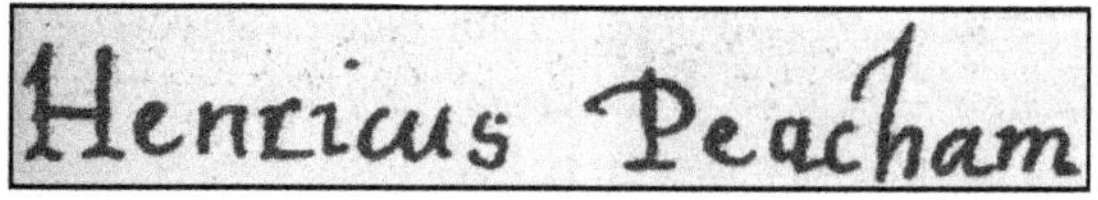

British Library. None, however, contain signatures that compare with that found on the *Emblemata Varia* c.1621.

Of the others, Schlueter notes that . . .

> *The first … reflects an unattractive hand and an undistinguished autograph … [which] bears little resemblance to the attribution in the Longleat manuscript ... The second … reflects a quite different but similarly unattractive hand and a signature, in English, that is a bit more like the carefully penned signature of the Longleat manuscript.* 42

There is one further autograph to consider. It appears on

Peacham's handwritten manuscript of *Basilicon Doron* (The Kingly Gift). It was published by Peacham c. 1610 as *A Book of Emblems illustrating the Basilicon Doron of James I*, and shows Peacham had decided to drop the 'a' from his name. He restored it later. But the problem with printing letters is that two people will very often write a lower-case letter so similarly that each example appears virtually indistinguishable from the other. It is the differences that occur to capital letters that are instructive, because these are always printed separately, and over time acquire the writer's individual characteristics.

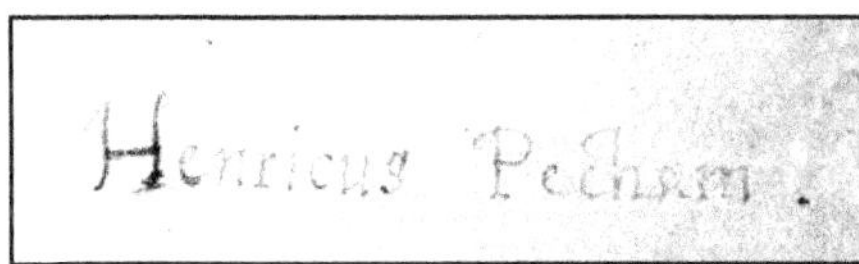

For example, although more than ten years separate the younger Peacham's two known signatures, he still draws a line to the right at the base of his 'r_'. This is absent on the manuscript.

Consider, too, the capital 'H'. Peacham *fils's* uprights are of near equal length. But not on the Titus manuscript, where the left upright begins with a lengthy flourish before extending downwards to form a hook. This contrasts with the one on the right-hand side, which is much shorter, and on a level with the letters of the copyist's forename.

The crossbar, too, is different. On Peacham's two signatures it is horizontal and very nearly of the same length as the uprights. Whereas, on the Longleat manuscript the crossbar inclines from left to right, in parallel with the slanting base of the 'P'; it is also of lesser size, being at most half the length of the shorter of the two uprights. Moreover, the capital 'P' is significant for other reasons. In both of Peacham *fils's* signatures: a forceful downward stroke is completed with a perpendicular line to the *right*. This does not occur on the Longleat manuscript, where the downward stroke is slightly curved before forming an obtuse angle at the base, which slants away to the *left*. Furthermore, the arc of the 'P' is also more flowing, more artistic on the Longleat manuscript, and clears the upright without touching: but, on the other two documents, the curve of the 'P' is semi-elliptical, and cuts the upright at two points.

There is also the added fact that neither one of Peacham *fils's* two signatures has been completed with the underlining flourish originating from the letter 'm'; but which appears quite distinct on the Longleat signature.

From these facts, it is evident that although Peacham *fils's* initials include the same characteristics on both of his known signatures, albeit separated by ten years, it is equally clear that the Peacham initials on the Longleat manuscript are significantly different in character from those appearing on the *Basilicon Doron* and the *Emblemata Varia*. The weight of evidence is unmistakeable. The Longleat manuscript was, without doubt, the work of the Reverend Peacham. And when this conclusion is taken in context with the accompanying date of 1574, two years before his son was born, it is difficult to envisage any other rational conclusion.

Despite this, there are still those who remain obstinately unconvinced. These are scholars for whom old habits die hard: they, having earlier persuaded themselves that the orthography on the Longleat MS is essentially from the same hand that wrote *Basilicon Doron* and *Emblemata Varia*. A comparison is therefore offered to allay even these doubts. Particular note should be given to the formation of the letter 'r'.

horreant ac reformident (quod vereor crimen an vlla devotio,) et
quid citimatius, e schola vbi hinc inde garritus & puerorum strepitus
(hoc enim sub onere ingemisco) nec per semihora otio frui liceat.
Sed quid non Principi, cui auram qua vescimur & vitam.
Illum supremum oro Regum Regem ut te orbi, iam ultimo in
extremis laboranti Augustum Christianum, Britannis tuis &
Ecclesiæ alumnum diutissime conservare velit.

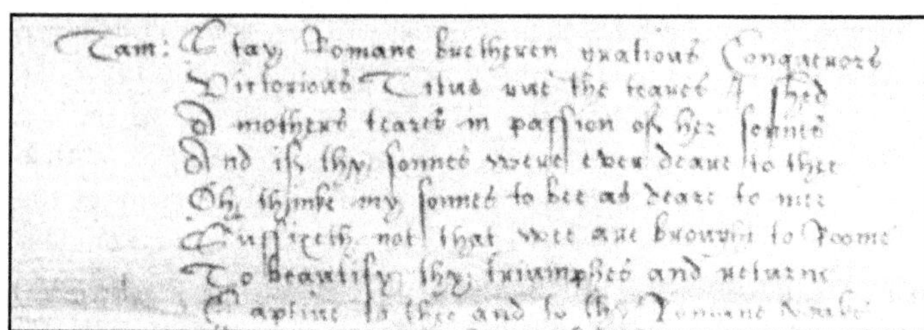

Tam: Stay, Romane bretheren gratious Conquerors
Victorious Titus rue the teares I shed
A mothers teares in passion of her sonne
And if thy sonnes were ever deare to thee
Oh thinke my sonnes to bee as deare to mee
Suffiseth not that wee are brought to Roome
To beautify thy triumphes and returne
Captive to thee and to thy Romane yoake

Peacham *fils's* habit of writing the letter 'r' with a horizontal base extending to the right was not confined to his name, but appears also in the handwritten manuscript of his *Basilicon* (See first of the two copies above). This is evident from examination of the original (second of the two copies above). However, Peter Croft, former Librarian at King's College Library, Cambridge was inclined to think Peacham *fils* used the Longleat manuscript as an exercise in 'writing fair' in the 'secretary script': as the emblem books were exercises in *"fair writing in the italic style."* [43]

In response to this, it should be pointed out there is no evidence whatever that Peacham had any such desire. Not only that, but very far from being an *"exercise in 'writing fair' in the secretary script"*, the lettering shows an accomplished hand at this form of writing. Nothing in Peacham *fils's* handwriting, even allowing that it was written later, compares with his alleged earlier effort.

However, Croft does make a valid observation when he *"notes that the italic 'Anno' [in the date] looks as though it is in the same hand as the text and also the same hand as the signature."* [44]

In support of this view, the 'A' in 'Anno' can be compared with the 'A' in TAMORA'S speech, where it will be seen as identical.

THE MANUSCRIPT'S DIALOGUE

It remains now to examine the play as Peacham described it. To begin with, the finely executed ink drawing at the top of the document (p. 420), includes a caption underneath. This explains the scene. But, because the caption is also a stage direction: *"Enter Tamora pleading for her sons going to execution"* and one that appears to explain the drawing, it should not to be confused with a compilation drawing. A compilation drawing does not carry a stage direction: a fact totally ignored by Bate, who with little hesitation remarked:

> *The text's conflation of passages from the first and last acts suggests that the drawing is a composite representation ... Indeed, I think that the illustration may offer an emblematic reading of the whole play from first act to fifth.* [45]

A compilation drawing is recognizable by its content, which is aimed at capturing the storyline with one illustration. The Peacham drawing is different, and does nothing more than show a single scene from the play: one that Schlueter recognized as being very similar to another occurring in the German version.

In this respect, the action depicted in the drawing would be seen as a visual aid for the dialogue that follows.

However, what is written below Peacham's illustration does not occur within any known edition of the play, as J. Dover Wilson queried: *"Why does the drawing seem to represent Tamora pleading for two sons, when in the play she has three sons and pleads for one only, her first-born Alarbus?"* [46] Furthermore, when TAMORA does make her plea, AARON is still a prisoner of war and should be absent from the scene. Yet, he is shown on the right, pointing a sword at TAMORA'S sons.

At the same time, TITUS'S own two sons should be on stage alongside him. In the drawing they are absent. The two figures on the left are merely soldiers, for they are not dressed in the regal gowns that would identify them as sons of TITUS.

The dialogue beneath the picture does nothing therefore to dispel the suspicion that this is an earlier version of the play.

Consider the stage direction: *"Enter Tamora pleading for her sons going to execution."* Wilson queried this direction by asking:

> *Why does he [Peacham] describe the Gothic princes as 'going to execution' when what happens in the play is not an execution but a sacrifice to the manes [souls of the dead] of the Andronici?* [47]

Also, in the present version of the play, TAMORA'S speech occurs in Act 1: scene i, and is then followed by the commencement of TITUS'S reply, which takes up six lines of dialogue. But these six lines do not occur on the Longleat manuscript. There, TAMORA'S speech is met with TITUS'S reply, in a single line; the first three words of which are: *"Patient yourself, madam"*. These are to be found in the first of the six lines of the known play. The last three words, which are *"die he must"*, are taken from the fifth line.

According to the Longleat manuscript, TITUS then turns his attention to AARON, who, according to the illustration is on stage, but in the play, as we now know it, he is still a prisoner-of-war. TITUS addresses him with two lines of dialogue that do not occur in any known version of the play. *"Aaron do you likewise prepare yourself / And now repent your wicked life."*

AARON replies to this with a speech of twenty lines, the words of which do occur in the known version of the play, but not until four Acts later. And, even there, although AARON answers a similarly accusing question: *"Art thou not sorry for these heinous deeds?"* This enquiry is posed by LUCIUS, and not TITUS. In fact, according to the illustrated manuscript, LUCIUS is not even on stage at this time.

To all these anomalies there is added one more: the insertion of a speaking part for ALARBUS, the eldest son of TAMORA. On the Longleat manuscript his name appears at the foot of the page as having a speaking role. But in each publication of the play, from its first printing in 1594 onwards, ALARBUS is mute. Yet, Peacham was about to enter his speaking part, when, having reached the bottom of the page, and with no space left to complete ALARBUS'S dialogue, he simply signalled him to be the next speaker.

That this was Peacham's intention is confirmed by the *et cetera* immediately preceding ALARBUS'S name. The ampersand and the abbreviated *cetera* is of material consequence, since together they verify that the dialogue was continuous; as would be the case if a single extract was copied from a more extensive script.

The catalogue of problems confronting the Stratford-based theory of Shakespeare has so far proved unanswerable. The suggestions put forward by well-meaning scholars, in an effort to weld some sort of theory together involving the facts relating to *Titus Andronicus*, and thereby conform to convention; have instead, resulted in one failure after another.

But when the play is considered in relationship to de Vere's authorship, these problems vanish. Moreover, by accepting the evidence above, it follows that Jonson's avowal on the Stratford monument that Edward de Vere should be tested for proof he was Shakespeare, and Oxford's own assertion that he was the poet who wrote Sonnet 76, confirms what has been said.

In conclusion, the foregoing evidence verifies that the completion of *Titus Andronicus* occurred in 1574, but the play may then have been known by the title, *Titus & Vespasian*. The storyline was based upon Roman tragedies: these being the best—in fact, only examples available to a playwright at that time.

The first performance took place in the same year, and was attended by Queen Elizabeth at her favourite palace, Hatfield House. Amongst the invited guests were Michael Hicks, working for Lord Burghley, and Henry Peacham, curate of the parish adjoining Hatfield House, and soon to publish his book, *The Garden of Eloquence*. After attending this performance, Peacham drew a scene from the play and accompanied it with appropriate dialogue, very likely copied from a prompt book or actor's script. Since Peacham signed and dated the manuscript, one may reasonably conclude it was gifted to Hicks as a suitable addition to his growing collection of Roman memorabilia.

In the following year, Edward de Vere left England to travel across Europe. He returned in 1576, more knowledgeable from his acquaintance with the artists and writers of the Renaissance, and with whom he had conferred while in Italy.

Several years after his homecoming, and with the intention of writing plays in the fashion newly learned from his travels abroad, he turned his attention once again to *Titus*. Observing certain defects in the play, yet retaining much of the original dialogue, he restructured it, scene by scene. By the middle of the 1580s, it was again being performed, this time in public. At the same time his original play, *Titus & Vespasian*, having been taken abroad by a travelling company of players, underwent certain changes that have since drawn commentators to observe . . .

> *Although in its plot this play is remarkably like the English Titus Andronicus it differs in the names of all its characters except the hero, in the absence of several episodes, and in several details. It seems more likely to derive from some other version of the story than from the English play as we have it ... It is impossible to be certain when the German tragedy was first performed, since various English players were in Germany from the 1580s into the seventeenth century.* [48]

There is a faint glow of evidence from the past to support its revision. It concerns a remark made by Edward Ravenscroft, a man who, in 1687, remodelled the tragedy after having heard from an old judge of stage matters that the piece came from another author, and that Shakespeare had only added *"some master-touches to one or two of the principal characters."*[49]

Because of the censorship surrounding Oxford's playwriting career, this other author is likely to have been *himself* during his earlier years. The *"master-touches"* are those he introduced before engaging the services of his allonym, Will Shaxpere; which enabled him to write under the penname, William Shakespeare. In this, we have the reason why Ravenscroft's informant was misled. For, so successfully had Oxford's authorship been kept from public knowledge, through the simple ruse of referring his work to a willing accomplice from one of the lower classes, that nearly a century later, the deception had become established fact.

SUMMARY

The explanations provided above satisfy all unanswered questions concerning the dating of *Titus Andronicus,* and they do so in a cogent and coherent manner. The explanations are also backed by facts and valid inferences. Stratford theorists have nothing that is remotely comparable to offer in their place.

The date 1574 on the Longleat manuscript, for example, defies their every attempt to explain it differently. Instead, the more careless among them posit muddle-headed excursions into mental arithmetic, which, although recognizing the positioning of the letters, representing *thousands, hundreds* and *units*, thereafter completely ignores the importance of the 'g' which occupies the place for *tens*. But, when this does become acknowledged, alongside Peacham's name, there can only be three possibilities; to wit, 'g' represents 70, 80, or 90. And since a 'g' has no connection in any form whatever with either 80 or 90, the one that remains, in line with classical convention, must be the truth.

Apart from the date on the manuscript, there is also the separate claim made by Shaxpere's Stratford fraternity that the Reverend Henry Peacham's son copied the Titus manuscript. This is refuted: if not by the difference in his handwriting or by the composition of his initials, when compared with the hand of his father, then certainly by reference to a speaking part for ALARBUS and the change in the play's structure.

At no time after 1594, the date of the play's first publication, does ALARBUS have a speaking part; nor does the illustration at the top of the Titus document take place on stage; nor are the alterations in the speaking parts observed in performance. Had they been Shakespeare's revisions, they would have emerged as such in a *later* quarto; that is after publication of the original text. The fact that these changes are already present in all these publications implies the play was written in its original form as early as 1574, when it was first performed, and that it was subsequently revised to its present structure in the years that followed: thereafter, gaining in popularity until ultimately this led to its publication in 1594. Consequent to this, only minor and insignificant changes occurred up until its appearance in the First Folio of 1623.

In this respect, it can be seen how easily an initial blunder gathers force with the passage of years. Eventually, a solid construction of erudition is built around it. But when the error is exposed to the truth, as in the present case, the structure must be expected to give way; otherwise scholarship becomes a vehicle of bias for the whims and vanities of those who achieve office.

The impact *Titus Andronicus* has upon the authorship debate is potentially profound. In 1574, the man credited with having written this play was a mere lad of ten or eleven; Christopher Marlowe was just one year older; Francis Bacon and William Stanley were both aged fourteen, Roger Manners was only three; and the recent newcomer to the authorship controversy Sir Henry Neville was himself just ten years old. The only serious contender for having written *Titus Andronicus* and, by implication, the plays and poems of Shakespeare, was Edward de Vere, aged twenty-four.

9

THE FIRST FOLIO'S DECEPTIVE TRIBUTES

Look here, upon this picture, and on this!
Hamlet

IN JANUARY 1616, Will Shaxpere, or Shackspeare as he then styled himself, was somehow persuaded to begin writing his last will and testament. He had apparently not thought to do so before: his health being good at the time, or so he maintained; *viz.*, *"I William Shackspeare, of Stratford upon Avon in the countie of Warr. gent., in perfect health and memorie, God be praysed."* But, just three months later, with the will having been finalised only a few weeks earlier, he was dead: the cause was not recorded.

An Unexpected Death

The conventional explanation for Shaxpere's death, it having followed so soon after declaring himself to be in *"perfect health"*, is that this had been just a lawyer's phrase, and that he was in fact desperately ill. Does that sound reasonable? Compare this with the will of actor Alexander Cooke, who died two years before. *"I, Alexander Cooke, sick of body but in perfect mind, do with mine own hand write my last will and testament."* [1] With his *"own hand"*, note! Something 'Shackspeare' was unable to declare.

Nine years earlier, fellow actor Augustine Phillips similarly confessed to being *"sick and weak in body"*, [2] shortly before his death. If both Cooke and Phillips could tell the truth about their condition on such an important document as their final farewell to the world, should we not suppose Shaxpere to be equally candid; that is, if he really were ill and dying? And why did he need a lawyer writing a lawyer's will, when the works of Shakespeare ring out with legal knowledge?

It is natural to believe that Shaxpere was the author of his own will, for this satisfies any lingering doubts concerning his penmanship and ability to spell. Indeed, why should he not have written it himself, if he were the playwright of popular belief? But the facts indicate otherwise.

Apart from his wishes being expressed in the dull legal jargon of a disinterested clerk, there is a far more obvious indicator that he did not write it himself. The will commences with the testator referring to himself as, *"I William Shackspeare";* further on, in the left margin, and now illegible under normal vision, is the name *"William Shakspere";* the document ends with the words *"By Me, William Shakspeare".*

It is a feature common amongst educated people that when referring to themselves in writing, they spell their name in a consistent manner. The fact that the document contains three variations of the name, suggests that the clerk(s) responsible for the testament had been completely unaware this was the final bequest of a man reputed to be the great London poet and playwright – William Shakespeare.

The house in which Shaxpere passed from this life had a tragic history: its two previous occupants having been poisoned there. It was this that had enabled Shaxpere to acquire the property at a lower price than would normally have been expected.

Like the two previous owners of New Place, Shaxpere's death was equally unexpected, but with more important implications: it cleared the way for the collected plays of *Shakespeare* to be published without fear of directing attention towards a living author. It would not have done for these great works of art to appear while Will Shaxpere lived: for, as the man credited with their authorship, he would have become a focus for attention in his hometown: especially from visitors. Questions would inevitably be directed at him and his neighbours, for which the replies would be seen as totally inadequate, if not ridiculous; thereby threatening to reveal the secret surrounding the true author and his family. Moreover, the publication of 'Shakespeare's' plays, credited to Oxford's allonym while still living, would require compensation be paid for the rest of his life. Shaxpere could then demand it be continued after his death, thus allowing his next of kin to benefit from the secret, with the ever-mounting risk that the cover-up would reach a wider public from a less committed keeper of the secret. All together, these would be seen as highly significant reasons why publication of Shakespeare's plays was to be deferred until after this man's death.

But deferring their publication raised a worrying problem. Suppose Shaxpere outlived those who wanted to ensure these great works were not lost to future generations? Were that to happen, the plays might never be published. The world of literature would then be much poorer for this missed opportunity. William Shaxpere's death in 1616 must therefore be considered most fortuitous, not only for everyone concerned at the time, but also for future generations. And that he had also signed his will shortly before dying, while being in perfect health and without mentioning a bequest relating to a continuation of the money he received for maintaining his pretence as Shakespeare: that too was providential.

There is also an interesting addition made to Shaxpere's will that continues to intrigue traditionalists. It was normal at that time, even though exceptions did exist, for two witnesses to attest a will, but Shaxpere's final testament required no less than *five* signatures, whereas two would have been sufficient. These were Francis Collins, Julius Shawe, John Robinson, Hamnet Sadler and Robert Whattcott. Might this not suggest that Francis Collins was keen to establish that Shaxpere's final words – *"And [I] do revoke all former wills and publish this to be my last will and testament,"* – would not be subsequently challenged? And, that of the five witnesses, at least two would still be alive to give evidence, should the will be challenged at a later date?

Jonson's Rise to Prominence

In 1616, the very same year Shaxpere unexpectedly died, Ben Jonson's fortunes dramatically changed. Lord Pembroke, one of the two brothers to whom *Shakespeare's* collected plays were to be dedicated, recommended to James I that Jonson be awarded a pension of £100 per annum (≈ £28,000). This left Jonson free from financial worry, thus enabling him to concentrate upon preparing the complete set of 'Shakespeare's' plays for what would become known as the First Folio edition.

In which case, it is understandable why – after completing the task of editing all 36 plays, and with the First Folio ready for sale – Jonson received a bonus. His annual pension was doubled to £200. The connection between these two amounts, and the timing of each award, cannot be separated from the work entailed in getting Shakespeare's plays into print.

In 1616 Jonson had published his own plays, which he called his *Works*; thus laying the foundation for the publication of 'Shakespeare's' works; something Oxford had been unable to do himself. Publishing his plays was not something new to Jonson. In April 1600, William Holme had printed a thousand copies of *Every Man Out of His Humour*. Before the year was out, it had been reprinted, and even undergone a third print run. In the following year Jonson published *Cynthia's Revels*. Yet, compared with Shakespeare, he was a newcomer to the stage; in fact, he was not even a shareholder in the Globe. But despite this, *"he apparently now reserved the right to print his work within a year or two of performance,"* [3] and he did so without even having to acknowledge the Lord Chamberlain's Men on the title page.

This gives the lie to those who suggest Will Shaxpere was unable to have done the same, because of his obligation to the Globe theatre. It does not appear to have occurred to those who offer this feeble line of excuse that for Shaxpere, a shareholder in the Globe – and especially if he were the plays' author – there would be no impediment to their publication. Some, in any case, had already become stale from past performances. It is therefore a contradiction to maintain Shaxpere could not publish, while agreeing that two other shareholders, Heminge and Condell, were able to do so, and without hindrance; particularly when some of the plays they published had not yet been staged?

The only response from orthodoxy that one can imagine is because Shaxpere did not want to publish them, while being perfectly content to see the fruit of his many labours *"stolen"*, *"maimed"* and *"deformed"* by the *"frauds"* of those who *"exposed them"*. Does that sound like the reaction of the litigant Shaxpere, who sued for the non-payment of even the smallest debt?

Introducing Heminge and Condell

John Hemynge, Richard Burbage and Henry Cundell, three actors from the Globe, were willed £1. 6s 8d each by Will Shaxpere: in remembrance of him. The bequest appeared as an interlineation on the will; that is, as an afterthought inserted on the revised and final version of the document after its completion. It seemed the lawyer drawing up the will had advised Shaxpere that he had failed to include anything in the document to suggest a previous connection with the theatre. When this was made known to Shaxpere he reluctantly agreed to the bare minimum being shared amongst the three named men.

No bequest was made to any writer: not even Jonson, who declared that he loved the man, this side of idolatry. If Will Shaxpere had been the person referred to by Jonson, then it is safe to say, the affection was not reciprocated.

Heminge and Condell did reciprocate, and in a manner far in excess of the bequest they received. But Burbage died in 1619, four years before the First Folio was published, and he is not credited with any part in the collection and editing of Shakespeare's plays. It is to the two surviving actors that the honour of having achieved this supreme task is given. As they say in their letter addressed to 'The Great Variety of Readers' . . .

> *we pray you do not envy his Friends, the office of their care, and pain, to have collected and published them ... cured, and perfect of their limbs; and all the rest, absolute in their numbers, as he conceived them.*

These words fall easy upon the ears of the faithful, and are frequently quoted with an almost semi-divine reverence. For in their eyes, Heminge and Condell gave the world Shakespeare's plays; without their aid, this treasure trove of literature might easily have been lost; hence, to cast doubt upon the integrity of these actors is the closest thing to sacrilege outside Church law.

Since there seems to have been no previous enquiry as to how Heminge and Condell managed to achieve so daunting a task, this now seems to be the appropriate time to look at what was involved.

The First Folio consists of thirty-six plays, written across a time span of approximately sixteen years; that is, if one accepts the Stratford chronology. This poses a real problem of retrieval. Where were Shakespeare's manuscript copies of his plays kept? Not in his house in Stratford-upon-Avon, for they are not mentioned in his will. Not at the Globe theatre for this was burnt to the ground on 29 June 1613, when all was lost. In whose house and keeping did Shaxpere entrust his manuscripts, and why?

What of the plays themselves? From where did Heminge and Condell obtain the manuscript of *King John*? Up until it made its appearance in the First Folio, the play was unknown. More to the point, why did these two theatrical managers not get the King's Men to stage the play before its publication? A new Shakespeare play, after more than a decade, would have surely brought them a good return. The fact they did not take this course of action tends to imply the play was not their property. Then, whose property was it?

The same inference can be drawn from *All's Well That Ends Well, Coriolanus*, and *Timon of Athens*. In each case, one is entitled to pose this question – 'Since there is no evidence that these plays were even known before they appeared in the First Folio, much less performed, from where did Heminge and Condell acquire them?' Who told them of their existence?

The popular answer is that Will Shaxpere sold them to his fellow shareholders before he died. In which case, why were they not staged? Is one to believe that the shareholders at the Globe paid good money for these manuscripts and then did nothing? Well, not quite nothing: one is also required to believe that Heminge and Condell, two shareholders, were allowed to take them away and publish them for the benefit of others.

The Stratford chronology, which lists the probable dates for the composition of Shakespeare's plays, is mostly based upon the record of each first performance closely following its composition. If the currently accepted chronology is to be relied upon as a consistent method of dating, then one must equally suppose that the plays mentioned above would have been performed soon after they were acquired. But evidence for this is lacking. And without consistency in reasoning, the Stratford chronology becomes shaky, and far too dependent upon special pleading.

Another problem facing Heminge and Condell was the geographical spread of Shakespeare's plays. The History plays, for example, began with performances by the Lord Admiral's Men who performed at the Theatre in north London before moving to the Rose in Southwark. As Peter Ackroyd admitted:

> *The theatrical records of this period are notoriously imprecise and muddled. The provenance and ownership of early plays are notoriously difficult to prove. Companies of players owned certain plays, as did*

> *the managers of the London theatres. There was a great deal of movement between companies, and actors sometimes brought plays with them. Companies also sold plays to one another.* [4]

Almost adjacent to the Theatre was the Curtain where Lord Strange's Men performed, and where *"Two of Shakespeare's earliest plays were already part of the repertoire."* [5] Quite apart from this, we also know that *Titus Andronicus* was passed from Lord Derby's Men to those of Lord Pembroke, and from there to Lord Sussex's Men. But, we are told . . .

> *When Shakespeare joined the Lord Chamberlain's, he brought with him all of his plays. This was their great advantage. From this time forward the Chamberlain's Men were the sole producers of Shakespeare's dramas.* [6]

How peculiar! On the one hand we are informed Shakespeare could not publish his own plays because they were *not his* to publish. Then we are told his plays *did belong to him*, allowing him to take them to a competing group of actors; as occurred when he joined the Chamberlain's Men. Amidst all this, Jonson, who was not even a shareholder in the Globe, was nevertheless allowed to publish his plays after they had been staged. One cannot escape the conclusion that the study of Shakespeare's life and works are frequently shown to be incompatible in the hands of Shaxpere's advocates.

In point of fact, before 1598, Shakespeare was never publicly associated with any of the plays that later became presented under that name. William Shakespeare was simply the poet who had written *Venus and Adonis* and *The Rape of Lucrece.* There was neither evidence, nor any obvious reason to associate this man with even one of the anonymously written plays being performed at that time. Any thought to the contrary exists entirely in the heads of those whose adulation for the man has subconsciously impelled them to project their own thoughts backwards in time, and impose these upon a situation acceptable to their private fancy. The manner, in which biographers of Shakespeare sell their story to the public, positively encourages these deceptively, imaginative scenarios to displace reality; whereafter, they merge into a world of myth and imagination.

Crucially, it was not until after Lord Burghley's death, when Francis Meres gave credence to 'Shakespeare' as the author of some twelve plays, that pirate publishers felt free to use this name on their stolen editions. Before 1598, all previously printed plays by Shakespeare were pirated, with the author unnamed.

Yet, the publishers of these fraudulent quartos must have known they had been written by a nobleman, for this meant there could be no legal redress brought against their person without disclosing the author's name to the public. It was this fact that allowed the frauds to continue, but with publishers ever careful not to identify the author.

However, when Meres gave the green light to 'Shakespeare' as the named author of twelve anonymous plays, the pirate publishers at last felt free to use that name to their own advantage: knowing that because Shakespeare was the nobleman-author's pseudonym, they were safe from prosecution: as indeed proved to be the case.

It is against this background of illegal publications that Will Shaxpere's advocates have concocted a tale involving a divided playwright. He is famous, but also anonymous; embryonic, yet accomplished; youthful, while being mature, and though tied to a company of actors, he is free to move his plays to other companies. Yet, although being free to move his plays, he has not the right to publish them.

Despite the contradictory nonsense promoted by self-seeking biographers', thirty-six plays were eventually collected together. Although it would make better sense if this were seen as having been achieved through the influence and direction of the Lord Chamberlain, the 3rd Earl of Pembroke, who was the brother-in-law of Susan Vere, Oxford's daughter, rather than to two inconsequential shareholders.

We now come to the editing of these plays. Since the First Folio consists of approximately 900 pages, this was to be no easy task. There were no typewriters in those days. Manuscripts had to be handwritten, and as Chettle discovered when he attempted to decipher Robert Greene's handwriting, errors, and misunderstanding were very easily committed by the unwary.

An early task faced by Heminge and Condell was that of deciding between plays that were Histories and those that were Tragedies. To confuse matters more, at least one play, *Hamlet*, was described as a *"Tragicall Historie"*; whereas, *Richard II* was not described in the *Stationers' Register* as a 'History', but as *The Tragedye of Richard the Second.*

Another question concerned the designation of *King Lear.* Shakespeare's title in the *Stationers' Register* affirmed it to be a History, but it was designated as a Tragedy in the First Folio. *Macbeth* was yet another example of the need for distinguishing between History and Tragedy. For, if *Richard II* is defined as a History, why has *Macbeth* been put amongst the Tragedies?

> *In spite however of this looseness of nomenclature Heminge and Condell could not have devised a better arrangement for the First Folio, unless they had been prepared to set out the plays in chronological order.* [7]

In presenting this opinion, Professor Alexander implicitly applauds the abilityinge and Condell by asserting . . .

> *Shakespeare's Histories do not indeed show the full range of Shakespeare's creative power as do the Tragedies; for the Tragedies are a later and maturer series, coming when all the Histories save one were already written and when Shakespeare's dramatic inspiration was at its flood.* [8]

In other words, Heminge and Condell correctly identified the difference between the Histories and Tragedies by placing them in an order which scholars have subsequently found to be acceptable. But the skill required for distinguishing between the two genres of Tragedy and History was only part of the huge problem that faced these two men; there was also the source material to be considered, and this, when collected together, we are told, arrived in a variety of forms.

> *The editors of the First Folio appear to have worked from several sources. They had the flawed texts of six plays, the so-called 'bad quartos'; one 'doubtful' quarto; and eleven 'good quartos'. They used Shakespeare's own manuscripts, known as 'foul papers' for a first draft, and 'fair copy' for an edited transcript; loose sheets kept by actors; and the 'prompt book' approved by the royal censor.* [9]

Without doubt, making sense of these sources and compiling them to accurately convey Shakespeare's intentions required extensive knowledge of the English language, combined with a lot of previous experience at writing prose and poetry. Plays, particularly those with classical references, needed to be recognized for what they were, and uniting different versions of the same play into a coherent whole, presented a challenge requiring not only intelligence, but also artistic aptitude of an extremely high order.

In the minds of the Stratford fraternity, Heminge and Condell were two men educated far above the normal run of actors. In Tudor England, the Poor Law had grouped players along with *"rogues, vagabonds and sturdy beggars:"* [10] a group at risk of being whipped out of town.

> *When the Act for the Punishment of Vagabonds was reinvoked in 1572 it presented groups of travelling players with a very serious problem. Unless they could prove that they belonged to an officially recognized patron or that they were licensed by local magistrates, they risked imprisonment, whipping, and even hanging.* [11]

In fairness, Heminge and Condell were of a higher class: both were churchwardens in their local parish, with income from sources outside the theatre, but this does not give them the ability to achieve what is said of them. There is also the fact that they both had very large families, with domestic chores to be attended to; and this, quite apart from their church duties and theatre commitments, would have left little time for the extra burden of collecting and editing the thirty-six plays of Shakespeare.

An actor at that time was a singular type of individual: one, who though belonging to the lowest class in society, might mingle with a higher class; for he earned his money by performing to audiences of different classes. Actors were also argumentative, and there are several accounts of duels, fights and killings between rival players. Heminge actually married the widow of an actor killed in a fight. Condell was from a similar background, but improved his status by making a good marriage.

Henry Condell was born in 1568, but not baptized until 5 September 1576. (One cannot help but recall the fuss made over Will Shaxpere's baptismal date and the inference drawn that it must have occurred three days earlier, thus coinciding with St. Georges Day.) Henry's father was Robert Condell, a fishmonger living in Norfolk. As with Will Shaxpere, there is no evidence of the boy's education, or any record of what he was doing to qualify him for the exacting task that lay ahead of him: that of editing Shakespeare's plays.

Upon reaching manhood, Condell appears to have had no occupation worth recording. This supposition is reinforced by the tradition that he was in London in 1592 as a member of Lord Strange's Men. In the same year, it is suggested he took part in *The Seven Deadly Sins:* a play allegedly written by Tarlton. But, Condell's name does not appear on the list of those belonging to Lord Strange's company, during the time they were licensed to play outside a seven-mile radius of London. This was during the Plague years of 1592-3; John Heminge, however, is listed.

One fact known for certain is that Condell had the good fortune to win the hand of Elizabeth Smart, the daughter of a wealthy London gentleman who made her his heiress. The marriage took place on 24 August 1596 in the parish of St Mary at Aldermanbury, where Condell was living at the time and where the newlyweds chose to live afterwards. Condell also became a churchwarden at St. Mary's, and it was in this church that the couple's nine children were baptized, although only three lived into adulthood.

Condell's name appears often in the cast lists of Jonson's plays; e.g., *Every Man In His Humour* (1598), *Every Man Out of His Humour* (1599), *Sejanus* (1603), *Volpone* (1605), *The Alchemist* (1610), *Catiline,* (1610) and *The Duchess of Malfi* (c.1613). A close and lasting relationship between playwright and actor is thus apparent, and one that also appears prominently in the prefatory poems and letters that front the First Folio. This poses the question – Did this relationship between the two men continue during preparation of the First Folio? If so, it may mean the letters bearing Condell's name were actually written by Jonson.

In 1605, Henry Condell and William Sly became co-owners of the Globe theatre.[12] We know from a subsequent lawsuit – Witter *v.* Heminge and Condell (1619) – that shares in the Globe had originally been divided up so that Richard and Cuthbert Burbage owned 50% between them, with the other 50% allotted equally in 10% shares to Augustine Phillips, John Heminge, Thomas Pope, William Kemp and Will Shaxpere.

In 1605, Phillips died, thus releasing his 10% shareholding in the Globe for either Condell or Sly to acquire. Since both became shareholders; then, from who was the other 10% acquired?

After the death of Oxford in June 1604, Shaxpere's role had

become largely redundant, and a problem for which no one wanted responsibility. From this time onwards, record of his association with the Globe theatre ceases, and he returns to Stratford to deal in real estate and agricultural produce. His last will and testament confirms that he held no financial interest in the Globe. In fact, any association with the theatre after Oxford's death would have been a potential embarrassment: hence, there was a reason to sell his 10% share before he died.

From 1605 onwards, Condell combined acting with theatre management. And in 1608, he extended this by purchasing a seventh part share in the Blackfriars Playhouse. There is no doubt that he was held in great respect. He received several legacies from fellow actors; Phillips, in particular, leaving him a *"thirty-shilling piece in gold."* He was also trustee for the estates of Nicholas Tooley and Alexander Cooke. His financial acumen having presumably been developed from the money inherited by his wife and the various properties this enabled him to buy.

In 1613 Condell's investment in the Globe received a serious setback when the theatre caught fire during a performance of *Henry VIII:* also known as *All Is True.* By the day following the fire, a ditty was already circulating in London describing the anxious activities of the shareholders as their investment burnt down around them: in fact, those named in the verse were the same three men who would be mentioned in the interlineation made on Shaxpere's revised will.

Out run the Knights, out run the Lords.
And there was great ado;
Some lost their hats, and some their swords —
Then out run Burbage too;
The reprobates, though drunk on Monday
Prayed for the Fool and Henry Condye,
⋮
Oh sorrow, pitiful sorrow, and yet all this is true.

The periwigs and drumheads fried
Like to a butter firkin
A woeful burning did betide
To many a good buff jerkin;

Then with swollen eyes, like drunken Fleming's
Distressed stood old stuttering Heminge. 13

After 1619, Condell's name ceased to appear on cast lists, leading to the assumption that he had retired from the stage. His retirement could well be seen as a preparation for the mammoth task of collecting and editing Shakespeare's plays, except that this would average out at approximately one play a month for three years without rest. Instead, it should be asked what is there in this profile of Henry Condell that had prepared him for the task that allegedly lay before him? One can see nothing beyond the fact that he was an actor with a head for business. The enormous undertaking of putting together each play from several different sources, deciding upon where the division into acts and scenes were to occur, understanding the structure of the unfolding drama, and being aware of the many errors in the bad quartos, and then being able to correct them would prove more than a challenge, even to a man of Jonson's genius. To imagine Condell having played a major role in this accomplishment is second only to supposing that Will Shaxpere wrote the plays in the first place.

What then of the other half of this partnership, *"old stuttering Heminge"* aged sixty-three in 1619?

John Heminge was born in Droitwich Spa, Worcestershire, in 1556, the son of George Heminge. In 1568, when aged only twelve, he travelled to the capital city to become apprenticed to James Collins, a London grocer, and a grocer he remained for the rest of his long life.

In 1587, he was presented to the Company of Grocers and became a freeman. Eight years later he was admitted as a full member of the Company, and bound ten apprentices to himself. Taking and bonding apprentices could be lucrative; since it often involved a parent paying the Master for the many years of training that lay ahead.

In November 1621, while supposedly immersed in the time-consuming, and intellectually demanding task of editing Shakespeare's 36 collected plays in preparation for their printing, Heminge paid in excess of twenty pounds ($\approx$ £5600), to be admitted to the company of Grocers' Livery. This entitled him to superintend at banquets held for special guests. Social climbing may have been behind this, for in 1629, he applied for and received his own coat of arms. The privilege was short-lived. A virulent outbreak of the Plague broke out in the following year, and on 9 October he suddenly made out his will. It was proved two days later, and he was buried on the following day in the church of St Mary at Aldermanbury, where his wife and Henry Condell were also interred.

Heminge was a family man. Although it was not until the age of thirty-two that he took a wife. She was Rebecca Knell, the sixteen-year-old widow of William Knell, an actor with the Queen's Men. Knell's death was the result of a duel he fought at Thame with a fellow player named John Towne. Towne was subsequently declared innocent of the death; it being considered an act of self defence. Heminge and his wife were to have fourteen children, but not all survived. One, however, did attend Westminster School where Ben Jonson had been educated.

After their marriage, Heminge and his wife moved from the parish of St. Michael, Cornhill, to Rebecca's home in Addle Street, which was owned by goldsmith Thomas Savage. The house was situated in the parish of St. Mary, Aldermanbury where, as with Condell, he too became active in the Church as a deputy churchwarden.

Heminge's association with the theatre can be traced back to 1593. In that year he appears on the cast list of Lord Strange's Men, for they had been granted a licence to go on tour: the Plague having closed the London theatres. Amongst the plays put on that year by Lord Strange's Men was 'Shakespeare's' *Henry VI*. But, neither the name Shakespeare nor Shaxpere is on the company's list of players: nor, indeed, any company of players for that matter. Yet, if Henry Chettle's reading of Robert Greene's scribble had been as accurate as the *Groatsworth of Wit* proclaimed, then Shakespeare's name, in whatever form, should have appeared on the list of players that were staging his play. Where else would it be, other than with the company that was performing his play? Surely, another divisive factor in the life and work of Shakespeare!

This, together with the fact that Philip Henslowe's journal also refers to *Henry VI* being performed, but omits reference to any payment for it, bemuses Shaxpere's advocates. Explanations are sometimes suggested for this anomaly, but they tend to amuse rather than educate. In fact, the non-occurrence of Shakespeare's name on any actors' list in 1592 is predictable. Oxford was the playwright Nashe called Will Monox and it was he who was responsible for writing *Henry VI.* Will Shaxpere was at that time still working as a theatrical odd job man in Shoreditch, and Oxford's penname, Shakespeare, had yet to emerge as the accredited author of *Venus and Adonis.* It is all perfectly logical.

In 1594, Heminge is said to have moved over to the Lord Chamberlain's Men. His career as an actor of any real status is dubious. Jonson mentions him on the cast list of a few plays, but the roles he played are unknown. A more reliable explanation is that he was appointed as the Chamberlain Men's business manager, playing bit parts when occasion required; stuttering is not an asset where fluent diction is paramount.

From 1596, Heminge's name is frequently found in the Court accounts as recipient of fees paid for performances by the Lord Chamberlain's Men, and thereafter the King's Men. His experience in the grocery trade and his trustworthiness would have stood him in good standing for this role.

Another point of interest resides in the fact that grocers do seem to have been obligatory during performances. Both James Burbage's Red Lion and Shoreditch projects were made *"in partnership with grocer John Brayne."* [14] And when the Rose was built, Henslowe made an agreement with grocer John Cholmley that he alone be given permission to sell his wares on the premises. Consequently, there can be little room for doubt that Heminge supplied and sold the drinks and snacks for audiences at the Globe. After the theatre's destruction by fire in 1613, and when a new building had been erected on the site in the following year, a house occupied by Heminge stood alongside: from where the old grocer reputedly sold ale.

One incident did cast a shadow over Heminge's otherwise blameless life. In 1615, he became involved in a lawsuit (*Ostler v. Heminge*). In the previous year, William Ostler, an actor for the King's Men, died intestate. His chattels should therefore have passed to his widow Thomasine, who was also Heminge's daughter. Part of Ostler's assets consisted of a shareholding in both the Blackfriars theatre and the Globe. Heminge seized these for himself. Presumably, he had gifted the shareholdings to Ostler after his daughter's marriage, but now that his son-in-law was dead, he wanted the shares returned, lest they fell into the wrong hands. Thomasine objected, and she sued her father to retain possession. The outcome is not recorded, perhaps due to an out-of-court settlement allowing Heminge to recover the shares.

Thus, once again, we become faced with a similar dilemma to that met with when viewing Condell's profile. Where is there any evidence of the literary skills required by Heminge for him to have edited the *Comedies, Histories, and Tragedies* of William Shakespeare? Since the Stratford professorship cannot invent the necessary skills for these two 'editors', they instead, turn to documentary evidence; Heminge and Condell said they did it, so it must be true.

> *Read the works of those who argue that the Earl of Oxford was the true author of Shakespeare's works, and of necessity the veteran editors of the First Folio are presented as liars and cheats for misrepresenting the plays' true authorship.* [15]

Not really! Heminge and Condell were actors, and they were simply playing a role written for them by someone they knew well – Ben Jonson. Oxford's association with the plays he had written, and which were subsequently assigned to his penname, William Shakespeare, was to be avoided. From this it follows that Heminge and Condell were lawfully obeying a ruling made by higher authority.

There can be no doubt, the Earl of Pembroke in his official position as Lord Chamberlain, knew what was taking place, but saw no incongruity in Heminge and Condell acting as editors to 'Shakespeare's' plays. After all, like Shaxpere, both actors came from the same level in society, which was at the lower end of the social spectrum. It therefore would have seemed reasonable that if one of their number had been paid to assume the role of author to the works of Shakespeare, there could be no obstacle in furthering this belief by including others from the same class to act as editors. To upper-class thinking, a connection between Shaxpere the 'author', and Heminge and Condell the 'editors' of his work, would seem appropriate. It still does, as may be witnessed by those who willingly and uncritically buy into it.

More realistically, Jonson was the editor. He has already been associated with the two letters signed by Heminge and Condell addressed to the *"Great Variety of Readers"* at the front of the First Folio. And the pension he received when the project began, and the addition to it, which he received when the project ended, allows money to speak louder than words. Over two hundred years ago, the great Shakespearian scholar Edmund Malone set out parallel columns with extracts on one side, drawn from these letters. On the other side he entered phrases taken from Jonson's works which mirrored those occurring in the letter. The comparisons were unmistakable.

E. K. Chambers was another Shakespeare scholar similarly persuaded: *"recalling that Malone's predecessor, George Steevens, [had also] 'called attention to some parallels between the epistle to the readers and the works of Ben Jonson'."* [16]

After reviewing Heminge's and Condell's lack of credentials for having edited the world's finest dramatic poetry, and then comparing this lack against those possessed by Jonson, coupled with the similarity in his style and phrasing, the only realistic conclusion to be reached is that Jonson wrote the two letters at the front of the First Folio, *per pro* Heminge and Condell.

This inference becomes even more apparent when seen against the background of what happened in 1635. The relatives of James Burbage petitioned Philip Herbert, Earl of Pembroke (formerly Earl of Montgomery), pleading for financial assistance on account of the heavy expenses that had been incurred since rebuilding the Globe. In their petition they said: – *"to ourselves we joined those deserving men Shakspere, Hemmings, Condell, Phillips and others"*.[17]

But, wait! Is this not inadvertently admitting that Shakspere (*sic*) was seen by the petitioners as just another *"deserving"* shareholder, on a par with those mentioned in the petition? How can it be otherwise? The real *Shakespeare* had been the playwright who so often delighted audiences at Court. But it now seems that Pembroke is being asked to remember a different *"Shakspere"*: someone who was just another shareholder; someone who helped manage the Globe. The Earl of Pembroke is emphatically not being asked to recall the *Shakespeare* whose First Folio of 36 plays was dedicated to him and his brother as: *"The Most Noble and Incomparable Paire of Brethren William Earle of Pembroke, &c … and Philip, Earle of Montgomery, &c"*: a folio edition which had been re-published in 1632, just three years before this appeal was made. Most decidely, the petitioners were unable to mention any connection between *"Shakspere"* and 'Shakespeare'. The reason for this is that Philip Herbert had married 'Shakespeare's' daughter, Susan Vere. It would have been ludicrous to mention Shaxpere as the author of the plays dedicated to him and his brother; since Philip Herbert was the real Shakespeare's son-in-law. And so the petitioners were confined to naming *"Shakspere"* as shareholder.

Contributors to the First Folio

The 3rd Earl of Pembroke's role in the publication of the First Folio is, itself, a feature that many consider to have been underestimated.

> *The Earl of Pembroke … became Lord Chamberlain in 1615 after having worked hard for several years to obtain the office. His object was not preferment, which he was too wealthy to need. He wanted that specific office in his hands. Though repeatedly offered higher positions, he as often rejected them. He would not consider parting with the Lord Chamberlainship except on the condition that his brother Philip succeeds him in it. The arrangement was made, but the succession did not take place until 1626 … Three years earlier, following the death of Sir George Buck, a young kinsman of Pembroke's, Sir Henry Herbert, had bought a lease on the office of the Master of the Revels. The public theatre was now hedged about with three Herberts.* [18]

As Lord Chamberlain, Pembroke exercised complete control over the theatre. The Master of the Revels was subordinate to him, and it was he who attended to the administrative details. Pembroke was also the brother-in-law of Lady Susan Vere, Countess of Montgomery, and Oxford's youngest daughter. Pembroke had once been engaged to Bridget, Susan's sister, but the premarital arrangement foundered over disagreement as to when the annuity promised to Bridget by Lord Burghley should commence. Despite this, the Herbert and de Vere families continued to remain close until the marriage of Philip and Susan made the bond permanent.

From 1615 onwards, Pembroke was in total control of the theatres; and it must have been soon after, that plans began to be made for the plays of his sister-in-law's father to be collected together for publication in what would become known as the First Folio. Only one obstacle stood in the way – Will Shaxpere. He was very much alive, and a potential hazard to the appearance of the plays, which in the public's mind, he had written.

It was therefore fortuitous that at the very beginning of 1616, within months of Pembroke taking office, Shaxpere, while being in perfect health, as he, himself, admitted, was persuaded to make out his last will and testament. It was to prove a fatal decision. No sooner had the will been finalised, albeit after a three-month period of indecisiveness, largely caused by the indiscretions of his daughter Judeth's fiancé, he was dead: leaving the way clear for publication of the plays, which for centuries to come would be described as his.

The First Folio was published in 1623 and is noticeable for the tributes that precede the plays. Amongst these is one from Leonard Digges.

> *Leonard Digges ... was an Oxford scholar; he was the stepson of Thomas Russell whom Shakespeare made the overseer of his will. Leonard Digges and his elder brother Sir Dudley Digges must have known Shakespeare, as Dr Hotson has shown, on familiar terms.* [19]

Hotson was probably correct, but for the wrong reason. In his poetic tribute, Digges begins by deliberately addressing his subject as '*SHAKE-SPEARE*', capitalised, and in its hyphenated form. This is in contrast to the heading of the tribute, which addresses the subject as, MAISTER W. SHAKESPEARE. Particular note should be made of the archaic use of 'MAISTER'. The reason being that Digges requires equally archaic meanings to be applied to the words in the third line, which read: *"And Time dissolues thy Stratford Moniment."*

As explained in Chapter 1 (p. 26), Digges was referring to a time when the riddle of the Stratford monument has been solved, and the truth it concealed is universally accepted. His hyphenated tribute to SHAKE-SPEARE is therefore not directed at Will Shaxpere, but dedicated to the Earl of Oxford.

Digges's subtle duplicity in registering the difference existing between Shakespeare and Shake(hyphen)speare suggests that what Hotson referred to as – *"his being on familiar terms"* with Shaxpere, had more to do with persuading him to write out his will than any conviviality existing between them. This would explain Digges having called upon his stepfather, who lived close to Stratford-upon-Avon, to become involved as an overseer. It also appears some form of persuasion was applied to Shaxpere in order to motivate him towards writing his will. Perhaps he had been assured that he could always rewrite it at a later date. For, judging by the time it took to finalise his list of bequests, it does not appear he had given much thought to the subject before then.

In the midst of making his bequests known, the pending marriage of his daughter Judeth, a beneficiary, unexpectedly entered a state of flux: it would therefore have been expedient for him to postpone further considerations until matters had become clearer and more settled in that direction. But, again, some urgency in the form of external pressure to finalise the will must have been exerted.

There are two further points to note. Firstly, with Thomas Russell acting as overseer, those involved with the First Folio had a direct link to Will Shaxpere, and were therefore able to rest content that no clause would find its way into the will that bequeathed a continuation of the money he received for his role as Oxford's allonym. Secondly, documentary evidence exists to support the suggestion that Shaxpere was continuing to receive hush money for his service to Oxford, even after the Earl's death.

The Countess of Oxford was buried at St Augustine's Church in Hackney on 3 January 1613, having succumbed to the effects of a virulent fever, referred to at the time as *"the new disease"*. In her will, made out six weeks earlier, she bequeathed a sum of money to be paid quarterly to a man she declined to name: calling him simply *"my dombe man."*[20]

Will Shaxpere had certainly earned the epithet, *"dombe man"* over the years in which he had allowed himself to be thought of as the author of plays and poems written by Lady Oxford's late husband. In fact, it is his dumbness that so perplexes those who attempt to connect him to the literary works of Shakespeare. For, quite apart from the similarity between the names Shaxpere and Shakespeare, there are no other substantive connections capable of withstanding careful scrutiny. Biographers have to make do with the sparse evidence that is available. This amounts to his commercial activities, his investment in the theatre, his family, his real estate, and his known associates: none of whom were literary men. By the careful use of language, these simple facts are wedded to the works of Shakespeare; then set to a scene of Elizabethan life in the capital city. And when Shakespeare's work does receive praise from contemporaries, as often occurs, it is Shaxpere who is given the credit. Yet, when Shaxpere died, not one person from the literary world so much as mentioned him.

While Shaxpere lived, a continuation of the reward he had enjoyed for his role in the cover-up would have been necessary. Consequently, if Shaxpere's silence was to be maintained after Lady Oxford's death, then further payments would have to be paid on a regular basis, and for as long as he remained alive; hence, the Countess' bequest to her *"dombe man":* a person she could never identify without divulging the connection this man had with her husband.

Shaxpere's will was intended to ensure the secret died with him, and was not passed on to enrich a member of his surviving family, who might inadvertently reveal the truth one day. The embarrassment, if not ridicule that threatened members of the Burghley, Oxford and Southampton households, if the scandal necessitating the concealment of Oxford's authorship became public knowledge, was a powerful force in ensuring all outlets to a wider domain were blocked. Providentially, Shaxpere's death followed almost as soon as the will was finalised. This not only guaranteed his perpetual silence, it also prevented him from altering his will at a later date. And, of course, it left those preparing the First Folio free to pursue their objective. There would no longer be the fear that Shakespeare's cover would be blown away by a confrontation between himself and a visiting member of the public, eager to question him about the plays.

Digges was not the only contributor to the First Folio who addressed Shakespeare by hyphenating his name. Another who did so, having identified himself as I. M., is assumed to have been James Mabbe, a fellow of Magdalen College. This may be doubted; Cambridge University was represented by Hugh Holland of Trinity College, who wrote his name in full. John Marston, representing the world of the theatre, is a more likely choice. In fact, Marston's name had previously appeared alongside that of Holland's when commending Jonson's publication of *Sejanus*; added to which, he had once before used the hyphenated form of Shake–speare in his title: *"To the Memorie of M. W. SHAKE-SPEARE"*. It would therefore be natural for him to reuse it in the First Folio, where, once again, it was directed at Oxford:

"We wondered (Shake–speare) that thou went'st so soone... "

The tributes appearing in the First Folio seem to follow a logical pattern. Leonard Digges and Hugh Holland represent the two great English universities, Oxford and Cambridge, and John Marston, who like Ben Jonson, gave only his initials, made his tribute on behalf of the world of theatre. Indeed, his poem is all about the theatre and its response to the author's death.

Marston had also written *Scourge of Villainy,* which is believed to include a coded aside to Oxford: *"Most, most of me beloved, whose silent name / One letter bounds. Thy true judicial style / I ever honour."* Marston then refers to this unnamed poet as *"my love"*, which, all told, makes him better qualified to be the I. M. of the First Folio, than James Mabbe, who has no part to play in the biographical accounts of Shaxpere: as is evident by the absence of his name in most indices relating to this man.

Jonson was the person closest to Oxford, as both a poet and a playwright, and it fell to him to act as the director and master of ceremonies when writing the main tribute to 'Shakespeare'. In this capacity, he first penned ten lines of verse beneath the engraving of an image, popularly believed to be a likeness of William Shakespeare. It is this that confronts the reader upon opening the First Folio. But Jonson was a master of double meanings. When circumstances required, he was well able to say what he meant, but without meaning what he appeared to say.

The Droeshout Engraving

The picture at the front of the First Folio, which supposedly represents William Shakespeare, is most unsatisfactory. It disappoints where most it should please. When one considers that the First Folio contains the greatest treasure of the English language; that it was dedicated to two of the highest-ranking members of the nobility: each of whom was a personal friend of King James; added to which, it was the most expensive book on the market, one can only look askance at why a hitherto unknown youth (he was born in 1601) was commissioned to portray a man who had died in far off Warwickshire, and who the artist was unlikely ever to have met. Yet, such was the case, and the reason for it seems bound up with the conditions imposed upon the young illustrator. In short, Martin Droeshout drew what he was instructed to draw: something an established artist with a reputation to protect would be unlikely to have agreed to, if the result was to be inartistic.

Martin Droeshout was the son of Flemish immigrants living in Southwark, close to the Globe; and he had yet to obtain a reputation in society. He was therefore a different proposition to an established artist. Moreover, he was unlikely to have met the subject of his engraving, which was of no consequence, because it was never intended that the figure he was commissioned to etch should be identifiable. Had he drawn a true likeness of Shaxpere, it would have attracted the attention of his London associates, some of whom had criminal connections. The picture would also have been recognised in the rural community where his family lived, especially by those with whom he did business. It was one thing to play the dumb man and allow people to believe he was Shakespeare. It was another matter to be portrayed in that role and be identified as the unlettered man he was.

Previous commentators have drawn specific attention to the curious, thick, unnatural line that extends upwards from beneath the chin of the figure to the lobe of the left ear. This, it has been suggested is the outline of an intended mask. The visage of the mask is understood to be that of Will Shaxpere, with Oxford's face concealed behind it. But the face is not that of Shaxpere (witness his image drawn by Dugdale), for it would have been too easily recognized by those able to expose his limitations and true character.

Since the visage is not that of Shaxpere, and cannot have been Oxford's: whose face is it? The answer is 'William Shakespeare': the man Oxford had invented to be the author of *Venus and Adonis,* and *The Rape of Lucrece.* In short, it is a symbolic cartoon that was intended to represent a person that existed in name only. It is an artist's invention. The figure therefore lends itself to a number of symbolic features.

The thick facial line, remarked upon above, divides the head in two: Shakespeare, forward-looking, presents his face to the public; the backward looking visage belongs to Oxford: turned away so that he cannot be seen in public. Thus, the two faces of Janus became Droeshout's model; aptly so, since: *"Janus, a dual-faced god, presided over all that is double-edged in life."* [21] It therefore made a fitting choice for representing the two faces of Oxford and Shakespeare.

To pursue this line of thought attention is drawn to the fact that the head of the figure is too large for the body. Artists and art connoisseurs alike have had no difficulty in arriving at the same conclusion. The result gives the figure's head an appearance of detachment, and this allows it to be seen as if separated from the torso; an important feature, as we shall soon discover.

Oxford's penname, William Shakespeare, operating behind the façade of Will Shaxpere, certainly fits this explanation. And the evidence for it being the correct interpretation is to be found within Droeshout's engraving. Principally, it is the doublet the figure is wearing, which commands most attention. For apart from the fact that the garment appears in the style of that worn by the subject of Hilliard's *Young Man With A Rose,* (shown inset), which was completed in 1617, Shaxpere's right arm is, without the least doubt, the rear view of the left arm. This, not unnaturally, is attached to the side back panel of the same garment, so that one half of the figure's attire appears to have its back turned to the viewer, while the figure's left arm and left breast panel face forward, as normal.

This observation was confirmed in two trade journals, *The Taylor and Cutter* (March, 1911), and the *Gentleman's Taylor* (April, 1911). Both agreed the figure was drawn from a composition of the front and back halves of the same doublet (p.449).

> *Gentlemen's Taylor, as long ago as 1911, had commented that the tunic "is so strangely illustrated that the right-hand side of the forepart*

is obviously the left-hand side of the back part and so gives a harlequin appearance to the figure which it is not unnatural to suppose was intentional, and done with express object and purpose."[22]

In other words, the doublet is displaying the Janus effect. One half is intended for the figure facing forwards, the other half is there to suggest what would be seen if the figure's back were turned to the observer. This is actually confirmed by the figure's ear. Instead of it being the lobe of the left ear, it is instead the rear part of the right ear.

The collar, too, is of interest. Until quite recently, it was believed to be a unique example. However the painstaking research of Derran Charlton, an English researcher, resulted in the discovery of a portrait found in a two-centuries-old book that referred to the Wentworth family. Thomas Wentworth, 1st Earl of Strafford (1593–1641), is seen wearing a starched, pleated collar that is virtually identical to the one drawn by Droeshout; the obvious difference being that Shakespeare's collar shows no observable means of fastening. By contrast, a ribbon tied in a bow secures that worn by Lord Wentworth. There is surely a subtle joke intended by choosing the Earl of Strafford as a model for Shakespeare. A paragram is a *"letter joke"*. By altering a single letter in a word or name, a *"low form of humour"* is achieved. Thus, the Earl of Strafford becomes the Earl of Stratford: a mocking dig at Stratford's Shaxpere who doubled for the Earl of Oxford.

Note the strange lack of any means for securing the collar in Droeshout's picture, which gives the impression of a shield. Presumably, this was intended to be a signal, alerting the more intellectually aware that the subject with his face turned away from the viewer was indeed being protected from sight. And since the Janus head is visibly shielded from the detached body, this piece of symbolism can be interpreted as a reference to the dual role of Oxford as Shakespeare, separated from, but shielded by, the body of his allonym, Will Shaxpere.

An opportunity to correct any inaccuracies was available to the editors of the *Poems Written by Wil. Shake-speare, Gent.* and published in 1640. This showed a re-drawing of the Droeshout engraving. But with the engraver retaining the Earl of Strafford's collar, and the shield-like effect it gave. He did, however, alter the doublet, since the face no longer suggests a Janus effect. Instead, he has added a cape to the figure's shoulder: attiring him as a gentleman of nobility. Lord Oxford can be seen wearing a similar cape (p.63). The figure also holds a sprig of hyssop: known also in France as belvedere. This was intended as a deliberate means of identifying Shakespeare as Oxford. When the second syllable of bel-ve-dere is inserted into the centre of the third syllable, it reads BEL DE VERE – Noble de Vere.

This method of naming the figure attests to the importance of the shield-like collar in the story of Shakespeare's double identity. As Charlton, remarked: *"I suggest that it would possibly have been most inappropriate for William Shakspere to have legally worn this type of nobleman-collar."*[23]

Charlton was correct. The figure's attire, by both Droeshout and Marshall, is inappropriate for a man of Shaxpere's class. And this was surely the whole point of the exercise. 'Shakespeare' was a nobleman, a courtier, and both illustrators express his status in their artistry, in the knowledge it was unlawful for a man of Shaxpere's class to wear an embroidered doublet or a cape.

> *In Elizabethan and Jacobean England, strict dress codes known as Sumptuary laws were well known by all the people. The penalties for violating sumptuary laws could be harsh. Heavy fines could be imposed for dressing out of one's class. The Renaissance culture required that everyone dress according to their status. ... Noblemen were allowed to wear a doublet of embroidered cloth ... According to Tarnya Cooper, curator of sixteenth-century portraits at the National Gallery in London, "the clothing a person wore was seen as a true reflection of his social status ... Only men above the rank of gentlemen could wear a cape over their clothing."*[24]

Portraits of Shakespeare's contemporaries, Jonson, Beaumont, Field, and Fletcher show each subject attired in the dress of their class. None wear an expensively embroidered doublet, such as that which adorns Droeshout's Shakespeare, and especially not the clothes engraved by Marshall in his illustration of the supposed author, for which he has actually added a cape; the prerogative of the nobility.

Fashion changes rather quickly, and it is therefore easy for later generations to take for granted a piece of apparel that was planned to be out of place when it was first illustrated. This appears to be true in the present case.

The evidence is overwhelming. Droeshout had been engaged to engrave a cartoon of the mythical 'Shakespeare' – resembling neither Oxford not Shaxpere – complete with a symbolic language that silently screamed the truth of what had taken place. A professional artist would have risked arrest for displaying the symbolism that appeared in the First Folio portrait of 'Shakespeare'. But Droeshout's apprentice status, and his never having met Shaxpere, was the reason for any 'innocent' errors that may have occurred. The symbolism was to be seen as the naïf mistakes of a beginner. Stratford dogma agrees upon this point. Nevertheless, the figure in the First Folio was specifically drawn to order, and it was for this reason that a young, previously unknown artist was chosen, instead of a more accomplished one, as would be expected for a book of such excellence.

When words are censored, a picture is left to tell the story, and that is precisely what Droeshout's engraving did by symbolising the underlying message found on the Stratford monument. William Shakespeare was the Earl of Oxford, as Jonson vowed to be the case, and others, like Thorpe, had confirmed in their own way. Even Oxford had identified himself in Sonnet 76 as the poet. Shaxpere was a provincial nobody, employed to deflect attention away from the nobleman and onto himself.

The professors' response to Droeshout is different, as expected; they condemn him for his ineptitude. Abandoning whatever principles of scholarship they once possessed, ignoring his proven prowess as an accomplished artist, they purposefully avert their gaze to avoid noticing the cryptic signals calling for their attention. Could it be they are fearful of coming to terms with the contradictions that would confront them, were they to reassess their ideas about Shakespeare in the light of this new evidence?

Despite his blackened reputation at the hands of modern-day 'experts', Martin Droeshout's career as an artist flourished, and he did not suffer from having received the commission to illustrate *Shakespeare* in a Janus pose. Instead, his reputation greatly prospered. Amongst men of note who later sat for him were the poet John Donne, the Duke of Buckingham, Lord Coventry, the Marquis of Hamilton, and the Bishop of Durham. And, in 1631, as a further mark of the respect afforded him, Droeshout was commissioned to make a set of engravings for the *Mikrokosmogrpahia*; this was a massive folio edition, running to more than a thousand pages.

Leonard Digges, like Thorpe, Jonson and Benson, was another, who was keenly aware that the use of Equi-distant Letter Sequencing, within a piece of text, could impart a secret message. When writing his tribute to Shakespeare for inclusion in the First Folio – it was actually set aside by Jonson in favour of his own poetic tribute – Digges made sure the leading sentence identified de Vere by name.

Digges' poem was not published until 1640, five years after his death, when it appeared alongside Benson's ELS encryption of E. de Vere and Mary Sidney (p. 254), and Marshall's nobly attired etching of 'Shakespeare', holding before him the sprig of belvedere that identifies the sitter as *'Noble de Vere'* (p. 450).

Remarkably, Benson's edition of *Poems Written by Wil. Shakespeare gent* contains three separate encryptions of de Vere by name: not to mention the question marks (? sic) that punctuate the lines beneath William Marshall's illustration of 'Shakespeare'.

Digges's poem begins with the lines:

> *Poets are borne not made, when I would prove*
> *This truth, the glad rememberance I must love*
> *Of never dying Shakespeare, who alone,*
> *Is argument enough to make that one.*
> *First, that he was a Poet none would doubt,*
> . . .

When these words are written into an 18-column grille, the result reveals a seven (or nine) letter vertical statement that repeats the now familiar name of E de Vere. The decryption was discovered by Art. Neuendorffer. The grille's setting is noteworthy, since it covers 18 columns; the key to this number being the number of letters that spell WILLIAM SHAKE-SPEARE, as it appears on the title page of Benson's book. At the same time de Vere's name is found in the 17th column, which coincides with Oxford's earldom.

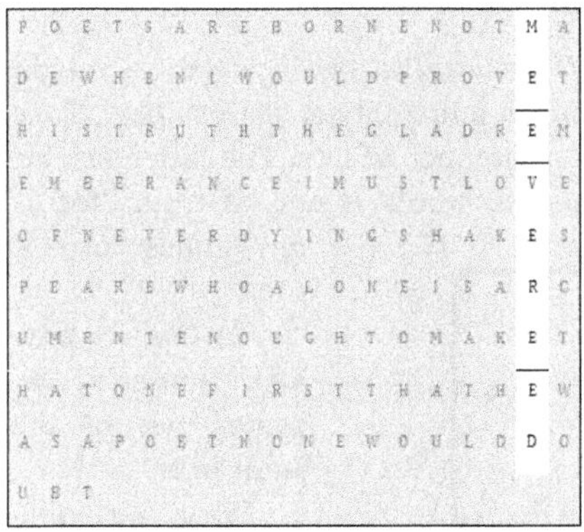

ME E VERE or ME E DE VERE

There was, in all of this undercover work, a consistency of purpose: put there to show the world at a later date, when these cryptic clues were seen and collected together, that William Shakespeare was Edward de Vere, and the secrecy surrounding it had once been paramount.

JONSON'S AMBIGUITY

Jonson had been taught by bitter experience to temper his style of writing after spending two terms of imprisonment for his part in penning *The Isle of Dogs* (1597), and *Eastward Ho*! (1605).

In the Isle of Dogs affair, he paid for his indiscretion with seven weeks' imprisonment, an experience that led him to 'temper' his style thereafter so that his targets were more ambiguous … [that is] by blending allusions … that could not be identified exclusively with specific victims. [25]

What, then, are these ambiguous allusions that occur in the tributes made to Shakespeare? And are there not to be found many straightforward expressions of fact that apply to Will Shaxpere, and which apply solely to him and no one else? A careful analysis of the letters and poems that precede the thirty-six plays by Shakespeare will answer that question.

Firstly there is Jonson's verse, which occurs opposite the Droeshout engraving. Little more may be said about this other than that Jonson disparages it as a likeness of the author. In his final couplet he exasperatingly exclaims: *"Reader, looke / Not on his Picture but his Booke."*

Jonson also admits: *"This figure, that thou here seest … was for gentle Shakespeare cut."* Jonson's ambiguity is at work here. Take note that it was *for* Shakespeare, not *of* him. The difference between the usage of these two words is one of truth; 'for' is ambiguous: 'of ' is not.

To the Reader.

This Figure, that thou here seest put,
It was for gentle Shakespeare cut;
Wherein the Grauer had a strife
with Nature, to out-doo the life:
O, could he but haue drawne his wit
As well in brasse, as he hath hit
His face, the Print would then surpasse
All, that was euer writ in brasse.
But, since he cannot, Reader, looke
Not on his Picture, but his Booke.

B. I.

To this, we may add Jonson's repeated use of the word 'brass'.

What was Jonson alluding to that had been *written in brass*? Engravings, such as that made by Droeshout, were etched on copper, not brass. However, if Jonson was using the word 'brass' as a synonym for 'effrontery', then 'writ in brass' makes perfect sense, *if* applied to Will Shaxpere. 'Shakespeare' had used 'brass' in a similar manner when writing dialogue for BEROWNE, in *Love's Labour's Lost*: *"Can any face of brass hold longer out?"* (Act 5, sc. ii). The OED describes this as the first example of 'brass' used to express *"insensibility to shame: hence Effrontery."*

Turning next to the first of the two letters signed by *"Iohn Heminge and Henrie Condell"*, the following statement stands out: *"he not having the fate, common with some, to be exequutor to his owne writings"*. Ben Jonson was executor to his own writings, which he published midway through his career. Had Will Shaxpere been the author Shakespeare, then he would certainly have been at leisure. While in retirement at Stratford-upon-Avon, from 1605 onwards, he had a great deal of time in those eleven years before his death, to have at least begun, if not finished, what Jonson had comfortably completed by 1616.

In the second of their letters, Heminge and Condell repeat the same longing. *"It had bene a thing, we confesse, worthie to haue bene wished, that the Author himselfe had liu'd to haue set forth, and ouerseene his owne writings."* This is followed by an admission: *"as where (before) you were abus'd with diuerse stolne, and surreptitious copies, maimed, and deformed by the frauds and stealthes of injurious imposters, that expos'd them."* Here we have a blatant admission that the previously published quartos of the plays, of which there were no less than fifty-one, were unauthorized, and that nothing had been done to remedy the situation.

Instead, these *"stolen and surreptitious copies, maimed and deformed by the frauds and stealth of injurious impostors"* had been allowed to continue unchecked from 1591 to 1623.

This neglect implicitly confirms that someone of Oxford's high birth had authored the plays, and that unscrupulous publishers had stolen his work, being well aware there could be no repercussions without revealing the true identity of the author.

Of these 51 quartos, 20 were published without naming the author, despite Shakespeare's popularity as the poet made famous by *Venus and Adonis* and *The Rape of Lucrece.* It was not until 1598, when Meres gave the green light to 'Shakespeare's' name appearing as author of twelve previously anonymous plays that publishers began appending Shakespeare's name to their pirate editions. Even then, many stopped short of naming him outright. Only fourteen quartos contain the name in full: of those remaining, fifteen hyphenate the surname; another presents it as William Shakespere, and one simply abbreviates it to W. Sh. (Statistics by Dr. Joachim Gerstenberg: *Willobie His Avisa,*

Baconiana, LIII, No. 170, November 1970, p. 58).

Foremost in importance of the tributes paid to Shakespeare is Ben Jonson's praise. It consists of forty couplets, but without divulging a single biographical fact that is attributable to Will Shaxpere; ambiguities are another matter.

The tribute commences with nine couplets that serve as an introduction to what follows. The tenth quickly refutes the plea made by William Basse that Shakespeare be allowed to share a tomb in Westminster Abbey with Chaucer, Spenser, and Beaumont. And, in case there was any doubt as to which of the two 'Shakespeares' Bass had in mind, he has conveniently identified his intended subject by adding the date of the man's decease – the one *"who died in April 1616"*.

Basse's poem was strategically written shortly before the First Folio was published, which gave Jonson just the time needed to make his reply public, and thus pre-empt any future attempt by popular appeal, urging for Will Shaxpere's interment amongst the great Englishmen of literature (p. 151).

My Shakespeare, rise; I will not lodge thee by
Chaucer, or Spenser, or bid Beaumont lye
A little further, to make thee a roome:
Thou art a Moniment, without a tombe,

Perhaps Jonson had in mind his own death one day, and had no wish to share eternity with an impostor, whom he had once caricatured as the clown, SOGLIARDO (p. 100).

A little further on, Jonson wrote these curious lines.

For, if I thought my judgement were of yeeres,
I should commit thee surely with thy peeres,
And tell, how farre thou didst our Lily out-shine,
Or sporting Kid, or Marlowes mighty line.

This is a strange admission. It claims that if Jonson's judgement had been conditional upon time (and why should it not have been?) he would have placed Shakespeare amongst the men of literature who had once been his own peer group; these, he identified as Lyly, Kyd and Marlowe.

John Lyly (c.1554 – 1606) was for many years a secretary to Oxford, and subsequently his theatre manager. While lodging at the Savoy, a tenement that seems to have been funded by Oxford for the benefit of promising writers, Lyly produced the much acclaimed *Euphues The Anatomy of Wit* (1578), followed by *Euphues and his England* (1580); he dedicated this second book to Oxford. Both works gave rise to a style of expression known as 'Euphuism': for which, Oxford became its leading exponent.

At a later date, Gabriel Harvey reminded Lyly of — *"thy old acquaintance in the Savoy, when young Euphues hatched the eggs that his elder friends laid."* [26] Lyly's response to Harvey's jibe occurs in his dedication to Oxford. There, he admits that the first of his *"two children was delivered before my friends thought me conceived,"* and that of these, *Euphues* was *"sent to a Nobleman to nurse, who with great love brought him up for a year."* [27] In common with these references is Oxford. He is firstly, Lyly's *"old acquaintance"*; secondly *"young Euphues"*, and thirdly the *"Nobleman"*.

A connection between Lyly's 'Euphuistic style' and Shakespeare is unavoidable, especially since Jonson refers to Lyly in the First Folio. Unsurprisingly, this leads Shaxpere's supporters to put the cart before the horse. It has to be Shakespeare who learnt from Lyly.

R. W. Bond, in his three-volume work (*Life, Essays, Notes in the Complete Works of John Lyly*, Oxford, 1902), devoted nine pages to the parallels existing between *Euphues* and Shakespeare, heading it as: *What Shakespeare Owes to Lyly.*

> *First of all he owes him very much for the example of intercourse between refined and well-bred folk, conducted with ease, grace, and naturalness; and especially of such among women, and of the flippant, tantalizing treatment of their lovers by women. As part of this he is his debtor for the example of a prose-dialogue, either brisk and witty or adorned with learning and fancy … [which] is yet as near the best talk of the day as was consistent with the literary heightening demanded for current effect and permanent vitality.* [28]

Despite Bond's glowing reference to Lyly as Shakespeare's mentor, there is no record that Lyly ever met Shaxpere, yet the opportunity was available. Lyly lived on until 1606, and was buried in London.

It was while in his position as Oxford's secretary that Lyly wrote a number of plays for boy actors to perform at Court. Amongst which are counted: *Alexander, Campaspe and Diogenes, Sapho and Phao*. But note!

The attractive songs in the plays, including such well known lyrics as 'Cupid and my Campaspe played' ... it is doubtful to what extent they are the work of Lyly. [29]

When one calls to mind the equally *"attractive songs in the plays"* of 'Shakespeare', the connection is too obvious to be ignored.

Before coming into contact with Oxford, Lyly had written nothing. After leaving his service, his inspiration faded and he produced nothing more of value.

Lyly was the most successful and fashionable of English writers, hailed as the author of "a new English," as a "raffineur de l'Anglois"; and, as Edward Blount, the editor of his plays, tells us in 1632, "that beautie in court which could not parley Euphuism was as little regarded as she which nowe there speakes not French." After the publication of Euphues Lyly seems to have entirely deserted the novel form ... and to have thrown himself almost exclusively into playwriting ... After 1590 his works steadily declined in influence and reputation; he died poor and neglected in the early part of James I's reign. [30]

One cannot help but draw a comparison with Will Shaxpere in the guise of Shakespeare. He came into contact with Oxford, judging from *Greene's Groatsworth of Wit, circa* 1592, having written nothing; at least, nothing that anyone has ever heard of. From that time onwards, until the death of Oxford twelve years later, the majority of 'Shakespeare's' plays and poems are said to have been written by him. After 1604, Shaxpere retires from the scene, and only special pleading by apologists encourages the belief that he continued writing in retirement.

Jonson's remaining two references are to Kyd who, like Lyly, also flourished in the 1580s, and Marlowe (1564 – 1593). Kyd is mostly associated with the anonymous play, *The Spanish Tragedy,* which was said to have competed with *Titus Andronicus* during the second half of that decade (p. 401). Kyd was arrested in 1593 and interrogated under torture. This is thought to have contributed to his early death in the following year. Under pain, he revealed Marlowe's atheism, while admitting that . . .

My first acquaintance with this Marlowe, rose from his bearing name to serve my Lord, although his Lordship never knew his service, but in writing for his players.

Dr Boas [*Christopher Marlowe*, Oxford, 1940], commented: [31]

> *It is one of the most tantalizing problems in Marlovian biography that Kyd omits to give a clue to the identification of this lord of whose household he had been a member in some capacity for nearly six years.*

Boas' gloom could have been lightened by awareness that shortly after Marlowe's departure from Cambridge, he arrived in London and took lodgings in the Norton Folgate district; he was then a short walk from Fishers Folly. Lord Oxford then owned this house, built in the style of a Folly, which stood close to Houndsditch, and was used as a centre for writers of promise.

This idea was based upon Renaissance art studios in Italy. A master would be in overall control, and apprentice artists, who variously contributed to each finished product, would produce works of art, with the master applying the finishing touches. If Oxford was applying the same principle, as it is believed, this would account for the Marlovian phrases found in the work of Shakespeare, and which have caused some to believe that Marlowe was either Shakespeare, or his instructor.

The truth is surely the other way round. The Marlovian phrases were actually coined by Oxford in his early plays, which he later revised in the 1590s. These then became known as the works of Shakespeare. In this sense, Shakespeare came after Marlowe, although Marlowe followed Oxford; that is, before Oxford adopted the penname Shakespeare, which dates from 1592.

One suspects it was Lyly who first arranged for Marlowe to meet Oxford. Both he and Lyly were from Canterbury. It would therefore be natural to suppose that upon arriving in London, Marlowe made contact with his fellow countryman in the hope of finding suitable employment. An introduction to Oxford's 'college' at Fishers Folly, followed by an invitation to join in the work produced there, seems the most likely course of events. It would certainly satisfy Kyd's remark that Marlowe was writing for the players of an unnamed Lord.

Let it be recalled, too, that Marlowe was a guest of Oxford in company with Thomas Nashe and Robert Greene, when all four dined together at a banquet held in the late summer of 1592, prior to William Shakespeare being launched as the author of *Venus and Adonis* (pp. 61-63). Marlowe would therefore have been a member of Oxford's group of writers.

Jonson's reference to Lyly, Kyd and Marlowe being the peer

group of 'Shakespeare' now makes better sense, but only because it can be understood as a reference to Oxford's penname. And it is this penname that takes us to the next part of Jonson's verse.

And though thou hadst small Latine and lesse Greeke,
From thence to honour thee, I would not seeke
For names; but call forth thund'ring Æschylus,
Euripides, and Sophocles to vs,

The opening remark is ambiguous. It can be read, firstly, as: 'And *although* you had very little Latin and even less Greek...' thus seeming to imply Jonson's superiority in recognizing that 'Shakespeare's early education did not seem adequate enough to prepare him for the plays he wrote. The Stratford fraternity prefer this interpretation because it allows them to cock a snoop at Jonson, by demonstrating their favourite's command of the classics, which is indicated in Shakespeare's plays and poetry.

The alternative interpretation is to read the phrase as: 'And *even if* you had very little Latin and even less Greek...' thus allowing the poet to have had an education on a par with Jonson. This makes uncomfortable reading for Shaxpere's advocates, since Jonson's education at Westminster School is well documented, whereas Shaxpere's schooldays in Stratford-upon-Avon require special pleading: the student rolls for that period having been conveniently 'lost'.

Professor Gervinus, a scholarly supporter of Shakespeare's erudition, believed Jonson most certainly did intend his comment to be a tribute to the poet's command of the classics:

> *This poem consists throughout of such boundless, well-nigh extravagant praise of Shakespeare that I do not believe that the line, 'And though thou hadst small Latine and lesse Greeke,' can be interpreted as detracting from his merits. The spirit of the whole passage is this: 'And even though thou hadst small Latin and less Greek, yet is there in that bygone age no lack of tongues to sound thy praise; for even Æschylus, Sophocles, and the rest would render a tribute of admiration to the power of thy words.'*[32]

In fact, the scholarship contained within Shakespeare's plays and poetry proves the truth of Gervinus's well-reasoned opinion. But in doing so, it undermines the case for Shaxpere, because there is not one shred of documentary evidence that he acquired even one of the books that inspired so many of Shakespeare's plays.

> *In the Comedy of Errors he has worked at a play of Plautus. In the Taming of the Shrew, the 'Supposes' of Ariosto is the foundation—a piece written in the spirit of the Latin comedies. Shakespeare was thoroughly acquainted with the works of Seneca; in his Cymbeline, after the manner of this poet, he makes the presiding divinity appear and speak in the same antique metre in which Heywood and Studley had imitated the Latin tragedist ... Which, however, of his contemporaries could have apprehended a piece of the old world with such a clear eye as he did the Roman nature in the three histories of Coriolanus, Cæsar, and Antony? ... but let us read Shakespeare's Troilus and Cressida, and ask ourselves whether this wonderful counterfeit imitation of the Homeric heroes were possible to any man who had not grasped thoroughly the substance and spirit of the old epic poets?* [33]

To suppose that Jonson would not have recognized these facts himself, and instead defied his own awareness by writing disparagingly about Shakespeare's grasp of the classics is absurd: the more so when everything else Jonson said about Shakespeare glowed with his honest admiration for the man. Nevertheless, the phrase has been deliberately constructed to allow a double meaning, since the ban on Oxford's identity as Shakespeare has still to be preserved.

As we approach the end of these fifty couplets, and still with nothing biographical to precisely identify the man vaunted as the supreme genius of the written word, Jonson's oft-repeated lines occur; these we are told fill that void.

> *Sweet Swan of Auon! What a sight it were*
> *To see thee in our waters yet appeare,*
> *And make those flights vpon the bankes of Thames*
> *That so did take Eliza and our Iames !*

Will Shaxpere, having been born in Stratford-upon-Avon, is naturally the principal candidate for the intended meaning of this expression. If this were the only truth behind the author's meaning, then little more could be said. But Jonson has gone to extraordinary lengths to be ambiguous in whatever could be construed as applying to 'Shakespeare'. The Stratford monument, erected in what appears to be the same year as publication of the First Folio, actually has a bust of its Stratford resident above an inscription containing two encryptions, each of which states – contrary to the figure it represents – that Edward de Vere was Shakespeare. How ambiguous is that? Consequently, the question must be asked: Does 'Sweet Swan of Avon' also have a second meaning: one, perhaps, that applies directly to de Vere?

Before answering this, let us consider the meanings attached to some alternative expressions. For example, the Prince of Wales and the Duke of Edinburgh are titles: neither of these require that the Prince or the Duke were born at these locations. George I and William III were both Kings of England, although both were raised on the Continent. The Merchant of Venice may have been born in that city, or he may have been born elsewhere; the importance to the story is that ANTONIO was trading in Venice at the time of the play's action.

The same can be said for *The Hunchback of Notre Dame*, or *The Tenant of Wildfell Hall*, or *The Jackdaw of Rheims*. Then there is *The Pied Piper of Hamlin;* he was a stranger to this German town until he arrived; and the *Hound of the Baskervilles* was not kept at Baskerville Hall. In each case, it is not where the subject of the expression was born or raised, but where they were known for what they achieved.

We have already seen firm evidence that Edward de Vere had been a welcome guest at Wilton House: a residence whose parkland is watered by the Avon and its tributary the Nadder. It was also where some of *Shakespeare's* best loved work was written.

In former times, Wilton House was a mansion celebrated for its contribution to literature, learning and scholarship. It was run by Lady Mary Herbert, sister of Sir Philip Sidney, the poet and soldier, killed in 1586. The house was also a place later frequented by Jonson, and where he was given accommodation to pursue his Court masques in partnership with Inigo Jones.

Wilton, we recall, was home to those two noble earls, William and Philip Herbert, to whom the First Folio was dedicated: Philip having married Lady Susan Vere, Oxford's daughter.

There is another interesting link between Jonson and Oxford; it occurs in the manner which the First Folio's tribute to 'Shakespeare' has been expressed. The late Ruth Loyd Miller referred to this in her *Oxfordian Vistas*, and Charlton Ogburn, too, noted it in his, *Mystery of William Shakespeare* (pp. 649-50).

In 1590 Edmund Spenser published his Faerie Queen. The work ... was preceded by half a dozen tributes in verse from other poets. The last is by Ignoto. ...

Thus then, to show my judgement to be such
As can discern of colours black and white
As else to free my mind from envy's touch,
...
I here pronounce this workmanship is such
As that no pen can set it forth too much.

IGNOTO, translated from Latin into English, means *"by the unknown"*. Miller identified this with Oxford; her reason being based upon the dedicatory sonnet that Spenser had addressed to the 17th Earl, in which he lavished unremitting praise upon his subject: declaring there to be a mutual relationship between him and the Muses.

Jonson had evidently noticed in this extract a similarity to the same admiration that he also wished to express. No doubt he thought that other eyes would eventually connect it to the IGNOTO verse, and from there, connect it to the Droeshout engraving with its supportive symbolism.

To draw no envy (Shakespeare) on thy name,
Am I thus ample to thy Book and Fame;
While I confess thy writings to be such,
As neither Man, not Muse, can praise too much.

By itself, this proves nothing. But taken as an integral part of everything else that was being done to point posterity towards the truth about Shakespeare's identity, it is entirely relevant.

In 1623, when the First Folio went on sale, Stratford-upon-Avon was a quiet and insignificant place: even unheard of by many people. It took one and a half centuries before the residents awoke one day to discover that people from the world outside were actively gathering on their doorsteps to celebrate a former local merchant as the great literary genius, William Shakespeare.

Why had the town not celebrated this before? Perhaps it was because the dignitaries of the town already knew the rumours surrounding their Shaxpere; and knew too well the limited education of his family and also that of the man himself. To have claimed honour for the town upon a false rumour would have held the whole community up to ridicule, if the truth came out; as they must have suspected would happen one day. But if the world called at their door and informed them of their former resident's literary background, then the fault was not of their making. They could stand back in all humility and beg acceptance for what they had been told. The sequence of events confirms this is what actually happened.

> *It was in 1769 that Stratford came into its own ... with a three-day jubilee staged there by David Garrick to make a suitable occasion of his presentation to the town of a cast of the Westminster statue. A century and a half after his death, Will Shakspere had finally and fully arrived.*[34]

The Westminster statue refers to the one in Poets' Corner, contrary to Jonson's best efforts to keep an impostor from being honoured in this hallowed place. *"Silliest ignorance",* coupled with *"blind affection"* had finally triumphed over truth.

Jonson does, however, cast one last glimmering ray of light upon the man he called *"Soul of the Age".* In the finale to his tribute, he writes: *"Shine forth, thou Starre of Poets,"* a fairly innocuous metaphor it may seem; that is, unless you happen to know that the de Vere coat of arms contains a lone star emblazoned on its upper left quadrant.

Peripheral Ambiguities

Of the remaining tributes, Hugh Holland's sonnet praises Shakespeare for his contribution to the stage. Leonard Digges, whom we met before with his obsolete English, which he used to draw attention to the riddle attached to the *Stratford Moniment,* has followed Holland by hyphenating the deceased's name twice, before adding further praise for the poet. I. M. completes the homage to Shakespeare by again, twice hyphenating his name, but adding nothing that would identify him as being the person from Stratford-upon-Avon. Devotees to the traditional image of Shakespeare should stop and wonder, even ask themselves: Why it is that within this magnificent tribute to the writer, his name repeatedly appears hyphenated? Yet, in church records, on legal documents, and in business records, the hyphen is absent.

Two letters signed jointly by the son of a fishmonger and a grocer accompany these poems. These two actors claimed it was they alone who had gone out to collect all of Shakespeare's thirty-six plays; and afterwards, had put their heads together and edited them. A story that is so ridiculous, it borders on the farcical. The cost of producing such a large book was estimated to be between £2340 and £5340 (≈ £650,000 – £1,500,000); well beyond the reach of two family men like Heminge and Condell.

Apart from this, there is that short verse by Jonson distancing himself from the accuracy of Droeshout's engraving. And although he accompanies this with a much longer tribute to the works of Shakespeare, this is completely devoid of anything about the author that could be called uniquely biographical.

Taken on trust, otherwise the contradictions and absurdities would undo years of creating Shaxpere in the guise of Shakespeare, the First Folio still provides the main pillar of support for the man identified as the wool merchant's son from Stratford-upon-Avon. It is an identification that academics from around the world are required to accept as dogma; to teach dogma, and defend dogma; that is, if they wish to prosper in their chosen field of English literature.[35]

Woe to dissidents who refuse to accept the establishment's paradigm; their career ambitions will be cut short with a snarl before they have had time to begin. No tutor or lecturer wishes to be awakened from their dreams of *"sweet Mr Shakspeare"*, only to discover that, like TITANIA, they have been enamoured with an ass. The universities are the culprits in perpetuating deceit. By offering tenure only to those with ambitions to pursue a single direction for their research, they embed a professorship that is guaranteed to maintain its stranglehold upon every truth that is potentially unfavourable to the accepted dogma.

It has been said that if one gives a lie sufficient start, it will never be caught. Well, the chase has certainly begun. It is time those who *are* concerned to see truth prevail, engage themselves to the fact that when a repressed people are made mute by authority, honest men will speak in the language of secrecy. That language, often expressed in cryptography, represents a far more honest account of suppressed truths within an authoritative society, than documents obedient to the regime.

Let the Folger Shakespeare Library, with its huge resources, now take a leading role in establishing the case for Oxford as the pen behind Shakespeare's name. In 1957, the Folger awarded America's great cryptographer and wartime hero William Friedman, its prize for the work he had done in explaining the conditions necessary for a valid cryptographic solution to exist, and why the claims made by Francis Bacon's support group failed to match these. But Friedman and his wife (also a noted cryptographer), also stated, categorically:

> *To be convinced that the authenticity of a literary idol could never be impugned even by a genuine cipher is an arbitrary attitude, and we do not share it.*
>
> (The Shakespearean Ciphers Examined, p. 14)

The Folger's course of action is therefore clear; that is, if it is not to impugn Jonson's avowal (p.14), or Oxford's personal declaration encoded in Sonnet 76 (p.201); supported as these are by the assertions of Thorpe (p.180), Benson (p.254), and Digges (p.453). The fact that Jonson, Thorpe, and Digges were contemporaries of Oxford, and they identify Oxford as Shakespeare by following the same cryptographic system made famous by Cardano's contribution to steganography in 1550, is more than suffient evidence that their statements are to be relied upon.

Moreover, the vow Jonson made on the Stratford monument is obliquely connected to his conversations with William Drummond (*Conv.*, 1, 658). Jonson had confided that, *"of all styles, he loved most to be named honest."* Those who deny Jonson's encryption, which includes the Folger Shakespeare Library, impugn his honesty; for the vow he encrypted into the sixaine below the bust of Shaxpere meets the requirements stipulated by the Friedmans. The Folger accepted the Friedmans' conclusions, because it was their 1957 book (re-issued in 2011), that earned the pair the Folger Shakespeare literary prize. This does mean the Folger must now prove to all, that it is not prone to double standards?

Jonson's passion for literature and his admiration for Shakespeare rebelled against the censorship made necessary to avoid the scandal which threatened to engulf the families of Burghley, Oxford, and Southampton. Playwrights and actors had not then acquired the elevated status they now enjoy, and suppression by the ruling class against the acting fraternity was commonplace. Jonson's response was to employ the latest method of secrecy invented by Girolamo Cardano, and use it to secrete the truth about Shakespeare into the inscription on the monument at Stratford-upon-Avon.

Added to this, he took virtual control of the dedications to Shakespeare that were to appear in the First Folio, and he saw to it that Droeshout's engraving complemented his own encrypted avowal of de Vere's authorship. At the same time, with one eye on the censors, he praised Shakespeare's work in glowing but ambiguous terminology. The facts are there; they all fit neatly together, acknowledgement of them is all that is required for the truth to finally prevail. Only an outdated dogma opposes it.

Apart from those who were directly involved in the financing and preparation of Shakespeare's collected *Comedies, Histories and Tragedies*, there were at least two others on the periphery of what was taking place. William Basse was one of these. It was he who proposed that Will Shaxpere (whom he thought necessary to identify by providing the man's date of death) should be laid to rest alongside Chaucer, Spenser and Beaumont inside Westminster Abbey. This prearranged set-up between Jonson and Basse was timed specifically to allow Jonson to publicly refute the suggestion at the front of the First Folio, where it would carry most weight and avoid neglect.

Another person on the periphery of the cover-up was Henry Peacham, the son of the Reverend Henry Peacham: the curate who had attended an early version of *Titus Andronicus* in 1574, and immortalised the occasion by drawing a scene from the play, complete with accompanying dialogue (Chapter 8). Without the least doubt, both father and son were well aware of who Shakespeare was in real life. In 1612 the younger of the two had published *Minerva Britanna*, (the British Minerva), a book of emblems. His choice of title is not without interest.

> *Minerva (in Greek, Athe'nē). The most famous statue of this goddess was by Phidias, the Greek sculptor. It was wood encased with ivory; the drapery, however, was of solid gold. It represented the goddess standing clothed with a tunic reaching to the ankles, a spear in her left hand, and an image of Victory (four cubits high = about six feet) in her right ... This statue was anciently one of the 'Seven Wonders of the World.'*[36]

Shakespeare as the British Minerva is not without appeal, the more especially since he was voted 'Man of the Millennium' at the turn of the last century.

A similar highflying notion may have occurred to Peacham, because he accompanied the title of his book with an illustration that has intrigued readers ever since. It shows a hand holding a pen with the forearm extended. But the man is concealed behind the arras of a discovery space (a curtained area occupying an alcove at the rear of the stage); the hand is in the process of completing a Latin inscription — MENTE. VIDEBOR˙ *"By the mind I shall be seen."*

Surrounding the illustration of the arm and hand is another scroll. This reads: VIVITUR. INGENIO. CAETERA. MORTIS. ERUNT: *"One lives by means of one's genius, the rest belongs to death"*. Both Latin mottoes are applicable to the man who secretly wrote the works of Shakespeare. This becomes even more revealing when it is understood that the declaration takes place on stage, inside the curtained area of the discovery space and that only the writer's hand and forearm are exposed to the audience.

It is important, too, to note that Peacham's book *"displays a dazzling preoccupation with word puzzles of various kinds—amongst them, prominently, anagrams."* [37] An anagram may therefore be suspected in the present case, particularly since the secretiveness of the figure is already implied by its concealed presence.

It is by rearranging the letters in MENTE. VIDEBOR˙ that TIB· NOM DE VERE is formed; so that by substituting an 'I' for the super-scripted dot, TIBI NOM DE VERE IS FORMED – *Thy name is de Vere,* which becomes a perfect anagram.

Perfect anagrams are specifically ones where the rearranged letters are connected to the meaning conveyed

MINERVA
BRITANNA
OR A GARDEN OF HEROICAL
Deuises, furnished, and adorned with *Emblemes* and *Impresa's* of sundry natures, Newly devised, *moralized, and published,*
By HENRY PEACHAM, Mr. of Artes.
LONDON
Printed in Shoe-lane at the signe of the Faulcon by Wa: Dight.

by original formation; for example, STATUE OF LIBERTY is a perfect anagram of BUILT TO STAY FREE.

In the Peacham anagram, because of the secrecy surrounding Shakespeare's authorship, the phrase: *"By the Mind I shall be seen"* connects logically to: *"Thy Name is de Vere"*. The scroll surrounding this epithet also refers to de Vere, because *"One lives by means of one's genius, the rest belongs to death"*, describes the relationship between the writer and his work.

Since Eva Turner Clarke first suggested this solution (*The Man Who Was Shakespeare,* New York, 1937), the anagram has been surrounded by controversy. The dispute centres upon the substitution of 'I' for the dot, which is required to complete 'TIBI'. Why, it is asked, should 'I' be especially chosen to fill the gap?

Observe the penned dot · immediately following VIDEBOR. This, the argument goes, implies that the letter 'I' was in the process of being written. However, against this, VIDEBORI is not a word existing in the Latin language. Had it been so, Peacham would have inserted the 'I' himself—and why not? Thirdly, the letters are all capitals, and a capital 'I' does not need to be dotted.

Let us therefore take note of the subtle clue that Peacham has introduced into his picture. It is the pen held by the mysterious figure, which is still attached to the motto, and next to the last letter of VIDEBOR˙, thus forming a dot. This is unusual, therefore suspiciously purposeful. The dot is most surely part of the solution: otherwise it would not be there. By placing the dot into the rearranged lettering; e.g. TIB· NOM DE VERE, it can now stand in for the missing 'I', which is required to complete TIBI, and thus complete a perfect anagram. Moreover, we are told by Peacham that we must mentally visualise the 'I', for this instruction is found in MENTE. VIDEBOR˙, (By the mind: **I** SHALL be seen).

This phrase thus carries a double meaning: as one would expect in a book, specialising in puzzles, riddles and anagrams. Both meanings of the phrase: BY THE MIND **I** SHALL BE SEEN are required to solve the identity of the unseen writer, whose arm protrudes from its concealment behind the theatrical curtain. Peacham's drawing has posed the question: Who is concealed in the discovery space? To provide an answer, the meaning behind the Latin mottos must first be understood. When this is achieved, the 'I' refers to the person who is the subject of the motto. At the same time, this 'I' refers to the ninth letter of the alphabet. When that is realised, and the letter 'I' is seen *by the mind* in place of the dot, which is used when rearranging the letters of MENTE. VIDEBOR´, the identity of the mysterious subject is revealed by name – *"de Vere;* [38] for which the accompanying mottos are entirely apt.

The hidden identity, the theatrical curtain, the discovery space, the hand holding a pen: these are all aptly symbolic of the secrecy attending the Earl of Oxford's authorship of Shakespeare's plays and poems. Because of this revelation, especially by a contemporary of Shakespeare's, attempts have been made to disprove the anagram. Three principal arguments stand out. The first of which is that the letters in MENTE. VIDEBOR´ are capable of different arrangements. But against this, none of the suggested alternatives form *perfect* Latin anagrams, unlike TIBI NOM DE VERE. The second objection is that MENTE. VIDEBOR´ contains only 12 letters, whereas TIBI NOM DE VERE has 13. The dot, which substitutes for 'I', is rejected on the grounds that Peacham left no precedent to validate it.

This is untrue; not only does a precedent exist, but Peacham also gave his name to it (*Minerva Britanna* p. 177). HINC SUPER HAC, MUSA (with 16 letters) is used for an anagram of HENRICUS PEACHAMUS (with 17 letters). Peacham's solution includes the additional letter 'E'. How is this justified? The answer is simple. Peacham introduced a comma after HAC, which he then uses as an 'E' to complete his name as the solution. In a similar manner, a dot was substituted by 'I' to complete the Vere anagram: identifying the absent letter by adding that 'I' was to be seen in the mind. Incidentally, HACE is not a Latin word; therefore the comma after HAC, only becomes an 'E' when it forms part of the solution.

The third objection is that the suggested anagram includes the word NOM. This, it is claimed, is not a recognised abbreviation for the Latin word NOMEN. Again this is false. Confirmation of the abbreviation NOM for NOMEN occurs in Adriano Capelli's *Dizionario De Abbreviature Latine* published in Italy in 1961.

So, once again, de Vere is seen within his society as a secretive figure: a man whose identity could only be revealed by symbols, subtle codes and riddles. Given that we now have solutions to the ELS devices of Thorpe, Jonson, Digges, Benson and Oxford, himself: we can add to these, Peacham's *Minerva Britanna* as yet another source revealing the identity of William Shakespeare.

Peacham's position was one he used to advantage. Not only did he publish *Minerva Britanna* (Minerva being the goddess of wisdom and the arts) with its enigmatic illustration on the title page alluding to Vere as a genius and playwright hidden from public view, he also published a collection of epigrams. These appeared in *The More The Merrier* (1608), and a further set in *Thalia's Banquet* (1620). Numbered amongst those to whom he dedicated a verse were Ben Jonson, Michael Drayton, John Seldon, William Byrd, and John Dowland. Exceptionally, since Peacham is the Stratford professors' unanimous choice for having copied the Titus Manuscript, he omitted writing an epigram for its author, William Shakespeare. Nor was this in any way due to his lack of scholarship. For Peacham followed *Thalia's Banquet* with *The Complete Gentleman ...*

> *his best-known work, and it occupies a significant place in the history of courtesy literature ... The learning displayed here offers ample justification for Peacham's claim "By profession I am a Scholler."* [39]

This book, published in 1622, was intended to coincide with the publication of the First Folio. In which case, let it be asked: Why does Peacham omit even a single mention of Shakespeare by name?

In a chapter on Poetry, Peacham extols those *"who honoured poesie with their pens and practice,"* men who had made Elizabeth's England *"a golden age (for such a world of refined wits and excellent spirits it produced whose like are hardly to be hoped for in any succeeding age)."* [40]

He then listed the names of those amongst the deceased who exemplified his report. At the very top of the list he placed *"Edward Earl of Oxford"*: a man who had died almost twenty years ago, leaving behind only a handful of juvenile poems and songs to his name. Unless, that is, Peacham's enigmatic illustration with its Latin mottos holds the reason for his neglect.

Both Peacham's *Minerva Britanna* and the Stratford monument appeared at about the same time; both contradicting in their own way the image of Shakespeare as it was to appear in the First Folio. Moreover, Droeshout's strange sartorial image of Shakespeare has nothing in common with the bust of Shaxpere the merchant, which was set in place at that time inside the parish church at Stratford-upon-Avon. Why the difference—if not because these images represented two different men?

The close proximity of the dates on which the First Folio and Peacham's book were intended for publication may have been purposefully contrived. For while the First Folio was appearing to confirm Shakespeare's authorship to the masses, Peacham's book was ignoring Shakespeare's name altogether.

Other great writers, such as Sir Philip Sidney and M. Edmund Spenser are referred to by Peacham, but never Shakespeare; he is omitted altogether. The author of two best-selling poems, as well as a collection of 154 sonnets, together with a magnificent volume of thirty-six plays, the greatest in the English language: and from a man whose stagecraft *"had so taken Eliza and our James,"* has been totally ignored by Peacham, the *"Scholler"* with a Master of Arts degree from Cambridge.

How easy it would have been for Peacham to remedy this oversight in his second edition, published in 1627, especially after the reception of Shakespeare's collected plays came on to the market. But apparently, he saw no need for this 'correction': since none appeared.

In 1634, Peacham published *The Complete Gentleman* for a third time, but even after eleven years, in which he must have been made aware of this omission; he still refused to name Shakespeare. Perhaps, by now, it is evident that Peacham did not consider Shakespeare to be anyone other than a person he had already named under a different title: the person, perhaps, who already headed his list of those who did most to make Elizabeth's reign a *"Golden Age"* of literature, and who by then had been dead for thirty years.

Peacham was not alone in the knowledge that Shakespeare's name in the First Folio did not automatically signify Shaxpere was the person who had written the plays. An edition of the First Folio, currently owned by Glasgow University,[41] originally belonged to a person fairly close to many of the actors named at the front of this edition. To signify his personal knowledge, the owner had annotated the list of names with a short pithy comment. For example, against John Lowine the word *"eyewitness"* is written; against Richard Burbage are the words *"by report";* this, presumably refers to the fact that Burbage died in 1619, four years before the First Folio went on sale. William Kemp had left the company in 1599 and so there is nothing against his name; William Ostler's name is adjoined by the word *"hearsay"*, and the words *"so to"* appear for Nathan Field who is next on the list. The real surprise is to read the annotation against the name William Shakespeare: it says, *"lease for making"*.

According to the OED, and *The Concise Etymology of the English Language (W. W. Skeat, Oxford, 1882 and 1936), "Leasing", means falsehood, from lēas, false"*. Thus, to use Shakespeare's own words:

CLOWN Now Mercury endue thee with leasing, for thou speak'st well of fools! (Act I; sc. v)

[May Mercury (the god of cheating) teach you to lie, since you speak well of fools (and in order to do that, one must needs lie).]

(*Twelfth Night* ed. J. M. Lothian and T. W. Craik 1988 p. 26)

The word *"making"* is conventionally defined as: *"to fashion, frame, construct, compose or form: to create, to bring into being... "* (*Chambers English Dictionary,* 1989). Shakespeare is therefore described by a contemporary of his time as *"lease for making;"* that is, 'false (or lying) for bringing into being'; that is, according to the original owner of Glasgow University's volume of the First Folio. And this was a person, judging from his comments about others on the list, who was contemporaneous with that age.

In view of what has preceded this last disclosure about Shakespeare, to be told that he was *"false for making"* is hardly a surprise. Jonson had said the same thing when he encrypted his avowal into the inscription on the Stratford monument; thereafter, reinforcing it with ambiguous phrases in his testimony to Shakespeare at the front of the First Folio.

Thorpe made a similar disclosure when he encrypted Vere's name into the Sonnets' dedication. Peacham's *Minerva Britanna,* Nashe's 'Will Monox', Barnfield's, play on the word 'ever', Marston's silent name bounded by a single letter, Chettle's cunning dig at Shakespeare by referring to him as the 'god of harbours', and Droeshout's clever engraving of a cartoon figure complete with symbolism, indicating Oxford to have been Shakespeare: these all point to two momentous facts. Edward de Vere was Shakespeare, and the connection between the two names was such a taboo subject, it could never be referred to publicly.

The original owner of Glasgow University's edition of the First Folio was clearly aware of this, and he recorded the information, perhaps to alert future readers of his own awareness. His private note against William Shakespeare's name, denouncing him as a playwright inside the very volume that suggested otherwise, is so matter of fact that there can be no viable reason for it, other than one of plain truth.

There is one further point to make. Glasgow's edition of the First Folio was one amongst a number published in 1623. It was dedicated to the Earls of Pembroke and Montgomery, yet contained a ridiculously etched figure of the supposed author, as well as a mixture of hyphenated and unhyphenated versions of the poet's name. There were also some questionable comments amongst the tributes that some might believe were inappropriate to the man they intended to identify. In short, there was a danger that the First Folio might excite a backlash of pamphlets or books containing scurrilous comments casting doubt upon the veracity of Shakespeare. These might lead to a revival of old rumours about the author of the plays and the possible reason behind a cover-up. To avoid this, the government issued in that same year, 1623, *"A Proclamation against Disorderly Books."* Its aim was to censor and suppress *"seditious, schismaticall, and scandalous Bookes and Pamphlets."* [42]

Writers and publishers now had their hands tied more firmly than ever before. Peacham, however, was able to avoid this proclamation by the simple strategy of publishing *The Compete Gentleman,* which in *three separate editions*, steadfastly refused to acknowledge that Will Shaxpere of Stratford-upon-Avon had anything to do with writing the plays appearing in the First Folio. At the same time, he placed Edward de Vere firmly at the head of those who had made Queen Elizabeth's era the golden age of literature.

10

SWEET SWAN OF AVON

Rara avis in terris nigroque similli.

A rare bird on the earth and very like a black swan.

Juvenal

IN THE ABSENCE of any direct proof that Shaxpere wrote Shakespeare, traditionalists have been compelled to call upon four main cornerstones to sustain their belief: these are the Stratford monument, *Greene's Groatsworth of Wit,* the First Folio, and Jonson's reference to Shakespeare as *"Sweet Swan of Avon"*.

The Cornerstones of Traditional Belief

By now it should be evident that the Stratford monument was constructed as a giant cryptogram. From start to finish, and in three different languages, visual, Latin, and English, it denounces Shaxpere as an impostor. The original monument, vouched for by Dugdale, Betterton, Rowe, Thomas, Grignion, and Hanmer, each one of whom was a gentleman commanding respect in society (Chapter 1), showed the effigy of Shaxpere not as a poet, but as a businessman trading in farm produce. It was a depiction that would have occasioned no surprise amongst his family, or among his neighbours. It was how he lived his life in rural Stratford.

The distich beneath the bust, with its obscure references to Pylos instead of Nestor, Maro instead of Virgil and the Greek philosopher Socrates, would have passed unremarked by his illiterate daughters. Even those educated would assume it to be no more than an obscure, classical tribute to the deceased: put there by his London friends. But, as shown in Chapter 1, these figures from antiquity were deliberately selected because they were able to provide, with cryptic exactness, the ambiguity needed to portray Shaxpere as a man of myth; a man who wrote nothing himself – relying upon others to declare his fame – and a man who acquired his reputation as a writer from another, whose secret he kept hidden.

The sixaine that follows does nothing overtly to dispel this view. The first half is spent in challenging each passer-by to discover who has actually been placed in this monument; which, because it is too small to contain a body, must be referring to a name.

The second half prefixes a reference to all that the author has written, with the German word for 'look', or 'see there!' and it closes with mention of 'his wit': something that was unlikely to have been disputed by those who had known him as a young man. All three couplets were written to form a cipher-text: one that was designed to conceal a Cardano grille: the most recent innovation in the art of secret writing at that time. Encrypted into the cipher-text is the vow by *"I. B."* (Ben Ionson) that *"E. de Vere"* was *"Shakspeare"*; while also urging every passer-by who decrypted this information to *"test him"* and validate the fact for themselves.

Both the encrypted avowal and the Latin distich occur beneath the effigy of Shaxpere, but not as the figure is presently shown, holding pen and paper; instead, the figure originally held fast to a sack of wool: confirmed by Dugdale, Betterton, Rowe, Thomas, Grignion and Hanmer. Shaxpere's family; his friends; his neighbours, would have had no difficulty recognising the man they had known in life, and therefore shown no surprise at his features or the symbolism of the woolsack, for wool was one of the commodities he and his father had traded in.

Consequently the Stratford monument, as a cornerstone for the proposition that Shaxpere is Shakespeare, can no longer be considered sufficient by those who understand the requirements of scholarship. To be sufficient, it is necessary that no alternative to a single interpretation exists.

Traditionalists need the monument to be unique to the memory of William Shakespeare, poet and playwright, in order to maintain their authority. Cryptology denies them this uniqueness with a perfectly viable alternative.

The second cornerstone, *Greene's Groatsworth of Wit,* was shown in Chapter 2 to have been a gross misunderstanding perpetrated by Henry Chettle. After Robert Greene's death, the wily publisher had discovered the dead man's scribbled notes, and understood them to refer to a new arrival on the literary scene. Thus far he was correct. What he did not, and could not know was that Greene had obtained this information from the errant Earl of Oxford, who was proposing to launch a mythical new arrival onto the literary scene, named William Shakespeare: a writer he had invented for his forthcoming epic poems, *Venus and Adonis* and *The Rape of Lucrece.* These, he intended to publish under the guise of a specially arranged patronage for his 'Shakespeare' by the teenage Lord Southampton: the youth to whom a number of his sonnets had already been addressed.

Greene, together with Marlowe and Nashe, had been warned in advance of what was afoot. These three had been invited to dine with Oxford (referred to as 'Will Monox' by Nashe p. 62), whose authorship of several well-received plays were already known to them. Over their meal it was explained to the three writers that a recent arrival in London from the midlands, named Shaxpere, working as an odd-job man inside the Theatre at Shoreditch, had agreed to play the role of 'Shakespeare' in real life. His true identity was therefore not to be revealed; for it would spoil the plans he was making to publish his poetry.

The scribbled notes Greene made after learning what was to happen, were discovered after his death by Chettle, who misunderstood them, and then published a pamphlet which damned Shakespeare before anyone even knew who he was. Oxford's well laid plans were therefore seriously jeopardised. His mythical Shakespeare had received a bad press before having given his name to a single piece of work. To rescue the situation, Oxford was forced to confront Chettle with assurances that he was mistaken about Shakespeare. Chettle was thus persuaded he had acted too hastily, and issued a grovelling apology aimed at restoring Shakespeare's good name.

Once this has been understood, and the evidence proposed is sufficiently clear to confer understanding, the second cornerstone in support of Shaxpere-is-Shakespeare collapses alongside the first. For yet again, the traditionalists' explanation has been proved to be insufficient. A completely viable alternative exists, and it confirms Jonson's vow that Oxford was Shakespeare.

Even so, it is anticipated that traditionalists will still insist that their interpretation is correct. Readers should therefore be aware it is possible to 'prove' almost any statement *if* conflicting evidence is omitted. This is very much the case with *Greene's Groatsworth of Wit,* where Chettle's interpretation assumes that Greene was ranting against Shakespeare as both an actor and a playwright. But there is no previous record of Shakespeare being either an actor or a writer. True, Chettle does paraphrase a line taken from *3 Henry VI,* but without realizing its provenance; he was to claim later that he had never heard of Shakespeare before reading Greene's scribbled notes, which is understandable since Oxford had only recently invented him as his penname.

The dogma attached to explaining *Greene's Groatsworth of Wit* also requires no mention be made of 'Will Monox', Nashe's mysterious companion who was present at the banquet preceding Greene's sudden death. This cunning little anagram conceals the fact that it was the Earl of Oxford who was the fourth member of the party that dined that evening; his purpose being to alert his three companions, before they found out for themselves, that plans were afoot to publish his poetry using a man named Shaxpere as an allonym for his penname.

There is also an aversion amongst Shaxpere's apologists to draw attention to the fact that Nashe had been praising performances of *Henry VI* earlier that year. For such praise to be lavished upon this play, Nashe must surely be credited with knowing who wrote it. Yet, according to Chettle's letter, Nashe's companion, Greene, was so ignorant of the author's identity that he was reduced to uttering curses at him on his death bed. None of this makes any real sense. But it is consequential to an acceptance of the traditional view put forward by those who insist upon their version of the Chettle-Greene letter.

Also contained in Chettle's apology is an unexplained reference to the offended party's many literary friends: those *"divers of worship"* who hurriedly rushed to Shakespeare's defence at the slightest word uttered against his reputation, happy to affirm *"his uprightness of dealing, which argues his honesty, and his facetious grace in writing"*. What writing is this? And where did these people come from? Equally importantly, where did they go? Greene had obviously never heard of them. And, as mysteriously as they appeared, they disappeared. They are never heard of again. Does this not strike the reader as strange, even beyond reason? Here is a man for whom there is no public record of his existence before publication of *Greene's Groats-worth of Wit*; who appeared on no actors list, and who had never published a single word; yet, he was still able to produce references from a class much above his own, and with such authority that it cowered Chettle into making a fawning apology? Where were these 'divers of worship' when his plays were being maimed and stolen by the frauds and stealth of imposters? Well might you ask!

The threat *Greene's Groats-worth of Wit* had posed to Oxford: it having seriously undermined his plans to present 'Shakespeare' as a scholar and a poet, explains the events that followed. But these continue to puzzle traditionalists when they attempt to make sense of the contradictions that oppose their view.

The second cornerstone has therefore been removed, leaving the First Folio next in line. But in the previous chapter, it was shown that Droeshout's engraving is yet another cryptic attempt at revealing the subterfuge surrounding Shakespeare's true identity; as, too, are the tributes that accompany this picture. These certainly praise 'Shakespeare,' but they never identify him other than by his work, as would be the case with a penname. Some also use the hyphenated form of his name – Digges actually uses both the hyphenated and the un-hyphenated form in adjacent lines – thus adding further to the mystery posed by Droeshout's enigmatic engraving.

Oxford's friends were desperate to attract as much dubiety to the man being falsely honoured in the First Folio, as caution would allow. And caution was essential if disfigurement was to be avoided. Amongst the atrocities suffered by those disobeying authority was the severing of ears. This penalty befell Stephen Vallenger, a contemporary of Nashe and Harvey while at Cambridge. Vallenger had been accused of libel, and suffered the consequence. Roland Jenks, an Oxford printer also suffered the loss of his ears for a seditious tongue. Ralph Emerson's fate was still worse. For trying to retrieve some books that had been impounded he was repeatedly tortured, and then imprisoned for nineteen years before being released in a paralysed state. John Stubbe and his publisher William Page were each sentenced to the severing of their hand for daring to make known an opinion concerning the marriage proposed between Queen Elizabeth and the French Prince, François de Valois. The amputation was performed with a butcher's knife placed at the wrist, which rested on a chopping-block. A mallet was then used to hammer down the blade until the hand came away. Those who doubt Oxford's authorship of Shakespeare's plays and poetry sometimes ask – Why did nobody make it known, instead of indulging in all this innuendo and cryptology? Had they lived in those days, would they still have asked?

Amongst the accolades appearing in the First Folio, nothing indicates that William Shaxpere of Stratford-upon-Avon was the poet and dramatist for whom this flow of esteem was intended. This may seem surprising, for it is often asserted that Jonson's reference to 'Sweet Swan of Avon' can only refer to the poet as a native of that town in middle England, which bestrides the river Avon. But this is to forget that Jonson was a master of double meanings. In the present case, he has failed to make it clear which Avon he is referring to; there exists more than one river Avon. Consequently, it is a case of each according to their needs. For those who believe Jonson was referring to the river Avon in Warwickshire, the case is clear: Shaxpere is the 'Swan of Avon'. But for those who knew Oxford's secret, they must then know that Jonson was referring to the river Avon that waters Wiltshire's countryside. This ambiguity protected Jonson's reputation for honesty, and was in keeping with the requirement that Oxford's authorship of the Shakespeare plays and poetry remained confidential: a secret to be shared only by those close to him.

Death and Insolvency

It was in 1588 that the Earl of Oxford lost his wife, and found himself close to becoming destitute as demands for money, totalling more than three million pounds, poured in.

> *In round sums, Oxford owed the Crown £3000 for his wardship, £4000 for his livery (apparently including a relatively negligible 'fine' for his marriage), a pittance for rents still unpaid from the time of his minority, and £4445 in penalties – in effect, accumulated interest.* [1]

Oxford responded by selling further assets. Fishers Folly was bought by the Cornwallis family. Ten acres of land next to the property were sold separately; as too was Vere House in Oxford Place. His company of actors, Oxford's Men, was disbanded, for they disappear from the records after performing in Maidstone, Kent, in 1589-90 (Ogburn, p. 644), and are not heard of again until the mid 1590s. He also disposed of all liability to maintain his ancestral home at Castle Hedingham by assigning it to Lord Burghley in trust for his three children. His abode from 1588 until his marriage at the close of 1591 is unknown.

It is, however, on record that he attended Queen Elizabeth's Eighth Parliament during February and March of '89. He was also present when Philip Howard was charged with treason in April that year. It is therefore likely that he was dwelling within easy reach of London. In which case, having eliminated his two main residences, the one that remains within a horse ride of London is Plaistow House, which was being renovated, even while he negotiated the sale of Fishers Folly.

Plaistow was then one of several villages lying on the outskirts of London, not far from Hackney, but has long since been absorbed by the capital's expanding boundary.

On the other hand, it was at this time that Oxford rented accommodation from Julia Penn, the mother of Michael Hicks, Lord Burghley's secretary. Having been forced to vacate Fishers Folly with his school of writers, his idea had apparently been to relocate them in alternative premises, and thus ensure the flow of literature would continue as before.

His old retainer, Thomas Churchyard, was charged with the renting of the premises at the Penn house on St Peter's Hill. The rental was £100 per annum (≈ £28,000 p.a.). The house was a large old building that had been the property of *"the Abbot of St Mary in York"*, and fit for the purpose Oxford had in mind. However, it very quickly became apparent that the tenancy was beyond Oxford's means, even on a quarterly basis, and Churchyard was forced to vacate the house in fear of being arrested for debt.

Mistress Penn responded by writing directly to Oxford: in doing so, she revealed that the tenancy had been a retreat for Oxford's group of writers.

> *My Lord of Oxford: The great grief and sorrow I have taken for your unkind dealing with me ... You know, my Lord, you had anything in my house whatsoever you or your men would demand, if it were in my house; if it had been a thousand times more I would have been glad to pleasure your Lordship withal.*[2]

Some idea of Oxford's parlous state also began to slowly emerge in the work authored by members of his former writing group. Tom Nashe wrote a pamphlet entitled *Pierce Penniless His Supplication to the Devil,* published some time before 8 September 1592, which discoursed upon the customs and vices of the day. [3] This led Gabriel Harvey to respond with *Pierces Supererogation* (1593), in which, with a telling passage, he may be said to have let slip that Oxford was Shakespeare.

> *Wit [did] bud in such as Sir Philip Sidney and M. [Edmund] Spenser — which were but the violets of March or the primroses of May. Til the one began to sprout in M. Robert Greene ... the other to blossom in M. Pierce Penniless, as in the rich garden of poor Adonis. Both to grow in perfection in M. Thomas Nashe.*[4]

Quite clearly, *Pierce Penniless* was not part of that class of society to which the university wits belonged, for Harvey has been careful not to name him, although he named the other writers. Nonetheless, *Pierce Penniless* was a distinguished man of letters, noticeably poor, and of a class above Greene and Nashe: for this is why his name has been shielded from the public.

There is a further clue; Harvey has referred to *"the rich garden of poor Adonis."* Harvey may have read *Venus and Adonis* – it was published shortly before he wrote his *Supererogation.* However, the phrase: *"Adonis' gardens"*, occurs in *I Henry VI* (act 1, sc. vi), which was publicly performed prior to Harvey's comment.

CHARLES KING OF FRANCE:	Thy promises are like Adonis' gardens, That one day bloom'd and fruitful were the next.

This was the 'Shakespeare' play performed in 1592, and from which its several declarations of *"St George"* helped identify 'Will Monox' as Oxford (p. 62). Harvey has also referred to Adonis as *"poor"* but his garden *"rich"*. At the time of Harvey's publication, *Venus and Adonis* was on sale, with its promise of *"some graver labour"* to follow; that is, *The Rape of Lucrece,* which was published in the following year. Those aware of Oxford's authorship, and how fast this 'rich fruit' had blossomed, as if grown in Adonis' gardens – despite its author's 'penniless' state – can understand what lay behind Harvey's covert comments. For it certainly implied that Harvey was aware that *Henry VI* and *Venus and Adonis* were written by the same person: an impoverished nobleman, for whom the mores of that time did not permit him to be identified. Harvey can only refer to him, therefore, as *Pierce Penniless* (pronounced P'erce Penniless). One does not have to seek far to discover the source of this knowledge; it is *Strange News,* published in 1592/93; after Tom Nashe returned to London, having recently been in the country accompanied by an unnamed Lord; but surely no longer unknown.

Nashe had used his pamphlet to defend the death of Greene against Harvey's cruel jibes. In it, Nashe included information Harvey would have understood, for it first reminded him of the *"angels"* bestowed upon him by Oxford, while they were both at Cambridge. Nashe had then disclosed that it was: – *"Will Monox (hast thou never heard of him and his great dagger?)"* with whom Greene had dined, shortly before his fatal illness. This reference to Oxford, albeit cryptic, was intended to remind Harvey of the indebtedness he had to his former benefactor, thereby putting him in his place. If 'Will Monox' had been George Peele, as some choose to believe (though what connection exists between these two names mystifies even those advocating it), Nashe's reference to Peele would have had no effect upon Harvey whatever.

Introducing Nashe and Spenser

Linking Oxford with Nashe and Greene is in agreement with a reading of the relevant facts. All three, joined by Marlowe, had dined together in the late summer of 1592, when Oxford may be assumed to have first announced that he had recently employed Will Shaxpere to act as an allonym for his publication of *Venus and Adonis* (Chapter 2). Moreover, by linking Nashe with Oxford in 1592, it throws new light upon several references that are found in *Pierce Penniless* and *Strange News;* as Professor McKerrow noted:

> *We have two references to a 'Lord' who was apparently Nashe's patron in the autumn of 1592: the first in Pierce Penniless, where Nashe mentions that "the feare of infection detained me with my Lord in the country". The other in Strange News, written in the*

winter of 1592-1593, where, replying to charges brought by Harvey, he says, "For the order of my life, it is as ciuil as a ciuil orange; I lurke in no corners, but converse in a house of credit, as well gouerned as any Colledge where there be more rare qualified men and selected good Schollers than in any Nobleman's house that I know in England." [5]

Nashe was most assuredly referring to Wilton House. Oxford was then in no position to finance such a *"well governed"* house in the country: and then play host to those *"rare qualified men and selected good scholars,"* that Nashe has referred to.

Mary Herbert, Countess of Pembroke, was in a different position. Her husband was immensely rich and well able to fund her wish to *"emulate the liberal culture of the Italian courts;"* something that would have greatly appealed to Oxford, for he was known as *"the Italianate Earl"*. Now compare Nashe's description of his recent whereabouts with that written by John Aubrey, who had this to say about Lady Herbert.

In her time, Wilton House was like a college, there were so many learned and ingenious persons. She was the greatest Patroness of wit and learning of any lady of her time. [6]

This places Oxford at Wilton House during the first half of 1592, with Nashe acting as his secretary. Recall that Nashe and Oxford were dining together later that year, after returning from the country. It would therefore have been in company with Oxford (the Lord he referred to), that Nashe was able to watch the staging of his employer's *Henry VI Part I*; for the play is referred to in *Pierce Penniless:* where Nashe states . . .

How it would have joyed brave Talbot (the terror of the French) to think that after he had lain two hundred years in his tomb, he should triumph again on the stage, and have his bones new embalmed with the tears of ten thousand spectators at least (at several time) who, in the tragedian that represents his person, imagine they behold him fresh bleeding. [7]

We therefore discover Nashe acting as Oxford's secretary in 1592, and writing a pamphlet with the title, *Pierce Pennilesse,* which just happened to describe his employer's impoverished state. No need to wonder why Harvey was quick to identify Oxford in his *Supererogation*: published soon after Nashe's *Strange News.* The question this poses is – What happened between 1589, when Oxford was in a state of despair, and 1592, when he had sufficiently recovered to spend time at Wilton House in company with Nashe?

Sonnet 66 would appear to provide the answer (p. 217). After the death of his first wife, sorrows came not as single spies, but in battalions, and these had reduced his spirits to the depth of despair. His wayward lifestyle, together with a host of problems, both financial and emotional, had at last caught up with him, and he even began to contemplate taking his own life: *"Tir'd with all these, from these would I be gone."*

Edmund Spenser was aware of Oxford's absence from London's literary life, and commented upon it in his *Teares of the Muses* (1591), where he allows THALIA to bemoan . . .

And he the man, whom Nature selfe had made
To mock her selfe, and Truth to imitate,
With kindly counter under Mimick shade;
Our pleasant Willy, ah is dead of late,
With whom all ioy and iolly merriment
Is also deaded, and in doleur drent.

. . .

But that same gentle Spirit, from whose pen
Large streams of honnie and sweet Nectar flowe,
Scorning the boldness of such base-borne men,
Which dare their follies forth so rashly throwe;
Doth rather choose to sit in idle Cell,
Than so himselfe to mockerie to sell.

Should dissent exist concerning Spenser's opinion of Oxford as a writer of quality verse, equal to the lines above, then let this doubt be referred to his *Faerie Queen* (1590), where such reservations may be set aside. In a sonnet addressed to Oxford, Spenser states precisely what other scholars were to deduce four centuries later. After paying tribute to the 17th Earl's long line of ancestry, he adds:

And also for the love which thou dost bear
To th'Heliconian imps—and they to thee—
They unto thee and thou to them most dear:
Dear as thou art unto thyself.

With these words Spenser has acknowledged that Oxford was most beloved by the Muses (the Heliconian imps – *"Helicon. The Muses Mount."* Brewer): the nine daughters of Jupiter and Mnemosyne, goddesses of the arts and sciences, who were responsible for inspiring artists with their greatest ideas.

But it seems Spenser was not the only poet to draw attention to Oxford's withdrawal from society. Thomas Lodge had been a member of Oxford's coterie attending Fishers Folly. In a poem that he attached to *Scilla's Metamorphosis* (1589), Lodge wrote a verse that seems particularly applicable to Oxford's state of mind at that time.

I will become a hermit now
And do my penance straight
For all the errors of mine eyes
With foolish rashness filled.

Scylla and Charybdis are two rocks situated off the northern shore of Sicily, both fatal to shipping. Scylla dwelt in a cave, and it was said that in avoiding one rock, the hapless seaman collided with the other. Shakespeare refers to this in *The Merchant of Venice* (Act 3; sc.v), where it means lurching from one disaster to another—an apt description of the life Oxford was experiencing at the time.

By Royal Command

It was during this bleak period of dejection that relief came from an old friend. The Queen, having learnt of Oxford's depressed state, may be said to have hit upon the perfect cure. She commanded that Oxford write a play showing FALSTAFF in love, and that it be finished within two weeks. The time for self-pity was brought to an end. Oxford needed to revitalise himself and begin work immediately. According to Professor Gervinus the haste in which the play was written, accounts of its lack of merit.

> *It is designed without any deeper background, without any merit of idea, without pathetic elevation, and without serious passages; it is almost entirely written in prose; it is the only piece of the poet's in which the plot decidedly outweighs the characterisation, the only one which moves in the stratum of plain, common and homely society.* [8]

Queen Elizabeth had obviously been greatly amused to see the character of FALSTAFF played in *Henry IV* parts 1 and 2, and desired to see how the author would portray him if he were in love. Evidence for the haste in which it was written comes from three separate sources.

John Dennis was first to leave a record of the play's hurried composition. In 1702, he produced the play under the title of *The Comical Gallant* and dedicated it to George Granville, to whom he wrote with assertion:

> *I knew very well, that it had pleas'd one of the greatest Queens that ever was in the World ... This Comedy was written at her Command, and by her direction, and she was so eager to see it Acted, that she commanded it to be finished in fourteen days, and was afterwards as Tradition tells us, very well pleas'd at the Representation.* [9]

Nicholas Rowe repeated the story in his condensed biography of Shakespeare (1709).

> *[The Queen] was so well pleas'd with that admirable Character of Falstaff, in the two Parts of Henry the Fourth, that she commanded him to continue it for one play more, and to shew him in Love. This is said to be the Occasion of his Writing The Merry Wives of Windsor. How well she was obey'd, the Play it self is an admirable Proof.* [10]

In the following year, another author, Gildon, included in his *Remarks on the Plays of Shakespeare*, this observation:

> *The Fairys in the fifth Act makes a Handsome Complement to the Queen, in her Palace of Windsor, who had oblig'd him to write a Play of Sir John Falstaff in Love, and which I am well assured he perform'd in a Fortnight; a prodigious Thing, when all is so well contriv'd, and carry'd on without the least Confusion.* [11]

Shakespearian scholar Edward Dowden, writing in 1911, was in no doubt that this play was given its final touches in 1592. However, it is not difficult to find traditionalist tongues eager to dispute this date. The reason is obvious. Based upon the premise that Will Shaxpere was Shakespeare, a date in 1592 would mean the plays in which FALSTAFF appears, including perhaps *Henry V*, in which his death is reported, were written earlier. But the writing of these plays would then clash with the composition of Shakespeare's 'first' tetralogy: for *Henry VI* was already being played in 1592. Suddenly, there is a logjam of plays, each clamouring for a date of composition that will tie in with the favoured view of Shakespeare's first efforts as a dramatist.

To avoid this, it becomes necessary to ignore Dowden and posit a much later date for the *Merry Wives of Windsor*. But the evidence for its composition in or before 1592 contradicts this.

> *In that year Count Mümpelgart, the prospective Duke of Württemberg, came to London, and the event lent itself to a comic interpolation about 'cosen-germans' and 'garmombles' that depended for its punch on the author's being up-to-the-minute, like a stand-in comedian today; dragged in years later it would have fallen flat.* [12]

Consider, for example, the quarto edition pirated in 1602. In this, the Welsh parson, SIR HUGH EVANS, passes this comment: *"there is three sorts of cosen garmombles, is cosen all the Host of Maidenhead and Readings."* [13] In the First Folio this has been edited to read: *"there is three cozen-Germans that has cozened all the hosts of Readins, of Maidenhead, of Colebrook, of horses and money."* [14]

The word 'cosen', which was a form of address between members of the nobility, has a second meaning, which is to cheat. When Count Mümpelgart visited England in 1592, there was an administrative blunder. Lord Howard had promised to provide a special warrant enabling the German visitors to obtain free post-horses. When the visitors arrived, they assumed their stopovers had been informed, and simply took the horses without payment. Not surprisingly, this caused a minor commotion, and resulted in the Germans being branded horse thieves. This is the source of a comical scene in the play, and would have raised a good laugh when it was performed at the time.

BARDOLPH: Sir, the German desires to have three
of your horses: the Duke will be tomorrow
at court, and they are going to meet him.

HOST: They shall have my horses, but I'll make
them pay: I'll sauce them. [Act 4: iii]

...

HOST: Where be my horses? Speak well of them,
varletto.

BARDOLPH: Run away with the cozeners: for so soon as
I came beyond Eton, they threw me off,
from behind one of them, in a slough of
mire; and set spurs and away, like three

German devils, three doctor Faustuses. [Act 5: v]

These comical allusions to events that took place in 1592 are plain, and would have been out of date five years later, which is the preferred date for its composition. Consider, also, the places mentioned in the play: Reading, Maidenhead and Colnbrook: all three are towns or villages at which the German party were known to have visited *en route* for Windsor Castle. Eton, which lies close to Windsor, is also mentioned in the play.

Consider, too, the reference to '*Doctor Faustus*'. Marlowe's play of that title is thought to have been written in 1592. It also includes a scene in which three men, who attempt to murder Faustus, are dragged through *"a lake of mud and dirt"*. [15] It would therefore have been a topical comment for inclusion in a play performed at court, where these facts would very likely have been known.

Included also in the play is a subtle joke that seems likely to have been aimed especially at Count Mümpelgart, and which would not have been missed by a Court audience.

CAIUS: I cannot tell vat is dat; but it is tell-a me dat you
make grand preparations for a Duke of Jamanie:
by my trot, dere is no Duke that the court is
know to come. [Act 4: sc. v]

Although DR. CAIUS is deemed to be a Frenchman (he lapses into this language several times), *"the clipped English of Dr Caius"* (Macauley) is pronounced with a distinct Germanic accent (as verified by a native German speaker and graduate lecturer in psychology). Even CAIUS' grammar conforms to the German tongue, where the infinitive of the verb (in the case cited above, 'to come') occupies the conclusion of a sentence; this is not at all common in French. But it is not only how CAIUS expresses himself that provides the humour, it is also what he says. Despite the preparations made at Court to receive this foreign nobleman, CAIUS claims to know of no such Duke. CAIUS is right. It was a Count that was expected: a Count who had to wait until his return to Germany before becoming a Duke.

Turning attention now to EVANS, as in the quarto of 1602, we find: *"three sorts of cosen garmombles"*. 'Garmomble' is obviously a made-up word derived by phonetically inverting 'Mümpel-gart';

it was subsequently replaced by *"cozen-Germans"* in the First Folio. By 1623, the pun of turning Mümpelgart's name around had lost its relevance, and so the editor replaced it with *"Germans"*, believing this to be more appropriate for subsequent performances.

Before then, in 1592, Nashe had decided to use this reference to Mümpelgart in his pamphlet: *Strange News, Of the Intercepting Certaine Letters.* It was while haranguing Harvey that he called him a *"fanaticall Phobetor, geremumble ... or what you will."* [16] The word re-emerged in 1599, again from Nashe; this time it was used as a verb 'geremumble', and occurs in *Nashes Lenten Stuffe.*

Two years earlier, Mümpelgart having been elevated to the title Duke of Württemberg, was finally made a knight of the garter by Elizabeth, but *in absentia.* It was not until 1603 and the accession of James I that the Duke was informed of the title.

However, the focus of attention for the composition of *The Merry Wives of Windsor* is decidedly fixed upon 1592. This, it may be recalled, was also the year when Nashe returned to London from time spent at Wilton House, *"in the country"* with *"my Lord,"* having served there as Oxford's secretary.

Consequently, there is very good reason to believe that this play was written in the amenable atmosphere provided by the Countess of Pembroke at her home by the river Avon: Nashe, acting as secretary. This would have enabled him to have picked-up on the punning reference to Mümpelgart's name, and seen it as a useful addition to his vocabulary. It would also explain his use of the word, twice: each time in close proximity to Mümpelgart's relationship with England.

This second reference to Württemberg has since become the slender twig upon which orthodoxy hangs its evidence for dating the play. To seek support for this date MISTRESS QUICKLY'S allusions to the Order of the Garter, which appear in Act 5: scene v, are proposed as evidence. However, these allusions may just as easily, and with greater reason, apply to 1592; especially as the play was to be part of the light entertainment ordered by Elizabeth to follow the more serious formalities of the Garter ceremony.

Tantalisingly, Nashe makes a reference to this play and its author in *Strange News,* entered in the *Stationers' Register* on 12 January 1592/3. In his *Epistle Dedicatorie,* Nashe wrote:

To the most copious Carminist of our time, and famous persecutor of Priscian, his verie friend Master Apis Lapis: Tho. Nashe wisheth new strings to his old tawnie Purse. [17]

There are a several points to make concerning this passage. Earlier in the year Nashe had been Oxford's companion and secretary during their sojourn in the country. Upon their return to London, he had dined with Oxford at a banquet made famous by Greene's death. Writing, as he did so soon after these events, it is natural to assume that any letter of dedication written by Nashe would be directed to his patron, Lord Oxford. The final phrase seems to leave no doubt this was the case. *"Tawnie"*, or to be precise, 'Reading Tawny', was the colour of Oxford's livery. Wishing *"new strings to his old tawny purse"*, at a time when Oxford's purse was all but penniless, is certainly confirmatory evidence that this was Nashe's subject. There is also a play on Vere, Oxford's family name; Nashe calls him *"his 'ver(i)e friend"*. But he also refers to him as *"Apis Lapis"*, the *"famous persecutor of Priscian"*.

"Priscian was a great grammarian of the fifth century, whose name is almost synonymous with grammar." [18] Nashe seized upon this fact and used it as a piece of polite humour that was unlikely to cause offence. In *Merry Wives of Windsor*, 'Shakespeare' introduces a comedy sketch involving a Latin lesson (Act 4: sc. i). Welsh parson SIR HUGH EVANS acts as a schoolmaster, with WILLIAM PAGE his pupil.

EVANS: William, how many numbers is in nouns?

WILLIAM: Two.

...

EVANS: . . . What is lapis, William?

WILLIAM: A stone.

EVANS: And what is 'a stone', William?

WILLIAM: A pebble.

EVANS: No, it is lapis: I pray you remember in your prain.

WILLIAM: Lapis

The lesson continues in the same vein with further points of Latin grammar introduced, some with sexual undertones, thus adding to the humour. Because it is a comedy sketch and some grammatical liberties have been taken, Nashe's accusation that his *"verie friend ... Apis Lapis"* is a *"persecutor of Priscian"*, can be seen as referring to this scene from *The Merry Wives of Windsor,* with its focus on the word 'Lapis'

As secretary to Oxford in 1592, Nashe may have penned the scene himself at his employer's dictation. In fact, the sketch was based upon a lesson taken from a book of Latin grammar that Edward VI had commanded for use in all schools. This was *A Shorte Introduction of Grammar,* written by William Lilly and John Colet, published in 1549.

> *In nouns be two numbers, the singular and the plural. The singular number speaketh of one, as lapis, a stone. The plural number speaketh of more than one, as lapides, stones.* [19]

The connection between *"persecuting Priscian"*, the scholar upon whose work Lilly and Colet's Latin grammar book was based, and the comedy scene involving *"lapis"* is at once obvious. It therefore requires only that 'Apis' be shown to possess some similar connection to *The Merry Wives of Windsor,* and Nashe's enigmatic reference will be complete.

For this, we refer to Egyptian mythology. *"Apis, in the form of a real black bull was believed to be the reincarnation or 'glorious soul' of Ptah."* [20] But, a sacred bull was also chosen by 'Shakespeare' for another comedy sketch in *The Merry Wives*: this one involved FALSTAFF.

> FALSTAFF: Now, the hot-blooded gods assist me!
> Remember Jove, thou wast a bull for thy
> Europa; love set on thy horns. (Act 5: sc. v)

FALSTAFF was referring to the Latin equivalent of Ptah: both Jove and Ptah were believed, by their respective followers, to have created the world. Like Ptah, Zeus (the Greek name for Jove) had also appeared as a bull: his intention having been an amorous desire to carry off Europa. It was this plan that gave FALSTAFF the same idea: he would adopt a similar strategy; but instead of a bull, he would disguise himself as a stag, and carry off Mistress Ford and Mistress Page, with whom he had arranged a tryst in the forest of Windsor.

'Apis Lapis' are therefore two words, each of which signifies a comedy sketch appearing in *The Merry Wives of Windsor.* The fact that Nashe was able to refer to these sketches at the end of 1592 is further evidence that this play had already been completed by then, and that he had firsthand knowledge of it.

The passage in *Strange News,* where Nashe makes these references, not only implies Oxford wrote *The Merry Wives of Windsor,* but it also yields a further clue. It is Nashe's comment concerning: *"the most copious Carminist of our time".* 'Carm/en–inis' is a Latin word, meaning poem, verse, and poetry. Nashe can therefore be seen as having dedicated his *Epistle* to the most copious poet or versifier of that time; which, of course, was the man currently referred to as Shakespeare.

Nashe will have had in mind Oxford's preparations for the forthcoming publication of *Venus and Adonis,* which went on sale soon after *Strange News.* This narrative poem, hugely popular in its day, consists of 199 stanzas, each containing six lines of rhyme in the pattern *ababcc.*

It is also arguable that *The Rape of Lucrece,* which went to print in the following year, had also been completed: or was then having the finishing touches put to it. This poem is even longer, with 265 stanzas, each having seven lines apiece. And, let us not omit to mention the majority of 'Shake-speares' (*sic*) 154 sonnets. By the end of 1592, most of these had been written and were circulating amongst his private friends. But when traditionalists think of Shaxpere, these literary friends always remain nameless.

Much Ado About Nothing

The publication of *Strange News* allowed Nashe to direct his comments at Gabriel Harvey. In one part of the pamphlet he wrote: *"For the order of my life, it is as civil as a civil orange".* [21] This is a peculiar simile and worth enquiring into, to discover what it means, and from where it was derived.

The play *Much Ado About Nothing* is conjectured to have been written in 1598, immediately following *The Merry Wives of Windsor* in 1597-8. By retaining this proximity in the dating of the two plays, it may be held that *Much Ado* was either written by 1592, or was then in the process of completion. There is evidence that this was, in fact, the case. In Act 2: sc. i, Beatrice exclaims:

"The Count is neither sad, nor sick, nor merry, nor well; but civil Count, civil as an orange, and something of that complexion."

Civil is a play on Seville and draws its humour from the Spanish city noted for its oranges and their colour. In the play, the colour is likened to jealousy.

Any literary critic who accepts that Oxford and Shakespeare were one and the same person, now has immediate access to a line of enquiry suggesting that *Much Ado About Nothing* was a revised version of the much earlier play *A historie of Ariodante and Genevora*. This was performed before the Queen on Shrove Tuesday, 12 February 1583 (Old Style). The similarity between the two plays is suggested for several reasons, one of which is the number of lines in *Ariodante and Genevora,* which appear to anticipate similarly expressed lines in *Much Ado.* [22]

The late Philip Johnson also drew attention to the existing connection between *Much Ado* and John Lyly's *Endymion,* which was published in 1591 and may have been performed before the Queen at Greenwich on 2 February 1587 O.S. Johnson pointed out that Arden editor A. R. Humphreys, had made the same connection between these plays. *"Humphries specifically links Much Ado About Nothing, to Endymion in a footnote on pp. 155-6."* [23]

When we consider that Lyly was also Oxford's secretary from 1580 to 1588, it is not altogether surprising to discover R. W. Bond declaring: *"In comedy Lyly is Shakespeare's only model: the evidence of the latter's study and imitation of him is abundant."* [24] Bond then pursues this line of thought with copious examples.

But Harvey, a contemporary of Lyly, did not agree. Five years after Lyly's departure from Oxford's service, Harvey called him: *"the fiddlestick of Oxford, now the very bauble of London".* [25] A violin is an instrument of sound; the bow or fiddlestick is merely the tool used for drawing music from it.

To pursue this analogy, we may judge that Lyly drew his 'music' from Oxford's 'violin', by playing on his employer's literary excellence; and by doing so, obtained his best compositions, one of which was *Endymion.*

The praise he received for this made him the 'bauble' of London. A 'bauble' is a foolish person. By using this word, Harvey indicated it was well-known in London that Lyly had not the artistic ability to have written *Endymion* without Oxford's help, and it made him look foolish by pretending otherwise.

In support of this interpretation, it may be noted that . . .

having written nothing before his association with Oxford, Lyly after its end wrote no more plays or anything else of the least merit though he desperately needed the kind of income his writing had brought. [26]

Yet, Lyly is supposed to have been a major influence in the development of Shakespeare's talent. In the likelihood of this being false, it provides a good lesson for accepting Oxford to have been Shakespeare's embryo. *Endymion* would therefore have been the predecessor of a version of *Much Ado About Nothing*. It would therefore have been a work derived in part from an earlier play written by Oxford, or at least written with his assistance.

One further advantage of assigning a revised version of *Much Ado About Nothing* to Oxford in 1591/2 is that it provides a possible solution to the reference made by Francis Meres' concerning *Loue labours wonne*, which is otherwise a lost Shakespeare play. Support for this idea comes from a suggestion that so much of Oxford's personal life could be identified in the play (Dr Richard Desper writing in *The Shakespeare Oxford Newsletter*, Vol. 42 No. 3 p. 21), that some wag referred to it as *"Much Ado About Oxford"*. And since the initial letter of Oxford is 'O' or otherwise, 'nought' meaning 'nothing', the play acquired its present name.[27]

A less contentious reason is more prosaic.

Much Ado About Nothing is a comedy of courtship and marriage, of a quick courtship that nearly comes to disaster and of a slow, reluctant one that is a complete success. [28]

In other words, this is a possible candidate for the lost play: *Love's Labour's Won*. The other possibility is that the missing work refers to *All's Well That Ends Well*. The location certainly favours this identification, since part of the action takes place at Rousillon: this being no great distance from Navarre, where the action in *Love's Labour's Lost* takes place.

Furthermore, 'Shakespeare' was several times careless when asked for the title of a play. Consider *Twelfth Night* or *What You Will* when asked to name this play. *As You Like It* is another possible response to a similar request for a title. It therefore seems fitting that *Love's Labour's Won* or *All's Well That Ends Well* might easily describe the same play, since after a series of reversals,

HELENA finally wins the love she laboured for.

Thus, by the close of 1592, Nashe suddenly found himself in a position to quote a memorable phrase from *Much Ado About Nothing,* and to allude to two scenes from *The Merry Wives of Windsor.* He was also privy to the copious verses of a poet who at that time was in the process of preparing two poems for publication, which together contained 3049 lines; and this is to omit any mention of the many sonnets from the same author's hand.

Hence, when Nashe returned from the country, after having been in service to Oxford, for he admits as much, it was from Wilton House he came, and to judge by the expressions he brought with him, his service to Oxford beside the river Avon that year had been extremely industrious. Jonson's reference to 'Shakespeare' as the *"Swan of Avon"* therefore loses nothing by positing it to mean time spent by Oxford on the Wilton estate.

INSTATING OXFORD AT THE AVON

The close relationship between Oxford and the Herberts of Wilton, which developed after 1588 when Lady Herbert emerged from her self-imposed withdrawal from society, was soon to take a more intimate course. Upon the evidence of cryptology, she entered into a brief sexual relationship with Oxford. This was the subject of a previous chapter (p. 252), and serves to reinforce Oxford's connection with the Avon, referred to by Jonson.

In 1597, a marriage was arranged which, if successful, would have united the de Veres with the Herberts. Pembroke's eldest son William, was to marry Oxford's daughter Bridget, who was then under the protection of her grandfather, Lord Burghley. Everyone seems to have favoured the match, but Burghley was unwilling to make the allowance he promised the couple available, until his death (p.191). Oxford was in no position to remedy the situation, and Lord Pembroke remained adamant the allowance should begin with the marriage. After much fruitless discussion, the engagement was called off.

It would be another eight years before a second engagement was announced; by then both Lord Pembroke and Lord Burghley were dead, and the dowry demanded was presumably met. On this occasion it was Philip Herbert who became engaged to Lady Susan Vere, and the couple were wed in 1605.

Two years before the wedding, and six months before his death, Oxford had made another visit to Wilton House. This was the occasion when *As You Like It* was performed before King James. The facts surrounding the performance are of especial note, because when news was brought to the King that *Shakespeare* had arrived at Wilton House, James at once changed his itinerary and returned to Lady Pembroke's home, having previously left there with his Court only eight weeks before.

The circumstances surrounding the King's return visit and his sudden change of plans are controversial, and to settle the dust that has been raised, it is necessary to focus solely upon the facts.

In 1603, London was again groaning beneath the assault of yet another bout of Plague. King James wisely retreated to the country, passing through Berkshire (Windsor), Surrey (Pyrford via Hampton Court), Oxfordshire (Woodstock), Hampshire (Winchester), Wiltshire (Wilton), and Hampshire again (Isle of Wight), before returning to Wiltshire (Salisbury). We know that during James' progress across this part of southern England, the Pembroke family *"entertained the king at Wilton on 29-30 Aug. 1603* (NICHOLS, *Progresses,* i.254)*,"*[29]

We know, also, that following this brief visit, James then travelled to the Hampshire coast, where he and his retinue crossed the Solent to visit the Isle of Wight. Upon his return to the mainland, the King changed his itinerary by unexpectedly returning to Wilton House. *"We know of this return visit because James' Court … stayed at Wilton between 24 October and 12 December."*[30]

Park Honan agreed, noting that *"after a voyage to the Isle of Wight, James at last reached Wiltshire for a prolonged stay at Wilton House with the young Earl of Pembroke."*[31] What had been the great attraction that brought about this change of mind?

The answer appears to be the recent arrival of *Shakespeare* at Wilton House, and a performance of *As You Like It*. Wilson confirmed that: *"Shakespeare's company performed … at Wilton on 2 December is a matter of firm historical record."*[32] The reason for this certainty, other than that given, is because the court records confirm the King's Men had indeed performed for James I and his court on the date mentioned.

> *John Heminges, one of his Majesty's players ... for the pains and expenses of himself and the rest of the company in coming from Mortlake in the county of Surrey unto the court aforesaid and there presenting before his Majesty one play. £30.* [33]

We can see from this record that Heminge was the business manager of the company, and the King's Men had been summoned from Mortlake (a village on the Surrey shore of the river Thames), to Wilton House: a journey of about 85 miles (136 kilometres). Prior to this, the King's Men had been settling down to see out the winter at Mortlake, and to prepare for the year ahead.

> *Provincial account books show Shakespeare's company having done their usual touring during the epidemic, performing in Bath, Shrewsbury, Coventry, and Ipswich on unspecified dates.* [34]

At Mortlake, the call from Wilton interrupted their plans, although it is unlikely Will Shaxpere was with 'his' company at the time; or, for that matter, had been on tour with the actors during the summer months. Not only is his name absent on the lists of players visiting those towns, but also: *"he spent part of most summers among his family, as the diarist Aubrey reported."*[35]

Thus, having spent most of the summer apart from the King's Men, the busiest time of the year for actors because of the increased number of daylight hours and the warm weather, there was even less reason for him to spend the winter in their company, for so it would follow. From this, we may conclude that Shaxpere was not one of those who made the journey from Mortlake to Wilton in the winter of 1603.

Does that mean he was already staying at Wilton as a guest of Lady Pembroke? Katherine Duncan-Jones thinks not (p.140).

> *Shakespeare was the King's Man, not the Countess of Pembroke's ... he was hardly in a position, either socially or legally to stay at Wilton House as an independent guest, as if for a country-house weekend.* [36]

Then who was it that made the decision to produce *As You Like It* at Wilton in December 1603? And who was it that informed the royal party of an event, so inviting that King James broke his journey to return to Wilton House, having only recently left there?

The short answer to both questions is contained in a letter that Lady Pembroke wrote to her son William, who was attending King James during his progress through southern England. The letter was retained in the family archives and subsequently shown to the Victorian poet and historian William Cory by Lady Herbert, the Baroness Lea, who was then the occupant at Wilton House.

Faith Compton Mackenzie, the daughter of Cory's niece, referred to this letter in her biography of Cory, having: *"depended as much as possible on other sources so far untouched, though it has been difficult to avoid an occasional quotation."*[37]

Mackenzie's account confirmed that it was during Cory's visit to the House in the summer of 1865, with the purpose of tutoring Lady Herbert's young son in the classics that the following incident was reported by her relative.

> *An interesting entry in his diary when he was staying at Wilton House, Salisbury, tells how Lady Pembroke showed him a letter from her forerunner to her son, urging him to bring the King (James I) from Salisbury to see As You Like It. "We have the man Shakespeare here," she added laconically.*
>
> *That would have been an agreeable occasion. The excellent play, the author present, and the King lured from Salisbury. To commemorate it a temple was built at Wilton, and known as 'Shakespeares House'.*[38]

The edited version of *Extracts from the Letters and Journals* of *William Cory*, published five years after his death, confirmed Mackenzie's accuracy, although somewhat laconically. However, note the quotation marks in the entry; thus proving Baroness Lea had shown Cory the letter, and he was quoting from it.

> *Aug. 5. The house (Lady Herbert said) is full of interest: above us is Wolsey's room; we have a letter, never printed, from Lady Pembroke to her son, telling him to bring James I from Salisbury to see As You Like It; "we have the man Shakespeare with us." She wanted to cajole the king in Raleigh's behalf—he came.*[39]

Edward Rose, who visited the House for an article that was to appear in the *Illustrated London News,* was another who referred to *"Shakespeare's House"*. Rose visited Wilton in 1887, twenty-two years after Cory's famous diary entry.

Straight from the terrace leads a pretty walk, between trees of infinite shades of delicate green; to its right is the great green-house; and to the left the gardens slope gently to the little river.

At the end of the shady walk is a little building which has been christened by Wilton … Shakespeare's House. For there is a story, in no way improbable, that once upon a time Shakespeare and his actors "gave a play" at Wilton House—before what a company one may imagine!

In memory of this a little temple has been built: classic as to its pillars, feudal as to the devices of arms above, with portrait busts, and an inscription on the wall from the wonderful lines in 'Macbeth'—

> *Life's but a walking shadow; a poor player,*
> *That struts and frets his hour upon the stage,*
> *And then is heard no more:*

Close to Shakespeare's House passes one of the three little rivers which pass through the park—not, as it might appropriately have been, the Avon, but the less romantic Nadder. An Avon is, however, the chief of the three streams, the other two being its tributaries; it is … a pleasant stream—the Upper Avon it is called—which comes through the downs of South Wiltshire, and goes past Salisbury into Hampshire. [40]

The structure referred to as Shakespeare's House presently stands in Lord Pembroke's private garden, and is not accessible to the general public. A recent archaeological survey carried out upon the building, as requested by the 17th Earl of Pembroke, confirmed that it dated back to the time of Mary Sidney.[41]

The Holbein Porch, as it is called, was originally attached to the House, but was dismantled in 1812 when the Cloisters were added. It was later reassembled at its present location in 1826. The copy of William Kent's statue of Shakespeare in Westminster Abbey, carved by Scheemakers (1743), and commissioned by the 9th Earl of Pembroke, includes the quotation from *Macbeth* referred to by Rose. But the original words described in his article, which he said were copied from the Holbein Porch, are no longer visible. And it is uncertain whereabouts on the building he saw them. However, the fact they were reportedly there when Rose viewed Shakespeare's House, would certainly confirm the story that it was constructed by Mary Sidney to commemorate the wonderful time at Wilton when *Shakespeare* was joined by King James and his Court for a festival of poetry and theatre.

An alternative explanation for the missing quotation is that Wilton's replicated statue of Shakespeare was placed inside the 'Temple' as a focus of attention for the construction of a shrine to the poet, and it was from the statue that Rose copied the words from *Macbeth*. It is known that in July 1849, the sculptures by Charles Newton were referred to in connection with the Holbein Porch. These, together with the statue of Shakespeare, would have made a fitting composition for the interior of the little building.

It would seem to be of added significance that the original effigy of Shakespeare in Westminster Abbey contains a different quotation: one taken from *The Tempest*. At Wilton, the quotation is from the Scottish play *Macbeth*. This does suggest the alteration was made in honour of James I, and his visit to the House to join *Shakespeare* in 1603. It is, of course, quite preposterous to suppose that Lady Mary Sidney would have considered erecting a building, however small, to the memory of a player from Shaxpere's background, and then endowing it with a quotation from his play. Duncan-Jones goes so far as to believe he would not even have been received as a house guest, and Sir Sidney Lee became incensed at the thought of Mary Sidney inviting the King to return to her home because Shakespeare had arrived, denouncing the letter Cory read as an *"ignorant invention"*.

It is quite certain, however, that King James and his Court were at Wilton in 1603, from late October to early December. Apart from the court's paymaster recording payment of £30 to the players, another record reported: *"Paid to m^r^ Sharppe for his layinges out vpon giftes and fees vnto the kinges seruantes £6. 5. 0."*[42]

Also, writing in 1873 when tradition was still very much alive, local historian W. Michael wrote that James I . . .

> *held a brilliant Court here in November 1603. The Earl was one of the great patrons of Shakspeare (sic) who is said to have assisted in some of his own plays which were performed at Wilton House in the presence of the King.*[43]

This would suggest that the letter sent by the Countess of Pembroke to her son, alerting him to the fact that *"Shakespeare"* had arrived, must be considered genuine; otherwise, how else could the King have learnt that *"Shakespeare"* had arrived?

Cory's hostess, the mother of the 13th and 14th earls of Pembroke, was certainly correct when informing her guest: *"She wanted to cajole the king in Raleigh's behalf—he came."* Why should she then be incorrect because of a remark made about Shakespeare's arrival at the House; which, in any case, was the inducement needed to bring James back to Wilton so she could pursue her plea on the behalf of Raleigh?

The Baroness also remarked to Cory that the letter had never before been printed, which, in itself, has an offhand naturalness about it.

In November 1603, Raleigh was on trial at Winchester charged with high treason. On the 17th of the month he was found guilty and sentenced to death. Lady Pembroke's plea on behalf of Raleigh, conjoined as it was to the festivities of that memorable occasion, may have had an effect. For, in the event, Raleigh mounted the scaffold on 13 December with the executioner at the ready: but moments before the axe fell, a reprieve from the King arrived. It was an event that out-staged even Shakespeare's dramatic moments. Raleigh was returned to his cell in the Tower, whereupon he began writing the *History of the World* in which he warned against pursuing the truth of his time too closely.

When considering the letter recorded in Cory's diary, it is well to remember that this was a man who, in 1860, had been recommended to Queen Victoria by her Prime Minister Lord Palmerston, for the position of Professor of Modern History at Cambridge. Except for Prince Albert's preference for Kingsley, this appointment would have confirmed him in the role of an established historian. Is it therefore reasonable to suppose that Cory would have bypassed the opportunity of examining, or at least seeing for himself, such a valuable document as the one described by Lady Herbert: especially since it had never before been printed? The quotation marks he made in his diary answer that question quite clearly.

The daughter of Cory's niece certainly claimed it had been shown to him, and she was present as a child on many occasions when Cory visited her parents' home to converse with her father. *"He was my mother's uncle, my father's comrade in scholarship ... I know that he was a specially loved guest in my family,"* she wrote.[44]

Like all the other documents capable of shedding light upon the reality of Shakespeare as the author of the works that bear his name, this letter can no longer be found. One does not have to look too far for a possible reason. Consider, Sir Sidney Lee's outburst: *"the 'tenor' of the letter, 'stamps it, if it exists, as an ignorant invention'."* And that of E. K. Chambers, who was more cautious: merely asserting, *"the apparent familiarity with which Shakespeare seems to have been referred to, is noteworthy."* [45] Both scholars realised that the countess of Pembroke would not have written to the King in such familiar terms about a man of Shaxpere's class. Therefore, in their mind, the letter had to be a forgery.

Since Cory was himself a writer of poetry, with important connections in society, and known for his interest in history and in Shakespeare (comments he made about the poet's plays appear in his biography), it is unlikely that he remained silent about Lady Pembroke's letter.

In 1865 the most prominent Shakespearian scholar of the day was James Orchard Halliwell-Phillipps. In the previous year he had attracted world interest by discovering a record informing that Shakespeare was one amongst others who had been awarded four and a half yards of *"skarlet red cloth"* to wear at King James' coronation procession, which was to take place between the Tower and Westminster. Did this discovery alert Cory into confiding that a further discovery awaited Phillipps at Wilton House? It would have been reasonable for Cory to do so, and negligent of him to have omitted passing on this information. On the other hand, the Baroness Lea may have shown Phillipps the letter herself, during his normal round of enquiries.

In the event this letter, embarrassing to the Stratford cause, disappeared. Phillipps cannot be excluded from suspicion. As Clare Asquith remarked, Phillipps was allowed to work *"unsupervised through various libraries and private collections,"* [46] and has been held jointly responsible with Collier for documents that have been "*stolen, forged and destroyed*": both men having tried to consolidate *"the legend of the English Bard"* by tampering with documents to further that cause.

When questioned about the letter many years later, Lady Herbert, by then quite elderly, is said to have replied she could no longer remember, but believed it had been lodged for safe keeping with the British Museum, or one other. If true, it suggests that this had been recommended to her by someone keen to get their hands on the letter, and with the promise of delivering it to a place of safety. But also with the intention of ensuring it would never be used to incriminate Shaxpere's reputation.

Oxford's first sojourn by the Avon at Wilton House would have occurred between 1589 and 1592. This seems to have been the time when he entered into a relationship with Lady Herbert. And it was in 1592 that Nashe recorded how he and his Lord had taken refuge from the Plague in the country: staying at a house run like a college.

Oxford's final visit to Wilton House occurred in the closing months of 1603, when Plague again forced city dwellers to take refuge in the country. During the twelve years between 1592 and 1604, the complete works of Shakespeare were either reworked from old plays, or in some cases newly written. How much he finished in the collegiate atmosphere of Countess Mary's home is impossible to say. The official guide book published by Wilton House provides the following information:

> *In the sixteenth and seventeenth centuries Wilton House was a centre of patronage for the arts, visited by many of the most famous literary figures, such as Sir Phillip Sidney, Ben Jonson, Aubrey and, in particular William Shakespeare.* (p. 5)

This echoes another report made concerning Wilton House during the quadricentennial celebrations of Shaxpere's birth.

> *There's history in every corner. King Charles the First spent many happy summers here. Shakespeare wrote a number of works here. Queen Elizabeth not only slept here, she left a lock of her hair, which is still a treasured heirloom.* [47]

Upon this evidence, we may suppose Oxford was not idle during time spent at Wilton House. In which case, *"Sweet Swan of Avon"* is appropriate to both the Wiltshire Avon and to Oxford. It is also ambiguous, for it appears to confirm 'Shaxpere's authorship; while those close to Oxford would have understood its alternative meaning. It was, after all, no less than one has come to expect from Jonson: 'Shakespeare's' most loyal and, let it be said, honest colleague.

11

DEBUNKING STYLOMETRIC 'PROOFS'

My desire is that mine adversary had written a book.

Job

WE SHALL NOW CONSIDER the argument that Oxford's earliest poetry shows no indication of the mature work Shakespeare produced in the 1590s. And for this, we shall begin with *Titus Andronicus*, described by Professor Gervinus as *"one of his earliest writings."*

In Chapter 8 it was shown from documentary evidence that the earliest version of this play dates from about 1574. This precludes Shaxpere as the author. But his acolytes are not so easily deterred. They have obtained a new weapon in their armoury – the computer. And, when armed with a program to analyse style, or so it is claimed, it will counter any argument that might show William Shaxpere's authorship of Shakespeare's work to have been the work of some other poet.

THE PROBLEM OF TITUS ANDRONICUS

The case of *Titus Andronicus* does, nevertheless, pose a problem for stylometry. *"It is startlingly different from the later plays, both in subject-matter and style."* [1] The reason for this is very simple; by force of circumstance, the author had modelled it upon plays by the Roman classicists.

In 1574, Oxford had yet to experience the work of the Italian Renaissance writers, and this is apparent in the earliest of his Roman plays. This fact has important ramifications. It divides his artistic output into two parts—work composed before setting off for Italy, and that which he composed after returning to England. Unfortunately for the stylometricists, the only poetry written by Oxford, which is now available, are the poems he wrote before he left England to tour Italy. These poems fall into the same category as *Titus Andronicus,* they were written too early for testing against the work he produced during his Renaissance period.

MENDENHALL'S PROBLEM

This setback, together with other considerations, poses a set of problems for those who believe that computer software offers an appropriate tool for use in the Shakespeare authorship debate. Current attempts to use numbers to settle the question of the authorship problem date back to the nineteenth century, and to Thomas C. Mendenhall, an American physicist. He had read about Augustus de Morgan's attempt to use mathematics to resolve a dispute concerning the authorship of certain texts in the *Bible.* Mendenhall therefore resolved to adapt a similar strategy in order to tackle the debate that was then raging at the time between advocates of Francis Bacon and traditionalists: both sides having declared Shakespeare to be their man.

Mendenhall's exhaustive study, involving the measurement of more than half a million words from both authors, and the frequency with which words of certain lengths occurred, was published in 1901. But its relevance to settling the authorship problem was soon impaired by the discovery that Christopher Marlowe shared the same characteristics of style as Shakespeare. This naturally led to the suggestion that Shakespeare had been strongly influenced by the plays of Marlowe. It is a suggestion that still continues to capture the imagination—and imagination is where most alleged 'facts' concerning Shakespeare occur.

Although at first sight the idea of Shakespeare being tutored by Marlowe may seem appealing, the facts do not support it. Marlowe's sole publication up to the time when 'Shakespeare' was known to have already written at least half a dozen plays was *Tamburlaine,* published in 1590. This is a gory tale of, blood cruelty, and conquest, set in the Middle East. Quite how this can be supposed as a tutorial for Shaxpere's early comedies is left for the advocates of stylometry to explain.

Nevertheless, Marlowe has included within *Tamburlaine* a phrase used by Shakespeare in *2 Henry IV,* (Act 2: scene iv), which occurs when PISTOL refers to the *"pampered Jades of Asia".*

For traditionalists, there is no question about it: Shakespeare picked up this phrase from Marlowe. But, as it has previously been explained, Marlowe became a student of the Earl of Oxford after leaving Cambridge with his Master's degree: at the time when he took lodgings in the Norton Folgate area within a short walk of Fishers Folly. This was where Oxford held sway over a gathering of writers: in the style of Renaissance artists. It is therefore far more likely that Marlowe 'borrowed' this phrase from Oxford. In which case, how, can stylometry resolve an authorship debate if Oxford is omitted from the equation? Yet, that is precisely what Robert Matthews and Tom Merriam did in their research paper, which was published in *Literary and Linguistic Computing* (1994).

THE MATTHEWS – MERRIAM PROPOSAL

The conclusion reached by Merriam and Matthews, based upon software that was designed to mimic the neural network of the brain, was that Shakespeare wrote the anonymous play *Edward III* under the supervision of Marlowe. They also concluded that *3 Henry VI* was a lost play, originally written by Marlowe and rewritten by Shakespeare. If we call Marlowe's lost play *Ur-Henry VI Part 3,* does this mean there were two other lost plays, *Ur-Henry VI Part One* and *Ur-Henry VI Part Two*? If not, why not, it is a reasonable inference to draw?

The astute reader will have discerned from these results by Matthews and Merriam that it is not the computer that decides the authorship question, but those in charge of the operation, for it is they who eventually apply a personal bias to their findings.

The same results in the hands of Oxford's supporters would happily conclude, not that Shakespeare wrote *Edward III* under the guiding supervision of Marlowe, but *vice versa*: Marlowe wrote this play under the influence of Oxford, during their work together at Fishers Folly. How can either Matthews or Merriam disagree? If they say there is no actual evidence that Marlowe was ever at Fishers Folly, one can reply neither is there evidence that Marlowe tutored, or even met Shakespeare. In essence, they have offered as scientific evidence conclusions that have been neither sufficiently nor adequately researched.

In 1994, when Matthews and Merriam made known their results, *The Mystery of William Shakespeare,* by Charlton Ogburn (Penguin Group, London 1988), had already cast sufficient doubt upon Shakespeare's true identity for a scientist, such as Matthews, to apply caution to his findings. It did not happen. Then, how can one trust evidence from stylometry if results simply mirror the ignorance or spin of the authors?

It seems Matthews and Merriam were carried away by the possibilities of their research, for they applied the same method of analysis to decide the authorship of *The Two Noble Kinsmen.* Not surprisingly, the conclusion they reached was that this had been a collaborative effort between Shakespeare and Fletcher.

Once again, it was *not* the computer 'speaking': instead, it was the voice of those running the research; they interpreted the results to accord with the dogma of orthodoxy. In doing so, they confirmed that parts of the play were in Fletcher's style while other parts were by 'Shakespeare'. But that does not have to be a collaborative effort. 'Shakespeare' may well have died before Fletcher appeared on the scene: he, having been commissioned to edit and fill in parts of the play that were incomplete. Alternatively, Fletcher may have decided to complete the play on his own initiative. This is not to deny that modern-day scriptwriters do collaborate, but they write well below the level of Shakespeare; and no genius, either musical or literary, has ever been willing to taint his work with the input of someone less able. Great artists, in any field, may improve upon the work of a lesser talent, but they will never submit to having that lesser talent meddle with their own work.

In the world of Matthews and Merriam, Shakespeare may rewrite a lost and hitherto unheard of play by Marlowe, but he collaborates with Fletcher. Of course, they may argue that they were simply following the authoritative view of Shakespeare's authorship. But then their conclusions were neither scientific nor sufficient, because other viable interpretations existed at the time. These they ignored; or, at least, left unexplored, despite the fact the information available, was capable of satisfying the same research findings.

The collaboration between Matthews and Merriam was that of a computer scientist and a historian. Perhaps men of science trust too much the prejudices adopted by their more literary associates, and fail to realise that rigour and detachment from bias are not as abundant in the humanities as they are meant to be in the science laboratory.

THE ELLIOTT – VALENZA PROPOSAL

Research findings from another collaborative effort, between Ward E. Y. Elliott, professor of American political institutions, and Robert J. Valenza, professor of mathematics and humanities, were recently made known and published in 2004 (*Oxford By The Numbers: What Are The Odds That The Earl of Oxford Could Have Written Shakespeare's Poems And Plays?*) Again, one can only wince at the sweeping statements with which they begin their paper.

They commence by quoting Alan H. Nelson and Steven W. May, both professors of English, and each committed to defend the traditional view of Shakespeare. From these two unbiased (did I say unbiased?) stalwarts, Elliott and Valenza confidently assert . . .

> *that, although many documents connect William Shakspere of Stratford to Shakespeare's poems and plays, no documents make a similar connection for Oxford. The documents, they say, support Shakespeare, not Oxford.*[2]

This statement is quite simply false. If it were correct, there would be no disputing Shakespeare's authorship. Since neither Elliott nor Valenza have appreciated this, and have simply taken Nelson and May on trust, a word of explanation is required.

Associating Shakespeare with Shaxpere's hometown of Stratford is their first error. No documents exist, whether on paper, stone, or brass, that are contemporaneous with Shakespeare's time, and which *unambiguously* connect Shaxpere with a career in letters; in fact, there are not even any letters. The Stratford monument, Digges' tribute contained in the First Folio, and Jonson's reference to the Swan of Avon were previously thought to fill this vacuum, but all three have now been shown to possess entirely different meanings; thereby destroying the uniqueness required for evidence supporting Shaxpere.

The second error is the two writers' failure to acknowledge the possibility they were supposedly investigating; could Oxford and Shakespeare refer to the same person? They betrayed their bias with their opening assertion; which, had it been true, is the solution to Shakespeare's identity.

Elliott and Valenza next proceeded to stress that . . .

Our ... stylometric tests provide no support for Oxford. In terms of quantifiable stylistic attributes, Oxford's verse and Shakespeare's verse are light years apart. [3]

Put differently, these 'light years' are the difference in time between the poet's youthful exuberance and the more mature contemplation that a true artist experiences in later life. If we search for a parallel in Beethoven – surely Shakespeare's musical equivalent – we are able to trace his development as a composer through a series of compositions. Yet, take away all he composed between the ages of twenty and forty, shroud his life in mystery, and it is no longer as clear that his teenage work had sufficient merit to establish him as the man who wrote the masterpieces that appeared after he turned forty. His early work continues in the style adopted by Haydn and Mozart. This is in contrast to his later compositions, which are uniquely individual.

What Elliott and Valenza have insufficiently considered is the distinct possibility, bearing in mind Oxford's retirement from court during the early 1590s, that Shakespeare's plays were actually Oxford's mature re-editing of those he had earlier written; especially since these appeared with such abundance during the 1590s. There were twenty-two 'new' plays in just eight or nine years, which suggests they were, indeed, edited editions of previously written work, rather than plays newly written. And, let it be noted, it was not until 1598 that a dozen of these plays, all of which had been the work of a nameless author up until then, suddenly became attributed to William Shakespeare: a man from whom nothing had been heard since the publication of *Lucrece,* five years earlier (Chapter 2).

Let it also not be forgotten that *The Troublesome Raigne of King John,* for which a quarto edition had been published in 1591, is claimed with justification to be the forerunner of Shakespeare's historical dramas:

. . . for its author ... reveals, were he indeed its creator, powers of construction and invention that Shakespeare himself was to acknowledge in what is regarded as his rehandling of the work ... the author

of The Troublesome Raigne may be fairly held to have anticipated Shakespeare and even to have instructed him; for Shakespeare's King John follows The Troublesome Raigne almost scene for scene ... Whatever his deficiencies the anonymous author of The Troublesome Raigne must be given high commendation for his constructive powers.

(Peter Alexander: Regius Professor of English Language and Literature).[4]

Elliott and Valenza's stylometric testing is no match for human cognition, such as that undertaken by Professor Alexander. Nor do the historical dramas stand alone in their supply of examples, where the work of 'Shakespeare' has supposedly been suborned from an earlier playwright: one, who is invariably described as anonymous.

One may also cite *Romeo and Juliet,* which contains *"many verbal resemblances"* to the poem of 3020 lines written by Arthur Brooke (*The Tragical History of Romeus and Juliet*). Brooke was, a teenager when he published this story, and it is thought possible, even likely, that Oxford, himself a teenager at the time, was the actual author; and that he arranged for the tale to be published under Brooke's name. Since Brooke drowned at sea, the authorship of the poem cannot be verified.

Elliott and Valenza next suggest: *"The odds that either [Oxford or Shaxpere] could have written the other's work are much lower than the odds of getting hit by lightning."*[5] Apart from the fact that – *"Over 40,000 thunderstorms occur throughout the world each day;"* in which case, being struck by lightning somewhere in the world is not as rare as we are being led to believe, there is a further presumption in this statement. It is that Shaxpere could actually write. It seems incredible that a man with no evidence of having penned anything other than a few badly blotted signatures – even these are of dubious origin – and who always excused himself when asked to write (an excuse still recalled many years after his death), could be used as a comparison to a man *known* to possess everything the other is only *imagined* to have possessed. But such is the mesmerizing power of the Shakespeare myth, that every objection concerning the identity of Shakespeare is always dismissed.

Let us look at the question of 'odds' mentioned by Elliott and Valenza. People are regularly struck by lightning somewhere in the world, But an examination of the many different arrangements of letters that comprise the words of Jonson's shortened avowal, SO TEST HIM I VOW HE IS E DE VERE, without even computing the probability that these letters will actually occur by chance, is still 1,496,065,783,500,288,000 (= 24! / 414720); that is, almost one and a half million, trillion different ways. And, when this is coupled with the probabilities derived from the confirmatory assertions made by 'Shakespeare' (p.201), Thorpe (p.180), Benson, (p.254), and Digges (p.453), Elliott and Valenza's crude analogy to being struck by lightning is relatively insignificant..

Jointly, the combined odds of Jonson's, 'Shakespeare's', Thorpe's, Benson's and Digges's encryptions being due to chance are of such inter-galactic magnitude, they even outnumber Simon Singh's comparative example, which refers to the entire human race examining 35 letters at the rate of one arrangement every second, over a time span one thousand times longer than the estimated age of the universe, currently thought to be 13·7 billion years (p. 172).

How could Elliott and Valenza's stylometric tests have failed so badly? Possibly, a lack of adequate data has produced results that have been too favourably interpreted: presumably, to align with their expectation. Experimental bias has a bad record for allowing results to be seen as a confirmation of the tests being performed. In the present instance, Elliott and Valenza began their work with an eye to the benchmark set by May and Nelson; and it was admiration for their work that became a target for the tests they were preparing. But, contrarily, Elliott and Valenza's results can no longer be considered fit for purpose. Oxford's admission that he wrote Sonnet 76; Jonson's avowal that Oxford was Shakespeare; Thorpe's further proof that Oxford was Shakespeare: these, put together, are more than sufficient to scupper stylometric evidence that Shakespeare was Shakespeare – whatever that means.

Mistaken evidence is not as uncommon as one might think. For instance, the astronomical observations recorded by the ancients, up to the time of Tycho Brahe, were interpreted to fit a geo-centric planetary system; whereas, the solar system suggested by Copernicus was scorned. To this, one may add phlogiston, abiogenesis, and the ether. These were at one time proposed as valid, evidential explanations for what was then being investigated. All have since been passed over. In recent time, Ludwig Bolzman's theory concerning atoms and molecules was so strongly opposed by physicists, who dogmatically stuck to the orthodox view, that it contributed to his suicide. Three years later Bolzman's work was never doubted.

Elliott and Valenza should take heed. In their case, a lack of sufficient data is very evident. In 1994, Valenza was on record as saying that the tests he had conducted, using the *Thisted-Efron* method, were remarkably poor at identifying some of Shakespeare's poems; and that Shakespeare's use of language differed significantly between his plays and poetry.[6]

Ten years later, this appears forgotten, for he uses poems by Oxford (in fact, half of them are not even poems, they are songs) to compare them with 'Shakespeare's' mature plays. He then unites with Elliott to conclude that upon this basis, Oxford could not have written the Shakespeare canon. Based upon previous findings, this U-turn does appear to be suspiciously contrived, to say the least.

What is at issue is the difference in number and genre, between Oxford's meagre collection of 16 early poems and the twenty-nine dramatic works of 'Shakespeare's' more mature period. These were specially selected to be the touchstone of authority. Incredible as it may seem for purposes of comparison, 50% of Oxford's poems were actually songs written before he had reached the age of sixteen. Of the other eight, these appear to have been composed not long afterwards. A more balanced approach would have been for Elliott and Valenza to have used Oxford's songs and poems to seek similarities between them and Brooke's poem, *The Tragical History of Romeus and Juliet.* But had they done so, and received a positive result, what impact would this have had upon their further tests?

It is also this scanty number of verses used for comparison that gives increasing concern, especially when Gabriel Harvey's speech to Queen Elizabeth is recalled.

In July 1578, Elizabeth stopped over at Audley End in Essex, the home of Sir Thomas Smith, while making a royal progress to Cambridge. Oxford was in attendance to the Queen, and it was to him that Harvey turned, when giving his welcoming speech.

> *Thy splendid fame, demands even more than in the case of others the services of a poet possessing lofty eloquence. Thy merit doth not creep along the ground, nor can it be confined within the limits of a song. It is a wonder which reaches as far as the heavenly orbs … thy glory will spread out in all directions beyond the Arctic Ocean … Pallas striking her shield with her spear shaft will attend thee. For a long time past Phoebus Apollo has cultivated thy mind in the arts. English poetical measures have been sung by thee long enough. Let that Courtly Epistle [to the reader of The Courtier] – more polished even than the writings of Castiglione himself – witness how greatly thou dost excel in letters. I have seen many Latin verses of thine, yea, even more English verses are extant; thou hast drunk deep draughts not only of the Muses of France and Italy, but hast learned the manners of many men, and the arts of foreign countries.* [7]

The remaining part of Harvey's speech is decidedly patriotic; it urges Oxford to renounce his passion for literature and take up arms to fight. Those giving their dissent to Oxford's credentials are forced to dismiss Harvey's remarks as nothing more than obsequiousness. But this is to miss the point. Harvey was appealing to Oxford, in the presence of Queen Elizabeth and her Court, to *"throw away the insignificant pen, throw away bloodless books, and writings that serve no useful purpose;"* [8] and take up the sword in defence of England: adding the assurance that Pallas would defend him.

In making his plea, Harvey found it wholly natural for the ears of the assembled audience to refer to Oxford's verses as far outnumbering his Latin ones, and to refer to his plays by scenes located in France and Italy. How else could he be known to have learned and *made known* the manners of men and the arts of foreign countries, other than by exhibiting that knowledge in his stage plays?

The point is also missed that if Harvey had been lying about Oxford's ability with the pen – a view implicitly suggested by the wounding remarks so often voiced by May and Nelson against Oxford – his speech would have been ridiculed for its absurd expressions. It is difficult to envisage Harvey writing such a vacuous speech to present before the Queen. She was too intelligent for statements to be made before her that lacked merit. If Harvey intended to praise Oxford before the assembled audience of the Court, he would certainly have chosen something for which his subject had genuine talent, and which his royal audience were fully aware of. May and Nelson believe Oxford lacked the talent Harvey refers to. Yet, note how Harvey attempts to persuade Oxford away from his books and the pen, and redirect his energy to arms and State affairs. Harvey was voicing the opinion of many at Court, who viewed Oxford's writing as unworthy of a highborn, educated member of the nobility. May and Nelson, writing four centuries after Oxford's death, and reduced to picking up the literary leftovers of Oxford's censored work in order to feed these to Elliott and Valenza, have, between them, created a complete hash, which they audaciously promote as 'proof'.

Harvey's speech, and his recognition and acknowledgement of Oxford's intelligence, education, and excellence in the arts stand out in contrast to Nelson's depiction of him as a halfwit; as does May, when referring to his few teenage songs, which, he thought proper to use as ammunition with which to denounce him. Harvey had known Oxford as a fellow scholar at Cambridge, and he would have been well aware of his talent for verse. It is therefore to Harvey that one looks for a contemporary's opinion of Oxford's early literary ability, in lieu of so much that is now missing, but of which the Court was aware.

The meagre number of poems and songs used by Elliott and Valenza, in order to distance Oxford from Shakespeare, were never going to be adequate for the task they had set themselves. Such a pitiful sample contradicts Mendenhall's basic guidelines for stylometric testing, in which . . .

> *he showed that large amounts of text are needed to make any progress . . . Only over lengthy passages—many hundreds, even thousands of words long—do stylistic characteristics stand any chance of rising above statistical noise.* [9]

'Statistical noise' is exactly what Valenza and Elliott are using to discredit Oxford with. There is also the importance of giving due consideration to the disparity in styles; especially between the *poems* and *songs* of a youth, and comparing them with the tragedies, romances and histories found in *plays* written, and perfected many years later, during the poet's greater maturity. Failure to compensate for the incongruity of this comparison is enough to discredit whatever results are forthcoming. It is hard to imagine how any informed person could allow themselves to accept results obtained this way. One is tempted to wonder if stylometry was being hijacked for the sole purpose of devising a tool just to discredit Oxford with; for without adequate data, a computer is ineffective. And, even when it is effective, the results have to be interpreted by a human agency. If that human agency is biased, then interpretations will be skewed in that direction.

Consider again Harvey's' reference to the many English verses written by Oxford. This implies the few songs and poems comprising Oxford's juvenilia may actually have been recognised by Elliott and Valenza as inadequate gauges, if used for comparative purposes. For they tendered their admission that if the seeds of Oxford's genius did exist during his early years, they needed sufficient time to germinate.

> *If you unconditionally accept the premise that the young Shakespeare must have been a grub, Oxford's many and great differences from Shakespeare do not damage his claim to be the True Shakespeare at all. On the contrary, they support the claim by showing that the young Oxford looks every bit the journeyman grub that the True Young Shakespeare must have been.* [10]

In this one extract, they hit upon the weakness of drawing inferences based upon using stylometry as a tool for deciding Shakespeare's credentials as an author; there are no youthful writings of any kind, whatsoever, attributable to this man. He is the butterfly that was never a grub. Instead, like Athene plucked from the head of Zeus, fully armed, and ready for battle, Shaxpere arrived in London, fully equipped with all the attributes necessary to write plays and poems of everlasting genius; but with no juvenilia to his name, and no known experience in theatrical production. This, many believe to be more credible than Oxford having developed his art over time. Even Mozart, the most often quoted example of a prodigy, born to compose music, had his juvenilia. Shakespeare? Nothing!

By opting for their preference of Shaxpere over Oxford, Elliott and Valenza cannot be comparing like with like. Let the early poetry of Will Shaxpere, were it to exist, be used in their stylometry tests: then, perhaps, comparisons to Shakespeare's plays, or more likely lack of them, might justify this exercise.

There is also a further point that appears to have eluded Elliott and Valenza. It is the claim that tests show Oxford did not have sufficient stylistic qualities during his youth to have composed the mature works of Shakespeare. But he did not compose them during his youth! What are they talking about? By what method did Elliott and Valenza extrapolate the youthful style of Oxford to show the results were incompatible with that of the older Shakespeare? Very obviously, they had no such method. Instead, they took the mature plays of Shakespeare, and using these, they claimed the style in which the plays had been written could not be extrapolated from the style of Oxford's teenage poetry. The same comparative judgement could be drawn between Beethoven's juvenilia and his final pieces. Put simply, the two stylometricists have no program with which to compute artistic development; and this contradicts the claims they are making. In place of this absence, they impose their own value judgments upon the results they obtained from their venture into stylometry, and then declare it was the computer that arrived at this conclusion.

Despite these deficiencies, who do Elliott and Valenza believe Shakespeare to have been? It would appear they have no way of telling. To separate Oxford from Shakespeare is one thing: to say who this man Shakespeare was, is a different matter. If Elliott and Valenza are so wedded to language as an arbiter of the truth, then they should pay greater attention to the words of Appleton Morgan. *Venus and Adonis* was *"the first heir of my invention"* wrote 'Shakespeare': the man to whom these two give their allegiance. In which case, they have failed to understand that . . .

> *To have written the poem Venus and Adonis, however inferior to the plays, genius itself would have been inadequate . . . it is absolutely impossible that the lad Shakespeare acquired or used any other dialect than the Warwickshire he was born to, and that his father, mother and neighbours spoke.* (p. 80)

Yet the poem, with its one-thousand-one-hundred-and-ninety-four lines, contains not so much as one word of Warwickshire dialect. Are we to assume, even though proof to the contrary is now surely conclusive, that William Shakespeare was Will Shaxpere? Elliott and Valenza certainly subscribe to that assumption despite this violation of Shakespeare's language occurring in his *"first"* poem. This absence of conformity to expectation is yet another defect in their program, which renders still further the inadequacy of their conclusion.

What then is to be made of these two stylometricists' one last throw of the dice? According to their claim, based as it is upon stylometry, Shaxpere has no opposition because their computer program rejects the work of all other aspirants. But Matthews and Merriam were also using stylometric testing, when they concluded Marlowe to be the author of some of Shakespeare's work. This contradicts Elliott's and Valenza's claim, as well as casting doubt upon a system giving contrary results.

Elliott and Valenza's tests also rejected *Titus Andronicus* and *Henry V* as Shakespeare's, which is understandable because both plays were originally written before Oxford's Renaissance period, but let that pass for the moment. Upon the basis of their results, the two stylometricists maintain William Shakespeare has to be Will Shaxpere. But where is Will Shaxpere's early work? Everyone else has been required to submit their poetry, songs, and plays to the criteria which have been set, so that these may be judged against work of the mature Shakespeare. Why should Will Shaxpere be exempt? It would seem that Elliott and Valenza are reduced to admitting that his early work, if it ever existed, has neither survived nor been remembered by anyone, and so it cannot be used for comparison. But that is the answer they said was unacceptable when applied to Oxford's later poetry. They laughingly compared it to those wags who claim their other car is a Porsche.[11] In other words, it doesn't exist. Now they are forced to plead exemption from the condition they, themselves, set as an absolute gold standard for acceptance, by anyone with a claim to have written the plays of Shakespeare.

Suppose, instead, an attempt is made to avoid this pitfall by claiming that Will Shaxpere was William Shakespeare, therefore the requirement of his absent juvenilia for testing is unnecessary. Alas, it will not do. Quite simply, it is begging the question. The authorship debate is all about *proving* that Shaxpere was Shakespeare: not stating it as a bare fact.

Ultimately, the use of stylometry as a means of trying to prove Shaxpere's authorship fails. Elliott and Valenza are forced back to the fundamentals of the controversy without hope of salvation. The only recourse is to *allege* Shakespeare must be Shaxpere, because he cannot be any other. But, why Shaxpere? There is nothing in writing to even suggest he could put pen to paper. Evidence of an education, either from documents or by word of mouth, is nonexistent; every member of his family before and after him was uneducated: even illiterate, or at best semi-literate; there is no record that he was ever employed or engaged in any of the professions that Shakespeare wrote about; no poet or playwright of his time ever said they had met him; he never addressed a single word to any writer contemporaneous with himself; the archives of the 3rd Earl of Southampton (a nobleman to whom two major poems and a great number of sonnets were dedicated) have been searched, without finding a single mention of either Shaxpere's or Shakespeare's name; his last will and testament contains nothing to connect him with a literary life; in death he was totally ignored as a man of fame; no one living in his native town ever made known they were aware he was other than a local businessman; the house in which he lived remained a family possession for fifty years after his burial, but no books or letters were reported there as having once belonged to him.

Conversely, the monument erected some six or seven years after Shaxpere's death contains a Cardano grille, encrypted by Jonson vowing that Shakespeare was actually Edward de Vere; *Shake-speares Sonnets* are preceded by a strangely worded dedication, unique in its composition, since it was written by the publisher, and when it is rearranged, forms a cryptogram that again asserts Edward de Vere to have been Shakespeare; Henry Peacham's *Minerva Britanna* contains an illustration that shows a concealed person behind the arras of a theatrical discovery space, and a Latin motto that refers to this mystery person as de Vere; Benson, Digges and Marshall each made it known that Oxford was Shakespeare; the tributes in the First Folio, some of which hyphenate the name Shake–speare, are ambiguous; as too is Droeshout's portrait of 'Shakespeare', which doubles as Oxford. And in Sonnet 76, whose subject matter is the poet himself; Oxford twice names himself as the author. So! Why Shaxpere?

One can guess the response. Shaxpere was associated with the theatre; he acted, and was a shareholder in the Globe. So what? Others fall into that category as well. Does that qualify them to have been Shakespeare?

All of which, leads to a major and rather obvious omission in the work conducted by stylometricists. It is the absence of *Shake-speares Sonnets*

Thomas Thorpe risked amputation by cryptically inserting into his dedication, Oxford's role as the author of these sonnets. Oxford's passion for the teenage Southampton, whom Thorpe also named in his cryptogram, is discussed in Chapters 3, 4 and 5, along with accounts of what was happening at that time.

It was also during this period that George Puttenham wrote his *Art of English Poesie* (1589), in which his reference to the Earl of Oxford is in total disagreement with Elliott's and Valenza's rush to judgement.

> *And in Her Maiesties time that now is, are sprong vp an other crew of Courtly makers Noble men and Gentlemen of Her Maiesties owne seruauntes, who haue written excellently well as it would appeare if their doings could be found out and made publicke with the rest, of which number is first that noble Gentleman Edward Earle of Oxford.* [12]

This reference to Oxford's poetry not only coincides with Harvey's speech at Audley End, in which he made reference to the excellence of Oxford's Latin verses, and even more to those in English, it also supports Spenser's allusion to his personal affinity with the Muses, *"the Heliconian imps"*.

Yet despite these affirmations and acclamations from major Elizabethan sources, all that remain of Oxford's verses, aside from those published towards the end of his life under the name of Shakespeare, are a handful that he initialled in the full flush of youth.

The Sonnets' Place in Stylometric Testing

Belief that Will Shaxpere – a recent arrival to London from the provinces, a member of the lower classes, with little money to call his own, and no history of either a university education or of any literary achievement – could gain access to the enclave of a pampered and protected aristocrat like the 3rd Earl of Southampton is nothing more than a daydream.

To further believe that this same uncouth fellow, with his rasping, Warwickshire patois and country manners to match, was then encouraged by the young nobleman's mother Lady Mary Brown, and his guardian Lord Burghley, to write poems to this youth in the hope it might turn the young man's thoughts to marriage, even though he was still only seventeen years of age, is so totally ridiculous, one can only look in bewilderment at any mind with the mentality to repeat such nonsense. But it does not end there. For the next logical step in this sequence of fantasies is that the teenage Earl of Southampton also allowed intimacies to occur between himself and this Warwickshire provincial, while his guardian, Lord Burghley, the most powerful man in England with a responsibility to the Queen for his ward's moral welfare, winked at what was happening. Yet, make no mistake: these are serious implications for which Elliott and Valenza have allowed themselves to be drawn into.

It is a realization of the consequences attending an amorous connection between Shaxpere and Southampton that impels apologists to invent their escape clause. The Sonnets, they declare, were merely imaginative exercises: The people Shaxpere wrote about were not living people; they existed in his imagination.

Let us put this into context. In 1593, Shaxpere supposedly published *Venus and Adonis.* In the year following, he published *The Rape of Lucrece*, again, supposedly. Both of these poems were dedicated to Henry Wriothesley, 3rd Earl of Southampton, and both poems met with enormous success. In the same period of time, Shaxpere was allegedly writing the Sonnets as a poetic exercise, and instead of publishing them, he was circulating them *"among his private friends"*: at least, according to Francis Meres, that is what he was doing. Exactly who were these 'private friends' of Shaxpere's? Their names remain as mysterious as so much else about the literary life of this man: and they are never identified in any of his biographies.

They were certainly not counted amongst the actors he mixed with, for they would have sold these 'poetic exercises' on to a pirate publisher for the price of a meal, especially when outbreaks of Plague closed the theatres. Nor were they amongst his business associates: their interests were purely financial. So, who were numbered amongst Shaxpere's 'private friends'? Why have they never surfaced in any of his biographies? And why was it that publisher William Jaggard could only lay hands upon two of these 'poetic exercises', when there were up to a 154 of a similar quality in circulation?

Then again, if they were 'exercises', would not Jaggard's inclusion of the two he published have set the ball rolling for the remainder to be made public? Shakespeare's name had already been made famous by *Venus and Adonis* and *Lucrece,* two poems carrying his name as works that he had dedicated to the young Earl of Southampton,: financial success was guaranteed.

It is perfectly clear from this analysis that to maintain the sonnets were merely poetic exercises, does not stand scrutiny. In fact, it took another ten years before Thorpe got hold of the entire set. He then printed them off with such haste that *"the text is very corrupt, being full of unintelligent blunders."*[13] It then took another thirty-one years before a second edition was published, and a complete century was to pass before a third edition appeared. Poetic exercises, they most certainly were not.

If *Shake-speares Sonnets* were not poetic exercises, then they were autobiographical; the people and the events he wrote about were real. This explains why publishers could not get hold of them, and when they were eventually obtained, under questionable circumstances, they were printed in such haste, as to be on sale before the censor could take action.

This serves to explain why there was no time to attend to corrections: as is evident from surviving copies. It explains, too, Thorpe's strained syntax, and the cryptogram it conceals. In short, Oxford's composition of these poems, and his intimate relationship with the teenage Earl of Southampton, for this was the person he wrote about, are revealed by the sonnets as the cause of the poet's dishonour. Thorpe remained safe from prosecution. To have arrested and charged him would have opened up the proverbial 'can of worms', even to the extent of identifying the person who had leaked them – probably Oxford's son.

Since these poems are the more mature fruit of Shakespeare, the *"grub",* which so preoccupied Elliott and Valenza, then it is to these verses, rather than Oxford's juvenilia, that they should have turned, which raises an interesting question:

> *Valenza found that Shakespeare's use of language differed significantly between his poetry and his plays. In retrospect, this is not*

surprising: language in poetry is clearly more tightly constrained than it is in plays. [14]

Why, then, did he imagine the situation would be any different if he tested Oxford's teenage verses against Shakespeare's plays? One assumes he would have anticipated this problem would recur. Or did experimental bias enter the equation?

This is not to decry the importance of stylometry in properly controlled experiments: those, where all factors are considered equally. In the 1960s, two statisticians, Frederick Mosteller and David Wallace successfully used stylometry to determine the authorship of the political essays printed in New York newspapers during 1787-8, which were designed to influence voters in the matter of the new United States constitution.

The conclusion they reached was that James Madison was the author, and this agreed with the opinion of historians. But it required samples to be taken of many tens of thousands of words before Mosteller and Wallace were able to claim they had achieved a satisfactory result.

Compare this with the derisory number of Oxford's words used by Valenza and Elliott. A computer can do no more than compute. It works solely upon the input of available data. If that is deficient or incomplete, then the resulting computation will be suspect, even false.

But, much to the point is the rather obvious fact that results arising from a stylometric test have to be assessed by human intelligence. If that intelligence is subject to the bias of an existing conviction – *"confirmation bias"* – then alternative beliefs will be outweighed, or set aside in the final analysis.

This is important, because there is a prevailing perception amongst some members of the public that whatever a computer 'says' must be true. It is a confusion that arises from uniting computed results, which will be correct subject to the input of data, with the conclusions drawn from those results, which need not be correct. Recall that Matthews and Merriam interpreted their results from stylometric tests, and concluded that Shakespeare wrote *Edward III* under considerable influence from Marlowe.

In other words, personally held convictions about the man being tested can become instrumental to the conclusion drawn.

Matthews and Merriam ignored the strongly held opinion by some that Oxford was Shakespeare. In which case, it would have been Marlowe receiving guidance from 'Shakespeare'. Let those in the future who receive 'proofs' based upon stylometry be very aware: the more so, when they refer to Shakespeare.

> *The discovery of truth is prevented more effectively, not by the false appearance of things present and which mislead into error, not directly by weakness of the reasoning powers, but by preconceived opinion, by prejudice.*
>
> Arthur Schopenauer

EPILOGUE

EDWARD DE VERE, 17th Earl of Oxford, undoubtedly wrote under the penname William Shakespeare. He admitted as much in Sonnet 76. Ben Jonson also vowed it was true, by declaring it factual in the verse inscribed on the Stratford monument. Thomas Thorpe was another who confirmed its truth in the asyntatic address he placed at the front of the Sonnets. Leonard Digges and John Benson repeated the same information, in a similar fashion, in the 1640 republication of Shakespeare's sonnets.

Henry Peacham, Thomas Nashe, Henry Chettle, Gabriel Harvey, John Marston, Richard Barnfield, William Barkstead, and the author of *Willobie His Avisa*, each gave hints of varying degree, to express their knowledge of Shakespeare's real identity.

The plays of Shakespeare are another source of knowledge to the same effect The congruence existing between scenes from *Hamlet, All's Well That Ends Well; The Merry Wives of Windsor, Taming of the Shrew, Comedy of Errors, Winter's Tale* and *Henry V* – to name only some – when compared with events that featured strongly in Oxford's personal life, are so exceptional that there is no other set of parallels which can be referred to as providing a similar example of repeated, unconnected, coincidences.

Does this mean the authorship controversy has been settled and Oxford will now be acknowledged as Shakespeare? The short answer, unfortunately, is negative. Although the evidence stands, and will do so for as long as men breathe, progress towards its wider acceptance will more likely come with funerals. The Establishment figures do not know how to give up their belief in the old teaching, and they will continue to repeat it as dogma. In this endeavour, they will be supported by viperish journalists who rely for source material upon their scholarly contacts, and know they must pay respect to the hands that feed them: else they may be refused contact in future.

A paradigm shift occurs in four stages, and the Shakespeare authorship controversy is likely to be no different. The first stage will be familiar. It consists of repeated denials that these new ideas put forward are too preposterous to be true. There is no time limit to this stage. The second stage occurs when sceptics concede these new ideas have a few points of merit, but overall the evidence is very weak, and not sufficiently interesting to spend time with. Stage three begins when established figures in the debate realise that these new ideas have much more to them than was previously thought possible, and that the implications are far-reaching in bringing a fresh approach to the subject. The final stage four is noticed when former critics of the new idea start to identify with it, essentially making it their own. The interested reader will therefore be able to conclude exactly which stage the Shakespeare authorship debate has reached, and by whom.

APPENDIX A

The following grilles, with words randomly distributed in vertical alignment, occur in no special order and form no sensible sentences. They are therefore in contrast to the 34-column grille, which produces three clusters of words; these, when read together, very clearly state SO TEST HIM, I VOW HE IS E. DE VERE AS HE SHAKSPEARE; ME I. B.

33

```
S T A Y P A S S E N G E R W H Y G O E S T T H O V B Y S O F A S T
R E A D I F T H O V C A N S T W H O M E N V I O V S D E A T H H A
T H P L A S T W I T H I N T H I S M O N V M E N T S H A K S P E A
R E W I T H W H O M E Q V I C K N A T V R E D I D E W H O S E N A
M E D O T H D E C K Y S T O M B E F A R M O R E T H E N C O S T S
I E H A L L Y T H E H A T H W R I T T L E A V E S L I V I N G A R
T B V T P A G E T O S E R V E H I S W I T T
```

32

```
S T A Y P A S S E N G E R W H Y G O E S T T H O V B Y S O F A S
T R E A D I F T H O V C A N S T W H O M E N V I O V S D E A T H
H A T H P L A S T W I T H I N T H I S M O N V M E N T S H A K S
P E A R E W I T H W H O M E Q V I C K N A T V R E D I D E W H O
S E N A M E D O T H D E C K Y S T O M B E F A R M O R E T H E N
C O S T S I E H A L L Y T H E H A T H W R I T T L E A V E S L I
V I N G A R T B V T P A G E T O S E R V E H I S W I T T
```

31

```
S T A Y P A S S E N G E R W H Y G O E S T T H O V B Y S O F A
S T R E A D I F T H O V C A N S T W H O M E N V I O V S D E A
T H H A T H P L A S T W I T H I N T H I S M O N V M E N T S H
A K S P E A R E W I T H W H O M E Q V I C K N A T V R E D I D
E W H O S E N A M E D O T H D E C K Y S T O M B E F A R M O R
E T H E N C O S T S I E H A L L Y T H E H A T H W R I T T L E
A V E S L I V I N G A R T B V T P A G E T O S E R V E H I S W
I T T
```

30

```
S T A Y P A S S E N G E R W H Y G O E S T T H O V B Y S O F
A S T R E A D I F T H O V C A N S T W H O M E N V I O V S D
E A T H H A T H P L A S T W I T H I N T H I S M O N V M E N
T S H A K S P E A R E W I T H W H O M E Q V I C K N A T V R
E D I D E W H O S E N A M E D O T H D E C K Y S T O M B E F
A R M O R E T H E N C O S T S I E H A L L Y T H E H A T H W
R I T T L E A V E S L I V I N G A R T B V T P A G E T O S E
R V E H I S W I T T
```

These grilles are reproduced with the permission of Professor A. W. Burgstahler Ph.D. The complete set can be accessed at: http://www2.chem.ku.edu/aburgstahler/stratmon/

APPENDIX B

A table of numbers in the order which the letters appear in the sixaine beneath the bust of William Shakspeare (*sic.*) inside the church of the Holy Trinity at Stratford-upon-Avon.

A	B	C	D	E	F	G	H	I	K	L	M	N	O	P	Q	R	S	T	V	W	Y
3	26	44	37	9	30	11	15	38	95	70	52	10	18	5	111	13	1	2	25	14	4
6	148	114	60	12	39	17	23	56	115	171	84	46	24	69		34	7	21	43	49	16
31	200	141	122	19	150	196	41	75	142	172	88	54	29	97		100	8	22	55	74	27
36		161	124	35		205	50	78		185	109	79	42	203		120	20	33	58	102	143
45			135	53			64	82		191	133	86	51			152	28	40	87	106	172
62			139	61			65	103			147	90	57			155	32	48	112	126	
66				89			68	113			153	116	85			181	47	63	119	180	
71				98			77	123				131	108			198	59	67	188	217	
94				101			81	166				160	128			211	72	73	193		
99				110			93	182				195	136				83	76	201		
117				121			105	192					146				92	80	212		
132				125			107	194					154				96	91			
151				130			127	215					162				129	104			
169				134			138	218					208				144	118			
177				140			158										163	137			
187				149			168										165	145			
197				156			174										190	157			
204				159			176										209	164			
				167			179										216	173			
				175			214											178			
				186														183			
				189														184			
				206														199			
				210														202			
				213														207			
																		219			
																		220			

THE EXPECTATION THAT "LO E DE VERE" WILL OCCUR IN 1 0R 2 COLUMNS AS A RANDOM FORMATION ABUTTING "MY NAME".

For 2 columns, there are 5 pairs of adjacent columns beneath the letters of "MY NAME". We can therefore examine one of these pairs for the possibile spaces in which "LO E DE VERE" could occur, reading downwards.

L	E
O	D
	E
	V
	E
	R
	E
7	1

L	D
O	E
E	V
	E
	R
	E
6	2

L	V
O	E
E	R
D	E
E	
4	4

V	L
E	O
R	E
E	D
	E
5	3

D	L
E	O
V	E
E	
R	
E	
3	5

E	L
D	O
E	
V	
E	
R	
E	
2	6

The numbers represent the possible arrangements the words can take when those occupying one column remain stationary. A single pair of columns, reading downwards, allows 48 arrangements. Since the words can also be read upwards, the total is 96 per pair. There are also 5 pairs. This increases the total to 480. Added to this is the possible arrangement of the words occurring in a single column, for which there are 6. This doubles to 12 to allow for reading upwards or downwards. The total is now 492. Since this entire procedure could be repeated above "MY NAME" the final number of possible spaces for "LO E DE VERE" to occur is 984.

There are 448 letters in the sonnet. To find the centre based value for this probability model, allow that half the available letters have previously been set down. At the same time, allow that half the frequencies attached to L O E D U R are amongst those letters already set down. The product of the remaining frequencies is then obtained from the half that remains.

$$\begin{matrix} L & & O & & E & & D & & E & & U & & E & & R & & E \\ \frac{12}{224} & x & \frac{18}{223} & x & \frac{28}{222} & x & \frac{13}{221} & x & \frac{27}{220} & x & \frac{8}{219} & x & \frac{26}{218} & x & \frac{12}{217} & x & \frac{25}{216} \end{matrix}$$

Equal to: $1{\cdot}097{,}914{,}662 \times 10^{-10}$. For which there are 984 positions available, in which the required words can be set down.

Hence: $1{\cdot}097{,}914{,}662 \times 10^{-10} \times 984 = 0{\cdot}000, 000, 108$ (3 sig. figs).

Equivalent to 1 expected success in 9,259,259 separate trials.

BIBLIOGRAPHY

ACKROYD, P. Shakespeare The Biography, London, 2006

ADAMS, J.Q. Shakespeare's Titus Andronicus The First Quarto 1594: London, New York, 1936

AKRIGG, G. Shakespeare and the Earl of Southampton, Cambridge Massachusetts, 1968

ALTROCCHI, P.H. Malice Aforethought: The Killing of a Unique Genius, Hawaii, 2010

AMPHLETT, H. Who Was Shakespeare? London, 1955

ANDERSON, M. Shakespeare By Another Name, New York, 2005

ANDERSON, V. The De Veres of Castle Headingham, Suffolk, 1993

ANNENBERG, W. Westminster Abbey, Annenberg School Press, 1972

ASQUITH, C. Shadowplay, New York, 2006

AUBREY, J. Aubrey's Brief Lives, ed. A. A. Clark, Oxford, 1898

BATE, J. The Genius of Shakespeare, London, 1998

BAUER, F. Decrypted Secrets Methods and Maxims of Cryptology, Berlin, 1997

BEAUCLERK, C. Shakespeare's Lost Kingdom, New York, 2010

BRAME, M. and POPOVA, G. Shakespeare's Fingerprints, Washington (State), 2002

BRINKWORTH, E. Shakespeare and the Bawdy Court of Stratford, Chichester, 1972

BRYSON, B. Shakespeare, London, 2007

CAIRNCROSS, A. The Problem of Hamlet: A Solution, London, 1936

CALLERY, S. Codes and Ciphers, London, 2006

CAMDEN, W. Annales: The True and Royal History of the famous Queene of England, France & Ireland, London, 1625

CAMPBELL, S. Only Begotten Sonnets, London, 1978

CHAMBERS, E. The Elizabethan Stage, Oxford, 1923

— William Shakespeare: A Study of Facts and Problems, 1930

— The Elizabethan and Caroline Stage, Oxford, 1941

CHILJAN, K. Book Dedications to the Earl of Oxford, private, 1994

CHUTE, M. Ben Jonson of Westminster, London, 1954

— Shakespeare of London, New York, 1949

— Stories from Shakespeare, London, 1996

CLARK, Eva T. Hidden Allusions in Shakespeare's Plays, 3rd revised edition, ed. Ruth Loyd Miller, Port Washington, 1974. See also: Shakespeare's Plays in the Order of Their Writing, London, 1930

— The Man Who Was Shakespeare, New York, 1937

COMPTON MACKENZIE, F. William Cory, London, 1950

COOK, J. Dr Simon Forman, London, 2001

COURTHOPE, W. A History of English Poetry, London, 1920

CRYSTAL, D. & B. The Shakespeare Miscellany, London, 2005
DAWSON, G. E. and KENNEDY-SKIPTON, L. Elizabethan Handwriting 1500-1650: London, 1966
DE LUNA, B. The Queen Declined: An Interpretation of Willobie His Avisa, Oxford, 1970
DONNE, J. Divine Poems, Ed. Helen Gardner, Oxford, 1978
DORAN, G, The Shakespeare Almanac, London, 2009
DOWDEN, E. The Sonnets of William Shakespeare, London, 1881
DUGDALE, Sir William, Antiquities of Warwickshire, 1656
DUNCAN-JONES, K. Shakespeare's Sonnets, London, 1997
— Ungentle Shakespeare, London, 2001
— Shakespeare's Life and World, London, 2004
FEUILLERAT, A. John Lyly: Contributions à l'Histoire de la Renaissance en Angleterre, Cambridge, 1910
FIDO, M. Shakespeare, London, 1988
FOWLER, W. P. Shakespeare Revealed in Oxford's Letters, Portsmouth, N.H., 1986
FOX, L. The Shakespeare Handbook, London 1988
FRIEDMAN, W. F. and E. S. The Shakespeare Ciphers Examined, Cambridge, 1957 (reprinted 2011)
GERVINUS, G. Shakespeare Commentaries, trans. F. E. Bunnėt, London, 1883
GOSSON, S. Schoole of Abuse, 1579, (reprinted for Shakespeare Society, London, 1841).
GREEN, M. Wriothesley's Roses, Baltimore, 1993
GREENWOOD, Sir George, The Shakespeare Problem Restated, London, 1908
— Is There A Shakespeare Problem? London, 1916
GRILLO, E. Shakespeare and Italy, Glasgow, 1949
HALLIWELL-PHILLIPPS, J. O. The Life of William Shakespeare, London, 1848
HAYNES, A. Sex in Elizabethan England, Stroud, Gloucs. 1997
— Walsingham Elizabethan Spymaster & Statesman, Stroud, 2004
HENSLOWE, P. Henslowe's Diary, second edition, ed. R.A. Foakes, Cambridge, 2002
HEYLIN, C. So Long As Men Can Breathe, Philadelphia, 2009
HOLMES, M. Shakespeare and Burbage, Chichester, 1978
HONAN, P. Shakespeare: A Life, Oxford, 1998
JAMES, B. and Rubinstein, W. The Truth Will Out, New York, 2006
JAMESON, R. The Story of the Learned Pig, London, 1786
JONES, E. & Guy, R. The Shakespeare Companion, London, 2005
JONSON, B. Epigrammes I. Booke, London, 1616
— Under-woods, Consisting of Diverse Poems, London, 1616
— Works of Ben Jonson, ed. C. H. Herford and P. E. Simpson, Oxford, 1947

KAHN, D. The Codebreakers The Story of Secret Writing New York, 1996
KAY, W. Ben Jonson A Literary Life, Basingstoke, 1995
KILROY, G. Edmund Campion Memory and Transcription, Aldershot, 2005
KITTLE, W. Edward de Vere 17th Earl of Oxford and Shakespeare, Baltimore, 1942
KNECHT, R. J. The French Religious Wars 1562-1598, Oxford, 2002
KREILER, K. Der Mann, der Shakespeare erfand, Freiburg, 2009
LAROQUE, F. Shakespeare, Court, Crowd and Playhouse, trans. A. Campbell, London, New York, 1993
LEE, Sir Sidney, A Life of William Shakespeare, New York, 1909
LOONEY, J. Shake-speare Identified in Edward de Vere Seventeenth Earl of Oxford, London, 1920
MATUS, I. Shakespeare In Fact, New York, 1994
MCDONNELL, K. Medieval London Suburbs, Chichester, 1978
MCMICHAEL, G. & GLEN, E. M. Shakespeare and His Rivals, New York, 1962
MICHAEL, W. History of Wilton House, Westbury, Wilts. 1873
MICHELL, J. Who Wrote Shakespeare? London, 1996
MILES, R. Ben Jonson His Life and Work, London, 1986
MILLER, R. L. Oxfordian Vistas, Jennings, 1975,
MONTAGUE, W. H. A New and Universal History of England, London, 1798
MORGAN, J. A. A Study In The Warwickshire Dialect, New York, 1900
NASHE, T. Works of Thomas Nashe, ed. R.B. McKerrow, revised, F.P. Wilson, Oxford. 1958
NELSON, A. Monstrous Adversary, Liverpool, 2003
NIMS, J. Metamorphosis, (Arthur Golding's translation), New York, 1965
O'CONOR, N. J. Godes Peace and the Queenes Vicissitudes 1539-1615, London, 1934
OGBURN, D. and C. This Star of England, New York, 1952
OGBURN, C. The Mystery of William Shakespeare, London, 1988
PEQUIGNEY, J. Such is My Love: A Study of Shakespeare's Sonnets, Chicago, 1985
PINCOCK, S & FRARY, M. Codebreaker: The History of Secret Communication, London, 2007
PRICE, D. Shakespeare's Unorthodox Biography, Westport, 2001
READ, C. Sir William Cecil and Queen Elizabeth, London, 1960
RENDALL, G. H. Shakespeare's Sonnets and Edward de Vere, London, 1930
ROPER, D. L. Shakespeare: To Be Or Not To Be? Truro, 2010
ROWE, N. Some Account of the Life &c, of Mr. William Shakespeare, London, 1709
ROWSE, A. Introduction to The Poems of Shakespeare's Dark Lady, by Emila Lanier, 1978
—— Shakespeare's Southampton, London, 1965
—— Eminent Elizabethans, London, 1983
—— Shakespeare The Man, London, 1988

SATINOVER, J. The Truth Behind the Bible Code, London, 1997
SCHOENBAUM, S. Shakespeare's Lives, Oxford, 1991
SEARS, E. Shakespeare and the Tudor Rose, private, 1991
SHAPIRO, J. 1599 A Year in the Life of William Shakespeare, London, 2005
— Contested Will, Who Wrote Shakespeare, London, 2010
SHEAVYN, P.A.B. The Literary Profession in the Elizabethan Age, Manchester, 1967
SINGH, S. The Code Book The Science of Secrecy from Ancient Egypt to Quantum Cryptography, London, 1999
SLATER, G. Seven Shakespeares, London, 1931
SOBRAN, J. Alias Shakespeare, New York, 1997
STONE, L. The Crisis of the Aristocracy, 1558-1641, Oxford, 1965
STOPES, C. Shakespeare's Environment, second issue, G. Bell, London, 1918
— The Life of Henry, Third Earl of Southampton, Shakespeare's Patron, Cambridge, 1922
STOW, J. The Survey of London, ed. Valerie Pearl, London, 1987, (1st ed. 1603)
STREITZ, P. Oxford Son of Elizabeth I, Darien, CT, 2001
TANNER, L. E. History of the Coronation, Andover, 1952
TROW, M. Who Killed Kit Marlowe? Sutton, 2002
WARD, B. The Seventeenth Earl of Oxford, 1550-1604, London, 1928
WHALEN, R. Shakespeare: Who Was He? Westport, CT, 1994
WARRE CORNISH, F. Extracts from the Letters and Journals of William Cory, Oxford, 1887
WHITTEMORE, H. The Monument: Shakespeare's Sonnets by Edward de Vere, 17th Earlof Oxford, Mass. 2008
WILLIAMS, E. N. Dictionary of English and European History 1485-1789 Middlesex, 1986
WILLIAMS, Neville: The Life and Times of Elizabeth I, London, 1972
WILLIAMS, Norman L: Sir Walter Raleigh, London, 1988
WILLIS, C. Behind Shakespeare's Mask, UPSO, 2006
WILSON, I. Shakespeare: The Evidence, London, 1993
WILSON, J. Titus Andronicus on the Stage in 1595 Shakespeare Survey: Cambridge & London, 1948
YOUNG Frances B. Mary Countess of Pembroke, London, 1912
YOUNG H. Mc. Sonnets of Shakespeare: A Psycho-Sexual Analysis: Wisconsin, 1937

SUNDRY REFERENCE MATERIAL

Arden Shakespeare Paperbacks, London, various dates for different plays
Arden Edition of the Works of William Shakespeare, London, various dates for different plays
Arden Shakespeare, Third Series, London, various dates for different plays

A Dictionary of Literary Terms, J. Cuddon, Revised Edition, London, 1982
Encyclopedia of World Mythology, ed. Emma Gray, London, 2006
Essential Shakespeare Handbook, Dunton-Downer, L & Riding, A., London, 2004
Great Oxford, Tunbridge Wells, 2004
Hampton Court Palace, Her Majety's Stationery Office, London, 1971
New Penguin Shakespeare, London, 1967 and variously dated
Oxford Compendium of English Literature, Oxford, 1989
Oxford Latin Dictionary, Oxford, 1968
Oxford National Dictionary of Biography, Vol. 43, ed. H.G.C. Mathew & B. Harrison, Oxford, 2004
Oxford Shakespeare, 'Titus Andronicus', Oxford, 1998
Scripta Mathematica, Vol. 6 (3), 'Cardan on Cryptography', Charles J. Mendelsohn, October 1939
Shakespeare Complete Works, Vol. 2, The Histories, ed. P. Alexander, London & Glasgow, 1988
Shakespeare's Titus Andronicus The First Quarto 1594, Folger Shakespeare Library, New York, 1936
The City of London Churches, ed. Elizabeth Drury, Collins & Brown Ltd., 1998
The Dictionary of Phrase and Fable, classic edition, E. Cobham Brewer, ISBN 0 86136 788 X, n.d.
The Oxford Companion to English Literature, ed. Margaret Drabble, Oxford, 1985
Tennessee Law Review, vol. 72: 1, Knoxville, 2004
Tourist Guide to St. Nicholas Church, Castle Hedingham, n.d.
United States Cryptologic History – Sources in Cryptologic History No. 3 *The Friedman Legacy*
Who's Who in Shakespeare, F. Stokes, New York, 2007
Wilton House: official booklet, Beric Tempest, n.d.
Wotton Baronetage: ed. Kimber & Johnstone, London, 1741

REFERENCES

INTRODUCTION

1 Friedman, W. F. and E. S. *The Shakespeare Ciphers Examined*, 1957, 14

2 Janis, I. *Victims of Groupthink: A Psychological Study of Foreign Policy Decisions and Fiascoes*, 1972, 9

1 THE MONUMENTAL TRUTH

1 *Tennessee Law Review* Vol. 72:1, 'Stratford Si! Essex No!' A. Nelson, 2004, 154-5

2 Stopes, C. C. *Shakespeare's Environment*, 2nd issue, 1918, 118.

3 ibid. 118

4 Matus, I. L. *Shakespeare In Fact*, 1994, 201,

5 ibid. (see Playbill), 200.

6 Stopes, 348.

7 ibid. 120-1

8 id 121

9 id

10 Wilson, I. *Shakespeare: The Evidence*, 1993, 397

11 Michell, J. *Who Wrote Shakespeare*, 1996, 97

12 *Shakespeare Oxford Society Newsletter*, Vol.30 : 3, Sir G. Greenwood, 9

13 Schoenbaum, S. *Shakespeare's Lives*, 1970

14 *Shakespeare Oxford Society Newsletter*, op. cit.

15 Matus, 204

16 Asquith, C. *Shadowplay The Hidden Beliefs and Coded Politics of William Shakespeare*, 2005, xvi

17 Kahn, D. *The Codebreakers*, 1996, 879,

18 Ogburn, C. *The Mystery of William Shakespeare*, 1988, 157

19 Callery, S. *Codes and Ciphers*, 2006, 115

20 ibid. 51

21 *Scripta Mathematica*, Vol. 6 (3), 'Cardan on Cryptography'. Charles J. Mendelsohn. October 1939, 166

22 Satinover, J. *The Truth Behind the Bible Code* 1997, 97

23 Kahn, 145

24 *Scripta Mathematica*, op. cit., 165

25 Friedman, W. and E. *The Shakespearian Ciphers Examined*, 1957, 280

26 *United States Cryptologic History – Sources in Cryptologic History No. 3 The Friedman Legacy: A Tribute to William and Elizebeth Friedman, second printing*, Center for Cryptologic History, National Security Agency, 1992, 22

27 Kahn, 879

28 *United States Cryptologic History*, op. cit., 22

29 *Confirmation bias*, Wikipedia

30 *Shakespeare Complete Works*, Vol. 4: 'Tragedies and Poems' ed. Peter Alexander: 1988, 15

31 Ionson, B. *Under-woods, Consisting of Diverse Poems*, An Epitaph on Henry L. La-ware, 1616, 227

32 Edward de Vere Newsletter No.9, ed. Nina Greene, with references from Donaldson, I. *Ben Jonson*, 1985

33 Kay, W. *Ben Jonson A Literary Life*, 1995, 10

34 Jonson, B. *Epigrammes I. Booke*, 1616, 767

35 Stopes, 109

36 Asquith, 20

37 Pincock, S & Frary, M. *Code Breaker The History of Secret Communication*, 2007, 39

38 *De Shakespeare Nostrati*, See Ogburn, 1988, 169

39 *Encyclopaedia Britannica*, CD Rom 2001: 'The Tudor Ideal of Government'

40 Kay, 70

41 ibid. 70

42 *Shakespeare Complete Works*, Vol. 4, 10

43 Dunton-Downer, L & Riding, A. *Essential Shakespeare Handbook*, 2004, 9

44 *Tennessee Law Review* Vol 72:1, *Evidence for a Literary Biography*, D. Price, 2004, 145

45 Nims, J. *Metamorphosis*, (Arthur Golding's translation), 1965, Introduction

46 *The Dictionary of Phrase and Fable*, classic edition, E. Cobham Brewer, ISBN 0 86136 788 X, n.d. 1276-7

47 Tourist Guide to St. Nicholas Church, Castle Hedingham, 9

48 Ogburn, 693

49 id.

50 *Encyclopaedia Britannica*, CD Rom 2001 de luxe: 'The Vere Family'

51 Ogburn, 692

52 *Encyclopaedia Britannica*, CD Rom 2001 de luxe: 'Dutch Language'

53 Kay, 161

54 id.

55 Ogburn, 25

56 ibid. 24

2 REINTERPRETING SHAKESPEARE

1 Ogburn, C. *The Mystery of William Shakespeare*, 1988, 16

2 ibid.

3 Wilson, I. *Shakespeare: The Evidence*, 1993, 56

4 ibid.

5 Ogburn, 27

6 Fido, M. *Shakespeare*, 1988, 12

7 Asquith, C. *Shadowplay*, 2006, 282-3

8 Ogburn, 27-8

9 Fox, L. *The Shakespeare Handbook*, 1988, 41

10 Michell, J. *Who Wrote Shakespeare?* 1996, 59

11 Jones, E. & Guy, R. *The Shakespeare Companion*, 2005, 52

12 Rowe, N. *Some Account of the Life &c, of Mr. William Shakespeare*, 1709
13 Ogburn, 655
14 *Tennessee Law Review*, vol. 72:1, 'The 1592 Groatsworth Attack', D. Carroll, Knoxville, 2004, 284-5
15 ibid. 291
16 Ogburn, 655
17 Ackroyd, P. *Shakespeare The Biography*, 2006, 198
18 Ogburn, 655
19 ibid. 633
20 Bate, J. *The Genius of Shakespeare*, 1998, 14
21 ibid. 19
22 Ogburn, 47
23 *Shakespeare Complete Works*, Vol.2, The Histories, ed. P. Alexander, 1988, 404
24 Ogburn, 55
25 Carroll, op. cit., 286
26 *Shakespeare Complete Works*, op. cit. 404
27 ibid. 401
28 ibid. 400
29 ibid. 404
30 id.
31 Wilson, 191
32 Ogburn, 51
33 Laroque, F. *Shakespeare, Court, Crowd and Playhouse*, trans. A. Campbell, 1993, 48
34 Rowe, N. *Some Account of the Life &c. of Mr William Shakespeare*, http://shakespeare.palomar.edu/rowe.htm [last visited: 19/1/2007]
35 Ogburn, 106
36 McMichael, G. & Glen, E.M. *Shakespeare and His Rivals*, 1962
37 Rowse, A. *Shakespeare The Man*, 1988, 64
38 Chute, M. *Ben Jonson of Westminster*, 1954, 58
39 Trow, M. *Who Killed Kit Marlowe?* 2002, 82
40 Kay, W. *Ben Jonson A Literary Life*, 1995, 49
41 Ogburn, 56
42 ibid. 56
43 Crystal, D & B. *The Shakespeare Miscellany*, 2005, 90
44 Wilson, 75
45 Michell, 249
46 ibid. 249
47 Wilson, 216
48 Michell, 249
49 Haynes, A. *Sex in Elizabethan England*, 1997, 62
50 Ogburn, 140
51 ibid. 113
52 id.
54 Ogburn, 30

55 Shakespeare Birthplace Trust Records Office, Misc. Doc. I, 106
56 Matus, I. *Shakespeare In Fact*, 1994, 38
57 Ogburn, 30
58 Laroque, 133
59 ibid. 133
60 Ogburn, 9
61 Nelson, A. *Monstrous Adversary*, 2003, 158
62 Ogburn, 10
63 *Shakespeare Complete Works*, Vol.2, 84
64 ibid. see 'King John', 25
65 ibid. 26
66 ibid. see '2 and 3 Henry VI', 406
67 ibid. 407
68 Gervinus, G. *Shakespeare Commentaries*, trans. F. E. Bunnėt 1883, 467
69 *Encyclopædia Britannica*, CD Rom de luxe; 'William Cecil 1st Baron Burghley — Assessment'.
70 Wilson, 242
71 Ogburn, 620
72 ibid. 621
73 Nelson, 2003, 386
74 Michell, 1996, 54-5
75 Ogburn, 1988, 142
76 ibid. 143
77 Wilson, 1993, 119-20
78 ibid. 70
79 Nelson, 2003, 386
80 ibid. 387
81 *Tennessee Law Review,* vol. 72:1, 'Stratford Si! Oxford No!' A. Nelson, 2004, 150
82 Wilson, 262-3
83 Looney, J. *Shake-speare Identified in Edward de Vere Seventeenth Earl of Oxford and the Poems of Edward de Vere* vol. 2 'Oxfordian Vistas' ed. Ruth Lloyd Miller, New York, London, 1975, 23
84 Ogburn, 354
85 ibid. 620-1
86 ibid. 151
87 *Troilus and Cressida*, ed. K. Palmer, Arden Shakespeare; 1981, 2
88 Ogburn, 152
89 *Love's Labour's Lost*, ed. R. David, Arden Shakespeare, 1981, xvi
90 ibid. xvi
91 Gervinus, G. 164
92 *Love's Labour's Lost*, xiii
93 Michell, 192
94 Gervinus, 298
95 Dunton-Downer, L. & A. Riding, *Essential Shakespeare Handbook*, 2004, 458

96 Wilson, 253
97 ibid. 254
98 ibid. 461-2
99 Crystal, 78
100 Ogburn, 94
101 Matus, 19
102 Wilson, 270
103 Cook, J. *Dr Simon Forman*, 2001, 109
104 Fido, 120
105 Wilson, 360
106 Cook, 109
107 Laroque, 131
108 Wilson, 361
109 ibid
110 Honan, P. *Shakespeare: A Life*, 1998, 328-9
111 Chute, M. *Ben Jonson of Westminster* 1954, 58
112 Wilson, 295
113 *The Dictionary of Phrase and Fable*, classic edition, E. Cobham Brewer, ISBN 0 86136 788 X, n.d.
114 Nelson, 2003, 8
115 id.
116 id.
117 *Encyclopædia Britannica*, CD Rom. 2001 de luxe: 'Armada'
118 Nelson, 2003, 317
119 ibid. 315
120 *De Vere Society Newsletter*, 'Melicertus', R. Detobel, April/May 2001, 17
121 *Encyclopædia Britannica*, 'Sidney'.
122 Quoted from 'On Shakespeare's Pastoral Name' in *Notes and Queries* 4th S. XII, Dec. 27, 1873, 509-10 see: *De Vere Society Newsletter*, 'Melicertus', R. Detobel, April/May 2001, 24
123 Ogburn, 561
124 Fido, 117
125 ibid. 118
126 Crystal, 124
127 Jones, E. & Guy R., *The Shakespeare Companion*, 2005, 150
128 Schoenbaum, S. *Shakespeare's Lives*, 1991, 303
129 http://www.wikipedia.org/Philip_Henslowe [last visited: 23/05/07]
130 Crystal, 105
131 Laroque, 110
132 ibid. 114
133 ibid. 115
134 Ogburn, 106
135 Bentley, R. *Shakespeare Cross Examination* (American Bar Association 1961 3rd printing 1974), see 'The Shakespeare Oxford Newsletter, vol.30 No.2A, spring 1994, 15
136 Laroque, 73; also Ogburn, 31

137 Wilson, 297
138 Fido, 115
139 Honan, 303
140 Duncan-Jones, K. *Ungentle Shakespeare*, 2001, 173
141 Ogburn, 33
142 *Shakespeare in the Public Records,*' Shakespeare's Will and Signatures', Jane Cox, 1964, 24-34
143 Wilson, 385
144 ibid. 386
145 ibid. 392
146 ibid. 310
147 Laroque, 134
148 Bentley, 15
149 *Shakespeare Complete Works*, Vol.4, op. cit., 12
150 Bentley, 15
151 Ogburn, 41; see Lansdowne MS. 777, fo. 67b., British Museum, from the reign of King James I.
152 *Shakespeare Complete Works*, Vol.4, op. cit., 13
153 Crystal, 127
154 Wilson, 297
155 Michell, 56-7
156 http://shakespeareauthorship.com/monrefs.html [last visited: 30/5/07].
157 Kay, 70
158 Price, D. *Shakespeare's Unorthodox Biography,* London, 2001
159 Ogburn, 19
160 ibid. 138

3 Thomas Thorpe's Cryptogram

1 Anderson, M. *Shakespeare By Another Name,* 2005, 363
2 Wilson, I. *Shakespeare: The Evidence,* 1993, 345
3 Gervinus, G. *Shakespeare Commentaries,* trans. F. E. Bunnètt, 1883, 442
4 Sobran, J. *Alias Shakespeare*, 1997, 144
5 id.
6 Michell, J. *Who Wrote Shakespeare,* 1996, 181
7 *Great Oxford,* see 'Secrets of the Dedication to Shakespeare's Sonnets', J. Rollett, 2004, 253ff
8 Michell, 181
9 *Great Oxford*, ibid. 265
10 Callery, S. *Codes and Ciphers,* 2006, 51
11 Bryson, B. *Shakespeare*, 2007, 10-11, 110
12 *Shakespeare Oxford Newsletter*, R. Horne, 1970, and Folger Shakespeare Library (documents).
13 id.
14 *Great Oxford*, op. cit. 265
15 id.
16 Cuddon, J. *A Dictionary of Literary Terms*, Revised Edition, 1982, 89

17 Ackroyd, P. *Shakespeare The Biography*, 2006, 288
18 id.
19 Singh, S. *The Code Book The Science of Secrecy from Ancient Egypt to Quantum Cryptography*, 1999, 7
20 Kilroy, G. *Edmund Campion Memory and Transcription*, 2005, 1
21 *Troilus and Cressida*, ed. K. Palmer, Arden Shakespeare, 1991, 2
22 *De Vere Society Newsletter*, February 2007: 'Elizabeth and ffrancis Trentham of Rocester Abbey', J. Crick, 29
23 Nelson, A. *Monstrous Adversary*: 2003, 438
24 Michell, 180
25 http://www.tudorplace.com.ar/Bios/RobertSouthwell(Father).htm [last visited: 14/6/2007]
26 Duncan-Jones, K. *Shakespeare's Sonnets*, 1997
27 *Shakespeare Oxford Newsletter*, Winter 2007, Vol.43 No.1, 13-21: James W. Brooks, Ph.D. A comparison of the 1609 and 1640 Texts of Shakespeare's Sonnets.

4 WHAT THE SONNETS TELL

1 Wilson, I. *Shakespeare: The Evidence*, 1993, 345
2 Fido, M. *Shakespeare*, 1988, 45
3 Holden, Anthony *Shakespeare's True Love*
4 Pequigney, J. *Such is My Love: A Study of Shakespeare's Sonnets*, 1985, 1
5 Nelson, A. *Monstrous Adversary*, 2003, 141
6 ibid. 215
7 *Shakespeare Oxford Newsletter*, Vol. 41 No.3, The Dark Lady and Her Bastard, J. Hamill, 8
8 Green, M. *Wriothesley's Roses*, 1993, 99ff
9 Anderson, M. *Shakespeare By Another Name*, 2005, 197
10 Sobran, J. *Alias Shakespeare*, 1997, 135
11 Ogburn, C. *The Mystery of William Shakespeare*, 1988, 284
12 Wilson, 146
13 Heylin, C. *So Long As Men Can Breathe*, 2009, 60
14 Crystal, D & B. *The Shakespeare Miscellany*, 2005, .13
15 http://www.luminarium.org/encyclopedia/wriothesley3.htm [last visited: 12/3/2011]
16 http://www.luminarium.org/result/raleighbio.htm [last visited: 25/6/2007]
17 Williams, Neville: *The Life and Times of Elizabeth I*, 1972, 152
18 *De Vere Society Newsletter*, February 2007, 24-35: Elizabeth and ffrancis Trentham of Rocester Abbey, J. Crick
19 Fido, 47
20 Campbell, S. *Only Begotten Sonnets*, 1978, 107
21 *The Oxford Companion to English Literature*, ed. Margaret Drabble, 1985, 1071
22 Feuillerat, A. *John Lyly: Contribution à l' Histoire de la Renaissance en Angleterre*, 1910

23 Nelson, 423
24 Akrigg, G. *Shakespeare and the Earl of Southampton*, Cambridge Massachusetts, 1968
25 Wilson, 25
26 *The Dictionary of Phrase and Fable*, classic edition, E. Cobham Brewer, ISBN 0 86136 788 X, n.d.
27 *Encyclopaedia Britannica* CD Rom. De luxe 2001: 'The Woman Ruler in a Patriarchal World'.
28 Montague, W.H. *A New Universal History of England, vol.2:* 1798, 84
29 ibid. 'James I (1603-25)'
30 Nelson, 357
31 Wilson, 55-6
32 Anderson, 135
33 Haynes, A. *Sex In Elizabethan England*, 1997, 39
34 ——. *Walsingham Elizabethan Spymaster & Statesman*, 2004, 87-8
35 Ogburn, 661
36 Haynes, 1997, 40
37 Nelson, 259
38 Anderson, 168
39 Bate, J. *The Genius of Shakespeare*, 1998, 90
40 *Great Oxford*, see 'Dating the Plays: Hamlet' Eddi Jolly, 2004, 173
41 Pequigney, 1
42 *Shakespeare Complete Works*, Vol. 2: 'Histories' ed. Peter Alexander: 1988, 80
43 Tanner, L. E. *History of the Coronation,* 1952, 43
44 ibid. 44
45 Chambers, E. K. *Elizabethan Stage,* vol.1 1923, Ch. 2
46 Bowen, Gwynneth *The Coronation Sonnet* Shakespeare Fellowship News-Letter Spring, 1956
47 Rendall, G. H. *Shakespeare's Sonnets and Edward de Vere* 1930
48 Amphlett, Hilda *Who Was Shakespeare,* 1955, 150
Kittle, W. *Edward de Vere 17th Earl of Oxford and Shakespeare,* 1942, 160
49 O'Conor, N. J. *Godes Peace & the Queenes Vicissitudes of a House 1539-1615,* 1934
50 Ogburn, 273
51 Dowden, E. *The Sonnets of William Shakespeare,* 1881
52 Fox, L. *The Shakespeare Handbook*, 1988, 217
53 Gervinus, G. *Shakespeare Commentaries*, transl. F. E. Bunnètt, 1883, 446
54 Williams, Norman: *Sir Walter Raleigh*, 1988, 49
55 ibid. 81
56 ibid. 106
57 ibid. 73
58 ibid. 79
59 ibid. 70
60 ibid. 109
61 Williams, Neville, *The Life and Times of Elizabeth I*, 1972, 197

62 Montgomery, W. *A Universal History of England*, Vol. 2, 1798, 68
63 Williams, Norman, 113
64 *What Was Life Like In The Realm of Elizabeth*, consultant, Professor Norman Jones, Time-Life, 144
65 *The Poems of Sir Walter Ralegh*, ed. Agnes M. C. Latham, 1951, 25
66 Williams, Norman: f.n. 115
67 Cook, J. *Dr Simon Forman*, 2001, 64
68 Williams, 105
69 ibid. 105-6
70 ibid. 118-9
71 Ogburn, 669
72 ibid. 661
73 id.
74 ibid. 671
75 *Dictionary of National Biography*
76 ibid.
77 Berkeley Young, F. *Mary Countess of Pembroke,* 1912, 139
78 Donne, J. *Divine Poems,* ed. H. Gardner, 1978, 34-5
79 Berkeley Young, F. 133
80 Aubrey, J. *Brief Lives,* ed. O. L. Dick, 1949, 139

5 A Shameful Cover-up

1 Bryson, B. *Shakespeare*, 2007, 9
2 Ogburn, C. *The Mystery of William Shakespeare*, 1988, 25
3 Wilson, I. *Shakespeare: The Evidence*, 1993, 21
4 ibid. 22
5 Asquith, C. *Shadowplay The Hidden Beliefs and Coded Politics of William Shakespeare,* 2005, 283
6 Ogburn 560
7 Asquith, xiv
8 *Shakespeare Complete Works*, Vol.2, The Histories, ed. P. Alexander, 1988, 80
9 Ogburn, 129
10 http://www.sirbacon.org/cecil.htm [last visited: 3/5/2007]
11 *Shakespeare Complete Works*, Vol. 4: 'Tragedies and Poems' ed. Peter Alexander: 1988 373
12 Ogburn, 634
13 Haynes, A. *Sex In Elizabethan England,* 1997, 101, 105
14 Nelson, A. *Monstrous Adversary,* 2003, 215
15 *The Observer Review* 21 April, 2002, 5, Portrait is exhibited at Hatchlands, Surrey, as part of the Cobbe collection.
16 Stopes, C. *Life of Henry Third Earl of Southampton, Shakespeare's Patron,* 1922, 65
17 Wilson, 349
18 Asquith, 12
19 ibid.

20 id.

21 Kay, D. *Ben Jonson A Literary Life*, 1995, 70

22 Dunton-Downer, L & Riding, A. *Essential Shakespeare Handbook,* 2004, 462

23 Nelson, A. op. cit., 214

24 Haynes, 107-8

25 Rictor Norton, "Anthony Bacon", *Gay History and Literature*, updated 14 June 2008 <http://rictornorton.co.uk/baconant.htm>.

26 ibid.

27 Heylin, C. *So Long As Men Can Breath,* 2009, 93 (Quoting J.M. Robertson: *The Problems of the Shakespeare Sonnets,* 1926)

28 Rollins, H. E. *A New Variorum Edition of Shakespeare – The Sonnets,* 1944, 327

29 Whittemore, H. *The Monument,* 2005, 20

30 Streitz, P. *Oxford Son of Queen Elizabeth I,* 2001, 239-40

31 *Ben Jonson Converssations with William Drummond,* ed. R.F. Patterson, 1923, 30

32 Montague, W. H. *A New and Universal History of England,* vol. 2, 1798, 39

33 Haynes, 31

34 ibid. 28

6 Shakespeare's Learning Curve

1 Nelson, A. *Monstrous Adversary,* 2003, 95

2 Clark, E. T. *Hidden Allusions in Shakespeare's Plays*, 1974, 11

3 ibid. 10

4 Wikipedia: 'Falstaff'

5 Rowe, N. *Some Account of the Life &c, of Mr. William Shakespeare*, 1709

6 Halliwell-phillips, J. O. *The Life of William Shakespeare*, 1848, 155

7 Gervinus, G. *Shakespeare Commentaries*, 1883, 299 fn

8 Clark, 15

9 Ogburn, C. *The Mystery of William Shakespeare*, 1988, 595

10 ibid.

11 Nelson, 74

12 Williams, N. L. *Sir Walter Raleigh*, London, 1988, 21

13 Ogburn, 568

14 Nelson, 238

15 ibid.

16 Wilson, M. *Sir Philip Sidney*, 1931, 168

17 Clark, 20

18 Gervinus, 164

19 ibid. 165

20 David, R. ed. *Love's Labour's Lost,* 1981, xxiii

21 ibid. xxix

22 Williams, E. N. *DictionaryofEnglish & European History1485-1789,* 1986, 215

23 David, xxx

24 Knecht, R. *The French Religious Wars 1562-1598,* 1986, 215
25 David, xxix
26 ibid. 36
27 Gervinus, 165
28 David, xxvii
29 ibid. xxv
30 ibid. xxx
31 Clark, 364
32 Williams, N. L. 23
33 ibid. 21
34 ibid. 22
35 Rowe, op. cit.
36 ibid.
37 Clark, 605
38 ibid. 475
39 www.earlofoxford.com/oo00.htm
40 Lamping, A. *Italian Grammar,* 83
41 Stokes, F. G. *Who's Who In Shakespeare*, 2007, 282.

7 Plays Sketched from Life

1 Sobran. J. *Alias Shakespeare*, 1997, 152
2 *The Tempest*, ed. F. Kermode, Arden Shakespeare, 1992, 137, 141
3 *The Tempest*, ed. V.M. and A.T. Vaughan, Arden Shakespeare, Third Series, 2007, 291-2
4 *Shakespeare Oxford Society Newsletter*, Vol. 32: 3. *The Tempest and the Bermuda Shipwreck of 1609*, P. Moore, 6
5 Miles, R. *Ben Jonson His Life and Work*, 1986, 99
6 *The Tempest*, op. cit. xv
7 *Works of Ben Jonson*, ed. C.H. Herford, and P. and E. Simpson, vol. 6, Oxford, 1925-52, 57-8
8 Vaughan, op. cit. 165 f.n.229
9 Nelson, A. *Monstrous Adversary*, 2004, 309
10 ibid. 418
11 Grillo, E. *Shakespeare and Italy*, 1949
12 *The Merchant of Venice*, ed. J. R. Brown, Arden Shakespeare, 1964, xxix
13 ibid. xxvii ; refer Hatfield House MSS, vii (1899), 440
14 Ogburn, 117
15 *As You Like It*, ed. Agnes Latham, Arden Shakespeare, 1993, f.n. 136
16 Dunton-Downer, L. & A. Riding, *Essential Shakespeare Handbook*, 2004, 275
17 Nelson, 46, 51
18 ibid. 43
19 id. 44
20 id. 71
21 id. 71
22 id. 107

23 id. 108,111
24 id. 81
25 *All's Well That Ends Well*, ed. G. K. Hunter, Arden Shakespeare, 1991, xlviii
26 Nelson, 311
27 ibid. 95
28 *As You Like It*, op. cit. xliv
29 Ogburn, 527
30 Nelson, 290
31 Chute, M. *Stories from Shakespeare*, 1996, 103
32 Gervinus, G. *Shakespeare Commentaries*, trans. F. E. Bunnètt, 1883, 180
33 Nelson, 71
34 Ogburn, 434
35 Nelson, 72
36 Stokes, F. *Who's Who in Shakespeare*, 2007, 242
37 *Shakespeare Oxford Society Newsletter*, Vol.38: 3: The Seven Ages of Man, C. Paul, 12
38 Bate, J. *The Genius of Shakespeare*, 1998, 8
39 *Merry Wives of Windsor*, ed. H. J. Oliver, Arden Shakespeare, 1987, f.n. 2
40 Bate, 8
41 id. 13
42 Stokes, 344
43 Bate, 73
44 id. 66
45 *King Henry VIII*, ed. R. A. Foakes, Arden Shakespeare, 1986, xxviii
46 id.
47 *Tennessee Law Review*, Vol. 72:1, Stratford Si! Essex No! A. Nelson, 2004, 150
48 *Great Oxford*, see 'Dating the Plays: *Hamlet*' Eddi Jolly, 2004, 170
49 Nelson, 35
50 Londré, F. H. *Hamlet As Autobiography: An Oxfordian Analysis*, Bulletin of faculty of Lettters, Hôsei University, No.39, 1993, 23
51 *Encyclopaedia Britannica* CD Rom. De luxe 2001: 'Diet of Worms'
52 Ogburn, 339
53 *Great Oxford*, op. cit. 170
54 Ogburn, 339
55 Dunton-Downer, L. & A. Riding, 325
56 Williams, Neville: *The Life and Times of Elizabeth I*, 1972, 252
57 Bate, 90
58 *Shakespeare Oxford Society Newsletter*, Vol.39: 2. Rosencrantz and Guildenstern in London, Lowell James Swank, 1
59 Nelson, 141
60 ibid. 145
61 id. 141
62 id. 177
63 Gervinus, 805
64 Fox, L. *The Shakespeare Handbook*, 1988, 172-3

65 Gervinus, 807
66 Chute, 115
67 *Othello,* ed. M.R. Ridley, 1986, 238
68 Nelson, 122
69 Ogburn, 512-13
70 ibid. 486
71 id. 504
72 Nelson, 145
73 Adams, S. *Leicester and the Commonwealth,* 2002, 52
74 ibid. 57
75 Nelson, 122
76 ibid. 122-23
77 Anderson, M. *Shakespeare By Another Name,* 2005, 116
78 ibid.
79 Nelson, 127
80 ibid. 174
81 Fox, 96-7
82 Nelson, 131
83 ibid. 129
84 Ogburn, 493
85 Smolin, L. *The Trouble With Physics,* 2006, 154
86 ibid. 115
87 Shapiro, J. *Contested Will,* 2010, p.301
88 ibid. 304
89 *Shakespeare Oxford Society Newsletter*, Vol.46: 1 Book Review, R. Whalen

8 Backdating Titus Andronicus

1 Gervinus, G.G. *Shakespeare Commentaries*: trans. by F.E. Bunnètt, 1883, 102-3
2 ibid. 102
3 Adams, J.Q. Shakespeare's Titus Andronicus The First Quarto 1594: 1936, 11
4 ibid. 10
5 ibid. 9
6 Wilson, I. *Shakespeare: The Evidence*: 1993, 8
7 Quarto is preferred to quinto in the belief that Peacham would have written 4 and 5 as qto and qo.
8 Dawson, G.E. and Kennedy-Skipton, L. *Elizabethan Handwriting 1500- 1650*: London, 1966, 18-19
9 *Oxford Latin Dictionary.*
10 De Vere left England in January 1575, but according to the Old Style of dating, New Year's Day began on 25 March each year. January would therefore still have been 1574.
11 Schlueter, J. Rereading the Peacham Drawing: Shakespeare Quarterly (50:2) 1999, 173

12 ibid. p174 & 176
13 ibid. 176
14 ibid. 178
15 id.
16 ibid. 175
17 id.
18 ibid. 180
19 ibid. 183
20 Adams, 11
21 *Wotton Baronetage*: ed. Kimber & Johnstone, (i.158), 1741
22 From a wooden tablet inside the porch at St. Mary's Church, North Mymms (photograph in Author's collection).
23 *What Was Life Like in the Realm of Elizabeth*: consultant, Norman Jones, Time-Life, London, N.D. 115
24 Adams, 34
25 Titus Andronicus, ed. E. M. Waith, Oxford Shakespeare, 1998, 23
26 id.
27 Titus Andronicus, ed. J. Bate, Arden Shakepeare, 1995, 40
28 Schlueter, 184
29 Berry, H. Date on the 'Peacham' Manuscript: Shakespeare Bulletin, Spring 1999, 5
30 ibid. 5
31 ibid. 6 footnote 3
32 Adams, 32-5
33 ibid. 35
34 ibid. 36
35 ibid. 35-6
36 ibid. 36
37 ibid. 36 f.n. 1
38 Berry, 5
39 Bate, 39 f.n. 1
40 Adams, 35
41 id.
42 Schlueter, 181
43 Waith, 25
44 ibid. 25
45 Bate, 41
46 Wilson, J. *Titus Andronicus on the Stage in 1595 Shakespeare Survey*: 1948
47 id.
48 Waith, 7
49 Gervinus, 102

9 The First Folio's Deceptive Tributes

1 Wilson, I. *Shakespeare: The Evidence,* 1993, 379
2 ibid
3 Kay, W. Ben Jonson A Literary Life, 1995, 51

4 Acroyd, Shakespeare The Biography, 2006, 143
5 ibid. 141
6 ibid. 208
7 Shakespeare Complete Works, Vol.2, The Histories, ed. Alexander, 1988, 7
8 ibid. 11
9 Dunton-Downer, L. & A. Riding, *Essential Shakespeare Handbook*, 2004, 33
10 *The Shakespeare Handbook*, ed. L. Fox, 1987, 56
11 ibid. 57
12 www.Globe-theatre.org.uk [last visited: 22/10/2007]
13 Chambers, E. *Elizabethan and Caroline Stage*, vol.2, 1941, 420-21
14 Wilson, 190
15 ibid. 401
16 Ogburn, C. The Mystery of William Shakespeare, London, 1988, 175
17 The Shakespearean Authorship Society (third edition), *'The Real Shakespeare'*, W. Kent, 1966, 4
18 Ogburn, 165
19 Shakespeare Complete Works, Vol.4, 9
20 Ogburn, 693
21 *The Encyclopedia of World Mythology*, ed. Emma Gray, London, 2006, 56
22 Ogburn, 173
23 Shakespeare Oxford Society Newsletter, Vol.43 No.1: D. Charlton, 27
24 ibid. Vol.45 No.3: J. Hamill, 21 (Quoting from, *Searching for Shakespeare* by T. Cooper, 2006, 114)
25 Kay, 20.
26 Ogburn, 568
27 ibid. 567-8
28 ibid. 569
29 Oxford Compendium of English Literature, 1989, 595
30 http://en.wikipedia.org/wiki/John_Lyly [Last visited 5 April 2011]
31 Ogburn, 627
32 Gervinus, G. *Shakespeare Commentaries*, transl. F. E. Bunnėt, 1883, 939
33 ibid. 66-7
34 Ogburn, 23
35 Tennessee Law Review, Vol. 72:1, Stratford Si! Essex No! A. Nelson, 2004,
36 *The Dictionary of Phrase and Fable*, classic edition, E. Cobham Brewer, ISBN 0 86136 788 X, n.d. 841
37 Shakespeare Oxford Society Newsletter, Vol.36:2 'The not-too-hidden key to Minerva Britanna', R. Stritmatter, 11
38 ibid. f.n. (14) p. 15 refers to a similar suggestion by Art Neuendorffer.
39 *Oxford National Dictionary of Biography*, Vol. 43, ed. H.G.C. Mathew & B. Harrison, Oxford, 2004 236-8
40 Ogburn, 695
41 I am indebted to Julia Cleave for bringing the subject of the annotations made in the First Folio, owned by Glasgow University, to the attention of members of the De Vere Society.

42 Heylin, C. So Long As Men Can Breathe, 2009, 215

10 Sweet Swan of Avon

1 Nelson, A. *Monstrous Adversary*, 2004, 334
2 ibid. 329
3 Nicholl, C. *Cup of News, The Life of Thomas Nashe,* 1984
4 Anderson, M. *Shakespeare By Another Name,* 2005, 270
5 Ogburn, C. *The Mystery of William Shakespeare*, 1988, 658
6 *Wilton House*: official booklet, Beric Tempest, N.D. 33
7 Chambers, E. *The Elizabethan Stage* vol iv. 1923, 198-9
8 Gervinus, G. *Shakespeare Commentaries,* translated F. E. Bunnètt, 1883, 378
9 *The Merry Wives of Windsor,* ed. H. J. Oliver, Arden Shakespeare, 1987, xliv
10 ibid. xlv
11 ibid. xlv
12 Ogburn, f.n. 436
13 *The Merry Wives of Windsor,* xlviii
14 ibid. 125-6
15 ibid. f.n.65 125
16 ibid. f.n.72 126
17 Ogburn. 656
18 *The Dictionary of Phrase and Fable*, classic edition, E. Cobham Brewer, ISBN 0 86136 788 X, n.d. 1008
19 Crystal, D. & B. *The Shakespeare Miscellany*, 2005, 125
20 Cotterell, A. and Storm, R. *The Encyclopedia of World Mythology*, 2006, 268
21 *Much Ado About Nothing*, ed. A. R. Humphreys, Arden Shakespeare, 1981, f.n.276 125
22 http://www.accessmylibrary.com/article/-1G1-168284993/much-ado-oxford-much.html
23 *Great Oxford*, see 'John Lyly's *Endimion*' Philip Johnson, 2004, 151
24 Ogburn, 569
25 ibid. 568
26 ibid. 569
27 Brame, M. and Popova, G. *Shakespeare's Fingerprints*, 2002, 3-9
28 Chute, M. *Stories from Shakespeare*, 1996, 83
29 *Dictionary of National Biography*, Vol IX, ed. Sir Leslie Stephen and Sir Sidney Lee, 679
30 Wilson, I. *Shakespeare: The Evidence,* 1993, 299-300.
31 Honan, Shakespeare*: A Life*, 1998, 301
32 Wilson, 299-300
33 ibid. 299
34 id.
35 Kay, D. *Shakespeare His Life, Work and Era*, 1992, 274
36 Duncan-Jones, K. *Ungentle Shakespeare,* 2001, 173
37 Compton Mackenzie, F. *William Cory*, 1950, xi
38 ibid. 88

39 Warre Cornish, F. *Extracts from the Letters and Journals of William Cory*, 1897, 168

40 *English Homes No. XI, Wilton House*, Edward Rose, (Illustrated London News August 6th 1887, 177)

41 Information provided personally by the Wilton House Manager, August 2003

42 Trowbridge Record Office, G25/1/91, Wiltshire, UK.

43 Michael, W. *History of Wilton House,* Westbury, Wilts. 1873, 7

44 Compton Mackenzie, xii

45 A New Variorum Edition of Shakespeare, *As You Like It,* edited by Richard Knowles 1977, Modern Language Association of America, 633-34

46 Asquith, C. *Shadowplay*, 2006, 283

47 *Glasgow Weekly News*, 19 May 1951

11 DEBUNKING STYLOMETRIC 'PROOFS'

1 Fox, L. *The Shakespeare Handbook*, 1987, 92

2 *Tennessee Law Review*, Vol. 72:1,'Oxford By The Numbers', W. Elliott and R. Valenza, 2004, 323

3 id.

4 *Shakespeare Complete Works*, Vol.2, The Histories, ed. Alexander, 1988, 25

5 *Tennessee Law Review*, op. cit., 323

6 *New Scientist* No. 1909, January 1994, 26: column 1

7 Ogburn, C. *The Mystery of William Shakespeare*, 1988, 543

8 id.

9 *New Scientist*, No. 1909, Jan. 1994, 23

10 *Tennessee Law Review*, op. cit. 394

11 Elliott, W. and Valenza, R. *The Oxfordian*, 2007; 10, 142-153

12 Nelson, A. *Monstrous Adversary*, 2003, 386

13 Stokes, F. *Who's Who in Shakespeare*, 2007, 302

14 *New Scientist*, op. cit., 26 col.

INDEX

A

B

D

E

F

G

H

I

J

K

L

M

N

O

P

Q

R

S

T

U

V

W

Y

Z

CPSIA information can be obtained
at www.ICGtesting.com
Printed in the USA
LVOW04s1622030416
481995LV00029B/235/P